THE PENGUIN BOOK OF

HEBREW VERSE

EDITED BY T. CARMI

ALLEN LANE

ALLEN LANE
Penguin Books Ltd
536 King's Road
London SW10 OUH

First published simultaneously by Allen Lane
'and Penguin Books 1981

ISBN 0 7139 1157 3

Set in Monophoto Ehrhardt

Printed in the U.S.A.
Set by Central Press, Jerusalem,
and Oliver Burridge & Co. Ltd, Great Britain

CONTENTS

PREFACE

This anthology spans the full range of Hebrew poetry, from the Bible to contemporary Israeli writing. To the best of my knowledge, it is the first such collection in English. More surprisingly, it is also the first comprehensive selection in Hebrew. This strange state of affairs is partially explained by the fact that the texts representing the first thousand years of post-biblical poetry came to light only at the turn of the century. Many of the major poets are not yet available in collected or critical editions. Scholars are still engaged in the arduous task of processing thousands of manuscripts from the hoard of the Cairo Genizah. No one can predict how much of this will prove to be of literary interest or how it will affect our overall view of the development of Hebrew poetry. Unknown poems, and even poets, are constantly being retrieved from the vast storehouse of undeciphered manuscripts. A comprehensive anthology of Hebrew poetry is, therefore, in the nature of a draft which should be revised periodically as new material is presented to the reader.

There are, to be sure, Hebrew editions of individual authors, especially from the Andalusian period onwards, and collections which encompass a specific age or geographical area. No student of Hebrew poetry can fail to be indebted to the monumental compilations of J. Schirmann: *Hebrew Poetry in Spain and Provence* (Jerusalem-Tel Aviv, 1956) and *Anthology of Hebrew Poetry in Italy* (Berlin, 1934). The innovative publications of H. Brody, M. Zulay and E. Fleischer have radically changed the picture of medieval Hebrew poetry. The collections of D. Yellin, A. M. Habermann, S. Mirsky, D. Yarden and others have acquainted us with a large variety of previously unknown texts.

In compiling this selection I have, of course, drawn on these, and many other, standard sources. However, the desire to present a comprehensive anthology obliged me to track down a multitude of scholarly publications in out-of-the-way journals and *Festschriften*, rare editions that have not been reprinted for centuries, and liturgical collections from all over the world which have never been ransacked for their poetic gems. As a result, this volume includes many poems which have never been previously anthologized or even published in critical editions; poems which have never been

7

dislodged from their original setting in a local liturgical rite; and even poems
(e.g., some of the *Hekhalot* hymns on pp. 195-201) which have never been
printed as poetry but, strange as it may seem, are printed as prose in the few
editions in which they are to be found. Early in the work of compilation – I
should add that, except in rare cases, I have limited myself to printed sources
– I realized that I must give chance a chance to proffer its unexpected gifts.
Such a moment of delight was the 'discovery' of the unusual 'Death of Moses
Sequence' (pp. 266-74) in an Italian rite (Bologne, 1538). The poems were
clearly lying in wait for me and testing my patience and persistence.

Although I have attempted a systematic review of the corpus of Hebrew
poetry, I am fully aware of the extent to which such an endeavour exceeds
the capabilities of a single person. Suffice it to mention that I. Davidson's
classic *Thesaurus of Mediaeval Hebrew Poetry* (New York, 1924-33) lists
about thirty-five thousand poems from printed sources, and since the index
was printed, thousands of additional poems have been published. Ideally,
the preparation of a comprehensive anthology should be undertaken by a
team of experts. Professor Schirmann has pointed out that

the study of Hebrew poetry demands a knowledge of many subsidiary subjects, such
as history, bibliography, palaeography, linguistics and liturgy. The full comprehension of Hebrew texts occasionally necessitates their comparison with texts written
in other languages . . . The research into their origins entails a knowledge of several
languages (e.g., Aramaic, Syriac, Byzantine Greek, Latin, Arabic, Spanish, Italian
and Provençal) and the closer we approach our own time, the more languages are
required.[1]

It goes without saying that I do not even faintly resemble this renaissance
figure. My main justification for rushing in where scholars fear to tread is
that I have read all this material as a poet, in search of the most rewarding
literary prizes.

Obviously, poems culled from such a wide variety of sources have presented serious textual problems. Many of the editions are corrupt, the readings are often suspect and the meanings obscure. I would not have been able
to cope with these problems without the help of the many scholars I consulted over the years. I am especially indebted to Professor Gershom G.

1. J. Schirmann, 'Problems in the Study of Post-Biblical Hebrew Poetry', *Proceedings of the
Israel Academy of Sciences and Humanities*, Vol. II, 1968, pp. 228-36.

Scholem for having placed his unpublished version of the *Hekhalot* hymns at my disposal; and to Professor Ezra Fleischer for his elucidations of many textual difficulties. Professor M. Greenberg, Dr J. Licht, Professor Y. Ben-Shlomo, Professor H. Blanc, Dr I. Gruenwald and Professor Y. Ratzaby all gave me valuable advice in their respective fields. Other acknowledgements are noted in the Table of Poems; but even a partial list of my benefactors would turn this preface into a 'Scroll of Thanksgiving'. I am, of course, solely responsible for all sins of omission and commission. 'Who can be aware of errors? Cleanse me from my unknown faults . . .' (Psalms 19.13).

While writing the Introduction, I was fortunate in being able to consult two pioneering works, recently published in Hebrew: E. Fleischer's *Hebrew Liturgical Poetry in the Middle Ages* (1975), and D. Pagis's *Change and Tradition: Hebrew Secular Poetry in Spain and Italy* (1976). Both these books are the first comprehensive surveys in their respective fields (secular poetry was especially neglected by Hebrew scholarship), and this is yet another indication of the state of research. My indebtedness to these books is very great, and were I to cite every instance of it, the Introduction would suffer from a serious case of footnote disease.

The biblical selection, as the reader will readily observe, is no more than a sampling of different genres of biblical poetry. Small as the selection is, I was surprised to notice how often it is echoed in the subsequent poems. Originally, I had planned to use one of the recent translations of the Bible. However, upon closer reading, some of them struck me as too 'poetic' for a volume of prose translations, while others were marred by idiosyncratic conjectures or a disregard for recent Hebrew research. I therefore felt duty bound to prepare my own eclectic versions, which would be consonant with the general tone of the volume. I have followed the translation of the Jewish Publication Society (*The Torah*, Philadelphia, 1962) in rendering the second person singular by 'You' or 'you' when referring to the Deity, rather than by 'Thou'. 'The biblical writers,' as Professor Orlinsky has pointed out, 'made no distinction between God on the one hand and man or animal on the other so far as the pronoun ('*attáh*, "Y/you") or verbal form (e.g., *nishbá'ta*, "Y/you vowed") was concerned. God and the serpent and Pharaoh – all are addressed directly by '*attáh*.'[1] The notes to the biblical translations in this anthology

1. H. M. Orlinsky, 'The Rage to Translate', *Genesis, the N.J.V. Translation*, Harper & Row, New York, 1966, p. xx.

are far from exhaustive. They are meant to indicate to the reader the surprising range of plausible interpretations advanced by authoritative biblical studies. My brief foray into the enchanting maze of biblical scholarship has convinced me of the truth of Professor Greenberg's conclusion: 'The beginning of wisdom in biblical study is the realization that the Bible is an exotic book about which modern readers understand very little.'[1]

The broad scope of the anthology has imposed severe limits on the modern section. Modern Hebrew poetry deserves a far more generous representation and I can only apologize for this discriminatory practice. Many poets whom I admire, and who would figure in any anthology of twentieth-century Hebrew verse, have of necessity been omitted. Nonetheless, the modern section does include poets born in the thirties, thus affording the reader a glimpse of contemporary Israeli poets against the background of a long and varied tradition. In translating the modern poems, I have consulted the verse translations listed in the Select Bibliography.

In choosing the poems, my main criterion has been literary merit. But this aesthetic bias had to be tempered throughout by a consideration of what would remain of the poem in an English prose translation. Many fine Hebrew poems have been omitted because their most admirable effects – a rich texture of sound or an intricate web of allusion and reference – would be totally lost in translation or would require a forbidding apparatus of notes and comments. The final selection was also affected by considerations of variety in genre, form, subject matter and geographical area. I have not included any poems in order to 'represent' a specific school of poetry, although I have attempted to offer as varied a selection as possible and to draw attention to lesser known centres, such as the Yemen, Turkey and North Africa. I realize that the most controversial omission is that of nineteenth-century Haskalah ('Enlightenment') poetry. Though this is an intriguing and crucial chapter of cultural history, the poems themselves are, to my taste, lacking in literary merit.

The monumental scope of many of the medieval poems has led me to excerpt and, sometimes, to abridge more than I had originally intended. Again, I am conscious of the fact that this procedure is open to question. As witnesses for the defence, I could summon some of the poets themselves. In the Spanish school, it was not uncommon for poets to move sections or

1. In *Ariel, A Quarterly Review of Arts and Letters in Israel*, No. 32, Jerusalem, 1973, p. 207.

verses from one poem to another, in keeping with the conventions of the particular genre. Thus Samuel Hanagid's poem (p. 295) appears both as an independent composition and as the introductory section to a long panegyric. Where the poems consist of independent, loosely linked sections, the presentation of judicious extracts can, I think, be defended. I have, however, also taken the liberty of excerpting long poems that are not constructed in this way. The length of these poems is often due to an extensive acrostic pattern which, in turn, dictates an accumulation of verses, a series of repetitions and variations, rather than the sequential development of a theme. Given the static nature of such poems, I felt that abridgement would not do too much violence to the original. At worst, the part would seem stronger than the whole, for the intensity of the short passage is not always maintained throughout the long work. Faced by the choice of total exclusion or partial presentation, I decided to make these poems available to the reader in an abridged form.

Although the translations are in prose, they are not word for word. I have tried to render the poems idiomatically and to capture something of their tone and movement, without 'betraying' their literal level. Occasionally, where I have felt that a more literal translation would prove too cumbersome, I have resorted to paraphrase. Doubtless, in the process, I have become one of Translation's thieves, as Marvell has it:

> He is Translation's thief that addeth more,
> As much as he that taketh from the store
> Of the first author.

I have aimed to keep the notes to the translations to a minimum and to supply the reader with essential background information in the Table of Poems.

Mr Stephen Mitchell reviewed the entire English manuscript with 'a cold eye'; I could not wish for a finer blend of critical severity and warm sympathy. Mr Dom Moraes edited some of my earliest drafts and, in fact, initiated the project by suggesting it to Penguin Books in 1963. Mr Hans Schmoller and Mr Nikos Stangos, formerly of Penguin, and Mr William Sulkin, the present poetry editor, have been unfailingly helpful and encouraging. To Dr Moshe Spitzer I am indebted for invaluable typographical, as well as scholarly, guidance. My deepest thanks are due to the Librarian and staff of the Schocken Institute, Jerusalem, and of the Oriental Reading Room of the Bodleian Library, Oxford, for their cooperation.

I should like to record my gratitude to the foundations and institutions that have generously assisted me over the years: in Israel, the President's Fund, the Office of the Prime Minister, the Ministry of Education and Culture and the America-Israel Foundation; in the United States, the National Translation Center, the Lucius N. Littauer Foundation, the Memorial Foundation for Jewish Culture and the Israel Matz Foundation; in England, the Arts Council of Great Britain. A two-year Visiting Fellowship at the Oxford Centre for Postgraduate Hebrew Studies enabled me to complete the project. It is a pleasure to acknowledge my thanks to the Principal and staff of the Centre. I am also grateful to Professor M. L. Rosenthal, Professor John Wain, Dr Harry Shukman, Mr Leon Wieseltier and Mr Jonathan Wilson for instructive comments concerning the English text; to Mr Stanley Burnshaw, Mrs Mollie Oren and Professor Ezra Spicehandler for their advice and help; to Professor Benjamin Hrushovski for kindly agreeing to write a special 'Note on the Systems of Hebrew Versification' for this volume; to Mr Curtis Arnson for editorial research and the preparation of the Glossary; and to Mr Y. Ben-David for vocalizing and proofing the Hebrew text. Although I would be happy to fulfil the dictum of the *Tractate of the Fathers* 6.6: '. . . whoever reports a thing in the name of the person who said it brings deliverance into the world', I fear I have overlooked the names of friends whose insights have been incorporated in the book.

Finally, I should like to dedicate this book to Dan Pagis. Though he is in no way responsible for my errors of judgement or fact, I must hold him accountable for his unflagging encouragement and active help at every stage of the work.

T. CARMI

INTRODUCTION

THE selection in this volume extends from the Song of Deborah, written some 3,000 years ago, to poems written in Israel by authors born in the 1930s. The reader is probably more aware of the point of departure and the modern scene than of the intervening periods of Hebrew poetry, with the possible exception of the medieval Spanish school. The first thousand years of post-biblical poetry are relatively unknown, even to the Israeli reader. Some of the later periods have also passed into oblivion. It is generally, and erroneously, believed that Hebrew poetry developed sporadically, that it was mostly liturgical and, moreover, written in a dead language. The main reason for these misconceptions lies in the peculiar fate and nature of Hebrew poetry.

Its distinctive historical features are its chronological span and geographical distribution. It has been written virtually without interruption from biblical times to the present day. Over the centuries its main centres were in Palestine and Spain, Babylonia and Italy and Germany and Eastern Europe. But it also had important branches in North Africa, the Balkans, Yemen and Holland.

This longevity and mobility involved several fresh and, sometimes, false starts. Centuries of continuity were followed by bouts of amnesia, and then a rediscovery of neglected treasures. This meant that Hebrew poetry could be at very different stages of its development, during the same period, in different geographical areas. The time-tables are far from synchronized: the classical period of liturgical poetry in Palestine extended from the sixth to the eighth century; the classical period of secular and liturgical poetry in Spain began in the eleventh century. In Germany and northern France, the Ashkenazi style emerged in the twelfth century; the characteristic Hebrew-Italian style took shape in the sixteenth century.

As it moved from one centre to another, Hebrew poetry assimilated the thematic and prosodic conventions of the surrounding culture. It borrowed the cutlery, and sometimes even the furniture, of the host country. Sonnets, for example, were being written in Hebrew at the beginning of the fourteenth century, a generation before Petrarch and some two hundred years before their appearance in English and in French. The sonnet fared well in

Hebrew; it enjoyed a long and varied history. Occasionally, however, the itinerant guest borrowed patterns that did not suit the climate and customs of the next location.

Yet despite dispersion in time and place, Hebrew poetry maintained its own internal tradition, which both absorbed and transformed the external influences. Once a centre is established, it begins to lead a life of its own and to interact with other centres of Hebrew creativity. Its development is then determined by a complex network of relationships and tensions: between its original matrix and the impact of the dominant literature; between the resultant fusion and the attraction of other Hebrew centres; between the prestige of a revered tradition and the need for innovation; between its inherited prosody and the local pronunciation of Hebrew. Radical techniques, which aroused fierce polemics in one centre, may be taken for granted in a different climate as conventional components of the 'tradition'. The nature of the poetry may also be drastically affected by a change in the social status of the poet and in the make-up of his public.

Post-biblical poetry developed in Palestine, under late Roman and Byzantine rule, in the centuries preceding the Muslim conquest (636). This is the period that witnessed the remarkable flowering of the *piyut*, that is, liturgical poetry, which made Palestine the centre of Hebrew letters until the late eighth century.

The *paytanim*,[1] liturgical poets, were generally cantors. On every Sabbath and festival, they surprised their congregations with new compositions which elaborated on the subjects of the biblical lection or the specific theme of the holy day. Many communities boasted their own 'house poets' and, consequently, their own anthologies of prayers in verse and rhythmical prose. The difference in the make-up of the congregations – some were more scholarly than others – may partially account for the varying levels of complexity in the *piyut* and even in the works of a particular *paytan*.

On the basis of the available material, Professor Ezra Fleischer has divided the long history of the Eastern *piyut* into three loosely-defined periods: the pre-classical *piyut*, covering the fifth and sixth centuries, and culminating with Yose ben Yose; the classical period, from the mid-sixth to the late

---

1. *Paytan* is a Hebrew form of the Greek *poiētes*, 'maker'. It appears in Hebrew sources of the second century C.E.

eighth century, which began with Yannai and was dominated by Eleazar ben Kallir; and the late Eastern period, *c*.750–1050, when Palestine ceased to be the dominant centre and the majority of poets lived in Babylonia (Iraq) and North Africa.

Little is known of the origin of the *piyut*. The first four or five centuries of post-biblical poetry are sparsely represented by the poems in the Talmud, the ecstatic hymns of the *Hekhalot* mystics, several alphabetic prayers of great antiquity, and fragments on parchment or papyrus from Dura Europus in Syria (early third century) and Oxyrynchus in Egypt (? third or fourth century). These are practically the only survivors. There is little doubt, however, that poetry was being written throughout this period, and that it had succeeded in evolving a new style no longer subservient to the biblical model. The extent of the change can easily be appreciated by comparing a hymn from the Thanksgiving Scroll with a stylized lament or a simple devotional poem from the Talmud. The fact that the vast corpus of the Talmud, which spans almost five centuries, contains so little poetry, testifies, at most, to the absence of a bond between the poetic creation of the period and standardized religious practice.[1]

Though the pre-classical *piyut* appears fully formed in the monumental *avodot* of Yose ben Yose, there are several links to the poetry that preceded it, such as the use of alphabetic acrostics and the prevalence of the 'quadripartite rhythm' (a line of verse composed of four units, each of which contains two heavily accented words). There are also apparent connections to early poetic *targumim*, the Aramaic paraphrases of the Bible that were improvised in the synagogue up to the end of the second century C.E.; to techniques of the *derasha*, the synagogue homily that replaced the Aramaic paraphrases; and to rhetorical devices employed in the Midrash.

In full or partial form, most of the major genres[2] are already encountered in the pre-classical period. They were, with very rare exceptions, unrhymed. The alphabetic acrostic set the limit of the line of verse. Word-metre was often the organizing rhythmic principle. The vocabulary was mainly biblical, though the *paytan* enlarged the semantic field of many words, and did not

---

1. E. Fleischer, *Hebrew Liturgical Poetry in the Middle Ages* (in Hebrew), Keter Publishing House, Jerusalem, 1975, pp. 41 ff.

2. A detailed description of some of these genres, such as the *avoda*, the *kerova* (*kedushta*) and the *yotser*, is given on pp. 51–5.

THE DISTRIBUTION OF HEBREW POETRY

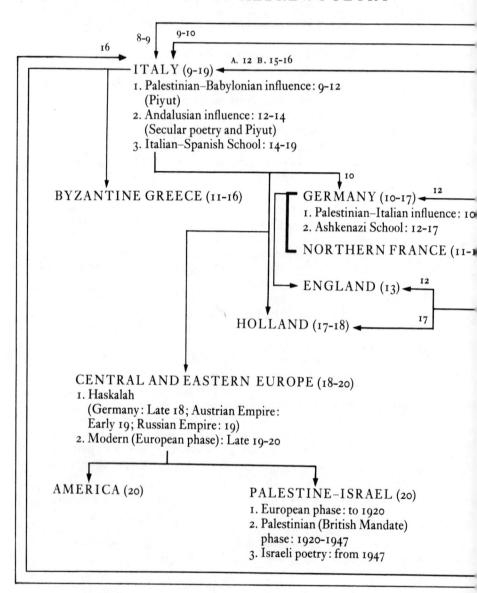

8-9 | 9-10

16

ITALY (9-19) ← A. 12 B. 15-16

1. Palestinian–Babylonian influence: 9-12
   (Piyut)
2. Andalusian influence: 12-14
   (Secular poetry and Piyut)
3. Italian–Spanish School: 14-19

10

BYZANTINE GREECE (11-16)

GERMANY (10-17) ← 12

1. Palestinian–Italian influence: 10
2. Ashkenazi School: 12-17

NORTHERN FRANCE (11-1

ENGLAND (13) ← 12

HOLLAND (17-18) ← 17

CENTRAL AND EASTERN EUROPE (18-20)

1. Haskalah
   (Germany: Late 18; Austrian Empire:
   Early 19; Russian Empire: 19)
2. Modern (European phase): Late 19-20

AMERICA (20)

PALESTINE–ISRAEL (20)

1. European phase: to 1920
2. Palestinian (British Mandate)
   phase: 1920-1947
3. Israeli poetry: from 1947

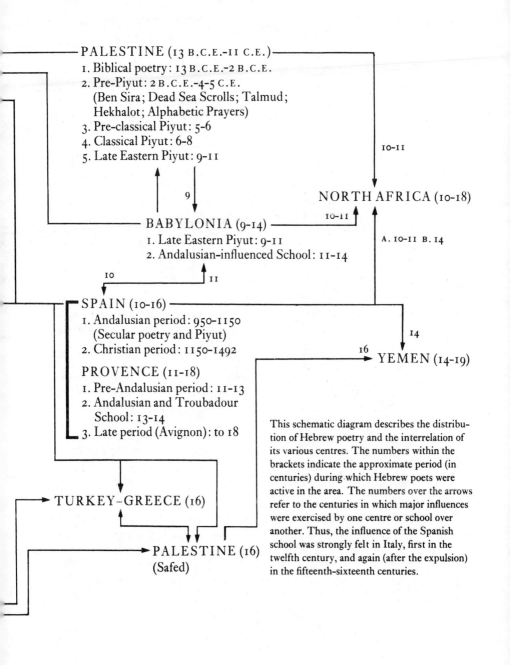

PALESTINE (13 B.C.E.-11 C.E.)
1. Biblical poetry: 13 B.C.E.-2 B.C.E.
2. Pre-Piyut: 2 B.C.E.-4-5 C.E.
   (Ben Sira; Dead Sea Scrolls; Talmud;
   Hekhalot; Alphabetic Prayers)
3. Pre-classical Piyut: 5-6
4. Classical Piyut: 6-8
5. Late Eastern Piyut: 9-11

10-11

9

NORTH AFRICA (10-18)

10-11

BABYLONIA (9-14)
1. Late Eastern Piyut: 9-11
2. Andalusian-influenced School: 11-14

10-11

A. 10-11 B. 14

10   11

SPAIN (10-16)
1. Andalusian period: 950-1150
   (Secular poetry and Piyut)
2. Christian period: 1150-1492

14

16   YEMEN (14-19)

PROVENCE (11-18)
1. Pre-Andalusian period: 11-13
2. Andalusian and Troubadour
   School: 13-14
3. Late period (Avignon): to 18

This schematic diagram describes the distribution of Hebrew poetry and the interrelation of its various centres. The numbers within the brackets indicate the approximate period (in centuries) during which Hebrew poets were active in the area. The numbers over the arrows refer to the centuries in which major influences were exercised by one centre or school over another. Thus, the influence of the Spanish school was strongly felt in Italy, first in the twelfth century, and again (after the expulsion) in the fifteenth-sixteenth centuries.

TURKEY–GREECE (16)

PALESTINE (16)
(Safed)

abstain from coinages. He was as yet restrained in his use of emblematic appellations (*kinuyim*) and of aggadic sources. Generally speaking, the pre-classical *piyut* and the poetry that preceded it are surprisingly 'modern' in tone. Their diction is unadorned and their rhythms are clear and forceful. The Hebrew reader requires no special training to appreciate the dramatic intensity of the earliest known poem on the binding of Isaac (p. 201):

... Benign One, when You said to him: / 'I desire your child as a fragrant offering' – / he rushed to fulfil the command, / he lost no time at all.

Quickly he split the wood, / took up the fire and the knife, / loaded his favoured one, Isaac, / with the faggot for the burnt offering.

Then he went on to build the altar, / stood up and placed his lamb upon it; / he took the sword in his hand / and took no pity at all . . .

The classical period established the intricate patterns of the major genres and intensified the use of existing devices. It created an extremely dense texture of epithets, neologisms and Midrashic allusions and gradually developed a specialized, inbred vocabulary that often makes the *piyut* seem abstruse and cryptic. The acrostics became highly intricate, sometimes spelling out not only the name of the author (this in itself was unknown in the previous period), but also his father's name, his place of residence, his occupation, and even concluding formulas such as *hazak*, 'be strong!'

Certainly the *paytan* needed strength to compose a *kedushta*, a sequence of 8 to 15 poems (or more, depending on the liturgical occasion), climaxed by the ecstatic rhymed prose of the 'sanctification'. The *kedushta* was the favourite genre of the classical period. Numbering anywhere from 150 to 300 verses, it made liberal use of anadiplosis, long alliterative chains, stereotyped transitional links, scriptural quotations as structural elements, and other formal devices. Nevertheless, it often achieved a moving simplicity, as in the following poem from a *kedushta* by Yannai, the first of the classical *paytanim*:

Our eyes are weak with longing for Your love, O Loving One, / for we are hated by the enemy. / Look how afflicted we are from within, / see how hated we are from with-out – / as You looked on the affliction of Leah / and saw her tormented by hate. / She was hated within the house / and detested without. / But not every loved one is loved, / nor every hated one hated: / there are some who are hated below, yet beloved above. / Those whom You hate are hated; those whom You love are loved. / We are hated because we love You, O Holy One!

The outstanding innovation of the classical period was the introduction of rhyme as a standard feature of liturgical poetry. Rhyme now set the boundary of the line of verse and of the strophe. There was only one rhyme to a strophe (e.g., aaaa, bbbb), and all the strophes of the same poem were, as a rule, identical in the number of lines, the metre, and the rhetorical pattern. The gain in resonance was, however, offset by a loss of rhythmical tautness.

The development of the *piyut* and the changes it underwent in the late Eastern period can be understood only in the context of its relationship to public prayer. During the pre-classical and classical periods, the obligatory benedictions which the congregation recited had assumed a fixed form. However, the overall pattern of the liturgy had not yet been standardized, and so the *paytanim* enjoyed a great deal of latitude. In fact, their monumental sequences, which were recited by the cantor or prayer-leader, could replace entire prose passages of the liturgy. The design of the poetic sequence was determined by the 'liturgical stations' – the obligatory benedictions or biblical verses – in the particular prayer to which the *piyut* was joined. In other words, each poem or group of poems in the sequence led up to a prescribed station or destination in the liturgy. The progression of poems within the sequence was governed by a clear pattern of strophic structure and acrostic development, but in certain sections the poet was given licence to expand *ad libitum*. The sequence, then, had a threefold obligation: to the subject of the biblical reading or holy day; to the liturgical stations of the prayer which it inhabited; and to the fixed pattern of the constituent poems.

The *piyut* forfeited its status as 'versified prayer' when the entire text of the liturgy became sanctified and the first prayer books were edited in ninth-century Babylonia. Henceforth, it could no longer serve as an alternative to passages of the codified rite; it had to content itself with being an ornamental insertion, an embellishment to a rigidly formulated text. The tension between the *piyut* and the established liturgy found expression in the antagonistic attitude of several Babylonian authorities. They viewed the *piyut* as a foreign body that was invading the precincts of a sacred territory and undermining the dominion of prayer.

This crucial change in status was partly responsible for the decomposition of the monumental forms. Where the classical *yotser*, for example, had consisted of seven or eight poems, each of which led to its liturgical station, the late Eastern *yotser* shrank considerably; and later generations of liturgical poets in Spain, Italy and Germany, no longer conscious of the architectonic nature of the genre, singled out some of its components and treated them as autonomous units.

Another major factor that contributed to the disintegration of the *piyut*'s compositional nature was the changeover from the Palestinian triennial cycle of biblical lections to the Babylonian annual cycle. In Palestine, the Pentateuch was divided into 154 or 167 sections and the entire cycle of readings was completed in about three and a half years. Yannai, for example, wrote *kerovot* for every section of the Palestinian cycle. In Babylonia, the weekly pericopes were enlarged (each one averaging approximately three Palestinian sections), their number was reduced to 54, and the full cycle was completed in one year.

Obviously, the Babylonian synagogue, even when it wished to preserve Palestinian customs, could not accommodate the three classical *kerovot* which now corresponded to its enlarged pericope. This would have been impossible for formal reasons: each *kerova* was a self-contained sequence; and undesirable for practical reasons: it would have taxed the patience of the congregation and of the heavenly hosts. It was at this point that local cantors began to edit and abridge classical compositions, creating their own collages which catered to popular taste. Since choirs played an increasingly important role in the synagogue, the cantors also enlivened the insertions with choral refrains. The most famous choral composer was surely a ninth-century *paytan*, known as 'The Anonymous', who wrote over five hundred *pizmonim* ('choruses'), which he grafted onto the *kerovot* of an earlier colleague (Simeon ben Megas, *c.* sixth century). The outcome of such editorial licence was that the overall structure, the logic of internal development, the relationship to the liturgy, and, of course, the authorship of the original composition, were often blurred beyond recognition. Scholars have, to their dismay, come across late Eastern *kedushta*-sequences which slowly reveal themselves to be the product of a dozen different pens.

Almost all of Hebrew poetry up to the tenth century is liturgical. This, however, does not mean that it is all 'religious' in the limited sense of the word, requiring the reader's consent to a system of belief or dogma. Since the *piyut* is generally linked to the biblical portion of the week, to the appropriate passages from the Prophetic books and, on special occasions, to the theme of the day, the range of subjects is almost unlimited. As long as the *paytan* observes the formal links, at the prescribed points, to the liturgical framework, he can, and does, digress at will. He can move, within the confines of the same sequence, from the lyrical to the dramatic, from narrative to supplication, from meditative poetry to mystical hymns. Thus a *kerova* sequence by Yannai can contain an invective against the oppressive Byzantine rule and Christian theology; or a detailed description of the mysterious growth of the human foetus; or a lethal condemnation of Woman:

Her sin is as bitter as death / . . . she dominates like death . . . / there is death in her eyes, death in her feet, and the angel of death dances before her.

A poet by the name of Samuel, using a verse from Habakkuk as his springboard, can describe the earthquake that shook Tiberias in 748 (though, admittedly, it is not often that one can glean such precise information from Eastern *piyutim*), and Kallir can write a blow-by-blow account of the terrible battle at the end of days between the mythical monsters Behemoth and Leviathan (p. 227).

Though the late Eastern period presided over the disintegration of classical genres and, in general, favoured a less rhythmical line and less demanding norms of rhyming, it also witnessed a classical revival in the works of its finest poets, Sa'adiah Gaon and Samuel Hashelishi. Samuel (fl. late tenth century) was a master of the taut and melodious Hebrew line. Sa'adiah (882–942), the most original poet and thinker of his time, was the major link between the Eastern and Spanish schools.

In several important respects, Sa'adiah prefigured the radical innovations of the Andalusian school, the most famous school in medieval Hebrew poetry. He was among the first to write secular verse on public issues, such as his fierce polemics against the Karaites. He introduced new rhyme-patterns: alternating rhyme (abab), and the four-unit line rhyming aaab, cccb, which later evolved into the characteristic Hebrew-Spanish quatrain. He paved the way for the introduction of philosophical themes into sacred poetry. But above all, it was his philological approach that left a lasting imprint on the Spanish school. Though the Spanish poets rejected his highly idiosyncratic system of analogical word-formation, they accepted his doctrine of the return to biblical Hebrew.

This doctrine was set forth in Sa'adiah's *Egron*, which he composed in Egypt in 902, some twenty-five years before he settled in Babylonia. The

Egron was the first Hebrew dictionary, the first rhyming dictionary and the first essay on Hebrew poetics. It was also the first formulation of the concept of *tsaḥot*, stylistic 'purity', which became one of the basic ideals of the Spanish school, from its earliest period in Muslim Andalusia to its last days in Christian Spain.

The enormous jigsaw puzzle of the *piyut* began to reveal its contours only with the discovery of the Cairo Genizah ('hiding place'). This momentous event – momentous for almost every branch of Hebrew scholarship – has been aptly described as a cluster of miracles. It was a miracle that the community in Fostat (Old Cairo), which is known to have bought its synagogue in the ninth century, perpetuated the customs and liturgy of the Palestinian rite. It was a miracle that they, and subsequent generations, held the written word in such esteem that any piece of writing in Hebrew could not simply be thrown away, but had to be stored in a special lumber-room. It was a miracle that hundreds of thousands of fragments were deposited in this windowless room in the synagogue's attic from the eleventh to the nineteenth century. And it was nothing less than a miracle that they were preserved from decay and were not discovered prematurely.

In 1896 two ladies from Cambridge, on a visit to Cairo, bought some Hebrew manuscripts as a memento. On their return, they showed them to Solomon Schechter, then Reader in Rabbinics at Cambridge University. He realized, to his amazement, that he was looking at a fragment of the Hebrew original of Ecclesiasticus.

Schechter immediately travelled to Cairo and, with the permission of the keepers, crated some 100,000 fragments and shipped them to England. In his account to the London *Times* in 1897 he recorded his lively impressions:

It is a battlefield of books, and the literary productions of many centuries had their share in the battle, and their *disjecta membra* are now strewn over its area. Some of the belligerents have perished outright, and are literally ground to dust in the terrible struggle for space, whilst others, as if overtaken by a general crush, are squeezed into big, unshapely lumps, which even with the aid of chemical appliances can no longer be separated without serious damage to their constituents. In their present condition these lumps sometimes afford curiously suggestive combinations; as, for instance, when you find a piece of some rationalistic work, in which the very existence of either angels or devils is denied, clinging for its very life to an amulet in which these same beings (mostly the latter) are bound over to be on good behaviour and not to interfere with Miss Jair's love for somebody. The development of the romance is obscured by the fact that the last lines of the amulet are mounted on some I.O.U., or lease, and this in turn is squeezed between the sheets of an old moralist, who treats all attention to money affairs with scorn and indignation. Again, all these contradictory matters cleave tightly to some sheets from a very old Bible . . .

When Genizah material began to be published, scholars were able to identify the provenance of other manuscripts, in both private and public collections, which had somehow stolen out of Cairo before Schechter's arrival. Today Genizah manuscripts are to be found in Budapest, Leningrad, Paris, London, Oxford, Manchester, New York, Philadelphia and other cities. The capital of the Genizah is, of course, Cambridge. Schechter's metaphor of a 'battlefield of books' is, unfortunately, still relevant. It is not uncommon for a researcher to discover that the fragment he is deciphering is part of a composition that is dispersed over three continents.

About forty per cent of the Genizah material consists of poetry, and the bulk of the poetry dates from the late Eastern period. It was among these manuscripts that Yannai was discovered (see p. 87), as were hundreds of other *paytanim*, and tens of thousands of unknown creations, some of monumental scope and unusual beauty. It was the Genizah that revealed the extent of Sa'adiah's achievement and 'resurrected' major poets of the Andalusian period, such as Ibn Khalfun. A great many questions remain unanswered and a vast quantity of material still awaits processing, not only in the boxes of the Genizah, but also in countless Hebrew manuscripts and early printed books stored away in libraries throughout the world.

The state of research and the magnitude of the task can be illustrated by two noteworthy examples. Samuel Hanagid and Solomon ibn Gabirol are among the greatest Hebrew poets of all time: yet the bulk of Hanagid's poems was published for the first time (by D. S. Sassoon) as late as 1934; and over forty unknown secular poems by Ibn Gabirol were first published only three years ago (edited by H. Brody and J. Schirmann). There can be little doubt that the Genizah and other manuscript collections hold many more revelations in their undeciphered leaves.

Up to the tenth century, the lineage of Hebrew poetry is fairly clear. All the *paytanim* of the classical period flourished in Palestine. From the middle of the ninth century, Babylonia, with its network of Talmudic academies and its highly organized Jewish community, superseded Palestine as the dominant centre of Jewish scholarship, setting the tone for the late Eastern period. Meanwhile, branches had sprung up in Egypt, North Africa and Syria, which, like Palestine, acknowledged the authority of Babylonia and its liturgical customs.

At the end of the ninth century Hebrew poetry made its first appearance on European soil, in southern Italy. The early Italian school was an offshoot of Palestine, and produced a distinctive synthesis of Palestinian (classical) and late Eastern elements. Germany, under the direct influence of Italy, produced its first major poet, Simeon the Great, in the tenth century. Here again, the Palestinian-Babylonian blend is clearly discernible.

The complexion of Hebrew poetry – one is tempted to say its physiognomy – was dramatically transformed in the tenth century with the emergence of the Andalusian school (Andalusia, at the time, encompassed most of the Iberian Peninsula) and the appearance of secular poetry. When Dunash ben Labrat of Cordoba – he was born in Fez and studied under Sa'adiah in Baghdad – first adapted the quantitative metres of Arabic to Hebrew; when he awkwardly imitated Arabic genres, forms and images; when he wrote the first, almost apologetic, secular poems and the first *piyutim* in the new style – he performed one of the most drastic operations in the history of Hebrew poetry. His opponents were quick to point out, in vicious polemical verse, that the quantitative metres of Arabic did violence to the nature of the holy tongue. But within decades Hebrew submitted to, and then quickly mastered, the techniques of the Andalusian school.

Hebrew poetry spans some five hundred years in Spain, which are divided into two major periods: the Muslim period (*c*.950–1150) and the Christian period (*c*.1150–1492). By the beginning of the eleventh century, the first of the giants of the 'golden age' (*c*.1020–1150) had arisen: Samuel Hanagid – Samuel the Prince, who for twenty years commanded the Muslim armies of Granada, and whose epic and lyrical accounts of military campaigns trace a sudden arc to the Song of Deborah. He was followed by three outstanding figures: Solomon ibn Gabirol, a passionate, introspective poet and major philosopher; Moses ibn Ezra, virtuoso technician and theoretician; and

Judah Halevi, 'the sweet singer of Zion', perhaps the finest poet of this school.

Secular Hebrew poetry was born at the courts of Jewish grandees who served as courtiers to Muslim rulers, at first in the caliphate of Cordoba (927–1013) and later, after the dissolution of the caliphate, in the smaller Muslim principalities. This aristocratic birth set its mark not only on the subjects of the poetry, but also on its style and character. Its main genres were panegyrics, laments on the death of the patron or his relatives, songs of self-praise, invectives aimed at the patron's rivals, the poet's rivals or, when the need arose, against the hard-fisted patron himself; aphoristic verse; stylized wine songs and love songs which, to the accompaniment of instrumental music, regaled the company gathered for a drinking session in the palace garden in springtime or the palace courtyard in winter. There were also genres of a more personal nature, such as complaints and meditative poems. The courtly milieu and the financial dependency of the poet (who was often well aware of the power of his pen) account for the rhetorical and epistolary nature of this poetry. It was urban and elegant, and it delighted in ornate metaphors.

There were other shaping forces as well, namely, the powerful attraction of Arabic verse, and the highly motivated desire to revive biblical Hebrew.

The unusual symbiosis of Hebrew and Arabic culture had begun in Babylonia and in other Muslim lands, where Jews wrote their Talmudic, philosophical and linguistic treatises in Arabic (though almost always in Hebrew script). It also had a preparatory stage of over two hundred years in Spain, beginning with the Muslim conquest and the ascendancy of the Umayyad dynasty (756).

Inspired by the model of Arabic poetry, especially that of the Abassid period (750–1258), secular Hebrew poetry was essentially limited to two forms: the non-strophic *qasida* (or *qit'a*, if it was less than ten verses long) and the strophic *muwashshah*. The *qasida* was the most common, or 'official', form. It employed a quantitative metre and a single rhyme throughout the poem; its line of verse consisted of two symmetrical hemistichs. 'In secular poetry . . . there is no trace of the paytanic strophic system, the Arabic forms reign supreme.'[1] The *muwashshah* (see p. 30), a varied and complex form,

---

1. S. M. Stern, *Hispano-Arabic Strophic Poetry*, Oxford University Press, 1974, p. 77.

relieved the monotony of the classical pattern and gave the poets scope to exhibit their structural inventiveness.

The revival of biblical vocabulary and images was stimulated by strong national sentiments and reflected a current of rivalry with the host culture. For the Arabs, the stylistic excellence of the Koran was proof of its veracity and divine inspiration. The Jews countered this by championing the Hebrew of the older Book of Books. Again and again poets expressly state that their intention is to glorify the ancient tongue, to demonstrate that it is equal, if not superior, to the reigning language. Judah Al-Ḥarizi (fl. early thirteenth century) announces this with great candour in his rhymed introduction to *Taḥkemoni*:

When I saw the work of Al-Ḥariri the heavens of my joy were rolled together and the rivulets of my mourning flowed, because every nation is concerned for its speech and avoids sinning against its tongue, whereas our tongue which was a delight to every eye is considered a brother of Cain [i.e. Abel, *Hevel*, meaning 'vanity'] . . . Like a sick person who suffers from an eye-infection and is unable to see the sun and believes the sun to be at fault, not realizing the defect in himself, so most of our fellow-Jews scorn the sacred tongue because its virtues are beyond them, and cannot see the light even if they have eyes . . . Therefore I compiled this book in order to display the force of the sacred tongue to the holy people.[1]

Earlier in the introduction, Al-Ḥarizi describes a beautiful maiden who, like Rebecca, comes to the well and offers him 'the liquid of her thoughts' and 'the milk and honey that are under her tongue'. When he asks who she is, she replies: 'I am your mistress, the holy tongue, and if I find favour in your eyes, I shall be your companion. Provided that . . . you sanctify my great name . . .' And, in fact, the poets were faithful to their mistress. Though they continued to write their theology, grammar and poetics in Arabic, well into the Christian period, they wrote their poetry almost exclusively in Hebrew.

Biblical purism was an ideal; it was never completely realized. It found its fullest expression in the secular poetry of Moses ibn Ezra, at the zenith of the 'golden age', then gave way to a more synthetic Hebrew in the Christian period. In actual practice, purism did not mean slavish imitation of biblical style, but rather an imposed limitation on the vocabulary and grammatical

---

1. Quoted by A. S. Halkin, in 'The Medieval Jewish Attitude Toward Hebrew', in A. Altmann (ed.), *Biblical and Other Studies*, Harvard University Press, 1963, pp. 235, 240.

forms in order to achieve maximum clarity. Secular poetry, which was stricter than the *piyut* in the observance of purism, did however enlarge the vocabulary of Hebrew by extending the semantic range of biblical words (a stratagem previously employed by the pre-classical *paytanim*), and by a widespread use of loan-translation. It was also considerably influenced by Arabic syntax and idiomatic usages.

The reinstatement of biblical Hebrew would not have been possible without the extensive philological research begun by Sa'adiah in his *Egron*. The quantitative metres of the Andalusian school demanded a thorough knowledge of the finer points of Hebrew grammar. Though all grammarians were not poets, all poets were, of necessity, accomplished philologists. Dunash ben Labrat, the founder of the Spanish school, and his bitter rival, Menahem ibn Saruk, were both 'court grammarians' in the service of Hisdai ibn Shaprut. Ibn Gabirol completed a long didactic poem on Hebrew grammar at the age of nineteen. Abraham ibn Ezra, the precursor of the Christian period, occupies a place of honour in the history of Hebrew linguistics.

Of the many ornamental techniques developed by the Andalusian school, one deserves special mention: the art of scriptural insertions. This consisted of an adroit and fluent weaving together of biblical quotations, from a short phrase to an entire verse. The quotation could be verbatim, slightly altered, or elliptical; it could create a broad spectrum of effects by assuming an altogether different, and even contradictory, meaning in its new setting. At times, an entire poem is chequered with quotations from a specific and relevant biblical passage. In such cases, the strands of quotations and allusions cease to be an ornamental device and become the very fabric of the poem, a sustained metaphorical texture.

The technique was used to great effect in humorous texts. Here, for example, are some of the biblical verses from which Al-Harizi weaves a descriptive passage:

Song of Songs 1.4	'Lead me! – We will follow you eagerly!'
Genesis 39.12	'He got away from her and fled outside'
Proverbs 23.4–5	'Do not toil to acquire wealth . . . When your eyes light upon it, it is gone, for suddenly it grows wings and soars like an eagle towards heaven'
Judges 5.30	'A wealth of dyed embroideries for the victors' necks'

Genesis 32.3	'And he called that place Mahanaim [i.e. Two Companies]'
Deuteronomy 22.28	'When a man chances upon a virgin who is not betrothed and forces her to lie with him'
Deuteronomy 22.27	'For the man came upon her in the open fields and, though the girl cried for help, there was no one to save her'
1 Samuel 1.8	'Why do you weep'
Genesis 39.17	'The Hebrew slave . . . came to me to dally with me'
Song of Songs 1.13	'My lover is for me a bag of myrrh as he lies on my breast'
Numbers 23.24	'He will not rest till he devours his prey and drinks the blood of the slain.'

These verses provide the materials for a rapid (and, in the original, brilliantly rhymed) catalogue of the exploits of a flea:

. . . And should you say: I will follow him eagerly, / he gets away and flees outside. / And even if you catch him once or twice, / he slips out of your hands, / suddenly grows wings / and soars like an eagle toward heaven. / Often he hides by the maidens beneath their embroidered cloth, / going from their loins to their thighs. / He conceals himself between their breasts / and calls that place the Two Companies. / When he chances upon a virgin who is not betrothed, / or upon a married woman, / he clings to her and lies with her / until his misdeeds make her scream; / and though the maiden cries for help, no one comes to save her. / And should you ask her: 'Why do you weep, why do you clamour?' / She replies: 'The pitch-black slave came to dally with me / and bedded in my bosom. / My lover is for me a bag of myrrh as he lies on my breast. / . . . All night long he fans the flames of battle / and will not rest till / he devours his prey and drinks the blood of the slain . . .'

Secular Hebrew poetry's aristocratic upbringing did not confine it within the palace walls; it quickly gained a wide and appreciative public in Spain and in distant lands. Its triumph was complete when it infiltrated the *piyut* and thus reached the masses in the synagogue. For the first time in Jewish history the *paytan* was not only a 'deputy' or 'delegate' of the congregation (*sheli'ah tsibur*), but a professional poet who was bound by the same conventions and judged by the same aesthetic criteria as the secular poet. The first two generations of *paytanim* after Dunash ben Labrat (d. *c*.990) hesi-

tated to accept his innovations, but from the time of Ibn Gabirol (b. 1021/
22) onwards, the greatest *paytanim* were also the greatest secular poets.

These poets, as Professor Dan Pagis has observed, 'actually related to
society in two different ways. In their secular poetry they were attached to a
reading or listening public, not to mention individual patrons. In their sacred
poetry they were attached to the congregation and the synagogue. In the
works of a particular poet and *paytan* there were stylistic affinities between
the two domains, but each domain was even more strongly related to the
corresponding domain in the works of fellow-practitioners. For example,
the secular poems of Moses ibn Ezra bear less resemblance to his own
piyutim than to the secular meditative poems of Samuel Hanagid, his predecessor in the Andalusian school.'[1]

In point of fact, the *piyut* led a double life in Spain. On the one hand, it
continued to evolve within the framework of its own long tradition, assimi-
lating new strophic patterns and thematic material. It also invented new
metrical schemes and even produced a specific syllabic system of its own. It
was far more varied and experimental than secular poetry. On the other hand,
it acceded to the conventions of secular poetry, in whole or in part. Its diction
tended to vary, depending on the tradition within which it was written. Only
those *piyutim* which accepted the secular modes without reservation tried to
observe the rigorous precepts of biblical purism.

A striking example of the marriage of the sacred and the profane is afforded
by a famous poem by Judah Halevi:

Ever since you were my home-of-love,
my love has camped where you have camped.
For your sake, I have delighted in the reproaches of my admonishers;
let them be, let them torment the one whom you tormented.
It was from you that they learned their wrath, and I love them
for they hound the wounded one whom you struck down.
From the day you despised me, I have despised myself,
for I will not honour what you have despised . . .

The poem is written in the classical monorhymed form (the hemistichs are
here printed as separate lines). Its vocabulary and imagery are typical of the

---

1. D. Pagis, *Change and Tradition: Hebrew Secular Poetry in Spain and Italy* (in Hebrew),
Keter Publishing House, Jerusalem, 1976, p. 4.

secular genre. The 'admonisher', for instance, is one of the stereotyped characters of love poetry; his function is to intensify the suffering of the languishing lover by abusing him. It is only with its last line –

> until Your anger has passed and again You will redeem
> Your own possession, which You once redeemed.

– that the poem reveals itself as a *piyut*. And it is even more surprising to learn that, except for the last line, this *piyut* is an adaptation of an eighth-century Arabic love poem.[1]

This is an extreme, though far from unique, instance of the infiltration of secular love imagery into sacred poetry. A more common and widespread example of the interaction can be seen in the enthusiastic adoption of the *muwashshah* form by the *paytanim*.

The *muwashshah*, or 'girdle poem', is an Arabic strophic poem (possibly for choral recital), which regularly alternates sections with separate rhymes and others with common rhymes (e.g., aa bbbaa cccaa, etc.). According to some scholars, its form was inherited from ancient Spanish folk poetry. Its themes were frankly hedonistic: celebrations of drink and love. It entered secular Hebrew poetry in the generation of Samuel Hanagid, shortly after its appearance in Arabic in Andalusia at the beginning of the eleventh century. Secular Hebrew girdle poems often conclude with a couplet in vulgar Arabic or Romance dialect, some of which were probably taken over in their entirety from Arabic or Romance folk songs. But despite its dubious ancestry and its suspect character (it was condemned by Maimonides for 'arousing the spirit of harlotry') it became one of the favourite vehicles of the *piyut* in Spain. Some of the most beautiful and moving medieval liturgical poems, not infrequently in the form of a dialogue between the lovers, God and Israel, were written as girdle poems. Moreover, the *piyut* outstripped secular poetry in the invention of novel and complex girdle patterns. The alacrity and ease with which the *paytanim* took to the *muwashshah* is partly due to the fact that the repertoire of the *piyut* already included a great variety of 'girdle-like' patterns.

The speed with which the Andalusian school imposed itself upon the centres of Hebrew poetry throughout the world is one of the most striking phenomena in the annals of Hebrew poetry. By the beginning of the eleventh

1. As pointed out by I. Levin, in *Hasifrut*, Vol. III, Tel Aviv University, 1971, pp. 118-19.

century, poets in Babylonia, Egypt, North Africa and Palestine were already writing in the Spanish style. From the middle of the twelfth century Provence became an adjunct of the Andalusian poetic empire. At the same time, poets in Italy abandoned the Palestinian paytanic style, and began to write secular and sacred poetry in the Hispano-Arabic manner. Greece, Turkey and Yemen followed suit. The conventions of the Spanish school became so pervasive that one is often hard put to identify the geographical provenance of a poem in the Andalusian style.

The only centre that did not pay total homage to the Andalusian school was the German-French, or Ashkenazi, centre. Some of its greatest poets, such as Ephraim of Regensburg and Ephraim of Bonn (twelfth century), did experiment with a limited range of quantitative metres, but little secular poetry was written in Ashkenaz (Germany) and the theory of ornamentation hardly influenced its poetry. From its very inception, as an offshoot of Italy, the Ashkenazi school jealously guarded its received tradition, which was predominantly Kallirian. An index of its veneration can be seen in the fact that it was the first centre to produce exegetical commentaries on the *piyutim* that figured in its rite. Though it produced great poetry in its classical period (tenth century) and during its typically Ashkenazi phase (twelfth and thirteenth centuries), it was probably the most 'provincial' centre of Hebrew poetry. Historical circumstances – the ravages of successive Crusades and the brutal pogroms during the year of the Black Death (1348-9) – partly account for this. The poetic efforts of the Ashkenazi school concentrated on passionate penitential verse (*seliḥot*) and dirges (*kinot*), many of which recorded the harrowing experiences of the Rhineland communities.

The golden age in Spain was brought to an abrupt end in 1140 with the invasion of the Almohads, a fanatical Berber sect from North Africa. After the destruction of the Jewish centres of Andalusia, the communities moved north, to Christian Spain. By the end of the thirteenth century, the Reconquest had spread southwards, leaving only the small kingdom of Granada under Muslim domination. New centres of Hebrew poetry now arose in Toledo, Saragossa and Barcelona, as well as in northern areas, such as Navarre, which had never been under Muslim rule. Meanwhile, an important centre of learning and poetry developed in Provence (which then designated the entire area of southern France between Spain and Italy).

The patronage of Hebrew poetry did not disappear in Christian Spain. There were Jewish princes, courtiers and administrators in the service of Christian kings, who, like their Andalusian predecessors, spread a protective wing over poets and scholars. However, the extent of patronage and the centrality of the court were considerably diminished. The poetry tended to become more personal, more realistic, reflecting larger areas of individual life and public experience. The language became more catholic, incorporating elements from rabbinic Hebrew and from the terminology introduced by the translators of Jewish Arabic classics. The tensions between the Jewish aristocracy and the masses found expression in social satire, intended for a large, popular audience.

Yet despite the radical change in social context – the poets were now living among Christians, and the vernacular was Spanish – the Andalusian school continued to exert a powerful influence. The assimilation of thematic and formal elements from Spanish and Troubadour poetry was very gradual and rarely resulted in extreme departures. This can be observed in the works of the greatest poets of the Christian period. Both Meshullam da Piera (d. after 1260) and Todros Abulafia (1247–after 1295) show signs of Troubadour influence. In the case of Da Piera, the changes are mainly stylistic. Abulafia, though he succeeded Da Piera, is far more traditional and occasionally shows the Troubadour imprint mainly in his choice of subject. To a certain extent this is also true of his contemporary Isaac Hagorni, the most original poet in Provence and one of the most intriguing figures of the Christian period.

The major innovation of the Christian period was the introduction of narratives in rhymed prose, interspersed with metrical poems. Of these works, the best known genre was the maqama. Although the first Hebrew maqama (by Solomon ibn Tsakbel) was apparently written shortly before the destruction of Andalusia, the genre reached its full stature in the work of Judah Al-Ḥarizi (c. 1170–after 1235).

The flowering of the maqama provides yet another example of the prestige enjoyed by the Andalusian school. The model was Arabic: it had been fashioned by two celebrated poets in the East, Al-Hamadani (967–1008) of Hamadan in Persia and Al-Ḥariri (1054–1122) of Basra in Iraq. Al-Ḥarizi first translated the classical maqamat of Al-Ḥariri and then proceeded to write his own maqama sequence, the Taḥkemoni. The majority of rhymed narratives deviated from the Arabic pattern. Many of them drew upon

European Christian sources and, in their use of structure and plot, resembled European stories of the time.

However, all the poems in the *maqamat* and in the related genres of rhymed narrative strictly adhered to the classical *qasida* form (quantitative metre and uniform rhyme). Though traditional, they had a far-reaching effect on the subject matter, tone and *dramatis personae* of secular poetry. The narrative and dramatic framework gave the poets licence to put poetic monologues in the mouths of lovelorn women, impotent greybeards, hospitable yokels, lecherous adulterers and even pathetic roosters fleeing the butcher's knife. The *maqama* framework also enabled the author to stage poetic duels; to appear in the double guise of counsel for the defence and the prosecution, alternately praising and condemning women or wine; and to record autobiographical experiences.

The intense persecutions of 1391 and the oppressive edicts and mass conversions that followed upon the Disputation of Tortosa (1413–14) gradually destroyed the fabric of Jewish life and letters in Spain. The Christian period of Hebrew poetry came to an end with the expulsion of the Jews from Spain in 1492 and from Portugal in 1497.

The expulsion signals the beginning of a new era in Hebrew poetry. The exiles and refugees flooded the shores of the Mediterranean and initiated a resurgence of poetic creativity in North Africa, Turkey, and Palestine. In Safed, the school of mystics which gathered around Isaac Luria in the sixteenth century provided Hebrew poetry with the inspiration of the Kabbalah, and this new source of energy quickly radiated out to Yemen, Holland and Italy.

While Hebrew poetry was being expelled from Spain – it had previously been expelled from England (1290) and France (1306, 1322 and 1394) – it was refining the *ottava rima* in Italy, in some of the most delicate lyrics ever written in Hebrew.

Italy, it will be recalled, was the first European host of Hebrew poetry. It was also, in many ways, the most hospitable. The history of Hebrew poetry in Italy extends from the ninth to the nineteenth century. It is of particular interest because in the course of this millennium, it mirrored all the existing schools, tried out all the Hebrew metrical systems, until finally achieving its distinctive style. This Italian style played an important role in shaping the poetry of seventeenth-century Turkey, Holland and Palestine, and, as we shall see, was bequeathed to the poets of nineteenth-century Austria, Germany and eastern Europe.

The first three centuries in Italy produced some major works, such as Amittai ben Shephatiah's *yotser* (p. 235), in the Palestinian-Babylonian manner. The Jewish community in Italy, the oldest in Europe, had had strong links with Palestine during the classical period of the *piyut*. In fact, some of the early Palestinian *piyutim* survived only because of their inclusion in the Italian rite. Subsequently, like all the Jewish communities of Europe, Italy accepted the spiritual leadership of Babylonia. As a result, it was never aware of the clash that had taken place in Babylonia between the sanctified obligatory ritual and the *piyut*. It treated both with almost equal reverence, and its *paytanim* proceeded to embellish those areas of the standardized liturgy that were less encumbered with poetic insertions. It was also oblivious to the linguistic tension that had existed between paytanic and rabbinic Hebrew in the late Eastern *piyut*. Loyal to both strata of the language, it produced a hybrid diction, peculiar to itself.

In the latter part of the twelfth century Hebrew poetry in Italy succumbed to the lures of the Andalusian school. In this case, the name of the missionary is known: Abraham ibn Ezra, the renowned poet, exegete, grammarian and astrologer from Tudela. He embarked on a voyage in 1140 and systematically introduced the Andalusian norms into Italy, Provence, France and England. It was during his stay in Italy that he wrote a scathing critique of the dominant paytanic style. His sarcastic polemic (inserted in his commentary to Ecclesiastes) reflected the classicistic, rationalistic ideals of the Andalusian school. He took the Kallir style to task for being hermetic and affected; for using imprecise metaphorical language; for ignoring the biblical context from which it derived its stereotyped emblematic appellations; for sacrificing clarity and grammatical decorum on the altar of rhyme; and, finally, for using Talmudic and Midrashic language as well as the specialized and, in his view, corrupt paytanic forms.

Ibn Ezra's critique and the chapter on Andalusian versification which he included in his 'Book of *Tsaḥot*' (Mantua, 1145) had a lasting effect on Hebrew poetry in Italy. It led to the banishment of the paytanic style and the disappearance of word-metre. It imposed the Andalusian conventions which, despite the subsequent emergence of rival systems, enjoyed official recognition almost until modern times.

A hundred years after Ibn Ezra's fateful visit, Italian elements began to assert themselves in Hebrew poetry, at first surreptitiously, and then in open defiance of the hallowed tradition. Immanuel of Rome (*c*. 1261-*c*. 1332), one of the wittiest and bawdiest of poets, introduced the sonnet into Hebrew around 1300. The thirty-eight sonnets which he interspersed in his famous *maqama* collection (*Maḥberot Imanu'el*) reflect both the *dolce stil nuovo* and the burlesque style then current in Italian letters. They also strike an original compromise between Andalusian and Italian prosody.

His sonnets adhered to a quantitative metre. In this respect, they were not disloyal to the Hispano-Arabic rule-book. But Immanuel chose an eleven-syllable line, corresponding to the standard Italian *endecasillabo*. Though he observed the regular pattern of 'long' and 'short' units, he no longer made a phonetic distinction between them. He was, in fact, writing quantitative-syllabic verse, that did not offend the traditionalists and, at the same time, pleased the Italian-oriented ear. This innovation affected the norms of rhyme and strophic pattern; it also introduced new notions of caesura and stress, borrowed from Italian prosody. By originating quantitative-syllabic metrics and by introducing the Italian sonnet into the Andalusian *maqama*, Immanuel sparked the fusion of Spanish and Italian elements.

From the fourteenth century onwards, Hebrew poetry increasingly assimilated Italian themes and strophic forms. Moses da Rieti (1388-after 1460) introduced the *terza rima* into Hebrew and was the first to use an overtly syllabic metre which disregarded the distinction between 'long' and 'short' and accorded with the Italian pronunciation of Hebrew. Joseph Tsarfati (d. 1527) reflected the high point of the Renaissance in his consummate love poems in *ottava rima*. The remarkable Frances brothers, Jacob and Immanuel (seventeenth century), were Baroque poets in their rhyme patterns, genres and subjects. Moses Ḥayim Luzzato (1707-47), the noted mystic and moralist from Padua, wrote dramatic poems in the Arcadian manner. His allegorical *Tower of Strength* was openly modelled on Guarini's popular pastoral drama *Il Pastor fido*. Luzzato's verse-plays (which are not represented in this selection) were far superior to his occasional verse and exercised a profound influence on Hebrew literature in eastern Europe a century after his death.

Throughout these centuries three metrical systems coexisted: the Spanish quantitative metre in monorhymed poems; the quantitative-syllabic metre in most of the strophic forms borrowed from Italian; and the syllabic metre which, despite its correspondence to Italian models, enjoyed only a limited vogue. A great many poets employed both the quantitative and quantitative-syllabic systems; and some did not hesitate to make use of all three systems.

The characteristic Hebrew-Italian style which evolved between the fifteenth and seventeenth centuries testified to an unusually close rapport between the two languages. At its extreme, this took the form of macaronic poems, alternating Hebrew and Italian lines; poems which paired Hebrew and Italian rhyme-words; echo-poems, in which the echo of the Hebrew word yields an Italian word (e.g. *yekara* ['dear one'] . . . *cara*); and even poems which could be read as both Hebrew and Italian. Needless to say, such *tours de force* were, as a rule, quite forced. But they illustrate the degree to which Hebrew poets felt at ease in both cultures.

Hebrew enjoyed a high status among the Humanists, some of whom studied under Jewish scholars and poets. Hebrew presses were founded in Italy as early as the fifteenth century, in the period of the incunabula. Unlike his predecessor in Spain, the Hebrew poet in Italy was not competing with the dominant culture; he saw himself as a collaborator in a joint venture. This collaboration was sorely tried, but not disrupted, by the severe oppressions that accompanied the Counter-Reformation in the latter part of the sixteenth century. Despite the harassing restrictions of the Roman Church, this was the period that witnessed the appearance of bi-lingual editions of original devotional poetry as well as translations of *piyutim*.

Hebrew poets often played an active role in Italian letters. Immanuel of Rome had no misgivings that he was betraying his 'Hebrew mistress' when he exchanged sonnets in Italian with Cino da Pistoia and Bosone da Gubbio. Judah Abrabanel (*c.* 1460-1530), who fled his native Portugal in 1483, was the celebrated author of *Dialoghi di Amore*, a classic of Italian philosophic prose. Judah Sommo (1527-92), author of the first known Hebrew drama, *The Comedy of Marriage*, was a renowned Italian playwright and producer at the Gonzaga court in Mantua, and author of a pioneering treatise on Renaissance stagecraft. His fame was such that he was exempted in 1580 from wearing the yellow badge required of the Jews. He was also admitted as a *scrittore*, though not as a full member, to the 'Academy of the Lovesick' (*Accademia degl' Invaghiti*), which was not open to Jews.

Similar Jewish academies, for the propagation of Hebrew poetry, music and drama, arose in Italy towards the end of the sixteenth and throughout the seventeenth century. Leon da Modena (1571-1648), a Rabbi and Italian playwright, was one of the moving spirits of the musical academy founded in the Venice ghetto in 1628. It bore a facetious Italian name, 'Academy of Boors' (*Accademia degli Imperiti*) and a resounding Hebrew name, 'When We Remembered Zion'. In Florence, the society known as the *Anelanti* ('Aspirants') commissioned Immanuel Frances to write a Hebrew text for an opera (1670) and a cantata which was performed in two synagogues. The eruption of messianic currents in Italy in the seventeenth century also gave rise to religious and mystical societies. *Shomrim Laboker* ('Association for Vigils') and *Me'irey Shahar* ('Those Who Arouse the Dawn') had branches in several cities and encouraged the composition of religious poetry which was sung to instrumental accompaniment. Such societies functioned until the nineteenth century and played an important role in the development of Hebrew poetry.

The devotional poetry inspired by these societies is not, strictly speaking, classed as *piyut*. The distinction that had once been clear-cut between poetry having a defined function in the liturgy and non-liturgical poetry had already begun to be obscured in the latter part of the Spanish period. In addition to secular poems on religious themes, there were a great many devotional poems that lacked any fixed liturgical 'address'. The same holds true for the enormous output of religious poetry, in later centuries, in North Africa, Greece, Turkey and Yemen. These works were in the margin of the ritual. They were often composed as occasional pieces to celebrate events in the private or public domain: weddings, circumcisions, or synagogue inaugurations. Few of them entered the prayer book or, to be more precise, the rites of the various Jewish communities throughout the world. These rites had assumed their final shape during the fourteenth and fifteenth centuries, and after the invention of printing, the 'editing' of the prayer books was essentially completed.

Given its enormous diversity, chronological range and geographical dispersion, what are the factors that give Hebrew poetry its cohesion and justify the use of that much abused word 'tradition'? First and foremost, the cement of biblical Hebrew. Though Hebrew poetry cultivated different stylistic prejudices at different periods – sometimes preferring the rabbinic idiom, or the specialized allusive usages of the classical *piyut* – biblical Hebrew remained, and continues to be, the base of the language. This is one of the reasons why Hebrew, despite its multi-layered formation, did not develop the schism that characterizes classical and modern Greek, or literary and vernacular Arabic. It is also the crucial factor that enables a Hebrew reader to choose a poem written in fifth-century Palestine, tenth-century Spain or fifteenth-century Italy, and to read it with pleasure and ease.

The long, sprawling tradition is held together not only by the infrastructure of biblical Hebrew, but also by the larger cultural frame of reference, the sources studied so intensively, committed to memory, commented upon and reinterpreted in each generation, until they become an almost subconscious layer of the national memory. It is further reinforced by the repetition of central themes and motifs, which are capable of transmitting the traumas of history, whether the martyrdom of entire communities during the Crusades, the *autos-da-fé* of the Inquisition, or the extermination of more than half of the Jewish population in Yemen in the seventeenth century. One could, for example, compile an extensive anthology of poems on the theme of the binding of Isaac (*akedot*), from Talmudic to modern times, that would mirror these and other events in the idiom of the respective periods. Even the limited selection in this volume indicates the recurrence of such themes as the death of Moses or the longing for Zion. It is as though one were walking through a house of mirrors, constantly catching glimpses of familiar scenes from different angles of vision.

A great many *piyutim* are, of course, inaccessible without the help of a critical key. Secular poems in the Spanish manner often require familiarity with their Arabic prototypes. Poems from Italy may exhibit peculiarities of syntax and gender that cannot be understood without reference to Italian. Poems from Yemen often wear a heavy Kabbalistic veil. But in every period of Hebrew poetry one finds poems of extreme complexity as well as of great simplicity – this is also true of the Bible – and much of this poetry, certainly more than is generally supposed, is readily available to the modern reader.

The extreme swings of the stylistic pendulum were possible precisely because Hebrew was not spoken. At a given moment in its history, it could summon up one of the strata of the language, invest it with renewed authority and make it the dominant diction of the period. The tendency towards a more eclectic language seems to manifest itself when the popular base of the poetry is broadened and writers are called upon to mine a more realistic vein.

The rabbinic idiom reasserted itself in the late Eastern period, when Hebrew poetry was no longer centralized in Palestine but was catering to the needs of far-flung communities throughout the East. A similar trend was evident in the poetry of Christian Spain, both secular and sacred, when the poetic scene was no longer as compact as it had been in Andalusia and when a large, popular audience had come into being. In this particular historical context, another important factor contributed to the emergence of a less 'aristocratic' style: the need to translate the Arabic classics of Jewish scholarship for the benefit of Jews in Christian lands. The concerted efforts of the translators in Provence and Christian Spain created a more heterogeneous diction, which became one of the strands of modern Hebrew.

The stylistic pendulum can be observed in action on the threshold of the modern period. Abraham Mapu (1808-67), the first Hebrew novelist and an important figure of the Haskalah ('Enlightenment') movement, cast his biblical romance *The Love of Zion* in archaic biblical Hebrew. But when he came to write a contemporary social satire, *The Hypocrite*, he apologized to his readers for having recourse to the 'black and comely Babylonian maiden', i.e. rabbinic Hebrew.

The Haskalah (1781-1881) was a movement that advocated the secularization of Jewish life and the emancipation of the Jewish people. It began in Prussia as a rationalist, cosmopolitan movement and, by the middle of the nineteenth century, assumed a romantic-nationalist aspect, as its major centres shifted to eastern Europe. The wave of pogroms that struck Russian Jewry in the 1880s tarnished the ideal of emancipation, undermined its feasibility, and initiated the earliest organized Zionist movement, known as *Ḥibat Tsiyon* ('The Love of Zion').

Though one must admire the courage and tenacity of epic poets such as Judah Lev Gordon (1830-93), and the gentle lyricism of poets such as Micah Joseph Lebensohn (1828-52), the poetry of the period is largely devoid of aesthetic interest.

It may be idle, or even suspect, to speculate on the reasons for the literary decline of a given era. Talent and genius are not predictable, and it is only hindsight that enables the literary historian to pigeon-hole his eagles. Still, in the case of the Haskalah, some of the contributing factors may have been the didactic, moralistic and nationalistic bias of its poetry; the relative isolation of the Jewish communities in eastern Europe from their host cultures; the sudden exposure of the Jews to foreign, and often antagonistic, social forces, and the resultant feelings of inferiority; the disregard of centuries of Hebrew poetry, of the enormous storehouse of potential poetic equipment;[1] and, finally, the legacy of the Hebrew-Italian school, which consisted of the syllabic system, a limited repertoire of feminine rhymes and a pseudo-biblical mannerism. The Ashkenazi pronunciation of Hebrew in Russia, Poland and Germany blurred the syllabic patterns and rhymes which had evolved organically within the Italian tonalities. The metrics of the Haskalah poets (their favourite was the eleven-syllable line) no longer had any relation to the actual sound of the language.

It was only with Ḥayim Naḥman Bialik (1873-1934) that Hebrew recovered from its stroke of amnesia, began to rediscover important chapters of its long history, and found its modern voice. In 1890 Odessa was the centre of Hebrew letters. By 1920 it was superseded by Palestine. This critical transition affected the prosody of Hebrew poetry, its musical key and, of course, its themes and locales.

Under the influence of Yiddish, Russian and German, the syllabic system was discarded in favour of the tonic-syllabic or accentual system (the alternation of stressed and unstressed syllables, as in English, German or Russian verse). This change was effected mainly by Bialik, the acknowledged leader of the Odessa circle.

It was a welcome and, in retrospect, natural change, since it renewed the link of Hebrew poetry to the patterns of stress that had marked biblical verse and parts of the early *piyut* in Palestine and Italy. This is not to imply that all these systems are identical. The precise metrical nature of biblical and early classical Hebrew poetry is still a subject of scholarly discussion. But the principle of stress, whether of phrases, words or feet, is common to all of them. Hebrew poetry, after having practised the quantitative metrics of

1. 'For when the poets of the Haskala or the era of Enlightenment set about reviving Hebrew, they found for their endeavours, in Berlin or Vienna, in Zolkiew or Vilna, no usable past. The masters of medieval song had long sunk into oblivion, and even their names faded from memory. "Who is Yannai?" asks in 1829 the best informed scholar of the times [S. J. Rapoport]. The choicest lyrics of Judah Halevi were clean forgotten until his *diwan* was recovered and parts thereof printed in 1840 and 1864 by S. D. Luzzatto.' (S. Spiegel, 'On Medieval Hebrew Poetry', in L. Finkelstein (ed.), *The Jews: Their Religion and Culture*, Schocken Books, New York, 1973, p. 112.)

Arabic in Spain and the syllabic metrics of Italian, was, in a sense, returning to its origins, to a quality inherent in the language, when it reverted to accentual rhythms. The change in musical key forced upon Hebrew when it moved to Palestine was, however, far more traumatic. This was the changeover from the Ashkenazi pronunciation, then current in Europe, to the Sephardic pronunciation that became standard in Palestine. Thus a line (from a poem by Bialik) that sounded something like

ḥsúl beyséynu óydoy hóyze

('our house-cat, still day-dreaming'), became:

ḥatúl beténu odó hozé.

The fluidity and flexibility of *ashkenázis* was replaced by the harsher, end-stressed beat of *sefaradít*. Many of the older poets, the founding fathers of modern Hebrew poetry in its European phase (1880-1920), were incapable of making the transition. Their ear was too finely attuned to the Ashkenazi musical patterns in which they had been reared. Bialik, who settled in Tel Aviv in 1924, only attempted *sefaradít* in his children's poems. A few of his contemporaries did try to transpose their earlier works into *sefaradít* so that they should make musical sense to younger readers and future generations. The attempt was rarely successful. Not surprisingly, those Ashkenazi poems that were written in free biblical cadences suffered least in transit.

Bialik had the distinction of providing Hebrew poetry with a new idiom which fused together the various strata of the language. These strata, as we have seen, tended to remain disparate, mainly because of the absence of living speech. Moreover, since the cultural sources were clearly demarcated, revered and rehearsed, words had difficulty in arriving unaccompanied; they were usually followed by a host of intrusive relatives. The result in Haskalah poetry was a mosaic technique, a patchwork quilt of involuntary quotations and allusions that stifled the individual voice.[1]

1. This florid, euphuistic style, known as *melitsa*, should not be confused with the deliberate and artful manipulation of biblical verses practised by the Hebrew-Spanish poets in the Middle Ages (see pp. 27-8). Bialik, in describing his younger contemporaries, wrote: 'The reign of *melitsa* [of Haskalah poetry] declined. The biblical verse no longer walked before them like a blind man's cane, but skipped after them playfully.'

History thoughtfully paired Bialik with Saul Tchernikhovsky (1875–
1943), the other major figure of the period. Bialik's biography, his *shtetl*
(small town) background, religious education and subsequent encounter
with secular culture (see p. 132), were typical of the East European Hebrew
writer. His poetry, his unerring linguistic instincts, seemed to recapitulate
successive stages of Jewish history. He was (at times, reluctantly) the voice
of the people at critical moments in their history.

When two walls collapse, they sometimes meet at the moment of falling and form an
arch. Bialik's poetry forms such an arch over the ruins of the traditional world into
which he was born; and it reflects the collapse of the tradition. The world of faith . . .
revealed itself as an absurdity; the certainty of accepted ideas disintegrated into
despair. It is the expression of this despair – in more or less old poetic forms reshaped
with great freedom – that gives Bialik's world its unique tension.[1]

Tchernikhovsky was far removed from the 'collapsing walls' of the traditional world. His upbringing was untypical: he received a secular Hebrew
education and a thorough grounding in Russian literature. The landscapes
of his childhood – the fertile fields and vast steppes of the border region
between Crimea and the Ukraine – were a powerful presence in his poetry
until his dying day. His nature poems have a wealth of detail, a breadth and
freedom of expression, that were unique in Hebrew poetry. He was by far
the most European Hebrew poet of his generation. His translations, from
fifteen languages, of national epics and of Renaissance and Romantic works
(see p. 133), reminded Hebrew poetry of the larger cultural frame of reference within which it had flourished in the Spanish and Italian periods. While
Bialik devoted endless energy and erudition to the in-gathering (*kinus*) and
editing of forgotten Hebrew sources, Tchernikhovsky was engaged in a
parallel venture: the in-gathering of European classics, from antiquity to his
time, from which Hebrew poetry had been severed in the ghetto-centuries.
He was acutely aware of the need to revitalize Hebrew poetry not only by the
infusion of new themes, but also by refocusing attention on formal and
aesthetic problems, and by cultivating European genres, such as the ballad,
the sonnet and the narrative idyll. In an affectionate monograph he paid
homage to Immanuel of Rome, the first Hebrew sonneteer, and in the preface

1. Tuvya Rübner, 'Chaim Nachman Bialik', in S. Burnshaw, T. Carmi and E. Spicehandler
(eds.), *The Modern Hebrew Poem Itself*, Schocken Books, New York, 1966, p. 18.

to his own sonnets, he bewailed the musical poverty of Hebrew poetry. Compared to Bialik, Tchernikhovsky was an outsider; he seemed to be more at home in the *Odyssey* and *Kalevala* than in the Talmud and *Zohar*. And though he consistently enlarged the vocabulary of Hebrew – some of his favourite areas were flora, fauna and the female anatomy – his idiom was far less flexible and resonant than Bialik's. The novelty of Tchernikhovsky's interests and the range of his cultural sources sometimes elicited extreme reactions. In retrospect, however, it is clear that he was neither the 'pagan' nor the 'Greek' that some of his critics made him out to be. It would be more accurate to say that Bialik and Tchernikhovsky provided Hebrew poetry with two basic models: the one intensely Jewish, steeped in the Yiddish and Hebrew lore of the East European milieu; the other more aware of European literature. In the works of later poets, each of these attitudes could be carried to extremes; but, on the whole, they complemented each other and contributed to the synthesis effected by Israeli poets.

Bialik's linguistic achievement is all the more remarkable when we remember that, unlike Pushkin, he did not have a nanny from whom he could learn the secrets of popular speech. Nor could he eavesdrop on the women at work in the kitchen, as did J. M. Synge, for the simple reason that the women in Odessa between 1890 and 1910 – when he was writing his greatest works – were not gossiping in Hebrew. He was, of course, aware of the challenge. In 1910 he wrote: 'I am now particularly taken by the folk genre. The Hebrew language has never experienced it, and there is something especially piquant about the situation: folk-songs in a language that is not spoken!'

But although Hebrew was not revived as a spoken language in Palestine until the end of the nineteenth century, it was not, as is commonly thought, 'dead'. It was, of course, the language of study and prayer, but prayer that was generally understood and not recited by rote. And it is important to remember that the prayer book is actually an anthology of the various layers of Hebrew. It was also the language of family observances and communal festivities, of legal and commercial documents, of historical chronicles, municipal records, tombstone inscriptions, and irreverent parodies of sacred texts; as well as the *lingua franca* of Jews from various countries.

Aharon Megged, the Israeli novelist, has admirably summed this up:

The revival of the Hebrew language is not like Lazarus arising miraculously from the dead. It is more like the Sleeping Beauty awakened by the Prince. She was not dead, she had only been dormant for a long time; and she was not rotten bones but a real beauty. Now when you betroth her and bring her into your house, your problem is how to make this noble, aristocratic princess, adorned with jewels and clad in purple, do all the domestic work, soil her hands, break her back cooking, washing and tending the garden in the back yard. Contrary to Eliza Doolittle of *Pygmalion*, she is quite all right at fancy parties, but she misbehaves in the market place . . .[1]

The 'market place' was Palestine. There Hebrew poetry faced one of its harshest trials: the need to adjust to a new geography, to a Mediterranean texture of light and seasons and sounds. The fact that this landscape was also 'familiar', that these hills and rivers had been sung before by poets who inhabited them in real life or in the life of the imagination, was both an advantage and an impediment. The literary memory had to make way for fresh, immediate vision; the individual memory had to contend with a new biography. Though Hebrew poetry had returned home and would gradually begin to recall its older, forgotten strata, the initial stages of the return were far from idyllic.

Some poets frankly admitted failure: 'A blossoming winter contrived to entice me / but I dreamed of the deserts of snow,' wrote David Shimoni, who first came to Palestine in 1909. There were poets who took refuge in childhood memories, writing from behind closed shutters in Tel Aviv or Jerusalem, just as the early painters in the bare Judean or Galilee hills continued to inhabit an imaginary, cloud-filled École de Paris. Others, and one can hardly blame them, latched on to the exotic, postcard aspects of the country: camel, desert and palm tree, snatching at mementos in the strange Oriental country, ransacking the Bible for glittering analogies.

Broadly speaking, it was the poets of the Palestinian period (1920–47), such as Karni, Greenberg, Lamdan, Shlonsky, S. Shalom and Alterman, who put the Sleeping Beauty to work in the fields. These were the poets who first introduced the rhythms of the spoken language into Hebrew poetry and brought it, somewhat belatedly, into the twentieth century. And as so often in the history of Hebrew poetry, the new surge of creativity was accompanied and catalysed by an influx of foreign influences; in this case, Russian Futurism and Symbolism, and German Expressionism. This, however, is only a partial list of the imported schools. A glance at the biographies of the poets, even in this limited selection, will give the reader an inkling of the

1. In 'How Did the Bible Put It?', *Encounter*, January, 1971, pp. 39–40.

varied cultural backgrounds, both Jewish and European, that were vying with each other. The Palestinian phase witnessed an unusual compression of poetic techniques and ideologies, and an accelerated, almost abnormal, rate of development and change. Processes that in literatures with a normal 'family life' may extend over many decades were here telescoped within a short, turbulent period.

Hebrew poetry's encounter with its homeland often produced poems of an ecstatic, almost messianic tone, such as Abraham Shlonsky's 'Toil' (p. 534), which was written around 1927, and forms part of a sequence named after Mount Gilboa in the Valley of Jezreel:

Dress me, good mother, in a glorious robe of many colours, / and at dawn lead me to toil.

My land is wrapped in light as in a prayer-shawl. / The houses stand forth like phylacteries . . .

Here the lovely city says the morning prayer to its Creator. / And among the creators / is your son, Abraham, / a road-building bard of Israel.

And in the evening twilight, father will return from his travails / and, like a prayer, will whisper joyfully: / 'My dear son Abraham, / skin, sinews and bones, / Hallelujah! . . .'

Shlonsky (1900-1973) was one of the leading modernists of his time: iconoclastic, aggressively secular, the *enfant terrible* who spearheaded the revolt against Bialik's 'classicism'. He translated the poems of Yesenin, Mayakovsky and Blok; he shocked the traditionalists by making 'Maimonides stare at a portrait of Bakunin'. Yet even he, when he came to celebrate his pioneering days, found himself drawn to sacred imagery. He appropriated the landscape by compounding biblical allusions with spoken rhythms and neologisms. He dressed himself in Joseph's coat of many colours – a very festive outfit for a day's work at tarring roads. And he summoned up a familiar scene from the traditional Jewish home: the blessing that the father bestows upon his children when he returns from the synagogue on the eve of the Sabbath. He does not see himself as an ordinary poet but rather as a 'road-building *paytan*' of Israel. Defiance and piety, innovation and tradition are played off against each other throughout the poem.

The trials of the pioneer, the spiritual and physical possession of the land (the landscape became one of the main protagonists of Hebrew verse and prose), the zeal of the return – these were prominent themes of the

Palestinian period. But the fervour was also counterpoised by a starker account of the realities of everyday life. Lea Goldberg (1911–70) shows us the darker side of the picture in her poem 'Tel Aviv 1935' (p. 553) – the year she emigrated to Palestine:

The masts on the housetops then, / were like the masts of Columbus' ships, / and every raven that perched on their tips / announced a different shore.

And the kit-bags of the travellers walked down the streets / and the language of an alien land / was plunged into the *ḥamsin*-days / like the blade of a cold knife . . .

Like pictures turning black inside a camera / they all turned inside out: pure winter nights, / rainy summer nights of overseas, / and shadowy mornings of great cities.

And the sound of steps behind your back drummed / marching songs of foreign troops, / and – so it seemed – if you but turn your head, there's / your town's church floating in the sea.

This is a far cry from Shlonsky's pioneering ecstasy. It is a violent poem: the earth heaves like a sea; disembodied kit-bags walk on the street; alien languages – those the poet hears and, presumably, those she carries within herself – slash at the parched eastern day; and the entire country is like the obscure interior of a camera, reversing all it sees and hears, turning white into black. In fact, the operative principle of the poem is the reversal of memory and of physical objects. The terror of the last stanza is heightened when one recalls the old Hebrew legend that at the end of days all the synagogues of the world will converge on the Land of Israel. This, too, is reversed: it is not the synagogue, but the town church that will float into view, the moment one dares look back. And for Lea Goldberg, the translator of Petrarch and Dante, the Church represented not only pogrom and persecution; it was also the repository of precious art and music.

By now there are several generations of Israeli poets who have not 'known the pain of hovering between two homelands' – a phrase taken from a poem by Lea Goldberg. Their perception of the desert was not impeded by the memory of soft European mists. They were born in, and into, Hebrew. They took much for granted and, for a time, revelled in their sense of primacy. It is doubtful whether any of them (and they are now in their forties or fifties) would write a hymn to the Hebrew language, as did Ḥayim Lensky from his prison in Leningrad, or Nathan Alterman from his sidewalk café in Tel Aviv.

The language is their birthright; it was not, consciously or unwittingly, competing with foreign models; it was not compensating or over-compensating for something lost or surrendered; it was not struggling to liberate itself from the gravitational pull of a many-layered tradition. The motto of the Israeli period, in the years following the War of Liberation of 1948, could have been a line from a poem by Ayin Hillel: 'I hate rhetoric (*melitsot*) as the forest hates the picnickers'; or a line from Yehuda Amichai: 'I, who use only a small part / of the words in the dictionary . . .'

The entire modern period could be studied in terms of the relationship of spoken Hebrew to written poetry. The rate of change, until some twenty years ago, was both exhilarating and unnerving. Shlonsky, the brilliant innovator, whose coinages fill an entire dictionary, had outrageously compared Bialik in the thirties to a huge bus, blocking a one-way street. But Shlonsky himself turned into a double-decker in his lifetime. Some of the younger poets and critics rediscovered other modernists, such as Avraham Ben Yitshak and David Vogel, who had developed a personal poetic idiom, having little to do with the Bialik tradition or with Shlonsky's rhetorical modernism. And the picture was further complicated in the fifties, when the younger poets turned to Anglo-American models.

This created a fairly distinct cleavage between the poetry – and, one might add, the criticism – of the modernizers and of their at first loyal, and then rebellious, progeny.

However, even the rebellious progeny soon discovered that fluency, immediacy and localism, though salutary and refreshing, could not substitute for historical depth; that the poetry would be impoverished if it did not regain its awareness of Jewish history and of Hebrew literature; and that, as Eliot pointed out, 'tradition cannot be inherited and if you want it, you must obtain it by great labour'.

Here again, one of the many wheels of Hebrew poetry came full circle: whereas the older writers attempted to free the language of involuntary associations, to silence – or, at the very least, to control – the background music of an obtrusive tradition, the younger writers in Israel have had to make a deliberate effort to repossess much that their forerunners had tried to repress.

Whether the poet wills it or not, there is often an element of counterpoint in Hebrew poetry. However colloquial the rhythms and even the diction, it is heard by the alert reader against the background of biblical poetry and of an uninterrupted poetic tradition. And some of the finest effects of modern

Hebrew poetry still result from the tension between everyday speech and the undertones and overtones of a shared heritage.

Here, for example, is the opening stanza of a poem by Yehuda Amichai, entitled 'A Sort of Apocalypse':

The man under his fig tree telephoned the man under his vine: / 'Tonight they will surely come. / Armour the leaves, / Lock up the tree, / Call home the dead and be prepared.'

The introduction of the anachronistic telephone into the body of a famous biblical idiom for peace and peace of mind – 'They shall sit every man under his vine and under his fig tree and none shall make them afraid' – is enough to jolt any Hebrew reader. But something is also happening on the physical, visual level. The peace-loving vine and fig tree shed their symbolic roles and are transformed into routine accessories of field camouflage.

Shlonsky, in his celebration of the road-building pioneers, heightened the meaning of the prosaic, investing it with religious significance. Amichai is dragging the familiar rhetoric down to earth. But in both cases, the underground waters of a great body of literature, having its source in the Bible, find their way into the channels that are being cut open by the spoken language.

Amichai's lines are representative of the individualistic, anti-dogmatic, anti-ideological tone of many of the younger poets. In some cases, this becomes a desperate attempt to step out of history. The individualization of Israeli society over the past twenty-five years has often led writers to rebel against the sentiment of collectivity, of being an exposed nerve within a very nervous system. And, needless to say, one often finds both impulses, pulling in opposite directions, within one and the same writer.

But it is still very much a case of conscious acceptance of, or resistance to, a shared history and a common heritage, even though the younger writers have rejected the eastern European view of literature as an agent of the national revival, a sort of audio-visual aid to communal morale.

A poem such as Amir Gilboa's 'Isaac', entirely modern in tone and technique, may serve as a final illustration of the way in which Hebrew, at a given moment, can draw on a wide range of linguistic and historical associations. The fact that this can be done with relative ease, that the memory cells of

Hebrew are constantly on the alert and react to the faintest impulses, imposes a responsibility upon the poet to exercise tact and restraint.

At dawn, the sun strolled in the forest / together with me and father / and my right hand was in his left.

Like lightning a knife flashed among the trees. / And I am so afraid of my eyes' terror, faced by blood on the leaves.

Father, father, quickly save Isaac / so that no one will be missing at the midday meal.

It is I who am being slaughtered, my son, / and already my blood is on the leaves. / And father's voice was smothered and his face was pale.

And I wanted to scream, writhing not to believe, / and tearing open my eyes. / And I woke up.

And my right hand was drained of blood.

The title of the poem alerts the reader to the biblical story, with which he is familiar from childhood. He is prepared to encounter overt or veiled references to the biblical narrative, but the opening stanza frustrates these expectations. A child-like voice tells of an idyllic stroll, together with the sun, through the forest. This scene is superimposed on the familiar biblical tableau. The innocence of the stroll seems to parallel the naiveté of Isaac's question in Genesis: 'Here are the fire and the wood, but where is the sheep for the holocaust?' And a fleeting allusion to the Song of Songs, like the sound of a distant pipe ('His left hand is under my head and his right arm embraces me') strengthens both the idyllic strain and the expectancy of dread.

The second stanza suddenly thrusts the poem back into focus. Two key words from the Isaac episode come out into the open: the 'knife' and the 'trees' (*etsim*). In Genesis 22, *etsim* means 'the wood [for the burnt offering]'; in the poem, as elsewhere in the Bible and in common usage, it refers to the 'trees' of the superimposed scene.

The opening line of the second stanza moves as swiftly as the flash it describes. It is fluent and literary and in marked contrast to the child's comment, which is intentionally awkward in Hebrew. Though the choice of words is not entirely colloquial, the syntax and rhythm are childlike and totally convincing. Such contrasts recur throughout the poem and give the literary usages an unquestioned tone of modernity and immediacy. *Abba*, here translated as 'father', is really the equivalent of the English 'daddy'; but *hatsila*, 'save', is a more stylized usage. These linguistic contrasts take place within an analogous juxtaposition of the traditional context and the intimate details of everyday life.

The intimacy of the child's voice, of *abba* and of the family reunion at lunch, is now grasped in its contemporary setting; it is a poem about the Holocaust, one of the dominant themes of modern Hebrew poetry. The father is both the legendary Patriarch, the Father of the tribe, and the poet's own father, who was murdered in the European forest.

In its language, images and events, the poem shuttles back and forth between the past and the present. The tableau and the real scene dissolve into each other. Personal biography, national memory – all become one in the childlike voice of the nightmare. The biblical motif ceases to be a 'subject', as it would have been even a generation before Gilboa. The identification is so total and, at the same time, so ambiguous, that it can hardly be paraphrased.

The simple, day-to-day history of Israel and of the Jewish people conspires to remind the Hebrew poet that he is a point in time, and that time has a way of exploding unexpectedly.

T. CARMI

NOTE ON MEDIEVAL HEBREW GENRES

THE following note is limited to an account of three of the major *piyut* genres: the *avoda*, the *kerova* and the *yotser*. Other genres which are represented in the anthology are discussed in the Introduction and Table of Poems.

I. THE AVODA

The *avoda* ('service'; pl. *avodot*) is a detailed description of the sacrificial service on the Day of Atonement in the Temple.

It begins with a brief review of the creation of the world, then sketches the history of humanity from Adam through the Patriarchs to the consecration of Aaron as High Priest. This serves as a transition to the second part: a vivid account of the priestly ritual in the Temple, mainly based on a tractate of the Mishnah entitled *Yoma* ('The Day'). Many of the *avodot* end with a rhapsodic picture of the High Priest – as he steps forth from the Sanctuary radiant and unharmed – modelled on Ben Sira's panegyric (p. 183). Yose ben Yose's unrhymed *avodot* (p. 87) established a pattern followed by *paytanim* for many centuries to come. I. Davidson's *Thesaurus of Mediaeval Hebrew Poetry* lists some forty different *avodot*, the last of which was composed (not for synagogal use) in the nineteenth century in Italy.

The *avoda* is the principal feature of the *Musaf* ('additional') prayers on the Day of Atonement.

2. THE KEROVA

The *kerova*[1] (pl. *kerovot*) is a sequence of poems related to, and inserted between, the benedictions of the *Amida* ('standing') prayer in the daily liturgy. The *Amida* (pl. *Amidot*) is the core of each of the prescribed daily services and was therefore also known as *Hatefila*, 'The Prayer' *par excellence*.

---

1. The origin of the name is uncertain. Some scholars maintain that it is derived from *karova*, the Aramaic designation of the reader who chanted the prayers.

There are various forms of *Amida* for different occasions and, accordingly, various forms of *kerova*. By far the most popular during the classical period was the *kedushta* (pl. *kedushta'ot*) which embellished the *Amidot* of Sabbaths and Holy Days. These *Amidot* enjoyed special prestige since their third benediction included the *Kedusha* (hence the name of the sequence, *kedushta*), the prayer of 'Sanctification', describing the exalted praise of God by the angels (as quoted in Isaiah 6.3 and Ezekiel 3.12).

The classical *kedushta* consists of three major sections which are demarcated by conventional devices and stereotyped liturgical formulas. They are subdivided into eight or more poems. Though the poems are intricately linked to the liturgy, to the readings from the Bible and the Prophets and to each other, they generally form independent, self-contained units.

The first section (poems 1–3) has a defined liturgical function: it corresponds to the first two benedictions of the *Amida* and to the beginning of the third benediction. The second section (poems 4–5) elaborates on the theme of the sequence. The third (poems 6–9) can be expanded at will by creating a chain of (often autonomous) poems: 7^1, 7^2, 7^3, etc. However, poem 8 is bound to introduce the *Kedusha*. Most *kedushta'ot* end at this point. Some of the *paytanim* added a ninth poem, which was inserted between the verses of the *Kedusha*, and was occasionally expanded into a small series: 9^1, 9^2, 9^3, etc.

As developed by Yannai (p. 87), the constituent poems of the *kedushta* adhere to the following pattern:

1. The *magen* ('shield'): three monorhymed quatrains, composing a partial alphabetic acrostic. The last line alludes to the first verse of the relevant portion from the Pentateuch and is then reinforced by several scriptural quotations related to the theme. A concluding stanza – a tercet or a quatrain – begins with the last word of the preceding quotation and closes with a reference to the first benediction, 'Shield of Abraham'.

2. The *meḥaye*: same structure; three quatrains complete the acrostic; they are linked by the second verse of the biblical portion to the concluding stanza, which leads into the second benediction, 'Who revives [*meḥaye*] the dead' (e.g. p. 218).

3. The *meshalesh* (from *shalosh*, 'three'): four couplets containing an acrostic of the author's name. The last couplet alludes to the first verse of the reading from the Prophets recited on this particular occasion and is again followed by several scriptural quotations.

4. This poem has no fixed pattern, though it is often made up of three quatrains. Its distinctive features are the concluding word 'Holy (One)' and the absence of any acrostic (e.g. p. 215).

5. Ten couplets with a partial alphabetic acrostic (e.g. pp. 219-20).

6. Eleven quatrains, complete alphabetic acrostic. The relevant biblical quotation precedes the poem and is sometimes designed as part of the opening line of each quatrain.

7. One to three poems, of varying length and form, in which the author displays his technical virtuosity by means of involved patterns of word-play, alliteration, acrostics and chain verse (e.g. p. 221).

8. The *siluk* ('conclusion') serves to introduce the *Kedusha* and is, therefore, the climactic point of the sequence. Varying in length and form, it is usually written in rhymed rhythmical prose (e.g. pp. 218-19). Its ecstatic account of the celestial domain is often reminiscent of *Hekhalot* hymns (pp. 195-201). The *siluk* always ends with 'As it is written: *And one called to another and said: Holy, holy, holy, is the Lord of Hosts*' (Isaiah 6.3).

9. The *Kedusha*, alternating rhythmical prose and alphabetic poetry (e.g. pp. 215-16). This central hymn, like other parts of the service, had not yet been standardized in Yannai's time and so he was able to compose a different version for each of his hundred and fifty *kerovot*.

Some of the classical *paytanim* after Yannai, and especially Eleazar ben Kallir (p. 89), modified the pattern of various components but did not alter the overall structure. In a typical Kallir *kedushta* the third poem is composed of monorhymed quatrains; the fourth is in cadenced, rhymed prose; the fifth is again composed of quatrains and includes an acrostic of the author's name; the sixth consists of rhymed tercets in some acrostic order, with a choral refrain after every third stanza, ending with the word 'holy' (e.g. pp. 221-3). Many of Kallir's innovations became standard practice in the composition of the *kedushta*.

The *kerova* disintegrated into its components after the classical period (see pp. 19-20) and was replaced by the *yotser* as the dominant genre of the late Eastern *piyut*.

3. THE YOTSER

The *yotser* (pl. *yotserot*) is a sequence of poems inserted in the 'Reading of the *Shema*' of the morning prayers. The 'Reading' consists of benedictions, liturgical verses, prayers and three extended passages from the Pentateuch. Its high point is the affirmation of the unity of God: 'Hear [*Shema*], O Israel, the Lord is our God, the Lord is One' (Deuteronomy 6.4). The sequence derives its name from the opening line of the first benediction before the *Shema*: 'Who creates [*yotser*] light and forms darkness'. In its expanded form, as a sequence for the Sabbath and Holy Days, the classical *yotser* consists of seven poems:

1. *Guf ha yotser* ('the body of the *yotser*') is the most important component of the sequence. It often celebrates the wonders of creation or hymns the specific festival or event (e.g. Amittai ben Shephatiah's '*Yotser* for a Bridegroom', p. 235), or takes its theme from the biblical portion. It is usually composed of rhymed tercets in alphabetic sequence, the last line of each stanza being a scriptural quotation. The acrostic is interrupted after every third tercet by a choral stanza (ending with the word 'holy'), which begins with the last word of the preceding tercet. The acrostic of the author's name is embedded in one or more of the choral stanzas. The final tercet or line alludes to the *Kedusha* which immediately follows the first poem.

2. The *ofan* ('wheel'; pl. *ofanim*) is the ecstatic angelological *piyut*, describing the heavenly host. It serves as a link between the first and the second verses of the *Kedusha*. Lacking a fixed pattern, it initiates a new alphabetic acrostic which may carry over to subsequent poems. (For various types of *ofanim*, see pp. 238-9, 243-4, 320-22 and 365-6; Judah Halevi's *ofan*, pp. 338-9, is in the Andalusian *muwashshah* form.)

3. The *me'ora* ('light'; pl. *me'orot*) precedes the closing formula of the first benediction before the *Shema* '. . . Creator of lights [*me'orot*]'. It generally interprets the 'light' symbolically as the light of the Torah, of Providence, or of the redemption of Zion (e.g. p. 364; for a *me'ora* in the *muwashshah* form, see pp. 420-21).

4. The *ahava* ('love'; pl. *ahavot*) introduces the second benediction before the *Shema*: 'Who has chosen His people with abounding love'. Like the preceding poem, it consists of four (or five) monorhymed verses which either continue an alphabetic acrostic or embody the author's name. The *me'orot* and *ahavot* are often the lyrical climaxes of *yotser* compositions (e.g. 'Resurrection', p. 254; for *ahavot* of the Spanish school, see p. 317 and 'To the Rivals', p. 335).

5. The *zulat* (pl. *zulatot*), the second most important component of the

sequence, is named after the conclusion of the prayer that follows the recitation of the *Shema*: '. . . there is no God besides [*zulat*] You'. Written in monorhymed quatrains, it begins a new alphabetic acrostic. The quatrains often end with scriptural quotations, taken in sequence from the appropriate reading from the Prophets. In the choral *zulat* (e.g. p. 233), each quatrain is followed by a couplet which introduces a second rhyme. (Other *zulat* patterns are found on pp. 255 and 377-9.)

6. The *mi kamokha*: a four-line stanza, containing an acrostic of the poet's name, which serves as a bridge between two liturgical verses from the Song of the Sea (Exodus 15.11 and 18): 'Who [*mi*] is like You [*kamokha*], O Lord, among the mighty?' and 'The Lord shall reign for ever and ever'.

7. The *ge'ula* ('redemption') is inserted before the final benediction of the *Shema* prayers: 'Who has redeemed [*ga'al*] Israel'. In the late Eastern period, this poem (then known as *adonai malkenu*, 'the Lord is our God') was 'doubled' by the addition of an eighth poem (e.g. p. 256) entitled *ve'ad matay* ('and how much longer'; the origin of the name is unknown).

The 'classical' pattern of the *yotser* was formulated during the late Eastern period. It was the preferred genre and many of the leading *paytanim* wrote monumental cycles of *yotserot* for each of the 54 pericopes of the annual Babylonian cycle. Towards the end of the period, apparently after the tenth century, the *yotser* decomposed as a result of the clash between the *piyut* and the standardized prayer. However, some of its components developed into separate and comprehensive *piyutim* in Spain and in Europe.

NOTE ON THE SYSTEMS OF HEBREW VERSIFICATION

by Benjamin Hrushovski

VERSE and rhyme, used in serious poetry as well as in a variety of other kinds of writing (e.g. grammars, historical chronicles, gravestone inscriptions and community annals), were an omnipresent feature of Hebrew culture in all periods and in all centres of the Jewish dispersion. Marked by strong tendencies of formalism and conservatism, the forms of Hebrew verse have nevertheless changed radically as Hebrew culture interacted with Greek rhetoric, Arabic secular literature, Italian Renaissance poetry, German eighteenth-century verse, Russian Romanticism and Futurism, Yiddish folklore, and English modernism. Almost all possible systems of rhythm and rhyme had been active in Hebrew literature in one period or another. Given a language with a stubborn core of vocabulary, morphology, spelling, imagery and basic mythology, the differences in formal systems were largely responsible for the great divergencies in the nature and poetics of Hebrew poetry in its major historical centres.

One must bear in mind that a Hebrew poet – in Rome, in Mainz, in Yemen, in Vilna, in Petersburg, in New York – was always placed at an intersection of at least three traditions: (a) the modes of Hebrew writing perpetuated in his own community; (b) the distinctly different poetic forms developed in his own language, Hebrew, in other cultural centres, either of his own time or in the past; (c) the poetic norms predominant in the language of the country in which he lived, the language which he read and spoke daily. A shift of orientation from one to another of these poetic systems was often responsible for the changes evolving in the forms or in the very nature of Hebrew verse.

Since in most periods the adherence to prevalent poetic norms was a rather strict one, it is possible to outline a number of major 'areas', or systems of genres and forms, which governed certain geographical and historical domains. The following simplified survey will present some typical features of the most important areas in the history of Hebrew poetic forms.

THE BIBLE

Biblical poetry, and perhaps biblical literature as a whole, provides a most flexible system of expressive form. The basic principle is parallelism. A poetic unit consists of two (or more) versets (or 'colas') displaying traits of equivalence in their rhythmical make-up (the number of stresses), their syntax and semantics, as well as in many additional features, such as syllable-numbers in parallel words, sound-repetition, and morphology. In most cases, however, there is neither a permanent nor a fixed parallelism of whole versets. Usually at least two or three kinds of parallelism will be applied, but we never know in advance which exactly, whether it will be complete or partial, word-for-word or verset-for-one-word, whether it will be based on synonymy, equivalence or opposition, in a direct or in a chiastic order. In any given pair of versets there is a mutual reinforcement of the overlapping patterns of parallelism – of meaning, syntax, and stress – all of which are based on the same unit: the major word, which alone carries the phrasal stress and the lexical meaning. Since each verset consists of a small and tightly compressed group of words (three or four), the effect is conspicuous and strong. (In translation these are not words but rather word groups, as in the English Bible.)

The system of this type of rhythm may be described as semantic-syntactic-accentual free parallelism. It is based on a cluster of shifting principles, the most prominent one being the semantic-rhetorical, the most obviously restricted one being the rhythmical. In later periods the rhythm of this poetry was taken to be basically accentual. Indeed, in biblical poetry the number of stresses per verset, though free, is clearly restricted – usually 2, 3, or 4, and quite often equal or similar in both versets of a pair (e.g. 3+2, the so-called 'dirge metre'). The number of syllables between these stresses, though perceived from the point of view of later and more rigorous metres as entirely free, was sometimes very much regulated as well: two adjacent stresses in one clause were precluded, and if a word was too long it had a secondary stress, thus providing usually 1 or 2 unstressed syllables between adjacent stresses. As a result, scholars have often perceived syllabic regularity in biblical versets. No systematic rhyme is to be found in the Bible, but there is a very pervasive usage of alliteration, sporadic end-rhyme, puns, acrostics and formulas, either embellishing or reinforcing the major principles of parallelism.

Here is an example of a poem of a rather ordered type:

וְתִשְׁמַע הָאָרֶץ אִמְרֵי־פִי.　　　　　　הַאֲזִינוּ הַשָּׁמַיִם וַאֲדַבֵּרָה

תִּזַּל כַּטַּל אִמְרָתִי,　　　　　　יַעֲרֹף כַּמָּטָר לִקְחִי

וְכִרְבִיבִים עֲלֵי־עֵשֶׂב.　　　　　　כִּשְׂעִירִים עֲלֵי־דֶשֶׁא

(1) Give ear, O ye heavens, and I will speak;
(2)　And hear, O earth, the words of my mouth.
(3) My doctrine shall drop as the rain,
(4)　My speech shall distil as the dew,
(5) As the small rain upon the tender herb,
(6)　And as the showers upon the grass.
　　　(Deuteronomy 32.1–4; the Authorized Version)

There are 3 + 3 stresses in each of the first two pairs of versets, and 2 + 2 stresses in the last pair (though here the first words are long and could have been pronounced as having a secondary stress, making the lines equivalent to the previous ones). The first two versets are almost entirely parallel. But the words הַאֲזִינוּ ('give ear') and וְתִשְׁמַע (literally 'and she will hear') are synonymous in meaning and not in morphology. 'I will speak' and 'the words of my mouth' are neither synonymous nor syntactically equivalent, but their meanings are parallel. The last pair is not an independent sentence, but each of its versets is parallel to the second word of the previous pair and is governed by the previous verb. There is variation in the equivalent words: 'heavens' and 'earth' are parallel by opposition; 'rain' and 'dew' both express fruition by water, but one is strong and the other subtle, rather like two poles of one scale. There is also a concatenation of the three pairs: versets 3 and 4 unfold the theme of the first pair (the unnamed object of the verb in 1 becomes the subject of phrases 3 and 4); versets 5 and 6 parallel the second word in 3 and 4. This almost perfect parallelism (changing in the following parts of the same poem) is variegated here too; thus the connotations of the words referring to water in the last four versets are chiastically ordered: the water is strong (3) – weak (4) – weak (5) – strong (6).

Many poetic texts in the Bible are, however, less symmetrical. The same principles are applied, though with greater freedom and flexibility, as one may observe in the opening of Isaiah 1 (p. 156). There is usually a greater variety in the number of versets in a group, as well as a second level of organization in which several groups of versets are combined in one long sentence. Symmetry, predominant in the previous example, is amply used by the prophets, but is usually engulfed in the wider flow of the argument. Thus, the formulaic opening of Isaiah 1.2, which is rather close to our previous example:

שִׁמְעוּ שָׁמַיִם	וְהַאֲזִינִי אֶרֶץ	כִּי יהוה דִּבֵּר
Hear, O heavens	and give ear, O earth:	for the Lord hath spoken

consists not of two but of three parts, the first two paralleling each other rigorously and the third remaining 'free', with the resultant structure *aab*. A thorough analysis of the whole passage will show a complex network of equivalence relationships in which every word participates in one way or another, and which is reinforced by the pervading imagery and prophetic tone.

THE POST-BIBLICAL PERIOD

During the first centuries after the close of the Bible, various rhythmical forms were developed, with no single established rigorous system. Parallelism of phrases, reinforced by rhetorical figures, is discernible everywhere. It seems, however, that several kinds of more regular rhythms evolved during that period. The basic tendency was to regularize the biblical accentual tradition, primarily into a 4-stress pattern. There were, however, three distinctly different interpretations of this basic rhythm:

(a) A permanent number of words per verset, e.g. four words as in some of the *Hekhalot* hymns (see pp. 195–6) and in a number of short Talmudic epigrams or poetic passages (e.g. גֹּזֵע יְשִׁישִׁים, p. 192); or three words as in the *akeda* אֵיתָן לִמֵּד דַּעַת (p. 201).

(b) A regular number of major stresses, whereby one stress often subordinated two words. Thus the *avoda* by Yose ben Yose (p. 209) lends itself to a reading in a regular pattern, as accepted by most scholars, of 4 + 4 (or 2 + 2/2 + 2) major stresses:

אַזְכִּיר גְּבוּרוֹת אֱלוֹהַּ / נֶאְדָּרִי בַּכֹּחַ // יָחִיד וְאֵין עוֹד, / אֶפֶס וְאֵין שֵׁנִי.

The rules for imposing one stress on two words are rhythmical rather than syntactic. The length of the poem and the very possibility of reading it in this manner support such a reading.

(c) A 4-stress pattern is imposed on the line, though there are often less than four words, the long words getting two stresses each. This system is clearly opposed to the one mentioned in type (b). It creates a kind of alternating metre, which can be seen while a modern metrical scheme is applied, e.g. (p. 192):

בָּאֲרָזִים נָפְלָה שַׁלְהֶבֶת –
מַה יַּעֲשׂוּ אֲזוֹבֵי־הַקִּיר ?
לִוְיָתָן בְּחַכָּה הוֹעֲלָה –
מַה יַּעֲשׂוּ דְּגֵי־הָרָקָק ?

By imposing two stresses on 3-syllabic words as in modern poetry (and disregarding some half-syllables) we get something similar to a modern 4-trochee line. Applying similar principles (the details of which cannot be given here) we find that this metre is predominant throughout the writings of Ben Sira. It creates a regularity in the number of syllables not unlike the one found in Syriac poetry. It was, however, by no means a rigid syllabic order in the sense of latter-day systems.

THE PIYUT

In Palestine under Byzantine rule, somewhere between the second and the sixth century, an entirely new kind of formal poetry developed, named *piyut*, which served for liturgical purposes. In this tradition, highly formalized poetic cycles (*kerovot, yotserot*) were composed for the Sabbaths and holidays. Basically these were complex cycles of strophic poems with rigid norms for a variety of formal devices assigned separately to each part of the cycle. Most of the poems were stringed on an acrostic of the 22 letters of the Hebrew alphabet (sometimes incomplete or containing the name of the poet).

The major forms developed in this poetry were: a strictly observed strophic structure, a permanent rhythm based on a fixed number of words in each line, and obligatory rhyme. At first rhyme was everywhere and of all kinds – at the beginning of lines, at the end of lines, or throughout a line (like English and Germanic alliteration), rhyme based on repetition of either morphological endings or of words of the same root, or of semantic properties (e.g. all lines ending with names of rivers; or pairs of oppositions, see, for example, some of the rhymes in Yannai's כלו עיניו, p. 215: [Loving One – enemy] אוֹהֵב – אוֹיֵב, [is loved – hated] אָהוּב – שָׂנוּי [from within – from without] מִבַּיִת – מִחוּץ, [below – above] בְּמַטָּה – בְּמַעְלָה), or of a whole word recurring in all lines of a strophe or a poem. The basic and predominant innovation, however, was end-rhyme based on sound parallelism. It was a highly complex rhyme involving most of the sounds of the rhyming words. There were two complementary requirements: (1) in each rhyming word two out of the three consonants of the Hebrew root had to participate in the rhyme (with the sounds between them varying); (2) the last syllable of each rhyming word had to be identical as well. Each rhyme was repeated at the end of all the lines of a strophe, i.e. 4, 5, 8 or 9 times. For example, SHiRaTI – kaSHaRTI – SHoRaRTI – SHeRiRuTI; in this case SH and R are the rhyming root consonants, and TI the rhyming last syllable.

This rhyme, based on a discontinuous group of sounds yet including the entire last syllable, may be called 'discontinuous-terminal'.

Thus a metre based on the number of words created a rhyming system based on the sound patterns covering the whole word. Such a system, of course, was very demanding for the poet and it was only made possible due to the highly 'difficult' style of the poetry of Eleazar ben Kallir (? sixth century) and his followers (especially in Italy in the tenth century) based on almost unlimited word innovations, allusions, and ellipses. With the transition to a simpler style the difficult requirements of rhyme had to be dropped and only the last syllable repeated in all lines of a strophe remained as an absolute norm of Hebrew medieval rhyme. This process was complete by the eleventh century.

The rhyming system of the Hebrew *piyut* was the earliest known massive, systematic and obligatory use of rhyme in poetry, and it is very plausible that through the Christian Syriac church employing Aramaic (a cognate language to Hebrew), and via Latin liturgy, the principle of rhyme was transferred to European poetry.

The basic forms of the Palestinian *piyut* were carried through Italy to the whole of medieval central and eastern Europe (Ashkenaz), where they dominated the creation of liturgical poetry until modern times (notably in the genre of the *seliha* – 'supplication', which favoured 5-word lines in 4-line strophes, rhyming *aaaa bbbb cccc*). In medieval Spain such strophic *piyutim* were also written, supplemented however by religious poetry employing the new metrical system.

HEBREW QUANTITATIVE POETRY IN SPAIN

The Hebrew poetry that flourished in Spain from the tenth to the fifteenth century was based on the Arabic system of poetics adapted to the Hebrew language. In secular poetry the metre was quantitative, i.e. there was a pattern of long and short syllables throughout a line repeated in all the lines of a poem (similar to the system used in classical Greek poetry). Under Arabic influence the Hebrew language here emphasized a difference between 'short' vowels (*shva*, *ḥataf*, and the conjunction *u*) and the regular vowels, considered as 'long'. This distinction disregarded the stress which was the major rhythmical factor in biblical poetry. The typical secular poem was a long poem (*qasida*) consisting of a chain of lines, each composed of two metrically equivalent versets (the *delet*, 'door', and *soger*, 'lock'). Each poem had only one rhyme repeated throughout its dozens of lines as a string of beads (the metaphor used by the theoreticians; the Hebrew word for 'rhyme' means literally 'bead').

It should be noted that the schemes of such quantitative metres were of two types: the regular type, in which a short syllable alternates with a fixed number of long ones throughout the line except at the end of each *delet* and *soger*. For example, the most widespread metre was (from left to right)

$$\cup - - - \, / \, \cup - - - \, / \, \cup - - \, // \, \cup - - - \, / \, \cup - - - \, / \, \cup - -$$

and the alternating type, such as Judah Halevi's Zionide (p. 347) where two basic feet alternate:

$$- - \cup - \, / - \cup - \, / - - \cup - \, / - \cup - \, //$$
$$- - \cup - \, / - \cup - \, / - - \cup - \, / - -$$

There was also a kind of free metre, with an irregular order of short and long syllables, which was, however, fixed in a permanent scheme and repeated in all the lines of a poem, as in many of the girdle poems (see below).

The Hebrew poets also employed a metre of 'long' syllables, avoiding the short ones altogether (*mishkal hatenu'ot*). On the other hand they developed a syllabic metre, based on a regular number of syllables per line (6 or 8), which allowed the free use of short vowels but disregarded them as syllables.

At the same time, however, Hebrew poets in Spain favoured a new form that had developed in Spanish-Arabic poetry and was possibly based on Romance strophic songs. This was the so-called *muwashshaḥ* or girdle poem, comprising two kinds of strophes: (1) each basic strophe had its own rhyme (or rhyme pattern), but was alternated with (2) girdles, strophes of a separate form (and metre) repeating one rhyme (or rhyme pattern) throughout the whole poem (see p. 30). The last girdle usually employed colloquial Arabic or colloquial Romance, thus indicating the melody to be used for the poem.

The girdle poem combined the effects of the string which unified the whole poem in a refrain-like manner with the love for variation in rhyming typical of European poetry as well as of the earlier Hebrew *piyut*. Thus the poem by Ibn Ghiyyat (p. 317) rhymes in the following manner (capitals represent the permanent, girdle rhymes; lower case letters – the changing rhymes of the basic strophes): AA/BA cd/cd/cd AA/BA ef/ef/ef AA/BA.

ITALY AND OTHER COUNTRIES

Italy was located at the centre of the Jewish world of the Middle Ages. Influences from all directions, from all Hebrew centres, were exerted on the writings of Hebrew poets there, with Italian poetry as a major influence. Rhymed and strophic Hebrew poetry written in Byzantine southern Italy in the ninth century in the vein of the Palestinian *piyut* appeared far earlier than rhymed poetry in Latin or Italian. The tradition of the *piyut* was predominant here until the fourteenth century. When Immanuel of Rome set out to write sonnets, much in the fashion of his Italian contemporaries, he found a language for secular poetry only in the Hebrew verse of Spain. As a result he transferred from Spain not only the poetic language and imagery but the quantitative metrical system as well, writing perfect ('Italian') sonnets in quantitative ('Arabic') metres. Sonnets, *ottava rima*, *terza rima*, and other Italian strophic forms combined with the language and metre of Arabic Spain for several centuries.

Little by little Hebrew poetry in Italy lost its requirement for quantitative metre and became purely syllabic, much as Italian poetry was. In this case, however, unlike the Hebrew syllabic metre of Spain, all short vowels were counted as syllables. In fact, though the number of words with feminine endings is very small in Hebrew, these became the predominant rhyming form, activating rather artificial and archaic words in rhyming positions, all under the influence of Italian poetry. This syllabic system was adopted by the new movement of secular poetry known as the *Haskalah* (Enlightenment) which developed in Germany in the late eighteenth century and moved to Austria and Russia in the nineteenth century and which laid the foundations of modern Hebrew literature.

Elsewhere, in the Byzantine Empire and after it in the Balkans, the Turkish Empire, northern Africa and other countries, Hebrew poetry showed strong influences on the one hand of the Spanish centre and on the other of the traditional *piyut*, one based on a rigorous syllable counting and the other, on the contrary, on a fixed number of words per line. There were also influences of Turkish strophic forms, especially in songs. Rhyme was obligatory throughout, with very few exceptions.

ACCENTUAL-SYLLABIC METRES IN THE MODERN PERIOD

While accentual syllabic (or tonic-syllabic) metre has dominated European poetry for several centuries now, it was accepted only recently, in about 1890, as the main form for Hebrew poetry. The first major poet consistently to use this metrical system, strongly influenced by Russian versification, was Bialik. In Hebrew, as in English, German and Russian poetry, it is based on a regular pattern of stressed and unstressed syllables. The Hebrew language, however, unlike English, has a vast number of long words of three or more syllables each. Thus rhythmical variation is achieved by skipping some of the metrical stresses rather than by stressing weak positions. For example, Iago's opening words in Act 1, Scene 2 of Shakespeare's *Othello* are, in English:

> Though in the trade of war I have slain men,
> Yet do I hold it very stuff o' the conscience
> to do no contriv'd murder: I lack iniquity . . .

and in Alterman's Hebrew translation:

> אָמְנָם בַּעֲבוֹדַת־הַמִּלְחָמָה
> שָׁפַכְתִּי דְּמֵי־אָדָם, אַךְ לְבָבִי
> סוֹלֵד מֵרֶצַח־בְּמֵזִיד. אֲהָהּ...

Iambic pentameter is used in both versions but the rhythm is quite different. The following diagram divides the actual graphic words of each language by bars and uses a dash for each possible stress:

English

```
| – | ∪ | ∪ | – | ∪ | – | – | – | – | – |
| – | – | – | – | – | –  ∪ | – | ∪ | –  ∪ |
| ∪ | – | – | ∪  – | –  ∪ | ∪ | – | ∪  –  ∪  ∪ |
```

Hebrew (from left to right)

```
| ∪  – | ∪  ∪  ∪  – | ∪  ∪  ∪  – |
| ∪  –  ∪ | – | ∪  – | ∪ | ∪  ∪  – |
| ∪  – | ∪  –  ∪ | ∪  ∪  – | ∪  – |
```

Clearly, whereas the first line in English has ten words, in Hebrew it has only three, and whereas in English it is possible to stress seven of these, in Hebrew only three stresses are allowed. Such an irregular line as the third in Shakespeare's original is not permitted in Hebrew metrical verse which complies with the rules of the very rigorous Russian tradition. Its great variety is achieved by skipping stresses in various places and changing the divisions between words from line to line.

The example given here is in the Israeli (or Sephardic) pronunciation now dominant in Israel. The revival, however, of accentual-syllabic metres in Hebrew poetry, with Bialik and Tchernikhovsky in the last decade of the nineteenth century, was in a different dialect, that of the Ashkenazi pronunciation developed in medieval Europe. The basic rule of that pronunciation is that whenever possible stress should fall on the penultimate syllable. When the penultimate syllable is a half-syllable the stress recedes to the third from the end; only monosyllabic words are ultimately stressed. Thus Bialik's poem (p. 509) should be read as follows:

עִם דִּמְדּוּמֵי הַחַמָּה אֶל־הַחַלּוֹן נָא־גֹּשִׁי
וְעָלַי הִתְרַפָּקִי
לִפְתִי הֵיטֵב צַוָּארִי, שִׂימִי רֹאשֵׁךְ עַל רֹאשִׁי –
וְכֹה עִמִּי תִדְבָּקִי.

In the Israeli pronunciation the reading would be:

עִם דְּמֻדּוּמֵי הַחַמָּה אֶל־הַחַלּוֹן נָא־גֹּשִׁי
וְעָלַי הִתְרַפָּקִי,
לִפְתִי הֵיטֵב צַוָּארִי, שִׂימִי רֹאשֵׁךְ עַל־רֹאשִׁי —
וְלֹה עָמִי תִדְבָּקִי.

and the metre is destroyed.

The shift from the Ashkenazi to the Israeli pronunciation caused an ex-tremely painful crisis in Hebrew poetry, especially since the poetic values of Hebrew poetry in its modern phase were placed heavily on metre and sound in the best Russian tradition. Though for centuries European Jews had prayed and studied Hebrew from early childhood in one of several Ash-kenazi dialects, the pioneers in the Land of Israel since the beginning of the twentieth century have spoken Sephardic. In Hebrew poetry, however, the Sephardic (or 'Israeli') dialect became dominant only in the late 1920s. The stress on the last syllables of most words sounded harsh and 'masculine' to the poets of the previous generation, who preferred 'melodious' poetry with feminine rhymes. Indeed, it was to them a new language and they wrote rather artificial poems in the spoken dialect. Some poets tried to translate their own poetry from Hebrew into new Hebrew, involving themselves in a reshuffling of sound-meaning relationships that rarely succeeded.

MODES OF MODERNISM

The dangers of a mechanical and overpronounced metre in a language with a strong ultimate stress were met by breaking away from the rigours of sym-metry. The freeing of rhythm in Hebrew poetry took two major directions. Under Russian influence, a verse-form was developed, employing a metrical scheme with a large number of deviations, as if hovering between anapests and iambs. This poetry, influenced by the poetics of Akhmatova, Blok, Yesenin and Mayakovsky, relied heavily on sound effects and rich rhyming. Though the norm for Hebrew rhyme accepted one stressed syllable at the end of a line (as is common in English), poets in the Shlonsky tradition excelled in highly complex and very rich and innovatory rhymes based on a discontinuous set of sounds going from the end of a line far back into its middle. For example, Alterman uses rhymes such as:

KSuMÁ HI – KoS HaMÁIm; LeKH uSHMÁ – haHaSHMÁL; SiPuNÉKHA – kaSe PaNÉKHA.

Again Hebrew poetry, as in the *piyut* of Yannai and Kallir, moulded its rhymes not on the last syllable but on the whole word, based on the nature of the Hebrew word, which has only consonants as part of its lexical core and vowels belong merely to the morphological system. This rhyming principle, founded on the nature of the Hebrew language, created a tension between richness of sound on the one hand and discord on the other, in the best tradition of Mayakovsky and Pasternak. As the rhyming sounds are discontinuous, and require identity of the stressed vowels but not necessarily of the final sounds, it may be called 'discontinuous-accentual' rhyme.

A different trend was the free verse based on a paucity of rhymes and a stronger deviation from any metrical background, playing essentially on variation of phrases, long and short lines, and in general on local rhythmical effects or on the rhythms of prose. The first wave of this development appeared in the 1920s (notably with David Vogel) under the impact of German Expressionism. A second wave developed in the late 1950s and 1960s with the transition from a Russian-oriented metrical poetry to a poetry based on understatement and imagery, primarily under the influence of English modernism.

RHYME: A SURVEY

Rhyme was dominant in Hebrew poetry from the sixth to the twentieth century. In the eighteenth century, under European influence, unrhymed poetic drama and epic poetry appeared, and in the early twentieth century Tchernikhovsky's unrhymed idylls and some of Bialik's quasi-biblical unrhymed poems. In the second decade of this century, with the impact of Expressionism, the predilection for systematic rhyming in lyrical poetry disappeared. This trend has strengthened in the last generation.

Though often highly inventive under the constraints of rhyme, poets were never free to select the rhyming principles. In the rhymed *piyut* (and only in some genres) one could either repeat the same word throughout or find as many rhyming words as lines in a strophe (4, 5, 8 or 9), according to the requirements of the discontinuous-terminal rhyme of the 'difficult' Kallirian tradition (see p. 62).

At a later stage of the *piyut* the requirement for rhyming two root-consonants was dropped and only the last syllable remained mandatory in rhyme, including however the preceding consonant (*consonne d'appui*) but disregarding stress. E.g., kaROV-la'aROV, shéLEG-medaLÉG (though in other languages OV, EG is perfectly sufficient). This terminal rhyme became the obligatory Hebrew rhyme in Spain and elsewhere throughout the medieval period. As stress was disregarded in the metre, so it played no role in rhyme. Only in Italy did rhyme become stress-bound, involving all sounds from the stressed vowel onwards, with a distinction between feminine rhyme (shÉLEG-pÉLEG) and masculine rhyme (medalÉG-orÉG). This, basically, has remained the rhyme of modern Hebrew poetry in accentual-syllabic metres to this day.

In modernism, however, especially under Russian influence, a rich rhyme was developed, inexact in its final syllable, discontinuous in its set of sounds, covering the whole word again (as in the *piyut*) or even several words, but stress-bound, as the metre depends primarily on stress (as in Alterman's examples above).

The four major rhyming possibilities shown in the following diagram, moving clockwise, were employed in Hebrew poetry throughout its history.

	− continuous	+ continuous
− stress	1. discontinuous-terminal (*piyut*) aReMÁ – heḥRíMA – RuMÁ	2. terminal (Spain) shéLEG – medaLÉG
+ stress	4. discontinuous-accentual (Modernism) SHÉLEg – SHokÉLEt	3. terminal-accentual (modern age) shÉLEG – pÉLEG/medalÉG – orÉG

Similar radical changes occurred in rhyme-patterning. The *piyut* developed a very rigorous system of strophic structures. Each strophe, however, allowed for only one rhyme: *aaaa bbbb cccc*. In Spain the major tradition required one rhyme throughout the whole poem (of 10, 40 or 60 lines). Under the impact of Italian strophic poetry (with some Spanish precursors) alternation of several rhymes in one strophe was introduced: e.g. *abab; aba bcb cdc*. Reinforced by the Russian tradition of masculine-feminine alternation in rhyme, this has remained the predominant rhyme pattern.

SYNOPSIS

Thus Hebrew poetry turned full circle (see Table, p. 71). It started in the Bible (I) with a system of phrase parallelism based on several of the major components of the phrase: semantics, syntax, phrasal stress. In the *piyut* (II) a metre of a fixed number of words and a rhyme based on the sound pattern of the whole word was developed. In medieval Spain (III) the system went down to the lower unit of syllable, and rhyme was based on the last syllable only. Syllabic metre in Hebrew shifted from a quantitative principle (in Spain) to the number of syllables (in Italy, IV) to an accentual syllabic system (in modern poetry, V). Hence the system moved back (at an accelerated speed): at first to a poetry leaning strongly on the number of major stresses in the line (in Russian-influenced Hebrew modernism, VI) and a rhyme covering the whole sound structure of the rhyming words, then to an English-influenced free verse (VII) based on a changing balance of phrase groups. Of course, this schematic cycle is extremely abstract and simplified; the subordinated factors always played an additional and often important role. And in recent years a kaleidoscope of forms has existed concurrently, competing with and complementing each other.

The awareness which a Hebrew poet may have of the relativity of systems of versification and rhyming does not help him in choosing whatever he needs for his particular poem. Indeed biblical verse does seem 'free' from the point of view of the modern reader trained on strictly syllable-counting accentual-syllabic verse. It is, however, impossible to imitate, except for small passages or for specific stylistic purposes, as much as it is impossible for an English dramatist to write Shakespearean iambic pentameters. Each system has evolved major verse forms with very typical combinations of syn-

The Major Systems of Hebrew Verse (in their logical and chronological order)

Length of Line / Basis of Metre	Free — Phrase	Fixed — Word	Fixed — Syllable
ANTIQUITY AND MEDIEVAL (From phrase to syllable)	I. *Bible*: free accentual metre — varying semantic–syntactic–rhythmic parallelism in phrase groups; *Rhyme*: sporadic	II. *Rhymed Piyut*: word-metre — number of words; rich, discontinuous, based on whole word	III. *Spain*: quantitative metre — number of syllables + order of long/short; based on last syllable
			IV. *Late Italy & Haskalah*: syllabic metre — number of syllables; *Rhyme*: stress-bound
			V. *Modern*: accentual-syllabic metre — number of syllables + order of stressed/unstressed; stress-bound
MODERN AGE (From syllable to phrase)	VII. *Modernist*: Free Verse — changing balance of phrase groups; *Rhyme*: not obligatory	VI. *Modernist*: accentual 'net' (in the Russian tradition) — number of major stresses + deviating from syllabic order; rich, discontinuous, based on whole word	

tactic and semantic, as well as rhythmical features. This combination, once automatized, has as it were 'exhausted' the possibilities of the system. Like their European and American contemporaries, Hebrew poets today either write basically free poetry, leaning heavily on the rhythmical formation of each line and passage, or are in search of a renewed form which would not sound epigonic on one hand and, at the same time, would be able to encompass the rhythms of the new spoken language.

NOTE ON THE TEXT

T HE phonetic transcription in this volume is generally based on the current Israeli pronunciation, which has been characterized by Haim Blanc as 'native, Europeanized, moderately formal, and non puristic'.[1] No attempt has been made to formulate an accurate, 'scientific' transcription, if only because the selection represents a very wide range of Hebrew pronunciations, current in different geographical areas at different periods.

The symbol *ḥ* has been used to designate the sound of the Hebrew letter ח ; *kh* has been used to represent כ . In current Israeli pronunciation both letters approximate the sound of Scottish lo*ch*, Spanish *j*unta. No distinction has been made between א and ע . The combination *ts* corresponds to the letter צ . Thus the name of the sixteenth-century poet צרפתי is transcribed *Tsarfati* (in the *Encyclopaedia Judaica – Żarfati*), even though the צ was then pronounced as an aspirated *s*.

'The vowel symbols (vowels in Hebrew are indicated by vowel points written below, above, or next to the letter . . .) and their approximate English equivalents are as follows:

a	f*a*ther
e	b*e*t
i	mach*i*ne
o	sh*o*re
u	s*ou*p'

'The diphthongs are formed by adding the sound of *y* to each of the foregoing vowel sounds. Thus, with English equivalents:

ay	m*y*, m*i*ne
ey	gr*ey*, n*ei*gh
oy	b*oy*

The diphthong *uy* is closer to that of the German *pfui* or that of the French

---

1. H. Blanc, 'How to Read the Phonetic Transcriptions of the Poems', in S. Burnshaw, T. Carmi and E. Spicehandler (eds.), *The Modern Hebrew Poem Itself*, Schocken Books, New York, 1966, pp. 191–5. With few exceptions, our transcription follows the principles outlined in the above essay, from which all the following quotations, and some of the examples, are taken.

73

fouille than to that of the English *hooey*. The diphthong *iy* is closer to the sound of the French *fille* than to that of the English *fee*.'

'When two vowels adjoin, they are pronounced separately, so that each is given its true value.' Thus *sheol* ('the underworld') is pronounced as *she* followed by *ol*.

The symbol ' (apostrophe) has often been used to indicate a 'catch' or slight pause between vowels or between a consonant and a vowel belonging to different syllables. Thus *amora'im* (Talmudic 'interpreters') is pronounced as *amora* followed by *im*.

'When two consonants adjoin, they are pronounced without any intervening vowel sound' (e.g. *zmora*, 'vine-twig').

Consistency has proved impossible. I have respected the conventional English spelling of certain Hebrew words, works and proper names (e.g. Shekinah, Mishnah, Yannai, Heber; instead of *Shekhina, Mishna, Yanay, Hever*), even when they deviate from the principles outlined above.

The spelling of post-biblical poetry has been modernized except for those cases in which the original form is dictated by metrical, or other, considerations. Some rules of biblical vocalization have not been consistently observed in post-biblical poetry. Many of the medieval poems originate in unvocalized manuscripts and the vocalization supplied by the various editors is, in some respects (e.g. pausal forms), a matter of choice.

All deletions are indicated in the Hebrew text by three dots enclosed in square brackets [. . .] and are usually noted in the Table of Poems.

No special mention has been made of the few instances in which I have incorporated conjectural readings (by the scholars who edited the texts) in the body of the Hebrew poems. Unfortunately, it has proved impracticable to include a full list of the many sources (though occasionally the information is provided under the relevant headings).

The translator's additions and glosses are enclosed in square brackets. Needless to say, the distinction between an 'addition' and a meaning that is implicit in the Hebrew and immediately grasped by the reader is not always clear-cut.

The division into verse paragraphs of non-strophic poetry has been made by the editor to clarify the poem's thematic development. Many of the long non-strophic poems, especially of the Spanish period, are composed of independent, loosely connected units (which are governed by the conventions of the specific genre). I have felt that the loss in fidelity would be offset by a gain in clarity for the English reader. For typographical reasons, the two hemistichs which compose a single line of verse in the *qasida* poems of the Spanish school have often been printed consecutively.

The italicized superscriptions were written either by the author or by an early compiler. This is usually apparent from the context or is explained in the Table of Poems.

Biblical references follow the numbering of chapter and verse in the authorized Hebrew text. Scriptural quotations that serve as structural devices in a poem (i.e. as a refrain, as a transitional link or as part of a pattern of scriptural insertions) are italicized in the English translation.

Some of the poems included in the 'Anonymous' sections contain an acrostic of the author's name (e.g., 'Rain Song' on p. 241 which yields YeHUDA). However, when nothing is known of the poet, except his name, it is customary to relegate him to the company of the 'Anonymous'.

Ben, bar and *ibn* mean 'son of'. *T.B.* refers to the Babylonian Talmud.

In the Table of Poems, all the poems are identified by their opening words in English and in Hebrew. In the body of the book, the Hebrew titles generally consist of the opening words, whereas the English titles are explanatory, with a view to setting the scene for the reader. In the modern section, the titles are those given by the authors, unless otherwise indicated by their inclusion in square brackets.

TABLE OF POEMS

THE BIBLE was composed and compiled over a period extending from the thirteenth to the second century B.C.E. The canon of the Hebrew Scriptures, completed around 100 C.E., is divided into three parts. The first, the Law (*Torah*), comprises the five books of Moses, the Pentateuch. The second, Prophets (*Nevi'im*), is subdivided into the Former Prophets, which chronicle Israel's history from the conquest of Canaan (*c* 1250 B.C.E.) to the destruction of the First Temple (587 B.C.E.); and the Latter Prophets, which include the great individual seers of the pre-exilic period, such as Amos, Isaiah, Micah, Jeremiah and Ezekiel. The third, Writings (*Ketuvim*), is a fairly random grouping of works, among them Psalms, Proverbs, Job, the five festival scrolls, and the apocalyptic book of Daniel (167–164 B.C.E.). The poetry of the Old Testament is rooted in the rich poetic literature of the ancient Near East: particularly Canaan (Ugaritic), Mesopotamia (Sumerian and Old Babylonian) and Egypt. The rhetorical forms and, to a certain degree, the content of Israelite poetry were derived from this milieu and adapted by Yahwism for its own purposes. The repertoire of literary types is extremely varied. G. Fohrer lists them under the following headings:

1. Songs of Everyday Life: vestiges of work songs, watchman's songs, drinking songs; elaborate taunt songs; love songs; war and victory songs; and personal or collective dirges. Early Israelite poetry was sung to the accompaniment of music and choral dancing.

2. Psalms: the two main literary types are the hymn (e.g. enthronement psalms, Zion songs, pilgrimage songs) and the communal or individual lament; there are also songs of thanksgiving, mainly of the individual, royal songs, and various forms belonging to the sphere of the priests and cult prophets. The psalms were chanted by the temple singers.

3. Wisdom Poetry and Didactic Poetry: these collections of sayings or single unified compositions, which embodied the views of the wisdom teachers, employ rhythmically structured proverbs, aphorisms, fables and allegories.

4. Prophetical Teaching: the prophets, whose messages were, for the most part, proclaimed orally, imitated many of the song types and often extended their use. They also introduced the prophetical dirge, which bewails a disaster to come, and developed distinctive rhetorical forms, such as the prophetical saying (oracles, threats and invectives; promises of divine intervention or salvation) and the prophetical report (of a vision, a call experience or a symbolic action). The various literary types of the Old Testament are often encountered in mixed form or are linked together to form a 'liturgy'. For example, the introduction of a lament may have hymnic character, or a thanksgiving song may often be formulated as a didactic poem. Some of the song types, such as the hymn, communal lament or royal song, were primarily composed for a specific cultic situation. However, religious or devotional

poetry written by individuals made its appearance very early and the distinction between cultic and non-cultic (or secular), or between communal and individual, is not always clear-cut.

The style of biblical poetry is characterized by a parallelism of line and thought and by the use of 'fixed pairs' of words set in parallel structure. The parallelism may be synonymous, antithetic, repetitive or synthetic (see Note on the Systems of Hebrew Versification, pp. 58 ff.). A verse can consist of one, two or three lines; the two-line verse, or bicolon, is the most common unit. Strophes, usually containing an equal or approximately equal number of verses, seem to have been common. Opinions concerning the character of Hebrew prosody are still divided. '. . . The correct pronunciation of ancient Hebrew, the syllabification of many words, and the quantity and accent of the syllables are uncertain' (S. Gevirtz). According to one major school of thought the metre is accentual: the verse is determined by the regular pattern of accented syllables; generally from one to three unaccented syllables fall between stresses. Some of the more common metric patterns are 3+2 (a bicolon with three stresses in the first colon and two in the second), 3+3 and 4+4. Other devices employed in biblical poetry include alliteration, vocalic and consonantal assonance, occasional rhymes, internal rhyme, key words and acrostics. The following examples of different types of biblical poetry are given in the sequence of the Hebrew canon:

'I shall sing to the Lord'   אָשִׁירָה לַיהוה   147

Exodus 15.1b–18. 'The Song of the Sea', which celebrates the crucial event in Israel's history, is a hymn, incorporating elements of the victory song and thanksgiving song. Its archaic diction and stylistic affinities with Canaanite poetry have led scholars to date it as early as the Mosaic period (thirteenth century B.C.E.); others, however, believe it to be of post-exilic origin. The dominant metre is 2+2 but there are occasional shifts to 3+3 and, in common with Ugaritic poetry, verses with an additional colon. The translation of the tenses and the division into strophes present serious difficulties. It is noteworthy that the Song omits any reference to Moses. Yahweh alone performed the miracle at the Sea of Reeds.

'For the warriors, in Israel'   בִּפְרֹעַ פְּרָעוֹת בְּיִשְׂרָאֵל   149

Judges 5.1–31. 'The Song of Deborah' (*c.* 1200 B.C.E.), noted for its dramatic vitality and rapid contrasts, is a religious victory song with a hymn-like beginning and conclusion, and motifs borrowed from taunt songs. It was composed soon after the battle it describes or it may have been sung while the campaign was still under way to muster the warriors. The archaic language and the 'impressionistic' technique – there is no attempt at logical, consecutive narration – often make the meaning and structure obscure. The verses are made up mainly of bicolons and tricolons, and the style is characterized by the urgency of repetitive, or 'climactic', parallelism. Scholars have pointed out the relationship of this song to nomadic war songs and to old Babylonian verse structure.

'All your glory, O Israel'   הַצְּבִי, יִשְׂרָאֵל   154

2 Samuel 1.19-27. 'David's Lament over Saul and Jonathan' (*c.* 1000 B.C.E.) is a deeply moving masterpiece of early Hebrew poetry. It is a personal dirge (*kina*), marked by the absence of religious character. There is no reason for doubting David's authorship. Though the text is partly corrupt, it is clear that 'How the heroes have fallen!' is the refrain of the lament, which was probably sung antiphonally. *Ekh* or *ekha*, 'Ah, how . . .', is the formulaic introduction to a dirge (see Isaiah's taunt dirge, p. 160, and Lamentations 4, p. 179). The measure is predominantly 2 + 2, and the lament employs a great many 'fixed pairs' or 'stock parallels' (e.g. 'do not tell'//'do not proclaim', 'blood'//'fat', 'swift'//'strong').

'Hear, O heavens, and listen, O earth'   שִׁמְעוּ, שָׁמַיִם   156

Isaiah 1.2-20 (second half of the eighth century B.C.E.). These verses are part of a collection of prophetic sayings which provide a cross-section of the prophet's message, and therefore have been placed at the beginning of the book (which actually comprises three independent groups of writings: Isaiah I, 1-39, Deutero-Isaiah, 40-55, and Trito-Isaiah, 56-66). Isaiah was probably of aristocratic origin and grew up in Jerusalem. His opening oracles consist of a 'prophetical judgement discourse' (lines 1-9), whose mode of speech is that of the law court. The invective (lines 10-39) was composed after the devastation of Judah by the Assyrian king Sennacherib (701 B.C.E.). The rejection of the cult as a means of salvation (lines 40-74) is a prophetical imitation of 'cultic torah', that is, instruction or advice given by a priest in questions involving cultic procedures. This section belongs to the first period of Isaiah's ministry (746/40-36 B.C.E.), in which he exposed the moral breakdown of Judah. The exhortation (lines 75-85) is another of the rhetorical forms employed by the great individual prophets.

'How the oppressor has met his end'   אֵיךְ שָׁבַת נֹגֵשׂ   160

Isaiah 14.4b-21. This is the finest example in the Bible of the mocking prophetical dirge – usually directed against a foreign power – which fuses the taunt song (*mashal*) with the funeral lament. The poem probably does not derive from Isaiah; it is part of a collection of anonymous oracles against foreign nations (Moab, Egypt, Edom) which date from the sixth or fifth century. The tyrant referred to in the superscription as 'the king of Babylon' cannot be identified with any certainty. The dirge draws heavily on mythological elements in its detailed account of the underworld (*sheol*), its mention of Canaanite deities (line 30) and its references to the mountainous abode of the gods. The metre is almost uniformly 3 + 2. The 'prophetic perfect' tenses express future events as though they had already come to pass.

'I thought: I shall depart'   אֲנִי אָמַרְתִּי : בִּדְמִי יָמַי   163

Isaiah 38.10-20. The so-called 'Psalm of Hezekiah' belongs to the category of individual songs of thanksgiving. Like 'The Song of the Sea' or Jonah's 'Thanksgiving
Song' it was already extant as a finished composition and was interpolated by the
compilers at a suitable place. It was probably added to the book of Isaiah during the
final stage of its composition (c. fifth century B.C.E.). The poor repair of the text,
especially in lines 9-27, has given rise to many conflicting interpretations.

'The Lord is my shepherd'   יהוה רֹעִי – לֹא אֶחְסָר   165

Psalm 23 (? post-exilic; sixth or fifth century B.C.E.), an individual song of confidence,
elaborates a motif that originally formed part of the introduction or body of a lament.
It is included in the 'Davidic Psalter' (Psalms 3-41), the largest original collection of
the five books into which the Psalter was divided, on the model of the Pentateuch.
The Psalter (*Tehilim*, 'hymns of praise') contains a varied selection of songs, including
wisdom poems, dating from several centuries. It assumed its final form in the fourth
century and served as the hymnal of the post-exilic Temple and synagogue. The
superscriptions are all secondary.

'As the deer longs for running waters'   כְּאַיָּל תַּעֲרֹג   166

Psalms 42-43 (? pre-exilic; eighth or seventh century B.C.E.) constitute a single song.
The division into strophes is clearly indicated by the regular repetition of the refrain
'Why are you so desolate . . .' This individual lament is part of the collection known
as the 'Elohistic Psalter', in which the divine name 'Yahweh' is regularly replaced by
the designation 'Elohim'. It has been suggested that this lament, 'unsurpassed in
tenderness and depth' (H. Gunkel), was written by a refugee, living in exile in
Northern Palestine (line 23). As in Psalm 23, the metre, with quite a few exceptions,
is 3+2.

'O my soul, bless the Lord'   בָּרְכִי, נַפְשִׁי   168

Psalm 104 (post-exilic) is a non-cultic devotional hymn, which derives many of its
metaphors from Babylonian and especially Canaanite mythology. It is typical of the
manner in which the Old Testament borrowed and demythologized pagan material.
Leviathan, here the plaything of God (line 58), is the primeval dragon Lotan who, in
Ugaritic literature, was the enemy of Ba'al. In the description of God's struggle with
the powers of chaos (lines 11-20), the 'abyss', *tehom*, recalls Tiamat of the Babylonian
Creation epic. It has been noted that this 'creation psalm' closely parallels the
Egyptian Hymn to the Sun of Amenhotep IV (fourteenth century). The metre, with
a few exceptions, is 3+3.

Job 28 (late post-exilic; fourth or third century B.C.E.), a wisdom poem with a characteristic refrain, was composed as an independent lyrical unit. It probably does not derive from the author of Job, who may have lived in Palestine in the fifth or fourth century. The personification or hypostatization of 'Wisdom' (*ḥokhma*), which seems to be rooted in a Gnostic myth, is also found in other Hebrew wisdom books, such as Proverbs 1–9 and Ecclesiasticus 24. The last verse 'was probably a later addition to bring to a practical conclusion this fine metaphysical flight' (E. P. Dhorme).

Song of Songs 5.2–6.3. The Song of Solomon (post-exilic; fifth or fourth century B.C.E.) comprises a collection of profane love songs and epithalamia composed in Palestine. Modern exegesis has rejected the many attempts to discover a coherent plot in the collection which would assign the various sections to a fixed cast of characters. The Song was probably taken into the canon as a result of the allegorical interpretation – still dominant in orthodox Judaism – which equates the 'lover' or 'bridegroom' with God, and the 'beloved' or 'Shulammite' with Israel. However '. . . in the second century A.D. the book still had to struggle for the recognition of its canonicity . . . according to Tosephta Sanhedrin 12, 10^2 . . . Rabbi Akiba (A.D. 137) cursed those who used to sing passages from the Song of Songs in the wine-shops – evidently still understanding it in its literal sense . . .' (O. Eissfeldt). The Song is used as the festival scroll for Passover. The first extract consists of a dream song (lines 1–31), a description of the lover's charms (lines 32–60) and a short dialogue.

Song of Songs 7.1–10. The Shulammite's dance is one of the many echoes in the Song of Syro-Palestinian marriage customs. On the eve of her wedding the bride performs a sword dance to the rhythm of a descriptive song (known in Arabic as the *waṣf*) that celebrates her beauty and her adornments. Then, during the 'royal week' following the wedding, the couple are fêted as king and queen. Close associations with ancient Egyptian love poetry have also been pointed out, especially in the presentation of the lovers or bridal pair in the disguises of 'shepherd', 'gardener', 'king' and 'queen'.

Song of Songs 8.5–7.

Lamentations 4 (c. 550 B.C.E.) is a collective dirge, bewailing the misery and destruction of Jerusalem after its capture by the Babylonians. Written (in Palestine ?) by an eye-witness, it is structured as an alphabetic song: the first word of each strophe (consisting of two bicolons) begins with the letter of the Hebrew alphabet in sequence.

This accounts for the relative looseness of the composition. Other alphabetic acrostics, of various types, which enable the author to display his skill and also serve as a mnemonic device, are found in Lamentations (1–3) and in Psalms (9–10, 25, 34, 111, 112). In Hebrew, the book is called by its initial word, *ekha*. Its dominant verse type is the '*kina* metre', 3+2, the 'rhythm that always dies away'. In fact, however, this metre is employed in a variety of poems having nothing to do with laments for the dead and, moreover, is not found in all funeral songs. Traditionally ascribed to Jeremiah, Lamentations is the festival scroll for the fast of the Ninth of Av, memorializing the destruction of Jerusalem.

SIMEON BEN SIRA or JESUS SIRACH (fl. late second century B.C.E.), a Jerusalemite scribe and scholar, was the author of a book of proverbial philosophy known since the fourth century as Ecclesiasticus. It is included in the Apocrypha. The original text had been lost, and the Wisdom of Ben Sira was preserved mainly through a Greek translation made by his grandson in Egypt. The first fragments of the Hebrew original were discovered in 1896 among manuscripts from the Cairo Genizah; within four years, two thirds of the Hebrew text was recovered. Additional fragments have turned up among the Dead Sea Scrolls and in the Masada excavations (1964). Though he probably spoke Mishnaic Hebrew, Ben Sira wrote his book in the idiom of biblical poetry, modelling himself on Psalms, Job, and especially the later sections of Proverbs. The following panegyric of the high priest, Simeon the Just, served as a paradigm for many later compositions commemorating the sacrificial service on the Day of Atonement in the Temple of Jerusalem.

'Chief among his brethren'   גְּדוֹל אֶחָיו   183

THE DEAD SEA SCROLLS (*c.* 170 B.C.E.–*c.* 68 C.E.) were first discovered in 1947 by a Bedouin shepherd in a cave at Qumran, on the north-western shore of the Dead Sea. Excavations in adjacent caves later yielded additional texts. These manuscripts, which include the most ancient fragments of the Hebrew Scriptures, are probably the remnants of an extensive library which the Essene Brotherhood left behind when its isolated settlement was destroyed by the Romans. The language of the Scrolls is based on biblical Hebrew, but shows the influence of the Hebrew and Aramaic spoken at the time. The poetic passages employ parallelism very loosely, often varying the length of the corresponding cola.

'. . . and they do not know the mystery to come'   וְלֹא יָדְעוּ רָז   186

Scholars have thus far been unable to elucidate this mysterious fragment. The 'birth-gates of evil' reappear, with slight variations, in the strange hymn describing the birth of the 'creatures of evil' (pp. 188–9).

This is the opening section of the sixteenth hymn of the *Hodayot* ('Thanksgiving Psalms'). These hymns imitate the style of the biblical Psalms, but their imagery is often over-elaborate and their vocabulary esoteric. The central religious experience of the *Hodayot*, which often have a personal tone, is the experience of election. The company of the elect, sequestered in the wilderness of Judea, is here represented by the tender 'Trees of Life', who are temporarily overshadowed by their thriving adversaries, the 'Well-Watered Trees'.

The birth of the Messiah, as described in the fifth hymn, will mark the onset of terrible pangs in the world's (or in Hell's) womb, culminating in the birth of the 'creatures of evil' and their final imprisonment. Like the preceding hymn, this one begins in the first person. But the incidental simile of the woman in labour is suddenly elaborated into an impersonal apocalyptic vision. J. Licht considers this to be 'undoubtedly the strangest and most difficult chapter of the Thanksgiving Scroll'.

THE TALMUD (completed *c.* 500 C.E.), a vast corpus of law, commentaries and legends, took shape in Palestine and Babylonia over a period of almost five centuries. It occasionally contains short poems: prayers designed for synagogal use, private devotions, elegies, and random snatches of popular verse. The personal prayers are often distinguished by great simplicity of diction and structure; the elegies, however, are highly stylized and because of their frequent use of epithets can sound like riddles. But both genres testify to a growing freedom from biblical models and to the evolution of new styles, under the impact of rabbinic Hebrew.

The *tanna* Abba Yose ben Ḥanin (second half of the first century) is said to have composed this complaint against the corruption and nepotism of the priestly ruling families.

Enumerates the woes which will precede the coming of the Messiah. Some scholars believe that this poem alludes to events that actually happened at the time of the Hadrianic persecutions, after Bar Kokhba's unsuccessful revolt (132–135).

A speech of condolence, improvised by the Palestinian *amora* Judah ben Naḥamani (third century) when he visited Hiyya bar Abba, whose child had died.

THE HEKHALOT HYMNS (*c.*third and fourth centuries) were composed by the *merkava* mystics in Palestine and later in Babylonia. The *hekhalot* ('palaces') are the seven heavenly halls through which the visionary aspires to pass; the *merkava* ('chariot') is the divine throne, situated in the inner recesses of the seventh heaven. Many of the hymns are addressed to the throne and to the divine glory seated upon it by 'the holy living creatures'; the mystic is instructed to recite them during his ecstatic ascent to heaven. The following sections are taken from the tract known as

The Greater Hekhalot, which describes – alternately in prose and verse – the angelic hosts in the 'Palaces of Silence', the celestial liturgy, and the techniques which enable the mystic to 'ascend' and 'descend' unharmed. The hymns have a characteristic rhythm and are often composed of double verses of 3 or 4 words to the line. They employ a consistent technical language, containing a great many bizarre words and phrases. In the opinion of G. Scholem, 'their immense solemnity of style is unsurpassed in Hebrew hymnology'.

'The beginning of praise'   תְּחִלַּת שֶׁבַח   195

Is prefaced by the following instruction: 'Rabbi Ishmael said: "Which song should a man chant when he is about to descend to the *merkava*? He should begin by reciting this one."' The expression 'to descend to the *merkava*' refers to the ecstatic *ascent* to heaven. No explanation has been found for this paradoxical expression.

'You who revoke decrees'   מְבַטְּלֵי גְזֵרָה   195

The 'living creatures' or 'heavenly beasts' (*hayot hakodesh*), who are the bearers of the throne in Ezekiel 1.5, are part of the angelic hierarchy at the celestial court. When they see that their King is angry at His children, they try to placate Him by invoking the memory of Abraham's devotion. They also 'hurl down their crowns, ungird their loins, beat their heads, fall on their faces and say, "forgive, forgive, O Holy One of Israel!"'

'Lovely face, majestic face'   פָּנִים נָאִים   196

Based on the belief that 'day by day ministering angels are created from the stream of fire. They sing a paean and then pass away . . .' They are stationed at their posts as the throne revolves, so that those on the left find themselves on the right, etc.

'Day after day, at the break of dawn'   בְּכָל יוֹם וָיוֹם   198

The celestial morning service. The last two lines refer to the belief that the angelic hosts are not permitted to sing in heaven before the congregation of Israel has begun to sing on earth.

'King of miracles, King of power'   מֶלֶךְ נִסִּים   198

Describes in rhythmical prose the throne's daily service to God. Zoharariel (line 19), who is also involved in the next passage, is one of the secret names of God in His splendour (*zohar*).

'A quality of holiness'   מִדָּה שֶׁל קְדֻשָּׁה   199

Celebrates the garment which God puts on when He descends to sit on His throne. From another hymn we learn that the stars and constellations were – and perhaps still are – created by the light that emanates from this cosmic robe.

'*King of Kings, God of Gods*'   מֶלֶךְ הַמְּלָכִים   200

Part of a long hymn which the throne addresses to God each day.

'*You who are crowned in grandeur*'   עֲטוּרֵי פְאָר   201

A recurrent theme of the *Hekhalot* is the danger facing the visionary of being consumed by fire as he ascends to the *merkava* sphere. Here, the mere mention of the
names of the 'holy creatures', who minister to the divine manifestation in the Holy of
Holies, calls forth the whirling flames. 'According to another fragment, the mystic
must be able to stand upright "without hands and feet", both having been burned'
(G. Scholem). Enoch, in one of the later *Hekhalot* manuscripts, was, more fortu-
nately, transformed into fire: '. . . forthwith my flesh was changed into flames, my
sinews into flaming fire, my bones into coals of burning juniper, my eye-lids into
sparks of lightnings, my eye-balls into firebrands, the hair of my head into hot flames,
all my limbs into wings of burning fire . . .' (translated by H. Odeberg).

ANONYMOUS (fourth century to the beginning of the seventh century). The *piyutim*
in this section originated in Palestine during the Byzantine rule. All of them, except
for the last one, are unrhymed and employ various forms of alphabetic acrostics. The
metre is largely based on word-count.

'*Abraham, the steadfast one*'   אֵיתָן לָמַד דַּעַת   201

This is the earliest known poem on the *akeda*, the binding of Isaac, which is one of
the favourite themes of medieval Hebrew poetry. The poem is remarkable for its unadorned language and its hammer-like rhythm, three words to a line. It follows the
narrative of Genesis 22, with occasional Midrashic allusions (e.g. the ten trials of
Abraham in stanza 2). The mention of the 'ashes' (stanza 7) recalls the Midrashic
statement that 'although Isaac did not die, Scripture regards him as though he had
died and his ashes lay piled on the altar'. Two later and more elaborate versions of the
akeda theme are printed on pp. 357 and 379.

'*I shall sing praises*'   אַבִּיעָה זְמִירוֹת   203

The opening section of a long poem on the advent of spring. Its simple, lyrical style
is typical of the pre-classical period of the *piyut*.

'*O You who know the times of the universe*'   זְמַנֵּי חָרוּץ   203

An excerpt from a prayer for rain, of which only a fragment has survived. Though
the language is simple, the exact meaning of certain expressions (e.g. 'the birthplace
of water') is uncertain.

'*How long will there be weeping*'   עַד אָנָה בְּכִיָה   204

The earliest known post-biblical dirge (*kina*) on the destruction of the Temple. It
includes many references to Lamentations. The refrain, here printed at the head of
the excerpts from the poem, is repeated after every two verses. The first eight signs
of the zodiac bewail the fate of Jerusalem, while the last four are practically accused
of betrayal. For some unknown reason, the author has changed the order of the signs
by placing Capricorn after Aquarius. This poem is traditionally recited on the eve of
the Ninth of Av.

'*What is frail man*'   אֱנוֹשׁ מַה יִּזְכֶּה   206

Takes many of its phrases from Job. Its style is rich in word-play and alliteration.

'*Now let us proclaim*'   וּנְתַנֶּה תֹּקֶף   207

This description of the heavenly court marks one of the most solemn moments in the
service for New Year and the Day of Atonement. According to a well-known legend,
the hymn was composed in the tenth century by Rabbi Amnon of Mainz, who,
having been mutilated by the Archbishop for refusing to convert, spoke its words as
he died in the synagogue on New Year's Day.

YOSE BEN YOSE (? fourth or fifth century) is the earliest Palestinian *paytan* known
by name. Practically nothing else is known of him; even his traditional epithet,
hayatom, 'the orphan', has not been clarified. He is best known for his masterful
avodot (see Note on Medieval Hebrew Genres, p. 51). It is presumed that he is the
author of many of the early, anonymous poems discovered in the Genizah. In contrast to the *paytanim* who follow him, his poetry is distinguished by its simplicity and
almost total lack of rhyme.

'*I shall proclaim the mighty deeds of God*'   אַזְכִּיר גְּבוּרוֹת אֱלוֹהַּ   209

(Excerpts.) The longest of Yose's three *avodot*. It consists of twenty-two ten-verse
stanzas (the last stanza has an additional eight verses), composing a tenfold alphabetic acrostic. The verses (here printed as two lines) are in the 'quadripartite rhythm',
previously encountered in Talmudic laments (p. 192). This is the most typical metre
of the pre-classical period. The rapid succession of verbs, the rich musical texture
and the asyndetic style enliven even the technicalities of the ritual. The prose passages
in the poem, including the high priest's confession, are taken verbatim from the
Mishnah.

YANNAI (? sixth century), the first *paytan* of the classical period, lived in Palestine
and was probably a cantor by profession. He was virtually unknown fifty years ago
when I. Davidson discovered several of his compositions among the Genizah manuscripts. Subsequently, the ingenious research of M. Zulay resulted in the publication

of over eight hundred poems, remarkable for their force, originality, and variety. One of the clues that led scholars to track Yannai down was a legend in a twelfth-century manuscript according to which he was the master of Eleazar ben Kallir (p. 89), 'but in all of Lombardy it [the only poem by Yannai preserved in the Ashkenazi ritual] is not recited, for it is said of Yannai that he grew jealous of his disciple Eleazar and planted a scorpion in his shoe that killed him'. However, the chronicler is careful to add: 'May God forgive all those who say this of Yannai – if it did not really happen.'

Yannai is the first *paytan* known to have employed rhyme, name-acrostics, and the complicated form of the *kerova* (especially the *kedushta*; see p. 52), which was to dominate liturgical poetry until the ninth century. The subject-matter of the *kedushta* is drawn from the biblical portion read on the particular Sabbath or feast-day for which the sequence was composed. Yannai's vocabulary is predominantly biblical, though he draws freely from the idiom of the Mishnah and the Midrash and excels in linguistic innovations. In many instances, his poems cannot be thoroughly understood without reference to their Midrashic sources. All of the following poems are taken from *kedushta* sequences:

'Our eyes are weak with longing'   כָּלוּ עֵינֵינוּ   215

Based on the story of the 'dulled-eyed' Leah who was unloved by Jacob, envied by her sister Rachel (Genesis 29.17ff.) and, according to the Midrash, hated even by sea-travellers and land-travellers for being deceitful.

'See how we stand before You'   רְאֵה עֲמִידָתֵנוּ   215
'Who are feared by faithful angels'   אֲשֶׁר אֵימָתָךְ   216

This well-known hymn, in double alphabetic acrostic, has been attributed to Yannai. It exhibits a brilliant use of elaborate phonetic patterns and structural devices.

'What have I gained?'   מַה יִּתְרוֹן לִי   218

When God reassured Abraham: 'Fear not . . . Your reward shall be very great' – Abraham countered: 'O Lord God, what can You give me, seeing that I continue childless . . .' (Genesis 15.1ff.). This monologue elaborates on the complaint of Abraham who, in anticipation, is already called 'the father'.

'From Heaven to the Heaven of Heavens'   מִשָּׁמַיִם לִשְׁמֵי הַשָּׁמַיִם   218

An unrhymed hymn in praise of God, whose mystery had been challenged by the builders of the Tower of Babel (Genesis 11). The hymn (whose conclusion has not been recovered) rises through the seven heavens, which are vaulted over the earth, and culminates in an agitated account of the metamorphoses of the angels when the moment comes for them to utter 'Holy, holy, holy!'

This is based on the episode of the burning bush in Exodus 3 and incorporates several Midrashic legends. Moses, tending a flock in the wilderness, is being tested as the future shepherd of his people. He and his sheep are miraculously transported (lines 3, 7) to the site of the burning bush on Mount Horeb-Sinai (line 9), where God fortifies him for his subsequent encounters with divine fire.

Enumerates the peculiar qualities of the celestial fire revealed to Moses in the unconsumed thorn-bush. This is the very same fire that, in years to come, would descend upon the altar in the Temple. The poem contained a complete alphabetic acrostic, but the manuscript is damaged in parts.

ELEAZAR BEN KALLIR or KILLIR (? sixth century), the outstanding representative of the classical *piyut*, probably lived in Palestine before the Arab conquest (635). Though his poems have figured prominently in printed rituals, and hundreds more have come to light in manuscript collections, his biography remains one of the great mysteries of Hebrew literary history. His radical innovations in the diction, style, and structure of the *piyut* had a great influence on the poets who succeeded him in Palestine and in other lands of the Near East and Europe. The 'Kallir style' involves a highly allusive use of language, packed with references to written and oral traditions. Accordingly, the *dramatis personae* of his poems, as well as various objects and place-names, are often designated by epithets and periphrases, many of which became the stock-in-trade of liturgical writing. The enigmatic nature of Kallir's language, which draws on the full range of post-biblical Hebrew, is further complicated by a wealth of neologisms and morphological oddities (which probably did not seem odd to his contemporaries). The structure of his *kerovot*, the patterns of rhyme, acrostic, repetition, and refrain, are far more complex than those of Yannai.

The 'Kallir style' was severely criticized in the twelfth century by Abraham ibn Ezra for having corrupted 'classical' (i.e. biblical) Hebrew and for being unduly obscure and esoteric (see p. 34). But Kallir – like other great innovators of the classical and late Eastern periods – was also capable of writing simple and direct poetry, both lyrical and dramatic, as some of the following selections demonstrate.

Part of a 'Kedushta for a Bridegroom', which was sung in the synagogue on the Sabbath following the wedding. In the fifth stanza, the bride and groom become personifications of Israel and of God. The metre (except for the refrain) is four words to a line.

The four-word verses of the monorhymed quatrains, composing an alphabetic acrostic, are paired off in parallelistic units. But a great deal of rhythmical variety is achieved by the shift of the caesura and the use of internal rhyme. God's 'garden bed' (line 14) is the Land of Israel.

One of a series of dirges (*kinot*) composed for the Ninth of Av and included in the Ashkenazi ritual.

The contrast between the upper and lower worlds is a common theme in medieval liturgical poetry (see pp. 216 and 263).

(Excerpts.) A rare example of extended narrative based on mythological subject matter. It is part of the final section of a monumental *kerova* for the Ninth of Av, whose complex design has not yet been fully clarified. The preceding sections combine lyrical, dramatic, and didactic elements in a description of the fall of Jerusalem. This is followed by an ecstatic account of the coming of the Messiah and the marvels of the 'end of days', when 'the seven classes of the righteous', seated under the Tree of Life in the garden of Eden, will be treated to the spectacle of a ferocious duel between the two monsters Behemoth and Leviathan. Afterwards both beasts, as well as the delicious Ziz, king of the birds, will be cooked and served to the pious. The gladiatorial contest and the banquet, as the Midrash points out, are meant to compensate 'the people who are near to Him' for having shunned unclean pagan sports and abstained from unclean flesh. The poem draws heavily on the description of the mythological monsters in Job 40 and 41. It is composed of irregular monorhymed sections, varying in length from three to twenty verses. The absence of any fixed metrical scheme, the frequent use of word-rhyme, and the introduction of a new rhyme even in the middle of a sentence – all enhance the free, flowing rhythm of the narrative.

PHINEHAS HAKOHEN (fl. late eighth century), the last of the classical *paytanim*, lived in the vicinity of Tiberias. A prolific poet, he wrote *kerovot* for the feast days and a series of poems commemorating each of the twenty-four classes (*mishmarot*) of priests who officiated in turn at the Temple.

An excerpt from a lengthy *siluk*. The 'male and female' (lines 3, 6) refer to the 'Male Upper Waters' and 'Female Lower Waters' which were separated from each other on the second day of creation.

'*You sold a brother*'　　　　　　　　　　אָח בְּנַעֲלֵיכֶם מְכַרְתֶּם　233

A choral *zulat* (part of a *yotser*-sequence; see Note on Medieval Genres, p. 53), and one of the finest examples of a ballad-like *piyut* in the classical period. It is based on the climactic encounter between Joseph, now Viceroy of Egypt, and his brothers, after the 'stolen' silver goblet turns up in Benjamin's bag (Genesis 43–45). Judah is terrified by the Viceroy's uncanny knowledge of their crime: the sale of Joseph to the Ishmaelites (Genesis 37) for twenty pieces of silver (with which, according to legend, each of the brothers bought himself a pair of shoes; line 16). The irony of the exchange is heightened by Joseph's refrain: 'the Revealer' is the all-knowing God, but Judah takes it to mean the avenging Viceroy who is using the silver cup for divination.

AMITTAI BEN SHEPHATIAH (late ninth century) was born in Southern Italy, the first European centre of Hebrew poetry in the Middle Ages. Both his grandfather and father had been noted *paytanim*, and he succeeded the latter as head of the yeshiva in his native Oria. His poems, which are among the best of the period, continue the tradition of the Palestinian school. In many hymns he inveighs against the oppressive edicts, especially the forcible conversions, imposed during the Byzantine rule.

'*The Lord, who revealed the end*'　　　　　אָדוֹן מַגִּיד מֵרֵאשִׁית　235

First section of a 'Bridegroom's *Yotser*' in which the six days of Creation are described as a series of preparations culminating in the First Marriage, with God in the role of host and best man. Written in rhymed tercets, with five words to a line, the poem contains a complete alphabetic acrostic. The fourth stanza, a quatrain which contains the poet's name, may have served as a refrain after every three stanzas.

'*When the humble one*'　　　　　　　　　　אֶל עִיר גִּבּוֹרִים　238

A dramatic account of the dangers that assailed Moses when he ascended to heaven to receive the Law. Angelology, derived from *Hekhalot* literature, is a favourite theme of early Hebrew poetry in Italy. According to the Midrashic source from which this *ofan* borrows many of its expressions, the Angel of Death (last stanza) taught Moses 'the secret of preserving life'.

'*A man draws a figure on a wall*'　　　　　אָדָם צָר בַּכֹּתֶל　240

An extract from a lengthy *siluk* describing the growth and movement of the foetus in the womb. It is part of the climax of a 'Bridegroom's *Kedushta*', which was sung on the Sabbath following the wedding.

ANONYMOUS (ninth to eleventh century). All the poems in this section, except for 'Open the gates' and 'We drew near', contain various types of alphabetic acrostics.

This beautiful poem is chanted as the sun is setting on the Day of Atonement, during the *ne'ila* ('closing') service. The name referred to the closing of the Temple gates at dusk and, by extension, to the closing of the heavenly gates. The poem may be a fragment.

Opening section of an unrhymed narrative of Palestinian origin which was patterned on an earlier Aramaic model. Like other hymns that celebrate Israel's miraculous passage through the Sea of Reeds, it was intended for the liturgy of the Seventh Day of Passover.

An intricate *ofan* for the Feast of Weeks. Each of the monorhymed stanzas – the first and last employ word-rhyme – ends with a scriptural quotation. Line 10 alludes to the legend that, upon hearing the first commandment, the Israelites 'flew back in horror twelve miles, until their souls fled from them'. The Lord then revived them with the dew that will, one day, bring the dead back to life.

A *piyut* for the Feast of Weeks, 'the festival of the giving of our Law'. When God decided to reveal the Torah, the mountains vied with each other for the honour of receiving His glory. Mount Carmel (stanza 4) moved down to the seashore so that the Shekinah could descend upon it whether it chose to rest on the sea or on the mainland. The refrain is repeated after each stanza.

In some Midrashic versions, the Angel of Death volunteers to seize Moses' soul, after the angels tearfully refuse to do so. His attempts end in humiliation; Moses almost batters him to death with his holy staff, when a heavenly voice is heard: 'Let him be, Moses, for the world is in need of him.' Infuriated, the Angel makes a third attempt, not knowing that God (last stanza) had already given Moses the kiss of death.

This unique poem echoes the tone of the Ten Commandments, but the imperatives are here addressed by the *paytan* to God.

'Mourning and weeping do not avail'   אֵבֶל וּבְכִי   248

A remorseless description, in rabbinic idiom, of the moment of death. The 'drop of poison' (line 23) falls from the tip of the sword that is brandished by the Plunderer. Lines 36-41 refer to the eschatological Aggadah of the 'beating in the grave', *ḥibut hakever*, according to which the Angel of Death revives the buried corpse and beats it with a chain which is 'half fire and half iron'.

'We drew near to find out'   נִגַּשְׁנוּ לָדַעַת   250

One of the earliest known Karaite *piyutim*, probably composed in Jerusalem in the ninth century. Its child-like simplicity contrasts sharply with the customary rabbinate style. The poem originated in the circle of the 'mourners for Zion' (*aveley Tsiyon*), a group of ascetics who spent their time lamenting the destruction of 'mother-Zion' and the dispersion of Israel.

'He wraps Himself in a cloak'   אוֹר נֹגַהּ   251

The quotations which conclude each stanza of this *Kedusha* follow the sequence of Isaiah 6.2-4.

SA'ADIAH GAON (882-942), the father of medieval Jewish philosophy, was born in the Faiyum district in Egypt. From 928, except for a period of conflict with the exilarch, he held the post of *gaon* ('eminence') of the Academy of Sura in Babylonia (Iraq). A bold innovator in many areas, he translated the Bible into Arabic (which had replaced Aramaic as the principal language spoken by the Jews); edited the first 'scientific' prayer-book; and compiled the first comprehensive Hebrew dictionary, including a rhyming dictionary for the use of poets. He was the first to wed Hebrew poetry and philosophy. He introduced alternating rhyme, new types of *piyut* and a complex diction which, though highly individual, reasserted the supremacy of biblical usages. The following excerpts are from a monumental philosophical hymn in ten sections (composed for the Day of Atonement), which is based on the opening verse of Psalm 104:

'You are far greater'   גָּדַלְתָּ מְאֹד   253

SAMUEL HASHELISHI (died after 1012) was 'the third' (*hashelishi*) in order of importance in the Jerusalem Academy. In some of his earlier poems, before he had risen to that rank, the acrostic reveals him as 'Samuel *Harevi'i*' ('the Fourth'). He died in Egypt, after having witnessed and recorded, in prose and verse, the Muslim riots against the Jews of Fostat. Though his poetry belongs to the 'Sa'adiah school', his musical qualities distinguish him as the finest lyricist of the late Eastern period. An extremely prolific poet, his favourite form was the classical *yotser*. Some of his *piyutim* observe a strict word count. The following selection consists of independent sections of *yotser* sequences:

(Excerpts.) The biblical verses that occur after every stanza and determine its recurrent rhyme are taken from the passage in I Kings 2.1–12 describing David's death.

EZEKIEL HAKOHEN (fl. late tenth century) is one of a large group of late Eastern *paytanim* of whom practically nothing is known. His euphemistic Arabic surname, Al-Baṣir ('the Seeing') would suggest that he was blind. Some of the allusions in the following poem are based on the allegorical interpretation of the Song of Songs. In the third stanza, for instance, 'the spice-bearing mountains' refer to Mount Moriah, the site of Isaac's sacrifice as well as of the Temple; the 'fawn' alludes to God who 'leapt from Egypt to the Red Sea . . . and from Sinai He leaps to the future redemption'; the 'myrrh and henna' represent Abraham and Isaac. Each stanza ends with a biblical verse which sets the rhyme for the quatrain. In addition to two acrostics (the complete alphabet and the author's name), the poem makes skilful use of the caesura and of internal rhyme.

JOSEPH ALBARDANI (tenth century) was chief *ḥazan* in the Great Synagogue of Baghdad, and was succeeded in this post by his son and grandson. The following poem, attributed to Albardani, is based on a Midrashic elaboration of the episode in Exodus 14:

MOSES BEN KALONYMUS (fl. late tenth century) is one of the first *paytanim* known in Germany. He was probably born in Lucca (Lombardy), where the extensive Kalonymus family had played a leading role in the development of Hebrew poetry. His family was moved by one of the Carolingian emperors to the Rhineland city of Mainz (Mayence, Magenza) and served as the link between the Italian and Central European *piyut*. Only two of his compositions have survived, including a long and spirited *kerova* for the last day of Passover, of which the concluding section is given here. The 'army of fire' (last line of stanza 4) recalls the legend that the Lord caused fiery steeds to swim out upon the sea in order to lure the Egyptian charioteers. The struggle between the 'Prince of the Sea' and the 'Prince of Egypt' (last stanza) accords with the tradition that God first vents his anger upon the 'guardian angels' before punishing the nations entrusted to their care.

SIMEON BEN ISAAC (b. *c.*950), a native of Mainz, was the outstanding synagogal poet of Ashkenazi Jewry. His distinctive style clearly reflects the influence of the Palestinian classical school, of *merkava* mysticism, and of his older contemporary, Moses ben Kalonymus. In several of his *piyutim*, he introduced his son's name in the acrostic. A venerated Talmudic authority, he became the hero of many folk legends. One tradition has it that his son embraced Christianity and rose to the rank of Pope. When Simeon the Great went to Rome to plead his people's cause, he played chess with the Pope and, by the style of his game, recognized him as his son.

Opening section of a penitential hymn, composed of four-word lines, for the afternoon service of the Day of Atonement. Line 7 borrows a Talmudic image: 'Man's evil inclination resembles a fly and is seated between the two valves of the heart.'

The subject-matter, structure and metre of these excerpts from a *kerova* for the New Year recall the famous hymn (p. 216) attributed to Yannai.

DAVID BEN NASI (? eleventh century). An Eastern *paytan* whose identity remains uncertain. His poems have been preserved in the Karaite prayer-book as well as in the 'Byzantine ritual' (*mahzor Roumania*) which was used by the Jews in the Balkans and in Constantinople. The metre of the following poem (excerpts) is four words to a line:

THE DEATH OF MOSES (eighth to eleventh century). The poems forming this unusual sequence, here given in abridged form, were written by various hands in the Near East. They were grouped in their present order by an anonymous later editor, and from the sixteenth century onwards have appeared in several synagogue rites printed in Italy. They are part of the liturgy of *Simhat Torah* ('Rejoicing of the Law') which marks both the conclusion and the renewal of the annual cycle of readings from the Pentateuch. The rejoicing is accompanied by laments over the death of Moses, a custom which was already current in Babylonia in the tenth century. The death of Moses (*petirat Moshe*), like the binding of Isaac, is one of the most popular subjects of liturgical poetry. (See also pp. 246 and 445.)

The first and last poems of the sequence, both of which have a popular flavour, are the only ones without some form of acrostic. The second stanza alludes to the legend (elaborated in the poem on p. 238) that the angels sought to scorch Moses with their fiery breath, but God spread His 'mantle' over him (Job 26.9) and told him to cling to the Throne of Glory.

'While I was yet in my mother's womb' אָז מֵרֶחֶם אִמִּי 266

The 'perfection' of Moses (line 2) refers to the tradition that he came forth circumcised from his mother's womb and on that very day began to walk and speak. In the *Italian Maḥzor* (1856), edited by S. D. Luzzatto, this *piyut* is prefaced by the remark that it is designed to move the worshippers to profuse weeping.

'All creatures were formed' אָז כָּל בְּרִיּוֹת 268

The dialogue form is often employed in the many Midrashim on the death of Moses which are woven into these poems. The last stanza (in which the 'staff of life' is, literally, the 'tree of life') is based on the legend that Moses will continue to be the great leader and teacher of his people in the world to come.

'I will not die!' לֹא אָמוּת 269

This has recently been identified by E. Fleischer as part of a *kedushta* written by Phinehas Hakohen (see p. 90) for the last portion of Deuteronomy. In the original 115-line poem, Moses is told that he must die for having struck the rock instead of speaking to it (Numbers 20.8–13). The final stanza reads: '. . . accept My constraint / and die by My kiss. / Even My loved and trusted ones must perish. / Say no more. / I have regretted My decree, / but what can I do? – This has been decreed!'

'This man, who was graced with light' אִישׁ אֲשֶׁר הֻקְרַן 270
'The road I am about to take' אֹרַח זוּ אֵלֵךְ 271
'Jokhebed went to Egypt' אָזְלַת יוֹכֶבֶד 273

A literal Hebrew translation of a much earlier Aramaic *piyut*, for which no source has been found in the Midrash. Jokhebed's futile search is closely paralleled by Samael's quest for Moses (p. 246).

PART TWO: FROM THE TENTH TO THE EIGHTEENTH CENTURY

MENAHEM IBN SARUK (fl. middle of the tenth century), apparently the earliest secular poet in Spain, was born in Tortosa and moved at an early age to Cordoba. There he engaged in important linguistic research under the patronage of Ḥisdai ibn Shaprut, the Jewish statesman and physician to the caliph 'Abd al-Raḥman III. For some unknown reason, possibly accusations of heresy, Ibn Saruk fell into disgrace.

His patron's agents broke into his house on the holy Sabbath, beat him mercilessly and led him off to prison where he composed an impassioned 'scroll' in epistolary form. The complaint, of which excerpts are given below, is written in cadenced biblical style, with occasional rhymed passages. It is prefaced by the words: 'I adjure you by the Lord, the God of heaven and earth, and by the bones of all the prophets and seers, that you read this scroll in its entirety until the very end.'

'I shall state my case'   אֲנִי אֶעֱרֹךְ מִשְׁפָּט   277

DUNASH BEN LABRAT (died *c*.990) changed the course of Hebrew poetry by introducing quantitative metres and secular genres, verse-forms and images borrowed from the Arabic. He was also the first to employ the new metrical technique in sacred poetry. A native of Fez, he studied in Baghdad under Sa'adiah Gaon and later settled in Cordoba, where he became the opponent of Ibn Saruk at Ibn Shaprut's court. His radical innovations aroused a fierce polemic, mostly in verse, between the disciples of the rival philologists, and he was accused of 'destroying the holy tongue'.

'He said: "Do not sleep!"'   וְאוֹמֵר: אַל תִּישַׁן   280

This is the first wine song, and reflects the new courtly setting of Hebrew poetry. Rhythmically, it testifies to the initial awkwardness of adapting Hebrew to quantitative metrics. Its rhyme scheme, aaab, cccb, became one of the preferred patterns of the Spanish school. It is conceivable that the moralistic conclusion was meant to forestall criticism.

JOSEPH IBN ABITUR (*c*. 950–after 1024) was born in Merida and achieved fame as a scholar in Cordoba. When his bid for the position of head of the yeshiva failed, he was placed under a ban by his opponents and fled to the East. He lived in Palestine and neighbouring countries from the end of the tenth century and is reported to have died in Damascus. The first great Spanish *paytan*, his many hundreds of *piyutim* continue the tradition of the Eastern school and are often indebted to Sa'adiah. Many of his formal and thematic innovations became standard practice in the Spanish *piyut*. He composed only one poem in the Arabic-inspired metre, a threnody on the persecutions that took place in Palestine when Bedouin tribes invaded the country in 1024. The following *seliha*, attributed to Ibn Abitur, is somewhat unusual for its personal tone. The rhyme of the first stanza is dictated by the biblical refrain, and recurs in the concluding 'couplet' of each subsequent stanza (bbbaa, cccaa).

'I know, my God'   יָדַעְתִּי, אֱלֹהַי   281

ISAAC IBN KHALFUN (*c*.965–after 1020). Born in Spain or North Africa, he lived in Cordoba for a long period, and travelled extensively, eking out a living by composing encomiums to capricious patrons. The first professional Hebrew poet, his verse is entirely secular and written in the Arabic *qasida* form (see Note on the Systems of Hebrew Versification, p. 63). He introduced a new note of elegance into Hebrew poetry and found biblical 'precedents' for motifs and metaphors taken from Arabic verse.

This was written to encourage his old friend Samuel Hanagid, after he had been deposed from a high-ranking post and two of his relatives had been murdered (1020). The 'spitting' and 'casting of the shoe' (lines 2–3) recall the degradation of the brother who refuses to perform a levirate marriage (Deuteronomy 25.9).

From a reply to a conciliatory 'song of friendship' by Hanagid, after the two had fallen out during a wine-feast. As was customary in such exchanges, the answer is cast in the same metre as the poem that prompted it.

SAMUEL HANAGID (993–1056), the first major poet of 'the golden age', was born in Cordoba and was among those who fled the capital when the Berber hordes destroyed it in 1013. A renowned Talmudist and statesman, he was the first Spanish Jew to be granted the title Nagid ('Prince'). He was appointed vizier shortly after the accession to the throne (1038) of Badis, the Berber ruler of Granada. In this capacity the Nagid, or Isma'il ibn Nagrela as he was known in Arab circles, commanded the armies of Granada in a series of victorious campaigns against Seville and her allies, which lasted from 1038 to 1056. The many poems he sent to his son from the battle-field constitute a unique poetic diary of his tempestuous life. He died after a strenuous campaign and was succeeded as vizier and commander by his son, Yehosef. Ten years later Yehosef Hanagid was assassinated and the Jewish community of Granada was massacred by the Muslims. Hanagid's vast knowledge of Hebrew and Arabic culture is apparent in his technical mastery and in his rich repertoire of forms and motifs. He excels in the fusion of epic and lyrical elements.

The conventional opening, as if in reply to an interlocutor, is also found in Ben Labrat's wine-song (p. 280). Here, the convention is somewhat modified by the poet's indirect answer.

Like the previous poem, this is taken from the collection *Ben Kohelet* ('Son of Ecclesiastes'), in which the dominant themes are the sorrows and vanities of life and the fear of death.

'Then Av – the month of ancient woe –'   וַיֵּצֵא אָב   286

From a poem describing his first major battle, against the army of Almeria, which was ruled by the Slav eunuch Zuhair and his fanatical Arab vizier Ibn Abbas. The Nagid, who prided himself on being 'the David of his generation', borrowed the title of this poem (*Shira*, 'Song') from Psalm 18. It consists of 149 lines in order to correspond with the number of chapters in Psalms. The war poems were grouped, in his lifetime, in *Son of Psalms*.

'See my distress today'   רְאֵה הַיוֹם בְּצָרָתִי   288

The son referred to in the last line is Yehosef, who, at his father's request, began to copy and arrange the Nagid's poems when he was eight and a half years old. The superscriptions were written by Yehosef in Arabic.

'Good herald, now tell me'   מְבַשֵּׂר טוֹב   289

The injunction at the end of these bloodthirsty verses, that they should be recited in synagogues and taught to children, stemmed from the Nagid's conviction that his personal success represented a triumph for the entire people. At the end of *Shira* he even requests that his victory be celebrated as a popular feast, 'a second Purim', throughout the Jewish world.

'Shall I forever live in a tent'   הֲלָעַד אֲנִי שׁוֹכֵן   291

'War is at first'   קְרָב דּוֹמֶה   291

From *Son of Proverbs*, a collection of over 1,000 aphorisms, many of which draw upon Arabic, Persian and Greek sources.

'No master will hire you'   לֹא יַעֲבִידְךָ מוֹשְׁלָךְ   292

'The earth is a prison'   אֶרֶץ לְאָדָם בֵּית כְּלוּא   292

'O you merry-makers'   אוֹהֲבֵי יָמִים   292

'Reflect, and you will realize'   שִׁית לִבְּךָ   292

'Is there a sea between me and you'   הֲיָם בֵּינִי וּבֵינֶךְ   293

One of a series of dirges on the death of his elder brother Isaac to whom he was particularly devoted.

'Are you asleep, my friend?'   רֵעִי, הֲתִישָׁן   293

(Opening section.) A younger Arab contemporary of the Nagid wrote that 'he was also proficient ... in the various branches of mathematics, and his lore of astronomy also surpassed that of the astronomers ...'. The long list of achievements is prefaced by the remark: 'This accursed Jew was in himself one of the most perfect men, although God had denied him His guidance' (quoted by J. Schirmann).

Appears both as an independent poem (in *Son of Ecclesiastes*) and as part of the 'introduction' or 'proem' to a panegyric (in *Son of Psalms*). It is a striking example of the autonomy of genres in the long poem, which often resembles a series of short poems on different themes.

Descriptions of nature often play an important role in the Nagid's wine songs, which are among the finest in Spanish Hebrew poetry.

The love poems are addressed not only to the female *ofra* or *tseviya* ('doe') but also, in the Arabic manner, to the male counterpart *ofer* or *tsevi* who, in this poem, is the cup-bearer. Apparently, there was still some opposition to love poems in the sacred tongue and Yehosef, in his Arabic introduction to the *diwan*, claimed that they were written allegorically (like Solomon's Song of Songs).

JOSEPH IBN ḤISDAI (fl. early eleventh century) was one of a group of scholars in Saragossa, which became a cultural centre after the destruction of Cordoba (1013). His son converted to Islam and served as vizier to three rulers of the Banu Hud dynasty. The following poem is the 'introduction' to a panegyric addressed to his childhood friend, Samuel Hanagid (who replied with a poem in the identical metre). Lines 21–24 are the surprising 'transition verse' which leads into the 'body', or actual theme, of the poem. Written around 1045, it is the only work of Ibn Ḥisdai which has survived. It was much admired for its involved rhetoric and, at a time when poems were rarely titled, came to be known as 'The Unique Song' (*Shira Yetoma*). This title was based on a bilingual pun in the poem, where *yetoma* means both 'orphan' (Hebrew) and 'unique' (Arabic).

HAYA GAON (939-1038), a halakhic scholar of immense authority, was the last *gaon* of the Academy in Pumbedita, a post which he held for forty years after succeeding his father, Sherira Gaon, in 998. All his secular poetry and some of his *piyutim* were written in quantitative metres. Though he may have been the first poet in Babylonia to employ the new Spanish prosody, he clearly adhered to the late Eastern tradition. The following *seliḥa* is one of a series of unrhymed, alphabetic compositions for the Ninth of Av, modelled after the Psalms. They describe the bitterness of exile with unusual power and boldness. He was the first to renounce rhyme in a composition intended for liturgical use.

ABRAHAM HAKOHEN (fl. early eleventh century), a Palestinian *paytan*, is known for his 'poems from prison', written in Egypt in 1024, after he was jailed for defaulting on a debt. These poems are of special interest because, like those of Samuel Hashelishi (p. 93), they record a personal experience in a classical, liturgical form, which could hardly have been intended for public service.

A striking description of the narcissus.

SOLOMON IBN GABIROL (1021/22–*c.* 1055), one of the greatest Hebrew poets of all time, was born in Malaga, lived most of his life in Saragossa and died in Valencia before 1058. Having decided to dedicate his life to the pursuit of poetry and philosophy, he depended on the precarious support of wealthy benefactors. He was conscious of his genius at an early age –

> I am the master and the song is my slave . . .
> and though I am only sixteen years of age
> my heart has the wisdom of an eighty-year old!

and his 'cantankerous soul' embroiled him in frequent conflicts. His secular poetry includes nature and love poems of unusual beauty; panegyrics, laments and riddles. But it was his turbulent personal poems, expressing his struggle against fate ('Time') and society, that struck a new note of introspective complexity. His liturgical poems, though entirely different in tone, are no less original. He was the first to introduce the full range of Hispano-Arabic conventions into the *piyut*. His compact and lyrical *reshuyot* (sing. *reshut*, 'prelude') served as a model for generations of poets. His monumental philosophic poem *Keter Malkhut* ('The Kingly Crown' – translated into English by B. Lewis) alternates rhymed, rhythmical prose and free, rhymed verse. It draws on early mystical Midrashim, neoplatonic cosmology and Muslim astronomy. His major theoretical prose work, *Mekor Ḥayim* ('The Source of Life'), enjoyed a curious history. Written in Arabic, but preserved only in a Latin translation (*Fons*

Vitae), it was attributed to Avicebron and regarded as the work of a Muslim or, in scholastic circles, Christian theologian. It was only in the nineteenth century that 'Avicebron' was shown to be a corruption of Gabirol's name.

(Excerpts.) The light of the moon is here equated with Wisdom. In an elegy on the death of his father, Wisdom appears and reproaches him for neglecting her by his prolonged mourning.

One of three elegies on the death of his friend and patron, Jekuthiel ibn Ḥasan, vizier in Saragossa, who was murdered by political rivals in 1040.

The opening and closing sections of a poem describing his illness, presumably a serious skin disease. In other poems he complains of his weak physique, small stature and ugliness.

'The paradox, which had served his predecessors as a rhetorical device, became in Gabirol's poems a means through which the poet expresses his divided soul' (D. Pagis).

Conclusion of a poem of self-praise. This was a conventional genre (see Ibn Khalfun's poem, p. 284), which suited Gabirol's temperament.

'Introduction' to a complaint on the departure of friends. Like the 'introductions' by Hanagid (p. 295) and Ibn Ḥisdai (p. 302), it has little to do with the theme of the poem.

This and the following five poems are *reshuyot* (preludes) to various prayers.

'*The gate that was shut*' שַׁעַר אֲשֶׁר נִסְגַּר 314

A dialogue between 'daughter-Zion' and God concerning the Messiah. According to Abraham ibn Ezra, Gabirol was among those who tried to predict the Day of Judgement on the basis of astronomical calculations.

'*Lord, You who reclined*' שׁוֹכֵב עֲלֵי מִטּוֹת זָהָב 314

The relationship between Zion, God and the Messiah is expressed in the form of a popular love poem. This seems to have been one of Gabirol's many innovations, like the direct address to the supreme 'soul' (Wisdom) in the following poem.

'*Bow down before God*' שְׁחִי לָאֵל 315
'*God Almighty, You who listen*' שַׁדַּי אֲשֶׁר יַקְשִׁיב 315
'*Morning and evening I seek You*' שְׁחַרְתִּיךָ בְּכָל שַׁחֲרִי 316

A prelude to *Nishmat*, the Sabbath morning prayer beginning 'The breath of (*nishmat*) every living being shall bless Your name . . .' As is customary, the last line of the *reshut* alludes to its liturgical function.

'*Before I was*' טֶרֶם הֱיוֹתִי 316

ISAAC IBN GHIYYAT (1038-89). As head of the yeshiva in his native town of Lucena, he was the teacher of the poets Joseph ibn Sahl and Moses ibn Ezra. His hundreds of *piyutim* (few secular poems have survived) are written almost entirely in the new Andalusian style. The last great innovator in the field of the *piyut*, he achieved special distinction in his melodious *muwashshaḥat* (girdle poems; see p. 30), a secular Arabic form first used as a vehicle for liturgical poetry by Gabirol.

'*O Lord, bring back*' שַׁדַּי, שׁוֹבְבָה 317

An *ahava* in the form of a girdle poem employing internal rhymes.

'*Have you heard, my friends?*' הַיְדַעְתֶּם, יְדִידִי 318

The language of love poetry is used in this girdle poem to deplore the flight of the 'gazelle' (God) from the poet's 'dwelling' (Zion).

LEVI IBN ALTABBAN (fl. late eleventh century) lived in Saragossa. Little is known of his life. His talent for harmonious lyricism is manifest in his short *reshuyot* and in *ahavot* and *me'orot* which occasionally take the form of a dialogue between God and Israel.

'*I shall turn*' לְקְרַאת מָקוֹר חַיָּי

Like others of his poems in which the acrostic yields LeVI, this philosophical *reshut* was mistakenly attributed to Judah Halevi.

'*Lord, our hearts are filled*' יְיָ, לְבָבוֹת נִמְהָרוּ

Drought is a frequent theme in Spanish *piyutim*. The acrostic is incomplete and it is possible that a few verses have been lost.

BENJAMIN BEN ZERAH (fl. late eleventh century) is generally listed as an Ashkenazi *paytan*, but his style seems to indicate that he lived in the Byzantine Empire. He was called *Ba'al Hashem* ('Master of the Divine Name') probably because of his extensive usage of the names of God and the angels in his *merkava* poems. In the following *ofan*, the third stanza refers to the tradition that the 'song-uttering' angels are instantly consumed by fire if they deviate from the tempo by so much as a 'hair's breadth'. The 'gigantic beast' (last stanza) is an angel named Israel ('on his forehead is engraved ISRAEL'), who is stationed in the middle of heaven and who initiates the angelic song.

'*Fashioned of fire and water*' בְּלוּלֵי אֵשׁ וּמֵימוֹת

JOSEPH IBN SAHL (died *c.* 1123) occupied the position of *dayan* in Cordoba for the last ten years of his life. Only a few of his poems have been preserved. Moses ibn Ezra praised him for his biting satires.

'*And the fleas charge*' וּפַרְעוֹשִׁים כְּפָרָשִׁים

MOSES IBN EZRA (*c.* 1055-after 1135), a consummate craftsman and the leading theoretician of the Spanish school, was born in Granada, where he was granted an honorific Arabic title. In 1090 the Jewish community was destroyed by the Berber Almoravids, and the members of his family dispersed. It is not known why Ibn Ezra, isolated and impoverished, remained in Granada. About five years later his life was endangered in a mysterious episode involving his elder brother's daughter, and he fled to Christian Spain. For the next forty years he wandered through 'the exile of Edom', an embittered refugee in search of patrons. Towards the end of his life he composed his Arabic treatise *The Book of Conversations and Memories*. This unique work, based on Arabic poetics, is an invaluable source for the history of Andalusian Hebrew poetry. It deals at length with poetics and the theory of 'ornamentation' and describes the rhetorical figures. In keeping with the ideal of *tsahot* ('purity' of rhetoric), these figures are primarily illustrated by reference to the Bible. Some of his long secular poems suffer from excessive ornamentation. However, his shorter meditative pieces and his sensual love poems are compact and beautiful. He was the first to write homonymic poems, on the model of the Arabic *tajnis*. In his extensive liturgical poetry, he deftly wove together Jewish religious and Arabic secular elements. He came to be known as *Hasalah* ('the supplicant') in acknowledgement of his moving *selihot*, many of which found a place of honour in synagogue rites.

This description of spring, in terms of a royal procession, makes fleeting allusions to Joseph's ornamental tunic (line 1; Genesis 37.3); to the release from prison of King Jehoiachim who 'took off his prison garb' (lines 4-5; 2 Kings 25.27-29); and, by inference, to Joseph's appointment as vizier (Genesis 41.40-43) after being released from the dungeon and dressed in fine robes.

Metaphors of growth and renewal in Ibn Ezra's poetry are almost always borrowed from the domain of the weaver or goldsmith (lines 5-6, 18). Many of these figures originate in biblical descriptions of the Tabernacle's ornaments and the priests' clothes.

This is, like the following poem, a *muwashshah*. The poet must have had such passionate works in mind when, in old age, he renounced his love poems as the 'mistakes of unbridled youth'.

The solution to this riddle is: a candle.

The influence of Hanagid's *Son of Ecclesiastes* can be felt in Ibn Ezra's reflective poems.

The description of the suffering and insomnia of the abandoned lover during the 'night of wandering' is a stock element in love poems and complaints. In this instance, it is part of the proem to a panegyric.

An invitation to a party in the poet's garden. The river is part of the conventional décor of wine feasts.

This address to the musician follows a detailed description of a wine feast. Lines 21-2 are the 'transition verse' which leads to an account of the poet's sorrows in exile.

A *pizmon* (strophic *seliḥa* with a refrain) for the Day of Atonement. Like many of the *piyutim* of the Spanish school, it is written in a syllabic, rather than quantitative, metre. Each line consists of nine syllables, divided into units of three and six. In the first three lines the shorter units are rhymed.

Excerpts from a *mustajab* (or *mustajib*) for the Day of Atonement. A Spanish type of *seliḥa*, it is composed of unmetrical, four-line stanzas. The biblical verse, which serves as the refrain, comes at the head of the poem. Its last word is then repeated in the rhyme position in the biblical quotation which concludes each stanza (x, aaax, bbbx). In the last stanza of this poem, 'my daughter' refers both to the soul and to the people of Israel; 'night' is also meant metaphorically as 'the darkness of exile'.

Opening of a meditative poem, written in exile. The Arabic superscription in Ibn Ezra's *diwan* reads: 'And he said when he was comforting his soul and turning to abstinence.'

JUDAH HALEVI (before 1075–after 1141) was born in Muslim Tudela, on the borders of Christian Spain. At an early age he travelled to the centres of Jewish scholarship in Andalusia. In Granada, he formed a lasting friendship with Moses ibn Ezra which is recorded in a moving exchange of poems. Later, Halevi settled in Toledo, the capital of Castile under Alfonso VI, where he practised medicine, apparently in the service of the king. However, the murder in 1108 of his benefactor, Solomon ibn Ferrizuel, at the hands of Christian mercenaries, and the attacks upon the Jews in Toledo in the following year, prompted him to return to the Muslim area, where he made his home in Cordoba. His personal experiences in Christian and Muslim Spain during the Reconquest ('Between the armies of Seir and Kedar my army is lost . . . when they fight their wars, we fall in their downfall'), and his philosophical views concerning the meaning of diaspora and the path to redemption, culminated in his decision to emigrate to the Holy Land. Shortly before his departure he completed his influential treatise *The Book of Argument and Proof in Defence of the*

Despised Faith. Translated from Arabic into Hebrew in the twelfth century, it came to be known as *The Book of the Kuzari* because it is composed as a dialogue between a Jewish scholar (the *ḥaver*) and the king of the Khazars, who had converted to Judaism in the eighth century. In September 1140, after an arduous voyage, Halevi arrived in Alexandria and was received with great acclaim. He died six months later, after a period of intensive creativity. His poetic corpus of secular and sacred works consists of over a thousand compositions which attest to an unrivalled mastery of language and musical patterns and a profound lyrical expression of religious and national themes. His 'songs of Zion' are, perhaps, his most famous works. No Hebrew poet since the Psalmists had sung the praises of the Holy Land with such passion. The longing for Zion, the pain of parting from his cultural environment, the perilous sea voyage – all these topics were uncommon in the poetry of the time.

This is the most extreme expression in Halevi's poetry of his view that the suffering of Israel is a sanctification of the name of God. In the *Kuzari* the *ḥaver* maintains that Israel could have hastened the deliverance by submitting willingly to the yoke of exile.

The opening line of this *reshut* refers to Song of Songs 5.2 which was allegorically interpreted to mean that Israel 'slept' in the darkness of exile but its heart yearned to rejoin the Shekinah. The 'star' (line 3; Numbers 24.17) represents the Messiah. Various messianic movements were active in Halevi's time and he once dreamt that the redemption would come in 1130.

An *ahava* which, like the previous poem, employs the phraseology of the Song of Songs. The 'lover' and 'gazelle' represent God.

A *reshut* for *Nishmat*.

A metrical *bakasha* ('supplication'), a type of personal *seliḥa* introduced by early Spanish *piyut*. Characteristically, its ending repeats its beginning.

Takes, as its point of departure, Psalms 36.10: 'With You is the fountain of life; by Your light do we see light.'

'Lord, where shall I find You?'   יָהּ, אָנָה אֶמְצָאֵךְ   338

An *ofan* in the rhyme-form of a *muwashshaḥ*, but written in the special syllabic metre which was exclusively used in Spain in strophic *piyutim*. In this case, there are twelve syllables to a line, divided into units of six and six by internal rhymes. It is based on Solomon's prayer (2 Chronicles 6.18), on a verse from the daily *Kedusha* ('Blessed be the glory of the Lord from His place'), and on the Midrashic paradox: 'The Lord is the place of His world, but the world is not His place'; that is, the world is contained in Him, not He in the world.

'Do these tears know'   הֲיֵדְעוּ הַדְּמָעוֹת   339

An epitaph for the tombstone of an unidentified 'Rabbi Abraham'.

'Alas, my daughter'   הָהּ, בִּתִּי, הֲשָׁכַחַתְּ   339
'On that day'   יוֹם אַכְפִּי הִכְבַּדְתִּי   340

This lament, in the *muwashshaḥ* form, for the Ninth of Av elaborates on a Talmudic legend concerning the murder of the prophet Zechariah, who was stoned in the Temple-court by order of King Joash (2 Chronicles 24.21-22).

'O graceful doe'   יַעֲלַת חֵן, רַחֲמִי לֵבָב   342

Vulgar Arabic – and sometimes Romance – was generally employed in the final couplet (*kharja*) of the secular Hebrew *muwashshaḥ*. The *kharja* was, in most cases, borrowed from popular Arabic or Romance songs.

'My love washes'   עָפְרָה תְכַבֵּס   343

The Arabic superscription in the *diwan* reads: 'An improvisation composed upon passing by a river where washerwomen were laundering.'

'Why, O fair one'   מַה לָּךְ, צְבִיָּה   343

Excerpts.

'O my fair youth'   בִּי הַצְּבִי   344

Another *muwashshaḥ*, in a characteristic popular vein.

'Gently, my hard-hearted'   אַט לִי, חֲזַק לֵבָב   346

Opening section of the reply to a song of friendship (by Solomon ibn al-Muallim) which had greeted Halevi's move to Granada.

'Why put your trust'   מַה תַּאֲמִין בִּזְמָן   346
'Th slaves of Time'   עַבְדֵי זְמָן   347
'My heart is in the East'   לִבִּי בְמִזְרָח   347

Zion was 'in the domain of Edom' (line 4) after the conquest of Jerusalem by the Crusaders in 1099.

Excerpts from the most famous of Halevi's Zion poems. Though not intended for the liturgy, it was soon included in the laments for the Ninth of Av and gave rise to scores of imitations ('Zionides'), many of which entered the Ashkenazi rite. The sixteenth-century legend, that Halevi was trampled to death by an Arab horseman as he was reciting this poem at the gates of Jerusalem, is widely known from Heine's portrayal in *Hebrew Melodies* (1851). The gates of Zion 'face the gates of heaven' (line 12) because, according to rabbinic belief, there was a celestial Temple corresponding to, and exactly opposite, the earthly one.

From a poem in which he exhorts himself to set forth on the voyage to Zion. The description of the storm at sea partly echoes Psalm 107.23-32.

The western wind brings him closer to his destination. This, and the following poems, were written during the long sea journey.

ABRAHAM IBN EZRA (1092-1167) was born in Tudela and lived for a time in Cordoba. In 1140 he left Spain and travelled extensively in Italy, Provence, Northern France and England. During these years he played a crucial role in disseminating the prosody and poetics of the Spanish school in Western Europe. His own poetry reveals some of the trends that began to emerge in the secular poetry of Christian Spain which, after the Almohad conquest of Andalusia, became the new centre of Hebrew creativity. In his liturgical poetry, Ibn Ezra favoured intricate varieties of the *muwash-shah*. He distinguished himself as a grammarian, biblical commentator and mathematician. He was also the author of a mystical allegory in rhymed prose.

Ibn Ezra introduced the character of the penniless roving bard into Hebrew poetry.

Both poems may reflect his belief in astrology, which he tried to reconcile with the faith in providence and free will; here, however, the tone is humorous.

'I have a cloak'   מְעִיל יֶשׁ לִי   353

Generally attributed to Ibn Ezra.

'I bow down'   אֶשְׁתַּחֲוֶה אַפַּיִם אַרְצָה   354

An unrhymed penitential prayer, in free biblical cadence (*rehuta*). The author's name is repeated twice in the acrostic.

ISAAC IBN EZRA (died middle of the twelfth century), one of Abraham's five sons, was born in Spain and seems to have accompanied Halevi on his voyage to Alexandria in 1140. He then proceeded to Baghdad where he converted to Islam (after 1143), probably under the influence of his patron, the philosopher-physician Abu al-Barakat, who had changed his faith at the age of sixty. Abraham composed two moving laments on his son's death.

'Go and weep'   בְּכִי תִשָּׂאוּ   356

Last section of a poem which was first published in 1965 by J. Schirmann in *New Hebrew Poems from the Genizah*, a collection of over 300 previously unknown compositions.

JUDAH SAMUEL ABBAS (died 1167), a native of Fez and resident of Aleppo, is the author of the most famous *akeda* in Hebrew poetry. It served as a model for many imitations, including one by Maimonides. It is chanted to an impressive melody in Sephardic communities before the blowing of the *shofar* during the New Year service.

'When the gates of mercy'   עֵת שַׁעֲרֵי רָצוֹן   357

The binding of Isaac is portrayed as a ritual sacrifice, with Abraham performing 'his priestly office' (line 19). Isaac asks to be bound securely (lines 51-2) lest he shrink from the knife and make the offering unacceptable to God. These Midrashic motifs also appear in the *akeda* by Ephraim of Bonn (p. 379). According to legend, Elijah (last line) girded his loins with the ram's skin and its right horn will be blown in the days of the Messiah to proclaim the end of exile. The poem is in the form of a metrical *pizmon*: the last line of the opening quatrain serves as the refrain, and the quatrain's rhyme is repeated in the last line of each stanza.

MOSES DAR'I (fl. *c.* 1200), the foremost poet of medieval Karaism, was born in Alexandria and spent time travelling in Syria and Palestine. He skilfully cultivated the poetic genres of the Spanish school. Some of his poems were written in Hebrew and Arabic.

'I said to the spying lady'   לַחֲבַצֶּלֶת שָׁרוֹן נָמִתִּי   360

TABLE OF POEMS

ANONYMOUS (eleventh to thirteenth century). This section is a miscellany of poems from Egypt, Spain, Italy, France and Germany.

A unique and unusually detailed description of woman's attributes by a poet who resided in Damietta, in northern Egypt. It serves as the 'introduction' to a song of friendship addressed to his benefactor.

According to the superscription, this was written as the poet took leave of his friend.

A *muwashshah* written by a member of the Spanish Ḥisdai family in praise of a fifteen-year-old 'fawn'.

A *me'ora* for the eighth day of the Feast of Booths.

An *ofan* for the fifth Sabbath after Passover.

An extract from a long moralistic meditation, *The Foundation of Religious Fear*, in rhymed tercets, written in Italy.

A series of variations patterned on Jeremiah 18.6: '. . . like clay in the hand of the potter, so are you in My hand, house of Israel'. This *piyut*, believed to be of French origin, is chanted before the open Ark during the evening service of Yom Kippur.

A lament for the Ninth of Av, probably of German origin, which contrasts the troops of the Crusaders with the Israelite camps in biblical times. The invitation to the 'smitten' daughter of Zion to join in the march to the Holy Land has not been found elsewhere in the literature.

'I shall give thanks' אוֹדֶה לָאֵל 370

A beautiful hymn which is included in the morning 'Prayer Before Prayer' of some rites. Lines 19-21 refer to the Midrash that God, unlike man, never confuses the deposits in His trust: 'Has a man ever risen at dawn and looked for his soul and not found it?' In Hebrew, each stanza ends with the word 'morning'.

'We pray You' אָנָּא, בְּכֹחַ 371

A mystical prayer traditionally attributed to the second-century *tanna* Neḥunya ben Hakana. It probably originated in the circles of *Ḥasidey Ashkenaz*, a pietist movement among the Jews of Germany and France. Each of the seven lines consists of six words; the forty-two words correspond to the forty-two-letter Name of God, which is formed by the initial letters of all the words.

'I shall speak out' אֲדַבְּרָה בְּצַר רוּחִי 372

Excerpts from a *seliḥa* describing the massacre of the Jews of Mainz by the Crusaders and burghers on 27 May 1096. After they had retreated to the bishop's fortified courtyard (stanza 5), more than 1,000 Jews met their deaths rather than submit to conversion.

DAVID BAR MESHULLAM OF SPEYER (twelfth century) was received in 1090 by the Emperor Henry IV as one of the representatives of the Jewish community. The following *seliḥa* for the eve of Yom Kippur describes the mass suicides in Speyer during the First Crusade (1096) in terms of ritual sacrifice. The 'royal purple' (line 6) is the garment which, according to tradition, God dips in the blood of the martyrs and which He will put on on the day of judgement. The joy of 'sanctifying the Name' (stanza 8) is a recurrent theme in the chronicles and *piyutim* of this period and is also found in late Midrashim on the *akeda*: ' While Abraham was building the altar, Isaac kept handing him the wood and the stones. Abraham was like a man who builds a wedding house for his son, and Isaac was like a man getting ready for the wedding feast . . .' (quoted by S. Spiegel).

'O God, do not let my blood' אֱלֹהִים, אַל דֳּמִי לְדָמִי 374

EPHRAIM OF REGENSBURG (1110-75), a renowned Tosafist, studied in France in his youth, lived in Speyer and Worms, and finally settled in Regensburg, where he became a member of the *bet din*. His poetry reflects the horrors of the Regensburg massacre (1137), when the Jews were dragged to the Danube and forced to accept baptism, and of the Second Crusade (1146-7). He was influential in introducing Spanish quantitative metres into Ashkenazi liturgical poetry. His *piyutim*, and those of his disciples Ephraim of Bonn and Barukh of Mainz, represent the finest artistic achievements of the late Ashkenazi school.

Last section of a long alphabetic *zulat* in rhymed tercets. The metre is three words to a line, and the last line of each stanza alludes to a biblical verse.

EPHRAIM OF BONN (1132-1200) was thirteen when the violence of the Second Crusade erupted. He and his relatives found refuge in the fortress of Wolkenburg, under the protection of the Bishop of Cologne. In old age he again narrowly escaped death by leaving Neuss only three days before its Jews were massacred (1186). His *Sefer Zekhira* ('Book of Remembrance'), in which he recorded the decrees and persecutions of the Second and Third Crusades, is an important historical source for the martyrology of the Jews in Germany, France, Austria and England. In characteristic Ashkenazi fashion, his *piyutim* draw heavily on Talmudic and rabbinic idiom and employ stylistic devices of the Palestinian school. At the same time, he occasionally uses a limited range of quantitative metres. He is the author of a commentary on ancient *piyutim*.

An elaborate *akeda*, which weaves together many aggadic elements and introduces a surprising variant: Abraham's *second* attempt to perform the sacrifice after Isaac's resurrection (stanza 16). S. Spiegel, who first published this poem in a masterful essay on the binding of Isaac (subsequently published in English, in book-form, as *The Last Trial*), quotes striking parallels from the chronicles of the time which relate how the martyrs were 'killed a second time' or removed from the grave and then buried again. The last line of each stanza is a biblical verse, not necessarily related to the story of Isaac or the ritual of sacrifice. The metre is four words to a line and all the stanzas, except the last, rhyme aabb. The initial letters of the first and third line in each stanza form an *atbash* (AZBY) acrostic followed by the signature: 'Ephraim bar Jacob, be mighty in Torah and good deeds.'

Concluding section of a long, emotional lament on the massacre at Blois (see following poem).

BARUKH OF MAGENZA (MAINZ) (*c.* 1150-1221) was a noted scholar and *dayan*. Many of his powerful *piyutim* deal with the persecutions in the years before and during the Third Crusade. The subject of the following *seliha*, of which only excerpts are given, is the massacre at Blois in 1171, when all the members of the Jewish community were burned at the stake following a blood libel.

ELIEZER BAR JUDAH OF WORMS (*c.*1165-*c.*1230) was the last major scholar of the *Ḥasidey Ashkenaz* movement. Born in Mainz, he studied in the centres of learning in Germany and Northern France, and wrote important works in the fields of ethics and esoteric theosophy. In his *piyutim*, as well as in his important commentary on the prayers and his short *Memoirs*, he recorded the widespread persecutions that followed the fall of Jerusalem to Saladin (1187). The following excerpts, from a simple narrative in rhymed couplets, describe the tragedy that struck the author in 1197. The deep piety that informs the poem is one of the distinguishing traits of *ḥasidut*.

JUDAH AL-ḤARIZI (*c.*1170-after 1235) was the master of the Hebrew *maqama*, a narrative in rhymed prose interspersed with metrical poems. A native of Christian Toledo, he lived for a while in Provence, then travelled extensively in the Near East. Before his departure from Spain (*c.* 1215) he completed his brilliant translation of the *maqamat* of the Arabic poet Al-Ḥariri (1054-1121), under the title *Maḥberot Iti'el* ('The Maqamas of Iti'el'). He then proceeded to use this form for his major work, *The Book of Taḥkemoni*, which shows the influence of his Arabic and Hebrew predecessors in this genre. Apart from its stylistic virtuosity, *Taḥkemoni* also records the author's impressions of Jewish communities in the Orient and his (often biased) evaluation of earlier and contemporary poets. The following poems are all taken from various episodes in *Taḥkemoni*, which consists of a series of fifty loosely-linked *maqamat*. The first three are part of a poetic duel between an old man, who claimed he could 'cleave rocks with his flinty tongue', and a young challenger. The youth sets the subject and the metre in the first two lines (ab), and the old man completes the quatrain with an appropriate simile and rhyme (cb).

Heber the Kenite, the roguish companion of the narrator of *Taḥkemoni*, chances upon a mountain village. His peasant host extends this rustic welcome.

This is the plea delivered by the 'big, soft, succulent' rooster, from the roof of a house of prayer, to the assembled villagers. The rooster was pursued for having kept Heber awake all night.

Heber is offered a beautiful young bride, sight unseen, for a price of 2,000 pieces of silver. When he unveils her after the wedding, he discovers that he has been duped, and addresses this song to her.

Al-Ḥarizi was a member of a wealthy family that became impoverished. He is known to have dedicated *Taḥkemoni* to four different patrons at different stages of his voyage through the East.

MEIR HALEVI ABULAFIA (*c.* 1170-1244), a renowned Talmudist and one of the early kabbalists of Toledo, wrote elegant secular verse which reflects his aristocratic background and his indebtedness to the works of Moses ibn Ezra. The following is an extract.

NAHMANIDES (1194-1270). Moses ben Naḥman, also known as RaMBaN (an acronym for Rabbi Moses Ben Naḥman), the highest religious authority of his time in Spain, was born in Gerona. As a young man he joined the ranks of the kabbalists, who drew their inspiration from the mystics of Provence. In 1263, at the command of King James I, he took part in a public disputation in Barcelona with the apostate Pablo Christiani. Though he emerged victorious from the confrontation and was even commended by the king, he was forced to flee for his life after the intervention of Pope Clement IV. He emigrated to Palestine in 1267, seven years after the invasion of the Tatar hordes, and was active in founding yeshivot and synagogues in Acre and Jerusalem. It was during these years that he composed most of his classic commentary on the Pentateuch.

Excerpts from a *mustajab* (see p. 106) which may have been the first *piyut* to employ the distinctive images and figures of speech of the Kabbalah. Naḥmanides believed that 'the special soul of man . . . the "over-soul", was pre-existent to the creation of the world, treasured up as a wave in the sea or fountain of souls – dwelling in the eternal light and holiness of God' (S. Schechter). After death, it returns to its source. It is 'clothed again' (line 39) in a celestial garment which it wove from its good deeds during its earthly stay.

DAVID HAKOHEN (fl. late thirteenth century) probably lived in Avignon. The four metrical hymns that have been preserved in French and North African rituals show a high degree of artistry. The following *reshut* is in the form of a *muwashshaḥ* with internal rhymes.

'*Bow down, my soul*' הִשְׁתַּחֲוִי וּבָרְכִי 396

ISAAC HAGORNI (fl. late thirteenth century) was born in Aire ('threshing floor', Hebrew *goren*, hence his name ha-*Gorni*). The most original of the Hebrew poets in Provence, he led the life of an impecunious troubadour, wandering through the Jewish communities of Southern France in search of patrons. He was hounded by his compatriots because of his amorous adventures and complained bitterly about their boorishness and parsimony. He also engaged in several harsh literary quarrels. Only eighteen of his poems have survived, in a single manuscript.

'*I shall now lament*' לְחִשְׁקִי הִנְנִי הוֹלֵךְ 397

The Andalusian tradition is apparent in the metre and form of this unusual poem, but the influence of the Christian environment is clearly felt, especially in the strange elaboration of the belief in relics.

'*From its very first day*' עִיר אַרְלְדִי 399

Opening section of a poem against the notables of Arles. Hagorni wrote in a similar vein against the communities of Aix-en-Provence, Apt and Draguignan.

MOSES BEN JOSEPH (fl. *c.* 1250) lived in Rome. The following *tokhaḥa* ('rebuke') is written in the form of an Italian *quartina* (abab). The last line of each stanza is a biblical quotation which often acquires a surprising meaning in the new context. The disputation between body and soul after death, in the presence of God, is a traditional motif, already found in the Talmud.

'*Listen to me, my limbs*' אִזְנוּ יְצוּרַי אֵלַי 400

IMMANUEL DEI ROSSI (late thirteenth century) also lived in Rome. His *tokhaḥa* follows one of the conventional Spanish patterns: it is written in rhymed tercets, each of which concludes with a biblical passage.

'*Doomed, man gives vent*' אֱנוֹשׁ אָנוּשׁ 405

MESHULLAM DA PIERA or DE PIERA (died after 1260) was one of the main figures in the circle of kabbalists in Gerona and was chosen to head the *consilium* of the community. Though he adhered to the metrics and uniform rhyme of the Andalusian school, his innovations affected the language, structure and subject-matter of secular poetry in Christian Spain. Unlike his predecessors, he made extensive use of rabbinic Hebrew and did not hesitate to borrow the vocabulary of scientific and philosophic translations. His poems are often intentionally enigmatic and bear an affinity to the hermetic style (*trobar clus*) of the Provençal poets. He modified the accepted form of the panegyric by enlarging the 'introduction', omitting the elegant 'transition verse' and reducing the actual laudation to a short *envoi*-like dedication.

Introduction to a panegyric addressed to Abraham ibn Ḥasdai of Barcelona, a noted translator and *maqama* writer.

Two sections from a long poem sent to his close friend Naḥmanides.

TODROS ABULAFIA (1247–after 1295), a native of Toledo, was presented before King Alfonso X and offered him panegyrics in Hebrew. In 1281 he was among the Jews of Castile arrested by order of Alfonso the Wise. It is not known how the poet, whose possessions were confiscated, regained his status at court. But by 1289 he was in the service of Sancho IV and later headed a group of Jewish financiers who received important monopolies. Todros arranged his copious works in *Gan Hameshalim Vehaḥidot* ('The Garden of Poems and Songs'), which presents an unusually candid picture of his love affairs, his experiences at court and his literary controversies. Though he introduced new themes into secular poetry, such as the troubadour theme of spiritual love, and initiated some mannerist forms, he was to some extent an epigone of the Andalusian school.

Abulafia's thematic innovations included love poems about Arab and Christian women. In the general mood of repentance that swept the community after the release of the Jewish prisoners, a ban (*ḥerem*) was proclaimed in the synagogue against those who maintained liaisons with non-Jewish women. Abulafia, however, did not mend his ways.

The last line is a typical example of the humour achieved by displacing a biblical phrase. In the original, Lamentations 1.14, the reference is to God's hand which 'plaits' or 'knots' the author's sins about his neck.

From a cycle of forty-seven girdle poems written in imitation of Arabic and Hebrew models. Almost all the poems were set to popular Arabic tunes. The *kharjas* are generally in vulgar Arabic and sometimes in Romance.

Like Meshullam da Piera, Abulafia made extensive use of Talmudic idiom, even including legalistic expressions in Aramaic (line 10).

The last line refers to the fact that the Jewish prisoners were deprived of food in an attempt to force them into conversion.

ABRAHAM ABULAFIA (1240-after 1291), the leading exponent of 'ecstatic' Kabbalah, was born in Saragossa and raised in Tudela. In 1260 he travelled to Palestine in search of the mythical river Sambatyon and the ten lost tribes. In Barcelona, at the age of thirty-one, he experienced a prophetic vision. Urged by an inner voice, he undertook a voyage to Rome in 1280 to confer with Pope Nicholas III 'in the name of Jewry'. The sudden death of the Pope, on the eve of his arrival, saved him from the stake. After a month in prison, he was released and returned to Sicily. His messianic revelations aroused strong opposition in rabbinic circles and he was forced to flee to the desolate island of Comino, near Malta. His kabbalistic manuals, many of which were written during the latter period of his life, are systematic guides to the theory and practice of meditation leading to mystical ecstasy. He also wrote over twenty 'prophetic works' of which only one, *Sefer Ha'ot* ('The Book of the Sign', 1288), is extant. The following two excerpts are taken from this abstruse, but undeniably poetic, apocalypse.

The numerical value of the Herald's name, *Zekharyahu* (line 6) is the same as that of the author's name *Avraham*. Gematria, the method of interpretation based on the numerical value of Hebrew words, plays an important part in Abulafia's system.

ABRAHAM BEN SAMUEL (thirteenth century), the author of the following *seliḥa*, which J. Schirmann considers 'one of the finest Hebrew poems of all time', has not been identified. Some scholars have conjectured that he is the famous mystic, Abraham ben Samuel Abulafia. The *seliḥa* is unrhymed (except for the last couplet) and written in free biblical cadence.

'To whom, among the avengers'   אֶל מִי מְגוֹאֲלֵי דָם   419

NAHUM (? late thirteenth century) is known as the author of a dozen *piyutim* in Sephardic liturgical collections. His delicate lyricism and feeling for nature achieve an unusual fusion of secular elements and religious ecstasy.

'Winter is gone'   הַסְּתָיו אָרַח   420

A *me'ora* in the form of a *muwashshah*. The spring landscape represents the time of redemption.

IMMANUEL OF ROME (*c.*1261-*c.*1332) was a source of inspiration for the Baroque poet Jacob Frances (p. 129), who called him 'the emperor of poets', as well as for Tchernikhovsky and Alterman in the twentieth century. Apparently he held the post of community scribe until he was forced to leave Rome temporarily because of some financial entanglement. He travelled extensively in Italy, devoting much of his time to writing biblical commentaries. In 1328 he returned to the home of his benefactor in Fermo and there edited his principal work *Maḥberot Imanu'el* ('The Maqamas of Immanuel'). It consists of twenty-eight *maḥbarot* (sing. *maḥberet*, Hebrew for *maqama*), alternating rhymed prose and metrical poetry, somewhat on the model of Al-Ḥarizi's *Taḥkemoni* (p. 114). The loose autobiographical framework of the book enabled Immanuel to group together poems, riddles, epigrams and epistles on a variety of subjects, written during different periods of his life. This work is unrivalled for its hilarious word-play and agile manipulation of the resources of the Hebrew language. The poetry combines the quantitative metres and ornaments of the Spanish school with strophic forms and motifs drawn from Italian verse. In the sonnet, a form which he introduced into Hebrew, he employed a new quantitative-syllabic metre. Known to his Christian friends as Manuello Giudeo, he also wrote poems in Italian and exchanged sonnets with his Italian colleagues. *Maḥberot Imanu'el* was among the first Hebrew books printed in Italy (Brescia, 1491). The following selection includes six sonnets, and two short poems in the Spanish style.

'Deep in my heart'   נַפְשִׁי בְּקִרְבִּי תַחֲשֹׁב   421

Like most of his thirty-eight sonnets, this is written in a Hebrew-Spanish metre, modified to correspond to the widespread Italian hendecasyllabic line. This became the favourite metrical scheme of Hebrew poetry in Italy.

This is prefaced by a long 'duel' in rhymed prose, in which the beautiful woman and the ugly woman (the daughter of the repulsive Gershom; line 2) are contrasted in great detail.

A love poem, written in the spirit of the *dolce stil nuovo*. In one of his sonnets, Immanuel included a final tercet adapted from Dante's *Vita Nuova*.

'Composed' by the virgin of the previous poem, after her marriage to an impotent mate.

Typical of Immanuel's ribald vein. Small wonder that the reading of his book 'on the Sabbath and even on week-days' was explicitly prohibited by the *Shulḥan Arukh* (The Standard Code of Jewish Law, *c.* 1569).

ISAAC ALḤADIB (died *c.* 1429), a native of Castile, was among the emigrants who sought refuge in Sicily towards the end of the fourteenth century. He lived in Syracuse and Palermo and gained fame as an astronomer. The following are excerpts from a thirty-five-stanza poem, extolling his mastery of all crafts, written in one of the Italian *ballata* forms (abababbccR). As in many of his satirical poems, the metre is eight 'long' syllables to the line.

DON VIDAL BENVENISTE (fl. early fifteenth century) was a member of a very influential family in Saragossa. The massacres of 1391, which destroyed practically all the Jewish communities of Catalonia and Aragon, by-passed Saragossa because of the king's presence in the town. It became the centre for the last circle of Hebrew poets in Spain, *Adat Nogenim* ('Band of Minstrels'), in which Vidal played the leading role. In 1413-14 he was one of the emissaries to the Disputation of Tortosa, initiated by the Antipope Benedict XIII. In the intensified persecution that followed the defeat of the Jews, Vidal and his teacher, the poet Solomon da Piera, were among the apostates. Vidal excels at satirical and aphoristic verse. His principal composition was the bawdy *maqama*, 'The Notebook of Epher and Dinah', from which the following poem is taken.

The beautiful but destitute Dinah is cajoled into marrying the old and impotent Epher. After objecting, 'Shall I in my youth ... lie with my forefathers' – a pun on the biblical phrase meaning 'to die' – she sings this song.

(Excerpts.) This was plagiarized in the middle of the sixteenth century by David Onkinerah of Salonika (p. 125).

SOLOMON BONAFED (died after 1445), the last prominent poet in Christian Spain, was the youngest member of the *Adat Nogenim* in Saragossa. The defection of many of his friends and the deterioration of the Jewish community filled him with a sense of futility which is expressed in his personal poetry. He engaged in bitter polemics with his opponents and in old age was forced to flee to the town of Belchite. There he wrote a scathing satire in rhymed prose against the notables of Saragossa. His compositions include outspoken love lyrics, philosophical poems and *reshuyot*, some of which are set to Spanish melodies.

Written to comfort a friend who had lost his fortune.

MOSES DA RIETI (1388–after 1460) practised as a physician in his native town of Rieti. Later he served as rabbi to the local community in Rome and became private physician to Pope Pius II. At the age of twenty-four he wrote his most important work, *Mikdash Me'at* ('The Little Shrine'), an adaptation in *terza rima* of the *Divine Comedy*. His decasyllabic line (*endecasillabo tronco*) marks the first appearance of overt syllabic metre in Hebrew poetry in Italy. One of the cantos from this work was adopted into the ritual and sung in the synagogue in his lifetime. The following sections are from the second part of the epic which describes the celestial court.

MOSES GABBAI (died *c.* 1443) served as rabbi in Teruel (Aragon) and later settled in Majorca. During the riots of 1391 he escaped to Algeria, where he was appointed rabbi of Honein. The following poem is partly based on the Mishnah (*Ta'anith* 2) which details the ceremonies for invoking rain in time of drought. On the last seven days of fasting, it was customary to 'put wood-ashes on the Ark and on the heads of the President and the Father of the court' (last stanza). An unusual feature of the poem is the use of a refrain (lines 1–2) and narrative technique traditionally associated with certain *avodot* (poems describing the service of the high priest in the Temple).

'Happy the eye that saw'   אַשְׁרֵי עַיִן רָאֲתָה   436

MOSES REMOS (*c.*1406–*c.*1430) was born in Majorca, studied science and philosophy in Rome and practised medicine in Palermo. At the age of twenty-four he was condemned to death, ostensibly for having poisoned a Christian patient. He rejected an offer of pardon on condition that he renounce his faith. The following elegy, of which excerpts are given, was written on the eve of his execution. In other sections of the poem he describes how the ten *Sefirot*, the Active Intelligence, the planets and the Sciences all join in the lament.

'Who could have believed'   מִי הֶאֱמִין כִּי כְמוֹת נָבָל   437

RAPHAEL DA FAENZA (fl. middle of fifteenth century) is known to have lived in Florence. The following poem may have been an adaptation of an Italian song.

'Hear my words, my dearest'   רַעְיָתִי, לִי אָזְנֵךְ הַטִּי-נָא   441

ANONYMOUS (thirteenth to sixteenth century). This section comprises a miscellany of poems from Spain (?), Provence, the Near East and Germany. The first four are written in classical Hispano-Arabic metres; the rest have a distinct popular tone.

'Lord, how much longer'   יָהּ, לְמָתַי פֵּרוּד יַנְחֵדֵנִי   443

An *ahava* for Passover, in the form of a *muwashshah* with internal rhymes, probably of Spanish origin.

'My heart goes out to Jokhebed'   לִבִּי לְיוֹכֶבֶד   445

Has been attributed to Samuel ben Moses Dayan of Aleppo (Syria). It is one of the laments on the death of Moses that were sung in Aleppo on the holiday of the Rejoicing of the Law. It is in the form of a *muwashshah*.

'When I see that the rains'   בִּרְאוֹתִי כִּי עָבַר   446

A melodious *piyut* for Passover which makes extensive use of secular love imagery. It is apparently of Provençal origin. It has a fixed line pattern of eight and seven syllables: $a_8b_7a_8b_7a_8b_7a_8a_8b_7a_4$. Two rhymes (a – masculine, b – feminine) recur throughout the poem. In line 11, the rhyme is formed by part of the word (*uvkir-*), a technique which is already found in eleventh-century Spanish poems.

JOSEPH HAKOHEN (1496-1578), a native of Avignon, practised medicine in
Italy. He is noted for his historiographical works. In the following monorhymed
poem he numerates the 'thirty-three conditions' of beauty in a woman. It is amusing
to compare it to an earlier poem on the same theme (pp. 360-61).

SIMEON LABI (died *c.* 1585) was brought to Fez, probably from Spain, in the year
of the expulsion. In 1549 he settled in Tripoli, where he engaged in teaching and
kabbalistic studies.

A kabbalistic hymn in honour of Simeon ben (bar) Yoḥai, the second-century *tanna*,
who, according to legend, hid from the Romans for twelve years in a cave, together
with his son Eleazar, buried up to the neck in sand and studying the Torah. He is the
classic hero of Jewish mysticism, to whom tradition attributed the authorship of the
Zohar and other pseudepigrapha. The hymn consists of ten stanzas corresponding to
the ten *Sefirot*, the powers that constitute the manifestations and emanations of God.
In describing Bar Yoḥai's ascent to the supreme mystery, each stanza employs the
highly charged symbols appropriate to the *Sefira* which it represents. This poem
became the most popular kabbalistic hymn; it is still sung today by Oriental Jews
during the festivities of *Lag Ba'omer* at the traditional site of Bar Yoḥai's tomb in
Meron, near Safed.

SA'ADIAH LONGO (sixteenth century), born in Turkey, was the senior member
of the *Ḥakhmey Hashir* ('Masters of Poetry'), a literary circle in Salonika. He was the
author of ribald poems and versified polemics. One of the more spiteful exchanges
was occasioned by his marriage, in old age, to a young wife. Like other members of
the Greek-Turkish group, his poems are written partly in traditional Spanish forms
and partly under the influence of the Italian school and local folk-songs.

This is set to the tune of a popular Ladino song. The opening verses serve as the
refrain. It has been suggested that Longo was facetiously referring to himself as the
'scoundrel'.

DAVID ONKINERAH (sixteenth century), perhaps a native of Istanbul, was the youngest and most gifted member of the Salonika 'Academy'. Strangely enough, the first poem he sent Longo as a 'visiting-card' was a plagiarism. The 'master' rebuked him in verse, Onkinerah wrote a witty confession, and the two became firm friends.

JUDAH ZARCO (sixteenth century) was born in Rhodes and for some time played an active role in the Salonika circle. The following poems are taken from his *maqama Lehem Yehuda* ('Judah's Bread', Istanbul, 1560). It has an unusually complex structure, both formal and allegorical, and abounds in original, and often difficult, conceits.

JOSEPH BIBAS (fl. early sixteenth century) lived in Constantinople. His jocular poem is written in syllabic metre, alternating lines of eight and seven syllables (abab):

SAMUEL ARCHEVOLTI (1515-1611) was born in Cesena and lived in Venice and Padua. He was influential as a grammarian and rhetorician. The last chapter of his major work, *Arugat Habosem* ('The Bed of Spices'), is devoted to theories of versification and cites many of his own poems to illustrate metrical forms.

The last tercet of this sonnet refers to Zachariah's prophecy (9.9): 'Lo, your king comes to you . . . humble and riding on an ass.'

MORDECAI DATO (1525-*c.*1600), an Italian kabbalist, wrote biblical commentaries, messianic propaganda, and memoirs of a visit to Safed.

ISAAC LURIA (1534-72) is referred to as *Ha'ari* ('the lion'), an anagram of his Hebrew appellation 'the Divine Rabbi Isaac'. He was the most important kabbalistic figure after the expulsion from Spain. Born in Jerusalem and brought up in Egypt, he spent the last two years of his life in Safed. Here he exercised a profound influence on his select disciples, who propagated the Lurianic system after his death. He was at first known as a poet; his mystical hymns for Sabbath meals, written in Aramaic, are found in most prayer books. However, only a few of his poems make use of kabbalistic symbolism.

ELIEZER AZIKRI (1533-1600) was one of the outstanding poets among 'the lion whelps', the circle of Luria's disciples in Safed. His classical work on kabbalistic ethics, *Sefer Ḥaredim* ('The Book of the Devout', Venice, 1601), was widely read. The following 'prayer for Unification', in syllabic metre, contains the Tetragrammaton in its acrostic. Its gentle tone and purity of feeling have made it one of the favourite hymns in the prayer book.

ISRAEL NAJARA (?1555-?1625), apparently a native of Damascus, was the most significant poet in the revival of religious poetry under the impact of the Kabbalah. He travelled extensively in the Near East, lived at times in Safed and, in old age, served as a rabbi in Gaza. An extremely prolific poet, his work is noteworthy for its musical fluency and inventiveness. His devotional poems are set to popular Turkish, Armenian, Spanish and new Greek melodies. This fact, coupled with his bohemian wanderings and his erotic-mystical imagery, aroused the opposition of some prominent rabbis. But Luria's enthusiastic endorsement silenced the critics and the poetry achieved unusually wide circulation among the Oriental communities, spreading as far as Aden, Calcutta and Cochin.

'Now I shall raise'   נְהִי נִהְיָה אֲעוֹרֵר   472

A ballad-like dirge for the Ninth of Av which is based on the following legend: '. . . Doeg ben Joseph died and left a young son to his mother, who used to measure him by handbreadths and give his weight in gold to the Temple every year. When, however, the besieging army [of Babylonia] surrounded Jerusalem, his mother slaughtered him and ate him' (*Midrash Rabbah: Lamentations*, 1.51).

'Sleep deserts my eyes'   תַּדַּד שְׁנַת עֵינִי   477
'Languishing in exile'   יְדִידִים לָאֵל נִבְחָרוּ   477

One of the many poems which reflect the feverish messianic currents of the time. Like most of his poems, it is written in a syllabic metre, in this case eight syllables to a line.

ANONYMOUS (fourteenth to seventeenth century). This section consists of poems written in Yemen. Early Yemenite poetry is dominated by the Spanish school. From the sixteenth century on, partly under the influence of the Kabbalah, it develops its distinctive regional flavour. All Yemenite poetry is meant to be sung, and certain categories are also accompanied by percussion and dancing.

'The love of the princely daughter'   אַהֲבַת בַּת נָדְבָה   478

This girdle poem was erroneously ascribed to Judah Halevi. It is included in W. Bacher's list of anonymous poems from Yemen.

'Shalom, I swear by you'   שָׁלוֹם, בָּךְ נִשְׁבַּעְתִּי   479

Stanzas 3 and 8 allude to the 'smooth words' of the adulteress in Proverbs 7.12-20. In a later manuscript version (*c.* 1661) these stanzas were deleted and the poem was read as a monologue addressed by a bride to her beloved.

'Old and grey as I am'   לִקְרַאת שָׁבָת   481

One of a group of Yemenite poems written in alternating Hebrew and Aramaic stanzas. Only the Hebrew is printed here.

'The star looked down'   כּוֹכָב אֲשֶׁר הִשְׁקִיף   481

Wholly secular poems, such as this song of friendship, are comparatively rare in Yemenite poetry.

SA'ADIAH BEN AMRAM (? sixteenth century) is the author of the following popular verses which are sung by Yemenite Jews to a merry Turkish tune. The meaning of the Arabic stanzas (3 and 4) is somewhat obscure. The majority of Yemenite poems were written in Hebrew-Arabic or entirely in Arabic. The poem is allegorical and employs kabbalistic terminology.

SA'ADIAH (c. sixteenth century) also signed his poems SA'ID or ḤaZMaK. The last two names are identical if the letters of the Hebrew alphabet are listed in *atbash* order (i.e. Z = A, Y = B). Many of his poems are devoted to the favourite Yemenite themes: the Sabbath and the festivals. The following *havdala* is still sung today.

SHALEM SHABAZI (died after 1681), the foremost Yemenite poet, was born in Ta'izz, in South Yemen, and probably earned his livelihood as an itinerant weaver. His hundreds of poems, written in Hebrew, Arabic or Aramaic, deal primarily with religious themes and reflect the messianic expectations of the Jews of Yemen and the persecutions of 1679-81, which destroyed more than half the Jewish population. His poetry draws its inspiration from pre-Lurianic Kabbalah and owes much to Najara. Though it employs simple, almost prosaic, rabbinic diction, avoiding the rhetorical flourishes of the classical Spanish school, the meaning is often puzzling because of the mystical allusions and the abrupt transitions from one subject to another.

An allegorical epithalamium. In the first stanza the poet speaks for the congregation of Israel. The terrestrial wedding symbolizes the nuptials of God and Israel, the renewal of the ancient covenant, and the joy of redemption.

The opening phrase, 'Who kissed me until/while I . . .' is a formula specific to Yemenite poetry. It usually introduces a religious allegory which, at first, seems to be a sensual love poem.

'From the far reaches'   שָׁמַעְתִּי מִפְּאַתֵי תֵימָן   489

Excerpts from a poem which Shabazi probably improvised during the ceremony of circumcision. The Yemenite *diwan* consists largely of such lyrical, semi-religious songs which are performed in the home on holidays and festivities.

JOSEPH JEDIDIAH CARMI (*c.* 1590–?) was appointed cantor of a private synagogue in Modena. For the 'Association for Vigils' (*Shomerim Laboker*) of this congregation he composed his kabbalistic *piyutim* and prayers in rhymed prose. The following is an excerpt from a rhythmical prayer. In his marginal glosses Carmi points out that the moon represents the people of Israel.

'Ehyeh-Asher-Ehyeh'   אֶהְיֶה אֲשֶׁר אֶהְיֶה   490

JUDAH ARYEH (LEONE) MODENA (1571–1648) was born in Venice and studied under the poet-grammarian Samuel Archevolti in Padua. A child prodigy, he translated passages from Ariosto's *Orlando Furioso* at the age of twelve. He became famous as a rabbi and preacher in Venice and was the author of the first autobiography in Hebrew, *The Life of Judah*. In this unusually revealing narrative he lists twenty-six professions at which he tried his hand, among them: *maestro di cappella*, author of an Italian comedy, *dayan*, alchemist (his son died of lead poisoning after one of the experiments), writer of amulets and talismans, and matchmaker. He was addicted to gambling and, as a result, was perpetually on the verge of penury. At the request of the English Ambassador in Venice, he wrote *Historia de riti ebraici* for presentation to King James I. An avid polemicist, he wrote famous tracts against Christianity, Karaism and the Kabbalah, and a condemnation of games of chance.

'On this day, may the weight'   יוֹם זֶה יְהִי מִשְׁקָל   491

A *seliha* for the eve of the new month, which, in the Hebrew calendar, coincides with the new moon. The custom of observing this day as a 'minor Day of Atonement' was instituted by the kabbalists of Safed towards the end of the sixteenth century. The poem is written in a quantitative-syllabic metre, alternating masculine and feminine rhymes, and has a *ballata*-like form.

JACOB FRANCES (1615–67) was the last major poet before the modern period. Born in Mantua, he acquired a thorough knowledge of Portuguese (which was his mother tongue), Italian, Aramaic and Latin. He courageously attacked the kabbalists and, later, the fervent followers of Shabbetai Tsevi (who proclaimed himself as the Messiah in 1665 and converted to Islam the following year). His anti-kabbalistic poems were banned and destroyed, he was stoned in the street and his house was ransacked. More than once, he was forced to seek refuge in Venice or Florence, where he eventually died. His collected works (published by P. Naveh in 1969 on the basis of a Bodleian autograph) comprise over 200 poems, including some fifty sonnets. However, only isolated poems were published during his lifetime. His satirical talent is matched only by that of Immanuel of Rome, whose influence he acknowledged. His love poems are among the finest in the baroque school of Hebrew poetry. A virtuoso technician, he employed many of the current Italian forms, but was equally skilful in the classical Spanish style. The close literary rapport between him and his younger brother, Immanuel, presents an unusual phenomenon: they collaborated in the writing of poems, and after Jacob's death, Immanuel added passages to some of his brother's poems, edited and revised them, and even completed them on the basis of rough drafts. He also compiled books which consisted of Jacob's poems and his own, suitably arranged and linked together by transitional passages in rhymed prose. There is still no definitive way of ascertaining the authorship of some of the poems by the Frances brothers.

One of several bitter poems against Rabbi Yeḥiel Norzi, a member of the Mantuan *bet-din* that banned his work. The sonnet is preceded by a note in Portuguese: 'For the death of Yeḥiel [the name is in code], a man who has not a single virtue, and is therefore the enemy of all good men.' Jacob often prefaced his poems with Portuguese comments and coded key words to avoid detection by the community's spies and investigators. The code was deciphered by the Italian scholar and poet S. D. Luzzatto (1800-1865).

The Portuguese note reads: 'For the marriage of two Germans.' It has been suggested that the sonnet refers to German Jews, whose excessive drinking was ridiculed by the Sephardim. The irony of this 'anti-epithalamium' is heightened by the bombastic biblical allusion in the last line (Exodus 15.11).

In Greek mythology, sleep (Hypnos) and death (Thanatos) are twin brothers.

Excerpts from a jesting epithalamium in *ottava rima*, written (and probably recited) in honour of his brother's second marriage in 1656. The superscription attributes the poem to a 'Hebrew Scapin', which, in Hebrew, is an anagram of the author's name. The poem, which employs popular Italian expressions, is a technical *tour de force*, alternating quantitative-syllabic and syllabic metrical patterns.

The sestet was written by Immanuel, probably after his brother's death. Jacob, it seems, had intended a different conclusion. The Portuguese note after the octave reads: 'Etc., to a beautiful portrait that will remain young forever.'

Written after seeing 'a beautiful woman kissing the body of her young husband, who was taken away by Heaven'.

IMMANUEL FRANCES (1618-*c.*1710) did not lag far behind his brother in poetic achievement. He was born and died in Leghorn. His wife – she was the sister of Jacob's wife – and two of his children died in 1654. Two years later he remarried (see Jacob's poem on p. 496). But the second wife and the son she bore him died in 1667. In the latter part of his life he served as a rabbi and highly regarded Talmudic authority in Florence. His poetry spans more than eighty years; it includes Italianate love poems, satirical dialogues against women and rabbis, and religious works of a dramatic and recitative character, some of which were commissioned by musical societies. Like Jacob, he set both secular and synagogal poems to popular Italian melodies. Though he occasionally used traditional Spanish patterns, he preferred Italian forms. He is best known for the collection of sarcastic poems *Tsevi Mudaḥ* ('The Banished Gazelle [*Tsevi*]'), a vehement denunciation of Shabbetai Tsevi and the messianic movement that engulfed the Jews of Italy. However, of the twenty-one poems in this book, seventeen are by Jacob. During a stay in Algiers in 1678 Immanuel composed the first draft of an important work on poetics and rhetoric, *Metek Sefatayim* ('Pleasing Speech'), which combined traditional and Baroque elements.

Recalls the rustic imagery of Al-Ḥarizi's peasant-host (pp. 389-90).

The seventh section of a long poem in *ottava rima*, sung by 'an evil old hag'.

This poem and the first of the following epitaphs are taken from 'The Dialogue of Itti'el and Ukhal', a mini-*maqama* against women. The 'Dialogue' consists of rhymed prose which links together sonnets, epigrams, and monorhymed verses in the Spanish manner. Six of the ten poems are by Jacob.

EPHRAIM LUZZATO (1729-92) was born in San Daniele and studied medicine in Padua. In 1763 he was appointed physician in London's Portuguese community hospital. His disregard for religious decorum (he wore his physician's sword on the Sabbath) attracted much criticism. He died in Lausanne, on his way back to Italy. In 1768 he published his collected poems in London in a limited edition of 100 copies. Entitled *Ele Bene Hane'urim* ('These Are the Sons of One's Youth') because most of them had been written in Italy, the volume contains over fifty poems, mostly sonnets in quantitative-syllabic metres. It was often republished and influenced the leading poets of the nineteenth-century Haskalah ('Enlightenment') movement. The lyrical quality of the love poems and the emphasis on individual experience made Luzzato a precursor of the modern period.

This sonnet limits itself to two alternating rhyme-words, 'water' and 'stone', and presents an amusing mosaic of scriptural allusions.

PART THREE: MODERN TIMES

HAYIM NAHMAN BIALIK (1873-1934) was acclaimed as 'the poet of the national renaissance' with the publication of his first book (Warsaw, 1901). He created a rich and flexible diction, which broke the stranglehold of Haskalah rhetoric (see p. 41) and was largely responsible for the abandonment of the syllabic system in favour of tonic-syllabic (accentual) metres. Born in Radi (Southern Russia), his large family was left destitute after the death of his father in 1880. In his sixteenth year he was sent off to prepare for the rabbinate in the yeshiva of Volozhin (Lithuania), where he came into contact with a clandestine Zionist group and with Russian poetry. The resultant crisis of faith, the clash between traditional Judaism and Western secularism, was to become a central theme of his poetry. In 1891 he went to Odessa, to join the literary circle that had gathered around the philosopher Ahad Ha'am. During the next two decades he composed all his major poems. His comprehensive anthology of rabbinic lore, *Sefer Ha'agada* ('The Book of Legends'), and his editions of medieval poets, all compiled in collaboration with H. J. Rawnitzki, played a crucial role in re-linking Hebrew literature to its older sources. In 1921 he was one of a group of Hebrew writers who, thanks to the intervention of Maxim Gorky, were permitted to leave the Soviet Union. After three years in Hamburg and Berlin, which had become centres for Jewish emigré writers, he settled in Tel Aviv, where he devoted most of his energy to publishing and public affairs. He died in Vienna, where he had gone for medical treatment. His poetry includes long descriptive and allegorical works, 'pro-phetic' denunciations of the passivity of the Jewish people, an enigmatic, mystical prose poem *Megilat Ha'esh* ('The Scroll of Fire'), folk-songs of unusual charm and, above all, lyrical verse which is often marked by acute despair. All his poetry, except for some of his children's poems, was written in the Ashkenazi accent.

This is the first section of the poem. Cosmic and mythic images are a recurrent element in his poetry.

Written after the pogrom in Kishinev (Bessarabia) in Easter, 1903. Shortly afterwards Bialik was sent there, on behalf of the Jewish Historical Commission in Odessa, to interview survivors and prepare a report on the atrocity. The title of the poem, 'On the Slaughter', is the concluding phrase of the blessing employed in ritual slaughter; this blessing was used by the martyrs in medieval Germany and Spain who sacrificed each other rather than submit to conversion (see, for example, p. 373, line 4). The poem is tightly structured; each stanza is identical in metre and rhyme. It draws heavily on Judges 6 and on Psalms, often creating tension by a reversal of biblical meaning.

SAUL TCHERNIKHOVSKY (1875-1943) was the most 'European' poet of the Odessa group. Unlike most of his eastern European contemporaries, who received a thorough religious education, he was privately tutored in Russian and modern Hebrew in his native village of Mikhalovka (near Crimea). His first book of poems (Warsaw, 1898) was notable for its variety of verse-forms and its Romantic nature imagery. After several years in Heidelberg, he completed his medical studies in Lausanne (1905). Upon returning to Russia, he was imprisoned for six weeks in Melitopol as a 'political agitator'. He served as an army doctor throughout the First

World War. In 1931, after having lived mainly in Odessa and Berlin, he settled in Tel Aviv, where he was appointed physician to the municipal schools. He translated works from fifteen different languages, including the *Iliad* and the *Odyssey*; poems by Anacreon, Horace, Goethe, Byron and Shelley; plays by Sophocles, Shakespeare and Molière; and a series of national epics (*Gilgamesh*, *Kalevala*, and sections from Siberian, Georgian and Icelandic verse narratives). The Hellenic ideal of beauty and the Canaanite cult, as opposed to the strictures of Diaspora Judaism, figure largely in his poetry. At the same time, he celebrated traditional Jewish village life in a series of idylls in dactylic hexameter. Some of his best work was written in old age; it was cast in the Sephardic accent and expressed his awareness of the physical presence of the land. .

This is the seventh sonnet of a corona sequence (*sonnet redoublé*) entitled 'To the Sun' (1919). The scene is an underground operating-room at the front. The opening line is a powerful echo of Numbers 17.13: 'And he [Aaron] stood between the dead and the living, and the plague was checked . . .'

Included in 'The Ballads of Worms', a series of seven poems based on episodes from medieval Jewish history. The entire Jewish community of Worms, 350 souls, destroyed itself by fire during the persecutions of 1349. The 'Ballads' were written in 1942, in response to the horrors of the Holocaust.

JACOB FICHMAN (1881–1958), a native of Belz (Bessarabia), ran away from home at the age of fourteen and afterwards lived in Odessa, where he came in contact with the 'Bialik circle'. After working in Warsaw and Vilna, he settled in Palestine in 1912. An influential editor and anthologist, he gained recognition for his impressionistic critical essays and his conscientious artistry. Like many of his contemporaries, he later 'transposed' some of his poems from the Ashkenazi to the Sephardic pronunciation.

AVRAHAM BEN YITSHAK (1883-1950) printed only eleven poems during his lifetime, nine of them before the First World War. Born in Przemysl (Galicia), he studied at the universities of Vienna and Berlin. After serving as general secretary of the Zionist Executive Council in London (1920), he headed the Hebrew Pedagogical Institute in Vienna up to the Nazi occupation of Austria, when he left for Jerusalem

(1938). His style is highly individual, combining biblical vocabulary with terseness and purity of expression and a rich musical texture. He wrote according to the Sephardic pronunciation long before it was adopted by other poets. He was 'rediscovered' with the publication of his collected poems in 1952, and 'is considered by many to be the first truly modern Hebrew poet' (Lea Goldberg).

This was the last poem he published (1930). The opening line evokes, and reverses the meaning of, Psalms 126.5 and Isaiah 32.20.

One of the few poems and fragments found among the author's effects.

JACOB STEINBERG (1887-1947), essayist and short-story writer, was born in Belaya Tserkov (the Ukraine). In Warsaw he wrote for Hebrew and Yiddish journals, and at the outbreak of the First World War emigrated to Palestine. Introspective and sceptical, his lyrical poetry reveals a persistent quest for the word that contains 'an epic of life'. Although he clung to Ashkenazi Hebrew and traditional techniques, his uncompromising individuality attracted the admiration of the poets of the fifties. The second of the following poems is typical of his passion for enigmatic affinities and paradoxes.

The first of a series of love poems.

DAVID VOGEL (1891-?1944), a native of Satanov (Russia), spent his youth in Vilna and Lvov, and settled in Vienna (1912). During the First World War he was imprisoned in Austrian detention camps as an enemy (Russian) national. From 1925 he lived mainly in Paris, and when the Second World War broke out, he was imprisoned by the French as an enemy (Austrian) alien. He was released after the capitulation of France (1941), then arrested by the Nazis (1944) and most likely perished in a concentration camp. Almost all his poems were written in free rhythm. Their imagery is startling and allusive, their tone restrained and dream-like. Like Ben Yitzhak and Steinberg, his poetry became an active influence in the fifties. He published only one volume of poems, *Lifney Hasha'ar Ha'afel* ('Before the Dark Gate', Vienna, 1923), a few stories and a novel set in a TB sanatorium.

Published posthumously. It was one of his last poems, written in Hauteville, near Lyons, after his release from the French detention camp.

ISRAEL EFRAT (b. 1891) was born in Ostrog (the Ukraine) and emigrated to the United States in 1905. He founded the Baltimore Hebrew College and held chairs in medieval Jewish philosophy and modern Hebrew literature at various American universities. In 1955 he settled in Israel and served as rector of Tel Aviv University. He has written some of his most intense lyrical poems in recent years.

URI ZVI GREENBERG (b. 1896), a native of Bialykamien (Galicia), received a Hasidic upbringing in Lvov. In 1915 he was drafted into the Austrian army and served on the Serbian front. Two years later he deserted and returned to Lvov, where he witnessed the Polish pogroms. He published poems in both Yiddish and Hebrew and was a prominent member of a Yiddish *avant-garde* expressionist group centred in Warsaw and Berlin. He emigrated to Palestine in 1923 as a sympathizer of the Socialist Labour movement, but in the wake of the Arab riots of 1929 joined the extremist Revisionist Party. Two protracted stays in Poland (1931-5, 1939) strengthened his premonition of the impending tragedy. During Israel's struggle for national independence, he was active in the ranks of the Irgun Tseva'i Le'umi, and in 1949 was elected to the Knesset as a member of the Herut Party. His poetry reveals a passionate identification of personal experience with Jewish messianic destiny, and a deep-rooted belief in the eternal enmity between 'the Star of David' and 'the Cross and the Crescent'. His heavily charged idiom draws on the resources of biblical prophecy, medieval dirges and kabbalistic symbolism. In early manifestos and in some of his poetry he sharply rejected 'European aesthetics'.

Appears in Greenberg's third book of Hebrew poetry, *Anacreon at the Pole of Melancholy* (1928).

The first of a series of poems entitled 'At the Rim of Heaven', from *Reḥovot Hanahar* ('The Streets of the River', 1951), a monumental series of laments for the loss of European Jewry.

Line 11 (except for the word 'hearts') is in Aramaic; 'over there' refers to the destroyed European home.

SIMON HALKIN (b. 1898) emigrated from Bolsk (White Russia) to the United States in his fifteenth year. Except for seven years in Tel Aviv (1932-9), he lived in America, holding various academic posts, until 1949, when he returned to Israel to take up the chair of modern Hebrew literature at the Hebrew University of Jerusalem. He has been influential as a novelist and critic. His translations include Whitman's *Leaves of Grass* and works by Shelley and Seferis. His compressed and densely textured poetry bears the mark of his Hasidic background and his intimate knowledge of American and European literature. The title of the following poem is part of a blessing ('Blessed be the *true judge*, who causes death and life') which is recited at the burial service.

ABRAHAM SHLONSKY (1900-1973) spearheaded the revolt against the 'school of Bialik' and made a major contribution to the modernization of Hebrew poetry. Born in Karyokov (the Ukraine), he was sent to Palestine at the age of thirteen to study at the first secondary school in Tel Aviv. He completed his studies during the First World War in Russia, and in 1921 returned to Palestine with a group of pioneers. A year's stay in Paris (1925) left a deep imprint on his writing. A brilliant and prolific translator, he influenced the development of Hebrew poetry with his classic renditions of Blok (*The Twelve*), Pushkin (*Eugene Onegin*), and Shakespeare (*Hamlet, King Lear*). As editor, polemicist, popular lyricist and author of children's literature, he set the literary tone for an entire generation. From the early forties he headed the literary Left, but his own poetry is rarely overtly political. Of the following poems, the first two were written in the early twenties, when he worked as a road builder in the Valley of Jezreel (see p. 45), and the last represents his later 'prosaic' tone.

YOKHEVED BAT-MIRIAM (1901-80), a native of Keplits (White Russia), grew up in a traditional Hasidic home and later received a modern education in Russian and Hebrew. She settled in Palestine in 1929, following a brief stay in Paris. Her poetry is often marked by the elusive style of the Russian Symbolists.

The first of a cycle of thirteen poems inspired by memories of childhood in Southern Russia. The unnamed feminine singular 'you' (*at*), to whom the poem is addressed, is the country that the poet left behind.

AVOT YESHURUN (b. 1904) was brought up in the devout Hasidic atmosphere of his grandfather's home in Krasnystaw (Poland). In 1925 he emigrated to Palestine, and for many years roamed the country's Jewish-Arab villages, working as a building-hand, fruit-picker and watchman. An identification of the eastern European Jew and the Palestinian Arab as victims of exile underlies much of his poetry, which is often studded with expressions in Yiddish and Arabic, bilingual puns and portmanteau words. Though his style is perhaps the most idiosyncratic in contemporary Hebrew poetry, his themes are often political and his tone ironically or elegiacally moralistic. The first three poems given below are extracted from *Thirty Pages¹ of Avot Yeshurun*, a series of letters exchanged between the poet and those in his home country whom he 'sentenced to the hard labour of endless longing':

ḤAYIM LENSKI (1905-?1942) was born in Slonim (White Russia). After two years (1921-3) at the Hebrew Teachers' Seminary in Vilna, he settled down in Leningrad, where he worked in a metal factory. In 1934 he was arrested for writing Hebrew and was sentenced to five years' hard labour in Siberia. While in the camps he continued to write lyrical poems, dramatic ballads and trenchant satires, remarkable for their bold imagery and musicality. He also translated the Vogul epic *The Tundra Book*. His poems managed to reach Palestine until 1937, when he was transferred to the notorious forced labour camp of Gornaya Shoriya, near the Mongolian border. Having served his time, he returned to Leningrad, but soon afterwards was again arrested and sent to the prison camp of Malaya Vyshera, and from there to Siberia, where, as far as can be ascertained, he died of hunger. His first collection was published in Palestine in 1939. In 1958 a manuscript in the poet's handwriting, containing 131 unpublished poems, reached Israel, and was published under the title *Beyond the River Lethe*. This title was taken from a late sonnet addressed to the Hebrew language:

1. Hebrew *amudim*, which also means 'synagogue lecterns' and 'pillars'.

'Queen! As I have transported your troops . . . beyond the Don, the Neva and the Neman . . . so will you transport my name beyond the river Lethe, like the names of the ancients, Heman [the singer] and Halevi.'

One of a series of ten sonnets written in Leningrad around 1931.

YONATAN RATOSH (b. 1908), a controversial political and literary figure, was brought up in a Hebrew-speaking home in Warsaw, and emigrated with his family to Palestine in 1921. In the mid-thirties he edited the Revisionist Party newspaper and was active in right-wing underground movements. In 1939 he founded 'The Young Hebrews', or, as it was popularly known, the 'Canaanite' movement. This group rejected both the Jewish religion and Zionism in favour of a new identity which would share in the cultural heritage of the Fertile Crescent. The literary expression of this ideology, in the work of Ratosh and his followers, was an archaic 'pre-biblical' style, inspired by Canaanite mythology and Ugaritic epics. Although the movement was never broad, its emphasis on myth and its stylistic mannerisms had considerable impact on contemporary poetry. In his later books Ratosh went to the other extreme and cultivated a very colloquial diction. The following dirge, written for the poet's father, is intended as a hymn for the pall-bearers. It describes how the dead man is borne westward to the palace of El, who presides over the Canaanite pantheon:

NATHAN ALTERMAN (1910-70), for a time the most influential poet since Bialik, was born in Warsaw and settled in Tel Aviv in 1925. After completing his secondary school studies, he specialized in agronomy in Nancy, but upon his return took up a journalistic post. A disciple of Shlonsky and of Russian and French Modernism, he soon became the leading 'imagist' poet of his generation. His five books of poetry, each of which marks a distinct stage in his development, are noteworthy for their exhilarating wit, their adroit manipulation of traditional forms, and sensitivity to the rhythms of the spoken language. From 1943 onwards he wrote a weekly satirical column in verse ('The Seventh Column') which played an important role in expressing and shaping public opinion. As a translator, he set a new standard in his versions of Shakespeare, Racine, Molière and old English and Scottish ballads.

This is the fourth and last section of a market-scene entitled 'As Evening Falls'.

Taken from Simḥat Aniyim ('The Joy of the Poor'), one of the major works of modern

Hebrew poetry. This poem is spoken by the dead lover, who is the central figure of the sequence, to his living beloved. Line 3 is patterned on a well-known Talmudic saying: 'The poor man is regarded as dead.'

LEA GOLDBERG (1911–70) was born in Koenigsberg and spent the early years of her life in Kovno (Lithuania). After receiving her Ph.D. in Semitic languages at the University of Bonn, she emigrated to Palestine in 1935. Together with Abraham Shlonsky she edited an influential anthology of Russian poetry in translation. Subsequently she was chairman of the Department of Comparative Literature at the Hebrew University. Her poetry is characterized by clarity, universality and lyrical delicacy. Some of her finest love poems – often conversational – take the form of sonnet sequences. In addition to Lithuanian folk-songs, she translated poems by Petrarch, Dante, Baudelaire and Rilke. She also excelled as a writer for children in prose and verse.

The grandmother wears a wig (stanza 3) in keeping with Orthodox Jewish custom.

The first of six poems entitled 'The Shortest Voyage', written in the early sixties (see p. 46).

GABRIEL JOSHUA PREIL (b. 1911), a native of Dorpat (Estonia), has lived in the United States since 1922, writing mainly in Hebrew, but also in Yiddish and English. His Hebrew translations include poems by Jeffers, Frost and Sandburg. His subtle, free-verse lyrical poetry is often set in the landscapes of New England.

ZELDA (MISHKOVSKY) (b. 1914) emigrated from Chernigov (the Ukraine) to Palestine in 1925. She taught in Orthodox schools for girls. Her first collection was

published in 1967 and brought her immediate recognition for its unique blend of deep
religious feeling, drawing on Hasidic lore, with a modern poetic sensibility.

AMIR GILBOA (b. 1917), a native of Razywilow (the Ukraine), studied in a Hebrew
gymnasium and came to Palestine in 1937 as an illegal immigrant. He worked inter-
mittently in kibbutzim, stone quarries and British army camps before joining the
Jewish Brigade (1942). His experiences during the campaigns in Egypt, North Africa
and Italy inspired many of the poems in his early books. He has consistently been one
of the most original and experimental Israeli poets, combining traditional elements
with colloquial usages, and personal concerns with national motifs.

This poem is discussed on pp. 48-50.

The title of the poem refers to the speaker's dead brother, to the biblical conqueror,
and to the moon. The latter allusion is based on a Talmudic comparison: 'The face
of Moses is like the face of the sun and the face of Joshua like the face of the moon.'

ABBA KOVNER (b. 1918). From his native Sebastopol (Crimea) he moved to Vilna,
where he graduated from the Hebrew Gymnasium. He was one of the organizers of
the armed revolt in the Vilna Ghetto and later commanded Jewish partisan units in
the neighbouring forests. He was imprisoned by the British in Cairo for his involve-
ment in the *beriha* (rescue immigration) operations. In 1946 he settled in a kibbutz,
and during the War of Independence served as a cultural officer. Most of his books of
poetry are lyric-dramatic sequences, written in a highly-coloured and allusive style.
The following poem is taken from the sequence *My Little Sister* (1967), which is set
in a Dominican convent in Vilna. Stanza 2 refers to the bowl of broth which the
newly-wed couple customarily drink after the ceremony. *Hala* (line 14) is the twisted
loaf of Sabbath bread.

TABLE OF POEMS

ḤAYIM GOURI (b. 1923) was born in Tel Aviv, studied at an agricultural school and served in the Palmaḥ. He was sent on various missions by the Haganah to the displaced persons' camps in Europe, and later saw active service in the Israeli forces during the War of Independence and succeeding campaigns. His later poetry is loosely-patterned and colloquial; it often reflects the volatile moods of the country.

TUVIA RUEBNER (b. 1924) was born in Bratislava (Czechoslovakia) and grew up under the influence of German literature. Soon after his arrival in Palestine, in 1941, he joined a kibbutz. A critic and university lecturer, he has translated medieval and modern German poets into Hebrew and Agnon's prose into German.

YEHUDA AMICHAI (b. 1924), a native of Würzburg, came to Jerusalem with his family in 1936. He served with the Jewish Brigade in the Second World War and as an infantryman in the War of Independence. He has played a leading role in the creation of the new idiom, which shows clear affinities to modern English poetry in its use of irony and understatement, and its juxtaposition of contrasting linguistic materials. His poems, novels and short stories have been widely translated.

The opening sonnet of a lengthy sequence from Amichai's first volume (1955).

The phrase *hakolot hanodedim* ('voices that are straying') in line 11 is a play on *haḥolot hanodedim*, meaning 'quicksand'.

This is included in the cycle 'Jerusalem 1967'. The letters of the Hebrew date (TASHKAḤ) in the opening line evoke the meaning 'you will [make] forget'.

AVNER TREININ (b. 1928), a native of Tel Aviv, is a professor of physical chemistry and Dean of the Faculty of Science at the Hebrew University. He has published three collections of poetry. His later work shows an increasing preoccupation with scientific themes.

DAN PAGIS (b. 1930) was born in Radautz (Bukovina). During the Second World War he was interned for several years in a Ukrainian concentration camp. He escaped in 1944 and two years later came to Israel. He now teaches medieval Hebrew literature at the Hebrew University. His publications include important studies on the aesthetics of medieval secular poetry, as well as a critical edition of Vogel's collected poetry. All of the following poems are taken from his third book, *Gilgul* ('Transformations', 1970), in which, for the first time, he wrote explicitly of his European experiences.

Line 5 can also be understood as 'Cain, the human being'.

Refers, in the last two lines, to Genesis 37.30: 'The boy is gone! And I – what am I to do?'

NATHAN ZACH (b. 1930), a native of Berlin, came to Palestine with his family in 1935. After serving in the Israeli army, he worked in a publishing house and lectured at Tel Aviv University. As an editor and critic, he took an active, and often controversial, part in the re-evaluation of Hebrew poetry. His translations include plays by Frisch, Brecht and Dürrenmatt, as well as Arabic folk-songs (in collaboration with Rashed Hussein).

DALIA RAVIKOVITCH (b. 1936). A native of Ramat-Gan, she was educated in Haifa and Jerusalem, and later worked as a journalist and teacher. She published her first poems while still serving in the army. In addition to four collections of poetry, she is the author of children's books in verse and prose.

THE POEMS

PART ONE
TO THE TENTH CENTURY

שִׁירִים מִן הַמִּקְרָא   *Biblical Poetry*

שִׁירַת הַיָּם   THE SONG OF THE SEA

אָז יָשִׁיר משה ובני ישראל את השירה הזאת
ליהוה ויאמרו לאמר :

*Then Moses and the Israelites sang this
song to the Lord :*

אָשִׁירָה לַיהוה,
כִּי גָאֹה גָּאָה :
סוּס וְרֹכְבוֹ
רָמָה בַיָּם.

I shall sing to the Lord, for He has
triumphed gloriously: horse and
chariot[1] He has hurled into the sea.

עָזִּי וְזִמְרָת–יָהּ,
וַיְהִי לִי לִישׁוּעָה.
זֶה אֵלִי וְאַנְוֵהוּ,
אֱלֹהֵי אָבִי וַאֲרֹמְמֶנְהוּ.
יהוה–אִישׁ מִלְחָמָה ;
יהוה שְׁמוֹ.

The Lord is my strength and my
protection ;[2] He has become my
salvation. This is my God, and I shall
praise Him; my father's God, and I
shall extol Him. The Lord is a warrior;
Lord is His name!

מַרְכְּבֹת פַּרְעֹה וְחֵילוֹ
יָרָה בַיָּם,
וּמִבְחַר שָׁלִשָׁיו
טֻבְּעוּ בְיַם סוּף.
תְּהֹמֹת יְכַסְיֻמוּ,
יָרְדוּ בִמְצוֹלֹת כְּמוֹ אָבֶן.

The chariots of Pharaoh and his army
He cast into the sea; the pick of his
officers were plunged into the Sea of
Reeds. The abyss engulfed them; they
went down into the depths like a stone.

יְמִינְךָ, יהוה,
נֶאְדָּרִי בַּכֹּחַ ;
יְמִינְךָ, יהוה,
תִּרְעַץ אוֹיֵב.

Your right hand, O Lord, is majestic in
power; Your right hand, O Lord,
shattered the enemy! In Your great

---

1. Or 'rider'.   2. Or 'song'.

וּבְרֹב גְּאוֹנְךָ
תַּהֲרֹס קָמֶיךָ,
תְּשַׁלַּח חֲרֹנְךָ –
יֹאכְלֵמוֹ כַּקַּשׁ.
וּבְרוּחַ אַפֶּיךָ
נֶעֶרְמוּ מַיִם,
נִצְּבוּ כְמוֹ־נֵד נֹזְלִים,
קָפְאוּ תְהֹמֹת בְּלֶב־יָם.

splendour You destroyed Your foes.
You let loose Your fury; it consumed
them like straw. At the blast of Your
nostrils, the waters were piled up, the
waves stood like a wall,[1] the abyss
congealed in the heart of the sea.

אָמַר אוֹיֵב :
'אֶרְדֹּף, אַשִּׂיג,
אֲחַלֵּק שָׁלָל,
תִּמְלָאֵמוֹ נַפְשִׁי ;
אָרִיק חַרְבִּי,
תּוֹרִישֵׁמוֹ יָדִי.'
נָשַׁפְתָּ בְרוּחֲךָ,
כִּסָּמוֹ יָם ;
צָלֲלוּ כַּעוֹפֶרֶת
בְּמַיִם אַדִּירִים.

The enemy said: 'I shall pursue, I shall
overtake them, I shall divide the spoils;
my lust will have its fill; I shall draw
my sword; my hand will ravage them.'
You blew with Your breath and the sea
engulfed them. They sank like lead in
the mighty waters.

מִי כָמֹכָה בָּאֵלִם, יהוה ?
מִי כָּמֹכָה נֶאְדָּר בַּקֹּדֶשׁ,
נוֹרָא תְהִלֹּת,
עֹשֵׂה פֶלֶא !

Who is like You among the gods, O
Lord? Who is like You, majestic in
holiness, awesome in fame, worker of
miracles!

נָטִיתָ יְמִינְךָ –
תִּבְלָעֵמוֹ אָרֶץ.
נָחִיתָ בְחַסְדְּךָ
עַם, זוּ גָּאָלְתָּ,
נֵהַלְתָּ בְעָזְּךָ
אֶל נְוֵה קָדְשֶׁךָ.

You stretched out Your right hand and
the earth[2] swallowed them. In Your
love, You led the people whom You
had redeemed; in Your strength, You
guided them to Your holy abode.[3]

---

1. Or 'mound, bank, dyke'.   2. The underworld or the sea's floor.   3. This may denote Zion or the whole of Canaan.

שָׁמְעוּ עַמִּים – יִרְגָּזוּן ;
חִיל אָחַז יֹשְׁבֵי פְּלָשֶׁת.
אָז נִבְהֲלוּ אַלּוּפֵי אֱדוֹם,
אֵילֵי מוֹאָב – יֹאחֲזֵמוֹ רָעַד,
נָמֹגוּ כֹּל יֹשְׁבֵי כְנָעַן.
תִּפֹּל עֲלֵיהֶם
אֵימָתָה וָפַחַד,
בִּגְדֹל זְרוֹעֲךָ
יִדְּמוּ כָּאָבֶן –
עַד יַעֲבֹר עַמְּךָ, יהוה,
עַד יַעֲבֹר עַם, זוּ קָנִיתָ.

The nations heard and quaked; anguish gripped the dwellers of Philistia. The clans of Edom were dismayed; trembling seized the tribes of Moab; all the dwellers of Canaan melted with fear. Terror and dread fell upon them; by Your mighty arm, they were struck dumb as stone – while Your people, O Lord, passed through, while the people whom You ransomed passed through them.

תְּבִאֵמוֹ וְתִטָּעֵמוֹ
בְּהַר נַחֲלָתְךָ,
מָכוֹן לְשִׁבְתְּךָ
פָּעַלְתָּ, יהוה,
מִקְּדָשׁ, אֲדֹנָי,
כּוֹנְנוּ יָדֶיךָ.
יהוה יִמְלֹךְ
לְעֹלָם וָעֶד !

You will bring them and plant them on the mount of Your inheritance, the place, O Lord, which You chose for Your dwelling, the sanctuary, O Lord, which Your hands established. The Lord will reign for ever and ever!

שִׁירַת דְּבוֹרָה   THE SONG OF DEBORAH

ותשר דבורה וברק בן אבינעם ביום ההוא לאמר :

On that day, Deborah and Barak, the son of Abinoam, sang this song:

בִּפְרֹעַ פְּרָעוֹת בְּיִשְׂרָאֵל,
בְּהִתְנַדֵּב עָם –
בָּרְכוּ יהוה !

For the warriors, in Israel, who have flowing locks,[1] for the people who are answering the call – praise the Lord!

---

1. Warriors consecrated themselves by dedicating their hair to God and letting it grow untrimmed. Or, this obscure phrase may mean, 'when there were leaders in Israel, when the people acted nobly . . .'

שִׁמְעוּ, מְלָכִים,
הַאֲזִינוּ, רוֹזְנִים!
אָנֹכִי לַיהוה,
אָנֹכִי אָשִׁירָה,
אֲזַמֵּר לַיהוה
אֱלֹהֵי יִשְׂרָאֵל.

Hear, O kings! Princes, give ear! I shall sing to the Lord, I shall sing to Him, I shall chant to the Lord, the God of Israel.

יהוה, בְּצֵאתְךָ מִשֵּׂעִיר,
בְּצַעְדְּךָ מִשְּׂדֵה אֱדוֹם –
אֶרֶץ רָעָשָׁה,
גַּם שָׁמַיִם נָטָפוּ,
גַּם עָבִים נָטְפוּ מָיִם.
הָרִים נָזְלוּ
מִפְּנֵי יהוה,
זֶה סִינַי מִפְּנֵי יהוה
אֱלֹהֵי יִשְׂרָאֵל.

Lord, when You set forth from Seir, when You marched from the land of Edom – the earth quaked and the heavens shook, the clouds poured down in torrents. Mountains melted before the Lord – even Sinai – before the Lord, the God of Israel.

בִּימֵי שַׁמְגַּר בֶּן עֲנָת,
בִּימֵי יָעֵל – חָדְלוּ אֳרָחוֹת;
וְהֹלְכֵי נְתִיבוֹת
יֵלְכוּ אֳרָחוֹת עֲקַלְקַלּוֹת.
חָדְלוּ פְרָזוֹן,
בְּיִשְׂרָאֵל חָדֵלּוּ –
עַד שַׁקַּמְתִּי, דְּבוֹרָה,
שַׁקַּמְתִּי אֵם בְּיִשְׂרָאֵל.
יִבְחַר אֱלֹהִים חֲדָשִׁים –
אָז לָחֶם שְׁעָרִים;
מָגֵן אִם יֵרָאֶה וָרֹמַח
בְּאַרְבָּעִים אֶלֶף בְּיִשְׂרָאֵל.

In the days of Shamgar, son of Anath, in the days of Jael – the highways were abandoned;[1] wayfarers went by round-about paths. The unwalled towns of Israel were abandoned,[2] all abandoned, until I,[3] Deborah, arose, until I arose, a mother in Israel. Because they had chosen new gods, there was fighting at their gates. Not a shield could be seen, nor a lance, among the forty thousand of Israel.

---

1. Or 'caravans ceased'.   2. Or 'there were no champions in Israel'.   3. Or 'you'.

לִבִּי לְחוֹקְקֵי יִשְׂרָאֵל,
הַמִּתְנַדְּבִים בָּעָם –
בָּרְכוּ יהוה !

My heart goes out to the captains of
Israel, who are answering the call
among the people – praise the Lord!

רֹכְבֵי אֲתֹנוֹת צְחֹרוֹת,
יֹשְׁבֵי עַל מִדִּין,
וְהֹלְכֵי עַל דֶּרֶךְ –
שִׂיחוּ !
מִקּוֹל מְחַצְצִים בֵּין מַשְׁאַבִּים,
שָׁם יְתַנּוּ צִדְקוֹת יהוה,
צִדְקֹת פִּרְזוֹנוֹ בְּיִשְׂרָאֵל ;
אָז יָרְדוּ לַשְּׁעָרִים עַם יהוה.

O you that ride on tawny donkeys, you
that sit on caparisoned camels, you that
voyage on foot – celebrate [His praises]!
What is that sound of archers by the
watering places?[1] There they recount
the triumphs of the Lord, His triumphs
that made Israel secure in the unwalled
towns.[2] For then the people of the
Lord marched down to the gates [to
wage war].

עוּרִי, עוּרִי, דְּבוֹרָה !
עוּרִי, עוּרִי, דַּבְּרִי שִׁיר !
קוּם, בָּרָק
וּשֲׁבֵה שֶׁבְיְךָ,
בֶּן אֲבִינֹעַם !

Rouse, rouse yourself, Deborah! Rouse
yourself, strike up a song! Arise, Barak!
Seize your captives, son of Abinoam!

אָז יְרַד שָׂרִיד
לְאַדִּירִים־עָם,
יהוה יְרַד לִי בַּגִּבּוֹרִים.
מִנִּי אֶפְרַיִם, שָׁרְשָׁם בַּעֲמָלֵק ;
אַחֲרֶיךָ בִנְיָמִין בַּעֲמָמֶיךָ.
מִנִּי מָכִיר יָרְדוּ מְחֹקְקִים,
וּמִזְּבוּלֻן מֹשְׁכִים בְּשֵׁבֶט סֹפֵר.
וְשָׂרַי בְּיִשָּׂשכָר עִם דְּבֹרָה,
וְיִשָּׂשכָר – כֵּן בָּרָק ;
בָּעֵמֶק שֻׁלַּח בְּרַגְלָיו.

Then down marched the nobles, the
chieftains of the people; the Lord
Himself marched down for me among
the valiant.[3] From Ephraim, the nobles
came in force,[4] followed by the clans of
Benjamin. From Machir, the captains
marched down, and from Zebulun,
those who bear the marshal's staff. The
nobles of Isaschar joined with Deborah,
and so did **Barak**; he sped into the
valley on foot.[5]

---

1. Or 'To the strains of the musicians at the wells, there . . .'   2. Or 'the triumphs of His rule in Israel'.
3. Or 'then down came the remnant [of Israel to wage war] against the mighty [of Canaan]. The people of
the Lord came down . . .'
4. Or 'came down to the valley'.   5. Or 'they rushed into the valley at his heels'.

בְּפַלְגוֹת רְאוּבֵן
גְּדֹלִים חִקְקֵי לֵב.
לָמָּה יָשַׁבְתָּ בֵּין הַמִּשְׁפְּתַיִם
לִשְׁמֹעַ שְׁרִקוֹת עֲדָרִים ?
לִפְלַגּוֹת רְאוּבֵן
גְּדוֹלִים חִקְרֵי לֵב.
גִּלְעָד בְּעֵבֶר הַיַּרְדֵּן שָׁכֵן ;
וְדָן – לָמָּה יָגוּר אֳנִיּוֹת ?
אָשֵׁר יָשַׁב לְחוֹף יַמִּים
וְעַל מִפְרָצָיו יִשְׁכּוֹן.

Among the factions of Reuben there was much heart-searching. Why do you sit idly by the sheep-folds[1] listening to the whistling of the shepherds? Among the factions of Reuben there was much heart-searching! Gilead remained beyond the Jordan; and Dan – why does he tarry aboard his ships? Asher lingers along the sea-shore, remaining beside its coves.

זְבֻלוּן – עַם חֵרֵף נַפְשׁוֹ לָמוּת.
וְנַפְתָּלִי – עַל מְרוֹמֵי שָׂדֶה.

Zebulun – this tribe defied death in battle; and so did Naphtali, on the heights of the battle-field.

בָּאוּ מְלָכִים, נִלְחָמוּ,
אָז נִלְחֲמוּ מַלְכֵי כְנַעַן
בְּתַעְנָךְ, עַל מֵי מְגִדּוֹ ;
בֶּצַע כֶּסֶף לֹא לָקָחוּ.
מִן שָׁמַיִם נִלְחָמוּ,
הַכּוֹכָבִים מִמְּסִלּוֹתָם
נִלְחֲמוּ עִם סִיסְרָא.
נַחַל קִישׁוֹן גְּרָפָם,
נַחַל קְדוּמִים, נַחַל קִישׁוֹן !
תִּדְרְכִי, נַפְשִׁי, עֹז !
אָז הָלְמוּ עִקְּבֵי סוּס
מִדַּהֲרוֹת, דַּהֲרוֹת אַבִּירָיו.

The kings came, they fought; then the kings of Canaan fought at Ta'anach and by the waters of Megiddo; they took no silver booty. From the heavens they fought, the stars from their courses fought against Sisera. The Kishon River swept them away; that ancient river – the river of Kishon! O my soul, stride ahead mightily![2] Then the hoofs of [their own] horses crushed [them],[3] their galloping, galloping steeds.

---

1. Or 'bonfires'.   2. Or 'bless the Lord's might'.   3. Or 'hammered [the ground]'.

152

אוֹרוּ מֵרוֹז,
– אָמַר מַלְאַךְ יהוה –
אֹרוּ אָרוֹר יֹשְׁבֶיהָ!
כִּי לֹא בָאוּ לְעֶזְרַת יהוה,
לְעֶזְרַת יהוה בַּגִּבּוֹרִים.

A curse on Meroz! – said the angel of the Lord – a bitter curse on its inhabitants! For they did not come to the help of the Lord, to the help of the Lord in the ranks of the valiant.[1]

תְּבֹרַךְ מִנָּשִׁים יָעֵל,
אֵשֶׁת חֶבֶר הַקֵּינִי,
מִנָּשִׁים בָּאֹהֶל תְּבֹרָךְ!
מַיִם שָׁאַל –
חָלָב נָתָנָה;
בְּסֵפֶל אַדִּירִים
הִקְרִיבָה חֶמְאָה.
יָדָהּ לַיָּתֵד תִּשְׁלַחְנָה,
וִימִינָהּ – לְהַלְמוּת עֲמֵלִים,
וְהָלְמָה סִיסְרָא, מָחֲקָה רֹאשׁוֹ,
וּמָחֲצָה וְחָלְפָה רַקָּתוֹ.
בֵּין רַגְלֶיהָ כָּרַע, נָפַל, שָׁכָב,
בֵּין רַגְלֶיהָ כָּרַע, נָפָל;
בַּאֲשֶׁר כָּרַע –
שָׁם נָפַל שָׁדוּד.

Blessed above women be Jael, the wife of Heber the Kenite, blessed above all women dwelling in tents! He asked for water: she gave him milk; she offered him curds in a lordly bowl. Her left hand reached for the tent-peg, her right, for the workman's mallet. And she struck Sisera, she crushed his head, she shattered his temple and pierced it. At her feet he sank and fell; where he sank down, there he fell, slain.

בְּעַד הַחַלּוֹן נִשְׁקְפָה וַתְּיַבֵּב
אֵם סִיסְרָא, בְּעַד הָאֶשְׁנָב:
'מַדּוּעַ בֹּשֵׁשׁ רִכְבּוֹ לָבוֹא?
מַדּוּעַ אֶחֱרוּ פַּעֲמֵי מַרְכְּבוֹתָיו?'
חַכְמוֹת שָׂרוֹתֶיהָ תַּעֲנֶינָּה,
אַף הִיא תָּשִׁיב אֲמָרֶיהָ לָהּ:

She peered through the window, sobbing, Sisera's mother peered through the lattice: 'Why is his chariot so long in coming? Why is the clatter of his chariots delayed?' The wisest of her ladies reply, and she, too, answers

1. Or 'to the help of the Lord as warriors'.

'הֲלֹא יִמְצְאוּ, יְחַלְּקוּ שָׁלָל –
רַחַם רַחֲמָתַיִם לְרֹאשׁ גֶּבֶר ;
שְׁלַל צְבָעִים לְסִיסְרָא ;
שְׁלַל צְבָעִים רִקְמָה,
צֶבַע רִקְמָתַיִם לְצַוְּארֵי שָׁלָל.'

herself in kind: 'They must be finding and dividing the spoils: a girl or two for each man; spoils of dyed cloth for Sisera; spoils of dyed, embroidered cloth, a wealth of dyed embroideries for the victors' necks.'[1]

כֵּן יֹאבְדוּ כָל אוֹיְבֶיךָ, יהוה !
וְאֹהֲבָיו – כְּצֵאת הַשֶּׁמֶשׁ בִּגְבֻרָתוֹ.

May all Your enemies perish thus, O Lord! But those who love Him – they shall be like the sun rising in all its might!

קִינַת דָּוִד עַל מוֹת שָׁאוּל וִיהוֹנָתָן

DAVID'S LAMENT OVER SAUL AND JONATHAN

וַיְקֹנֵן דוד את הקינה הזאת על שאול ועל יהונתן בנו :

Then David chanted this lament over Saul and his son Jonathan:

הַצְּבִי, יִשְׂרָאֵל,
עַל בָּמוֹתֶיךָ חָלָל !
אֵיךְ נָפְלוּ גִבּוֹרִים !

All your glory, O Israel, lies slain upon your heights![2] How the heroes have fallen!

אַל תַּגִּידוּ בְגַת,
אַל תְּבַשְּׂרוּ בְּחוּצֹת אַשְׁקְלוֹן,
פֶּן תִּשְׂמַחְנָה בְּנוֹת פְּלִשְׁתִּים,
פֶּן תַּעֲלֹזְנָה בְּנוֹת הָעֲרֵלִים.

Do not tell of it in Gath, do not proclaim it in the streets of Ashkelon, lest the daughters of the Philistines rejoice, lest the daughters of the uncircumcised exult.

---

1. Or 'on the necks of the spoils', referring to the captive maidens; or 'for the queen', referring to Sisera's mother.

2. According to a different emendation: 'Raise up a dirge over your slain bodies'.

הָרֵי בַגִּלְבֹּעַ,
אַל טַל וְאַל מָטָר עֲלֵיכֶם
וּשְׂדֵי תְרוּמֹת!
כִּי שָׁם נִגְעַל מָגֵן גִּבּוֹרִים,
מָגֵן שָׁאוּל, בְּלִי מָשִׁיחַ בַּשָּׁמֶן.

You mountains of Gilboa – let there be no dew or rain upon you, no fertile fields![1] For there, the hero's shield[2] was defiled, the shield of Saul no longer anointed with oil.

מִדַּם חֲלָלִים,
מֵחֵלֶב גִּבּוֹרִים
קֶשֶׁת יְהוֹנָתָן לֹא נָשׂוֹג אָחוֹר
וְחֶרֶב שָׁאוּל לֹא תָשׁוּב רֵיקָם.

From the blood of the slain,[3] from the fat of the heroes – the bow of Jonathan never recoiled, the sword of Saul never returned unstained.

שָׁאוּל וִיהוֹנָתָן,
הַנֶּאֱהָבִים וְהַנְּעִימִם,
בְּחַיֵּיהֶם וּבְמוֹתָם לֹא נִפְרָדוּ.
מִנְּשָׁרִים קַלּוּ,
מֵאֲרָיוֹת גָּבֵרוּ.

Saul and Jonathan, beloved and cherished – in life and death they were not parted. They were swifter than eagles, stronger than lions.

בְּנוֹת יִשְׂרָאֵל, אֶל שָׁאוּל בְּכֶינָה,
הַמַּלְבִּשְׁכֶם שָׁנִי עִם עֲדָנִים,
הַמַּעֲלֶה עֲדִי זָהָב עַל לְבוּשְׁכֶן!

Daughters of Israel, weep for Saul, who dressed you in scarlet and finery, who decked your clothing with adornments of gold.

אֵיךְ נָפְלוּ גִבֹּרִים
בְּתוֹךְ הַמִּלְחָמָה!
יְהוֹנָתָן – עַל בָּמוֹתֶיךָ חָלָל!

How the heroes have fallen in the thick of the battle! O Jonathan – slain upon your heights!

---

1. Or 'no upsurging of the depths', that is, no water from springs or wells.
2. Or 'the shields of the heroes'.   3. Or 'of the valiant'.

155

צַר לִי עָלֶיךָ,
אָחִי יְהוֹנָתָן,
נָעַמְתָּ לִּי מְאֹד.
נִפְלְאַתָה אַהֲבָתְךָ לִי
מֵאַהֲבַת נָשִׁים.

I grieve for you, my brother, Jonathan.
You were most dear to me. Your love
for me was more wonderful than the
love of women.

אֵיךְ נָפְלוּ גִבּוֹרִים
וַיֹּאבְדוּ כְּלֵי מִלְחָמָה !

How the heroes have fallen and the
weapons of war perished.[1]

חֲזוֹן יְשַׁעְיָהוּ בֶן־אָמוֹץ

THE INDICTMENT OF ISRAEL

שִׁמְעוּ, שָׁמַיִם,
וְהַאֲזִינִי, אֶרֶץ –
כִּי יהוה דִּבֵּר :

Hear, O heavens, and listen, O earth,
for the Lord has spoken:

'בָּנִים גִּדַּלְתִּי וְרוֹמַמְתִּי,
וְהֵם פָּשְׁעוּ בִי.
יָדַע שׁוֹר קֹנֵהוּ,
וַחֲמוֹר – אֵבוּס בְּעָלָיו ;
יִשְׂרָאֵל לֹא יָדַע,
עַמִּי לֹא הִתְבּוֹנָן.'

'I have raised children and reared them,
but they have rebelled against me. The
ox knows its owner and the ass its
master's stall; but Israel does not know,
My people has no understanding!

1. Saul and Jonathan are referred to as the 'instruments of war' which have been destroyed.

הוֹי, גּוֹי חֹטֵא,

עַם כֶּבֶד עָוֹן,

זֶרַע מְרֵעִים,

בָּנִים מַשְׁחִיתִים !

עָזְבוּ אֶת יהוה,

נִאֲצוּ אֶת קְדוֹשׁ יִשְׂרָאֵל,

נָזֹרוּ אָחוֹר.

O sinful nation, people heavy with crime, brood of evildoers, depraved children! They have forsaken the Lord, they have spurned the Holy One of Israel and turned their backs on Him.

עַל מֶה תֻכּוּ –

עוֹד תּוֹסִיפוּ סָרָה ?

כָּל רֹאשׁ לָחֳלִי

וְכָל לֵבָב דַּוָּי.

מִכַּף רֶגֶל וְעַד רֹאשׁ

אֵין בּוֹ מְתֹם :

פֶּצַע וְחַבּוּרָה

וּמַכָּה טְרִיָּה,

לֹא זֹרוּ וְלֹא חֻבָּשׁוּ

וְלֹא רֻכְּכָה בַּשָּׁמֶן.

אַרְצְכֶם שְׁמָמָה,

עָרֵיכֶם שְׂרֻפוֹת אֵשׁ ;

אַדְמַתְכֶם – לְנֶגְדְּכֶם

זָרִים אֹכְלִים אֹתָהּ ;

וּשְׁמָמָה כְּמַהְפֵּכַת זָרִים.

וְנוֹתְרָה בַת־צִיּוֹן

כְּסֻכָּה בְכָרֶם,

Where can you still be struck, if you persist in your revolt?[1] Every head is diseased and every heart is in pain.[2] From head to foot there is not a sound spot: nothing but wounds and welts and festering sores which have not been drained or bandaged or softened with oil. Your country is desolate, your cities burnt to ashes; strangers devour your land before your very eyes; it is as desolate as Sodom[3] overthrown. Only the daughter of Zion[4] remains – like a watchman's hut in a vineyard, like a

1. Or 'Why would you be struck again? Why do you persist in your rebelliousness?'
2. Or 'The whole head . . . the whole heart . . .'
3. Lit. 'strangers, aliens'; 'Sodom' is conjectural. Or, the meaning could be: 'God has wreaked such desolation as He wreaks upon strangers.'
4. A common term for Jerusalem, 'daughter-Zion'.

בִּמְלוּנָה בְמִקְשָׁה,
כְּעִיר נְצוּרָה.
לוּלֵי יהוה צְבָאוֹת
הוֹתִיר לָנוּ שָׂרִיד כִּמְעָט –
כִּסְדֹם הָיִינוּ,
לַעֲמֹרָה דָּמִינוּ.

shed in a cucumber-field – a city under siege. If the Lord of hosts had not left us a scanty remnant, we should have been like Sodom, we should have become like Gomorrah.

שִׁמְעוּ דְבַר יהוה,
קְצִינֵי סְדֹם!
הַאֲזִינוּ תּוֹרַת אֱלֹהֵינוּ,
עַם עֲמֹרָה!
'לָמָּה לִּי רֹב זִבְחֵיכֶם?'
יֹאמַר יהוה.
'שָׂבַעְתִּי עֹלוֹת אֵילִים
וְחֵלֶב מְרִיאִים;
וְדַם פָּרִים וּכְבָשִׂים וְעַתּוּדִים
לֹא חָפָצְתִּי.
כִּי תָבֹאוּ לֵרָאוֹת פָּנָי –
מִי בִקֵּשׁ זֹאת מִיֶּדְכֶם
רְמֹס חֲצֵרָי?
לֹא תוֹסִיפוּ הָבִיא מִנְחַת שָׁוְא.
קְטֹרֶת – תּוֹעֵבָה הִיא לִי.
חֹדֶשׁ וְשַׁבָּת קְרֹא מִקְרָא –
לֹא אוּכַל אָוֶן וַעֲצָרָה.
חָדְשֵׁיכֶם וּמוֹעֲדֵיכֶם
שָׂנְאָה נַפְשִׁי,
הָיוּ עָלַי לָטֹרַח,
נִלְאֵיתִי נְשֹׂא.
וּבְפָרִשְׂכֶם כַּפֵּיכֶם,
אַעְלִים עֵינַי מִכֶּם;

Hear the word of the Lord, rulers of Sodom! Listen to the teaching of our God, people of Gomorrah! 'What need do I have of your countless sacrifices?' says the Lord. 'I have had my fill of burnt offerings of rams and the suet of fatlings; I take no delight in the blood of bulls, lambs and he-goats. When you come to appear before Me – who has required of you that you trample My courts? Bring no more worthless offerings; your incense is an abomination to Me. New moons and sabbaths and sacred assemblies – I cannot endure solemn congregations joined with evil. Your new moons and your festivals fill me with loathing; they have become a burden to me, I can bear them no longer. And when you spread out your hands, I shall avert My

גַּם כִּי תַרְבּוּ תְפִלָּה,
אֵינֶנִּי שֹׁמֵעַ;
יְדֵיכֶם דָּמִים מָלֵאוּ.

eyes from you. Though you pray continuously, I shall not listen: your hands are full of blood!

רַחֲצוּ, הִזַּכּוּ,
הָסִירוּ רֹעַ מַעַלְלֵיכֶם
מִנֶּגֶד עֵינָי!
חִדְלוּ הָרֵעַ,
לִמְדוּ הֵיטֵב,
דִּרְשׁוּ מִשְׁפָּט,
אַשְּׁרוּ חָמוֹץ,
שִׁפְטוּ יָתוֹם,
רִיבוּ אַלְמָנָה!'

'Wash yourselves, cleanse yourselves, put your evil deeds out of my sight! Cease doing evil, learn to do good, seek justice, sustain the oppressed, defend the fatherless, plead the widow's cause!

'לְכוּ נָא וְנִוָּכְחָה!'
יֹאמַר יהוה.
'אִם יִהְיוּ חֲטָאֵיכֶם כַּשָּׁנִים –
כַּשֶּׁלֶג יַלְבִּינוּ,
אִם יַאְדִּימוּ כַתּוֹלָע –
כַּצֶּמֶר יִהְיוּ.
אִם תֹּאבוּ וּשְׁמַעְתֶּם –
טוּב הָאָרֶץ תֹּאכֵלוּ;
וְאִם תְּמָאֲנוּ וּמְרִיתֶם –
חֶרֶב תְּאֻכְּלוּ' –
כִּי פִּי יהוה דִּבֵּר.

'Come now, let us settle our accounts,' says the Lord. 'Though your sins be like scarlet, they can yet turn white as snow; though they be red as crimson, they can yet become like wool. If you consent and obey, you will eat the fat of the land; but if you refuse and rebel, you will be consumed by the sword' – for the mouth of the Lord has spoken!

הַמָּשָׁל עַל מֶלֶךְ בָּבֶל

TAUNT DIRGE

וְהָיָה בַּיּוֹם הָנִיחַ יהוה לְךָ מֵעָצְבְּךָ וּמֵרָגְזֶךָ, וּמִן הָעֲבֹדָה הַקָּשָׁה אֲשֶׁר עֻבַּד בָּךְ – וְנָשָׂאתָ הַמָּשָׁל הַזֶּה עַל מֶלֶךְ בָּבֶל, וְאָמַרְתָּ:

When the day comes that the Lord gives you relief from your sorrow and anguish, and from the cruel servitude imposed upon you, you will take up this song of derision against the king of Babylon:

אֵיךְ שָׁבַת נֹגֵשׂ,
שָׁבְתָה מַדְהֵבָה !
שָׁבַר יהוה מַטֵּה רְשָׁעִים,
שֵׁבֶט מֹשְׁלִים.
מַכֶּה עַמִּים בְּעֶבְרָה
מַכַּת בִּלְתִּי סָרָה,
רֹדֶה בָאַף גּוֹיִם –
מֻרְדָּף בְּלִי חָשָׂךְ.
נָחָה, שָׁקְטָה כָּל הָאָרֶץ,
פָּצְחוּ רִנָּה ;
גַּם בְּרוֹשִׁים שָׂמְחוּ לְךָ,
אַרְזֵי לְבָנוֹן :
'מֵאָז שָׁכַבְתָּ – לֹא יַעֲלֶה
הַכֹּרֵת עָלֵינוּ'.

How the oppressor has met his end! How his arrogance[1] has come to an end! The Lord has broken the staff of the wicked, the rod of the ruler, that struck peoples down in wrath, with ceaseless blows, and drove the nations in fury, with relentless tyranny. The whole earth is relieved and peaceful; all things break into song. Even the cypresses rejoice at your fate, even the cedars of Lebanon: 'Now that you have been laid to rest, no one will come to hew us down.'

שְׁאוֹל מִתַּחַת רָגְזָה לְךָ
לִקְרַאת בּוֹאֶךְ ;
עוֹרֵר לְךָ רְפָאִים,
כָּל עַתּוּדֵי אָרֶץ ;
הֵקִים מִכִּסְאוֹתָם
כֹּל מַלְכֵי גוֹיִם.
כֻּלָּם יַעֲנוּ
וְיֹאמְרוּ אֵלֶיךָ :

Sheol was all astir, awaiting your arrival: it roused the shades for you, all the leaders of the earth; it made the kings of all the nations rise from their thrones. They all speak out and say to

---

1. Or 'tyranny'; or 'imposition of taxes'.

'גַּם אַתָּה חֻלֵּיתָ כָמוֹנוּ,
אֵלֵינוּ נִמְשָׁלְתָּ.
הוּרַד שְׁאוֹל גְּאוֹנֶךָ,
הֶמְיַת נְבָלֶיךָ;
תַּחְתֶּיךָ יֻצַּע רִמָּה,
וּמְכַסֶּיךָ תּוֹלֵעָה.'

you: 'So you, too, have been enfeebled by disease, like us; you have become one of us. Your pomp has been brought down to Sheol, and the music of your lutes. Maggots will be your bedding, and worms your covering.'

אֵיךְ נָפַלְתָּ מִשָּׁמַיִם,
הֵילֵל בֶּן שָׁחַר!
נִגְדַּעְתָּ לָאָרֶץ,
חוֹלֵשׁ עַל גּוֹיִם!
וְאַתָּה אָמַרְתָּ בִלְבָבְךָ:
'הַשָּׁמַיִם אֶעֱלֶה,
מִמַּעַל לְכוֹכְבֵי אֵל
אָרִים כִּסְאִי,
וְאֵשֵׁב בְּהַר-מוֹעֵד,
בְּיַרְכְּתֵי צָפוֹן;
אֶעֱלֶה עַל בָּמֳתֵי עָב,
אֶדַּמֶּה לְעֶלְיוֹן.'
אַךְ אֶל שְׁאוֹל תּוּרָד,
אֶל יַרְכְּתֵי בוֹר.

How you have fallen from heaven, O radiant star of the dawn![1] How you have been felled to the ground – you who mowed down the nations! And you had said in your heart: 'I shall scale the heavens. I shall set my throne higher than the stars of God, and take my seat on the Mount of Assembly,[2] in the farthest reaches of the north. I shall scale the pinnacles of the clouds,[3] I shall be equal to the Most High!' But you have been brought down to Sheol, to the farthest reaches of the pit!

רֹאֶיךָ – אֵלֶיךָ יַשְׁגִּיחוּ,
אֵלֶיךָ יִתְבּוֹנָנוּ:
'הֲזֶה הָאִישׁ מַרְגִּיז הָאָרֶץ,
מַרְעִישׁ מַמְלָכוֹת?

Those who see you stare at you, peer at you closely: Is this the man who shook the earth and made kingdoms tremble?

---

1. Lit. 'Shining One (*Helel*) son of Dawn (*ben Shaḥar*)', a minor Canaanite deity.
2. A mountain which, according to Mesopotamian belief, served as the meeting place of the gods.
3. Or 'I shall mount the backs of the clouds'.

שָׁם תֵּבֵל כַּמִּדְבָּר
וְעָרָיו הָרָס ?
אֲסִירָיו לֹא פָתַח בָּיְתָה ?'

Who turned the world into a desert,
and razed its cities? Who never set his
captives free, to let them go home?

כָּל מַלְכֵי גוֹיִם כֻּלָּם
שָׁכְבוּ בְכָבוֹד אִישׁ בְּבֵיתוֹ ;
וְאַתָּה הָשְׁלַכְתָּ מִקִּבְרְךָ
כְּנֵצֶר נִתְעָב ;
לְבֻשׁ הֲרֻגִים מְטֹעֲנֵי חָרֶב,
יוֹרְדֵי אֶל אַבְנֵי בוֹר
כְּפֶגֶר מוּבָס.
לֹא תֵחַד אִתָּם בִּקְבוּרָה
כִּי אַרְצְךָ שִׁחַתָּ,
עַמְּךָ הָרָגְתָּ.

All the kings of the nations were laid to
rest with honour, each in his sepulchre,
but you were cast aside, unburied, like
a rotten branch;[1] your clothes like
those who are slashed to death by the
sword; those who go down into a stony
pit[2] like trampled carrion. You will not
share their [royal] burial because you
ravaged your land, you murdered your
people!

לֹא יִקָּרֵא לְעוֹלָם
זֶרַע מְרֵעִים.
הָכִינוּ לְבָנָיו מַטְבֵּחַ
בַּעֲוֹן אֲבוֹתָם —
בַּל יָקֻמוּ וְיָרְשׁוּ אָרֶץ,
וּמָלְאוּ פְנֵי תֵבֵל עָרִים.

Let his brood of evildoers never again
be named! Prepare a slaughterhouse
for his sons, for the guilt of their
father; lest they rise to possess the
earth and cover the face of the world
with despots![3]

---

1. Lit. 'contemptible branch'; the expression has also been interpreted as 'untimely birth' or 'loathsome carcass, putrefaction'.
2. A common grave in the battle-field.
3. This word has been variously translated as '[fortified] cities', 'ruins', or 'enemies'.

162

מִכְתָּב לְחִזְקָיָהוּ

HEZEKIAH'S HYMN OF THANKSGIVING

מכתב לחזקיהו מלך יהודה בחלתו, ויחי מחליו :

A psalm by Hezekiah, king of Judah,
upon recovering from his illness:

אֲנִי אָמַרְתִּי :
בִּדְמִי יָמַי אֵלֵכָה,
בְּשַׁעֲרֵי שְׁאוֹל פֻּקַּדְתִּי
יֶתֶר שְׁנוֹתָי.
אָמַרְתִּי : לֹא אֶרְאֶה יָהּ,
יָהּ בְּאֶרֶץ הַחַיִּים ;
לֹא אַבִּיט אָדָם עוֹד
עִם יוֹשְׁבֵי חָדֶל.
דּוֹרִי נִסַּע וְנִגְלָה מִנִּי
כְּאֹהֶל רֹעִי.
קִפַּדְתִּי כָאֹרֵג חַיַּי,
מִדַּלָּה יְבַצְּעֵנִי.
מִיּוֹם עַד לַיְלָה תַּשְׁלִימֵנִי.
שִׁוִּיתִי עַד בֹּקֶר,
כָּאֲרִי כֵּן יְשַׁבֵּר כָּל עַצְמוֹתָי.
מִיּוֹם עַד לַיְלָה תַּשְׁלִימֵנִי.
כְּסוּס, עָגוּר – כֵּן אֲצַפְצֵף,
אֶהְגֶּה כַּיּוֹנָה.
דַּלּוּ עֵינַי לַמָּרוֹם :
אֲדֹנָי, עָשְׁקָה לִּי – עָרְבֵנִי !

I thought: I shall depart in the midst[1]
of my days; I am consigned to the
gates of Sheol for the rest of my years.
I thought: I shall never see the Lord
again,[2] the Lord in the land of the
living; I shall no more behold the face
of men among the inhabitants of the
earth. My dwelling,[3] like a shepherd's
tent, is being pulled up and taken away
from me. You are cutting off[4] my life,
as a weaver severs the thrum. Between
morning and nightfall, You will put an
end to me. I cried out until daybreak:
'Like a lion, He[5] is crushing all my
bones!' Between morning and nightfall, You will put an end to me. I
twittered like a swallow, like a wryneck,
I moaned like a dove. My wearied eyes
were raised to heaven: 'O Lord, I am
in misery, be my surety!' But what

---

1. Or 'stillness'.
2. I.e., visit His Temple.
3. Possibly, a reference to his body.
4. Or 'folding up'.
5. Or 'it [the illness]'.

מָה אֲדַבֵּר ? – וְאָמַר לִי;
וְהוּא עָשָׂה.
אֲדַדֶּה כָל שְׁנוֹתַי
עַל מַר נַפְשִׁי.
אֲדֹנָי! עֲלֵיהֶם יִחְיוּ,
וּלְכָל בָּהֶן חַיֵּי רוּחִי,
וְתַחֲלִימֵנִי וְהַחֲיֵנִי!
הִנֵּה לְשָׁלוֹם –
מַר לִי מָר!

more can I say? He told me [this would
come to pass], this is His doing.[1] I
shall spend all my years wandering
[through the underworld] with a bitter
soul. 'O Lord, the days of my life are
Yours, and Yours is the life of my
spirit – restore me, bring me back to
life! O give me peace, my lot is most
bitter!'[2]

וְאַתָּה חָשַׁקְתָּ נַפְשִׁי
מִשַּׁחַת בְּלִי,
כִּי הִשְׁלַכְתָּ אַחֲרֵי גֵוְךָ
כָּל חֲטָאָי.
כִּי לֹא שְׁאוֹל תּוֹדֶךָּ,
מָוֶת – יְהַלְלֶךָּ;
לֹא יְשַׂבְּרוּ יוֹרְדֵי בוֹר
אֶל אֲמִתֶּךָ.
חַי, חַי – הוּא יוֹדֶךָ
כָּמוֹנִי הַיּוֹם;
אָב לְבָנִים יוֹדִיעַ
אֶל אֲמִתֶּךָ.

Then, loving me, You spared my life
from the pit of destruction, when You
cast all my sins behind Your back. For
Sheol cannot praise you, Death cannot
acclaim You. Those who sink into the
pit cannot hope for Your kindness.[3] It
is the living, only the living, who can
give You praise, as I do this day. The
[living] father proclaims Your kindness[3] to his sons.

יהוה לְהוֹשִׁיעֵנִי,
וּנְגִינוֹתַי נְנַגֵּן
כָּל יְמֵי חַיֵּינוּ
עַל בֵּית יהוה.

The Lord has come to my rescue, and
we shall sing His praises, all the days of
our life, in the House of the Lord.

---

1. Or 'What more can I say or tell Him? He has done it!' According to some interpretations, Hezekiah
begins to celebrate his recovery at this point, and the following verses are rendered differently.
2. Or 'My great bitterness was transformed into peace'.
3. Or 'faithfulness, grace, truth'.

164

יהוה רֹעִי

THE LORD IS MY
SHEPHERD

מִזְמוֹר לְדָוִד:

A psalm of David:

יהוה רֹעִי – לֹא אֶחְסָר:
בִּנְאוֹת דֶּשֶׁא יַרְבִּיצֵנִי,
עַל מֵי־מְנֻחוֹת יְנַהֲלֵנִי.
נַפְשִׁי יְשׁוֹבֵב,
יַנְחֵנִי בְמַעְגְּלֵי צֶדֶק
לְמַעַן שְׁמוֹ.
גַּם כִּי אֵלֵךְ
בְּגֵיא צַלְמָוֶת –
לֹא אִירָא רָע,
כִּי אַתָּה עִמָּדִי.
שִׁבְטְךָ וּמִשְׁעַנְתֶּךָ
הֵמָּה יְנַחֲמֻנִי.

The Lord is my shepherd, I lack
nothing at all. He lays me down in
green pastures, He leads me to calm
waters.[1] He refreshes my soul. He
guides me in straight paths for His own
sake. Even when I walk through a
valley of pitch darkness,[2] I fear no
danger, for You are beside me. Your
rod and Your staff – they give me
comfort.

תַּעֲרֹךְ לְפָנַי שֻׁלְחָן
נֶגֶד צֹרְרָי;
דִּשַּׁנְתָּ בַשֶּׁמֶן רֹאשִׁי,
כּוֹסִי רְוָיָה.
אַךְ טוֹב וָחֶסֶד יִרְדְּפוּנִי
כָּל יְמֵי חַיָּי,
וְשַׁבְתִּי בְּבֵית יהוה
לְאֹרֶךְ יָמִים.

You spread a table for me in full view
of my enemies. You anoint my head
with oil; my cup is brim-full. Only
goodness and mercy will follow me all
the days of my life, and I shall live in
the Lord's house for many, many years.

---

1. Or 'waters in places of repose'.
2. Or 'the valley of the shadow of death'.

כְּאַיָּל תַּעֲרֹג עַל אֲפִיקֵי־מָיִם

YEARNING FOR GOD

לַמְנַצֵּחַ מַשְׂכִּיל לִבְנֵי קֹרַח:

For the choirmaster; a maskil *of the Korahites:*[1]

כְּאַיָּל תַּעֲרֹג עַל אֲפִיקֵי־מָיִם,
כֵּן נַפְשִׁי תַעֲרֹג אֵלֶיךָ, אֱלֹהִים!
צָמְאָה נַפְשִׁי לֵאלֹהִים,
לְאֵל חָי – מָתַי אָבוֹא וְאֵרָאֶה
פְּנֵי אֱלֹהִים?

As the deer longs for[2] running waters,
so does my soul long for You, O God!
My soul thirsts for God, for the living
God; when shall I come before God?

הָיְתָה לִּי דִמְעָתִי לֶחֶם
יוֹמָם וָלָיְלָה,
בֶּאֱמֹר אֵלַי כָּל הַיּוֹם:
'אַיֵּה אֱלֹהֶיךָ?'
אֵלֶּה אֶזְכְּרָה
וְאֶשְׁפְּכָה עָלַי נַפְשִׁי:
כִּי אֶעֱבֹר בַּסָּךְ,
אֶדַּדֵּם עַד בֵּית־אֱלֹהִים
בְּקוֹל רִנָּה וְתוֹדָה,
הָמוֹן חוֹגֵג.

My tears have been my food day and
night, as people taunt me, day after
day: 'Where is your God?' I pour out
my soul when I recall [the old days]:
how I marched in the procession
moving slowly[3] towards the house of
God, with joyous shouts of praise,
amid the festive throng.

מַה תִּשְׁתּוֹחֲחִי, נַפְשִׁי,
וַתֶּהֱמִי עָלָי?
הוֹחִלִי לֵאלֹהִים!
כִּי עוֹד אוֹדֶנּוּ,
יְשׁוּעֹת פָּנָיו.

Why are you so desolate, my soul, why
so distraught within me?[4] Hope in
God. For I shall still praise Him for
His saving presence.

---

1. *Maskil* is a type of song, perhaps 'artistic song, didactic poem'. The Korahites, or 'sons of Korah', were a guild of temple singers in the post-exilic period.
2. Or 'cries out for'.
3. The meaning of the Hebrew is uncertain.
4. Or 'why do you moan within me?'

אֱלֹהַי, עָלַי נַפְשִׁי תִשְׁתּוֹחָח —
עַל כֵּן אֶזְכָּרְךָ
מֵאֶרֶץ יַרְדֵּן וְחֶרְמוֹנִים,
מֵהַר מִצְעָר.
תְּהוֹם אֶל תְּהוֹם קוֹרֵא
לְקוֹל צִנּוֹרֶיךָ.
כָּל מִשְׁבָּרֶיךָ וְגַלֶּיךָ
עָלַי עָבָרוּ.

O God, my soul is desolate within me,
and so from this land of the Jordan, the
ranges of Hermon and Mount Mizar,
I turn my thoughts to You. [Here] deep
calls to deep in the roar of Your
cataracts. All Your breakers and Your
floods have swept over me.

יוֹמָם יְצַוֶּה יהוה חַסְדּוֹ,
וּבַלַּיְלָה שִׁירֹה עִמִּי:
תְּפִלָּה לְאֵל חַיָּי.
אוֹמְרָה לְאֵל־סַלְעִי:
'לָמָה שְׁכַחְתָּנִי ?
לָמָּה קֹדֵר אֵלֵךְ
בְּלַחַץ אוֹיֵב ?'
בְּרֶצַח, בְּעַצְמוֹתַי
חֵרְפוּנִי צוֹרְרָי,
בְּאָמְרָם אֵלַי כָּל הַיּוֹם:
'אַיֵּה אֱלֹהֶיךָ ?'

May the Lord bestow his steadfast love
by day, and may His song be with me
every night: a prayer to the God of my
life. I say to God, my Rock: 'Why have
You forgotten me? Why must I go
about in squalid black, tormented by
the enemy?' My foes revile me, their
jeers shatter my bones, as they taunt
me, day after day: 'Where is your
God?'

מַה תִּשְׁתּוֹחֲחִי, נַפְשִׁי,
וּמַה תֶּהֱמִי עָלָי ?
הוֹחִילִי לֵאלֹהִים !
כִּי עוֹד אוֹדֶנּוּ,
יְשׁוּעֹת פָּנַי וֵאלֹהָי.

Why are you so desolate, my soul, why
so distraught within me? Hope in God.
For I shall still praise Him, my ever-
present saviour, my God.

שָׁפְטֵנִי, אֱלֹהִים,
וְרִיבָה רִיבִי
מִגּוֹי לֹא־חָסִיד ;

Grant me justice, O God, and champion my cause against impious people.

167

מֵאִישׁ מִרְמָה וְעַוְלָה תְפַלְּטֵנִי.
כִּי אַתָּה אֱלֹהֵי מָעוּזִּי,
לָמָה זְנַחְתָּנִי ?
לָמָּה קֹדֵר אֶתְהַלֵּךְ
בְּלַחַץ אוֹיֵב ?

Save me from treacherous and evil
men. For You are my God, my stronghold; why, then, have You rejected
me? Why must I go about in squalid
black, tormented by the enemy?

שְׁלַח אוֹרְךָ וַאֲמִתְּךָ —
הֵמָּה יַנְחוּנִי,
יְבִיאוּנִי אֶל הַר קָדְשְׁךָ
וְאֶל מִשְׁכְּנוֹתֶיךָ.
וְאָבוֹאָה אֶל מִזְבַּח אֱלֹהִים,
אֶל אֵל שִׂמְחַת גִּילִי,
וְאוֹדְךָ בְכִנּוֹר, אֱלֹהִים אֱלֹהָי !

Send forth Your light and Your truth;
they will guide me and bring me to
Your dwelling place. Then I shall come
to the altar of God, the God of my joy
and my delight, and I shall praise You
with the lyre, O God, my God!

מַה תִּשְׁתּוֹחֲחִי, נַפְשִׁי,
וּמַה תֶּהֱמִי עָלָי ?
הוֹחִילִי לֵאלֹהִים !
כִּי עוֹד אוֹדֶנּוּ,
יְשׁוּעֹת פָּנַי וֵאלֹהָי.

Why are you so desolate, my soul, why
so distraught within me? Hope in God.
For I shall still praise Him, my ever-
present saviour, my God.

בָּרְכִי, נַפְשִׁי, אֶת יהוה

IN PRAISE OF THE CREATOR

בָּרְכִי, נַפְשִׁי, אֶת יהוה !

O my soul, bless the Lord!

יהוה אֱלֹהַי, גָּדַלְתָּ מְּאֹד,
הוֹד וְהָדָר לָבָשְׁתָּ:
עֹטֶה אוֹר כַּשַּׂלְמָה,
נוֹטֶה שָׁמַיִם כַּיְרִיעָה ;

O Lord, my God, You are very great,
clothed in majesty and splendour: You
wrapped yourself in light as in a cloak;
You spread out the heavens like a tent;

הַמְקָרֶה בַמַּיִם עֲלִיּוֹתָיו;
הַשָּׂם עָבִים רְכוּבוֹ,
הַמְהַלֵּךְ עַל כַּנְפֵי־רוּחַ;
עֹשֶׂה מַלְאָכָיו רוּחוֹת,
מְשָׁרְתָיו – אֵשׁ לֹהֵט.

You laid the beams of Your high chambers upon the waters;[1] You take the clouds for Your chariot, You ride on the wings of the wind; You make the winds Your messengers, and flaming fires Your servants.

יָסַד אֶרֶץ עַל מְכוֹנֶיהָ,
בַּל־תִּמּוֹט עוֹלָם וָעֶד.
תְּהוֹם כַּלְּבוּשׁ כִּסִּיתוֹ,
עַל הָרִים יַעַמְדוּ מָיִם.
מִן גַּעֲרָתְךָ יְנוּסוּן,
מִן קוֹל־רַעַמְךָ יֵחָפֵזוּן –
יַעֲלוּ הָרִים, יֵרְדוּ בְקָעוֹת,
אֶל מְקוֹם זֶה יָסַדְתָּ לָהֶם.
גְּבוּל שַׂמְתָּ, בַּל־יַעֲבֹרוּן,
בַּל־יְשֻׁבוּן לְכַסּוֹת הָאָרֶץ.

You fixed the earth on its foundations, so that it should never totter. You covered it with the abyss[2] as with a garment; the waters stood above the mountains. Then, at Your rebuke, they fled; at the blast of Your thunder they rushed away, streaming up the mountains and down into the valleys[3] to the place You had assigned them. You fixed their bounds: they may not pass them or cover the earth again.

הַמְשַׁלֵּחַ מַעְיָנִים בַּנְּחָלִים:
בֵּין הָרִים יְהַלֵּכוּן,
יַשְׁקוּ כָּל חַיְתוֹ־שָׂדָי,
יִשְׁבְּרוּ פְרָאִים צְמָאָם;
עֲלֵיהֶם עוֹף־הַשָּׁמַיִם יִשְׁכּוֹן,
מִבֵּין עֳפָאִים יִתְּנוּ קוֹל.

You send forth springs into the gullies: they wind their way between the mountains, giving drink to all the animals; there the wild asses quench their thirst; the birds of the air dwell beside them, singing their songs from among the branches.

מַשְׁקֶה הָרִים מֵעֲלִיּוֹתָיו,
מִפְּרִי מַעֲשֶׂיךָ תִּשְׂבַּע הָאָרֶץ:
מַצְמִיחַ חָצִיר לַבְּהֵמָה
וְעֵשֶׂב – לַעֲבֹדַת הָאָדָם

You water the mountains from Your high chambers, the earth abounds with the fruit of Your works. You make grass grow for the cattle and grains for the service of man, bringing food out of

1. The royal palace of God was founded on the upper waters, above the firmaments.
2. Or 'You covered the depths [with water] as with a garment'.
3. Or 'as the mountains rose, they went down into the valleys'.

לְהוֹצִיא לֶחֶם מִן הָאָרֶץ;
וְיַיִן יְשַׂמַּח לְבַב־אֱנוֹש,
לְהַצְהִיל פָּנִים מִשָּׁמֶן,
וְלֶחֶם לְבַב־אֱנוֹש יִסְעָד.
יִשְׂבְּעוּ עֲצֵי־יהוה,
אַרְזֵי־לְבָנוֹן אֲשֶׁר נָטָע,
אֲשֶׁר שָׁם צִפֳּרִים יְקַנֵּנוּ.
חֲסִידָה – בְּרוֹשִׁים בֵּיתָהּ;
הָרִים הַגְּבֹהִים – לַיְּעֵלִים,
סְלָעִים – מַחְסֶה לַשְׁפַנִּים.

the earth; and wine that gladdens man's heart, oil that makes his face shine, and bread that strengthens man's heart. The trees of the Lord drink their fill, the cedars of Lebanon which He planted, where the birds build their nests. The stork makes her home among the junipers; the high mountains are for the wild goats; the cliffs are a refuge for rock-badgers.

עָשָׂה יָרֵחַ לְמוֹעֲדִים,
שֶׁמֶשׁ יָדַע מְבוֹאוֹ.
תָּשֶׁת חֹשֶׁךְ – וִיהִי לָיְלָה,
בּוֹ תִרְמֹשׂ כָּל חַיְתוֹ־יָעַר:
הַכְּפִירִים שֹׁאֲגִים לַטָּרֶף
וּלְבַקֵּשׁ מֵאֵל אָכְלָם;
תִּזְרַח הַשֶּׁמֶשׁ – יֵאָסֵפוּן
וְאֶל מְעוֹנֹתָם יִרְבָּצוּן;
יֵצֵא אָדָם לְפָעֳלוֹ
וְלַעֲבֹדָתוֹ – עֲדֵי עָרֶב.

You made the moon to mark the seasons; the sun knows when it must set. You bring on darkness, and night comes; then all the beasts of the forest prowl. The young lions roar for prey, looking to God for their food. When the sun rises, they steal away to lie down in their lairs. Then man goes out to his work and to his labours until nightfall.

מָה רַבּוּ מַעֲשֶׂיךָ, יהוה!
כֻּלָּם בְּחָכְמָה עָשִׂיתָ,
מָלְאָה הָאָרֶץ קִנְיָנֶךָ.
זֶה הַיָּם גָּדוֹל וּרְחַב־יָדַיִם –
שָׁם רֶמֶשׂ וְאֵין־מִסְפָּר,
חַיּוֹת קְטַנּוֹת עִם גְּדֹלוֹת;
שָׁם אֳנִיּוֹת יְהַלֵּכוּן,
לִוְיָתָן זֶה־יָצַרְתָּ לְשַׂחֶק־בּוֹ.

How manifold are Your works, O Lord! You made them all with wisdom; the earth is full of Your creatures. There is the sea, vast and wide, with innumerable beings in it, living things both small and great. There ships[1] move about, and Leviathan whom You created as Your plaything.

---

1. Some scholars read *emot* ('dreadful things, monsters') for the Masoretic text *oniyot* ('ships').

כֻּלָּם אֵלֶיךָ יְשַׂבֵּרוּן
לָתֵת אָכְלָם בְּעִתּוֹ.
תִּתֵּן לָהֶם – יִלְקֹטוּן,
תִּפְתַּח יָדְךָ – יִשְׂבְּעוּן טוֹב;
תַּסְתִּיר פָּנֶיךָ – יִבָּהֵלוּן,
תֹּסֵף רוּחָם – יִגְוָעוּן
וְאֶל עֲפָרָם יְשׁוּבוּן;
תְּשַׁלַּח רוּחֲךָ – יִבָּרֵאוּן,
וּתְחַדֵּשׁ פְּנֵי אֲדָמָה.

They all look hopefully to You, to give them their food in due time. When You give it to them, they gather it up; when You open Your hand, they eat their fill of it. When You hide Your face, they are appalled; when You take away their breath, they perish and return again to the dust. When You send forth Your breath, they are created; thus You renew the whole earth.

יְהִי כְבוֹד־יהוה לְעוֹלָם,
יִשְׂמַח יהוה בְּמַעֲשָׂיו!
הַמַּבִּיט לָאָרֶץ – וַתִּרְעָד,
יִגַּע בֶּהָרִים – וְיֶעֱשָׁנוּ.
אָשִׁירָה לַיהוה בְּחַיָּי,
אֲזַמְּרָה לֵאלֹהַי בְּעוֹדִי.
יֶעֱרַב עָלָיו שִׂיחִי,
אָנֹכִי אֶשְׂמַח בַּיהוה.
יִתַּמּוּ חַטָּאִים מִן הָאָרֶץ,
וּרְשָׁעִים עוֹד אֵינָם.

May the glory of the Lord endure forever! May the Lord rejoice in His works: He looks at the earth and it trembles; He touches the mountains and they smoke. I shall sing to the Lord all my life; I shall chant hymns to my God as long as I live. May my prayer be pleasing to Him; I shall rejoice in the Lord. May sinners disappear from the earth and the wicked be no more.

בָּרְכִי, נַפְשִׁי, אֶת יהוה!
הַלְלוּיָהּ!

O my soul, bless the Lord! Hallelujah!

וְהַחָכְמָה – מֵאַיִן תִּמָּצֵא ?

THE INACCESSIBILITY OF
WISDOM

כִּי יֵשׁ לַכֶּסֶף מוֹצָא,
וּמָקוֹם לַזָּהָב יָזֹקּוּ.
בַּרְזֶל מֵעָפָר יֻקָּח,
וְאֶבֶן – יָצוּק נְחוּשָׁה.
קֵץ שָׂם לַחֹשֶׁךְ
וּלְכָל תַּכְלִית הוּא חוֹקֵר
אֶבֶן אֹפֶל וְצַלְמָוֶת.
פָּרַץ נַחַל מֵעִם גָּר,
הַנִּשְׁכָּחִים מִנִּי רָגֶל,
דַּלּוּ מֵאֱנוֹשׁ נָעוּ.
אֶרֶץ, מִמֶּנָּה יֵצֵא לָחֶם,
וְתַחְתֶּיהָ נֶהְפַּךְ כְּמוֹ אֵשׁ.
מְקוֹם־סַפִּיר אֲבָנֶיהָ,
וְעַפְרֹת זָהָב לוֹ.
נָתִיב – לֹא יְדָעוֹ עָיִט,
וְלֹא שְׁזָפַתּוּ עֵין־אַיָּה,
לֹא הִדְרִיכוּהוּ בְנֵי שָׁחַץ,
לֹא עָדָה עָלָיו שָׁחַל.
בַּחַלָּמִישׁ שָׁלַח יָדוֹ –
הָפַךְ מִשֹּׁרֶשׁ הָרִים.
בַּצּוּרוֹת יְאֹרִים בִּקֵּעַ
וְכָל יְקָר רָאֲתָה עֵינוֹ.
מִבְּכִי נְהָרוֹת חִבֵּשׁ
וְתַעֲלֻמָהּ יֹצִא אוֹר.

There is a source for silver, and a place
where gold is refined. Iron is extracted
from the earth and copper is smelted
from stone. Man puts[1] an end to
darkness, he probes the farthest confines for the stone [that is hidden in]
gloom and pitch darkness. He breaks
open a shaft far from human habitation,
in sites forgotten by men's feet,
forsaken by those who have wandered
away. The very earth, from which
bread comes forth, is convulsed under-
neath as if by fire. Its stones yield
sapphires, its dust has gold in it.[2] No
bird of prey knows the path to it, nor
has the falcon's eye seen it; the proud
beasts have not set foot on it, nor has
the lion ever trodden it. Man sets his
hand to the flinty rock, and overturns
mountains by their roots. He hews out
channels in the rocks and his eyes
behold all that is precious. He dams[3]
the springs of rivers, and brings hidden
things to light.

---

1. Lit. 'He put'. The passage is obscure.
2. Or 'A place where stones are sapphires and whose dust is gold'.
3. Or 'probes, explores'.

וְהַחָכְמָה – מֵאַיִן תִּמָּצֵא,
וְאֵי זֶה מְקוֹם בִּינָה?
לֹא יָדַע אֱנוֹשׁ עֶרְכָּהּ,
וְלֹא תִמָּצֵא בְּאֶרֶץ הַחַיִּים.
תְּהוֹם אָמַר: 'לֹא בִי הִיא,'
וְיָם אָמַר: 'אֵין עִמָּדִי.'

But where can Wisdom be found, and where is the home of understanding? No man knows the way to it[1] nor can it be found in the land of the living. The Abyss says 'It is not in me,' and the Sea says 'I do not have it.'

לֹא יֻתַּן סְגוֹר תַּחְתֶּיהָ,
וְלֹא יִשָּׁקֵל כֶּסֶף מְחִירָהּ.
לֹא תְסֻלֶּה בְּכֶתֶם־אוֹפִיר,
בְּשֹׁהַם יָקָר וְסַפִּיר.
לֹא יַעַרְכֶנָּה זָהָב וּזְכוֹכִית,
וּתְמוּרָתָהּ – כְּלִי פָז.
רָאמוֹת וְגָבִישׁ לֹא יִזָּכֵר;
וּמֶשֶׁךְ חָכְמָה – מִפְּנִינִים.
לֹא יַעַרְכֶנָּה פִּטְדַת־כּוּשׁ,
בְּכֶתֶם טָהוֹר לֹא תְסֻלֶּה.

It cannot be gotten in exchange for choice gold, nor can its price be weighed out in silver. It cannot be balanced against gold of Ophir, against precious onyx or sapphires. Gold and glass cannot equal it, nor can vessels of fine gold match its value. Coral and jasper are of no account; it is harder to acquire Wisdom than pearls. Arabian topaz cannot equal it, nor can it be balanced against pure gold.

וְהַחָכְמָה – מֵאַיִן תָּבוֹא,
וְאֵי זֶה מְקוֹם בִּינָה?
וְנֶעֶלְמָה מֵעֵינֵי כָל חָי
וּמֵעוֹף הַשָּׁמַיִם נִסְתָּרָה.
אֲבַדּוֹן וָמָוֶת אָמְרוּ:
'בְּאָזְנֵינוּ שָׁמַעְנוּ שִׁמְעָהּ.'

Where, then, does Wisdom come from, and where is the home of understanding? It is hidden from the eyes of all the living, and concealed from the birds of the air. Hell and Death say 'We have heard of it, but only by rumour.'

אֱלֹהִים הֵבִין דַּרְכָּהּ
וְהוּא יָדַע אֶת מְקוֹמָהּ,
כִּי הוּא לִקְצוֹת הָאָרֶץ יַבִּיט,

Only God understands the way to it. He alone knows where it is, for He looks to the ends of the earth and

---

1. Lit. 'its worth' (*erka*). *Darka*, 'its way', is an accepted emendation.

תַּחַת כָּל הַשָּׁמַיִם יִרְאֶה.
לַעֲשׂוֹת לָרוּחַ מִשְׁקָל,
וּמַיִם תִּכֵּן בְּמִדָּה,
בַּעֲשֹׂתוֹ לַמָּטָר חֹק,
וְדֶרֶךְ לַחֲזִיז־קֹלוֹת –
אָז רָאָהּ וַיְסַפְּרָהּ,
הֱכִינָהּ וְגַם חֲקָרָהּ.
וַיֹּאמֶר לָאָדָם:
'הֵן יִרְאַת אֲדֹנָי – הִיא חָכְמָה,
וְסוּר מֵרָע – בִּינָה.'

surveys all that is under the heavens.
When He determined the weight of the
wind and set a measure to the waters;
when He decreed a limit to the rain[1]
and a path for the thunderstorm – it
was then that He looked at Wisdom
and appraised it, He established[2] it and
fathomed its depths. And to man He
said: 'To fear the Lord, that is
Wisdom, and to avoid evil, that is
understanding.'

אֲנִי יְשֵׁנָה – וְלִבִּי עֵר   THE LOST LOVER

אֲנִי יְשֵׁנָה – וְלִבִּי עֵר.
קוֹל דּוֹדִי דוֹפֵק:

I was asleep, but my heart was awake.
I heard my lover knocking:

'פִּתְחִי לִי, אֲחֹתִי,
רַעְיָתִי, יוֹנָתִי תַמָּתִי!
שֶׁרֹּאשִׁי נִמְלָא טָל,
קְוֻצּוֹתַי – רְסִיסֵי לָיְלָה.'

'Let me in, my sister, my darling, my
dove, my perfect one! For my head is
wet with dew, my curls with the mist
of the night.'

'פָּשַׁטְתִּי אֶת כֻּתָּנְתִּי –
אֵיכָכָה אֶלְבָּשֶׁנָּה?
רָחַצְתִּי אֶת רַגְלַי –
אֵיכָכָה אֲטַנְּפֵם?'

'I have already taken off my robe –
shall I put it on again? I have bathed
my feet – shall I now soil them?'

---

1. Or 'when he made rules for the rain'.   2. Or 'discerned'.

174

דּוֹדִי שָׁלַח יָדוֹ מִן הַחוֹר,
וּמֵעַי הָמוּ עָלָיו.
קַמְתִּי אֲנִי לִפְתֹּחַ לְדוֹדִי,
וְיָדַי נָטְפוּ מוֹר,
וְאֶצְבְּעֹתַי – מוֹר־עֹבֵר
עַל כַּפּוֹת הַמַּנְעוּל.
פָּתַחְתִּי אֲנִי לְדוֹדִי –
וְדוֹדִי חָמַק, עָבָר.
נַפְשִׁי יָצְאָה בְדַבְּרוֹ!
בִּקַּשְׁתִּיהוּ – וְלֹא מְצָאתִיהוּ,
קְרָאתִיו – וְלֹא עָנָנִי.

My lover drew back his hand from the
latch, and my heart beat wildly for him.
I rose to let my lover in; my hands
dripped with myrrh, my fingers flowed
with myrrh upon the handles of the
bolt. I opened to my lover, but he had
slipped away and was gone. My soul
longed for his words![1] I looked for
him, but could not find him; I called to
him, but he did not answer me.

מְצָאֻנִי הַשֹּׁמְרִים,
הַסֹּבְבִים בָּעִיר,
הִכּוּנִי, פְצָעוּנִי,
נָשְׂאוּ אֶת רְדִידִי מֵעָלַי
שֹׁמְרֵי הַחֹמוֹת.
הִשְׁבַּעְתִּי אֶתְכֶם,
בְּנוֹת יְרוּשָׁלָ͏ִם,
אִם תִּמְצְאוּ אֶת דּוֹדִי,
מַה תַּגִּידוּ לוֹ?
שֶׁחוֹלַת־אַהֲבָה אָנִי!

The watchmen, making the rounds of
the city, came upon me; they beat me,
they wounded me, they tore off my
mantle – these guardians of the walls.
I adjure you, daughters of Jerusalem, if
you should find my lover, what will
you say to him? Tell him that I am
sick with love.

'מַה דּוֹדֵךְ מִדּוֹד,
הַיָּפָה בַּנָּשִׁים?
מַה דּוֹדֵךְ מִדּוֹד,
שֶׁכָּכָה הִשְׁבַּעְתָּנוּ?'

'O fairest of women, how does your
lover excel other men, that you adjure
us in this way?'

---

1. Or 'My soul had grown faint when he spoke'.

'דּוֹדִי צַח וְאָדוֹם,
דָּגוּל מֵרְבָבָה.
רֹאשׁוֹ כֶּתֶם פָּז,
קְוֻצּוֹתָיו תַּלְתַּלִּים,
שְׁחֹרוֹת כָּעוֹרֵב;
עֵינָיו כְּיוֹנִים
עַל אֲפִיקֵי מָיִם —
רֹחֲצוֹת בֶּחָלָב,
יֹשְׁבוֹת עַל מִלֵּאת;
לְחָיָו כַּעֲרוּגַת הַבֹּשֶׂם,
מִגְדְּלוֹת מֶרְקָחִים;
שִׂפְתוֹתָיו שׁוֹשַׁנִּים,
נֹטְפוֹת מוֹר־עֹבֵר;
יָדָיו גְּלִילֵי זָהָב,
מְמֻלָּאִים בַּתַּרְשִׁישׁ;
מֵעָיו עֶשֶׁת־שֵׁן,
מְעֻלֶּפֶת סַפִּירִים;
שׁוֹקָיו עַמּוּדֵי שֵׁשׁ,
מְיֻסָּדִים עַל אַדְנֵי פָז;
מַרְאֵהוּ כַּלְּבָנוֹן,
בָּחוּר כָּאֲרָזִים;
חִכּוֹ מַמְתַקִּים,
וְכֻלּוֹ מַחֲמַדִּים —
זֶה דוֹדִי וְזֶה רֵעִי,
בְּנוֹת יְרוּשָׁלָם!'

'My lover is fair and radiant, he is peerless among ten thousand. His head is the finest gold; his locks are palm fronds, black as the raven. His eyes are like doves beside flowing brooks: milk-white doves, perched by a brimming pool. His cheeks are like beds of spices, exhaling perfumes. His lips are lilies, flowing with liquid myrrh. His arms are rods of gold, inlaid with topaz. His body is a pillar of ivory, covered with sapphires. His legs are marble columns, set in sockets of fine gold. His bearing is like the trees of Lebanon, lofty as the cedars. His mouth is most sweet; all of him is pure delight. Such is my lover, such is my friend, O daughters of Jerusalem!'

'אָנָה הָלַךְ דּוֹדֵךְ,
הַיָּפָה בַּנָּשִׁים?
אָנָה פָּנָה דוֹדֵךְ? —
וּנְבַקְשֶׁנּוּ עִמָּךְ.'

'Where has your lover gone, O fairest of women? Which way has your lover turned? Let us seek him together.'

'דּוֹדִי יָרַד לְגַנּוֹ,
לַעֲרֻגוֹת הַבֹּשֶׂם,
לִרְעוֹת בַּגַּנִּים
וְלִלְקֹט שׁוֹשַׁנִּים.
אֲנִי לְדוֹדִי וְדוֹדִי לִי,
הָרוֹעֶה בַּשּׁוֹשַׁנִּים.'

'My lover has gone down to his garden, to the beds of spices, to tend his flock in the garden and to gather lilies. My lover is mine, and I am his; he tends his flock among the lilies.'

שׁוּבִי, שׁוּבִי, הַשּׁוּלַמִּית!

THE MAIDEN'S DANCE

'שׁוּבִי, שׁוּבִי, הַשּׁוּלַמִּית,
שׁוּבִי, שׁוּבִי, וְנֶחֱזֶה בָּךְ!'

'Return, return, O Shulammite, return, return, let us gaze at you!'

'מַה תֶּחֱזוּ בַּשּׁוּלַמִּית
כִּמְחֹלַת הַמַּחֲנָיִם?'

'What will you see in the Shulammite as she dances between the companies?'[1]

'מַה יָּפוּ פְעָמַיִךְ בַּנְּעָלִים,
בַּת נָדִיב!
חַמּוּקֵי יְרֵכַיִךְ כְּמוֹ חֲלָאִים,
מַעֲשֵׂה יְדֵי אָמָּן;
שָׁרְרֵךְ אַגַּן הַסַּהַר
אַל יֶחְסַר הַמָּזֶג;
בִּטְנֵךְ עֲרֵמַת חִטִּים,
סוּגָה בַּשּׁוֹשַׁנִּים;
שְׁנֵי שָׁדַיִךְ כִּשְׁנֵי עֲפָרִים,
תָּאֳמֵי צְבִיָּה;
צַוָּארֵךְ כְּמִגְדַּל־הַשֵּׁן;
עֵינַיִךְ בְּרֵכוֹת בְּחֶשְׁבּוֹן,

'How beautiful are your sandalled feet, O royal daughter! Your curved thighs are like jewels fashioned by a master. Your navel is a round goblet, brim-full of wine.[2] Your belly is a heap of wheat, ringed with lilies. Your breasts are like two fawns – the twins of a gazelle. Your neck is like a tower of ivory. Your eyes are the pools of Heshbon, by the gate

1. Lit. 'the dance of Mahanaim'; the meaning is uncertain.
2. Or '– may it never lack mixed wine!'

177

עַל שַׁעַר בַּת־רַבִּים ;
אַפֵּךְ כְּמִגְדַּל הַלְּבָנוֹן,
צוֹפֶה פְּנֵי דַמָּשֶׂק ;
רֹאשֵׁךְ עָלַיִךְ כַּכַּרְמֶל,
וְדַלַּת רֹאשֵׁךְ כָּאַרְגָּמָן ;
מֶלֶךְ אָסוּר בָּרְהָטִים !'

of Bath-rabbim. Your nose is like the
tower on Lebanon that looks towards
Damascus. Your head rises like Mount
Carmel,[1] your flowing locks are
[lustrous] as purple; a king is held
captive in these tresses!'

'מַה יָּפִית וּמַה נָּעַמְתְּ
אַהֲבָה בַּתַּעֲנוּגִים !
זֹאת קוֹמָתֵךְ דָּמְתָה לְתָמָר,
וְשָׁדַיִךְ – לְאַשְׁכֹּלוֹת.
אָמַרְתִּי : "אֶעֱלֶה בְתָמָר,
אֹחֲזָה בְּסַנְסִנָּיו !
וְיִהְיוּ נָא שָׁדַיִךְ
כְּאֶשְׁכְּלוֹת הַגֶּפֶן,
וְרֵיחַ אַפֵּךְ כַּתַּפּוּחִים,
וְחִכֵּךְ כְּיֵין הַטּוֹב !"'

[The Lover:] 'How fair you are, how
pleasing, O rapturous love![2] Here is
your figure, stately as a palm tree, and
your breasts like clusters of fruit. I say:
"Let me climb the palm tree and take
hold of its branches! May your breasts
be like clusters of grapes on the vine,
the fragrance of your breath like apples,
and your mouth like choice wine –"'

'הוֹלֵךְ לְדוֹדִי לְמֵישָׁרִים,
דּוֹבֵב שִׂפְתֵי יְשֵׁנִים.'

[The Maiden:] '– that will flow
smoothly for my lover, gliding over his
sleeping lips.'[3]

---

1. Or 'Your head adorns you like crimson'.
2. Or 'How beautiful you are, how pleasant, O Love with its delights!'
3. Or 'gliding over his lips and teeth'. The verse has also been understood as part of the lover's speech:
'. . . choice wine that flows to give lovers vigour and stirs the lips of those who sleep'.

מִי זאת עָלָה   THE SEAL OF LOVE

מִי זֹאת עֹלָה מִן הַמִּדְבָּר,
מִתְרַפֶּקֶת עַל דּוֹדָהּ ?

Who is this coming up from the wilderness, leaning tenderly upon her lover?

'תַּחַת הַתַּפּוּחַ עוֹרַרְתִּיךָ —
שָׁמָּה חִבְּלַתְךָ אִמֶּךָ,
שָׁמָּה חִבְּלָה יְלָדַתְךָ,
שִׂימֵנִי כַחוֹתָם עַל לִבֶּךָ,
כַּחוֹתָם עַל זְרוֹעֶךָ,
כִּי עַזָּה כַמָּוֶת אַהֲבָה,
קָשָׁה כִשְׁאוֹל קִנְאָה;
רְשָׁפֶיהָ רִשְׁפֵּי אֵשׁ,
שַׁלְהֶבֶתְיָה.
מַיִם רַבִּים לֹא יוּכְלוּ
לְכַבּוֹת אֶת הָאַהֲבָה,
וּנְהָרוֹת לֹא יִשְׁטְפוּהָ.
אִם יִתֵּן אִישׁ
אֶת כָּל הוֹן בֵּיתוֹ בָּאַהֲבָה —
בּוֹז יָבוּזוּ לוֹ.'

[The Maiden:][1] 'Under the apple-tree I aroused you; it was there that your mother conceived you, there she conceived you and brought you forth. Set me as a seal upon your heart, as a seal upon your arm;[2] for love is as fierce as death, passion is as harsh as the grave; its flashes are raging fires, violent flames. Vast floods cannot quench love, nor can rivers sweep it away. If a man were to offer all his wealth for love, he would be laughed to scorn.'

אֵיכָה יוּעַם זָהָב   DIRGE ON THE FALL OF JERUSALEM

אֵיכָה יוּעַם זָהָב,
יִשְׁנֶא הַכֶּתֶם הַטּוֹב —
תִּשְׁתַּפֵּכְנָה אַבְנֵי־קֹדֶשׁ
בְּרֹאשׁ כָּל חוּצוֹת!

How the gold was tarnished, the finest gold debased! How the sacred gems[3] were strewn about at every street

---

1. Some translations ascribe the following verse to the Lover. The maiden's reply begins with 'Set me . . .'
2. Or 'like the seal which is upon your hand'.
3. I.e., the people of Jerusalem. Or 'the sacred stones [of the sanctuary]'.

corner! The precious sons of Zion, once worth their weight in gold – how they were disparaged as earthenware from a potter's hand! Even jackals bare their breasts and suckle their young; but the daughter of my people became as cruel as the desert ostrich. The tongue of the suckling cleaved to its palate for thirst; infants begged for bread, but no one offered them a crumb. Those who once fed on dainties lay stunned in the streets; those who were brought up in purple, clung to garbage-heaps. The punishment of the daughter of my people was far greater than the penalty of Sodom, which was overthrown in an instant, untouched by human hands. Her nobles were purer than snow, whiter than milk; their bodies were ruddier than coral, their limbs[1] were sapphire. Then their faces turned blacker than soot; none could recognize them in the streets. Their skin shrivelled on their bones, it became as dry as wood. Those who died by the sword were luckier than

בְּנֵי צִיּוֹן הַיְקָרִים,
הַמְסֻלָּאִים בַּפָּז –
אֵיכָה נֶחְשְׁבוּ לְנִבְלֵי־חֶרֶשׂ,
מַעֲשֵׂה יְדֵי יוֹצֵר!
גַּם תַּנִּים חָלְצוּ שַׁד,
הֵינִיקוּ גּוּרֵיהֶן;
בַּת עַמִּי לְאַכְזָר,
כַּיְעֵנִים בַּמִּדְבָּר.
דָּבַק לְשׁוֹן יוֹנֵק
אֶל חִכּוֹ בַּצָּמָא;
עוֹלָלִים שָׁאֲלוּ לֶחֶם,
פֹּרֵשׂ אֵין לָהֶם.
הָאֹכְלִים לְמַעֲדַנִּים –
נָשַׁמּוּ בַּחוּצוֹת;
הָאֱמֻנִים עֲלֵי תוֹלָע –
חִבְּקוּ אַשְׁפַּתּוֹת.
וַיִּגְדַּל עֲוֹן בַּת עַמִּי
מֵחַטַּאת סְדֹם,
הַהֲפוּכָה כְמוֹ־רָגַע,
וְלֹא חָלוּ בָהּ יָדָיִם.
זַכּוּ נְזִירֶיהָ מִשֶּׁלֶג;
צַחוּ מֵחָלָב;
אָדְמוּ־עֶצֶם מִפְּנִינִים,
סַפִּיר גִּזְרָתָם.
חָשַׁךְ מִשְּׁחוֹר תָּאֳרָם,
לֹא נִכְּרוּ בַּחוּצוֹת;,
צָפַד עוֹרָם עַל עַצְמָם,
יָבֵשׁ הָיָה כָעֵץ.
טוֹבִים הָיוּ חַלְלֵי־חֶרֶב

1. Meaning uncertain.

180

מֵחַלְלֵי־רָעָב;

שֶׁהֵם יָזֻבוּ מְדֻקָּרִים

מִתְּנוּבוֹת שָׂדָי.

יְדֵי נָשִׁים רַחֲמָנִיּוֹת

בִּשְּׁלוּ יַלְדֵיהֶן;

הָיוּ לְבָרוֹת לָמוֹ

בְּשֶׁבֶר בַּת עַמִּי.

כִּלָּה יהוה אֶת חֲמָתוֹ,

שָׁפַךְ חֲרוֹן אַפּוֹ,

וַיַּצֶּת־אֵשׁ בְּצִיּוֹן

וַתֹּאכַל יְסֹדֹתֶיהָ.

לֹא הֶאֱמִינוּ מַלְכֵי אֶרֶץ,

כֹּל יֹשְׁבֵי תֵבֵל,

כִּי יָבֹא צַר וְאוֹיֵב

בְּשַׁעֲרֵי יְרוּשָׁלָם.

מֵחַטֹּאת נְבִיאֶיהָ,

עֲוֹנֹת כֹּהֲנֶיהָ,

הַשֹּׁפְכִים בְּקִרְבָּהּ

דַּם צַדִּיקִים.

נָעוּ עִוְרִים בַּחוּצוֹת,

נְגֹאֲלוּ בַּדָּם;

בְּלֹא יוּכְלוּ יִגְּעוּ

בִּלְבֻשֵׁיהֶם.

'סוּרוּ, טָמֵא!' – קָרְאוּ לָמוֹ –

'סוּרוּ, סוּרוּ, אַל תִּגָּעוּ!'

כִּי נָצוּ גַם נָעוּ, אָמְרוּ בַּגּוֹיִם:

'לֹא יוֹסִפוּ לָגוּר!'

פְּנֵי יהוה חִלְּקָם,

those who died of hunger; those who bled to death from their wounds than those who were deprived of all food.[1] Tender-hearted women cooked their children with their own hands; this was their fare when the daughter of my people met with disaster. The Lord vented all His wrath, He poured out His fury. He kindled a fire in Zion that consumed its foundations. The kings of the earth, all the world's inhabitants had never imagined that enemies could penetrate the gates of Jerusalem. But the sins of her prophets brought this to pass, the crimes of her priests, who in her midst shed the blood of the righteous! Defiled by blood, they staggered blindly through the streets; no one could bear to touch their garments. 'Away! Unclean!' people shouted at them,[2] 'Away! Away! Do not come near!' So they wandered, fugitives, and the nations said, 'They will never find a dwelling place.' The Lord Himself dispersed them, He no

---

1. Lit. 'the fruits of the field'.
2. Another possible interpretation is that they themselves are sounding the leper's cry; cf. Leviticus 13.46.

181

לֹא יוֹסִיף לְהַבִּיטָם ;
פְּנֵי כֹהֲנִים לֹא נָשָׂאוּ,
וּזְקֵנִים לֹא חָנָנוּ.
עוֹדֵינוּ תִּכְלֶינָה עֵינֵינוּ
אֶל עֶזְרָתֵנוּ הָבֶל ;
בְּצִפִּיָּתֵנוּ צִפִּינוּ
אֶל גּוֹי לֹא־יוֹשִׁעַ.
צָדוּ צְעָדֵינוּ
מִלֶּכֶת בִּרְחֹבֹתֵינוּ.
קָרַב קִצֵּנוּ, מָלְאוּ יָמֵינוּ,
כִּי בָא קִצֵּנוּ.
קַלִּים הָיוּ רֹדְפֵינוּ
מִנִּשְׁרֵי שָׁמָיִם ;
עַל הֶהָרִים דְּלָקֻנוּ,
בַּמִּדְבָּר אָרְבוּ לָנוּ.
רוּחַ אַפֵּינוּ, מְשִׁיחַ יהוה,
נִלְכַּד בִּשְׁחִיתוֹתָם —
אֲשֶׁר אָמַרְנוּ:
בְּצִלּוֹ נִחְיֶה בַגּוֹיִם.

longer took notice of them. He showed no regard for the priests, no favour to the elders. And still our eyes wasted away as we looked in vain for help; anxiously we watched for a nation[1] that would not save us. Men dogged our steps – we could not walk through our streets. Our end drew near; our days were numbered; our end had come. Our pursuers were swifter than eagles in the sky, they pursued us in the mountains, they waylaid us in the desert. The Lord's anointed[2] – the very breath of our life – was caught in their snares; it was under his wing that we had hoped to live on among the nations.

שִׂישִׂי וְשִׂמְחִי, בַּת אֱדוֹם,
יוֹשֶׁבֶת בְּאֶרֶץ עוּץ !
גַּם עָלַיִךְ תַּעֲבָר־כּוֹס,
תִּשְׁכְּרִי וְתִתְעָרִי.
תַּם עֲוֹנֵךְ, בַּת צִיּוֹן,
לֹא יוֹסִיף לְהַגְלוֹתֵךְ.
פָּקַד עֲוֹנֵךְ, בַּת אֱדוֹם,
גִּלָּה עַל חַטֹּאתָיִךְ !

Rejoice and be glad, O daughter of Edom, you who dwell in the land of Uz! The cup will yet pass to you as well; you will become drunk and expose your nakedness. Your punishment is now completed,[3] O daughter of Zion; He will not exile you again. But you, O daughter of Edom – He will make you pay for your crimes, He will lay bare all your sins!

1. Egypt, which gave no aid against Babylon.
2. King Zedekiah, who was captured in flight near Jericho, and afterwards blinded and imprisoned by Nebuchadnezzar (Jeremiah 52.7-11).
3. Or 'Your crime is absolved'.

בֶּן סִירָא *Simeon ben Sira*

שִׁמְעוֹן כֹּהֵן גָּדוֹל SIMEON THE HIGH PRIEST

גָּדוֹל אֶחָיו וְתִפְאֶרֶת עַמּוֹ,
שִׁמְעוֹן בֶּן יוֹחָנָן הַכֹּהֵן :
אֲשֶׁר בְּדוֹרוֹ נִבְדַּק הַבַּיִת
וּבְיָמָיו חֻזַּק הֵיכָל ;
אֲשֶׁר בְּיָמָיו נִבְנָה קִיר,
פִּנּוֹת מָעוֹז בְּהֵיכַל מֶלֶךְ ;
אֲשֶׁר בְּדוֹרוֹ נִכְרָה מִקְוֶה,
אֲשִׁיחַ בַּיָם בַּהֲמוֹנוֹ ;
הַדוֹאֵג לְעַמּוֹ מֵחֶתֶף
וּמְחַזֵּק עִירוֹ מִצָּר.

Chief among his brethren and pride of
his people, Simeon son of Yohanan the
priest: in whose time the House was
repaired and in whose days the Temple
was fortified; in whose days the wall
was built, with battlements to secure
the King's palace; in whose time a
reservoir was dug, a cistern thundering
with water like the sea. He safeguarded
his people from marauders and
strengthened his city against siege.

מַה נֶּהְדָּר בְּהַשְׁגִּיחוֹ מֵאֹהֶל
וּבְצֵאתוֹ מִבֵּית הַפָּרֹכֶת !
כְּכוֹכַב אוֹר מִבֵּין עָבִים
וּכְיָרֵחַ מָלֵא בִּימֵי מוֹעֵד ;
כְּשֶׁמֶשׁ מַשְׁרֶקֶת אֶת הֵיכַל הַמֶּלֶךְ
וּכְקֶשֶׁת נִרְאָתָה בֶעָנָן ;
כְּנֵץ בַּעֲנָפִים בִּימֵי מוֹעֵד
וּכְשׁוֹשָׁן עַל יִבְלֵי מָיִם ;
כְּפֶרַח לְבָנוֹן בִּימֵי קָיִץ
וּכְאֵשׁ לְבוֹנָה עַל הַמִּנְחָה ;
כַּזַיִת רַעֲנָן מָלֵא גַרְגֵּר
וּכְעֵץ שֶׁמֶן מַרְוֶה עָנָף ;
כִּכְלִי זָהָב בְּבֵית אָצִיל
הַנֶּאֱחָז עַל אַבְנֵי חֵפֶץ –

How glorious he was as he looked out
from the Tent of the Presence, as he
emerged from the curtained shrine!
Like a star shining through the clouds,
or the full moon on feast days; like the
sun glittering on the King's palace or
the rainbow seen in the cloud; like a
blossom on the bough at spring time,
or a lily by a flowing stream; like a
flower of Lebanon on a summer's day,
or the fire of frankincense upon the
offering; like a spreading olive-tree
laden with fruit, or an oleaster whose
branches drink their fill; like a golden
vessel in the house of a nobleman,
encrusted with precious stones.

בְּעֲטוֹתוֹ בִּגְדֵי כָבוֹד
וְהִתְלַבְּשׁוֹ כְּלִיל תִּפְאָרֶת;
בַּעֲלוֹתוֹ עַל מִזְבַּח הוֹד
וַיֶּהְדַּר עֲזָרַת מִקְדָּשׁ;
בְּקַבְּלוֹ נְתָחִים מְיַּד אֶחָיו
וְהוּא נִצָּב עַל מַעֲרָכוֹת;
סָבִיב לוֹ עֲטֶרֶת בָּנִים
כִּשְׁתִילֵי אֲרָזִים בַּלְּבָנוֹן;
וַיַּקִּיפוּהוּ כְּעַרְבֵי נָחַל
כָּל בְּנֵי אַהֲרֹן בִּכְבוֹדָם
וְאִשֵּׁי אֲדֹנָי בְּיָדָם,
נֶגֶד כָּל קְהַל יִשְׂרָאֵל —
עַד כַּלּוֹתוֹ לְשָׁרֵת מִזְבֵּחַ
וּלְסַדֵּר מַעַרְכוֹת עֶלְיוֹן.
וַיִּשְׁלַח יָדוֹ עַל הַקַּשְׂוָה
וַיַּסֵּךְ מִדַּם עֵנָב,
וַיִּצֹק עַל יְסוֹד הַמִּזְבֵּחַ
לְרֵיחַ נִיחֹחַ לְמֶלֶךְ עֶלְיוֹן.

When he clothed himself in his splendid robes and put on his glorious diadem; when he ascended the majestic altar and filled the Temple Court with his splendour; when he received the portions of the offering from his fellow-priests as he stood by the wood-stacks on the altar; a garland of sons was around him, like shoots of a cedar in Lebanon; all the sons of Aaron in their priestly garments surrounded him like willows of the brook, with the Lord's offerings in their hands, before the whole assembly of Israel, until he completed the rites at the altar and set in order the fire for the Most High. Then he held out his hand for the libation cup and poured out the blood of the grape, poured it at the base of the altar, as a soothing odour to the Most High King.

אָז יָרִיעוּ בְּנֵי אַהֲרֹן הַכֹּהֲנִים
בַּחֲצֹצְרוֹת מִקְשָׁה.
וַיָּרִיעוּ וַיַּשְׁמִיעוּ קוֹל אַדִּיר,
לְהַזְכִּיר לִפְנֵי עֶלְיוֹן.
כָּל בָּשָׂר יַחְדָּו נִמְהָרוּ
וַיִּפְּלוּ עַל פְּנֵיהֶם אָרְצָה
לְהִשְׁתַּחֲווֹת לִפְנֵי עֶלְיוֹן,
לִפְנֵי קְדוֹשׁ יִשְׂרָאֵל.
וַיִּתֵּן הַשִּׁיר קוֹלוֹ
וְעַל הָמוֹן הֶעֱרִיבוּ רִנָּה.
וַיָּרֹנּוּ כָּל עַם הָאָרֶץ

At this, the sons of Aaron, the priests, blew their trumpets of beaten silver, sounding a mighty fanfare as a reminder before the Most High. Instantly all the people as one man fell on their faces to worship before the Most High, the Holy One of Israel. Then the song [of the Levites] resounded, sweetly sung to the sound of instruments. And all the common people cried out in prayer

בִּתְפִלָּה לִפְנֵי רַחוּם —
עַד כַּלּוֹתוֹ לְשָׁרֵת מִזְבֵּחַ
וּמִשְׁפָּטָיו הִגִּיעַ אֵלָיו.

to the Merciful One, until he completed the rites at the altar and placed the offerings upon it in due order.

אָז יָרַד וְנָשָׂא יָדָיו
עַל כָּל קְהַל יִשְׂרָאֵל,
וּבְרְכַּת אֲדֹנָי בִּשְׂפָתָיו
וּבְשֵׁם אֲדֹנָי יִתְפָּאָר.
וַיִּשְׁנוּ לִנְפֹּל שֵׁנִית
הָעָם כֻּלּוֹ מְפָנָיו.

Then he came down from the altar and, raising his hands over the whole assembly of Israel, he pronounced the Lord's blessing,[1] he gloried in the Name of the Lord. And a second time they all prostrated themselves before Him.

עַתָּה, בָּרְכוּ־נָא אֶת אֲדֹנָי אֱלֹהֵי יִשְׂרָאֵל
הַמַּפְלִיא לַעֲשׂוֹת בָּאָרֶץ,
הַמְגַדֵּל אָדָם מֵרֶחֶם
וַיַּעֲשֵׂהוּ כִּרְצוֹנוֹ.

Now bless the Lord God of Israel who works wonders on the earth, who raises a man from the womb and moulds him as He wills.

יִתֵּן לָכֶם חָכְמַת לֵבָב
וִיהִי בְשָׁלוֹם בֵּינֵיכֶם.
יֵאָמֵן עִם שִׁמְעוֹן חַסְדּוֹ
וְיָקֶם־לוֹ בְּרִית פִּינְחָס:
אֲשֶׁר לֹא יִכָּרֵת לוֹ וּלְזַרְעוֹ
כִּימֵי שָׁמָיִם.

May He give you wisdom of the heart and may peace reign among you. May His gracious word stand fast with the house of Simeon, may He make good His promise to Phinehas: that neither he nor his descendants shall be cut off [from the priesthood] for as long as the heavens endure.

---

1. The 'Lord's blessing' is found in Numbers 6.24-26.

שִׁירִים מִן הַמְּגִלּוֹת הַגְּנוּזוֹת   *Poems from the Dead Sea Scrolls*

וְלֹא יָדְעוּ רָז נִהְיָה   THE MYSTERY TO COME

. . . וְלֹא יָדְעוּ רָז נִהְיָה
וּבְקַדְמוֹנִיּוֹת לֹא הִתְבּוֹנָנוּ.
וְלֹא יָדְעוּ מָה אֲשֶׁר יָבוֹא עֲלֵיהֶמָה
וְנַפְשָׁמָה לֹא מִלְּטוּ מֵרָז נִהְיָה.

. . . and they do not know the mystery to come; they have not brooded over the past; they do not know what will befall them; they have not saved their lives from the mystery to come.

וְזֶה לָכֶם הָאוֹת,
כִּי יִהְיֶה בְּהִסָּגֵר מוֹלְדֵי־עַוְלָה:
וְגָלָה הָרֶשַׁע מִפְּנֵי הַצֶּדֶק
כִּגְלוֹת חֹשֶׁךְ מִפְּנֵי אוֹר;
וּכְתֹם עָשָׁן וְאֵינֶנּוּ עוֹד —
כֵּן יִתַּם הָרֶשַׁע לָעַד
וְהַצֶּדֶק יִגָּלֶה כַּשֶּׁמֶשׁ,
תְּכוֹן תֵּבֵל.
וְכָל תּוֹמְכֵי רָזֵי־פֶשַׁע אֵינָמָה עוֹד
וְדֵעָה תִּמְלָא תֵבֵל
וְאֵין שָׁם לָעַד אִוֶּלֶת.

And this shall be the sign for you, for it will come to pass when the birth-gates of evil are shut: wickedness will then fly before righteousness as darkness flies before light; and as smoke disappears and is no more, so shall wickedness disappear forever and righteousness be revealed like the sun. The earth will be fixed and firm. All those who support the mysteries of sin will be no more. Knowledge will fill the earth, and never again will there be folly on earth.

נָכוֹן הַדָּבָר לָבוֹא וֶאֱמֶת הַמַּשָּׂא !

This word is sure to come; this oracle is true!

וּמִזֶּה יִוָּדַע לָכֶמָה כִּי לֹא יָשׁוּב אָחוֹר:
הֲלֹא כָּל הָעַמִּים שָׂנְאוּ עָוֶל ?
וּבְיָד כֻּלָּמָה יִתְהַלָּךְ.
הֲלֹא מִפִּי כָל לְאֻמִּים שֵׁמַע הָאֱמֶת ?
הֲיֵשׁ שָׂפָה וְלָשׁוֹן מַחֲזֶקֶת בָּהּ ?
מִי גּוֹי חָפֵץ אֲשֶׁר יַעַשְׁקֻנּוּ חָזָק מִמֶּנּוּ ?
מִי יַחְפֹּץ כִּי יִגָּזֵל בְּרֶשַׁע הוֹנוּ ?

And by this shall you know that it will not fail: Do not all peoples hate injustice? Yet all of them commit it. Do not all nations mouth the praises of truth? But is there a lip or tongue that keeps it? Which nation would wish to be oppressed by a stronger rival? Who would wish to have his wealth wickedly plundered? Which nation has not

מִי גּוֹי אֲשֶׁר לֹא עָשַׁק רֵעֵהוּ?
אֵיפֹה עָם אֲשֶׁר לֹא גָּזַל הוֹן לְאַחֵר . . .

oppressed its neighbour? Where is the
people that has not plundered another's
wealth? . . .

מְשַׁל הַגָּן

THE PARABLE OF THE TREES

אוֹדְךָ, אֲדֹנָי,
כִּי נְתַתַּנִי בִּמְקוֹר נוֹזְלִים בַּיַּבָּשָׁה
וּמַבּוּעַ מַיִם בְּאֶרֶץ צִיָּה
וּמַשְׁקֶה גַּן רָוֶה אֲשֶׁר נָטַעְתָּ,
מַטַּע בְּרוֹשׁ וְתִדְהָר עִם תְּאַשּׁוּר יַחַד לִכְבוֹדֶךָ :
עֲצֵי חַיִּים בְּמַעְיַן רָז,
מְחֻבָּאִים בְּתוֹךְ כָּל עֲצֵי מָיִם.

I will praise You, O Lord, for You
have put me by a source of streams on
the dry ground, by bubbling springs on
the parched land, by the waters that
irrigate Your luxuriant garden – a
grove of pine together with fir and box
– which You planted for Your glory.
These are the Trees of Life, set beside
a secret spring, concealed among all the
Well-Watered Trees.

וְהָיוּ לְהַפְרִיחַ נֵצֶר לְמַטַּעַת־עוֹלָם,
לְהַשְׁרִישׁ טֶרֶם יַפְרִיחוּ
וְשָׁרְשֵׁיהֶם לְיוּבָל יְשַׁלֵּחוּ.
וַיִּפְתַּח לְמַיִם חַיִּים גִּזְעוֹ
וַיְהִי לִמְקוֹר־עוֹלָם,
וּבְנֵצֶר עָלָיו יִרְעוּ כָּל חַיַּת יָעַר,
וּמִרְמָס גִּזְעוֹ לְכָל עוֹבְרֵי דֶרֶךְ,
וְדָלִיָּתוֹ לְכָל עוֹף כָּנָף.

One day the Trees of Life will put
forth a shoot which will become the
Everlasting Plant, for they take root
before they grow and extend their
roots towards the stream. And the
Plant will open its stem to the living
waters; it will become an everlasting
source [of blessing]. All the wild
creatures will graze among its fallen
leaves; all the wayfarers will pass by its
stem; all the winged birds will nest in
its boughs.

וַיִּרֹמּוּ עָלָיו כָּל עֲצֵי־מָיִם
כִּי בְמַטָּעָם יִתְשַׂגְשָׂגוּ,
וְאֶל יוּבָל לֹא יְשַׁלְּחוּ שֹׁרֶשׁ.
וּמַפְרִיחַ נֵצֶר־קֹדֶשׁ לְמַטַּעַת־אֱמֶת סָתָר,
בְּלֹא נֶחְשָׁב וּבְלֹא נוֹדַע חוֹתָם רָזוֹ.

But now all the Well-Watered Trees
tower over it, for they grow as soon as
they are planted; but their roots do not
extend towards the stream. And the
trees that will one day put forth the
holy shoot of the Plant of truth – these
trees are hidden away; their secret is
sealed, it is not valued, it is not known.

וְאַתָּה, אֵל, שַׂכְתָּ בְּעַד פְּרִיו
בְּרָז גִּבּוֹרֵי כֹחַ וְרוּחוֹת קֹדֶשׁ
וְלַהַט אֵשׁ מִתְהַפֶּכֶת.
בַּל יָבוֹא זָר בְּמַעְיַן־חַיִּים
וְעִם עֲצֵי־עוֹלָם לֹא יִשְׁתֶּה מֵי־קֹדֶשׁ.
בַּל יְנוֹבֵב פִּרְיוֹ עִם מַטָּע־שְׁחָקִים
כִּי רָאָה בְּלֹא הִכִּיר
וַיַּחְשׁׁב בְּלֹא הֶאֱמִין לִמְקוֹר־חַיִּים
וַיִּתֵּן יָדוֹ בְּפֶרַח־עוֹלָם.

For You, O God, have hedged in its
fruit on every side with the mystery of
angels, creatures of might, and of holy
spirits, with a whirling, flashing fire.
No stranger can approach the spring of
life; he cannot drink the holy waters
together with the everlasting trees; he
cannot bear fruit together with the
heavenly Plant – because he saw but
did not understand, he considered but
did not believe in the source of life, he
dared to lay hands upon the eternal
flower.

חֶבְלֵי מָשִׁיחַ

THE BIRTH OF THE MESSIAH

וַיָּשִׂימוּ נַפְשִׁי כָּאֳנִיָּה בִּמְצוּלוֹת יָם,...
וּכְעִיר מִבְצָר מִלִּפְנֵי אוֹיֵב.
וָאֶהְיֶה בְּצוּקָה כְּמוֹ אֵשֶׁת לֵדָה מַבְכִּירָה
כִּי נֶהֶפְכוּ צִירֶיהָ
וְחֵבֶל נִמְרָץ עַל מִשְׁבָּרֶיהָ
לְהָחִיל בְּכוּר־הָרִיָּה,
כִּי בָאוּ בָנִים עַד מִשְׁבְּרֵי־מָוֶת.

They have made my life like a ship in
the depths of the sea, like a fortified
town facing the enemy. I was in
anguish, like a woman bearing her first
child, when her labour suddenly begins
and she is seized with cruel pangs
which hasten the birth in her womb,[1]
when the child is about to be born with
deadly pangs.

וְהָרִיַּת גֶּבֶר הֵצֵרָה בַּחֲבָלֶיהָ
כִּי בְמִשְׁבְּרֵי־מָוֶת תַּמְלִיט זָכָר,
וּבְחֶבְלֵי־שְׁאוֹל יָגִיחַ מִכּוּר־הָרִיָּה
פֶּלֶא יוֹעֵץ עִם גְּבוּרָתוֹ.
וְיִפָּלֵט גֶּבֶר מִמִּשְׁבָּרִים.

Then she who bears the man will be
gripped by spasms, for she will give
birth to a son in deadly pangs. He will
burst from her womb[1] in hellish spasms
– a wonderful, mighty counsellor. Thus
will the man spring forth amid pangs.

---

1. Lit. 'crucible of pregnancy'.

בְּהָרִיתוֹ הֶחִישׁוּ כָּל מִשְׁבָּרִים
וְחֶבְלֵי־מֶרֶץ בְּמוֹלָדֵיהֶם
וּפַלָּצוֹת לְהוֹרוֹתָם.
וּבְמוֹלָדָיו יֵהָפְכוּ כָּל צִירִים בְּכוּר־הָרִיָּה.

At his conception all the [world's]
pangs will redouble; wherever they
spring up there will be cruel spasms,
wherever they are bred there will be
agony. At his birth, the womb [of
Hell] will suddenly be gripped by all
its throes.

וְהָרִיַת אֶפְעֶה לְחֵבֶל נִמְרָץ
וּמִשְׁבְּרֵי־שַׁחַת לְכָל מַעֲשֵׂי פַלָּצוּת.
וַיֵּרָעוּ אַשֵּׁי־קִיר כָּאֳנִיָּה עַל פְּנֵי מָיִם
וַיֵּהֱמוּ שְׁחָקִים בְּקוֹל הָמוֹן.
וְיוֹשְׁבֵי עָפָר כְּיוֹרְדֵי יַמִּים
נִבְעָתִים מֵהֲמוֹן מָיִם,
וַחֲכָמֵיהָ כָּלְמוֹ כְּמַלָּחִים בִּמְצוּלוֹת
כִּי תִתְבַּלַּע כָּל חָכְמָתָם
בַּהֲמוֹת יַמִּים,
בִּרְתֹחַ תְּהוֹמוֹת עַל נְבוּכֵי מָיִם.
וְיִתְרַגְּשׁוּ לְרוּם גַּלִּים
וּמִשְׁבְּרֵי־מַיִם בַּהֲמוֹן קוֹלָם.
וּבְהִתְרַגְּשָׁם יִפָּתְחוּ שְׁאוֹל וַאֲבַדּוֹן,
וְכָל חִצֵּי־שַׁחַת עִם מִצְעָדָם
לִתְהוֹם יַשְׁמִיעוּ קוֹלָם.
וְיִפָּתְחוּ שַׁעֲרֵי־שְׁאוֹל לְכָל מַעֲשֵׂי־אֶפְעֶה.

Then she who bears evil will suffer
cruel spasms, as the infernal pangs
bring forth all the creatures of havoc.
The earth's foundations will rock like
a ship upon the waters, the skies will
roar with a thunder of waters. All the
inhabitants of the dust, like men who
sail the sea, will be terrified by the roar
of waters. All the wise men will be like
sailors on the ocean; their seamanship
will be in vain, as the sea thunders and
the abyss boils with swirling waters, as
billows are cast up and breakers roar.
Then, as they rage, Hell and Perdition
will gape open, and the arrows of the
Pit, let loose, will cry out to the abyss.
Thus will the gates of Hell open up to
all the creatures of evil.

וְיִסָּגְרוּ דַּלְתֵי־שַׁחַת בְּעַד הָרִיַת־עָוֶל
וּבְרִיחֵי־עוֹלָם בְּעַד כָּל רוּחֵי־אֶפְעֶה.

But then the doors of the Pit will shut
upon the children of wickedness, and
the eternal bolts will close upon all the
spirits of evil.

שִׁירִים מִן הַתַּלְמוּד *Poems from the Talmud*

אוֹי לִי מִבֵּית בַּיְתוֹס

SONG OF PROTEST

אוֹי לִי מִבֵּית בַּיְתוֹס,
אוֹי לִי מֵאַלָּתָן.
אוֹי לִי מִבֵּית קַתְרוֹס,
אוֹי לִי מִקֻּלְמוֹסָן.
אוֹי לִי מִבֵּית חָנָן,
אוֹי לִי מִלְּחִישָׁתָן.
אוֹי לִי מִבֵּית יִשְׁמָעֵאל בֶּן פְּיָאבִי,
אוֹי לִי מֵאֶגְרוֹפָן —
שֶׁהֵם כֹּהֲנִים גְּדוֹלִים,
וּבְנֵיהֶם גִּזְבָּרִין,
וְחַתְנֵיהֶן אֲמַרְכָּלִין,
וְעַבְדֵּיהֶן בָּאִין
וְחוֹבְטִין עָלֵינוּ בְּמַקְלוֹת.

Woe to me from the house of Boethus: woe to me from their cudgels. Woe to me from the house of Kathros: woe to me from their quills. Woe to me from the house of Hanin: woe to me from their slanders. Woe to me from the house of Ishmael son of Phabi: woe to me from their fists. For they are the High Priests, their sons are the treasurers, their sons-in-law are the trustees, and their slaves come and beat us with their sticks.

בְּעָקְבוֹת מְשִׁיחָא

THE ADVENT OF THE MESSIAH

בְּעָקְבוֹת מְשִׁיחָא
חֻצְפָּא יִסְגֵּא
וְיֹקֶר יַאֲמִיר.
הַגֶּפֶן תִּתֵּן פִּרְיָהּ,
וְהַיַּיִן בְּיֹקֶר.
וְהַמַּלְכוּת תֵּהָפֵךְ לְמִינוּת,
וְאֵין תּוֹכָחַת.
בֵּית־וַעַד יִהְיֶה לִזְנוּת,
וְהַגָּלִיל יֶחֱרַב

At the advent of the Messiah, impudence will increase and prices will soar. The vine will yield its fruit, yet wine will be costly. The empire will fall into heresy, and no one will protest. The meeting-place of scholars will be given over to harlotry; the Galilee will

וְהַגּבְלָן יִשֹׁם.
וְאַנְשֵׁי־הַגְּבוּל
יְסוֹבְבוּ מֵעִיר לְעִיר,
וְלֹא יְחוֹנֵנוּ.
וְחָכְמַת־סוֹפְרִים תִּסְרָח,
וְיִרְאֵי־חֵטְא יִמָּאֵסוּ,
וְהָאֱמֶת תְּהֵא נֶעְדֶּרֶת.
נְעָרִים פְּנֵי זְקֵנִים יַלְבִּינוּ,
זְקֵנִים יַעַמְדוּ מִפְּנֵי קְטַנִּים.
בֵּן מְנַבֵּל אָב,'
בַּת קָמָה בְאִמָּהּ,
כַּלָּה בַּחֲמֹתָהּ,
אֹיְבֵי אִישׁ אַנְשֵׁי בֵיתוֹ.'
פְּנֵי הַדּוֹר כִּפְנֵי הַכֶּלֶב.
הַבֵּן אֵינוֹ מִתְבַּיֵּשׁ מֵאָבִיו.
וְעַל מִי יֵשׁ לָנוּ לְהִשָּׁעֵן?
עַל אָבִינוּ שֶׁבַּשָּׁמָיִם!

be laid waste, the Golan made desolate.
Those who live on the frontier will
roam from town to town, and no one
will take pity on them. The wisdom of
the scribes will decay, sin-fearing men
will be despised, and truth will be
gone. The young will shame their
elders; the aged will stand up in the
presence of youngsters. *For son maligns
father, daughter rebels against mother,
daughter-in-law against mother-in-law,
and a man's household are his enemies.*[1]
The face of this generation is like a
dog's face; the son feels no shame
before his father. On whom then can
we rely? On our Father in heaven!

אַחֵינוּ הַמְיֻגָּעִים   ON THE DEATH OF A CHILD

אַחֵינוּ הַמְיֻגָּעִים,
הַמְדֻכָּאִים בָּאֵבֶל הַזֶּה,
תְּנוּ לְבַבְכֶם לַחְקֹר אֶת זֹאת —
זֹאת הִיא עוֹמֶדֶת לָעַד,
נָתִיב הוּא מִשֵּׁשֶׁת יְמֵי בְרֵאשִׁית:
רַבִּים שָׁתוּ, רַבִּים יִשְׁתּוּ,
כְּמִשְׁתֵּה רִאשׁוֹנִים כָּךְ מִשְׁתֵּה אַחֲרוֹנִים.
אַחֵינוּ,
בַּעַל הַנֶּחָמוֹת יְנַחֵם אֶתְכֶם!

O wearied brethren, weighed down by
this grief, set your hearts to consider
this, for this is eternally so, the way of
the world since the six days of creation:
many have drunk, many will drink, and
the last will drink as the first drank.
Our brethren, may the Master of
Comfort comfort you!

1. Micah 7.6.

191

גֶּזַע־יְשִׁישִׁים　　FUNERAL ORATION

גֶּזַע־יְשִׁישִׁים עָלָה מִבָּבֶל
וְעִמּוֹ סֵפֶר מִלְחֲמוֹת אֲדֹנָי.
קָאַת וְקִפּוֹד הָכְפְּלוּ לִרְאוֹת
בְּשֹׁד וָשֶׁבֶר הַבָּא מִשִּׁנְעָר.
קָצַף עַל עוֹלָמוֹ וְחָמַס נְפָשׁוֹת,
וְשָׂמַח בָּהֶם כְּכַלָּה חֲדָשָׁה.
רוֹכֵב־עֲרָבוֹת שָׂשׂ וְשָׂמֵחַ
בְּבוֹא אֵלָיו נֶפֶשׁ צַדִּיק !

The Scion of an Ancient Stock has
come from Babylon together with the
Book of the Wars of the Lord. Both
vulture and raven rush to see this
ravage and ruin, which has come from
Shinear.[1] When He raged at His world,
He plundered souls, then delighted in
them as in a new bride. He who rides
upon the highest heaven rejoices and
exults when the souls of the righteous
come to Him.

בָּאֲרָזִים נָפְלָה שַׁלְהֶבֶת　　LAMENT

בָּאֲרָזִים נָפְלָה שַׁלְהֶבֶת —
מַה יַּעֲשׂוּ אֵזוֹבֵי־הַקִּיר ?
לִוְיָתָן בְּחַכָּה הֹעֲלָה —
מַה יַּעֲשׂוּ דְּגֵי־הָרְקָק ?
בְּנַחַל שׁוֹטֵף נָפְלָה חֲרָבָה —
מַה יַּעֲשׂוּ מֵי־גֵבִים ?

If the cedars have caught fire, what
hope is there for the moss on the wall?
If Leviathan has been hauled in by a
fish-hook, what hope is there for the
minnows? If the mighty river has been
struck by drought, what hope is there
for the waterholes?

אֱלֹהַי, נְשָׁמָה שֶׁנָּתַתָּ בִּי　　THANKSGIVING UPON
　　　　　　　　　　　　　　　　AWAKENING

אֱלֹהַי,
נְשָׁמָה שֶׁנָּתַתָּ בִּי — טְהוֹרָה.
אַתָּה בְרָאתָהּ,
אַתָּה יְצַרְתָּהּ,

My God, the soul which You set
within me is pure. You created it, You

1. Babylon.

192

אַתָּה נְפַחְתָּהּ בִּי
וְאַתָּה מְשַׁמְּרָהּ בְּקִרְבִּי.
וְאַתָּה עָתִיד לִטְּלָהּ מִמֶּנִּי
וּלְהַחֲזִירָהּ בִּי לֶעָתִיד לָבוֹא.

formed it, You breathed it into me, and
You preserve it within me. One day
You will reclaim it from me, but then
You will restore it to me in the days to
come.

כָּל זְמַן שֶׁהַנְּשָׁמָה בְּקִרְבִּי,
מוֹדֶה אֲנִי לְפָנֶיךָ,
יהוה אֱלֹהַי וֵאלֹהֵי אֲבוֹתַי,
רִבּוֹן כָּל הַמַּעֲשִׂים,
אָדוֹן כָּל הַנְּשָׁמוֹת:
בָּרוּךְ אַתָּה יהוה
הַמַּחֲזִיר נְשָׁמוֹת לִפְגָרִים מֵתִים.

As long as the soul is within me, I shall
give thanks to You, Lord my God and
God of my fathers, Master of all
creation, Lord of all souls. Blessed are
You, O Lord, who restore souls to dead
bodies.

אֱלֹהַי, נְצֹר לְשׁוֹנִי מֵרָע

PRAYER

אֱלֹהַי,
נְצֹר לְשׁוֹנִי מֵרָע
וּשְׂפָתַי מִדַּבֵּר מִרְמָה.
וְלִמְקַלְלַי נַפְשִׁי תִדֹּם
וְנַפְשִׁי כֶּעָפָר לַכֹּל תִּהְיֶה.
פְּתַח לִבִּי בְּתוֹרָתֶךָ
וּבְמִצְוֹתֶיךָ תִּרְדֹּף נַפְשִׁי.
וְתַצִּילֵנִי מִפֶּגַע רָע,
מִיֵּצֶר הָרָע וּמֵאִשָּׁה רָעָה,
וּמִכָּל רָעוֹת הַמִּתְרַגְּשׁוֹת בָּעוֹלָם.
וְכָל הַחוֹשְׁבִים עָלַי רָעָה —
מַהֵר הָפֵר עֲצָתָם
וְקַלְקֵל מַחְשְׁבוֹתָם!

My God, keep my tongue from evil and
my lips from speaking guile. May my
soul be silent before those who revile
me; may my soul be as lowly to all as
the dust. Open my heart to Your law,
so that my soul may pursue Your
commandments. Deliver me from
mishap, from the evil urge and from an
evil wife, from all the misfortunes that
occur in the world. And as for those
who scheme against me — quickly
thwart their counsels and frustrate
their designs!

הַמַּפִּיל חַבְלֵי־שֵׁנָה   PRAYER BEFORE SLEEP

בָּרוּךְ אַתָּה יהוה
אֱלֹהֵינוּ מֶלֶךְ הָעוֹלָם,
הַמַּפִּיל חַבְלֵי־שֵׁנָה עַל עֵינַי
וּתְנוּמָה עַל עַפְעַפָּי.
וִיהִי רָצוֹן מִלְּפָנֶיךָ,
יהוה אֱלֹהַי וֵאלֹהֵי אֲבוֹתַי,
שֶׁתַּשְׁכִּיבֵנִי לְשָׁלוֹם
וְתַעֲמִידֵנִי לְשָׁלוֹם.
וְאַל יְבַהֲלוּנִי רַעְיוֹנַי
וַחֲלוֹמוֹת רָעִים וְהִרְהוֹרִים רָעִים,
וּתְהִי מִטָּתִי שְׁלֵמָה לְפָנֶיךָ.

Blessed are You, Lord our God, king
of the universe, who weigh down my
eyes with bonds of sleep and my
eyelids with slumber. May it be Your
will, Lord my God and God of my
fathers, to lay me down in peace and
raise me up in peace. Do not let my
thoughts, or evil dreams, or sinful
fancies alarm me. Grant that [the fruit
of] my bed be perfect before You.

וְהָאֵר עֵינַי
פֶּן אִישַׁן הַמָּוֶת,
כִּי אַתָּה הַמֵּאִיר לְאִישׁוֹן בַּת־עָיִן.
בָּרוּךְ אַתָּה יהוה,
הַמֵּאִיר לָעוֹלָם כֻּלּוֹ בִּכְבוֹדוֹ.

Give light to my eyes lest I sink into
the sleep of death, for it is You who
illuminate the pupil of the eye. Blessed
are You, O Lord, whose glory illumi-
nates all the world.

רָנִּי, רָנִּי הַשִּׁטָּה!   THE COWS' HYMN TO THE
ARK OF THE LORD

רָנִּי, רָנִּי הַשִּׁטָּה!
הִתְנוֹפְפִי בְּרֹב הֲדָרֵךְ —
הַמְחֻשֶּׁקֶת בְּרִקְמֵי־זָהָב,
הַמְהֻלָּלָה בִּדְבִיר־אַרְמוֹן,
הַמְפֹאָרָה בַּעֲדִי־עֶדָיִים.

Sing, oh sing, acacia! Tower in all your
splendour, you who are decked with
golden embroidery, praised in the
inmost sanctuary, resplendent with the
finest adornments!

שִׁירִים מֵהֵיכָלוֹת רַבָּתִי   *Hekhalot Hymns*

תְּחִלַּת שֶׁבַח   HYMN FOR THE DESCENT TO THE MERKAVA

תְּחִלַּת שֶׁבַח וְרֵאשִׁית שִׁירָה,
תְּחִלַּת גִּילָה וְרֵאשִׁית רַנָּה
מְשׁוֹרְרִים הַשָּׂרִים הַמְשָׁרְתִים
בְּכָל יוֹם לַיהוה אֱלֹהֵי יִשְׂרָאֵל.
לְכִסֵּא כְבוֹדוֹ הֵם מְנַשְּׂאִים :
'גִּיל, גִּיל, כִּסֵּא כָבוֹד,
רַנֵּן, רַנֵּן, מוֹשַׁב־עֶלְיוֹן !
הָרִיעַ, הָרִיעַ, כְּלִי־חֶמְדָּה,
שֶׁנַּעֲשָׂה בְּהַפְלֵא וָפֶלֶא.
שַׂמֵּחַ תְּשַׂמַּח מֶלֶךְ שֶׁעָלֶיךָ
כְּשִׂמְחַת חָתָן בְּבֵית חֻפָּתוֹ !'

The beginning of praise and the start of
song, the beginning of joy and the
start of jubilation – these are sung by
the princes[1] who daily serve the Lord
God of Israel. They exalt His throne
of glory: 'Rejoice, rejoice, throne of
glory! Sing, sing for joy, seat of the
Most High! Exult, exult, O precious
vessel, so marvellously fashioned! You
will gladden the king upon you, as a
bridegroom is gladdened in his bridal-
chamber!'

מְבַטְּלֵי גְזֵרָה   HYMN TO THE HOLY LIVING CREATURES

מְבַטְּלֵי גְזֵרָה, מְפֵרֵי שְׁבוּעָה,
מַעֲבִירֵי חֵמָה, מְשִׁיבֵי קִנְאָה,
מַזְכִּירֵי אַהֲבָה, מְסַדְּרֵי רֵעוּת
לִפְנֵי הֲדַר־גְּאוֹן־הֵיכַל־נוֹרָא :

You who revoke decrees, undo vows,
remove wrath, soothe fury, recall love,
restore friendship before the splendour
of the glory of the palace of the Dread
One –

מַה לָּכֶם שֶׁאַתֶּם נוֹרָאִים,
וּפְעָמִים לָכֶם שֶׁאַתֶּם שְׂמֵחִים ?

Why is it that sometimes you take
fright and at other times you are merry?

---

1. The Holy Living Creatures.

מַה לָכֶם שֶׁאַתֶּם מְרַנְּנִים,
וּפְעָמִים לָכֶם שֶׁאַתֶּם מְבֹהָלִים ?

Why is it that sometimes you exult and at other times you are terrified?

אָמְרוּ : 'כְּשֶׁפְּנֵי גְבוּרָה מַקְדִּירִין,
עוֹמְדִים אָנוּ בְּבֶהָלָה גְדוֹלָה ;
וּכְשֶׁזָּהֲרֵי שְׁכִינָה מְאִירִין,
אָנוּ שְׂמֵחִים שִׂמְחָה רַבָּה !'

They said: 'When the face of the Divine Majesty grows dark, we stand in great terror. But when the sparks of the Shekinah[1] radiate, we are full of mirth!'

פָּנִים נָאִים   THE FACE OF GOD

פָּנִים נָאִים, פָּנִים הֲדוּרִים,
פָּנִים שֶׁל יֹפִי, פָּנִים שֶׁל לֶהָבָה,
פְּנֵי יהוה אֱלֹהֵי יִשְׂרָאֵל
כְּשֶׁהוּא יוֹשֵׁב עַל כִּסֵּא כְבוֹדוֹ
וְסַלְסוּלוֹ מְתֻקָּן בְּמוֹשַׁב הֲדָרוֹ.
יָפְיוֹ נָאֶה מִיָּפְיֵי גְבוּרוֹת,
הֲדָרוֹ מְעֻלֶּה מֵהֲדַר חֲתָנִים וְכַלּוֹת
בְּבֵית חֻפָּתָם.

Lovely face, majestic face, face of beauty, face of flame, the face of the Lord God of Israel when He sits upon His throne of glory, robed in praise upon His seat of splendour. His beauty surpasses the beauty of the aged, His splendour outshines the splendour of newly-weds in their bridal chamber.

הַמִּסְתַּכֵּל בּוֹ מִיָּד נִקְרָע,
וְהַמֵּצִיץ בְּיָפְיוֹ מִיָּד מִשְׁתַּפֵּךְ כְּקִיתוֹן.
הַמְשָׁרְתִים אוֹתוֹ הַיּוֹם
שׁוּב אֵין מְשָׁרְתִים אוֹתוֹ לְמָחָר,
וְהַמְשָׁרְתִים אוֹתוֹ לְמָחָר
שׁוּב אֵין מְשָׁרְתִים לְפָנָיו –
כִּי תָּשַׁשׁ כֹּחָם וְהֻשְׁחֲרוּ פְּנֵיהֶם,
תָּעָה לִבָּם וְנֶחְשְׁכוּ עֵינֵיהֶם
אַחַר הֲדַר־זִיו־יֹפִי שֶׁל מַלְכָּם.

Whoever looks at Him is instantly torn; whoever glimpses His beauty immediately melts away.[2] Those who serve Him today no longer serve Him tomorrow; those who serve Him tomorrow no longer serve Him afterwards; for their strength fails and their faces are charred, their hearts reel and their eyes grow dim at the splendour and radiance of their king's beauty.

---

1. God's 'immanence' or 'indwelling' in the world.
2. Lit. 'is emptied out like a ladle'.

מְשָׁרְתִים אֲהוּבִים, מְשָׁרְתִים נָאִים,
מְשָׁרְתִים מְמַהֲרִים, מְשָׁרְתִים קַלִּים!
הָעוֹמְדִים עַל אֶבֶן כִּסֵּא הַכָּבוֹד
וְהַנִּצָּבִים עַל גַּלְגַּל הַמֶּרְכָּבָה;
כְּשֶׁאֶבֶן כִּסֵּא הַכָּבוֹד מְחַזֵּר עֲלֵיהֶם,
כְּשֶׁגַּלְגַּל הַמֶּרְכָּבָה מַחְטִיף אוֹתָם –
הָעוֹמְדִים לְיָמִין,
חוֹזְרִים וְעוֹמְדִים לִשְׂמֹאל;
וְהָעוֹמְדִים לִשְׂמֹאל,
חוֹזְרִים וְעוֹמְדִים לְיָמִין;
וְהָעוֹמְדִים לְפָנִים,
חוֹזְרִים וְעוֹמְדִים לְאָחוֹר;
וְהָעוֹמְדִים לְאָחוֹר,
חוֹזְרִים וְעוֹמְדִים לְפָנִים.

Beloved servants, lovely servants, swift servants, light-footed servants, who stand before the stone of the throne of glory, who wait upon the wheel of the chariot. When the sapphire of the throne of glory whirls at them, when the wheel of the chariot hurls past them, those on the right now stand again to the left, those on the left now stand again to the right, those in front now stand again in back, those in back now stand again in front.

הָרוֹאֶה אֶת זֶה, אוֹמֵר: זֶה הוּא זֶה.
וְהָרוֹאֶה אֶת זֶה, אוֹמֵר: זֶה הוּא זֶה.
כִּי קְלַסְתֵּר פָּנָיו שֶׁל זֶה
דּוֹמֶה לִקְלַסְתֵּר פָּנָיו שֶׁל זֶה;
וּקְלַסְתֵּר פָּנָיו שֶׁל זֶה
דּוֹמֶה לִקְלַסְתֵּר פָּנָיו שֶׁל זֶה.

He who sees the one says, 'That is the other'. And he who sees the other says, 'That is the one'. For the visage of the one is like the visage of the other; and the visage of the other is like the visage of the one.

אַשְׁרֵי הַמֶּלֶךְ שֶׁאֵלּוּ מְשָׁרְתָיו,
וְאַשְׁרֵי מְשָׁרְתִים שֶׁזֶּה מַלְכָּם.
אַשְׁרֵי עַיִן הַנִּזּוֹנֶת וְהַמִּסְתַּכֶּלֶת
בָּאוֹר הַמֻּפְלָא הַזֶּה,
רְאִיָּה מֻפְלָאָה וּמְשֻׁנָּה מְאֹד.

Happy the King who has such servants, and happy the servants who have such a King. Happy the eye that sees and feeds upon this wondrous light – a wondrous vision and most strange!

בְּכָל יוֹם וָיוֹם

THE CELESTIAL MORNING SERVICE

בְּכָל יוֹם וָיוֹם בְּהַגִּיעַ עֲלוֹת־הַשַּׁחַר,
מֶלֶךְ הָדוּר יוֹשֵׁב וּמְבָרֵךְ לַחַיּוֹת:
'לָכֶם, חַיּוֹת, אֲנִי אוֹמֵר,
לָכֶם, בְּרִיּוֹת, אֲנִי מַשְׁמִיעַ –
חַיּוֹת, חַיּוֹת נוֹשְׂאוֹת כִּסֵּא כְבוֹדִי
בְּלֵב שָׁלֵם וּבְנֶפֶשׁ חֲפֵצָה –
תִּתְבָּרֵךְ הַשָּׁעָה שֶׁבְּרָאתִי אֶתְכֶם בָּהּ,
יִתְרוֹמֵם הַמַּזָּל שֶׁיְּצַרְתִּי אֶתְכֶם בּוֹ;
יָאִיר אוֹרוֹ שֶׁל אוֹתוֹ הַיּוֹם
שֶׁעֲלִיתֶם בַּמַּחֲשָׁבָה עַל לְבָבִי;
שֶׁאַתֶּם כְּלִי־חֶמְדָּה שֶׁהֲכַנְתִּי
וְשִׁכְלַלְתִּי אֶתְכֶם בּוֹ.
הַחֲרִישׁוּ לִי קוֹל כָּל יְצוּרִים שֶׁבָּרָאתִי
וְאֶשְׁמַע וְאַאֲזִין לְקוֹל תְּפִלַּת בָּנַי.'

Day after day, at the break of dawn, the majestic King sits and blesses the Holy Beings: 'To you, Holy Beings, I say; to you, Living Creatures, I proclaim – Holy Beings, Holy Beings, who carry My throne of glory with whole heart and willing mind – blessed be the hour in which I created you; exalted be the zodiacal sign under which I fashioned you; radiant be the light of the day on which you first occurred to Me. For you are the precious vessels that I prepared and perfected on that day. Now silence the voice of all the heavenly beings I have made, so that I may listen to the voice of My children praying.'

מֶלֶךְ נִסִּים

THE THRONE OF GLORY ADDRESSES THE KING

מֶלֶךְ נִסִּים, מֶלֶךְ גְּבוּרוֹת,
מֶלֶךְ נִפְלָאוֹת, מֶלֶךְ פְּרִישׁוֹת –
כִּסְאָךְ מְעוֹפֵף וְעוֹמֵד תַּחְתָּיו
מִשָּׁעָה שֶׁתָּקַעְתָּ יָתֵד אֲרִיגַת הַמַּסֶּכֶת,
שֶׁשִּׁכְלוּל הָעוֹלָם וּמִסְלוּלוֹ עוֹמֵד עָלֶיהָ
שָׁנִים רַבּוֹת, דּוֹרוֹת עַד אֵין קֵץ.
וַעֲדַיִן לֹא הִנִּיחַ רַגְלָיו
עַל קַרְקַע עֲרָבוֹת רָקִיעַ
אֶלָּא כְּעוֹף מְעוֹפֵף וְעוֹמֵד תַּחְתָּיו.
גֵּאֵי־גֵאִים, קְשׁוּרֵי־כְתָרִים

King of miracles, King of power, King of wonders, King of marvels: Your throne hovers yet does not move, ever since You set the peg of the loom which fixes the world's course and its perfection, all these many years and endless generations. Your throne has never set foot on the floor of the seventh heaven, but hovers like a bird and does not move. The proudest of the proud, adorned with crowns, and

198

וְכָל מַלְכֵי רָאשֵׁי־מְדוֹת שֶׁבָּרֶאתָ
חֲבוּשִׁים וְעוֹמְדִים תַּחַת כִּסֵּא כְבוֹדֶךָ
וְהָיוּ מְנַטְּלִין אוֹתוֹ בְּעֹז, תֹקֶף וּגְבוּרָה.
וְאַף הֵם לֹא הִנִּיחוּ רַגְלֵיהֶם
עַל קַרְקַע עֲרָבוֹת רָקִיעַ
אֶלָּא בָּעוֹף מְעוֹפְפִים וְעוֹמְדִים תַּחְתֵּיהֶם.
וְשָׁלֹשׁ פְּעָמִים בְּכָל יוֹם נָיוֹם
כִּסֵּא כְבוֹדֶךָ מִשְׁתַּטֵּחַ לְפָנֶיךָ וְאוֹמֵר לְךָ:
'זְהָרָרִיאֵל יהוה אֱלֹהֵי יִשְׂרָאֵל,
הִתְכַּבֵּד וְשֵׁב עָלַי, מֶלֶךְ מְפֹאָר,
לְפִי שֶׁמַּשָּׂאֲךָ חָבִיב עָלַי וְיָקָר
וְאֵין כָּבֵד עָלַי.'

all the royal living creatures whom You
created stand close together beneath
Your throne of glory, bearing it with
might, strength, and power. They too
have never set foot upon the floor of
the seventh heaven, but hover like a
bird and do not move. Thrice daily
Your throne of glory prostrates itself
before You and says: 'Zoharariel,
Adonai, God of Israel, sit upon me in
glory, resplendent King, for Your
burden is most dear to me and does not
weigh me down.'

מִדָּה שֶׁל קְדֻשָּׁה   GOD'S ROBE OF GLORY

מִדָּה שֶׁל קְדֻשָּׁה, מִדָּה שֶׁל גְּבוּרָה,
מִדָּה נוֹרָאָה, מִדָּה מְבֹהָלָה,
מִדָּה שֶׁל רֶתֶת, מִדָּה שֶׁל זִיעַ,
מִדָּה שֶׁל בַּהַל, מִדָּה שֶׁל חַלְחָלָה –
מִדָּה שֶׁל חָלוּק
שֶׁל זְהָרָרִיאֵל יהוה אֱלֹהֵי יִשְׂרָאֵל,
שֶׁמְּעֻטָּר וּבָא עַל כִּסֵּא כְבוֹדוֹ,
וְחָקוּק וּמָלֵא כֻּלּוֹ, מִבְּפָנִים וּמִן הַחִיצוֹן,
יהוה יהוה.
וְעֵינֵי כָל בְּרִיָּה אֵינָהּ יְכוֹלָה לְהִסְתַּכֵּל בּוֹ,
לֹא עֵינֵי בָשָׂר וָדָם וְלֹא עֵינֵי מְשָׁרְתָיו.
כִּי הַמִּסְתַּכֵּל בּוֹ וְהַמֵּצִיץ וְהָרוֹאֶה אוֹתוֹ,
אוֹחֲזוֹת מַחְזוֹרִיּוֹת לְגַלְגַּלֵּי עֵינָיו,
וְגַלְגַּלֵּי עֵינָיו מְפַלְּטִין וּמוֹצִיאִין לַפִּידֵי אֵשׁ

A quality of holiness, a quality of
power, a fearful quality, a dreaded
quality, a quality of awe, a quality of
shuddering, a quality of dismay, a
quality of terror – such is the quality of
the garment of Zoharariel, Adonai, God
of Israel, who, crowned, comes to the
throne of His glory; His garment is
engraved inside and outside and
entirely covered with YHWH YHWH.
No eyes are able to behold it, neither
the eyes of flesh and blood nor the eyes
of His servants. Whoever beholds it,
whoever glimpses and sees it, his eye-
balls are seized by balls of fire, his
eye-balls discharge fiery torches which

וְהֵן מְלַהֲטִין אוֹתוֹ וְהֵן שׂוֹרְפִין אוֹתוֹ;
כִּי הָאֵשׁ הַיּוֹצֵא מִן הָאָדָם הַמִּסְתַּכֵּל
הִיא מְלַהֶטֶת אוֹתוֹ וְהִיא שׂוֹרֶפֶת אוֹתוֹ.
מִפְּנֵי מָה?
מִפְּנֵי דְמוּת עֵינַיִם שֶׁל חָלוּק
שֶׁל זָהֲרָרִיאֵל יהוה אֱלֹהֵי יִשְׂרָאֵל,
שֶׁמְּעַטָּר וּבָא עַל כִּסֵּא כְבוֹדוֹ.

burn him and consume him. For the very fire that springs out of the man beholding the garment burns him and consumes him. Why? Because of the image of eyes in the garment of Zoharariel, Adonai, God of Israel, who, crowned, comes to the throne of His glory.

מֶלֶךְ הַמְּלָכִים

CREATION HYMN

כיון שעמד לפני כסא כבוד, פותח ואומר שירה שכסא כבוד משורר בכל יום ויום:

מֶלֶךְ הַמְּלָכִים,
אֱלֹהֵי הָאֱלֹהִים וַאֲדוֹנֵי הָאֲדוֹנִים –
הַמְסוֹבָב בְּקִשְׁרֵי כְתָרִים,
הַמֻּקָּף בְּעַנְפֵי נְגִידֵי נֹגַהּ,
שֶׁבַּעֲנַף הוֹדוֹ כִּסָּה שָׁמַיִם
וּבַהֲדָרוֹ הוֹפִיעַ מִמְּרוֹמִים.
מִיָּפְיוֹ נִתְבַּעֲרוּ תְהוֹמוֹת,
וּמִתָּאֳרוֹ נִתְּזוּ שְׁחָקִים.
וְגֵאִים מַפְלִיט תָּאֳרוֹ,
וְאֵיתָנִים מְפוֹצֵץ כִּתְרוֹ,
וִיקָרִים טוֹרֵד חֲלוּקוֹ.
וְכָל עֵצִים יִשְׂמְחוּ בִּדְבָרוֹ,
וִירַנְּנוּ דְשָׁאִים בְּשִׂמְחָתוֹ –
וּבְדַבְּרוֹ יִזְּלוּ בְשָׂמִים.

When [the man who has made the ascent] *stands before the throne of glory, he begins by reciting the hymn that the throne of glory sings each day:*

King of Kings, God of Gods and Lord of Lords, encircled by wreaths of crowns, surrounded by boughs of glowing princes – He who covered the heavens with His glorious bough and appeared from the heights in His majesty. The deeps were set ablaze by His beauty, the firmaments were kindled by his radiant stature. The proud angels burst out of His stature, the mighty explode from His crown, the precious erupt from His garment. And all the trees rejoice in His word, the grasses exult in His joy, and as He speaks perfumes flow forth.

עֲטוּרֵי פְאָר

THE ATTENDANTS OF THE INNERMOST CHAMBER

עֲטוּרֵי פְאָר, מְכֻתְּרֵי כְתָרִים,
מְרַנְּנֵי עֶלְיוֹן בְּשִׁיר גִּילָה –
רוֹמְמוּ אַתֶּם לַאֲדוֹן לֶהָבָה,
כִּי בִשְׁכִינַת שְׁכִינָה, הֲדַר הַדְרֵי
חַדְרֵי חֲדָרָיו אַתֶּם חוֹנִים.
הִפְלִיא אֶת שִׁמְכֶם מִשֵּׁם מְשָׁרְתָיו,
הִבְדִּיל אֶתְכֶם מִמְּשָׁרְתֵי מֶרְכָּבָה.
הַמַּזְכִּיר שֵׁם אֶחָד מִכֶּם –
אֵשׁ לוֹהֶטֶת, לֶהָבָה סוֹבֶבֶת, שַׁלְהֶבֶת מַקֶּפֶת,
גַּחֲלֵי אֵשׁ, גַּחֲלֵי רוּחַ, גַּחֲלֵי זִיו מְנַתְּזוֹת.

You who are crowned in grandeur,
who are wreathed in crowns, who
celebrate the Most High with hymns of
jubilation – now glorify the Master of
flame, for you are stationed within the
very heart of the Shekinah, in the
innermost glory of the chamber of
chambers. He has exalted your names
above those of His other servants; He
has singled you out from among the
servants of the chariot. Whoever
mentions any of you by name – fire
consumes him, flames surround him,
torches whirl about him and glaring
coals, coals of wind, coals of splendour
shower upon him!

עֲלוּמֵי שֵׁם

Anonymous

אֵיתָן לִמַּד דַּעַת

AKEDA: THE SACRIFICE OF ISAAC

אֵיתָן לִמַּד דַּעַת
בְּטֶרֶם יְדָעֲךָ כֹּל,
גִּלָּה לְכָל יָצוּר
דֶּרֶךְ לְהִתְהַלֶּךְ־בָּהּ.

Abraham, the steadfast one, made You
known, before You were known by the
world; he revealed to all creatures the
path which they should take.

הֻבְחַן מֵעֶשְׂרִים דּוֹר,
וְעָמַד בְּכָל נִסָּיוֹן.
זֶה, נִסִּיתוֹ בְּעֶשֶׂר,
חֲנַנְתּוֹ לְמֵאָה פְרִי.

He was designated from among twenty
generations[1] and withstood every trial.
Lord, you put him to the test ten
times; You granted him offspring in
his hundredth year.

---

1. The book of Genesis records twenty generations from Adam to Abraham.

טוֹב, בְּאָמְרְךָ לוֹ:
'יֶלֶד לְנִיחוֹחַ חָשַׁקְתִּי' —
כַּמָּה צִוּוּי שָׁקַד,
לֹא אֵחַר דָּבָר!

Benign One, when You said to him:
'I desire your child as a fragrant
offering' – he rushed to fulfil the
command, he lost no time at all.

מִהַר וּבְקַע עֵצִים,
נָשָׂא אֵשׁ וּמַאֲכֶלֶת,
שָׂם עַל יְחִידוֹ
עָרֶךְ עֲצֵי עוֹלָה.

Quickly he split the wood, took up the
fire and the knife, loaded his favoured
one, Isaac, with the faggot for the
burnt offering.

פָּנָה וּבָנָה מִזְבֵּחַ,
צָג וְהֶעֱלָה כֶבֶשׂ;
קַח בְּיָדוֹ חֶרֶב —
רַחֲמָיו לֹא נִכְמָרוּ.

Then he went on to build the altar,
stood up and placed his lamb upon it;
he took the sword in his hand and took
no pity at all.

שַׁדַּי הִשְׁמִיעַ לוֹ:
'הֶרֶף יָדְךָ מְהֵרָה!
תְּמוּר בִּנְךָ רָצִיתִי
תָּפוּשׂ בַּסְּבַךְ בְּקֶרֶן.'

The Almighty cried out to him: 'Drop
your hand at once! Instead of your son,
I desire the ram caught by his horns in
the thicket.'

תֵּפֶן, אֵל, בָּאֵפֶר,
תִּזְכָּר־לָנוּ בְּרִיתוֹ,
תִּנְצָר־לָנוּ עֲקֵדָתוֹ,
תַּעַן עִנּוּי נַפְשֵׁנוּ.

O God, heed these ashes, credit us
with his covenant, favour us for his
binding, reward our self-denial!

תִּגְאָלֵנוּ גָּאוֹל, חָזָק.

Redeem us, Mighty One!

אַבִּיעָה זְמִירוֹת

GO IN PEACE, COME IN PEACE

אַבִּיעָה זְמִירוֹת בְּהַגִּיעַ עֵת זָמִיר
וּבְזִמְרָה אֶעַן :
לֵךְ לְשָׁלוֹם גֶּשֶׁם.
בְּמִפְעֲלוֹת צוּרִי אַבִּיטָה כִּי נָעִימִים בְּעִתָּם
וּבְנֹעַם אֲמַלֵּל.
בֹּא בְשָׁלוֹם טַל.
גֶּשֶׁם חָלַף וּסְתָיו עָבַר
וְהַכֹּל בְּצִבְיוֹן נוֹצָר :
לֵךְ לְשָׁלוֹם גֶּשֶׁם.
דּוּדָאִים נָתְנוּ רֵיחַ בְּגִנַּת דּוֹדִים
וְחָלְפוּ דְוָיִים :
בֹּא בְשָׁלוֹם טַל.
הָאָרֶץ עֻטְּרָה דָּגָן וְתִירוֹשׁ
וְכָל יָצוּר צֹוֵחַ :
לֵךְ לְשָׁלוֹם גֶּשֶׁם. [...]

I shall sing praises now that the time of the singing of birds has come, and I shall answer in song: go in peace, rain. I shall look at the deeds of my God, so pleasant in their season, and sweetly say: come in peace, dew. The rains are over and gone, the winter is past; everything is created with beauty: go in peace, rain. The mandrakes give forth their perfume in the lovers' garden; sorrows are past: come in peace, dew. The earth is crowned with new grain and wine, and every creature cries: go in peace, rain!

זְמַנֵּי חָרוֹן

PRAYER FOR RAIN

זְמַנֵּי חָרוֹן תִּמְחֶה מֶנּוּ,
יוֹדֵעַ זְמַנֵּי עוֹלָם,
וְנִדְבוֹת פִּינוּ קַבֵּל מֶנּוּ,
בּוֹרֵא מַיִם בְּיַלְדּוּת־מָיִם.

O You who know the times of the universe, avert from us the times of wrath. Accept our offerings of praise, You who create water in the birthplace of waters.

זַךְ בְּלִי עָווֹן אַתָּה
וְחַי בְּלִי מָוֶת אַתָּה,
זַכֵּנוּ לְמַעֲנָךְ וְהַחֲיֵנוּ
וְהַרְאֵנוּ בְּנִדְבַת מָיִם.

You are pure, untouched by sin; You are alive, untouched by death. Purify us[1] for Your sake, and revive us. Let us see bounteous waters.

---

1. Also: 'acquit us'.

וְאֵין אֵל יְקַדְּמֶךָ
וְאֵין מֶלֶךְ מוֹלְכֶךָ,
מַלְכוּתָךְ מוֹשְׁלָה בַכֹּל,
מוֹלִיךְ בַּלַּהַב וּבַמָּיִם.

There is no god before You, no king
who reigns over You. Your kingdom
has dominion over all – You who lead
us through fire and through water.

וְאֵין לָךְ גּוֹי כָּמוֹנוּ,
וְאֵין לָנוּ אֵל כָּמוֹךְ,
פּוֹתֵחַ יָדוֹ לִתְשׁוּבָה,
וְאַחֶרֶת לְאוֹצָר מַיִם.

You have no other people like us; we
have no other god like You, who open
Your one hand to those who repent,
while the other opens the storehouse
of water.

הִלּוּכָךְ בְּלַהֲבֵי אֵשׁ,
יִשְׁבָךְ בְּנַהֲרֵי מַיִם,
קְדֻשָּׁתָךְ בְּרִבְבוֹתֵי אֵשׁ,
סְפִירָתָךְ בְּנִטְפֵי מָיִם.

Your path is in flames of fire, Your
dwelling in streams of water. You are
sanctified by myriad fires, Your Sefira[1]
is in drops of water.

הֵן מַלְאָכִים לָךְ יַמְלִיכוּ
וְגַם שָׂרִים לָךְ יָשִׁירוּ,
מְלֹךְ מְהֵרָה בְּצִיּוֹן,
וְנָגִיל בְּמַלְקוֹשׁ מָיִם. [...]

Angels crown You; princes enthrone
You. Reign speedily in Zion, and let us
rejoice in showers of water.

עַד אָנָה בְּכִיָּה בְּצִיּוֹן

DIRGE FOR THE NINTH
OF AV

עַד אָנָה בְּכִיָּה בְּצִיּוֹן וּמִסְפֵּד בִּירוּשָׁלַיִם?
תְּרַחֵם צִיּוֹן וְתִבְנֶה חוֹמוֹת יְרוּשָׁלָיִם!

How long will there be weeping in Zion
and lamentation in Jerusalem? Have
mercy on Zion and build anew the
walls of Jerusalem!

---

1. The ten Sefirot are the ideal numbers which contain the forces of creation. The third and fourth Sefirot are water and fire. In later kabbalistic usage (e.g. Simeon Labi, pp. 124, 457) the term was understood differently.

אָז בַּחֲטָאֵינוּ חָרַב מִקְדָּשׁ
וּבַעֲווֹנוֹתֵינוּ נִשְׂרַף הֵיכָל.
בָּעִיר שֶׁחֻבְּרָה לָהּ קָשְׁרוּ מִסְפֵּד
וּצְבָא הַשָּׁמַיִם נָשְׂאוּ קִינָה: [...]

Because of our sins the Temple was destroyed, because of our crimes the Palace was burnt. In the city that once was bound firmly together[1] lamentations were heard, and the host of heaven sounded a dirge.

טָלֶה רִאשׁוֹן בָּכָה בְּמַר גֶּפֶשׁ
עַל כִּי כְבָשָׂיו לַטֶּבַח הוּבָלוּ:
יְלָלָה הִשְׁמִיעַ שׁוֹר בַּמְּרוֹמִים
כִּי עַל צַוָּארֵנוּ נִרְדַּפְנוּ כֻלָּנוּ:

The Ram, first of all, wept bitterly, for his sheep were being led to the slaughter. The Bull howled on high, for we were all driven hard, with yokes upon our necks.

כּוֹכַב תְּאוֹמִים נִרְאָה חָלוּק
כִּי דַם אַחִים נִשְׁפַּךְ כַּמָּיִם.
לָאָרֶץ בִּקֵּשׁ לִנְפֹּל סַרְטָן
כִּי הִתְעַלַּפְנוּ מִפְּנֵי צָמָא.

The Twins were seen to split asunder, for the blood of brothers was shed like water. The Crab would have fallen down to earth, for we were fainting from thirst.

מָרוֹם נִבְעַת מִקּוֹל אַרְיֵה
כִּי שַׁאֲגָתֵנוּ לֹא עָלְתָה לַמָּרוֹם.
נֶהֶרְגוּ בְתוּלוֹת וְגַם בַּחוּרִים
כִּי עַל כֵּן בְּתוּלָה קָדְרוּ פָנֶיהָ.

The Lion's roar filled heaven with terror, for our cry did not ascend to heaven. Virgins and young men were slaughtered, and the Virgin's face grew dark with grief.

סָבַב מֹאזְנַיִם וּבִקֵּשׁ תְּחִנָּה
כִּי נִבְחַר לָנוּ מָוֶת מֵחַיִּים.
עַקְרָב לָבַשׁ פַּחַד וּרְעָדָה
כִּי בְעַקְרַבִּים יִסְּרוּנוּ צָרֵינוּ.

The Balance tipped in supplication, for we preferred death to life. The Scorpion shuddered, for our enemies whipped us with lashes.[2]

פְּנֵי הַקֶּשֶׁת נֶהֶפְכוּ לְאָחוֹר
כִּי צוּר דָּרַךְ קַשְׁתּוֹ כְּאוֹיֵב.
צָפוּ מַיִם עַל רֹאשֵׁנוּ
וּבִדְלִי מָלֵא חִכֵּנוּ יָבֵשׁ.

The Archer turned his bow away, for the Lord had drawn His bow like an enemy. The water rose high above our head, yet in the month of the Water Bearer[3] our palates were parched.

---

1. Jerusalem (see Psalms 122.3).
2. In Hebrew, 'scorpions'.
3. Lit. 'in a full pail'. 'Pail' is the Hebrew sign of the zodiac for the rainy month.

קָרַבְנוּ קָרְבָּן וְלֹא נִתְקַבֵּל.
וּגְדִי פָּסַק שָׂעִיר חַטָּאתֵנוּ.
רַחֲמָנִיוֹת בִּשְּׁלוּ יַלְדֵיהֶן
וּמַזַּל דָּגִים הֶעֱלִים עֵינָיו.

We offered a sacrifice, but it was not
accepted; the Goat would not present
a he-goat as our sin-offering.[1] Tender-
hearted women boiled their own
children, yet the Fish turned a blind
eye.

שָׁכַחְנוּ שַׁבָּת בְּלִבּוֹת שׁוֹבְבִים —
שַׁדַּי שָׁכַח כָּל צִדְקוֹתֵינוּ.
תְּקַנֵּא לְצִיּוֹן קִנְאָה גְדוֹלָה
וְתָאִיר לְרַבָּתִי עָם מְאוֹר נָגְהֶךְ!

With wayward hearts we forgot the
Sabbath, and so the Lord did not
remember our merits. O Lord, be most
jealous for Zion's honour, and let Your
radiance shine upon the city once so
full of people!

אֱנוֹשׁ מַה יִּזְכֶּה   BEAR THIS IN MIND

אֱנוֹשׁ מַה יִּזְכֶּה — וּצְבָא דֹק לֹא זַכּוּ בְעֵינֶיךָ?
בַּלֶּחֶם אִם תִּבְעַר הָאֵשׁ — מַה בְּחָצִיר יָבֵשׁ?
גָּלוּי לְךָ חֹשֶׁךְ כְּמוֹ אוֹר, מְשׁוֹטֵט כֹּל בָּעָיִן.
דִּרְכְּךָ בַּסֵּתֶר, וּגְלוּיוֹת לְךָ כָּל נִסְתָּרוֹת.
הַדָּן יְחִידִי, וְהוּא בְאֶחָד וּמִי יְשִׁיבֶנּוּ,
וְעַל גּוֹי וְעַל אָדָם יַחַד יִנְטֶה קָו וְאֵין מִי יַרְשִׁיעַ.
זֹאת יָבִין יְצִיר, וְלֹא יַתְעוּ יֵצֶר — לַחֲטֹא לְיוֹצֵר:
חֶתְלַת בְּאֵרוֹ, חֲפִירַת בּוֹרוֹ, חֶשְׁבּוֹן בּוֹרְאוֹ;

What is frail man, that he should be
innocent when even the host of heaven
are not innocent in Your sight? If fire
consumes the green trees, surely the
withered grass will perish. Darkness is
as clear to You as light; Your eyes
range over all the earth. Though Your
dwelling is hidden, all hidden things
are revealed to You. He alone is judge;
He decides, and who can turn Him
from His purpose? Upon nations and
men alike He stretches His measuring
line, and no one can condemn Him.
Man would not be tricked by his
passions into sinning against his Maker,
if he bore these things in mind: that he
was swaddled in his mother's womb,[2]
that a grave will be dug for him, that
he will have to answer to his Creator;

1. See Leviticus 16.6 ff.
2. Lit. 'his well'.

206

טָמֵא מְשְׁאֵרוֹ, וּמְטַמֵּא בְּעוֹדוֹ, וּמְטַמֵּא בְּמוֹתוֹ;
יְמֵי חַיָּיו תֹּהוּ, וְלֵילוֹתָיו בֹּהוּ, וְעִנְיָנָיו הֶבֶל;
כַּחֲלוֹם מֵהָקִיץ נִדְמֶה, בַּלָּהוֹת יְבַעֲתוּהוּ תָמִיד;
לַיְלָה לֹא יִשְׁכַּב, יוֹמָם לֹא יָנוּחַ, עַד יְרַדַּם בַּקָּבֶר.
מַה יִּתְאוֹנֵן אָדָם חָי – דַּיּוֹ אֲשֶׁר הוּא חָי! [...]

that his flesh exudes impurity: alive –
he becomes defiled, dead – [his body]
defiles others; that the days of his life
are desolate, and his nights are chaos,
and all his labours come to nothing;
like a dream when a man awakens, he
is always beset by the terrors of death.
He finds no rest at night, no repose
during the day, until at last he is put to
sleep in the grave. Why, then, should
any man who is alive complain? It
should be enough for him that he is
alive!

וּנְתַנֶּה תֹּקֶף   THE DAY OF JUDGEMENT

וּנְתַנֶּה תֹּקֶף קְדֻשַּׁת הַיּוֹם
כִּי הוּא נוֹרָא וְאָיֹם
וּבוֹ תִּנָּשֵׂא מַלְכוּתֶךָ
וְיִכּוֹן בְּחֶסֶד כִּסְאֶךָ
וְתֵשֵׁב עָלָיו בֶּאֱמֶת.

Now let us proclaim how majestic is
the holiness of this day, for it is a day
of terror and of awe. On this day, Your
kingdom is lifted high, Your throne
established in mercy, as You sit upon
it in truth.

אֱמֶת כִּי אַתָּה הוּא דַיָּן
וּמוֹכִיחַ וְיוֹדֵעַ וָעֵד
וְכוֹתֵב וְחוֹתֵם וְסוֹפֵר וּמוֹנֶה
וְתִזְכֹּר כָּל הַנִּשְׁכָּחוֹת
וְתִפְתַּח סֵפֶר הַזִּכְרוֹנוֹת
וּמֵאֵלָיו יִקָּרֵא
וְחוֹתָם יַד כָּל אָדָם בּוֹ.

Truly it is You who are judge and
plaintiff, knower and witness; You
record and set the seal; You count and
number; You recall all forgotten
things; You open the Book of Remembrance, which reads itself aloud; the
signature of every [dying] man is in this
book.

וּבְשׁוֹפָר גָּדוֹל יִתָּקַע
וְקוֹל דְּמָמָה דַקָּה יִשָּׁמַע
וּמַלְאָכִים יֵחָפֵזוּן

Then a great trumpet is sounded; a
still, small voice is heard; angels scurry,

וְחִיל וּרְעָדָה יֹאחֵזוּן
וְיֹאמְרוּ: 'הִנֵּה יוֹם הַדִּין
לִפְקֹד עַל צְבָא־מָרוֹם בַּדִּין' –
כִּי לֹא יִזְכּוּ בְעֵינֶיךָ בַּדִּין.

seized with pain and trembling, as they declare: 'Behold the Day of Judgement, come to punish the host of heaven in judgement!' – for they are not innocent in Your sight, when You sit in judgement.

וְכָל בָּאֵי־עוֹלָם יַעַבְרוּן לְפָנֶיךָ כִּבְנֵי־מָרוֹן:
כְּבַקָּרַת רוֹעֶה עֶדְרוֹ,
מַעֲבִיר צֹאנוֹ תַּחַת שִׁבְטוֹ –
כֵּן תַּעֲבִיר וְתִסְפֹּר וְתִמְנֶה
וְתִפְקֹד נֶפֶשׁ כָּל חָי,
וְתַחְתֹּךְ קִצְבָּה לְכָל בְּרִיָּה
וְתִכְתֹּב אֶת גְּזַר דִּינָם.

And all that come into the world pass before You like troops[1] on parade: as a shepherd seeks out his sheep, then passes his flock under the counting rod, so do You parade, count, number and remember the life of every living thing, as you sentence all creatures and record their verdict.

בְּרֹאשׁ הַשָּׁנָה יִכָּתֵבוּן
וּבְיוֹם צוֹם כִּפּוּר יֵחָתֵמוּן:
כַּמָּה יַעַבְרוּן וְכַמָּה יִבָּרֵאוּן
מִי יִחְיֶה וּמִי יָמוּת
מִי בְקִצּוֹ וּמִי לֹא בְקִצּוֹ
מִי בַמַּיִם וּמִי בָאֵשׁ
מִי בַחֶרֶב וּמִי בַחַיָּה
מִי בָרָעָשׁ וּמִי בַמַּגֵּפָה
מִי יָנוּחַ וּמִי יָנוּעַ
מִי יַשְׁקִיט וּמִי יִטָּרֵף
מִי יִשָּׁלֵו וּמִי יִתְיַסָּר
מִי יָרוּם וּמִי יִשָּׁפֵל
מִי יַעֲשִׁיר וּמִי יַעֲנִי:

On New Year's Day their fate is inscribed, and on the Fast-Day of Atonement it is sealed:[2] how many will pass away, and how many will be born; who is to live, and who is to die; who will come to the end of his time, and who to an untimely end; who will perish by fire, and who by water; who by the sword, and who by wild beasts; who by earthquake, and who by plague; who will rest, and who will stagger; who will be serene, and who will be harassed; who will be at ease, and who will suffer; who will be lifted up, and who will be brought low; who will be rich, and who will be poor.

וּתְשׁוּבָה וּתְפִלָּה וּצְדָקָה
מַעֲבִירִין אֶת רֹעַ הַגְּזֵרָה!

But penitence, charity, and prayer can revoke the harsh decree.

---

1. Or 'flocks of sheep'.
2. There are ten 'days of awe' or 'penitence' between the first day of the year and the Day of Atonement.

[...] אֱמֶת כִּי אַתָּה הוּא יוֹצְרָם
וְיוֹדֵעַ יִצְרָם
כִּי הֵם בָּשָׂר וָדָם:
אָדָם יְסוֹדוֹ מֵעָפָר
וְסוֹפוֹ לֶעָפָר,
בְּנַפְשׁוֹ יָבִיא לַחְמוֹ.
מָשׁוּל כַּחֶרֶס הַנִּשְׁבָּר
כְּחָצִיר יָבֵשׁ וּכְצִיץ נוֹבֵל
כְּצֵל עוֹבֵר וּכְעָנָן כָּלָה
וּכְרוּחַ נוֹשֶׁבֶת וּכְאָבָק פּוֹרֵחַ
וְכַחֲלוֹם יָעוּף!

Truly it is You who fashioned them and You know their nature: they are but flesh and blood; man comes from dust and to dust returns; he gets his food at the peril of his life; he is like broken earthenware; like withering grass and fading flowers; like a fleeting shadow and a driven cloud; like a puff of wind, like vanishing dust, like a dream that flies away.

וְאַתָּה הוּא מֶלֶךְ, אֵל חַי וְקַיָּם.

But You are the King, the living, everlasting God!

יוֹסֵי בֶּן־יוֹסֵי   *Yose ben Yose*

סֵדֶר עֲבוֹדַת יוֹם הַכִּפּוּרִים

AVODA: THE SERVICE ON THE DAY OF ATONEMENT

[פתיחה בשבח האל]   *Prologue: In Praise of God*

אַזְכִּיר גְּבוּרוֹת אֱלוֹהַּ נֶאְדָּרִי בַּכֹּחַ,
יָחִיד וְאֵין עוֹד, אֶפֶס וְאֵין שֵׁנִי.
אַחֲרָיו אַיִן בַּחֶלֶד, לְפָנָיו בַּשַּׁחַק,
אֵין בִּלְתּוֹ קֶדֶם, זוּלָתוֹ בְּעֵקֶב.
אָדוֹן לַחֲשֹׁב, אֱלֹהִים לַעֲשׂוֹת,

I shall proclaim the mighty deeds of God, who is glorious in power. He alone is God and there is no other; there is none besides Him, none second to Him; there will be none after Him on earth, there was none before Him in heaven; there was none but He of old, nor shall there be in the end. Lordly in thought, godly in action –

נִמְלָךְ וְאֵין נֶעְדָּר, שָׂח וְאֵין מְאַחֵר.
אוֹמֵר וְעוֹשֶׂה, יוֹעֵץ וּמֵקִים,
אַמִּיץ לָשֵׂאת וְגִבּוֹר לִסְבֹּל.
אֲשֶׁר לוֹ רְנָנוֹת מִפִּי יְצוּרָיו,
מִמַּעְלָה וּמִמַּטָּה יִשָּׂא תְהִלָּה.
אֵל אֶחָד בָּאָרֶץ וְקָדוֹשׁ בַּשָּׁמַיִם,
אַדִּיר בַּמָּרוֹם – מִמַּיִם יִשָּׂא שִׁיר,
אֶדֶר מִתְּהוֹמוֹת, שֶׁבַח מִמְּאוֹרוֹת,
אֹמֶר מִיָּמִים, זֶמֶר מִלֵּילוֹת;
אֵשׁ תּוֹדִיעַ שְׁמוֹ, עֲצֵי-יַעַר יְרַגֵּנוּ,
בְּהֵמָה תְּלַמֵּד עֱזוּז נוֹרְאוֹתָיו.

when He takes counsel,[1] no one is
absent; when He orders, no one delays.
He speaks and does, designs and fulfils,
bearing the world with strength,
carrying it with might. He is celebrated
in song by His creatures; from above
and from below He is given praise. The
only God on earth, the Holy One in
heaven, the Mighty One on high – He
receives songs from the waters, paeans
from the deeps, adoration from the
luminaries, speech from the days,
melody from the nights. Fire shouts
out His name, the trees of the forest
sing for joy, the animals teach the
might of His terrible acts.

[אהרן, משה ומרים]

Aaron, Moses, and Miriam

יֵחַד שְׁלִישִׁי לִרְאוֹת פְּנֵי-מֶלֶךְ,
לְשׁוֹרֵר, לְשָׁרֵת, לָבוֹא חֲדָרָיו.
כְּגֶפֶן אַדֶּרֶת, יְפַת פְּרִי וְעָנָף,
הִצְמִיחַ עַמְרָם מִשֹּׁרֶשׁ לֵוִי,
כִּי שָׁלְחָה שְׁלֹשֶׁת שָׂרִיגֵי חֶמֶד:
מְכַהֵן וְרוֹעֶה וְאִשָּׁה נְבִיאָה.
כְּגֶשֶׁת עֵת דּוֹדִים, פִּרְחוֹ הוּקָם
לִשְׁבֹּר מוֹסְרוֹת צַעַן, לִפְרָץ גֶּדֶר שֹׁעַל.
כֻּסָּה בֶּעָנָן וְנִתְקַדַּשׁ שָׁבוּעַ,
נִצַּב בַּתָּוֶךְ בְּעֵת מַתַּן אֹמֶר.
כֹּחַ אַדִּירִים לְפָנָיו נִכְנָעוּ,
מִמּוֹרָאוֹ לֹא עָמַד אִישׁ.
כְּלַכֵּל צֹאן קֹדֶשׁ שְׁאֵר בִּישִׁימוֹן,

Levi, the third son of Jacob, was
singled out to see the face of the King,
to sing, to serve, to enter His chambers.
Like a noble vine, lovely with fruit and
branch, Amram – of the root of Levi –
blossomed, putting forth three
beautiful branches: priest, shepherd,
and prophetess. When the hour of
deliverance came, Moses, the flower of
Amram, arose to break the bonds of
Egypt, to breach the wall of the Sea.
He was hidden by the cloud [on Mount
Sinai] for a week and was purified, then
stood between God and Israel when
the word was given. The mighty
angels yielded before him; no mortal
could withstand his awe. He fed the
holy flock with flesh in the desert and
bread from the skies, until they came

---

1. A reference to the Midrashic legend that God consulted the ministering angels before creating Adam.

מִלְחֶם שְׁחָקִים עַד בּוֹאָם לָאָרֶץ.

כְּרְתָה בְרִית עִם עַלְמָה תּוֹפֵפֶת,

גּוָעָה וְנֶאֶסְפָה וְלֹא הָיָה מָיִם.

to the land. A covenant was made with the girl who played on the tambourine; when she breathed her last and was gathered to her kin, there was no more water.[1]

[בגדי הכהן הגדול]

The Vestments of the High Priest

שַׂר פָּקִיד, נְגִיד מְלֶאכֶת הַקֹּדֶשׁ

שָׁלַח לְקָדִים צִירֵי אֱמוּנָה,

שָׂח לָמוֹ: 'הַבִּיטוּ אִם עָלָה הַשַּׁחַר,

אִם הֵפִיץ אוֹר קָדִים עֲלֵי אָרֶץ.'

סִפְּרוּ לוֹ כִּי בָרַק נֹגַהּ —.

וְרָץ לְמִקְוֶה טֹהַר לְבֵית הָעֲזָרָה;

סָכוּ מְחִיצַת שֵׁשׁ בֵּינוֹ לְבֵין עָם

לְנָהַג־בּוֹ בְּגֹדֶל, בְּלִי חָזוֹת מַעֲרֻהוּ.

שְׁמַלַת עוֹרוֹ יְמַהֵר וְיִפְשֹׁט,

וַיֵּרֶד וְיִטְבֹּל וְיַעַל וְיִסְתַּפָּג.

סְגַן הַמַּלְבּוּשׁ יַעֲטֵהוּ בַדִּים,

וְיוֹסִיף לְגַדְּלוֹ בַּעֲדִי בִגְדֵי־פָז.

שָׂשׂ בְּמַעֲטֵה הוֹד וְלֵב לֹא יַגְבִּיהַּ,

לְבֵשָׁם לִכְבוֹד אֵל, וְלֹא לַמַּעֲנֵהוּ.

סֵדֶר מִלְחָמוֹת בָּהֶם יִשְׁאָל,

וְעֵינָיו לְמוֹרֵהוּ כְּתַלְמִיד לָרַב.

סוֹד יְגַלֶּה לּוֹ בְּמִשְׁפַּט הָאוּרִים,

אִם עָלֹה אִם חָדֹל, אִם לְחֶרֶב אִם לְיֶשַׁע.

סֹלּוּ לֵאלֹהִים, בְּנֵי גוֹי גָּדוֹל,

קָרוֹב בְּכָל עֵת לְבַשֵּׂר עֵת יְשׁוּעוֹת!

Then the officer, the overseer in charge of the holy service, sends faithful messengers to the East, saying to them: 'See if the dawn has risen, if light from the East has spread over the earth.' As soon as they tell him that the light is gleaming, the high priest rushes to the pool of purification in the Temple court. They spread a screen of fine linen between him and the people, thus dignifying him, so that none should see his nudity. Quickly he strips off his clothes, goes down and bathes, comes up and dries himself. The prefect, in charge of his vestments, clothes him in linen, then further adorns him with golden ornaments. He rejoices in his majestic garments but does not become proud, having put them on for the glory of God, not for his own. He consults the Urim[2] about the order of battle, raising his eyes to his Master, as a pupil to his teacher. Then He reveals the secret to him in the decision of the Urim: should they go forth or desist; will they fall by the sword or be victorious. Oh, sing out God's praise, sons of a great nation, for He is always close at hand, bearing tidings of salvation!

---

1. According to legend, a well, granted because of the merits of Miriam, followed the Israelites for forty years on their wanderings through the desert and disappeared when she died.

2. A kind of oracle, set within the 'breastpiece of decision', worn by the high priest over his heart.

עָלַץ כְּמַלְאָךְ בְּשִׁבּוּץ מִכְנְסֵי־בָד,
כְּפָרָשׁ מוּכָן, צִיר אֱמֶת לְשׁוֹלְחָיו:
עֶרְוַת זִמָּה בָּהֶם יְכַסֶּה,
כִּי כֵן מִצְוָתָם לְכַסּוֹת עֶרְוָה.
עַלְמוּת קוֹמָה יְמַלֵּא בְּכֻתֹּנֶת
כְּפוּלָה, מְשֻׁבֶּצֶת עַד פַּסֵּי יָד:
עֲוֹן בֵּית יַעֲקֹב יְכַפֵּר בָּזֹאת,
מוֹכְרֵי צַדִּיק עַל כְּתֹנֶת פַּסִּים.
עֹז אַבְנֵט הִתְאַזַּר בְּמֶזַח אֲרוּג־בָּד,
וְלֹא כִלְאַיִם כְּכָל יְמֵי שָׁנָה.
עֲטֶרֶת רֹאשׁוֹ כַּהֹוד הַמְּלוּכָה,
צְנִיף צְפִירַת שֵׁשׁ לְכָבוֹד וּלְתִפְאָרֶת.
עָטוּי מְעִיל תְּכֵלֶת כְּזֹהַר הָרָקִיעַ,
מְמַלֵּא בֵית־יָד גְּלִילֵי זְרוֹעוֹתָיו;
עָגֹל שְׂפַת־פִּיו, רֹאשׁוֹ כְתַחְרָא,
מֵסַב קָלַע, בְּלִי לְהִקָּרֵעַ;
עַל פְּאַת שׁוּלָיו רִמּוֹנֵי צְבָעִים,
וּפַעֲמוֹנֵי פָז סָבִיב בַּתָּוֶךְ:
עֵת יַשִּׁיקוּ קוֹל זֶה בָּזֶה,
יְכַפֵּר בְּעַד קוֹל מַכֵּה רֵעַ בַּסָּתֶר.

He exults in the fringed linen pants –
like an envoy, like a horseman on the
alert, a messenger faithful to those who
dispatch him. By wearing the pants he
atones for lechery, for they were
prescribed[1] to cover his nakedness. He
completes the concealment of his body
with a double tunic, fringed, reaching
down to the wrists. Thus he atones for
the sin of the house of Jacob, who sold
the righteous Joseph because of his
ornamented tunic.[2] Then he girds
himself with a splendid sash, a belt
entirely woven of linen, and not of
linen mixed with wool as is the custom
throughout the year. The crown on his
head is like a sovereign's glory, a
turban-diadem of fine linen, for dignity
and beauty. Wrapped in a robe of blue,
bright as the firmament, his rounded
arms fill the sleeves. The opening for
the head has a binding around it, as in
a coat of mail, which deflects the
slingstones, without being torn. All
around the hem there are multicoloured pomegranates, with golden
bells between them; when they strike
each other and tinkle, the high priest
atones for the voice of him who strikes
down his neighbour in secret.[3]

[הַוִּדּוּי וַהֲטָלַת הַגּוֹרָלוֹת]

The Confession and Casting of Lots

קָרַב אֵצֶל פַּר חַטָּאתוֹ,
וְהוּא עוֹמֵד בֵּין הָאוּלָם וְלַמִּזְבֵּחַ —

He draws near to the bull, his sin-
offering, which stands between the
porch and the altar and,

---

1. Exodus 28.42.
2. Joseph's 'coat of many colours' (Genesis 37.3).
3. I.e., the sin of slander.

וסומך שתי ידיו עליו ומתודה. וכך היה אומר :
'אנא השם, חטאתי עויתי פשעתי לפניך, אני וביתי.
אנא בשם, כפר נא לחטאים ולעוונות ולפשעים
שחטאתי ושעויתי ושפשעתי לפניך, אני וביתי.
ככתוב בתורת משה עבדך מפי כבודך :
"כי ביום הזה יכפר עליכם לטהר אתכם.
מכל חטאתיכם לפני יי – '"
והכוהנים והעם העומדים בעזרה,
כשהיו שומעים את השם הנכבד והנורא
מפורש יוצא מפי כוהן גדול בקדושה ובטהרה,
היו כורעים ומשתחוים ונופלים על פניהם
ואומרים : 'ברוך שם כבוד מלכותו לעולם ועד !'
ואף הוא היה מתכון לגמור את השם כנגד המברכים
ואומר להם : '"תטהרו !"'

laying both his hands upon it, con-
fesses; and he says: 'O Lord,[1] I have
sinned, I have committed iniquity, I
have transgressed against You, I and
my household. I beseech You, by Your
Name,[1] absolve me of the sins,
iniquities, and transgressions which I
have committed against You, I and my
household, as it is written in the Law
of Your servant Moses[2] from the mouth
of Your Glory: *For on this day atonement shall be made for you to cleanse
you, of all your sins before the Lord.*'
And when the priests and the people,
who stand in the court, hear the
glorious and awesome Ineffable Name
come forth from the mouth of the high
priest, in sanctity and purity, they
kneel, bow down and prostrate themselves, saying: 'Blessed be the name of
His glorious kingdom for ever and
ever!' – while the high priest takes care
to complete the utterance of the Name
as they end the blessing, and then says
to them: '– *you shall be clean!*'

קָדְמָה לְשַׁעַר אֵיתָן, לִצְפוֹן הַמִּזְבֵּחַ,
יְלֻוּהוּ בְּכָבוֹד כֹּהֲנֵי מִשְׁנֶה.
קִימַת שְׂעִירִים הֲלוֹא שָׁם הָיְתָה
וּכְלִי בֵּית הַנַּחַת גּוֹרָלוֹת זָהָב.
קוֹבְצָם עַל־יָד וְטוֹרֵף וּמַעֲלֶה :
זֶה לְחֵי עוֹלָם, וְזֶה לְמִיתַת צוֹק.
קַחְתּוֹ בְיָמִין פּוּר חָקוּק לַשֵּׁם,
סֶגֶן יַשְׁמִיעַ לוֹ : 'הַגְבֵּהַ יְמִינֶךָ !'
קָשִׁי מַעֲלְלֵי־דוֹר בִּשְׂמֹאל אִם יַעַל,

Then he goes towards the Eastern gate
[of the Temple court], to the north of
the altar, accompanied with pomp by
his lieutenants. For there the two he-
goats stand in waiting and the casket in
which the golden lots are kept. He
takes them in his hand, shuffles and
draws them out – one marked for the
Eternal and the other for death in a
ravine. If he takes up the lot inscribed
'For the Lord' in his right hand,[3] the
prefect says to him: 'Raise your right
hand.' But if this lot[4] comes up in his

---

1. The high priest uttered the Tetragrammaton.
2. Leviticus 16.30.
3. This was considered a good omen.
4. Lit. '[the lot marked for] the stubbornness of the generation's doings'.

רֹאשׁ בֵּית אָב יָשִׂיחַ לוֹ: 'הַגְבַּהּ שְׂמֹאלָךְ!'
קָפַץ וּנְתָנָם עַל שְׁנֵי הַשְּׂעִירִים
וְהִצְרִיחַ בְּקוֹל רָם: 'לַשֵׁם חַטָּאת!'
קָשַׁר שְׁנֵי בְרֹאשׁ הַמִּשְׁתַּלֵּחַ,
דְּחָפוֹ לְמִדְבָּר – וְזֶה לְבֵית שְׁחִיטָה.

left hand, the chief of the priestly
division tells him: 'Raise your left
hand.' At once he places the lots on the
two goats, crying with a loud voice: 'A
sin offering to the Lord!' He binds a
thread of scarlet wool onto the head
of the scapegoat, dispatching it to the
wilderness, and the other to the place
of slaughter.

[הַמּוֹפֵת]

The Sign

תַּכְלִית מַעֲשִׂים – גֵרוֹת הַבְּעִיר,
פָּרַשׂ כַּפַּיִם, קִדֵּשׁ וּפָשַׁט.
תִּלְבֹּשֶׁת שְׁאֵרוֹ חֲנִיכָיו יָרִיצוּ,
לְבֵשָׁם בְּכָבוֹד וְיָצָא בְּמָשׁוֹשׁ.
תָּאֲרוֹ הִקְרִין כְּצֵאת הַשֶּׁמֶשׁ בִּגְבוּרָתוֹ,
מְשַׁלֵּחַ לְשׁוֹלְחָיו צְדָקָה וּמַרְפֵּא.
תְּחִלָּה הִשְׁמִיעָם: 'לְכוּ שְׁתוּ בְּלֶב טוֹב,
אֵל נוֹשֵׂא עָוֹן וְעוֹבֵר עַל פֶּשַׁע!'
תְּמִימִים יְשָׁרִים לְנָוֵהוּ יְלַוּוּהוּ,
שִׂמְחָה יַעֲשׂוּ בְּצֵאתוֹ בְּלִי פֶגַע.
'תֶּן לָנוּ מוֹפֵת', בְּאָזְנָיו יֹאמְרוּ,
'וְנֵדַע בַּמֶּה יְכֻפַּר עָוֹן.'
תִּתּוֹ צִיר שָׂעִיר, וְהוּא מְבַשֵּׂר יְשׁוּעוֹת:
'הִלְבִּין כַּשֶּׁלֶג אֹדֶם הַשָּׁנִי!'

Finally, he lights the lamps, spreads his
hands, laves and removes the golden
garments. His acolytes quickly bring
him his own clothes; he puts them on
triumphantly and joyously steps forth.
His face is radiant, like the sun rising
in all its grandeur, as he grants
deliverance and healing to those who
dispatched him. At first he says to
them: 'Go drink with a good heart, for
God has forgiven iniquity and pardoned
transgression!' Now, perfect and pure
of heart, they accompany him to his
house, rejoicing that he has come forth
from the Sanctuary without mishap.
'Give us a sign,' they say to him, 'by
which we shall know that our sins have
been atoned for.' Whereupon he shows
them the messenger who dispatched
the goat; he bears tidings of salvation:
'The scarlet thread has turned as white
as snow[1]!'

---

1. The thread of scarlet yarn was tied to the door of the Sanctuary; when the scapegoat reached the
wilderness, the thread would turn white.

זַּנַּי _Yannai_

כָּלוּ עֵינֵינוּ לְאַהֲבָתָךְ PRAYER FOR LOVE

כָּלוּ עֵינֵינוּ לְאַהֲבָתָךְ, אוֹהֵב,
נִשְׂנָאִים מִשֹּׂנְאָת אוֹיֵב.
רְאֵה־נָא בְּעָנְיֵנוּ מִבַּיִת
וְשׁוּר שְׂנָאָתֵנוּ מִבַּחוּץ,
כְּלֵאָה אֲשֶׁר רָאִיתָ בְּעָנְיָהּ
וְשַׂרְתָּ בְּשִׂנְאַת עֻנּוּיָהּ;
מִבַּיִת הָיוּ לָהּ שׁוֹנְאִים,
וּבַחוּץ הָיוּ לָהּ מַשְׂנִיאִים.
וְלֹא כָּל אָהוּב אָהוּב
וְלֹא כָּל שָׂנוּי שָׂנוּי —
יֵשׁ שְׂנוּאִים בְּמַטָּה וַאֲהוּבִים בְּמָעְלָה.
שְׂנוּאֶיךָ שְׂנוּאִים וַאֲהוּבֶיךָ אֲהוּבִים.
שְׂנָאָתֵנוּ כִּי אֲהַבְנוּךְ, קָדוֹשׁ!

Our eyes are weak with longing for
Your love, O Loving One, for we are
hated by the enemy. Look how afflicted
we are from within, see how hated we
are from without – as You looked on
the affliction of Leah and saw her
tormented by hate. She was hated
within the house and detested without.
But not every loved one is loved, nor
every hated one hated: there are some
who are hated below, yet beloved
above. Those whom You hate are
hated; those whom You love are loved.
We are hated because we love You,
O Holy One!

רְאֵה עֲמִידָתֵנוּ FROM SOUL TO FLESH

רְאֵה עֲמִידָתֵנוּ מִכַּף וְעַד קָדְקֹד,
מִגִּיד וְעַד עֶצֶם, מִנֶּפֶשׁ וְעַד בָּשָׂר:

See how we stand before You from
foot to head, from sinew to bone, from
soul to flesh:

יָחֵף כַּפֵּינוּ, נָגוּף אֶצְבְּעוֹתֵינוּ.
נָדוּ רַגְלֵינוּ וְהָלְמוּ עֲקֵבֵינוּ.
מָעֲדוּ קַרְסֻלֵּינוּ וְדַלְיוּ שׁוֹקֵינוּ.
כָּשְׁלוּ בִּרְכֵּינוּ וְקָטְנוּ יְרֵכֵינוּ.
חָלְחֲלוּ מָתְנֵינוּ וְעָצְבוּ כְּסָלֵינוּ.
הָמוּ מֵעֵינוּ וְנִתַּר לִבֵּנוּ.

The soles of our feet are sore, our toes
bruised; our feet wobble, our heels are
battered; our ankles totter, our legs
hang useless; our knees stagger, our
thighs are thin; our hips quiver, our
loins are in anguish; our entrails howl,
our heart leaps out; our arms are fallen,

מָטָה זְרוֹעֵנוּ וְלֹא הִשִּׂיגָה יָדֵנוּ.
הֻכְחַשׁ שִׁכְמֵנוּ בְּעֹל צַוָּארֵנוּ.
נִסְקַד גְּרוֹנֵנוּ בְּמַכַּת לְחָיֵינוּ.
יָבְשׁוּ שְׂפָתֵינוּ וְקֵהוּ שִׁנֵּינוּ –
וְתִפְאַרְתָּךְ בְּפִינוּ וְצִדְקָךְ בִּלְשׁוֹנֵנוּ.

our hands grasp nothing; our shoulders
are shrunken because of the yoke upon
our neck; our throat is twisted, because
of the blows upon our cheeks; our lips
are parched, our teeth set on edge. Yet
Your praise is in our mouths and Your
righteousness on our tongues.

קָצַר גֶּשֶׁם־אַפֵּינוּ וְצָלוּ אָזְנֵינוּ.
נִכְלַם מִצְחֵנוּ וְחָוְרוּ פָּנֵינוּ.
כָּלוּ עֵינֵינוּ וְנֶעֶצְבוּ רַקּוֹתֵינוּ.
אַגְמַן רֹאשֵׁנוּ וְסָמַר שַׂעֲרֵנוּ.
נִבְהֲלוּ עֲצָמֵינוּ וְצָפַד עוֹרֵנוּ.
נָקְטָה נַפְשֵׁנוּ, קָפְדָה רוּחֵנוּ.
נִצְרַפְנוּ בָּאֵשׁ, וְנִבְחַנְנוּ בַּמַּיִם.
בְּשִׂמְחָה, בְּצָרָה, בַּבַּיִת וּבַגָּלוּת,
הַשְׁכֵּם וְהַעֲרֵב פַּעֲמַיִם אוֹמְרִים:
'שְׁמַע יִשְׂרָאֵל יהוה אֱלֹהֵינוּ יהוה אֶחָד.'

The breath of our nostrils is cut short,
our ears ring; our forehead is shamed,
our face is pale; our eyes dim, our
temples are in pain; our head bends
down, our hair stands on end; our
bones are frightened, our skin is
shrivelled; our soul is sick, our spirit is
restless; we have been tried by fire and
tested by water. Yet in joy and sorrow,
at home and in exile, morning and
evening, twice daily, we proclaim:
*'Hear O Israel! The Lord is our God,
the Lord alone.'*

אֲשֶׁר אֵימָתָךְ
AND THAT IS YOUR GLORY

וְלָךְ כֹּל יַכְתִּירוּ:

And all shall wreathe crowns for You –

אֲשֶׁר אֵימָתָךְ
בְּאֶרְאֵלֵי אֹמֶן, בְּאַבִּירֵי אֹמֶץ,
בִּבְרוּאֵי קֶרַח, בִּבְלוּלֵי קֶדַח –
וּמוֹרָאָךְ עֲלֵיהֶם;

who are feared by faithful angels,
mighty heroes, creatures of ice mingled
with fire – and Your dread is upon
them;

וְאָבִיתָ תְּהִלָּה
מִגְּלוּמֵי גוּשׁ, מִגָּרֵי גַיְא,

yet You desire glory from those made
of dust, sojourners of the valley,

מִדְּלוּלֵי פֹּעַל, מִדַּלֵּי מַעַשׂ –
וְהִיא תְּהִלָּתָךְ.

destitute of deeds, lacking in good
works – and that is Your glory;

אֲשֶׁר אֵימָתָךְ
בַּהֲמוֹן מַלְאָכִים, בְּהִלּוּךְ מַחֲנוֹת,
וּבְאַלְפֵי אֲלָפִים וּבְרִבְבֵי רְבָבוֹת –
וּמוֹרָאָךְ עֲלֵיהֶם;

who are feared by multitudes of angels,
armies on the move, thousands of
thousands, myriads of myriads – and
Your dread is upon them;

וְאָבִיתָ תְּהִלָּה
מִזִּיו שׁוֹנֶה, מִזֹּהַר כָּבֶה,
מֵחַסְרֵי שֵׂכֶל, מֵחוֹרְשֵׁי רֶשַׁע –
וְהִיא תְּהִלָּתָךְ [...]

yet You desire glory from those whose
radiance changes, whose lustre fades,
devoid of sense, devising evil – and that
is Your glory;

אֲשֶׁר אֵימָתָךְ
בִּשְׁבִיבֵי אֵשׁ, בִּשְׁבִילֵי מַיִם,
בִּתְלוּלֵי רוֹם, בִּתְלוּיֵּי גֹבַהּ –
וּמוֹרָאָךְ עֲלֵיהֶם;

who are feared by flaming fires, watery
paths, celestial steeps, suspended stars
– and Your dread is upon them;

וְאָבִיתָ תְּהִלָּה מִבְּשַׂר דָּם,
מֵהֶבֶל וָתֹהוּ, מֵחָצִיר יָבֵשׁ,
מִצֵּל עוֹבֵר, מִצִּיץ נוֹבֵל;
מַשְׁלִימֵי נֶפֶשׁ וּמַפְרִיחֵי רוּחַ
וּמְעִיפֵי חַיָּה וְחוֹנְטֵי נְשָׁמָה
וּמוֹצִיאֵי יְחִידָה וְנִשְׁמָעִים בַּדִּין
וּמֵתִים בְּמִשְׁפָּט וְחַיִּים בְּרַחֲמִים –
וְנוֹתְנִים לָךְ פְּאֵר, חֵי עוֹלָמִים!

yet You desire praise from flesh and
blood, vanity and nothingness, withering grass, fleeting shadow, fading
flower; from those who surrender their
soul, fling away their breath, cast up
their life, disgorge their spirit, expel
their soul; who are heard in judgement,
die by Your sentence, live by Your
mercy, and acclaim Your splendour,
O Life Eternal!

מַה יִּתְרוֹן לִי   ABRAHAM'S COMPLAINT

'מַה יִּתְרוֹן לִי?' אָב נִתְחַנֵּן,
'נַפְשִׁי עֲגוּמָה וְלִבִּי מִתְאוֹנָן.
שִׂמְחָה בְּלִבִּי מַה יְרַנֵּן?
עֵץ סָרָק אָנֹכִי וְלֹא רַעֲנָן.

'What have I gained?' the father cried.
'My soul is mournful and my heart
laments. How can joy sing in my heart?
I am a barren tree, bearing no fruit.

פָּעֳלִי מַה בְּכָל יְקָרִי?
צִיץ עִקָּרִי עֲקָרִי בִּמְקוֹרִי.
קִנְיַן בִּרְכָתִי יִירַשׁ אָרוּרִי,
רֵיק אִם אֶפְנֶה וַעֲרִירִי.

'What does all my honour avail me?
The blossom of my root is cut off at the
source. The accursed one[1] will inherit
all the wealth given to me as a blessing
if I die empty and childless.

שֵׁם צֶדֶק יֵשׁ לִי,
שֶׁתֶל צֶדֶק אֵין לִי.
תַּתִּי לָךְ וְנָחַתָּ לִי –
מָה אֶתֵּן לָךְ וּמַה תִּתֵּן לִי?'

'I have a good name but have no good
seedling. You have given to me, I have
given to You – what can I give You,
what can You give me?

אָזְנֶיךָ קַשּׁוּבוֹת
לְכָל מַחֲשָׁבוֹת
מַטְלִיל תֶּחִי בְּרוּחוֹת נְשָׁבוֹת!

'Your ears are attentive to all thoughts,
O You who revive us with dew carried
on the wind!'

מִשָּׁמַיִם לִשְׁמֵי הַשָּׁמַיִם   HYMN FROM THE HEAVENS

מִשָּׁמַיִם לִשְׁמֵי הַשָּׁמַיִם,
מִשְּׁמֵי שָׁמַיִם לַעֲרָפֶל,
מֵעֲרָפֶל לִזְבוּלָה,
מִזְּבוּלָה לִמְעוֹנָה,
מִמְּעוֹנָה לִשְׁחָקִים,

From Heaven to the Heaven of
Heavens; from the Heaven of Heavens
to the Dark Clouds; from the Dark
Clouds to the Abode; from the Abode
to the Dwelling-place; from the
Dwelling-place to the Skies; from the

---

1. His servant, Eliezer.

מְשֻׂחָקִים לַעֲרָבוֹת,
מֵעֲרָבוֹת לְרוּם כִּסֵּא,
וּמֵרוּם כִּסֵּא לְמֶרְכָּבָה —

Skies to the Plains; from the Plains to
the height of the Throne; and from the
height of the Throne to the Chariot —

מִי יִדְמֶה לָךְ, מִי יִשְׁוֶה לָךְ,
מִי רָאָה, מִי הִגִּיעַ,
מִי יִתְלֶה רֹאשׁ, מִי יָרִים עָיִן,
מִי יַקְשֶׁה, מִי יָעֵז,
מִי יָזִיד, מִי יְחַשֵּׁב בַּלֵּב,
מִי יִגְאֶה, מִי יָגֵס,
מִי יַעֲרֹךְ —

who can be compared to You, who is
Your equal? who has seen You, who
has reached You? who can hold his
head high, who can lift up his eyes?
who can question, who can defy? who
can fathom, who can calculate? who
can be proud, who can be haughty?
who is like You?

וּרְכוּבָךְ עַל כְּרוּב וְדִיאָתָךְ עַל רוּחַ,
וְאָרְחָךְ בְּסוּפָה וְדַרְכָּךְ בִּסְעָרָה,
וּשְׁבִילָךְ בְּמַיִם וּשְׁלִיחוּתָךְ בְּאֵשׁ —
אֶלֶף אֲלָפִים וְרִבֵּי רְבָבוֹת,
נַעֲשִׂים אֲנָשִׁים, נַעֲשִׂים נָשִׁים,
נַעֲשִׂים רוּחוֹת, נַעֲשִׂים זִקִים,
נַעֲשִׂים כָּל דְּמוּת וְעוֹשִׂים כָּל שְׁלִיחוּת,
בְּאֵימָה, בְּיִרְאָה, בְּפַחַד, בְּרַעַד, בְּרֶתֶת, בְּזִיעַ
יִפְתְּחוּ . . .

For You ride on a cherub and fly on a
wind; Your road is in whirlwind, Your
way is in storm; Your path is through
waters. Fires are Your emissaries —
thousands of thousands and myriads of
myriads, who are changed into men,
changed into women, changed into
winds, changed into demons; who
assume all shapes and fulfil every
mission, with fear, dread, awe,
trembling, terror, trepidation, they
open . . .

אַחַר הַמִּדְבָּר

MOSES THE MESSENGER

אַחַר הַמִּדְבָּר צִיר נָהַג צֹאן;
אַחַר הַמִּדְבָּר הִנְהִיג עַמּוֹ כַּצֹּאן.

Into the wilderness the Messenger
drove his flock; into the wilderness he
would lead his people like a flock.

בְּלֹא רַגְלַיִם רָץ וְהֵרִיץ מַרְעִיתוֹ,
לָלֶכֶת לִמְקוֹם חֲזִיוֹן מַרְאִיתוֹ.

Without feet he ran, rushing his herd
to the place where he would see his
vision of God.

גִּדּוּלֵי דֶשֶׁא הָיוּ נִבְרָאִים לְפָנָיו
וְאַחַר כָּךְ הָיוּ נִבְלָעִים מִלְפָנָיו.

Green crops sprang up before him,
then were swallowed in his wake.

דֶּרֶךְ גְּדוֹלָה לְיוֹם אֶחָד הָלֵךְ
כִּי אוֹהֵב מֵישָׁרִים יִשֵּׁר לוֹ הֵלֶךְ.

In a single day he travelled a long
distance, for He who loves straightness
straightened the path before him.

הַר הָאֱלֹהִים עֵת כִּי הִגָּע,
מִטָּרְחוֹ הוּנַח וּמִיגִיעוֹ הֻרְגָּע.

When he reached the mountain of God,
he was eased of his hardship and
relieved of his toil.

וּתְחִלָּה נִרְאָה לוֹ כִּדְמוּת מַלְאָךְ,
לַעֲשׂוֹת דְּמוּתוֹ כִּדְמוּת מַלְאָךְ.

At first an angel appeared before him to
change his form into that of an angel.

זֶה, לְפִי דַרְכּוּ חִנְּכוֹ לִרְאוֹת,
לִהְיוֹת בָּקִי בְּכָל מַרְאֵי מַרְאוֹת:

Then the Lord taught him to look at
fire, to be expert in fiery visions.

חִזֵּק לִבּוֹ כְּשָׁר לַבַּת אֵשׁ –
בַּעֲבוּר לְלַבְּבוֹ בְּכָל מִינֵי אֵשׁ.

His heart was strengthened by looking
at the flame, so that he might be able to
withstand all manner of fire.

טָהוֹר בְּתוֹךְ טֻמְאָה יְקָרוֹ הוֹפִיעַ,
גָּבַהּ עַל סְנֶה כְּבוֹדוֹ הוֹדִיעַ;

The Pure One revealed His splendour
in the midst of Egypt's defilement; the
High One proclaimed His glory from
the lowly bush –

יַעַן כִּי צָרַת עַמּוֹ הִיא צָרָתוֹ
וִישׁוּעָתָם הִיא יְשׁוּעָתוֹ.

For His people's distress is His distress,
and their salvation is His own.

אֵשׁ אֲשֶׁר הִיא   THE CELESTIAL FIRE

וּבְכֵן וַיֵּרָא מַלְאַךְ יהוה אֵלָיו בְּלַבַּת אֵשׁ:

Now an angel of the Lord appeared to
Moses in a blazing fire –

אֵשׁ אֲשֶׁר הִיא אוֹכְלָה אֵשׁ
אֵשׁ בּוֹעֶרֶת בְּיַבֵשִׁים וּבְלַחִים
אֵשׁ גּוֹחֶלֶת בְּשֶׁלֶג וְקִיטוֹר
אֵשׁ דּוֹמָה לַאֲרִי רוֹבֵץ
אֵשׁ הַמַּרְאָה כַּמָּה מַרְאוֹת
אֵשׁ וַדַּאי כִּי לֹא כָבָה
אֵשׁ זוֹרַחַת וּמְשׁוֹטֶטֶת
אֵשׁ חוֹשֶׁשֶׁת וּמִתְלַקַּחַת
אֵשׁ טָסָה בְּרוּחַ סְעָרָה
אֵשׁ יוֹקֶדֶת בְּאֶפֶס עֵצִים
אֵשׁ כִּי כָל יוֹם מִתְחַדֶּשֶׁת
אֵשׁ לֹא נֻפְּחָה מֵאֵשׁ
אֵשׁ מַעֲלָה לוּלַבִּין
אֵשׁ נִיצוֹצֶיהָ הֵם הַבְּרָקִים [...]
אֵשׁ שְׁחוֹרָה כָּעוֹרֵב
אֵשׁ תַּלְתַּלִּים כְּצִבְעֵי קֶשֶׁת.

a fire that devours fire; a fire that burns
in things dry and moist; a fire that
glows amid snow and ice; a fire that is
like a crouching lion; a fire that reveals
itself in many forms; a fire that is, and
never expires; a fire that shines and
roars; a fire that blazes and sparkles; a
fire that flies in a storm wind; a fire
that burns without wood; a fire that
renews itself every day; a fire that is
not fanned by fire; a fire that billows
like palm branches; a fire whose sparks
are flashes of lightning; a fire black as
a raven; a fire, curled, like the colours
of the rainbow!

אֶלְעָזָר בֵּירַבִּי קַלִּיר (קִילִיר)   *Eleazar ben Kallir*

אֲגוּדִים בְּשִׂמְחָה   EPITHALAMIUM

'אֲגוּדִים בְּשִׂמְחָה, תָּעֵצַם שִׂמְחַתְכֶם
בְּאַהֲבָה וּבְגִיל הַיּוֹם בְּהִתְחַתֶּנְכֶם;
גִּילוּ וְשִׂמְחוּ בַּיָי אֱלֹהֵיכֶם.

[The Poet:] 'Bound by affection, may
your joy increase, as you are wed today
in love and gladness; be glad and
rejoice in the Lord your God.

דּוּץ חָתָן בְּחֻפַּת הֲדָרֶךָ
הַנָּוֶה בְּיָפִי בֵּין חֲבֵרֶיךָ,
וְיִשְׂמַח לִבְּךָ מֵאֵשֶׁת נְעוּרֶיךָ.

'Bridegroom, delight in your glorious marriage chambers; excel in beauty among your companions; may your heart rejoice in the wife of your youth.

זֹהַר פָּנַיִךְ יַצְהִיר כְּיַיִן.
חוֹרְשַׁיִךְ יִהְיוּ כְאֶפֶס וּכְאַיִן.
טִירָתִי, טֹבוּ דֹדַיִךְ מִיַּיִן.'

'Your radiant face [O bride,] shall glow like wine; your enemies shall be as nothing; My [silver] parapet,[1] your love is sweeter than wine.'

כְּהַשֹׁתֶפַת עָסִיס,
כְּעָגוּר נָסִיס,
שׂוֹשׂ אָשִׂישׂ בְּקָדוֹשׁ!

Like one drinking wine or hearing the song of a swallow or a crane, I shall revel in the Holy One!

'יוֹנָתִי בְּחֵן וָחֶסֶד אֲכַלְלָה,
כְּהִגָּלוֹתִי בְּלַהַב אֵשׁ אוֹכְלָה;
לָכֵן לִבַּבְתִּנִי, אֲחוֹתִי כַלָּה.

[God to Israel:] 'I shall crown My dove with grace and kindness, as once I did when I revealed Myself in the flame of the consuming fire [on Mount Sinai]; for you have ravished My heart, My sister, My bride.

מְקוֹם מַיִם חַיִּים מַעְיָנַיִךְ.
נִעַרְתִּי מִמֵּךְ כָּל מְעַנַּיִךְ.
סְגֻלָּתִי, שְׂאִי סָבִיב עֵינַיִךְ.

'Your fountains are a place of running water; I have shaken all your tormentors from you; My treasured one,[2] lift up your eyes and look about you.

עוֹלָה-מִמִּדְבָּר טוֹבוֹת אֲדַשֵּׁן.
פִּנָּתִי בְּעַנְנֵי כָבוֹד אֲעַשֵּׁן.
צַוָּארֶךְ דִּמִּיתִי כְּמִגְדַּל הַשֵּׁן.

'I shall shower her who comes up from the wilderness[2] with favours; I shall envelop My cornerstone[3] with clouds of glory; I have likened your neck to an ivory tower.'

כְּהַשֹׁתֶפַת עָסִיס,
כְּעָגוּר נָסִיס,
שׂוֹשׂ אָשִׂישׂ בְּקָדוֹשׁ!

Like one drinking wine or hearing the song of a swallow or a crane, I shall revel in the Holy One!

---

1. An epithet for the bride (Song of Songs 8.9).
2. Epithets for the people of Israel, derived from biblical expressions.
3. Jerusalem.

קוּמִי, רַעְיָתִי, בְּאַהֲבָה הִתְחַתַּנְי,
רַנָּה וְתוֹדָה לְמַלְכֵּךְ תְּנִי.
שִׁיר הָפִיקִי בְּחֶפַּת חַתּוּנִי,
תּוֹפְפִי : "תַּחַת הַתַּפּוּחַ עוֹרַרְתַּנִי.'"

'Arise, My beloved, and be married in
love; give hymns and thanks to your
King; sing and make music in My
bridal chamber: "under the apple tree
You have awakened me!"'

אֵם הַבָּנִים

THE DIALOGUE OF ZION AND GOD

אֵם הַבָּנִים כְּיוֹנָה מְנַהֶמֶת,
בַּלֵּב מִתְאוֹנֶנֶת וּבַפֶּה מִתְרַעֲמֶת,
גּוֹעָה בְּבְכִי וּבְמַר נוֹאֶמֶת,
דְּמָעוֹת מַזֶּלֶת וְדוֹמֶמֶת וְנִדְהֶמֶת:

The mother of children moans like a
dove; she mourns in her heart and
complains out loud; she cries bitterly,
calls out desperately; she sheds tears,
she is silent and stunned:

'הִשְׁלִיכַנִי בַּעְלִי וְסָר מֵעָלַי,
וְלֹא זָכַר אַהֲבַת כְּלוּלַי,
זֵרְנִי וּפִזְּרַנִי מֵעַל גְּבוּלַי,
חִדָּה עָלַי כָּל תּוֹלָלַי.

'My husband has abandoned me and
turned away, and has not remembered
my love as a bride; he has scattered
and dispersed me far from my land; he
has let all my tormentors rejoice at my
downfall.

טְרָפַנִי כְּנִדָּה וּמִפָּנָיו הִדִּיחַנִי,
יְקָשַׁנִי בְּכֶלֶב וְלֹא הֱנִיחַנִי,
כָּלּוּ עֵינַי בְּתוֹכָחוֹת וְכִחֲנִי,
לָמָּה לָנֶצַח עֲזָבַנִי, שְׁכֵחַנִי ?'

'He has cast me off like an unclean
woman, banished me from his presence;
he has harshly ensnared me, given me
no respite; he has chastised me till my
eyes failed. Why has he forsaken me,
forgotten me forever?'

'מַה תִּתְאוֹנְנִי עָלַי, יוֹנָתִי,
נֶטַע חֶמֶד עֲרוּגַת גַּנָּתִי ?
שִׂיחַ פִּלּוּלַיִךְ כְּבָר עָנִיתִי,
עָטוּר בָּךְ כְּאָז חָנִיתִי.

'O my dove, O plant of delight in my
garden bed, why do you cry out against
me? I have already answered your
prayer, as I did in days of old, when I
dwelt crowned in your midst.

פָּנִיתִי אֵלַיִךְ בְּרַחֲמֵי הָרַבִּים,
צָעֹד בְּשַׁעַר בַּת רַבִּים,
קָמַיִךְ, אֲשֶׁר עָלַיִךְ מִתְרַבִּים,
רַעֲשְׁתִּי הֱיוֹת כֶּעָשָׁן כָּבִים.

'I have turned to you with great compassion, and now I march through the gate of Bath-Rabbim [Jerusalem]. Your enemies, ever more numerous – I shook them till they were snuffed out like smoke.

שְׁחוֹרָתִי, לָעַד לֹא אֶזְנָחֵךְ,
שֵׁנִית אוֹסִיף יָד וְאֶקָּחֵךְ.
תַּמּוּ וְסָפוּ דִּבְרֵי וִכּוּחֵךְ,
תַּמָּתִי, לֹא אֶעֶזְבֵךְ וְלֹא אֶשְׁכָּחֵךְ.'

'My dark one, I shall never desert you; I shall reach out again and take you to myself. Your complaint has come to an end: my perfect one, I shall not forsake you or forget you.'

אָז בִּמְלֹאת סֶפֶק

JEREMIAH AND THE BEAUTIFUL WOMAN

אָז בִּמְלֹאת סֶפֶק יָפָה כְּתִרְצָה,
הֵן אֶרְאֶלָּם צָעֲקוּ חוּצָה.
בֶּן חִלְקִיָּהוּ מֵאַרְמוֹן כְּיָצָא,
אִשָּׁה יְפַת תֹּאַר מְנֻוֶּלֶת מָצָא:

Then, when she had had her full measure of grief – she who was as beautiful as Tirzah[1] – the valiant angels cried aloud. As Jeremiah son of Hilkiah came out of the Temple, he met the beautiful woman, in filthy attire.

'גּוֹזְרַנִי עָלַיִךְ בְּשֵׁם אֱלֹהִים וְאָדָם –
אִם שֵׁד לַשֵּׁדִים אַתְּ אוֹ לִבְנֵי אָדָם?
דְּמוּת יָפְיֵךְ כִּבְשַׂר דָּם,
פַּחְדֵּךְ וְיִרְאָתֵךְ כְּמַלְאָכִים לְבַדָּם.'

'In the name of God and man, I charge you to tell me: are you a demon among demons or a human being? Your beauteous form is like that of flesh and blood; but the dread and fear of you is like that of angels alone!'

'הֵן לֹא שֵׁד אֲנִי וְלֹא גֹלֶם פַּחַת.
יְדוּעָה הָיִיתִי בְּשׁוּבָה וָנַחַת.
וְהֵן לְשָׁלוֹשׁ אֲנִי, וּלְשִׁבְעִים וְאֶחָד,
וְלִשְׁנֵים עָשָׂר, וְשִׁשִּׁים, וְאֶחָד.

'I am neither a demon nor a thing of base matter. I was renowned for my peace and repose; for I belonged to *three* and to *seventy-one*, to *twelve*, to *sixty* and to *one*.

---

1. Song of Songs 6.4.

זֶה הָאֶחָד – אַבְרָהָם הָיָה,
וּבֶן הַשְּׁלוֹשָׁה – אֲבוֹת שְׁלִישִׁיָּה;
חֹק שְׁנֵים עָשָׂר – הֵן הֵן שִׁבְטֵי יָהּ,
וְשִׁשִּׁים – רִבּוֹא, וְשִׁבְעִים וְאֶחָד – סַנְהֶדְרֵי יָהּ.'

'The *one* was Abraham, who was one of the *three*, the Patriarchs three; the *twelve* were the tribes of the Lord; the *sixty* were the myriads [who came out of Egypt]; and the *seventy-one* were the elders of the Lord.'[1]

'טַעֲמִי הַקְשִׁיבִי וַעֲשִׂי תְשׁוּבָה.
יַעַן הֱיוֹתֵךְ כָּל כָּךְ חֲשׁוּבָה,
יָפֶה לִיךְ בְּעֶלֶץ וְלִשְׂמֹחַ בְּטוֹבָה
וְלֹא תִקָּרֵא עוֹד "בַּת הַשּׁוֹבֵבָה".'

'Heed my advice and repent. Since you were once so esteemed, it is fitting that you exult and rejoice in goodness, so that you may no longer be called "the faithless daughter".'[2]

'כִּי אֵיךְ אֶשְׂמַח וְקוֹלִי מָה אָרִים –
הֵן עוֹלָלַי נִתְּנוּ בְּיַד צָרִים!
לָקוּ נְבִיאַי וְהֻגָּם מֻגָּרִים,
גָּלוּ מְלָכַי וְשָׂרַי, וְכֹהֲנַי בְּקוֹלָרִים.

'How can I rejoice, how sing out loud? My infants are delivered into the enemies' hands, my prophets beaten and dragged away, my kings and nobles exiled, my priests in chains.

מְלוֹן מִקְדָּשִׁי בַּעֲווֹנִי נִבְדָּד,
דּוֹדִי מֵאָז בָּרַח וַיִּדָּד,
נֹעַם אָהֳלִי בְּעַל-כָּרְחִי שֻׁדָּד,
רַבָּתִי עָם – אֵיכָה יָשְׁבָה בָדָד.

'On account of my sins my abode is desolate; my beloved[3] of old was driven away and fled; my lovely tabernacle was ravaged; she that was full of people, *how lonely she dwells!*[4]

סִיחַ לֵאלֹהֶיךָ, נָבִיא יִרְמְיָה,
בְּעַד סֹעֲרָה, מֻכָּה, עֲנִיָּה,
עַד יַעֲנֶה אֵל וְיֹאמַר: "דַּיָּה".
וְיַצִּיל בָּנַי מֵחֶרֶב וְשִׁבְיָה.'

'Pray to your God, prophet Jeremiah, for the one who is storm-tossed, flogged, afflicted – till God hearken and say, "She has had her fill!"; till He save my children from captivity and the sword.'

פִּלֵּל תְּחִנָּה לִפְנֵי קוֹנוֹ:
'מָלֵא רַחֲמִים, רַחֵם כְּאָב עַל בְּנוֹ!'

Whereupon he entreated his Creator: 'O You who are full of pity, have pity – as a father upon his son!' Then God

1. The members of the *Sanhedrin*, the Supreme Council.
2. Jeremiah 31.22.
3. The Shekinah (Divine Majesty), which accompanied Israel wherever they went as exiles.
4. I.e. Jerusalem: Lamentations 1.1.

צָעַק: 'אוֹי לָאָב שֶׁהֶגְלָה נִינוֹ
וְגַם אוֹי לַבֵּן שֶׁבִּשְׁלְחַן אָב אֵינוֹ!

cried out: 'Woe to the father who has
banished his son, and woe to the son
who is not at his father's table!

קוּם לָךְ, יִרְמְיָה, לָמָּה תֶחֱשֶׁה?
לֵךְ קְרָא לָאָבוֹת וְאַהֲרֹן וּמֹשֶׁה.
רוֹעִים יָבוֹאוּ קִינָה לְהַנָּשֵׂא
כִּי זְאֵבֵי עֶרֶב טָרְפוּ אֶת הַשֶּׂה.'

'Arise, Jeremiah! Why are you so
silent? Go summon the Patriarchs and
Aaron and Moses. Let the shepherds
come and raise a lament, for desert
wolves have devoured the lamb.'

שׁוֹאֵג הָיָה יִרְמְיָה הַנָּבִיא,
עַל מַכְפֵּלָה נוֹהֵם כְּלָבִיא:
'תְּנוּ קוֹל בִּבְכִי, אֲבוֹת הַצְּבִי,
תָּעוּ בְנֵיכֶם, הֲרֵי הֵן בַּשֶּׁבִי!'

Then the prophet Jeremiah growled
out loud; by the Double Cave[1] he
roared like a lion: 'Weep aloud, you
fathers of splendour; for your children
have strayed, and are captives!'

מֶלֶךְ הָאוֹמֵר לַיָּם   HE SHALL BE KING!

לְךָ יהוה הַמַּמְלָכָה וְהַמִּתְנַשֵּׂא לְכֹל לְרֹאשׁ:

*Yours, O Lord, is the sovereignty and
You are exalted over all.*

מֶלֶךְ הָאוֹמֵר לַיָּם: 'עַד פֹּה תָבוֹא' —
הוּא יִמְלֹךְ מֶלֶךְ!
מֶלֶךְ הַתָּעוּב, מְלֵחָה סְרוּחָה וְעַד בּוֹר יָבוֹא,
לָמָּה יִמְלֹךְ מֶלֶךְ?

A king who says to the sea: 'Thus far
shall you come' – He shall be king!
A king of abomination, who comes
from a stinking drop and goes no
further than the grave – why should he
be king?

מֶלֶךְ הַבּוֹנֶה בַשָּׁמַיִם מַעֲלוֹתָיו וְכֵס רְכוּבוֹ,
הוּא יִמְלֹךְ מֶלֶךְ!
מֶלֶךְ הַשָּׁב לַעֲפָרוֹ כַּנֵּר בְּהִכָּבוֹ,
לָמָּה יִמְלֹךְ מֶלֶךְ?

A king who builds his upper chambers
and his chariot-throne in the heavens –
He shall be king! A king who returns
to the dust like an expiring candle –
why should he be king?

---

1. The Cave of *Makhpelah* in Hebron, the burial place of the Patriarchs and their wives.

מֶלֶךְ הַגּוֹאֵל מִכָּל רָע כַּל בּוֹטְחֵי בוֹ,
הוּא יִמְלֹךְ מֶלֶךְ!
מֶלֶךְ הָרָדוּף כְּעָלֶה נִדָּף מִפַּחַד לְבָבוֹ,
לָמָה יִמְלֹךְ מֶלֶךְ?

A king who redeems from harm all those who trust in him – He shall be king! A king who flees like a driven leaf because of his heart's dread – why should he be king?

מֶלֶךְ הַדָּגוּל מֵרְבָבָה בְּהַאֲלִיפוֹ וּבְהַרְבִּיבוֹ,
הוּא יִמְלֹךְ מֶלֶךְ!
מֶלֶךְ הַקֵּץ נָעָר, וְיָרֵא מִדִּין רִבּוֹ,
לָמָה יִמְלֹךְ מֶלֶךְ?

A king distinguished among ten thousand, who brings forth thousands and ten thousands of angels – He shall be king! A king who fears, dreads, and is terrified at the judgement of his Master – why should he be king?

מֶלֶךְ הֶהָיָה וְהוּא יִהְיֶה בְּחַסְדּוֹ וּבְטוּבוֹ,
הוּא יִמְלֹךְ מֶלֶךְ! [...]

A king Who ever was and shall be, in His grace and in His bounty – He shall be king!

וְיִפָּתְחוּ שַׁעֲרֵי עֵדֶן גָּן

THE BATTLE BETWEEN BEHEMOTH AND LEVIATHAN

וְיִפָּתְחוּ שַׁעֲרֵי עֵדֶן גָּן,
וְשֶׁבַע כִּתִּים מְשׁעָרִים בַּגָּן,
וְעֵץ הַחַיִּים בְּתוֹךְ הַגָּן.
וְיִשְׁמְעוּ קוֹל צוּרָם בַּגָּן;
וּכְמוֹ לְשֶׁעָבַר נִתְהַלֵּךְ בַּגָּן
כֵּן יִתְהַלֵּךְ בְּתוֹכָם בְּתוֹךְ הַגָּן.

Then shall the gates of the garden of Eden be opened, and the seven pre-ordained companies of righteous men shall be revealed within the garden, and the tree of life in the middle of the garden. They shall hear the sound of their Creator in the garden; and as once He moved about in the garden, so shall He now move amongst them in the garden.

וְיִרְאוּ וְיַרְאוּ בְּאֶצְבַּע וּבְדְמוּת
וְיֹאמְרוּ: 'זֶה אֱלֹהִים אֱלֹהֵינוּ וְלֹא נָמוּת.
הוּא יְנַהֲגֵנוּ עַל מוּת!'

They shall see, and pointing a finger at His likeness, they shall say: 'Such is God, our God, and we shall not die. He shall be our guide forever!'

וְאָז יַרְאֵם שָׁלוֹשׁ נֶחָמוֹת:
זִיו וְלִוְיָתָן וּבְהֵמוֹת.

Whereupon He shall show them the three rewards: Ziz, Leviathan and

זִיז הַמַּטְעִים כָּל מִין מַטְעַמּוֹת,
פּוֹרֵשׂ כְּנָפָיו בְּתַעֲצוּמוֹת
וּמַכְהֶה מְאוֹרוֹת עַד תְּהוֹמוֹת.
וְיוֹצִיא לָהֶם בְּכֹחַ בְּהֵמוֹת —

Behemoth. Ziz: his flesh has many
different flavours; when, with great
might, he unfurls his wings, he darkens
the lights of heaven, down to the very
deeps. And then, for their pleasure, He
shall bring out Behemoth by force.

אֲשֶׁר רִבְצוֹ אֶלֶף הָרִים
וַאֲבוּסוֹ מֵאֶלֶף הָרִים;
מַשְׁקֵהוּ מֵאֹסֶם נְהָרִים,
יוּבַל הַיּוֹצֵא מֵעֵדֶן לְאַרְבַּעַת נְהָרִים;
מִגְעָיָתוֹ מְפָרֵק הָרִים.

Behemoth: his lair is upon the Thousand Mountains; he daily feeds upon
the produce of the Thousand Mountains; and he drinks from the abundant
waters of the River Yuval, which issues
from Eden to become four rivers; his
roar rends the mountains.

הִנֵּה נָא בְמָתְנָיו כֹּחוֹ
וּמְעִידִין מַעֲשָׂיו עַל כָּרְחוֹ
וְאוֹנוֹ בְּשָׁרִירֵי בְטְנוֹ מוֹכִיחוֹ.
וּמִי יוּכַל לַעֲמֹד נִכְחוֹ?

See the strength in his loins; his deeds
testify to his might; the power in the
muscles of his belly proves it. Who can
stand up to him?

יַחְפֹּץ כְּמוֹ אֶרֶז לְהַגְבִּיהַּ זְנָבוֹ
וְכָל חַיְתוֹ שָׂדַי יִשְׁכְּנִין לְקַנֵּן בּוֹ.
וְאַחֲרֵי כֵן יוֹרִיד בְּנַחַת זְנָבוֹ
וְיַשְׁכִּין מְעוֹפְפִים בְּאָבּוֹ,
לְבַל יִנָּזְקוּ מֵחַיּוֹת הַיּוֹשְׁבוֹת בְּקִרְבּוֹ.
כִּי רַחֲמָן הוּא בְּכָל מִדּוֹת שֶׁבּוֹ,
וְיוֹשֵׁב כַּמֶּלֶךְ בְּמֶסְבּוֹ —
עַד בּוֹא יוֹם מוּכָן לְשַׂחֶק בּוֹ
וְיִגָּלֶה לָעָם קְרוֹבוֹ.

When he so wills, he raises his tail like
a cedar, making room for all the beasts
of the field to nestle there. Then he
gently lowers his tail, in the thicket of
which he shelters the birds of the air, so
that none shall be harmed by the beasts
dwelling within him – for he is merciful
in all his ways. Thus he reclines like a
king on his couch, till the appointed
day, on which God shall sport with him
and reveal him to the companies of the
pious.[1]

וְנֶגְדּוֹ יֻצַּג לִוְיָתָן —

And against him shall Leviathan be
pitted:

1. Lit. 'the people who are near to Him'.

228

מִלְמַטָּה יְחוֹלֲלוּ לוֹ דָגִים גְּדוֹלִים
וּמִלְמַעְלָה יְצַלְצְלוּ לוֹ אֶרְאֶלִים,
הוֹדוֹ וּשְׁבָחוֹ מְמַלְלִים.

Big fish dance for him below, angels
sing for him above, chanting his glory
and his praise.

תַּחְתָּיו חַדּוּדֵי חֶרֶשׂ,
סְנַפִּירָיו מַכְהֶה גַּלְגַּל חֶרֶס,
יִרְפַּד חָרוּץ עַל טִיט חֶרֶס.

His undersides are jagged shards; his
radiant fins obscure the sun; he sprawls
on the mud like a threshing-sledge.

מִנְּחִירָיו יֵצֵא עָשָׁן,
מַרְתִּיחַ כָּל מֵי בָשָׁן.
מַטְרִיד בְּעָקְצוֹ וּמַדְאִיג חַיּוֹת וְרוֹמְסָן
וּמֵהֶן יִשְׂבַּע וְיִדָשָׁן.
יַחְשֹׁב תְּהוֹם לְשֵׂיבָה בּוֹ לְכָבְשָׁן.

Smoke issues from his nostrils, making
all the waters of Bashan seethe; he
lashes the sea-beasts with his tail,
terrifies and tramples them, then eats
them and grows fat; he makes the ocean
foam and look white-haired, as he
crushes the beasts with his tail.

כְּעַפְעַפֵּי שַׁחַר מְכֻנֶּה בְעֵינַיִם.
בִּשְׁלוֹשׁ מֵאוֹת וְשִׁשִּׁים וְחָמֵשׁ עֵינַיִם.
סָבוּב אֵימוֹת שִׁנַּיִם.
מְשֻׁבָּח בְּמִינִים שִׁשִּׁים וּשְׁנַיִם
וְיֵשׁ לוֹ זוּגִים שְׁנַיִם:
בָּרִיחַ, עֲקַלָּתוֹן וְתַנִּינִים שְׁנַיִם;
וְהוּא עֲלֵיהֶם כְּמֶלֶךְ בְּמַחֲנַיִם,
מוּכָן לְמִשְׁתֶּה־נִצָּחִים, לְבֶן שִׁנַּיִם.

His three hundred sixty-five eyes gleam
like the shimmer of dawn;[1] he has rings
of terrifying teeth; he is the finest of
the sixty-two species; he has two
couples in his retinue: the Fleeing
Serpent and the Coiled Serpent, and a
pair of dragons; he is over them like a
king over two armies, and open-
mouthed[2] awaits the final banquet.

וְהוּא מִכֻּלָּם כָּבֵד וְגָדוֹל.
זְנָבוֹ סְמוּכָה בְּפִיהוּ בְּחַיִל גָּדוֹל,
מַסְבִּיב כְּטַבַּעַת הַיָּם הַגָּדוֹל.
וּבְבוֹא יוֹם הַגָּדוֹל,
יֹאמַר מֶלֶךְ הַגָּדוֹל

He is the heaviest and greatest of them
all. His tail, mightily gripped in his
mouth, girds the Great Sea like a ring.
And when the great day comes, the
great King will ordain that he be served

1. Lit. 'are called "the eyelids of dawn"'; a reference to Job 41.10.
2. Lit. 'whose teeth are white'.

לִתְּגְּנּוּ מַאֲכָל לְגוֹי גָּדוֹל.
וְיִשְׁלַח בּוֹ הַשַּׂר הַגָּדוֹל
— וְאִתּוֹ גְדוּדִים הֲמוֹן גָּדוֹל,
לִפְרֹס עָלָיו חֵרֶם גָּדוֹל,
לְמָשְׁכוֹ בְחַכָּה בְּכֹחוֹ הַגָּדוֹל.

up as a delicacy to the great people. He will dispatch the great prince Gabriel against him, accompanied by a great throng of hosts, to spread a great net over him and, with great force, to draw him out with a hook.

— וְיִרְמְחוּ בוֹ רְמָחִים
וַיַחְשֹׁב לְתֶבֶן בַּרְזֶל מֶרְמָחִים.
וְעוֹד יַרְתִּיחוּ בוֹ רְתָחִים
וּלְקַשׁ נֶחְשְׁבוּ לוֹ תוֹתָחִים.

They throw spears at him, but he regards the iron spears as straws; they batter him and beat him, but he considers the clubs as splinters.

— וְיוֹרוּ חִצֵּי קֶשֶׁת
וְלֹא יַבְרִיחֻנּוּ בֶן־קֶשֶׁת;
לְעֵץ רָקָבוֹן נְחֹשֶׁת.

They shoot arrows at him, but no arrow can put him to flight; bronze to him is rotten wood.

— וִיקַלְּעוּ בוֹ אֲבָנִים כְּסָלַע
וּלְקַשׁ נֶהְפְּכוּ לוֹ אַבְנֵי קֶלַע.
וְאָז יֶחֱרֶה לְשִׂיתָם לְבֶלַע!

They sling stones at him, huge as rocks, but slingstones turn to chaff on him. Then, seized with rage, he rears about to slaughter them.

וַיַגְבִּיהַּ רֹאשׁ מוּל אֵלִים,
וּמִשֵּׂתוֹ יָגוּרוּ אֶרְאֵלִים
וּמִפָּנָיו בְּחִיל נִבְהָלִים.

He raises his head against the mighty ones, and at his majesty the angels are struck with dread and flee from him in dismay.

וְיִוָּדַע אֶל מָעוֹז
וְיִתֵּן בְּקוֹלוֹ, קוֹל עֹז,
לִשְׁלֹחַ בּוֹ מַתַּן עֹז,
— לְהִתָּפֵשׂ בְּלִי מָעוֹז
בְּצַוָּארוֹ יָלִין עֹז.

When this becomes known to God the Stronghold, He sends forth His voice, His mighty voice, to assault him with great force. Leviathan, in whose neck dwells strength, can find no refuge and is caught.

וְאֶחָד בְּאֶחָד יִגְּשׁוּ שְׁנֵיהֶם
וְרוּחַ לֹא יָבֹא בֵינֵיהֶם;
וּקְדוֹשִׁים יִרְאוּם בְּעֵינֵיהֶם
אֵיךְ יִנָּצוּ לִפְנֵיהֶם
וְצוּר יְשַׂחֶק בָּם לִפְנֵיהֶם.

Now they press so close to each other,
that air cannot pass between them.
The holy ones, with their own eyes,
behold the combat, as the Lord sports
with the beasts.

וְיַתְחִיל מַקְרִין לְנַגַּח בּוֹ בְּקַרְנָיו,
וְזֶה בְּגַאֲוַת אֲפִיקֵי מָגִנָּיו.
וְיִבְעַר אֵשׁ עֲשָׁנוֹ
וְיֹּאחֵז בַּגִּזָּה אֲשֶׁר בְּמָתְנָיו
וְיָנוּס מְצַעֵר לְבֵין עֲצֵי עֲדָנָיו
וְיָרוּץ וְיִבְרַח מִפָּנָיו;
וְיֹּאחֵז בְּקִיטוֹר עֲשָׁנָיו
בַּעֲצֵי בֹשֶׂם וְשׁוֹשַׁנָּיו
וְיַעֲלֶה רֵיחַ קְטֹרֶת עַד שְׁמֵי מְעוֹנָיו
וְכָל גַּן תֶּעְשַׁן בְּעִנְיָנָיו.

The horned Behemoth begins by
thrusting with his horns, and Leviathan
parries with the rows of shields on his
back. Then his smoking fire flares up,
catching hold of the fleece on Behemoth's loins. In pain, he runs away to
the shelter of Eden's trees, and escapes
from Leviathan. But the smoke
billowing out of him kindles the spice
trees and lilies of Eden, and the odour
of incense is wafted to His heavenly
abode. The whole garden fills with
smoke because of Behemoth.

וּבַת קוֹל תְּפוֹצֵץ מִמְּרוֹמָיו:
'הָפִיחִי גַנִּי, יִזְּלוּ בְשָׂמָיו!'
לְהָפִיחַ בּוֹ רֵיחַ סַמָּיו.

Whereupon a divine voice calls out
from the heights: 'Blow upon my
garden, let its fragrance be wafted
abroad'[1] to disperse the odour of its
perfumes.

וְאָז יְעוֹרְרוּ צָפוֹן וְתֵימָן
וִיסוֹבְבוּ לְאוֹת וְסִימָן.
וְיֶאֱזֹר עָז־חַיִל וְיֶאֱמָן
וְיָשׁוּב עַל בָּרִיחַ מְזֻמָּן
וְיֵצֵא לִקְרָאתוֹ מְיֻמָּן.
וְיִלָּפְתוּ שֵׁנִית בּוֹ בַזְּמָן:
וְיִתְמַרְמַר אֵלָיו מְכֻמָּן

Then, at this signal, the north wind and
the south wind awake and blow in all
directions. Behemoth girds himself
with strength and, gaining courage,
turns back to Leviathan,[2] who is
prepared for battle. He moves at him,
tensed for the combat, and again they
grapple with each other. Behemoth,[3]
mad with rage, encircles him with his

---

1. Song of Songs 4.16.   2. Lit. 'the fleeing [serpent]'.   3. Lit. 'the concealed one'.

וַיְסַבִּיבוּ בְקַרְנָיו כְּאַמָּן ;
וְדָג לְעֻמָּתוֹ יִתְיַמָּן
וּסְנַפִּירָיו יַשְׁחִיז לְזַמָּן
וּלְשַׁחֲטוֹ בָם יִתְאַמָּן ;
זֶה קַרְנָיו לְמוּלוֹ יַעַקְּמָן,
וְזֶה סְנַפִּירָיו לְמוּלוֹ יְקִימָן –
וּמִתּוֹךְ כָּךְ שְׁנֵיהֶם יַשְׁלִימָן
לְשָׁחֲטָם וּלְטַבְּחָם וּלְהַחֲרִימָן.
וְיִנָּתְנוּ מַאֲכָל לְעַם נֶאֱמָן
וְיָבִינוּ כִּי לֹא אַלְמָן,
וְיֹאמְרוּ: 'בָּרוּךְ הַנֶּאֱמָן !
כִּי כָל דָּבָר אֲשֶׁר מֵאָז זְמָן,
הֵקִיצוּ לְקֵץ וּזְמָן.'

horns like a master warrior; while the
Fish, facing him, wheels to the right,
whetting his fins again and again, as he
tries to gash him. Behemoth arches his
horns, Leviathan rears his fins – but
now He makes an end of the pair, to
slaughter, prepare, and consecrate
them. They shall be served up as a dish
to the faithful people. Seeing that
Israel has not been forsaken, they shall
say: 'Blessed is the Steadfast One. For
everything that he ordained long ago,
he accomplishes now, at the end of
time!'

פִּינְחָס הַכֹּהֵן

Phinehas Hakohen

וּמֵהַיּוֹם וָהָלְאָה

WATER

וּמֵהַיּוֹם וָהָלְאָה יֵרָאוּ הֲמוֹנֵי מַיִם:
מִלְמַטָּה סִילוֹנֵי מַיִם וּמִלְמַעְלָה קִילוֹנֵי מַיִם ;
זְכָרִים וּנְקֵבוֹת עֵרוּבֵי מַיִם ;
מְתוּקִים, מְלוּחִים – מַיִם עִם מַיִם.
וּבִשְׂאֵת עֲנָנִים מַיִם –
יָרִיקוּ זְכָרִים עַל נְקֵבוֹת, לְהַרְבִּיעַ מַיִם ;
מְתוּקִים עַל מְלוּחִים, לְהֵיטִיב מַיִם.
וּמֵהֶם תְּעֻבַּר אֶרֶץ, מֵעֲרוּבֵי מַיִם,
לְהוֹלִידָהּ וּלְהַצְמִיחָהּ מִשְּׁמֵי שָׁמַיִם. [...]

And from this day on, teeming waters
shall be seen: jets of water from below
and torrents of water from above; male
and female – mingled waters; sweet and
salty – waters with waters. And when
the clouds are laden with water, they
shall empty the male upon the female
waters, to inseminate the waters; the
sweet upon the salty, to improve the
waters. And by them shall the earth
conceive, by these mingled waters, to
give birth and to sprout, from the
heaven of heavens.

232

אָח בְּנַעֲלֵיכֶם — JOSEPH REVEALS HIMSELF TO HIS BROTHERS

'אָח בְּנַעֲלֵיכֶם מְכַרְתֶּם.
בְּשִׂטְמַתְכֶם עַל דָּמוֹ קַמְתֶּם.
גְּדִי עִזִּים בְּמִרְמָה שְׁחַטְתֶּם.
דְּאַגְתֶּם לֵב אֲבִיכֶם וְסוֹד הֶעֱרַמְתֶּם.
אוֹי לָכֶם מִדִּין חוֹשֵׂף!'
אָמַר לָהֶם יוֹסֵף.

'You sold a brother for the price of shoes. Full of hate, you set upon him to shed his blood. Deceitfully, you slaughtered a kid. You pained your father's heart, you plotted to delude him. Woe to you from the judgement of the Revealer!' – said Joseph to them.

'הֶאָח, חָלִילָה לְךָ מֵעֲשׂוֹת זֹאת,
וְתָמַהְנוּ כְּשָׁמַעְנוּ מִמְּךָ כָּזֹאת.
זְקֹף עֵינֶיךָ לַמָּרוֹם וְאַל תְּגַלֶּה רָזוֹת.
חוֹבָתֵנוּ גָרְמָה, עַל כֵּן בָּאָה עָלֵינוּ הַצָּרָה הַזֹּאת.
בִּי אֲדוֹנִי, בִּדְבָרֶיךָ הֲמַמְתָּנוּ בִּרְעָדָה!'
אָמַר לוֹ יְהוּדָה.

'O far be it from you to do such a thing! We are amazed to hear all this from you. Lift your eyes to heaven; do not reveal the secrets [of our past]. It is our crime that has brought this trouble upon us. My lord, your words have filled us with trembling!' – said Judah to him.

'טְרַחְתּוּהוּ בְּיַד עוֹשֵׂי חֲבָלִים.
יְעַצְתֶּם לָשׂוּם רַגְלוֹ בִּכְבָלִים.
כְּאַכְזָרִים מְכַרְתּוּהוּ לַאֲנָשִׁים מְחַבְּלִים,
לַיִּשְׁמְעֵאלִים, בַּעֲבוּר נְעָלִים.
אוֹי לָכֶם מִדִּין חוֹשֵׂף!'
אָמַר לָהֶם יוֹסֵף.

'You tormented him at the hands of schemers. You conspired to have his feet shackled. Merciless, you sold him to violent men, to the Ishmaelites, for shoes. Woe to you from the judgement of the Revealer!' – said Joseph to them.

'מִלַּלְנוּ אֵלֶיךָ כְּדַל וָרָשׁ.
נִדַּנוּ כְּנִמְצָא הַגָּבִיעַ הַדֻּרָשׁ.
סוֹדֵנוּ אַל תְּגַל, וְרִיבְךָ יְפָרֶשׁ.
עַל דָּמֵנוּ אַל תַּעֲמֹד, כִּי הַדָּם מִיַּד מַאֲבִידוֹ יִדָּרֵשׁ.
בִּי אֲדוֹנִי, בִּדְבָרֶיךָ הֲמַמְתָּנוּ בִּרְעָדָה!'
אָמַר לוֹ יְהוּדָה.

'Most humbly we pleaded with you. We grieved when the sought-for goblet was found. Do not disclose our secret, or mix our past in this [present] quarrel. Do not allow our blood to be spilled, for blood shall be revenged on the murderer's head. My lord, your words have filled us with trembling!' – said Judah to him.

'פָּתַר לָכֶם אֶת חֲלוֹמוֹ.
צְפִיתֶם בְּקִנְאַתְכֶם לְהַחֲרִימוֹ.
קַמְתֶּם וְהִתְמַכַּרְתֶּם לִשְׁפֹּךְ אֶת דָּמוֹ.
רִמִּיתֶם אֲבִיכֶם בְּ"זֹאת מָצָאנוּ", וְקַמְתֶּם לְנַחֲמוֹ.
אוֹי לָכֶם מִדִּין חוֹשֵׂף !'
אָמַר לָהֶם יוֹסֵף.

'שִׁנַּנְתָּ לְשׁוֹנְךָ כְּחִצִּים לְשַׁכֵּל.
תָּמַהְנוּ מִדְּבָרֶיךָ וּלְהָשִׁיב לֹא נוּכַל.
פְּנֵה אֶל בּוֹרְאֶךָ, אַל תֵּלֶךְ בָּנוּ רָכֵל.
נָא, בִּי אֲדוֹנִי, רִיבָה רִיבֵנוּ בְּשֵׂכֶל.
בִּי אֲדוֹנִי, בִּדְבָרְךָ הֲמַמְתָּנוּ בִּרְעָדָה !'
אָמַר לוֹ יְהוּדָה.

'חַיַּבְתֶּם מִיתָה מְשֻׁנָּה.
שָׁב – דַּרְכּוֹ סְכַרְתֶּם מִשְּׁכִינָה.
הָאֵל יִמְחַל לָכֶם מִשְּׁמֵי מְעוֹנָה.
כֻּלְּכֶם בֹּאוּ אֵלַי גֹּשְׁנָה.
הֵן לְמִחְיָה שְׁלָחַנִי חוֹשֵׂף.'
נָם : 'אֲנִי אֲחִיכֶם יוֹסֵף !'

חָלְחָלוּ כְּשָׁמְעוּ מִלָּתוֹ.
זָעוּ וְנִבְהֲלוּ וְלֹא יָכְלוּ לַעֲנוֹתוֹ.
קוֹל נָתַן בִּבְכִי וּבָכוּ לְעֻמָּתוֹ.
וְאַחֲרֵי כֵן דִּבְּרוּ אֶחָיו אִתּוֹ.

'He interpreted his dream to you.
Envious, you lay in wait to destroy him.
Then you eagerly rose to shed his blood.
You deceived your father, saying:
"*We found this*",[1] and then sought to
comfort him. Woe to you from the
judgement of the Revealer!' – said
Joseph to them.

'You have sharpened your tongue like
arrows to destroy us. We are terrified
by your words and cannot answer.
O turn to your Creator, and do not
bear old tales against us. If you please,
my lord, contend with us reasonably.
My lord, your words have filled us with
trembling!' – said Judah to him.

'You have merited an unnatural death.
You blocked the old man's way to the
prophetic spirit.[2] May God, in his
heavenly abode, forgive you. Now
come, all of you, to Goshen; it was the
Revealer who sent me ahead to save
men's lives.' And he said: 'I am your
brother Joseph!'

They shuddered at his words. They
shook, dumbfounded, and could not
answer him. Then he wept aloud, and
they too wept. *And afterwards his
brothers talked with him.*

---

1. Joseph's ornamental tunic, dipped in the kid's blood; Genesis 37.32.
2. Legend has it that the spirit of prophecy deserted Jacob as long as he was separated from Joseph.

אֲמִתַּי בַּר־שְׁפַטְיָה   *Amittai ben Shephatiah*

אָדוֹן מַגִּיד מֵרֵאשִׁית   FOR THE MARRIAGE OF
CASSIA, THE POET'S
SISTER

אָדוֹן מַגִּיד מֵרֵאשִׁית אַחֲרִית שָׁנִים
וּמִקֶּדֶם אֲשֶׁר לֹא נַעֲשׂוּ מְזֻמָּנִים,
אוֹמֵר : 'עֲצָתִי תָקוּם לְדוֹרוֹת אַחֲרוֹנִים.'

The Lord, who revealed the end from
the beginning and from ancient times
prepared what is yet to be, says: 'My
design shall last for generations to
come.'

בְּמַחֲשַׁבְתּוֹ אָז כְּעָלָה לִבְרֹאות חֲתָנִים,
בְּטֶרֶם יְצָרָם הִקְדִּים כָּל תִּקּוּנִים
לְלַמֵּד תַּכְסִיסֵי חֻפָּה לִבְנֵי־בָנִים.

When He resolved to create the Bridegroom and Bride, He first made all the
necessary provisions, so that their
descendants would be instructed in the
order of marriage.

גָּדַר וְקֵרָה בָּרֵאשׁוֹן גַּג תִּקְרָתָם,
תָּכַף וְיָסַד אֶת בֵּית חֲתֻנָּתָם,
וְאוֹר לְהָאִיר עֲלֵי הֲסִבַּת סְעֻדָּתָם.

He built the frame of the celestial roof
and laid its beams; then quickly
constructed their bridal bower and
created light to shine upon their
banquet.

אֱמֶת, מַה גּוֹרָאִים מַעֲשֶׂיךָ, נוֹרָא !
מִדַּת בָּשָׂר דָּם צָר צוּרָה –
תְּפִיסַת רֵיק בְּלֹא רְאוּת וַחֲקִירָה ;
יוֹצֵר צָר צוּרָה בְּתוֹךְ צוּרָה. קָדוֹשׁ !

In truth, most fearsome are Your
deeds, O Fearful One! When a human
being makes a form, he can do nothing
without sight and study; but You,
O Creator, can make a form within a
form [in the womb], O Holy One!

וְרִבֵּק בַּשֵּׁנִי עֲלִיָּה נָאָה וּמְיֻפָּה
וּבָהּ הֵכִין שׁוֹשְׁבִינִים לְצַלְצֵל וּלְתוֹפְפָה
וְהִסִּיק אַתּוּנָא מְעַרְבְּבֵי סְעֻדָּתָם לְשָׂרְפָה.

On the second day, He added an upper
storey, beautifully adorned, and
created the groomsmen,[1] to sing and
strike the timbrels; and He stoked a
fiery furnace to burn the adulterers.[2]

הִקְנָה בַּשְּׁלִישִׁי וּפִנָּה תִיאַטְרוֹן לִמְשַׂחֲקִים
וְהֵצִיץ אִילָנוֹת תְּמוּר פַּרְפְּרָיוֹת וּפִנּוּקִים
וְגַנַּת בִּיתָן גְּנוּנִים בּוֹ לְהָקִים.

On the third day, He assembled the
waters, thus clearing a stage for the
players; He brought forth trees, for
pleasure and delight, and made a royal
garden for their bridal chambers.

---

1. Angels.   2. Lit. 'those who disrupt their feast'.

235

וּבְרְבִיעִי הִדְלִיק שְׁנֵי גֵרוֹת כְּפָנָסִיּוֹת
מִלְּהַכָּבוֹת מֵהֲפַחַת רוּחַ וּמְטַר מֵיוֹת
וְהַשְּׁאָר לָנוֹי כְּעִטּוּרֵי סֻכָּה לִהְיוֹת.

On the fourth day, He lit up two
torch-like lamps, which even gusts of
wind and pouring rain could not put
out; and He lit all the others for
beauty's sake, to adorn the bridal
canopy.

זִמֵּן בַּחֲמִישִׁי מִינֵי עוֹפוֹת וְדָגִים
וְהִתְקִין מֵהֶם לְמַאֲכָל יְשִׁישִׁים וּמְעֻנָּגִים
וְזִיז וְלִוְיָתָן לְחַמְבָּא לַחֲבוּרַת זוּגִים.

On the fifth day, He summoned every
kind of bird and fish, with which He
would prepare a meal for the venerable
celebrants; and He hid away Ziz and
Leviathan for the companies of the
pious.[1]

חַיֵּל בַּשִּׁשִּׁי מִינֵי חַיָּה וּבְהֵמָה
תַּבְשִׁילֵי שָׁבוּעַ וְהוֹתֵר לַעֲשׂוֹת מֵהֵמָּה
וּבְהֵמוֹת גָּנַז לַצַּדִּיקִים לְיוֹם נֶחָמָה.

On the sixth day, He mustered all kinds
of beasts and cattle to provide abundant
food; and He stored away Behemoth
for the righteous on the day of redemption.[1]

טוֹב שָׂר וְהִנֵּה הַכֹּל נִתְיַפָּה
וְכָל מִינֵי סְעֻדָּה צְרוּרִים בַּמַּפָּה
וַעֲדַיִן אֵין חָתָן וְכַלָּה בַּחֻפָּה.

The Benign One saw that everything
was now beautiful, and the table set
with many fine dishes, but as yet no
bride and groom stood under the
canopy.

יִפֶּה זִיו חָתָן מִגַּלְגַּל חַמָּה
נִשָּׂא גָלְמוֹ מֵהֲדוֹם וְעַד רוּמָה
וְאַחֲרֵי כֵן הֶעֱמִידוֹ לְאֶלֶף אַמָּה.

He made the groom more radiant than
the globe of the sun, made his body
tower from earth to heaven; but later
[after the Fall] reduced him to a
thousand ells.

כּוֹנֵן שְׁתֵּים עֶשְׂרֵה חֻפּוֹת מָלוֹן
שֶׁל אֹדֶם פִּטְדָה זָהָב תַּרְשִׁישׁ וְיָהֲלֹם
וְהִכְרִיזוּ לוֹ מַלְאָכִים : 'בֹּאֲךָ לְשָׁלוֹם !'

He set up twelve bridal chambers of
carnelian, topaz, gold, chrysolite and
diamond; and the angels called to him:
'Welcome!'

לְעֵת הַכְנִיסוֹ בְּכַלַּת חֲתָנִים הַמְיֻקָּרָה
הִרְדִּימוֹ וְלָקַח צַלְעוֹ וְקִשְּׁטָהּ כְּנַעֲרָה
הִרְחִיצָהּ וְסָכָהּ וּפִרְכְּסָהּ וְקָלַע שְׂעָרָהּ.

Then, placing him in the precious
bridal bed, He put him to sleep. He
took one of his ribs and dressed it up
as a girl; He bathed her, anointed and
adorned her, and plaited her hair.

---

1. To be eaten by them at the end of time; see 'The Battle Between Behemoth and Leviathan', p. 232.

מְסָרָהּ לַאֲלָפִים וְלִרְבָבוֹת לַהֲבִיאָהּ בִּזְמִירוֹת
וְכָל שַׁמָּשִׁים עוֹמְדִים שׁוּרוֹת־שׁוּרוֹת
חַמָּה וּלְבָנָה לְעֻמָּתָם מְרַקְּדוֹת כִּנְעָרוֹת.

He entrusted her to the thousands and myriads of angels who ushered her in with song. All the attendants arranged themselves in rows, the sun and the moon dancing like maidens before them.

נָשְׂאָה חֵן וָחֶסֶד לִפְנֵי בַעְלָהּ
וְהוּא בִּכְבוֹדוֹ בֵּרְכָם בְּרָכָה מְכֻלָּלָה
וְהַכֹּל עָנוּ: "יִשְׂמַח חָתָן עִם כַּלָּה!"

Her husband found her lovely and delightful, and God Himself gave them His perfect blessing. And all responded: 'Let the groom rejoice with his bride!'

סָח לְשׁוֹשְׁבִינִים לְסַדֵּר שֻׁלְחָן שֶׁל מַרְגָּלִיּוֹת
וְסָבִיב־סָבִיב הוֹשֵׁב סַפְסָלִים וְקֻתֶדְרָיוֹת
וּלְשַׁמֵּשׁ בְּבָשָׂר וְלִמְזֹג יַיִן עֲסִיסִיּוֹת.

He told His groomsmen to set the jewelled table, to put benches and soft chairs all around it, to serve the meat and pour out fine wine.

עוֹדָם בְּחֶפָּתָם הִתְרָם הַתְרָיָה אַחַת
וְלֹא קִיְּמוּהָ וְכִמְעַט יָרְדוּ לַשַּׁחַת
לוּלֵי מִזְמוֹר שִׁיר לְיוֹם נָחַת.

While still in their bridal bower, He imposed upon them a single prohibition [not to eat of the tree of knowledge]. They did not heed it and, but for the intervention of the Sabbath-Day,[1] would have been doomed to the Pit.

פָּקַד זְמַנָּם וְגָע קֵץ עִתָּם
וּמֵאָז וְעַד עַתָּה נִמְסַר לְתוֹלְדוֹתָם
לִפְרוֹת וְלִרְבּוֹת וְסוֹף לָמוּת אַחֲרִיתָם.

A limit was set to their time, and the end of their life arrived. Ever since then their offspring are fated to be fertile and increase, and then in the end to die.

צְנוּעִים נָהֲגוּ אֵלֶּה לְדוֹרֵי דוֹרוֹתָם
לְשַׁדֵּךְ בְּעֵת אֵרוּסִין וּלְקַדֵּשׁ בְּטַבַּעְתָּם
וּבְעֵת חֻפָּתָם לִשְׂמֹחַ בְּשִׂמְחַת חֲתֻנָּתָם.

The 'pure ones'[2] have made this their custom for all generations: to betroth, to consecrate with a ring, and to rejoice in their marriage within the bridal chamber.

---

1. The Sabbath persuaded God not to send Adam to Gehenna. In gratitude he composed 'A Psalm, a Song for the day of rest' (Psalm 92).
2. Epithet for the children of Israel.

קְרֵבִים בְּשִׂמְחָתָם עָדֶיךָ עֲמוּסֵי מֵעַיִם,
לָגִיל בְּמוֹרָא וְלֹא בְּעַזּוּת אַפַּיִם,
מְסַיְּמִים בְּרְכָתָם : 'כְּהַיּוֹם הַזֶּה בִּירוּשָׁלָיִם !'

Now, 'those whom You carried since birth'[1] approach You joyfully to celebrate – with awe, not with arrogance – and they conclude their blessing thus: 'If only we were in Jerusalem on this day!'

רַחֲמִים מְבַקְשִׁים מִמְּךָ, נוֹרָא וְנִקְדָּשׁ,
לֶאֱסֹף נִדָּחִים וְלָשִׁיר שִׁיר חָדָשׁ,
שָׂשִׂים וּשְׂמֵחִים בְּבִנְיַן בֵּית הַמִּקְדָּשׁ.

They beg You for mercy, O Hallowed and Fearful One. Gather the exiles, so that they may sing a new song as they rejoice in the restored Temple.

שֶׁבַח וּגְדֻלָּה לְשִׁמְךָ, אֵלִי זֶה,
אֲשֶׁר רִחַמְתָּ דּוֹר עָנִי וְנִבְזֶה,
וְנֹאמַר : 'שֶׁהֶחֱיָנוּ וְהִגִּיעָנוּ לַזְּמָן הַזֶּה !'

Praise and glory to Your name, O my God, for You have shown mercy to a lowly, wretched generation. Now let us say: 'He has kept us alive, He has brought us to the present moment!'

תָּמִיד הֵיטִיבָה אַחֲרִית עֲלֵי יְדִידִים
לְדוֹרֵי דוֹרִים הֱיוֹת שִׁמְךָ מְיַחֲדִים ;
לְהַקְדִּישְׁךָ בְּרַעַד וּבִרְתֵת כֻּלָּם עוֹמְדִים.

May You always grant Your loved ones a happy end, so that they may declare Your unity forever. Now all rise to sanctify You with fear and trembling.

אֵל עִיר גִּבּוֹרִים

MOSES' JOURNEY THROUGH HEAVEN

אֵל עִיר גִּבּוֹרִים כְּעָלָה עָנָו,
פָּגְעוֹ קְמוּאֵל, הַשּׁוֹעֵר, עִם צָבָא שִׁנְאַנָּיו.
גָּעַר בּוֹ נֶאֱמָן וְנָס מִפָּנָיו,
וְהוּא מִתְהַלֵּךְ בָּרָקִיעַ כְּבִשְׁכוּנַת שְׁכֵנָיו.
וּמֵאַחוֹרֵי הַפַּרְגּוֹד שָׁמַע קוֹל-רַעַשׁ בְּאָזְנָיו,
אוֹמְרִים : 'קָדוֹשׁ קָדוֹשׁ קָדוֹשׁ יְיָ צְבָאוֹת !'

When the humble one scaled the city of the mighty angels, he was met by Kemuel, the gate keeper, with his dread legions. The faithful one rebuked him and he fled. Then Moses walked about on the firmament as a man walks in his own neighbourhood. And he heard tumultuous voices from behind the Curtain, saying: '*Holy, holy, holy is the Lord of hosts!*'

---

1. Epithet for the children of Israel.

מַרְאֵה הַדַרְנִיאֵל כְּחָז, נִבְהַל מִתָּאֲרוֹ,
שֶׁשְּׁמוֹנֶה מֵאוֹת פַּרְסָה גָּדוֹל מֵחֲבֵרוֹ
וּשְׁנַיִם־עָשָׂר בְּרָקִים יוֹצְאִים מִפִּיו בְּדַבְּרוֹ.
וּלְבַסּוֹף הָלַךְ לְפָנָיו כְּתַלְמִיד לִפְנֵי מוֹרוֹ,
וּבַת קוֹל שָׁמַע מֵהֵיכַל דְּבִירוֹ,
אוֹמְרִים : 'קָדוֹשׁ קָדוֹשׁ קָדוֹשׁ יְיָ צְבָאוֹת !'

When he beheld Hadarniel, he was terrified by his stature, for he was taller than his fellows by eight hundred parasangs, and twelve lightning flashes leapt from his mouth as he spoke; but in the end, he went before him as a disciple goes before his master. And Moses heard a divine voice from within the palace sanctuary, saying: '*Holy, holy, holy is the Lord of hosts!*'

תְּמוּנַת סַנְדַלְפוֹן כְּרָאָה, אֲחָזוּהוּ חֲבָלִים,
שֶׁאִשּׁוֹ שׂוֹרֶפֶת לַפִּידִים וְגֶחָלִים
וְהוּא מִשְׁתַּמֵּשׁ אַחַר־הַמֶּרְכָּבָה בְּכֶתֶר הִלּוּלִים.
וּבְשָׁעַת הַכֶּתֶר כָּל חֵילֵי מָרוֹם חָלִים
וְכָל אַדְנֵי שְׁרַפְרַף רוֹעֲשִׁים וּמִתְגַּלְגְּלִים,
אוֹמְרִים : 'קָדוֹשׁ קָדוֹשׁ קָדוֹשׁ יְיָ צְבָאוֹת !'

When he saw the figure of Sandalfon, anguish struck him, for his fire consumes torches and burning coals. He stands behind the Chariot, wreathing a crown of praises for Him, and when the crown rests on His head, all the armies of heaven shudder. The supports of His footstool roar and roll, saying: '*Holy, holy, holy is the Lord of hosts!*'

יְפִי־כַנְפֵי גַלִּיצוּר נֶגֶד הַחַיּוֹת מַעֲמָדָם
שֶׁלֹּא יִשָּׂרְפוּ מַלְאָכִים מִלַּהַב לַפִּידָם.
וְאוּדֵּי־רִגְיוֹן אוֹחֵז מוּל מַלְכֵי אָדָם
לְהַפִּיל עַל כֹּל אֵימָתָם וּפַחְדָּם —
וּכְקוֹל מַיִם רַבִּים שָׁמַע מֹשֶׁה כְּנֶגְדָּם,
אוֹמְרִים : 'קָדוֹשׁ קָדוֹשׁ קָדוֹשׁ יְיָ צְבָאוֹת !'

The glorious wings of Gallizur screen the creatures of the chariot, so that their fiery torches shall not consume the angels. He holds fire-brands from the Rigyon[1] up to the faces of human kings, so that their radiant faces strike the world with terror and dread. And Moses heard a sound there like the rush of many waters, saying: '*Holy, holy, holy is the Lord of hosts!*'

חַשְׁרַת מַיִם מִתְוַעֲדִים בַּחֲבוּרָתָם
זִקּוּק נוּר וְלַפִּידִים בְּשׁוּב אִשּׁוֹתָם ;
קוֹרְאִים שַׂר הַחֹשֶׁךְ לְהִתְוַעֵד בְּוִעִידָתָם,
קוֹפֵץ מַלְאַךְ הַמָּוֶת לְהִזְדַּוֵּג אִתָּם —
וְכָל צְבָאוֹתָם בִּקְרִיאָתָם עוֹנִים לְעֻמָּתָם,
אוֹמְרִים : 'קָדוֹשׁ קָדוֹשׁ קָדוֹשׁ יְיָ צְבָאוֹת !'

Masses of water merge with the angelic companies. Torches and flares, back from their missions, join them. They call on the Prince of Darkness to enter their ranks. The Angel of Death leaps forward to be united with them. And the heavenly legions all cry out in answer, saying: '*Holy, holy, holy is the Lord of hosts!*'

---

1. The river of fire which is formed by the sweat of the creatures of the chariot (see p. 244, line 13).

אָדָם צָר בַּכֹּתֶל　　GOD THE ARTIST

אָדָם צָר בַּכֹּתֶל צוּרָה, [. . .]
מְיַפֶּה בְּסַם וּבְסִקְרָא.
בַּאֲשֶׁר שָׂמָהּ שָׁם דָּרָה,
וְאֵינָהּ זָזָה מִמְּקוֹם סְדוּרָהּ,
כִּי רַגְלָהּ מְקֻפַּחַת וּשְׁבוּרָה
וְלֹא שׁוֹמַעַת קוֹל אֲמִירָה
וְאֵינָהּ רוֹאָה וְלֹא מְדַבְּרָה –
אֲבָל צוּר צַיָּר הַנּוֹרָא,
צָר צוּרָה בְּתוֹךְ צוּרָה,
בְּכָל מִדּוֹתֶיהָ שְׁלֵמָה וּגְמוּרָה,
בְּמַרְאֶה וּבְמִשְׁמָע סְדוּרָה
וְגַם בַּהֲלִיכָה וּבַחֲזִירָה,
שֶׁהוּא צָר וָלָד בִּמְעֵי־עֻבָּרָה.

A man draws a figure on a wall, embellishing it with yellows and with reds. Where he has put it, there must it stay. It cannot move from its fixed place, for its foot is twisted and broken; it cannot hear speech, or see, or speak. But God is an awesome artist who can shape form within form, flawless and perfect in all its dimensions, able to see and hear, to move back and forth. Thus does he shape the embryo in the womb of a pregnant woman.

אָדָם הוֹלֵךְ אֵצֶל צַיָּר לְהַשְׁכִּירוֹ,
אִיקוֹנִין שֶׁל אָבִיו לְצַיְּרוֹ:
וְהוּא מְשִׁיבוֹ כָּכָה בְּדִבּוּרוֹ:
'מִיָּמַי לֹא רְאִיתִיו וְאֵינִי מַכִּירוֹ,
הַרְאֵנִי דְמוּתוֹ וַאֲנִי אַתְאִירוֹ' –
אֲבָל צוּר צַיָּר יוֹצֵר יְצָרוֹ:
מַטִּיף מֵאִישׁ טִפַּת מְקוֹרוֹ
וּפוֹתֵחַ רֶחֶם לִקְלֹט הֵרָיוֹן עֻבּוּרוֹ
וּמַקְרִישׁ עֲצָמָיו וּמַגְלִיד עוֹרוֹ
וּמְדַמֶּה פָנָיו כְּנֶגֶד פַּרְצוּף הוֹרוֹ. [. . .]

A man goes to an artist to commission a portrait of his father. This is what he says in reply: 'I have never seen him and do not know him, but if you show me his likeness, I will make an image of him.' But God is an artist who can make his creation: He makes a man emit a drop of semen from his source, makes the womb open to conceive the embryo, makes its bones congeal, coats it with skin, and forms its features in the father's image.

עֲלוּמֵי־שֵׁם   *Anonymous*

פְּתַח לָנוּ שַׁעַר   THE CLOSING OF THE GATES

פְּתַח לָנוּ שַׁעַר
בְּעֵת נְעִילַת שַׁעַר,
כִּי פָנָה יוֹם.

Open the gates to us when the gates are being closed, for the day is about to set.

הַיּוֹם יִפְנֶה,
הַשֶּׁמֶשׁ יָבוֹא וְיִפְנֶה,
נָבוֹאָה שְׁעָרֶיךָ.

The day shall set, the sun shall go down and set – let us enter Your gates!

יְמֵי הַקַּיִץ עָבְרוּ   RAIN SONG

יְמֵי הַקַּיִץ עָבְרוּ.
הַסְּתָיו בָּא, מְטְרוֹתָיו יֵחָשְׁרוּ
וְעַל הָאָרֶץ יָרִיקוּ וְיִגְבְּרוּ.
דָּגָן, תִּירוֹשׁ וְיִצְהָר מְהֵרָה יִפְרוּ.
הֶעָבִים גֶּשֶׁם יַמְטִירוּ,
חֶלֶד עֲשָׂבִים לָצֵאת יְמַהֲרוּ.
זְרְעוֹנֶיהָ וְנִצֶּיהָ יְשַׁפְּרוּ.
קוֹלוֹת רְעָמִים יְבַשְּׂרוּ:
'הַזּוֹרְעִים בְּדִמְעָה בְּרִנָּה יִקְצֹרוּ!'

The days of summer are gone. The rainy season is here. Its showers will gather, then pour themselves, more and more, upon the earth. Grain, wine, and oil will flourish quickly. The clouds will send down rain, and urge the earth to bring forth grass. Seeds and buds will grow in beauty. Voices of thunder will herald: '*Those who sow in tears shall reap with songs of joy!*'

אֲשֶׁר גִּלָּה חָכְמָה   MOSES OVERCOMES THE SEA

אֲשֶׁר גִּלָּה חָכְמָה לְיַעֲקֹב
וְהִתְקִין בִּינָה לִבְנוֹ בְּכוֹרוֹ –

He who revealed wisdom to the sons of Jacob and bestowed knowledge upon

241

בַּחֲרוֹן אַפּוֹ עַל מִצְרַיִם הִשְׁקִיף,
הוֹפִיעַ בְּחֵמָה עַל בְּכוֹרֵיהֶם,
גָּזַר יַם־סוּף לִגְזָרִים
וּבֵין חוֹמוֹת־מַיִם עָבְרוּ שְׁבָטִים.

His first-born,[1] He looked down in anger upon the Egyptians, appeared in wrath to their first-born, split the Red Sea asunder, so that the tribes could pass between walls of water.

דִּינִים אָמַר הַיָּם לְמֹשֶׁה:
'לָמָּה, מֹשֶׁה, מַּעֲשֶׂה לִי כָּכָה?
הֲלֹא אֲנִי נִבְרֵאתִי בַּיּוֹם הַשְּׁלִישִׁי
וְאַתָּה נִבְרֵאתָ בַּיּוֹם הַשִּׁשִּׁי,
וַאֲנִי גָדוֹל מִמָּךְ בִּשְׁלֹשֶׁת יָמִים,
וְאַתָּה מְבַקֵּשׁ לַעֲבֹר בְּתוֹכִי?
זְכָר־נָא מֹשֶׁה שֶׁאֲנִי הֶחָכַמְתִּיךָ.
וּמַדּוּעַ תֹּאמַר: "הִבָּקְעָה לִי!"'

The sea berated Moses: 'Why, Moses, are you doing this to me? After all, I was created on the third day, while you were created on the sixth; I am three days older than you, and yet you wish to pass through me? Remember, Moses, that I am wiser than you. Then how dare you say: "Divide before me!"'

חָרָה אַף מֹשֶׁה וְהֵשִׁיב כְּנֶגְדּוֹ:
'שְׁמָעֵנִי, הַיָּם, וְקַבֵּל אֲמָרִי!
טַפֵּי יַעֲקֹב רָאָה אֱלֹהִים
נְתוּנִים בְּצָרָה לִפְנֵי אוֹיֵב —
יַעַמְדוּ מֵימֶיךָ חוֹמָה גְבֹהָה,
וּבְדֶרֶךְ סְלוּלָה, יָמִין וּשְׂמֹאל.
כִּי הוּא אָמַר, אֶעֱבֹר בְּגַלָּךְ.
הִבָּקְעָה לִי וְאַל תִּתְעַכָּב!'

The anger of Moses was kindled and he replied: 'Listen to me, O sea, and heed my words! God has seen that the children of Jacob are imperilled by the enemy. So let your waters arise like a great wall, on the right and on the left, with a paved path in their midst. For He has ordained that I shall pass through your waves. Now divide before me and do not delay!'

לֵאלֹהִים נַעֲשָׂה הַיָּם,
וּמֶרְכְּבוֹת כְּרוּב אֵלָיו נִגְלָה.
מִמְּקוֹם תָּקְפּוֹ הִתְמוֹטְטָה אֶרֶץ,
כִּי פְדוּיֵי יהוה רָאוּ אֲפִיקִים.

God, Who had created the sea, now revealed Himself to it, riding on a cherub. From His mighty seat He made the earth heave, and the children of the Lord, redeemed, beheld the sea's

1. The people of Israel.

ANONYMOUS

נִלְכָה סִינַי לִשְׁמֹעַ תּוֹרָה!'
אָמְרוּ פְדוּיִים לְמֹשֶׁה יָדִיד.
סָגַר הַיָּם בִּתְפִלָּתוֹ
וְעַל יַד שְׁלוּחוֹ חֲרוֹן־אַף הֵשִׁיב.
עָנָהוּ יהוה מִתּוֹךְ לַהֲבֵי אֵשׁ וַיֹּאמֶר לְעַמּוֹ:
'אָנֹכִי יהוה אֱלֹהֶיךָ אֲשֶׁר הוֹצֵאתִיךָ
מֵאֶרֶץ מִצְרַיִם מִבֵּית עֲבָדִים.' [...]

bed. 'Let us go to Sinai to hear the
Law!' said the redeemed ones to
Moses, the beloved, whose prayer had
closed the sea,[1] whose emissary[2]
placated His wrath. Then the Lord
spoke to him from the midst of blazing
fires and said to His people: "*I am the
Lord your God who brought you out of
Egypt, out of the land of slavery!*"[3]

אַרְבָּעָה רָאוּ — FOUR SAW VISIONS OF GOD

אַרְבָּעָה רָאוּ מַרְאוֹת אֱלֹהִים:
עָנָיו וּבֶן אָמוֹץ וּבֶן בּוּזִי וְאִישׁ חֲמוּדוֹת –
בִּדְבַר הָאֱלֹהִים;
וְלֹא יָכְלוּ אַרְבַּעְתָּם לִרְאוֹת דְּמוּת אֱלֹהֵי הָאֱלֹהִים
כִּי אֵל גָּדוֹל יְיָ וּמֶלֶךְ גָּדוֹל עַל כָּל הָאֱלֹהִים.

Four saw visions of God – the humble
one (Moses), the son of Amoz (Isaiah),
the son of Buzi (Ezekiel), and the man
greatly beloved (Daniel) – at the
command of God. Yet none of the four
could see the image of the God of gods,
*for the Lord is a great God, and a great
king over all gods.*

עָנָיו, אֱמָר־נָא מָה רָאִיתָ!
'רָאִיתִי אֵשׁ בַּסְּנֶה וְאֵינָהּ בּוֹעֲרָה.
בְּהִסְתַּכְּלִי לִרְאוֹת חַלְתִּי וָאִירָא.
גֵּאֶה קוֹלוֹ בְּהַר חָמַד קָרָא,
דְּבַר יְיָ נָכוֹן וְהִרְתִּיעָה בָרָה.
וְלֹא יָכֹלְתִּי לִרְאוֹת דְּמוּת אָיֹם וְנוֹרָא,
מוֹנֶה מִסְפָּר לַכּוֹכָבִים, לְכֻלָּם שֵׁמוֹת יִקְרָא.'

O humble one, tell what you saw. 'I
saw a flame in the thorn-bush, but it
did not burn. When I gazed at it, I
recoiled in fear. The Proud One called
out from His cherished mountain. The
word of the Lord rang out and the
people drew back. But I could not see
the image of Him, dread and terrible,
*who numbers the stars one by one, and
calls each one by its name.*'

בֶּן אָמוֹץ, אֱמָר־נָא מָה רָאִיתָ!
'רָאִיתִי הַיּוֹשֵׁב עַל כֵּס, מְשׁוֹטֵט חִקְרֵי נְשִׁיָּה,
וְשׁוּלָיו מְלֵאִים הֵיכַל שְׁמֵי עָלִיָּה.

O son of Amoz, tell what you saw.
'I saw Him who sits upon a throne,
scanning the limits of the earth, as His
train filled the temple of the uppermost

1. Over the drowning Egyptians.
2. Aaron, who later checked the plague; Numbers 17.11.
3. Exodus 20.2; the first sentence of the Ten Commandments.

243

זֶה לָזֶה קוֹרְאִים קְדֻשָּׁתוֹ לִשְׁעָיָה,
חִתִּים אַמּוֹת הַסִּפִּים מֵאֵימָתוֹ בְּיִרְאָה.
וְלֹא יָכֹלְתִּי לִרְאוֹת אֱלוֹהַּ כָּל בְּרִיָּה,
גְּדֹל הָעֵצָה וְרַב הָעֲלִילִיָּה.'

heavens. The seraphim called one to
another, saying the Thrice Holy[1] so
that He should heed them. For fear of
Him, the threshold trembled to its
foundations. But I could not see the
God of all creatures, who is *great in
counsel and mighty in deed*.'

בֶּן בּוּזִי, אֱמָר־נָא מָה רָאִיתָ!
'רָאִיתִי טַפְסְרֵי חַיָלֵי גְדוּדֵי צְבָאוֹת,
יַחַד כְּמַרְאֶה הַבָּזָק רָצוֹא וָשׁוֹב בְּנוֹרָאוֹת.
כְּקוֹל מַיִם רַבִּים כַּנְפֵיהֶם דָּאוֹת.
לְמוּלָם נִרְאוֹת נוֹשְׂאוֹת וְהֵם נִשָּׂאוֹת,
וְלֹא יָכֹלְתִּי לִרְאוֹת דְּמוּת עוֹשֵׂה נוֹרָאוֹת,
קָדוֹשׁ קָדוֹשׁ קָדוֹשׁ יְיָ צְבָאוֹת.'

O son of Buzi, tell what you saw. 'I saw
the angels – legions, armies, and hosts –
like a flash of lightning, all fearfully
darting to and fro, their beating wings
like the sound of many waters. And the
holy creatures, facing them, seemed to
be bearing the throne though they were
borne by it. But I could not see the
image of Him who does awesome
deeds, the *holy, holy, holy Lord of
Hosts*.'

אִישׁ־חֲמֻדוֹת, אֱמָר־נָא מָה רָאִיתָ!
'רָאִיתִי מִזֵּעַת חַיּוֹת נַהֲרֵי לַהַב מוֹשְׁכִים,
נִשְׁגָּב חָן עַל כִּסְאוֹ – מִפַּחְדּוֹ הֵם נִמְשָׁכִים;
שְׂעַר רֵאשֵׁהּ כַּעֲמַר נְקֵא וְהוּא מַחֲלִיף
וּמַעֲבִיר מְלָכִים,
עַל חוּג הָאָרֶץ יוֹשֵׁב מֶלֶךְ מַלְכֵי הַמְּלָכִים.
וְלֹא יָכֹלְתִּי לִרְאוֹת דְּמוּת הַנּוֹתֵן תְּשׁוּעָה לַמְּלָכִים,
מַשְׁגִּיחַ מִן הַחַלּוֹנוֹת, מֵצִיץ מִן הַחֲרַכִּים.'

O man greatly beloved, tell what you
saw. 'I saw fiery rivers streaming from
the sweat of the holy creatures. The
Lofty One rested upon His throne; it
was His dread that made them stream
forth. The hair of His head was like
pure wool. He replaced kings, removed
kings – the King of all kings, throned
on the vaulted roof of the earth. But I
could not see the image of Him who
gives victory to kings, *who looks in at
the windows, gazes through the lattice*.'

מִימִינוֹ אֵשׁ דָּת וּמִשְּׂמֹאלוֹ אֵשׁ
וּלְפָנָיו אֵשׁ וְאַחֲרָיו אֵשׁ
וְהוּא אֵשׁ אוֹכְלָה אֵשׁ, וְעַמּוֹ בֵּית אֵשׁ
וּמַלְאָכָיו חֶצְיָם מַיִם וְחֶצְיָם אֵשׁ
וְהֵם טוֹבְלִים בְּנַהֲרֵי אֵשׁ
וְעוֹנִים וְאוֹמְרִים: בָּרוּךְ כְּבוֹדוֹ מִמְּקוֹמוֹ!'

There are flaming fires at His right and
fires at His left; fire before Him and
fire behind Him; He is a fire that
devours fire, His people are a house of
fire; his angels are half water and half
fire; they immerse themselves in rivers
of fire, then proclaim: *Blessed be His
glory from His place!*'

---

1. The *Kedusha*: 'Holy, holy, holy is the Lord of Hosts' (Isaiah 6.3).

אַדְנֵי אֲדָמָה

THE CONTEST OF THE MOUNTAINS

אַדְנֵי אֲדָמָה הָיוּ מִתְפָּרְקִים
בְּרֶדֶת מְשָׁמַיִם שׁוֹכֵן שְׁחָקִים.
בָּנִים, מִקּוֹל בְּרָקִים, לֹא הָיוּ יוֹנְקִים
בְּשָׁמְעָם דְּבַר אֵל חַי מְפָרֵשׁ חֲקוּקִים.

The earth's foundations shook when
He who dwells in the clouds descended
from heaven. At the sound of the
lightning, infants ceased suckling, as
they heard the word of the living God
pronounce the Law on the Tablets.

יַקֵּר תְּיַקֵּר בַּבֹּקֶר בַּבֹּקֶר
כְּנִיהִי בַיּוֹם הַשְּׁלִישִׁי בְּחִית הַבֹּקֶר;
וְכֵן לְעֵת עֶרֶב יִהְיֶה אוֹר בֹּקֶר
לַמְתַנִּים שְׁבָחָךְ עֶרֶב וָבֹקֶר.

You shall be cherished ever more,
morning after morning, as *on the third
day, when morning came.*[1] And in the
evening, let there be morning light for
those who say Your praise evening and
morning.

גָּעֲשׁוּ וְרָעֲשׁוּ מִמְּקוֹמָם הָרִים
וְנָמוּ: 'אַיֵּה שׁוֹקֵל בְּפֶלֶס הָרִים?'
דִּבֶּר תָּבוֹר: 'אֲנִי גָבֹהַּ מִכָּל הָרִים
וְעָלַי נָאֶה לַחֲנוֹת יוֹצֵר הָרִים.'

The mountains heaved and quaked,
leaped from their places and said:
'Where is He who weighs the mountains on a balance?' Mount Tabor
declared: 'I am the highest of the
mountains; by right, the maker of
mountains should rest upon me.'

הָמָה כַרְמֶל וּבְתוֹךְ יָם בָּא
וְנָם: 'בִּי יַחֲנֶה נַעֲרָץ בְּסוֹד קְדוֹשִׁים רַבָּה.'
וְגַבְהוּתוֹ אוֹתוֹ תִּעֲבָה,
וְלֹא נֶאֱמַר לוֹ 'בָּרוּךְ הַבָּא'.

Mount Carmel spoke softly, as it moved
down to the sea, and said: 'He who is
feared in the council of the holy ones,
He shall rest upon me!' But, for his
pride, he was spurned and was not told
'Welcome'.

זָע סִינַי וְלֹא דִּבֶּר מְאוּמָה
וְנָם: 'אֵיךְ בִּי יַחֲנֶה שׁוֹכֵן רוּמָה?'
חַי הֱשִׁיבוֹ: 'עָלֶיךָ אֲקַדְּמָה,
כִּי הִשְׁפַּלְתָּ אֶת עַצְמָךְ אוֹתָךְ אָרִימָה.'

Mount Sinai shuddered but did not
speak. 'How could He who dwells on
high rest upon me?' The Living One
answered him: 'Upon you shall I greet
my people. Since you lowered yourself,
I shall raise you up.'

---

1. The day the Lord came down upon Mount Sinai (Exodus 19.16) to give the Torah.

טָהוֹר מָאַס כָּל הֶהָרִים הַגְּדוֹלִים,
כִּי מִקּוֹל אֵימָתוֹ נָפְלוּ חֲלָלִים.
יָרַד לְסִינַי וְעִמּוֹ כָּל חֲיָלִים
וְהִנְחִיל לְמֹשֶׁה פְּרָטִים וּכְלָלִים.

The Pure One disdained all the high
mountains. At His dread voice, they
were struck down. Then He descended
upon Sinai, with all His host, and
bestowed the Law[1] upon Moses.

יֵקַר תְּיֻקַר בַּבֹּקֶר בַּבֹּקֶר
כִּנְיִהִי בַיּוֹם הַשְּׁלִישִׁי בִּהְיֹת הַבֹּקֶר;
וְכֵן לְעֵת עֶרֶב יִהְיֶה אוֹר בֹּקֶר
לַמְחַנִּים שְׁבָחֲךָ עֶרֶב וָבֹקֶר.

You shall be cherished ever more,
morning after morning as *on the third
day, when morning came.* And in the
evening, let there be morning light for
those who say your praise evening and
morning.

מַלְאַךְ הַמָּוֶת   THE ANGEL OF DEATH SEEKS MOSES

[...] מַלְאַךְ הַמָּוֶת שָׁלַח בְּמֹשֶׁה:
׳אִם פִּיּוּסִים דַּבֵּר לְמֹשֶׁה,
אֱמָר־לוֹ: ״רַבָּנִי, רַבָּךְ אֶצְלְךָ שְׁלָחַנִי
נַפְשְׁךָ לְבַקֵּשׁ.״׳
וְלֹא קָם נָבִיא עוֹד בְּיִשְׂרָאֵל כְּמֹשֶׁה.

The Angel of Death was dispatched
against Moses: 'Speak soothing words
to Moses. Say to him, "O master, your
Master has sent me to you to request
your soul."' *Never again did there arise
in Israel a prophet like Moses.*[2]

סָעוּר יָצָא הַמַּלְאָךְ וְהָלַךְ אֶל הַסְּנֶה,
עָן: ׳שֶׁמָּא רָאִיתָ לְמֹשֶׁה רֹאשׁ רַבָּנִי?׳
פָּתַח לוֹ: ׳מִיּוֹם שֶׁהִלְהִיבָנִי בָּאֵשׁ לֹא רְאִיתִיו לְפָנָי.׳
וְלֹא קָם נָבִיא עוֹד בְּיִשְׂרָאֵל כְּמֹשֶׁה.

The Angel stormed forth, came to the
bush of thorns and said: 'Have you,
perchance, seen Moses, the chief
master?' It answered him: 'I have not
seen him since the day I was set
ablaze.' *Never again did there arise in
Israel a prophet like Moses.*

---

1. Lit. 'specific and general [precepts]'.
2. Deuteronomy 34.10.

246

צָעַד וְהָלַךְ אֶל הַיָּם הַגָּדוֹל,
קָרָא: 'שֶׁמָּא רָאִיתָ לְמֹשֶׁה הָרַב הַגָּדוֹל?'
רָחַשׁ: 'לֹא רְאִיתִיו מִיּוֹם שֶׁקְּרָעַנִי
וְהִרְעִיץ הַתַּנִּין הַגָּדוֹל.'
וְלֹא קָם נָבִיא עוֹד בְּיִשְׂרָאֵל כְּמֹשֶׁה.

He marched and came to the Great
Sea, shouting: 'Have you, perchance,
seen Moses, the great teacher?' It
murmured: 'I have not seen him since
the day he tore me apart and shattered
the Great Serpent (Pharaoh).' *Never
again did there arise in Israel a prophet
like Moses.*

שָׁאַג וְהָלַךְ אֶל הַר סִינַי,
שָׁאֲלוֹ: 'שֶׁמָּא רָאִיתָ לְמֹשֶׁה הֶעָנְוָנִי?'
תֵּנָּה לוֹ: 'לֹא רְאִיתִיו מִיּוֹם שֶׁקִּבֵּל תּוֹרָה מִסִּינַי.'
וְלֹא קָם נָבִיא עוֹד בְּיִשְׂרָאֵל כְּמֹשֶׁה.

Roaring, he went on to Mount Sinai
and asked: 'Have you, perchance, seen
Moses, the humble one?' It told him:
'I have not seen him since the day he
received the Law on Sinai.' *Never again
did there arise in Israel a prophet like
Moses.*

וְנַפְשׁוֹ בִּנְשִׁיקָה קִבֵּל הַמְּקֻדָּשׁ בְּפִי חַיּוֹת וְאוֹפַנִּים.

But He had already taken his soul with
a kiss – He who is hallowed by the
holy creatures and the angels of the
chariot.

לֹא תְאַחֵר לְהָשִׁיב
THE POET'S COMMAND-MENTS TO GOD

לֹא תְאַחֵר לְהָשִׁיב שְׁאֵלַת קוֹרַאֲךָ בְּכָל לִבּוֹ.
לֹא תִבְזֶה עֱנוּת עָנִי בְּהִתְחַנְנוֹ אֵלֶיךָ בְּנִיבוֹ.
לֹא תִגְעַר בְּרָשׁ וְאִישׁ תְּכָכִים לְפָנֶיךָ בְּהִתְיַצְּבוֹ.
לֹא תִדְחֶה אֶת יְצוּרְךָ מִפִּתְחֲךָ רֵיקָם לַהֲשִׁיבוֹ.
לֹא תַהַכְּרֵהוּ וְתַכְלִימֵהוּ עַל חַטָּאתוֹ וְחוֹבוֹ.
לֹא תוֹכִיחֶנּוּ בְּאַפְּךָ אֶת דְּרָכָיו בְּעָזְבוֹ.
לֹא תִזְכָּר־לוֹ עֲווֹנוֹתָיו הָרִאשׁוֹנִים הַטְּמוּנִים בְּחֻבּוֹ
לֹא תַחֲבֹל עֲבוֹטוֹ עַל פְּשָׁעוֹ אֲשֶׁר נִגְאַל בּוֹ.
לֹא תִטְרֹד הָרָחוֹק בְּשִׁיבָתוֹ, כִּי קָרוֹב תְּקָרְבוֹ.

You shall not withhold Your answer
from him who cries to You with all his
heart. You shall not despise the afflicted
wretch when he implores You for
mercy. You shall not berate the poor
and downtrodden, when he appears
before You. You shall not turn Your
creature away from Your door empty-
handed. You shall not grieve him or
shame him for his sin and guilt. You
shall not rebuke him in Your anger
once he forsakes his ways. You shall
not remember against him his early
sins, buried in his bosom. You shall not
take his pledge in pawn for having
defiled himself with crime. You shall
not banish him who strays afar, but

לֹא תְיַסְּרֵנּוּ בַחֲמָתֶךָ, כִּי רַפּוֹא תִרְפָּא מַכְאוֹבוֹ.
לֹא תְכַלֶּה רָשָׁע וְסוֹרֵר מִדְּרָכָיו בְּשׁוּבוֹ.
לֹא תִלְחָצֶנּוּ לְגָמְלוֹ כְּרֹעַ מַעֲלָלוֹ וְאַרְבּוֹ.
לֹא תִמְשֹׁךְ אַפְּךָ עַל עַמְּךָ בְּדוֹר וָדוֹר בְּעַצְבּוֹ.
לֹא תִנְטְשֵׁהוּ וְתַזְנִיחֵהוּ כִּי גָדַל לִמְאֹד כְּאֵבוֹ.
לֹא תַסְגִּירֵהוּ לָעַד בְּיַד צָרוֹ וְאוֹיְבוֹ.
לֹא תַעֲזֹב אֶת נְוֵה קָדְשְׁךָ לְשַׁמְּמוֹ וְחָרְבּוֹ.
לֹא תָפִיג אֶת שֵׁם קָדְשְׁךָ לְחַלְּלוֹ בְּיַד לוֹעֲבוֹ.
לֹא תַצְמִית וּתְבַיֵּשׁ מִסַּבְרְךָ יִשְׂרָאֵל עַם קְרוֹבוֹ.
לֹא תָקוּץ בְּשִׂיחִי בְּעָמְדִי לְפָנֶיךָ כְּעָנִי לָבוֹא.
לֹא תִרְחַק מֶנִּי, אֵלִי צוּרִי אֶחֱסֶה בּוֹ.
לֹא תִשְׁכַּח אֶת צָרוֹתַי אֲשֶׁר עָבְרוּ עָלַי
וְעֶלְבּוֹנִי מִי יַחְשְׁבוֹ!
לֹא תִתְעַלַּם מִתְּחִנָּתִי, וְאֶנְקָתִי אֵלֶיךָ תָבוֹא!

shall draw him near when he returns. You shall not chasten him in anger, but shall remedy his pain. You shall not destroy the wicked and rebellious when he turns from his course. You shall not oppress him and requite him for his evildoing and deceit. You shall not prolong Your anger with Your sorrowing people to all generations. You shall not forsake them or cast them off, for their suffering is very great. You shall not deliver them forever into the hands of their foes. You shall not abandon Your holy abode to desolation and ruin. You shall not enfeeble Your holy name, and let it be profaned by those who flout it. You shall not frustrate or put to shame the hope placed in You by the people of Israel, who are close to You. You shall not abhor my complaint when I come to stand before You like a pauper. You shall not be far from me, my God, my Rock, in whom I take refuge. You shall not forget the troubles that have swept over me, for who can measure my humiliation? You shall not hide Yourself when I beseech You: let my sighs come before You!

אֵבֶל וּבְכִי
DEATH THE PLUNDERER

אֵבֶל וּבְכִי
אֵין מוֹעִילִין לוֹ לְאָדָם בִּמְלֹאוֹת סִפְקוֹ.
בְּזָהָב לֹא יִפָּדֶה וּבְכֶסֶף לֹא יִנָּצֵל מִיּוֹם הַדִּין.
בִּרְאוֹתוֹ שׁוֹדֵד לוֹבֵשׁ אַף וּמְכֻסֶּה חֵמָה,
גַּם הוֹכִיחוֹ
עֵקֶב לִבּוֹ וּפֹעַל כַּפָּיו.
דְּמָעוֹת מוֹרִיד
בְּשָׁמְעוֹ תַּחְבּוּלוֹתָיו מִפִּי שׁוֹדְדוֹ.

Mourning and weeping do not avail a man when his measure is full. Gold cannot ransom him or silver save him from the Day of Judgement. He beholds the Plunderer clothed in anger, covered in wrath, rebuking him for his heart's deceit and the works of his hands. He weeps as he hears his treacherous acts from the mouth of the

Plunderer. He begs him: 'Oh, take
ransom and do not destroy me.' But
the Plunderer replies: 'Don't be foolish.
Has a man ever been redeemed by
ransom? This is the rule and the road
for all who are born of the seed of man:
none may be saved from death.' Then
the throes of death overtake him, the
pangs of death beset him from all sides.
About to perish, he fixes his gaze on
the Plunderer, and his face changes.
He reaches out and signs everything
that is read to him. Then the Plunderer
draws near and stands at the head of
his bed. When he sees the drawn
sword, he knows. Trembling, he opens
his mouth. A drop of poison is thrust
into his mouth, more bitter than any
bitterness. From that drop he dies,
from that he putrefies, from that his
face turns green. His friends and
kinsmen mourn over him as he lies
there like a stone. He is carried on a
bier and led to the grave. Two ministering angels – his escorts during his
lifetime – now escort him to the grave.
They turn here and there, listening to
what is said around his bier. They note
down his just deeds and his falsehoods,
and affix their seal; this will be part of
the final reckoning. As he approaches
the grave, all the organs of his body[1]

הוּא מִתְחַנֵּן :
'לְקַח־נָא כֹּפֶר וְאַל תַּשְׁחִיתֵנִי !'
וּמֵשִׁיח לוֹ שׁוֹדֵד :
'מַה לְּךָ לְשְׁטוּת ? מִי זֶה אָדָם שֶׁנִּפְדָּה בְּכֹפֶר ?
זוֹ הִיא מִדָּה וְזֹאת הִיא דֶּרֶךְ
לְכָל בְּנֵי זֶרַע אָדָם, שֶׁלֹּא יִנָּצֵל מִן הַמִּיתָה.'
חֲבָלִים מַשִּׂיגִין אוֹתוֹ,
צִירֵי מָוֶת מִפֹּה וּמִפֹּה.
טֶרֶם אָבָד,
וְנוֹתֵן בּוֹ עֵינָיו וּמַרְאִיתוֹ נֶהְפָּכֶת.
יָדוֹ מוֹשִׁיט וְחוֹתֵם עַל כָּל מַה שֶּׁקּוֹרִין לְפָנָיו.
בְּגִשְׁתּוֹ אֵלָיו, יַעֲמֹד מְרַאֲשׁוֹתָיו.
כִּרְאוֹתוֹ חֶרֶב שְׁלוּפָה – כְּיוֹדֵעַ, זָע וּפוֹתֵחַ פִּיו.
לְתוֹךְ פִּיו מֻשְׁלָךְ
טִפָּה מָרָה, שֶׁהִיא עֲצוּמָה מִכָּל מָר :
מִמֶּנָּה מֵת,
מִמֶּנָּה מַסְרִיחַ וּמִמֶּנָּה פָּנָיו מוֹרִיקוֹת.
נֶאֱנָחִים עָלָיו
אוֹהֲבָיו וּקְרוֹבָיו וְהוּא מֻשְׁלָךְ כְּאָבֶן.
סָאִין אוֹתוֹ עַל הַמִּטָּה
לְהוֹלִיכוֹ לַקֶּבֶר.
עִמּוֹ מִתְלַוִּין
שְׁנֵי מַלְאֲכֵי שָׁרֵת שֶׁמְלַוִּין לוֹ בְּחַיָּיו.
פּוֹנִין הֵנָּה וָהֵנָּה,
מַקְשִׁיבִין מַה מְּשִׂיחִין אַחֲרֵי מִטָּתוֹ,
צִדְקוֹ וְכִזְבוֹ
כּוֹתְבִין וְחוֹתְמִין וּמַעֲלִין לְחֶשְׁבּוֹן.
קָרַב לַקֶּבֶר –
רָעֲשׁוּ מָאתַיִם וְאַרְבָּעִים וּשְׁמוֹנָה אֲבָרָיו.

1. Lit. 'his 248 organs', a conventional Talmudic phrase.

רַעַד וָפַחַד אוֹחֲזוֹ
בְּהַסִּיעוֹ מִן הַמִּטָּה לְהוֹרִידוֹ לַקֶּבֶר.
שְׁכְנוּהוּ בַקֶּבֶר וְהִשְׁלִיכוּ עָפָר עַל פָּנָיו.
שִׁבְעַת יָמִים קָשִׁין לַגּוּף יוֹתֵר מִן הַמִּיתָה.
תָּמְהוּ וְנֶחְפְּזוּ
כָּל טוֹמְנָיו וְחוֹזְרִין מֵאַחֲרָיו.

quiver. Terror and trembling seize him
when he is removed from the bier to be
lowered into the grave. They lodge him
in the grave, throw dirt on his face.
The seven days to come are more
painful to the body than the moment
of death. All those who buried him
now shudder and run away from him.

זְכָר־זֹאת, אֱלוֹהַּ מָעֻזֵּנוּ,
וְהִתְנַהֵג עִמָּנוּ בְּמִדַּת רַחֲמִים.
אַתָּה רַחֲמָן, מָלֵא רַחֲמִים!

Remember this, God our Stronghold,
and favour us with Your mercy. For
You are merciful, Most Merciful One!

נִגַּשְׁנוּ לָדַעַת   LAMENT FOR ZION

נִגַּשְׁנוּ לָדַעַת אֶת שְׁלוֹם אִמֵּנוּ,
עָמַדְנוּ עַל פִּתְחָהּ וּבָכִינוּ.
מְצָאוּנוּ הַשּׁוֹמְרִים, הִכּוּנוּ, פְּצָעוּנוּ —
'סוּרוּ, טָמֵא!' קָרְאוּ לָנוּ.

We drew near to find out how our
mother was faring. We stood at her
door and wept. The watchmen found
us, beat us, wounded us: 'Away,
unclean ones!' they shouted.

אָתָאנוּ שֵׁנִית וְלֹא נִגַּשְׁנוּ,
וְעַל רֹאשׁ הָהָר מֵרָחוֹק עָמַדְנוּ.
יוֹשֶׁבֶת־בָּדָד יָצְאָה לִקְרָאתֵנוּ,
נִשְׁקְפָה מִכִּלְאָהּ וְעָמְדָה נֶגְדֵּנוּ.

Again we came but did not draw near;
from afar, we stood at the top of the
Mount [of Olives]. The solitary one[1]
appeared before us; she looked out
from her prison as she faced us.

נָשָׂאנוּ עֵינֵינוּ לִרְאוֹתָהּ
וְלֹא הִכַּרְנוּהָ מֵרֹעַ מַרְאִיתָהּ.
סָר תָּכְנִיתָהּ וְכָל תַּבְנִיתָהּ,
אֲסוּרָה בַכֶּבֶל וְהִכְבִּידוּ נְחֻשְׁתָּהּ.

We raised our eyes to see her but could
not recognize her, so wasted did she
look. She had lost her shape, her form
was gone; she was bound in chains and
weighed down by her fetters.

---

1. An epithet for the captive Zion, derived from Lamentations 1.1.

נָשָׂאנוּ קוֹלֵנוּ בִּבְכִיָּה
עַל חִלּוּל הַר הַמּוֹרִיָּה
וְעַל אִמֵּנוּ הָעֲנִיָּה,
כִּי לֹא נִשְׁאַר לָהּ מִחְיָה.

We raised our voices in lament for the
desecration of Mount Moriah and for
our poor mother, who had nothing left
to sustain her.

צַעֲקָתֵנוּ עָלְתָה בְּאָזְנָהּ,
אַף הִיא קוֹלָהּ נָתָנָה.
בָּכְתָה בְּתַחֲנוּנִים וְנָשְׂאָה קִינָה:
'הִנְנִי יוֹשֶׁבֶת כְּאַלְמָנָה.

Our cries reached her ears and she too
wept aloud. She wept and implored and
lamented: 'How like a widow am I!

בָּנַי הָלְכוּ בַשִּׁבְיָה
וּמִקְדָּשִׁי נִתַּן לִשְׁאִיָּה
וְנִשְׁאַרְתִּי עֵרֹם וְעֶרְיָה –
עַל אֵלֶּה אֲנִי בוֹכִיָּה.'

'My children have gone into captivity,
my sanctuary is laid waste, and I am
left naked and bare – *for these things do
I weep!*'[1]

אוֹר נֹגַהּ   THE SANCTIFICATION

אוֹר נֹגַהּ עֹטְיָה מְעִילוֹ,
בָּרוּךְ שֵׁם כְּבוֹד גָּדְלוֹ,
גִּבּוֹר כֹּחַ וְשַׂגִּיא חֵילוֹ:
שְׂרָפִים עוֹמְדִים מִמַּעַל לוֹ.

He wraps Himself in a cloak of morning
light. Blessed is the name of His great
glory. His hosts are very mighty.
Seraphim stand above Him.

דָּר בְּשִׁבְעָה וְהוּא בְאֶחָד:
הוּא לְבַדּוֹ בְּיִחוּד נִתְיֶחָד,
וְעִמּוֹ צְבָא הַמְשֵׁל וָפַחַד,
שֵׁשׁ כְּנָפַיִם שֵׁשׁ כְּנָפַיִם לְאֶחָד.

He dwells in the seven heavens, yet is
one. No one but He is one. With Him
are the legions of dominion and fear.
Each has six wings.

1. Lamentations 1.16.

זָהֲרֵי שְׁבִיבֵי אוּר בִּפְנִינָיו,
חֶסֶד וֶאֱמֶת יְקַדְּמוּ פָנָיו,
טְכוּסֵי גַּלְגַּל הֵם אוֹפַנָּיו,
בִּשְׁתַּיִם יְכַסֶּה פָנָיו.

Flames glow in his angels of pearl.
Love and truth herald His coming. His
ofanim[1] are arrayed like wheels. *With
two he covers his face.*

יְקוֹד סוּפָה וָסַעַר מַעְגָּלָיו,
כִּלּוּל עָנָן אָבַק רַגְלָיו,
לַהֶטֶת אֵשׁ בּוֹעֶרֶת גַּלְגַּלָּיו,
וּבִשְׁתַּיִם יְכַסֶּה רַגְלָיו.

Flaming storm and whirlwind are His
paths. The crests of clouds are the dust
at His feet. His wheels are blazing fire.
And with two he covers his feet.

מַלְאָךְ בְּתֻפֵּי לַהַב מְתוֹפֵף,
נְגִינוֹת חֲדָשׁוֹת לְחַדֵּשׁ וּלְנוֹפֵף;
שִׂיחַ כַּנֶּשֶׁר יַשְׁמִיעַ וִיצַפְצֵף,
וּבִשְׁתַּיִם יְעוֹפֵף.

An angel beats fiery drums, waving
new songs to Him, soars screaming like
an eagle. *And with two he flies.*

עִמּוֹ כָּל מִינֵי זֶמֶר,
'פֶּלְאִי' הוּא שְׁמוֹ, נֶאֱמַר;
צִלְצוּל קְדֻשָּׁתוֹ לַעֲנוֹת וְלוֹמַר:
וְקָרָא זֶה אֶל זֶה וְאָמַר.

Singing of every kind attends Him. It
is written[2] that 'His name is a mystery'.
To celebrate His sanctity in song, *one
calls to the other and says –*

קוֹל יַשְׁמִיעוּ מֵאַרְבַּע תּוֹצָאוֹת,
רְבוּעִים וּמְרֻבָּעִים לְכָל יְצִיאוֹת;
שׁוֹאֲגִים בְּקוֹל צָבָא וָאוֹת:
'קָדוֹשׁ קָדוֹשׁ קָדוֹשׁ יְיָ צְבָאוֹת'.

Four-sided, facing in all directions,
they cry out from the four quarters.
Legions and standards roar: *Holy, holy,
holy is the Lord of the hosts.*

תַּחַת וָמַעַל יָסְדָה יָדוֹ,
תּוֹלֶה תֵבֵל בִּזְרוֹעַ יָדוֹ,
תַּקִּיף, וְאֵין עוֹד מִלְבַדּוֹ:
'מְלֹא כָל הָאָרֶץ כְּבוֹדוֹ'.

His hand founded earth and heaven.
The universe hangs upon His mighty
arm. The power is His, there is no
other. *The whole earth is full of His
glory!*

---

1. Angels attending the chariot.   2. Judges 13.18.

252

סְעַדְיָה נָאוֹן *Sa'adiah Gaon*

גָּדַלְתָּ מְאֹד YOU ARE GREAT INDEED!

גָּדַלְתָּ מְאֹד מִכָּל הַתּוֹכְנִים,
כִּי הֵמָּה יְתַכְּנוּ הַתַּחְתּוֹן וְעָלָיו יִבְנוּ הָעֶלְיוֹן –
וְאַתָּה תִכַּנְתָּ הַשָּׁמַיִם תְּחִלָּה וְתַחְתֵּימוֹ
רָקַעְתָּ הָאָרֶץ לַחֲבִיוֹן.
יְיָ אֱלֹהַי, גָּדַלְתָּ מְאֹד !

You are far greater than all architects:
for they fix the lower, then erect the
upper part above it; but You first fixed
the heavens, then stretched the earth
beneath them as a haven. *O Lord my
God, You are great indeed!*

גָּדַלְתָּ מְאֹד מִכָּל הַשּׁוֹמְעִים,
כִּי כֻלָּם לֹא יָבִינוּ דִּבְרֵי שְׁנַיִם מְדַבְּרִים
כְּאֶחָד לְמוּלָם –
וְאַתָּה שׁוֹמֵעַ דִּבְרֵי כָל קַצְוֵי אֶרֶץ וְאִיֵּי הַיָּם,
וְדָבָר מִמְּךָ לֹא נֶעְלָם.
יְיָ אֱלֹהַי, גָּדַלְתָּ מְאֹד !

You are far greater than all those who
have hearing: for they cannot grasp the
words of two people who address them
at the same time; but You hear what is
said by all the ends of the earth, as well
as the islands of the sea; nothing
escapes You. *O Lord my God, You are
great indeed!*

גָּדַלְתָּ מְאֹד מִכָּל הָרָמִים,
כִּי הֵמָּה רוּמָם וְגָבְהָם יֵשׁ לְמַעְלָה מִמֶּנּוּ
רוּם וָגֹבַהּ –
וְאַתָּה רָם עַל כָּל רָמִים, וְאֵין רוּם לְפָנֶיךָ לְכָל גֹּבַהּ.
יְיָ אֱלֹהַי, גָּדַלְתָּ מְאֹד !

You are far greater than all the lofty
ones: for though they are lofty and
high, yet is there loftiness and height
beyond them; but You are the highest
of the high; no loftiness is high to You.
O Lord my God, You are great indeed!

גָּדַלְתָּ מְאֹד מִכָּל הַקּוֹבְעִים מַחַן,
כִּי כֻלָּם בָּאָרֶץ יִקְבָּעוּן, וּבְהָרֵי תּוֹעָפוֹת –
וְאַתָּה קָבַעְתָּ בָּאֲוִיר מַחַן לְכָל עֵיט צִפּוֹר וְלָעוֹפוֹת.
יְיָ אֱלֹהַי, גָּדַלְתָּ מְאֹד !

You are far greater than all those who
set up encampments: for they set them
up on the earth, even on steep mountains; but You made the birds of prey
and winged creatures encamp in the
air. *O Lord my God, You are great
indeed!*

גָּדַלְתָּ מְאֹד מִכָּל הַצַּיָּרִים,
כִּי הֵמָּה יָצוּרוּ בָאוֹר וּבְפַלְדוֹת אוּרִים –

You are far greater than all artists: for
they can only make forms by the light
of day or fire; but You form all life

253

וְאַתָּה צָרַפְתָּ אֶת כָּל הַחַיִּים בְּמֵעַיִם וּבְסְתָרִים
וּבְחַדְרֵי חֲדָרִים.
יְיָ אֱלֹהַי, גָּדַלְתָּ מְאֹד! [...]

within the entrails, in the hidden
recesses and innermost chambers.
O Lord my God, You are great indeed!

שְׁמוּאֵל הַשְּׁלִישִׁי

Samuel Hashelishi

שָׁאַפְנוּ צֵל

THE MESSAGE

שָׁאַפְנוּ צֵל מְקַוִּים לִישַׁעֲךָ,
כִּשְׂכִיר פָּעֳלוֹ יְקַוֶּה.
מְצַפֶּה הֶעֱמַדְנוּ,
אֲשֶׁר יִרְאֶה – יַגִּיד, יְחַוֶּה.
וַנְּיַחֲלָה לְהִתְבַּשֵּׂר: 'בָּא גוֹאֵל
כְּמַסְתִּיר פָּנָיו בַּמַּסְוֶה.'
אָמוֹר אָמַר: 'שׁוּבוּ אֶחָיו,
וְאִם אַיִן – בְּעִתּוֹ יִנְוֶה.'
לִבֵּנוּ אֲזַי נִשְׁבָּר
וְכָל הַדָּוֶה – עַל כָּךְ יִדְוֶה.

We longed for Your salvation as one
sighs for the shade, as a servant pines
for his wages. We posted a lookout who
would report whatever he saw. We
hoped to hear good tidings: 'The
redeemer has come! He is like the one
who covered his face with a veil!'[1]' But
the lookout said: 'Come back again;
and if he is not yet here, he will appear
in due time.' Then our hearts broke.
All those who grieve – it is this that
they grieve for.

דַּכָּא תָּשֵׁב אֱנוֹשׁ

RESURRECTION

דַּכָּא תָּשֵׁב אֱנוֹשׁ וְתָשׁוּב פָּחֹן וְתַחֲנֹן.
גְּרָמִים תְּדַבֵּק, גִּידִים תִּמְתַּח, וְגֹנֵן תִּגְנֹן,
בָּשָׂר תַּעֲלֶה, וְהָעוֹר תַּקְרִים בְּנוֹף יִצֹּן.
אֲהוּבְךָ יִפְרַח כַּשּׁוֹשַׁנָּה, יַךְ שָׁרָשָׁיו כַּלְּבָנוֹן.

You turn man back into dust, but You
will turn to him again with compassion.
You will join his bones, stretch his
sinews and protect him. You will put
flesh upon him, cover him with skin –
when the Messiah comes. Then Your
loved one will blossom like the lily, and
strike root like the poplar.

1. I.e. Moses; Exodus 34.33 ff.

אִישׁ מְשׁוֹרֵר   DAVID'S LAST WORDS TO SOLOMON

אִישׁ מְשׁוֹרֵר,
שַׁחַר מְעוֹרֵר,
צֶדֶק בּוֹרֵר
וּתְמִימוּת;
בְּבוֹא קִצּוֹ
פְּנוֹת לְרִבְצוֹ,
הֵיטִיב יְעָצוֹ
בִּנְאִימוּת;
גִּלָּה חֶפְצוֹ
וְחִזֵּק נִצּוֹ
הֱיוֹת בְּמַעֲרִיצוֹ
עָמוּת.
'וַיִּקְרְבוּ יְמֵי דָוִד לָמוּת' [...]

On his last day, about to go to his resting place, the singer who awoke the dawn with song, who cherished justice and righteousness, raised his voice to give good counsel. He disclosed his heart's desire and urged his offshoot to cling to his dread God. *Then the time of David's death drew near.*

'יְרָא בְּרַעַד
מְשׁוֹכֵן עַד,
הַמְכוֹנֵן מִצְעַד
גָּבֶר.
כָּל דְּבָרַי אֵלֶּה
נְצֹר וּמַלֵּא,
וְכַנְּשָׁרִים תַּעֲלֶה
אֵבֶר.
לְדַכָּא מְיַחֶלֶת
הַלְאָט מְנַהֶלֶת,
וְתִמְצָא תּוֹחֶלֶת
וָסֵבֶר.'
'לְמַעַן יָקִים יְיָ אֶת דְּבָרוֹ אֲשֶׁר דִּבֶּר' [...]

'Fear and tremble before the Dweller of Eternity, who orders the steps of man. If you heed all my words, you will grow wings like an eagle. The Daughter of Zion is contrite, filled with longing; lead her gently, so that she may find hope and cheer' *so that the Lord may fulfil the promise that He made.*

תַּצְמִיחַ חָטְרוֹ
וְתָחֹק מִשְׁטְרוֹ
וְנֵזֶר תְּעַטְּרוֹ
בְּמֵישָׁרִים.
תְּהַדֵּר מוֹשָׁבוֹ
וּבֶטַח תּוֹשִׁיבוֹ
וְיִמְסֹךְ מַשְׁאַבּוֹ
לַיְשָׁרִים.
תִּזְכֹּר לְשָׁכוּלָה
אַהֲבַת כְּלוּלָה
וְתַעְדֶּה כַּכַּלָּה
קִשּׁוּרִים.
תּוֹצִיא בַּכְּשָׁרוֹת
בַּכּוֹשָׁרוֹת,
וִיקַדְּמוּךָ שָׁרוֹת
וְשָׁרִים.

Oh spread David's branch, impose his
rule, and crown him with his rightful
diadem. Glorify his throne, make him
sit securely. Let him water the righteous
from his wellspring. The Daughter of
Zion is bereaved; remember the love of
her bridal days, and let her adorn
herself with ribbons like a bride. When
the time has come, bring out the
prisoner safe and sound. Then will men
and women, singing, welcome You.

יִפָּתְחוּ קִבְרוֹת מְתֵי מִסְפָּר

PRAYER FOR RESURRECTION

יִפָּתְחוּ קִבְרוֹת מְתֵי מִסְפָּר,
יִגֶּלֶה מֵעֵינֵיהֶם עָפָר.
זָב גּוּפָם וְנִתְעַפָּר,
וְצַף עַצְמָם וּפֻרְפָּר.
כִּלְאָם – עַד אָנָה יוּפָר?
כֶּהְיָם – מָתַי יָצְפַּר?
הַעִירֵם בְּקוֹל שׁוֹפָר,
הֵן בְּיָקְצָם שִׁבְחֲךָ יֻסְפָּר.
'וִידַעְתֶּם כִּי אֲנִי יְיָ בְּפָתְחִי אֶת קִבְרוֹתֵיכֶם.'

Let the graves of the few[1] be opened;
let the dust be removed from upon
their eyes. Their bodies have wasted
away in the dust; their bones have been
crushed and battered. When will their
prison crumble? When will their
darkness turn to dawn? Arouse them
with a trumpet blast; for when they
awaken, Your glory will be told.
'*You shall know that I am the Lord
when I open your graves.*'

---

1. The children of Israel.

יְחֶזְקֵאל הַכֹּהֵן   *Ezekiel Hakohen*

אָמַרְתִּי לָאֲבָנִים   I SAID TO THE STONES

אָמַרְתִּי לָאֲבָנִים בְּשָׂגֵּין גָּלוּי, לֹא לָחוּשׁ:
'הָבוּ לִי מִכֹּחֲכֶם, אוּלַי אוּכַל לָחוּשׁ,
כִּי יְגוֹנִים כִּלּוּנִי וַיְשִׂימוּנִי כָּחוּשׁ —
אִם כֹּחַ אֲבָנִים כֹּחִי, אִם בְּשָׂרִי נָחוּשׁ ?'

I said to the stones distinctly, not in a whisper: 'Give me of your strength, so that I may feel again; for griefs have consumed me and made me lean. *Is my strength the strength of stones? Is my flesh made of bronze?*'

אָמַרְתִּי לְגִבְהֵי נֶשֶׁר הַדָּאִים לְכָל פִּנָּה:
'הַדְאוּנִי עִמָּכֶם וְאֶרְאֶה דּוֹדִי אָנָה פָּנָה,
כִּי חוֹלַת אַהֲבָה אֲנִי וְנַפְשִׁי מְסֻכָּנָה —
מִי יִתֶּן לִי אֵבֶר כַּיּוֹנָה, אָעוּפָה וְאֶשְׁכֹּנָה !'

I said to the loftiest eagles, who soar in all directions: 'Lift me with you in flight, so that I may see where my Beloved is gone; for I am faint with love, and my soul is in agony. *If only I had the wings of a dove, to fly away and find rest!*'

אָמַרְתִּי לְהַרְרֵי בְשָׂמִים, מְקוֹם דִּלּוּג הָעֹפֶר:
'הִזָּסְרוּ וְאַל תִּתְגָּאוּ בַּאֲשֶׁר מִכֶּם הַמֹּר וְהַכֹּפֶר,
כִּי זְרוֹעוֹתַי נָטְפוּ מֹר בְּדוֹד הֶחָסֹן וְהַשֶּׁפֶר —
וַיְגָרֵס בֶּחָצָץ שִׁנָּי, הִכְפִּישַׁנִי בָאֵפֶר.'

I said to the spice-bearing mountains, where the fawn leaps: 'Take heed; do not be proud that you are favoured with myrrh and henna. My arms too once dripped with myrrh for my strong and graceful lover, *but he broke my teeth on gravel, and trampled me in ashes.*'

אָמַרְתִּי לְזֹרְמֵי עָבוֹת אֲשֶׁר צִיָּה מְמוֹגְגוֹת:
'הָחִישׁוּ וּרְאוּ אֵיךְ עֵינַי מַזְלִיגוֹת,
כִּי קָדַח בָּרָק בְּכוֹתַי, לְבָבִי שָׁם כִּפְלָגוֹת —
עֵינִי נִגְּרָה, וְלֹא תִדְמֶה, מֵאֵין הֲפֻגוֹת.'

I said to the flowing clouds that soften deserts: 'Come quickly, see how my eyes are streaming; for lightning has seared my eyeballs, and split my heart into runnels of water. *My eyes flow unceasingly, without respite.*'

אָמַרְתִּי לְטַרְפֵּי אִילָנוֹת וָאַשְׁבִּיעֵם בְּאֵלִי:
'הֱיוּ סֵתֶר לִי פֶּן הַחֶרֶב יְשַׁכְּלִי,
כִּי אָהֳלִי שֻׁדָּד וְנֶהֱרַס הֵיכָלִי —
בָּנַי יְצָאַנִי וְאֵינָם, אֵין נֹטֶה עוֹד אָהֳלִי.'

I said to the leaves of the trees, I adjured them by my God: 'Be my refuge, lest the sword destroy me; for my tent[1] is despoiled, my temple in ruins. *My sons have left me and are gone; there is none to pitch my tent again.*'

1. The land of Israel.

אָמַרְתִּי לַכְּפִירִים וּלְכָל בְּנֵי לָבִיא :
'הַלְווּנִי מִכֹּחֲכֶם אוּלַי אֲכַלְכֵּל כְּאֵבִי,
כִּי לִבִּי נָמֵס בְּקִרְבִּי, לֹא יִשָּׂא עָצְבִּי —
כִּי עָנִי וְאֶבְיוֹן אָנֹכִי וְלִבִּי חָלַל בְּקִרְבִּי.'

I said to the lions and to all their young:
'Lend me your prowess, so that I may
endure my pain; for my heart is melted
within me, and cannot bear my anguish.
*I am downtrodden and poor; my heart is
sorely tormented.*'

אָמַרְתִּי לִמְלוֹנֵי מִדְבָּר וּמִקְלְטֵי בוֹרְחִים :
'הַנְווּנִי בַּלֵּילוֹת מִקֹּרֶי קָרָחִים,
כִּי הָיִיתִי כִּצְבִי מֻדָּח מִפְּנֵי אֹחִים —
מִי יִתְּנֵנִי בַמִּדְבָּר מְלוֹן אֹרְחִים.'

I said to the desert havens and places
of refuge: 'Shelter me at night from the
freezing cold; for I am like a gazelle
pursued by howling beasts. *If only I
could find a haven in the desert!*'

אָמַרְתִּי לִסְפִינוֹת הַיָּם בִּנְהִי וּמַאֲמַר מָר :
'הַעֲבִירוּנִי עִמָּכֶם וַאֲבַקֵּשׁ צָרֵי לִבְשָׂרִי הַנִּסְמָר,
כִּי כְסָלַי מָלְאוּ נִקְלֶה, עַל כֵּן אֶזְעַק כְּתוֹא מִכְמָר —
הַיָם אָנִי, אִם תַּנִּין, כִּי תָשִׂים עָלַי מִשְׁמָר ?'

I said to the sailing ships, crying out
bitterly: 'Take me with you to seek a
balm for my bristling flesh; for my
loins burn with fever, and I shriek like
an antelope trapped in a net. *Am I the
sea or the Serpent, that you build
barriers around me?*'

אָמַרְתִּי לִפְלִיאֵי הַדּוֹר הַמְרַשְּׁלִים אֶזְרוֹעִי :
'הָצִינוּ וְהַרְאוּנִי הַדֶּרֶךְ אֲשֶׁר בָּהּ נָסַע דּוֹדִי וְרֵעִי,
כִּי הָרִים סְבָכוּנִי וָאֶשְׁכַּח אָרְחִי וְרִבְעִי —
דּוֹדִי נָסַע וְנִגְלָה מִנִּי כְּאֹהֶל רֹעִי.'

I said to the illustrious men of my
generation, who have crushed my
spirit:[1] 'Set up sign-posts; show me the
path that my Beloved, my Darling, has
taken; for I am bewildered by mountains, and have forgotten my journey
and my resting place. *My home has been
taken from me, pulled up like a shepherd's
tent.*'

אָמַרְתִּי לַקּוֹנְנוֹת בַּשַּׁחַר לְהַשְׁכִּים :
'הַרְבֵּינָה עָלַי נְהִי כְּיוֹנֵי חֲרַכִּים,
כִּי נִכְסָף אֲנִי לְקוֹלְכֶן וְאֶל נְהִיכֶן אַסְפִּים —
וַיְהִי לְאֵבֶל כִּנֹּרִי וְעֻגָבִי לְקוֹל בֹּכִים.'

I said to the wailing-women who rise at
dawn: 'Raise a long lament for me, like
doves moaning in a lattice. I long to
hear your voices, to join in your lament.
*My harp is tuned to a dirge, my flute to
the voice of those who weep.*'

---

1. Lit. 'who weaken my arm'. The meaning is not clear.

אָמַרְתִּי לְשׁוֹמְרֵי פֶּתַח אֵל מַצִּיל וּפוֹדֶה :
'הִתְעַשְּׁתוּ לְפָדוֹתִי מִפֶּתַח צוֹדֶה,
כִּי תוֹעֲבוֹתַי וּפִשְׁעֵי בָאתִי לְהִתְוַדֶּה —
פִּתְחוּ לִי שַׁעֲרֵי צֶדֶק אָבֹא בָם אֹדֶה !'

I said to the door-keepers of God the
Saviour: 'Devise a way to free me from
the evil at my door; for I have come to
confess my abominations and my
crimes. *Open to me the gates of righteous
ness; I will enter through them and
praise Him.*'

יוֹסֵף אַלְבַּרְדָּאנִי   *Joseph Albardani*

אָמְנָם שָׁלוֹשׁ כִּתּוֹת   THE THREE FACTIONS

אָמְנָם שָׁלוֹשׁ כִּתּוֹת נֶחְלְקוּ עַמּוֹ
בְּצֵאתָם מִמִּצְרַיִם וּרְדָפָם פַּרְעֹה בְּעַצְמוֹ.
גַּלֵּי יָם כְּחָפָה צְבָיֶיהֶם, שׁוֹרְרוּ לִשְׁמוֹ :
'יהוה אִישׁ מִלְחָמָה יהוה שְׁמוֹ.'

As they were leaving Egypt, pursued by
Pharaoh himself, His people divided
into three factions. But when the waves
of the sea engulfed Egypt's armies,
they all sang to His name: '*The Lord,
the warrior — Lord is His name!*'

כִּתָּה רִאשׁוֹנָה דִּבְּרָה : 'נִטְבַּע בְּמֵי זֵידוֹנִי',
הִגִּידָה : 'כִּי רַבִּים רַחֲמָיו, נִפְּלָה נָא בְיַד יְיָ.'
וְאָמַר לָהֶם מֹשֶׁה עֶבֶד יְיָ :
'הִתְיַצְּבוּ וּרְאוּ אֶת יְשׁוּעַת יְיָ.'

The first faction spoke up: 'Let us
drown in the seething waters.' They
insisted: 'Let us fall into the hands of
the Lord, for His mercy is great.' But
Moses, the servant of the Lord, replied:
'*Stand firm and see the Lord's deliverance.*'

כִּתָּה שְׁנִיָּה זָמְמָה לַחֲזֹר לְמִצְרַיִם וּלְשִׁעְבּוּדָם וְעָלָם.
חַי הֵשִׁיבָם : 'אֲנִי תַּחְתֵּיכֶם אַשְׁפִּילָם'.
טָהוֹר נָם לָהֶם : 'זֹאת קָשָׁה מִכֻּלָּם,
כִּי אֲשֶׁר רְאִיתֶם אֶת מִצְרַיִם הַיּוֹם
לֹא תֹסְפוּ לִרְאֹתָם עוֹד עַד עוֹלָם.'

The second faction wanted them to go
back to Egypt, back to servitude and
the yoke. To them the Eternal spoke:
'I shall strike down the Egyptians
before you.' And Moses, the pure one,
said to them: 'What you wish is worst
of all; *but as sure as you see the Egyptians
now, you will never see them again.*'

כִּתָּה שְׁלִישִׁית יָזְמָה : 'נַעֲשֶׂה מִלְחָמָה בַּיָּם וְיֵבוֹשׁוּן,
כֻּלָּם עַל צַוָּארֵיהֶם דְּגָלֵינוּ יִרְגָּשׁוּן.'
לָהֶם הֵשִׁיב עָנָו : 'נִפְלָאוֹת אֵל תַּרְחִישׁוּן,
יהוה יִלָּחֵם לָכֶם וְאַתֶּם תַּחֲרִשׁוּן.'

The third faction proposed: 'Let us
give battle in the sea and abase them;
our standards will rage above their
necks!' To them the humble Moses
said: 'Rather extol God's wonders;
*the Lord will fight for you; so you hold
your peace!*'

שָׁלוֹשׁ כִּתּוֹת נֶחְלְקָה אֲיֻמָּה.
אַחַת נָמָה: 'נִתְּנָה רֹאשׁ וְנָשׁוּבָה מִצְרָיְמָה.'
וְאַחַת נָמָה: 'נִטְבַּע בְּתוֹךְ הַיָּמָּה.'
וְאַחַת נָמָה: 'נַעֲשֶׂה בָם מִלְחָמָה.'
הֵשִׁיב עָנָו בְּשָׂפָה נְעִימָה:
'יְמִין יהוה רוֹמֵמָה.'

Thus did the noble people split up into
three factions, the one saying: 'Let us
head back for Egypt'; the other: 'Let
us drown in the sea'; and the last: 'Let
us give them battle'. To all of which
the humble one joyfully replied: '*The
right hand of the Lord raises up!*'

מֹשֶׁה בַּר־קָלוֹנִימוֹס

Moses ben Kalonymus

אָז פָּתַח אוֹצָרוֹת

PHARAOH PURSUES THE
ISRAELITES

[...] אָז פָּתַח אוֹצָרוֹת גִּנְזֵי מַטְמוֹנִים,
אֲשֶׁר גָּנַז הוּא וּמְלָכִים קַדְמוֹנִים,
וְהוֹצִיא כְּלֵי יְקָר וְדַרְכְּמוֹנִים
וְחִלַּק לְכָל אֶחָד וְאֶחָד כְּפִי הֲגוּנִים
וְשִׁדְּלָם בִּדְבָרִים וְהִסְבִּיר לָמוֹ פָנִים.
וְכֹה אָמַר לָהֶם בְּשִׂיחַ מַעֲנִים:
'מִשְׁפַּט הַמֶּלֶךְ – כָּל הָעָם בּוֹזְזִים וּלְפָנָיו נוֹתְנִים,
וַאֲנִי כְּאֶחָד מִכֶּם אֶטֹּל מָנִים;
מִשְׁפַּט הַמֶּלֶךְ – עֲבָדָיו יוֹצְאִים רִאשׁוֹנִים,
וַאֲנִי אֵצֵא רִאשׁוֹן וְאַתֶּם צְאוּ אַחֲרוֹנִים;
מִשְׁפַּט הַמֶּלֶךְ – עֲבָדָיו אוֹסְרִים
מֶרְכַּבְתּוֹ וּמְתַקְּנִים,
וַאֲנִי בְּעַצְמִי אֶאֱסֹר רִכְבִּי וְאָשִׂים רְסָנִים!'

Then he opened the hoards of hidden
treasures which he and kings of old had
stored away. He brought out precious
vessels and gold Darics and presented
them to his chieftains, to each according
to his rank. He enticed them with
words, with a show of kindness, and
appealed to them thus: 'It is the royal
custom that all the people yield their
plunder to the king; but I shall share
with you on equal terms. It is the royal
custom that subjects go first into battle;
but I shall go first and you will follow
me. It is the royal custom that subjects
harness the king's chariot and make it
ready; but I shall harness my chariot
and secure the reins with my own
hands.'

וְנִתְרַצּוּ יַחַד גְּדוֹלִים וּקְטַנִּים
וַיָּשִׂימוּ כּוֹבַע עַל רָאשֵׁיהֶם וְלָבְשׁוּ שִׁרְיוֹנִים
וַיַּחְגְּרוּ אִישׁ חַרְבּוֹ וְנָטְלוּ כִידוֹנִים

Then all of them, the lowly and the
high alike, assented. They put helmets
on their heads, arrayed themselves in
armour, girt on their swords, seized

וַיִּקְחוּ אִישׁ רֹמַח בְּיָדוֹ וַיַּחֲזִיקוּ מָגִנִּים
וְנָשְׂאוּ קֶשֶׁת וּמִלְאוּ שִׁלְטֵיהֶם חִצִּים שְׁנוּנִים,
וְהַקַּלָּעִים, אִישׁ קַלְעוֹ בְּיָדוֹ, לְקַלַּע בָּאֲבָנִים.
וַיֵּצְאוּ יַחַד בְּלֵב שָׁלֵם וּבְצִבְיוֹנִים,
וְלֹא נִכְשַׁל אֶחָד מֵהֶם וְלֹא אֵרְעוּהוּ סִימָנִים,
– לְבִלְתִּי לְנַחֵשׁ לָשׁוּב לִמְלוֹנִים –
כִּי חֻקּוֹת הָעַמִּים מְנַחֲשִׁים וּמְעוֹנְנִים.

their javelins, gripped their lances,
equipped themselves with shields.
They took their bows, filled their
quivers with keen arrows, and the
slingers held their slings ready to cast
stones. Thus did they set forth
together, eagerly and wholeheartedly.
None met with any accident, none was
beset by evil omens, lest they turn back
because of some foreboding (for the
heathen resort to augurs and to soothsayers).

וְאִישׁ יִשְׂרָאֵל עַל שְׂפַת יָם חוֹנִים.
וַיִּשְׂאוּ עֵינֵיהֶם וְהִנֵּה מִצְרַיִם נוֹסְעִים כַּעֲנָנִים
וְאֵין מָקוֹם לָנוּס, לֹא לְאָחוֹר וְלֹא לְפָנִים,
– וְאַף לֹא מִדְּפָנוֹת מִפְּנֵי חַיּוֹת וּפְתָנִים –
וַיִּצְעֲקוּ אֶל יְיָ וְהִפִּילוּ לְפָנָיו תַּחֲנוּנִים.
וַיִּמָּצֵא לָהֶם הַמָּצוּי בְּכָל עִדָּנִים
וַיִּגְעַר בְּיַם סוּף וְחָרְבוּ זֵידוֹנִים,
וַיֵּלְכוּ בַּתְּהוֹמוֹת כְּעַל דְּרָכִים מְפֻנִּים.
מִזֶּה וּמִזֶּה הֶעֱלָה אִילָנוֹת טְעוּנִים
וּבְתוֹךְ תְּהוֹמוֹת הִמְתִּיק לָמוֹ מַעְיָנִים
וְעִשֵּׁן לִפְנֵיהֶם קְטֹרֶת סַמְמָנִים
וַיַּנְחֵם אֶל מָחוֹז חֶפְצָם שַׁאֲנַנִּים. [...]

The Israelites were encamped on the
sea-shore. When they looked up, they
saw the Egyptians advancing like
clouds. There was nowhere to flee,
neither in front nor in back nor to the
sides, which were blocked by vipers
and wild beasts. They cried out to the
Lord, appealing to Him; and He, who
is ever-present, presented Himself to
them. He rebuked the Red Sea, and
the seething waters dried up. Then
they walked through the deeps as
through cleared paths. On either side
He raised up trees laden with fruit;
within the deeps He made sweet fountains flow. He perfumed their way with
clouds of incense; and He led them,
safe and serene, to their destination.

וְהִנֵּה כְּבוֹד יְיָ אֱלֹהֵי יִשְׂרָאֵל בָּא בְּרֹב לִגְיוֹנִים.
וַיִּרְכַּב עַל כְּרוּב וַיֵּדֶא מוּל בַּעֲלֵי מְדָנִים
וְעָמְדוּ שַׂרְפֵי הַקֹּדֶשׁ וְחַיּוֹת וְאוֹפַנִּים
וְאֶלֶף אַלְפִין וְרִבּוֹ רִבְבָן גְּדוּדֵי שִׁנְאַנִּים
וְרֶכֶב אֵשׁ וְסוּסֵי אֵשׁ וְכָל דִּמְיוֹנִים,
כַּמַּרְאֶה אֲשֶׁר רָאָה צִיר בְּחֶזְיוֹנִים:
סוּסִים אֲדֻמִּים וְסוּסִים שְׁחֹרִים, שְׂרֻקִּים וּלְבָנִים.

And the glory of the Lord God of
Israel appeared among a multitude of
legions. Riding on a cherub, He
swooped down upon the men of strife.
In His company were the seraphim, the
holy creatures, the ofanim,[1] and
thousands upon thousands, myriads
upon myriads of angelic troops, with
fiery chariots, fiery horses, and all the
other apparitions which the prophet[2]
beheld in his ecstatic vision: red horses

---

1. A class of chariot-angels.   2. Zechariah; see 1.8.

וַיַּחֲנוּ אֵלֶּה נֹכַח אֵלֶּה אֱפוּנִים :

מַחֲנֵה אֵשׁ מוּל מַחֲנֵה קַשׁ פָּנִים בְּפָנִים. [...]

and black, sorrel and white. Thus they camped opposite each other, wheels ready to roll, face to face: an army of fire and an army of straw.

וְאָז שַׂר יָם עִם חָם שַׂר יַחַד נְדוֹנִים :

זֶה לְעֻמַּת זֶה נֶאֶבְקוּ בַּמְּעוֹנִים.

וַיֶּחֱזַק רַהַב עַל שַׂר אֲוֵינִים

וַיַּשְׁלִיכֵהוּ אַרְצָה וַיִּרְמְסֵהוּ בְּעֶזְרַת דָּר אוֹפַנִּים.

וְעַם וּוֹ בִּשׁוּרָם בְּאֵלֶּה דִינִים,

עוֹזֵר וְעָזוּר בְּקוּ נְדוֹנִים,

פָּתְחוּ פִיהֶם בְּשִׁיר וּבִרְנָנִים :

'עָזִּי וְזִמְרָת יָהּ!' פָּצְחוּ בְרַנּוּנִים,

לְרָם עַל רָמִים וּמִתְגָּאֶה עַל גֵּיוְתָנִים,

לְשׁוֹמֵעַ אֶנְקַת אֶבְיוֹנִים,

לְמַשְׁפִּיל רָמִים וּמֵרִים מִסְכֵּנִים.

וְקִדְּמוּ שָׁרִים אַחַר נוֹגְנִים

וּבְתוֹךְ עֲלָמוֹת תּוֹפְפוּ נְגוּנִים.

וְאַחַר כָּךְ הֻרְשׁוּ שְׁנְאַנִּים.

Then the Prince of the Sea and the Prince of Egypt[1] came to grips, struggling with each other in the heavens. Rahav, the Prince of the Sea, with the help of the Chariot-Dweller, overpowered the Prince of the Egyptians, hurled him down to earth and trampled him. And when the Israelites witnessed these judgements, how the protector and those he protected met their doom, they shouted and sang songs of praise. 'The Lord is my refuge and my defence,' they chanted, in honour of the highest of the high, who rules over the proud, who heeds the groans of the needy, who brings down the haughty and raises up the poor. The singers went first, then came the musicians, and among them maidens playing timbrels. Only afterwards were the angels permitted to sing.

שִׁמְעוֹן בַּר־יִצְחָק

Simeon ben Isaac

אֱוִילִי הַמִּתְעֶה

AGAINST THE EVIL INCLINATION

אֱוִילִי הַמַּתְעֶה, מַרְגִּיז וּמַחֲטִיא –

בַּלְּעֵהוּ, קַלְּעֵהוּ וְעוֹד בַּל יַסְטִיא.

גְּעוֹל הַמְגֹאָל וּמְטַנֵּף טְהוֹרִים –

This fool who tricks and provokes and seduces to sin – destroy him, cast him away, so that he may no more mislead us! This abomination that defiles and

1. The tutelary angel of the Egyptians.

דְּחֵהוּ, מְחֵהוּ מִלִּבּוֹת וְהַרְהוֹרִים.
הוּחַל הַמֲהַתֵּל וּמְפַתֵּל יְשָׁרִים –
וַבְּחֵהוּ, שֶׁכְּחֵהוּ וְלֹא יַטֶּה אֲשׁוּרִים.
זְבוּב הָאוֹרֵב בְּמִפְתְּחֵי הַלֵּב –
חַנְּקֵהוּ, נַקֵּהוּ, וְלֵב חָדָשׁ תְּלַבְלֵב. [...]

befouls the pure – repulse it, erase it
from heart and mind. This dupe who
deludes and perverts the righteous –
punish him, obliterate him, so that he
may not lead us astray. This fly that
lurks in the doorway of the heart –
strangle it, blot it out, and make a new
heart blossom forth!

מֶלֶךְ עֶלְיוֹן

THE TWO KINGS

ובכן נמליכך, מלך.

Let us declare Your dominion, O King!

מֶלֶךְ עֶלְיוֹן:
אַמִּיץ הַמְנַשֵּׂא, לְכֹל לְרֹאשׁ מִתְנַשֵּׂא,
אוֹמֵר וְעוֹשֶׂה, מָעוֹז וּמַחְסֶה,
נִשָּׂא וְנוֹשֵׂא, מוֹשִׁיב מְלָכִים לַכִּסֵּא –
לַעֲדֵי־עַד יִמְלֹךְ.

Supreme King: mighty, exalted, raised
over all; ordaining, fulfilling; refuge
and stronghold; lofty, bearing the
world aloft; setting kings on their
thrones – He shall reign for ever!

מֶלֶךְ אֶבְיוֹן:
בָּזוּי וּמְשֻׁסֶּה, פְּשָׁעָיו מְכַסֶּה,
בָּהוּל וּמַחְתָּשֶׁה, עָווֹן פּוֹשֶׂה,
נִבְחָן בְּכָל מַעֲשֶׂה, וְאוֹצָרוֹ יִשָּׁסֶה –
וְאֵיךְ יִמְלֹךְ? [...]

Abject king: vile, despoiled; concealing
his crimes; frantic, enfeebled, spread in
sin; tested at every step, his treasure
doomed to plunder – how shall he
reign?

מֶלֶךְ עֶלְיוֹן:
טָהוֹר בִּזְבוּלָיו, אוֹת הוּא בְּאַרְאֶלָּיו,
אֵין עָרֹךְ אֵלָיו, לִפְעַל כְּמִפְעָלָיו,
חוֹל שָׂם גְּבוּלָיו כַּהֲמוֹת יָם לְגַלָּיו –
לַעֲדֵי־עַד יִמְלֹךְ.

Supreme King: pure in His dwelling;
eminent among his legions; none can
compare with Him, none match His
works; He bounded the sea with sand,
even as its waves roared – He shall
reign for ever!

מֶלֶךְ אֶבְיֹן:
יָהִיר בְּזָדוֹן, מְגָרֶה מָדוֹן,
בְּחַיָּיו נִדּוֹן, בְּמוֹתוֹ לַאֲבַדּוֹן,
רוּחוֹ יָדוֹן וְיֵדַע שֶׁדּוּן —
וְאֵיךְ יִמְלֹךְ ? [...]

Abject king: haughty, wilful, stirring
up discord; alive – he is judged, dead –
the pit awaits him; his spirit lives on to
know that there is a judgement – how
shall he reign?

מֶלֶךְ עֶלְיֹן:
שׁוֹמֵעַ אֶל אֶבְיוֹנִים וּמַאֲזִין חַנּוּנִים,
מַאֲרִיךְ רְצוֹנִים וּמְקַצֵּר חֲרוֹנִים,
רִאשׁוֹן לָרִאשׁוֹנִים וְאַחֲרוֹן לָאַחֲרוֹנִים —
לַעֲדֵי־עַד יִמְלֹךְ.

Supreme King: He listens to the poor,
heeds their pleading; prolongs His
favour, curtails His wrath; first of the
first, last of the last – He shall reign for
ever!

מֶלֶךְ אֶבְיֹן:
תּוֹחַלְתּוֹ נִכְזָבָה, תִּקְוָתוֹ נֶעֱלָבָה,
גְּוִיָּתוֹ נִרְקָבָה, נִשְׁמָתוֹ נִכְאָבָה,
נִשְׁבָּר וְנִשְׁבָּה מִלַּהַט הַיּוֹם הַבָּא —
וְאֵיךְ יִמְלֹךְ ?

Abject king: his hopes are empty, his
wishes put to shame; his body rots, his
soul is in pain; he is broken and captive,
dreading the flames of the day that will
come – how shall he reign?

אֲבָל מֶלֶךְ עֶלְיֹן:
שׁוֹפֵט הָאֱמֶת, מַעֲבָדָיו אֱמֶת,
עוֹשֶׂה חֶסֶד וֶאֱמֶת וְרַב־חֶסֶד וֶאֱמֶת,
נְתִיבָתוֹ אֱמֶת וְחוֹתָמוֹ אֱמֶת —
לַעֲדֵי־עַד יִמְלֹךְ.

But the Supreme King is a truthful
judge, His works are truth; He does
right, with unfailing love, ever constant
and true; truth is His way and truth
His seal – He shall reign for ever!

דָּוִד בֶּן־נָשִׂיא   *David ben Nasi*

אֲמוּלָה לִבָּתִי   A REPROACH

אֲמוּלָה לִבָּתִי כְּמוֹ אֵשׁ מִתְלַהֶטֶת,
וְנֹכַח תּוֹעֲבוֹתַי עֵינִי מַבֶּטֶת,
לַעֲשׂוֹת אוֹתָם בָּאוֹר וּבָעֲלָטֶת,
מַעֲשֵׂה אִשָּׁה זוֹנָה שַׁלָּטֶת.

My poor heart burns, as if it were on
fire, when I look at my own abominations, done in darkness and in light –
the deeds of a bold-faced whore!

בְּפִי וּבִלְשׁוֹנִי פַּתּוּיֵי קַשּׁוּב,
וְתַחַת שְׂפָתַי חֲמַת עַכְשׁוּב.
וְשָׂרַי וּזְקֵנַי וְכָל נִכְבָּד וְחָשׁוּב
הֶחֱזִיקוּ בַּתַּרְמִית, מֵאֲנוּ לָשׁוּב. [...]

Lures lie in wait in my mouth, on my
tongue; on my lips is spiders' poison;
my lords and elders, all the honoured
and important men *cling to deceit,
refusing to repent.*

זְקֵנַי וְישִׁישַׁי, שַׁחֲרִית וְעַרְבִּית,
זוֹלְלֵי בָשָׂר וְסוֹבְאֵי יֵין חָבִית.
וְסוֹחֵר וּמוֹכֵר, לְהוֹסִיף מַגְבִּית,
מַרְבֶּה הוֹנוֹ בְּנֶשֶׁךְ וְתַרְבִּית. [...]

From morning to evening my aged
leaders gorge themselves on meat and
guzzle wine from the barrel; while the
dealers and merchants augment their
hoard, *grow rich by lending at discount
or at interest.*

דְּחֵה מְזֵי רָעָב מִבָּתִּים וּמִתְחוּמִים,
וְכַבֵּה רֶשֶׁף וְגַם קֶטֶב לְחוּמִים.
יְהִי־נָא חַסְדְּךָ לְשַׂבְּעֵנוּ מִמְּרוֹמִים
דְּבָרִים טוֹבִים, דְּבָרִים נְחוּמִים.

Oh, banish the pangs of hunger from
our homes and realms, and quench the
burning heat, the ravaging pestilence.
May Your never-failing love nourish
us from on high, *with kind words, with
words of consolation.*

עֲלוּמֵי־שֵׁם   *Anonymous*

פְּטִירַת מֹשֶׁה   THE DEATH OF MOSES
SEQUENCE

מי עלה למרום   *1. The Angels Try to Block His Way*

מִי עָלָה לַמָּרוֹם,
מִי עָלָה לַמָּרוֹם,
מִי עָלָה לַמָּרוֹם,
וּמִי הוֹרִיד עֹז מִבְטָחָה ?

Who went up to heaven? Who went up
to heaven? Who went up to heaven and
brought down the mighty mainstay?[1]

הִתְקַבְּצוּ מַלְאָכִים זֶה אֶל זֶה,
לְקֵבָל־זֶה,
וְאָמַר זֶה אֶל זֶה :
'מִי הוּא זֶה וְאֵיזֶה הוּא,
מְאַחֵז פְּנֵי כִסֵּה,
פַּרְשֵׁז עָלָיו עֲנָנוֹ ?'

The angels banded together against
this man; and they said one to another:
'Who is he and what is he, that he
dares cling to the Throne, and God
spreads His radiant cloud over him?'

מֹשֶׁה עָלָה לַמָּרוֹם,
מֹשֶׁה עָלָה לַמָּרוֹם,
מֹשֶׁה עָלָה לַמָּרוֹם,
וְהוּא הוֹרִיד עֹז מִבְטָחָה !

Moses went up to heaven. Moses went
up to heaven. Moses went up to heaven
and brought down the mighty mainstay!

אז מרחם אמי   *2. He Pleads with God for His Life*

'אָז מֵרֶחֶם אִמִּי
בָּחַנְתָּ תֻמִּי
וּבָחַרְתָּ נְאֻמִי —
וְלָמָה אֲנִי מֵת ?'

'While I was yet in my mother's womb
You marked my perfection and chose
me as Your spokesman – why then

---

1. I.e. the Torah, in which the angels put their trust and which they refused to relinquish to mortals.

266

פֶּן יֵאָמֵר : אִישׁ הָאֱלֹהִים
עָלָה אֶל הָאֱלֹהִים,
וְהִנּוּ כֵּאלֹהִים.'

should I die?' 'Lest it be said: the man of God went up to God, and he has become like God.'

'בְּעֵת טִיט וָחֹמֶר
נֻתַּתִּי בְּתֵבַת גֹּמֶא,
וְשָׁמַרְתִּי אֹמֶר –
וְלָמָה אֲנִי מֵת ?'
'פֶּן יֵאָמֵר : בִּיטָה אֶל פָּנִים בְּפָנִים,
וְקָרַן לוֹ עוֹר פָּנִים,
וְהִנּוּ כֵּאלֹהִים.'

'When Israel laboured with clay and with mortar, I was put into a wicker basket. And I fulfilled Your word – why then should I die?' 'Lest it be said: He spoke to God face to face and then the skin of his face shone, and he has become like God.'

'גַּם הֻשְׁלַכְתִּי לַיְאוֹר
מִפְּנֵי מוֹרְדֵי אוֹר,
וּדְבָרְךָ הָיָה לִי אוֹר –
וְלָמָה אֲנִי מֵת ?'
'פֶּן יֵאָמֵר : גָּדַע חָם בְּעֶשֶׂר מַכּוֹת,
וְגָאַל עֵינֶיהָ-בְּרֵכוֹת,
וְהִנּוּ כֵּאלֹהִים.'

'I was cast into the Nile for fear of those who rebelled against the light, but Your word was my light – why then should I die?' 'Lest it be said: He felled Egypt with ten plagues and redeemed her whose eyes are like pools,[1] and he has become like God.'

'דִּהַרְתָּ בַּת מַפְרִיךְ
עַל יַד הַיְאוֹר לְהַדְרִיךְ,
יָמַי לְהַאֲרִיךְ –
וְלָמָה אֲנִי מֵת ?'
'פֶּן יֵאָמֵר : דָּץ כְּנִשְׁתַּלַּח אֶל סְגֻלָּה
וְהוֹצִיאָם בְּגִילָה,
וְהִנּוּ כֵּאלֹהִים.'

'You led the tyrant's daughter to the Nile, brought her in haste, so that my life might be prolonged – why then should I die?' 'Lest it be said: He exulted when he was sent to the treasured people and brought them out of Egypt joyfully, and he has become like God.'

---

1. Israel; see Song of Songs 7.5.

אז כל בריות

3. God Bargains with Him

'אָז כָּל בְּרִיּוֹת נוֹצְרוּ מֵאֲדָמָה,
וְסוֹפָם לְתוֹלֵעָה וְרִמָּה.
בִּי נִשְׁבַּעְתִּי:
בְּגוּפְךָ לֹא תִשְׁלֹט רִמָּה,
וְלֹא כְּמוֹת כָּל הָאָדָם תָּמוּת.'

'All creatures were formed out of earth and are doomed to be food for maggots and worms. By My own self I swear: no maggot shall have sway over your body, and you shall not die as all men die.'

'וְאֵיךְ אָמוּת?'

'How then shall I die?'

'גְּדוּדִים וּשְׂרָפִים יַעַמְדוּ מִפֹּה וּמִפֹּה
וְיַעֲשׂוּ שֵׁרוּתֶךָ,
וַאֲנִי אַצְהִיר בְּתוֹךְ שׁוּרָתֶךָ.
בִּי נִשְׁבַּעְתִּי:
וְלֹא יֵדַע אִישׁ אֶת קְבוּרָתֶךָ,
וְלֹא כְּמוֹת כָּל הָאָדָם תָּמוּת.'

'Bands of angels and seraphim, standing on either side, shall wait upon you, and My splendour shall shine in your ranks. By My own self I swear: no one shall know your burial place, and you shall not die as all men die.'

'וְאֵיךְ אָמוּת?'

'How then shall I die?'

'הֵן אֲנִי בִּכְבוֹדִי אֶשָּׂאֲךָ אַרְבָּעָה מִילִים,
וְתַרְשִׁישִׁים חַסְדְּךָ יִהְיוּ גוֹמְלִים.
בִּי נִשְׁבַּעְתִּי:
וְאַנִּיחֲךָ אֵצֶל שְׁלֹשֶׁת הַגְּדוֹלִים,
וְלֹא כְּמוֹת כָּל הָאָדָם תָּמוּת.'

'I Myself will carry you for four miles, and gleaming angels shall shower you with favours. By My own self I swear: I will place you next to the three Patriarchs, and you shall not die as all men die.'

'וְאֵיךְ אָמוּת?'

'How then shall I die?'

'מַלְאֲכֵי־מַעַל אֲשֶׁר בֵּינֵיהֶם שָׁלוֹם
יֵצְאוּ לִקְרָאתְךָ בְּדִבְרֵי שָׁלוֹם.
בִּי נִשְׁבַּעְתִּי:

'The angels on high, who dwell in peace, shall go forth to greet you with words of peace. By My own self I

נוֹאֲמִים לְפָנֶיךָ: "יָבוֹא שָׁלוֹם" —
וְלֹא כְּמוֹת כָּל הָאָדָם תָּמוּת.'

swear: they shall salute you: "Enter
into peace!", and you shall not die as
all men die.'

וְאֵיךְ אָמוּת?'

'How then shall I die?'

'קְדוֹשֵׁי מַעְלָה יֹאמְרוּ: "מָתַי יָבוֹא בְּרֹאשׁ עַם
לִתְשׁוּעַת עֲדָתוֹ,
הָאִישׁ אֲשֶׁר לֹא קָם בְּיִשְׂרָאֵל כְּמוֹתוֹ?"
בִּי נִשְׁבַּעְתִּי:
רוֹגְשִׁים וְאוֹמְרִים: "יְהִי שָׁלוֹם בִּמְנוּחָתוֹ" —
וְלֹא כְּמוֹת כָּל הָאָדָם תָּמוּת.'

'The holy ones on high shall say:
"When will he come again at the head
of his flock to bring salvation to all his
people – this man, whose like has never
yet arisen in Israel?" By My own self
I swear: they shall all cry out: "Peace
be upon his resting place!", and you
shall not die as all men die.'

וְאֵיךְ אָמוּת?'

'How then shall I die?'

'שְׁמוּרָה תִהְיֶה אֶצְלְךָ דָּת עֵץ הַחַיִּים,
וְאַתָּה תָבוֹא בְּרֹאשׁ חֲבוּרָתְךָ בְּבִנְיַן
מוֹצָא מַיִם חַיִּים.
בִּי נִשְׁבַּעְתִּי:
תִּשְׁמַע מִפִּי "תְּהִי נִשְׁמָתְךָ צְרוּרָה בִּצְרוֹר הַחַיִּים",
וְלֹא כְּמוֹת כָּל הָאָדָם תָּמוּת.'

'The Law, that staff of life, shall be
entrusted to you; you shall come at the
head of your company when Jerusalem,
the source of living waters, is rebuilt.
By My own self I swear: you shall hear
Me say: "May your soul be treasured
in the treasury of life", and you shall
not die as all men die.'

וְאֵיךְ אָמוּת?'

'How then shall I die?'

לא אמות

4. He Refuses to Die

'לֹא אָמוּת! לָמָה אָמוּת?

'I will not die! Why should I die?

אִם גָּרַמְתִּי בַּעֲוֹל פֶּה
בַּסְּנֶה בְּדִבּוּר פֶּה,

'If it is because of my perverse words,
spoken at the burning bush, when I

כְּשָׁמְעִי פֶּה אֶל פֶּה
"וְאַתָּה תִּהְיֶה לּוֹ לְפֶה",
בְּעַצּוֹתִי כִּי כְבַד פֶּה
לֵחַר בְּמִי שָׂם פֶּה –
אִם עָוֹן הוּא מְחֵהוּ,
וְאַל תִּזְכְּרֵהוּ.'

heard You say, mouth to mouth, "You
shall put the words in Aaron's mouth";
when I sinfully answered: "I am slow
of speech", and angered You who give
man speech – if this is my crime, blot
it out and do not call it to mind!'

וְהֵשִׁיבוֹ אָיֹם
בְּעֶצֶם הַיּוֹם:
'דְּבָרֶיךָ חָחְמְדוּ
בַּסְּנֶה, וְאִם כָּבְדוּ,
לְדוֹרוֹת יִתְמָדוּ.
וְאֵיךְ לְעָוֹן יִפָּקְדוּ?

And the Dread One answered him that
very day: 'Your words were sweet to
me, and though they faltered at the
bush they will be remembered for many
generations. How can such words be
counted a crime?

זֹאת לֹא זֹאת.'

'That is not why.'

'לָמָּה זֹאת – אֵין זֹאת?'

'If that is not why, why then should I
die?'

'מֹשֶׁה, עֲלֵה וָמוּת,
כִּי גְזֵרָה הִיא שֶׁתָּמוּת!'

'Moses, go up and die, for it has been
decreed that you shall die!'

איש אשר הקרן

5. He Cries Out to His Mother

אִישׁ אֲשֶׁר הַקְרַן לוֹ אוֹרָה,
אִישׁ בָּחֲרוֹ אֵל נוֹרָא,
אִישׁ גַּשׁ לְעַרְפְּלֵי־נוֹרָא –
יֵאָמֵר לוֹ: 'עֲלֵה וּמוּת בָּהָר'?
צָעַק צְעָקָה גְדוֹלָה וּמָרָה:
'יוֹכֶבֶד, אִמִּי!'

This man, who was graced with light,
who was chosen by the dread God,
who approached the dark clouds of
terror – shall he now be told: 'Go up
and die on the mountain'? He cried
out, loud and bitter: 'Jokhebed, my
mother!'

אִישׁ דָּשׁ עַנְנֵי נְהוֹרָא,
אִישׁ הֵשֵׁךְ עֶבְרָה,
אִישׁ וְחֵר מֵעָם עֶבְרָה –
יֵאָמֵר לוֹ: 'עֲלֵה וּמוּת בָּהָר'?
צָעַק צְעָקָה גְדוֹלָה וּמָרָה:
'יוֹכֶבֶד, אִמִּי!'

This man, who walked on the glowing
clouds, who stilled God's anger, who
averted His wrath from the people –
shall he now be told: 'Go up and die
on the mountain'? He cried out, loud
and bitter: 'Jokhebed, my mother!'

אִישׁ קָרָא עַל הַיָּם שִׁירָה,
אִישׁ רָאָה וַיִּירָא,
אִישׁ שְׁכִינָה שָׂרָה,
אִישׁ תִּנָּה מִשְׁנֵה תוֹרָה –
יֵאָמֵר לוֹ: 'עֲלֵה וּמוּת בָּהָר'?
צָעַק צְעָקָה גְדוֹלָה וּמָרָה:
'יוֹכֶבֶד, אִמִּי!'

This man, who sang out by the shores
of the Red Sea, who looked, terrified,
at the burning bush, who beheld the
Shekinah, who expounded the Law[1] –
shall he now be told: 'Go up and die
on the mountain'? He cried out, loud
and bitter: 'Jokhebed, my mother!'

אֹרח זו אלך

6. He Takes Leave of His People

'אֹרַח זוּ אֵלֵךְ
גָּזַר עָלַי הַמֶּלֶךְ.
הִנְנִי הַיּוֹם מֻבְדָּל וְהוֹלֵךְ.
קָהָלִי, הֱיֵה לְשָׁלוֹם.'

'The road I am about to take was
decreed by the King; I am set apart
today, and take my leave. My people,
be at peace.'

'בְּזֹאת לֹא גֵדַע מַה נַּעֲשֶׂה,
כִּי כָל אֲשֶׁר יַחְפֹּץ יַעֲשֶׂה,
וְאֵין מִי יֹאמַר לוֹ: "מַה תַּעֲשֶׂה?"
רוֹעֵנוּ, לֵךְ לְשָׁלוֹם.'

'As for this, we do not know what to
do, for He does what He chooses, and
none can say to Him: "What are you
doing?" Our shepherd, go in peace.'

---

1. Lit. 'a copy of the Law', the traditional name of the fifth book of Moses, Deuteronomy.

'הַיּוֹם לִי אַחֲרוֹן,
חַק לִי רִאשׁוֹן וְאַחֲרוֹן.
אֵאָסֵף כְּנֶאֱסַף אָחִי אַהֲרֹן.
קְהָלִי, הֱיֵה לְשָׁלוֹם.'

'וְנָתִיב מוּכָן הוּא,
קָטֹן וְגָדוֹל שָׁם הוּא.
מִי יִחְיֶה וְלֹא יִרְאֶהוּ?
רוֹעֵנוּ, לֵךְ לְשָׁלוֹם.'

'זֶה הוּא לִי אָמַר:
"עֲלֵה וּמוּת בָּהָר" —
וְנַפְשִׁי לִמְאֹד הֵמַר.
קְהָלִי, הֱיֵה לְשָׁלוֹם.'

'חָקַק לִבְנֵי אָדָם מִיתָה.
לַחֲסִידָיו יָקָר הַמָּוְתָה —
וַעֲנוּתְךָ לָעָם הִבָּעְתָּ.
רוֹעֵנוּ, לֵךְ לְשָׁלוֹם.'

'כָּבֵד עָלַי רָעָה,
כִּי הַמָּוֶת לִי הִגֵּעָה.
מַה אֶעֱשֶׂה — לֹא אֵדָעָה.
קְהָלִי, הֱיֵה לְשָׁלוֹם.'

'לֹא יִחַר לָךְ
וְלֹא יֵצֶר לָךְ,
כָּבוֹד בְּגַן עֵדֶן מוּכָן לָךְ,
רוֹעֵנוּ, לֵךְ לְשָׁלוֹם.'

'This day is my last; thus has He ordained, who is both First and Last; I shall be gathered to my kin as was my brother Aaron. My people, be at peace.'

'Such is the fated course; both high and low must take it; who shall live and not see death? Our shepherd, go in peace.'

'This is what He said to me: "Go up and die on the mountain"; and He made my soul most bitter. My people, be at peace.'

'He has doomed all men to death, but the death of His faithful ones is precious in His sight. Now that you have told the people of your grief, our shepherd, go in peace.'

'Disaster weighs me down, for death is close upon me. What shall I do? I do not know. My people, be at peace.'

'Do not be angry, do not be grieved; glory awaits you in the Garden of Eden. Our Shepherd, go in peace.'

וַיִּקְבֹּר אֹתוֹ בַגַּי בְּאֶרֶץ מוֹאָב מוּל בֵּית פְּעוֹר,
וְלֹא יָדַע אִישׁ אֶת קְבֻרָתוֹ עַד הַיּוֹם הַזֶּה.

*He was buried in a valley in Moab
opposite Beth-peor, but to this day no one
knows his burial-place.*[1]

אֵזְלַת יוֹכֶבֶד

7. His Mother Looks for His Grave

אָזְלַת יוֹכֶבֶד מְפַיֶּסֶת לְמִצְרַיִם:
'מִצְרַיִם, מִצְרַיִם, אוּלַי רָאִיתָ לִי לְמֹשֶׁה?'
'בְּחַיַּיִךְ, יוֹכֶבֶד, לֹא רָאִיתִי אוֹתוֹ
מִן הַיּוֹם שֶׁהָרַג כָּל בְּכוֹר.'

Jokhebed went to Egypt and implored
it: 'Egypt, Egypt, have you by chance
seen Moses?' 'On your life, Jokhebed,
I have not seen him since the day he
slew all my first-born.'

אָזְלַת יוֹכֶבֶד וְשָׁאֲלָה לְנִילוֹס:
'נִילוֹס, נִילוֹס, אוּלַי רָאִיתָ לִי לְמֹשֶׁה?'
'בְּחַיַּיִךְ, יוֹכֶבֶד, לֹא רָאִיתִי אוֹתוֹ
מִן הַיּוֹם שֶׁהָפַךְ מֵימַי לְדָם.'

Jokhebed went to the Nile and asked it:
'Nile, Nile, have you by chance seen
Moses?' 'On your life, Jokhebed, I
have not seen him since the day he
turned my water to blood.'

אָזְלַת יוֹכֶבֶד מְפַיֶּסֶת לַיָּם:
'יָם, יָם, אוּלַי רָאִיתָ לִי לְמֹשֶׁה?'
'בְּחַיַּיִךְ, יוֹכֶבֶד, לֹא רָאִיתִי אוֹתוֹ
מִן הַיּוֹם שֶׁהֶעֱבִיר בִּי שְׁנֵים עָשָׂר שְׁבָטִים.'

Jokhebed went to the Red Sea and
implored it: 'Sea, sea, have you by
chance seen Moses?' 'On your life,
Jokhebed, I have not seen him since
the day he led the twelve tribes
through me.'

אָזְלַת יוֹכֶבֶד וְשָׁאֲלָה לַמִּדְבָּר:
'מִדְבָּר, מִדְבָּר, אוּלַי רָאִיתָ לִי לְמֹשֶׁה?'
'בְּחַיַּיִךְ, יוֹכֶבֶד, לֹא רָאִיתִי אוֹתוֹ
מִן הַיּוֹם שֶׁהִמְטִיר עָלַי מָן לְיִשְׂרָאֵל.'

Jokhebed went to the desert and asked
it: 'Desert, desert, have you by chance
seen Moses?' 'On your life, Jokhebed,
I have not seen him since the day he
showered manna upon me for Israel.'

אָזְלַת יוֹכֶבֶד מְפַיֶּסֶת לְסִינַי:
'סִינַי, סִינַי, אוּלַי רָאִיתָ לִי לְמֹשֶׁה?'
'בְּחַיַּיִךְ, יוֹכֶבֶד, לֹא רָאִיתִי אוֹתוֹ
מִן הַיּוֹם שֶׁהוֹרִיד עָלַי שְׁנֵי לוּחוֹת הַבְּרִית.'

Jokhebed went to Mount Sinai and
implored it: 'Sinai, Sinai, have you by
chance seen Moses?' 'On your life,
Jokhebed, I have not seen him since
the day he descended upon me with the
two tablets of the Law.'

1. Deuteronomy 34.6.

אָזְלַת יוֹכֶבֶד וְשָׁאֲלָה לַסֶּלַע :
'סֶלַע, סֶלַע, אוּלַי רָאִיתָ לִי לְמֹשֶׁה ?'
'בְּחַיַּיִךְ, יוֹכֶבֶד, לֹא רָאִיתִי אוֹתוֹ
מִן הַיּוֹם שֶׁהִכָּה עָלַי שְׁנֵי שַׁרְבִיטִין.' [...]

Jokhebed went to the rock and asked it:
'Rock, rock, have you by chance seen
Moses?' 'On your life, Jokhebed, I have
not seen him since the day he struck
me twice with the staff.'

ולא קם נביא עוד בישראל כמשה
אשר ידעו יהוה פנים אל פנים.

There has never yet arisen in Israel a
prophet like Moses, whom the Lord knew
face to face.[1]

1. Deuteronomy 34.10.

PART TWO

FROM THE TENTH TO THE
EIGHTEENTH CENTURY

מְנַחֵם אִבְּן־סָרוּק   *Menahem ibn Saruk*

אֲנִי אֶעֱרֹךְ מִשְׁפָּט

THE POET PLEADS HIS CASE

[...] אֲנִי אֶעֱרֹךְ מִשְׁפָּט וְיָדַעְתִּי כִּי אֲנִי אֶצְדָּק.
כֹּה חֻקּוֹת לִי בִּתְשׁוּבַת אִגַּרְתִּי
אֲשֶׁר שָׁלַחְתָּ אֵלִי לֵאמֹר:
– 'אִם הֶעֱוֵיתָ –
כְּבָר הֲבִיאוֹתִיךְ לְמוּסָר,
וְאִם לֹא הֶעֱוֵיתָ –
כְּבָר הֲבִיאוֹתִיךְ לְחַיֵּי הָעוֹלָם הַבָּא'.
הֲזֹאת חָשַׁבְתָּ לְמִשְׁפָּט? הֲלְהוֹכַח מִלִּין תַּחְשֹׁב?
הֲלֹא אֱלֹהִים יַחֲקָר־זֹאת,
הֲנוֹטַע אֹזֶן הֲלֹא יִשְׁמָע,
אִם יוֹצֵר עַיִן הֲלֹא יַבִּיט!
וְכִי תַחְסֹם אֶת פִּי בְּרוּחַ קָדִים
וְתַאֲלִים אֶת לְשׁוֹנִי בְּהַבְלֵי מַהֲתַלּוֹת?
הֲלֹא מֵעֲפָרְךָ עֲפָרִי וֵאלֹהֶיךָ אֱלֹהַי,
חוֹפֵשׂ כָּל תַּעֲלוּמוֹת וְחוֹפֵשׂ כָּל חַדְרֵי בָטֶן. [...]

I shall state my case, and I know that I shall be acquitted. This is what you wrote in reply to my letter, this is what you dispatched to me: 'If you have sinned, I have already repaid you as you merit; but if you have not sinned, I have made you merit eternal life in the world beyond.' Do you consider this a judgement? Do you think such words are proof enough? Will not God find this out? He that planted the ear, will He not hear? He that moulded the eye, will He not see? Will you muzzle my mouth with an east wind, and silence my tongue with taunting lies? Is not my dust the same as yours, and your God mine – He who searches out all secrets and delves into man's inmost being?

שְׁמַע נָא, בֶּן אָדָם, כִּי עוֹד יֵשׁ לְעַבְדְּךָ מִלִּים.
דַּע אַתָּה, אֲדוֹנִי, כִּי אֱלֹהִים הָיִיתָ בְּמִשְׁפָּטִי,
מִשְׁפָּט אֱלֹהִים שְׁפַטְתָּנִי, דִּין עֶלְיוֹן דַּנְתָּנִי:
אֲשֶׁר הוּא הָעֵד – הוּא הַדַּיָּן,
וְלוֹ הַנִּסְתָּרוֹת וְהוּא יוֹדֵעַ מַעֲלוּמוֹת לֵב.
וְלֹא צִוָּה כֵן לְנוֹחֲלֵי מִשְׁפָּט לַעֲשׂוֹת פְּלִילָה.
וַאֲנִי יָדַעְתִּי כִּי לֹא יְיָ הֱסִיתְךָ בִי,
כִּי אִם בְּנֵי הָאָדָם,
כִּי גֵרְשׁוּנִי הַיּוֹם מֵהִסְתַּפֵּחַ בְּנַחֲלַת יְיָ. [...]

Listen, man, for your servant still has something more to say. Know, my lord, that you have taken the role of God in my trial. You have judged me as though you were God, sentenced me as though you were the Most High, who is both witness and judge. All the hidden things are His; He knows the secrets of the heart. But this is not how He ordained that mortal judges should sit in judgement. I know that it is not God, but men, who set you against me; it is they who have deprived me of my share in the Lord's inheritance.

עַל חֲמַס עוֹשְׁקַי אָשִׂיחַ אֶל אָרֶץ:
אָרֶץ, אַל תְּכַסִּי דָמִי! [...]
מֵאַרְבַּע הָרוּחוֹת בּוֹאִי, רוּחַ,
אֲשֶׁר מִמֶּנָּה רוּחִי נָפָחָה!
הִתְאַבְּלִי – הַיְמִינִי, הַאֲנִינִי – הַשְׂמִילִי,
לִבְשִׁי עָלַי שָׂק וְהִתְפַּלְּשִׁי בָאֵפֶר.
עַל תּוּגַת מְחֻצָתֵךְ – הַרְחִיבִי קַרְחָתֵךְ,
וְעַל מַר רוּחִי – חוּלִי וָגֹחִי.
אֵלַי נָא עָלַי כָּל יְמֵי הָאָרֶץ
וְחָלִילָה לָךְ תֵּת לְזַעֲקָתֵךְ דֹּמִי.
שְׂאִי עַל כַּפַּיִךְ – אוּלַי תּוּכְלִי הוֹעֵיל,
וְגַם שִׁפְכִי שִׂיחַ – אוּלַי תַּעֲרִצִי:
כִּי גוֹאֲלִי חַי, לֹא שָׁכַח חַנּוֹת,
וּלְהַסְתִּיר פָּנִים – לֹא גָמַר אֹמֶר.

My oppressors have done me violence,
and I shall cry out to the earth: O
earth, cover not my blood! From the
four quarters come, O wind, from
which my spirit drew its breath!
Mourn, turn right. Lament, turn left.
Put on sackcloth for me, roll in ashes.
In grief for me, who am half of you,
pluck out your hair. Lie writhing on
the ground for my embittered soul.
Wail for me through all the years of the
earth. Never let your cry abate. Lift up
your hands on high: you may yet help.
Pour out your complaint: you may
inspire awe. For my vindicator lives,
He has not forgotten to be gracious,
He has not resolved to hide His face.

גַּם קוֹלִי אֵלֵי מַיִם עַל יַבֶּשֶׁת לְחוּתִי –
הֲלֹא בְמֵימֵי מוּצָק בְּצֵקִי הוּלָשׁ.
גַּם אַתֶּם צַעֲקוּ בְּקוֹל שָׁאוֹן
וְאַל תִּדֹּם הֶמְיַת צְוַחְתְּכֶם.
גַּם אַתֶּם לוּ שְׁמַעוּנִי,
הֵן לָכֶם יְכֹלֶת לִנְקֹם נִקְמָתִי:
בִּשְׁתוֹת אֶתְכֶם חוֹמְסַי – הֱיוּ נָא לְמָרִים,
בְּבוֹאֲכֶם בְּמֵעֵימוֹ – הֱיוּ לַצָּבוֹת בֶּטֶן,
וְכָל מַשְׁקֶה אֲשֶׁר יִשְׁתֶּה – יֵמַר לְשׁוֹתָיו,
וְעוֹלְלוּ לָמוֹ – וְיִהְיוּ כָמוֹנִי!

I shall cry out to the waters too, for my
body has been parched. Was not my
dough kneaded from the waters that
freeze fast? Now you too roar and
boom; let your thundering cry never
cease. Oh, if only you too would heed
me, for you have it in your power to
avenge me. When my despoilers drink
you, turn bitter; when you enter their
bowels, swell their bellies. Let every
liquid that they drink be bitter to them.
Torment them till they become like me!

וְלִשְׁמֵי קֶדֶם אָמַרְתִּי: שְׁמַעוּנִי!
וְלִצְבָא מְרוֹם חַנּוֹתִי בְּמוֹ פִי,
וּלְגִבּוֹרֵי כֹחַ, אֵלֵי פֶלֶא,
אֲשֶׁר מִשְׁכְּנוֹתָם גָּבְהֵי מְרוֹמִים –

And to the ancient heavens I shall say:
listen to me! I shall entreat the host of
heaven, the creatures of night, the
wondrous angels who dwell in the
uppermost heavens. To all of them I

לְכֻלָּם אֶפְרֹשׁ כַּפַּי וְאֶשְׁפֹּךְ שִׂיחִי:
אוּלַי יָעִידוּ חֲמָתִי לְשָׁהֲדִי בַּמְּרוֹמִים
הַשַׁלִּיט עַל כֻּלָּם !

shall spread out my hands and pour out
my prayer: may they attest my wrath
before my Witness on high, who rules
over all!

וְגַם לְשׁוֹכְנֵי עָפָר עֵינִי דוֹמַעַת,
הָעֲתִידִים לַעֲמֹד בַּדִּין לִפְנֵי יוֹצֵר כֹּל.
– הָעֲשׁוּקִים כָּמוֹנִי הַיּוֹם –
דִּמְעוֹת אַנְחוֹתַי יֵשׁוּ לְדִמְעוֹתָם,
וְעַל חֲמָסִי אֶל אֵל יְשַׁוֵּעוּ:
אוּלַי מִמֶּנִּי אוֹ מֵהֶם יַקְשִׁיב אֹזֶן.

They that sleep in the earth, they that
are destined to stand on trial before the
Creator of all – to them too will my
tears flow. And they that are wronged
as I am today – Let them join my tears
and my sighs to their weeping, and
bemoan the violence done to me before
God. Perhaps He will listen to me, or
to them.

עוֹד אֲנִי מְדַבֵּר וְאֶעֱרֹךְ מִלִּים – וְלֹא לְהוֹכִיחַ ;
וְאַזְכִּיר קַדְמוֹנִיּוֹת – לֹא לְהוֹעִיל.
אַךְ עַתָּה הֱצִיקַתְנִי רוּחִי:
עוּרָה, אֲדוֹנִי, וְהִתְבּוֹנֵן וְהַט אֹזֶן לְשַׁוְעַת מִתְחַנֵּן,
וְלֵב עָגוּם תַּרְנִין, אִם פָּנֶיךָ לֹא תַעֲנִין !
מְאוּמָה לֹא אֲבַקֵּשׁ – בִּלְתִּי קֶשֶׁב.
וְאִם אֶל כָּמוֹנִי יִפְנֶה כָמוֹךְ – אֵינֶנּוּ תָמֹהַּ,
וְאִם תֵּט אֵלַי סְכוֹת חִין עֶרְכִּי – כְּבוֹדְךָ לֹא יֵחָל
וְאֵין לְמַעֲלָתְךָ גֵּרָעוֹן.
אָעִיר זִכְרוֹנֵי קֶדֶם אֲשֶׁר צִדְקִי בָם,
וְאִם תִּבְחַר אֱמוּנָה, תּוֹדֶה לִי עֲלֵיהֶם. [...]

Though I am still speaking, stringing
words together, it is not to rebuke you.
Though I recall days gone by, it is not
to profit by them.[1] But now my spirit
constrains me to say: Arise, my lord,
and behold, listen to the suppliant's
cry. You will make the sad heart sing
for joy if you do not cover your face
with clouds. I ask nothing but an
attentive ear. If a man of your rank
were to turn to the likes of me, none
would wonder. And if you were to
bend down to me and heed my prayer,
your glory would not be diminished,
nor your eminence lessened. I shall
awaken memories of the past in which
my righteousness is manifest. If you
choose the path of truth, you will thank
me for having done so!

---

1. A reminder of the services he rendered Ḥisdai as his court poet and secretary.

279

דּוּנָשׁ בֶּן־לַבְרָט **Dunash ben Labrat**

וְאוֹמֵר : אַל תִּישַׁן

וְאוֹמֵר : 'אַל תִּישַׁן! שְׁתֵה יַיִן יָשָׁן,
עֲלֵי מֹר עִם שֵׁשׁ שׁוֹשָׁן וְכֹפֶר וַאֲהָלִים,
בְּפַרְדֵּס רִמּוֹנִים וְתָמָר וּגְפָנִים
וְנִטְעֵי נַעֲמָנִים וּמִינֵי הָאֲשָׁלִים,
וְרֶגֶשׁ צְנוֹרִים וְהֶמְיַת כִּנּוֹרִים
עֲלֵי פֶה הַשָּׁרִים בְּמִנִּים וּנְבָלִים.
וְשָׁם כָּל עֵץ מוּנָף, יְפֵה פֶרִי עָנָף,
וְצִפּוֹר כָּל כָּנָף יְרַנֵּן בֵּין עָלִים,
וְיֶהְגּוּ הַיּוֹנִים כְּהוֹגִים נְגוּנִים,
וְהַתּוֹרִים עוֹנִים וְהוֹמִים כַּחֲלִילִים.
וְנִשְׁתֶּה בַעֲרוּגוֹת בְּשׁוֹשַׁנִּים סוּגוֹת,
וְנָגִיס הַתּוּגוֹת בְּמִינֵי הַלּוּלִים,
וְנֹאכַל מַמְתַּקִּים וְנִשְׁתֶּה מְזָרְקִים
וְנִנְהַג בַּעֲנָקִים וְנִשְׁתֶּה בְסָפָלִים.
וְאָקוּם בַּבְּקָרִים אֲנִי לִשְׁחֹט פָּרִים
בְּרִיאִים נִבְחָרִים, וְאֵילִים וַעֲגָלִים,
וְנִמְשַׁח שֶׁמֶן טוֹב וְנַקְטִיר עֵץ רָטֹב.
בְּטֶרֶם יוֹם קָטֹב יְבוֹאֵנוּ – נַשְׁלִים!'

גְּעַרְתִּיהוּ : 'דֹּם, דֹּם! עֲלֵי זֹאת אֵיךְ תִּקְדֹּם –
וּבֵית קֹדֶשׁ וַהֲדֹם אֱלֹהִים לָעֲרֵלִים!
בְּכִסְלָה דִּבַּרְתָּ וְעַצְלָה בָחַרְתָּ
וְהֶבֶל אָמַרְתָּ כְּלֵצִים וּכְסִילִים,
וְעָזַבְתָּ הֶגְיוֹן בְּתוֹרַת אֵל עֶלְיוֹן
וְתָגִיל – וּבְצִיּוֹן יְרוּצוּן שׁוּעָלִים.
וְאֵיךְ נִשְׁתֶּה יַיִן וְאֵיךְ נָרִים עַיִן –
וְהָיִינוּ אַיִן, מְאוּסִים וּגְעוּלִים!'

THE POET REFUSES AN INVITATION TO DRINK

He said: 'Do not sleep! Drink old wine, amidst myrrh and lilies, henna and aloes, in an orchard of pomegranates, palms, and vines, full of pleasant plants and tamarisks, to the hum of fountains and the throb of lutes, to the sound of singers, flutes and lyres. There every tree is tall, branches are fair with fruit, and winged birds of every kind sing among the leaves. The doves moan melodiously, and the turtle-doves reply, cooing like reed pipes. There we shall drink among flower-beds fenced in by lilies, putting sorrow to rout with songs of praise. We shall eat sweets as we drink by the bowlful. We shall act like giants, drinking out of huge goblets. And in the mornings I shall rise to slaughter fat choice bulls and rams and calves. We shall anoint ourselves with fragrant oil and burn aloe incense. Oh, before doom overtakes us, let us enjoy ourselves in peace!'

But I reproached him thus: 'Silence! How dare you – when the Holy House, the footstool of God, is in the hands of the gentiles. You have spoken foolishly, you have chosen sloth, you have uttered nonsense, like the mockers and fools. You have forsaken the study of the Supreme God's law. Even as you rejoice, jackals run wild in Zion. Then how could we drink wine, how even raise our eyes – when we are loathed and abhorred, and less than nothing?'

יוֹסֵף אִבְּן־אֲבִיתוֹר **Joseph ibn Abitur**

יָדַעְתִּי, אֱלֹהַי — CONFESSION

יָדַעְתִּי, אֱלֹהַי, כִּי אֲנִי חָמַסְתִּי נַפְשִׁי
וְאָנֹכִי סַבֹּתִי חָרְבָּן עַל מִקְדָּשִׁי.
פְּשָׁעַי הֵם לְכָדוּנִי וַיָּקֶם בִּי כַחֲשִׁי,
כִּי עֲוֹנוֹתַי עָבְרוּ רֹאשִׁי.

I know, my God, that I have done
violence to myself, that I have brought
destruction upon my Temple. My own
crimes have trapped me, my lies have
risen up against me; *for my sins have
swept over my head.*

אָנֹכִי הַחוֹטֵא וְהָרַע מִתְּחִלָּתִי,
בִּי לְבַדִּי הֶעָוֹן וְאֵין בְּאַחֵר זוּלָתִי,
גַּם לֹא יִתְעָרַב זָר עִמִּי בְּנַפִילָתִי
וְהַבֹּשֶׁת הִיא סוּתִי וּכְלִמָּה מַלְבּוּשִׁי
כִּי עֲוֹנוֹתַי עָבְרוּ רֹאשִׁי.

I am the sinner, the evil-doer, from my
very inception. I alone am guilty, no
other is at fault; no stranger shall have
any part in my downfall. Shame is my
garment, disgrace my clothing; *for my
sins have swept over my head.*

דְּבָרַי יַרְשִׁיעוּנִי וּשְׂפָתַי יַעֲנוּ בִי,
הֵן בְּעָוֹן חוֹלָלְתִּי וְעַמִּי נוֹלַד חוֹבִי,
וּבוֹ יֶחֱמַתְנִי אִמִּי וּבוֹ גִּדְּלַנִי אָבִי.
אֵין פֶּשַׁע כְּמוֹ פִשְׁעִי אֲשֶׁר הוּא לִי לְמוֹקְשִׁי
כִּי עֲוֹנוֹתַי עָבְרוּ רֹאשִׁי.

My very words convict me, my lips
bear witness against me. Indeed, I was
brought to birth in iniquity, and my
guilt was born with me. My mother
conceived me in guilt, my father reared
me in it. There is no crime like mine,
it sets a snare for me; *for my sins have
swept over my head.*

זוּלָתִי עָוֹן כָּל יוֹם, דַּיֵּנִי עָוֹן הַיּוֹם.
חֶטְא יוֹם אֶחָד אִלּוּ פָקַד עָלַי אָיֹם,
טָבַעְתִּי בְּאֵין מָקוֹם וְלֹא אֶמְצָא לִי פִדְיוֹם.
רְאוּ מֶה עָשָׂה חֶטְאִי וּמַה שִׁלַּם לִי טִפְשִׁי
כִּי עֲוֹנוֹתַי עָבְרוּ רֹאשִׁי.

This day's crimes alone – not even
counting those of other days – would
suffice. If the Dread One were to
punish me for the sins of a single day,
I would sink without any foothold, and
would find no redemption. See what
my crime has done, how my folly has
repaid me; *for my sins have swept over
my head.*

יַד אוֹיְבִי מְצָאַתְנִי וְנָפַלְתִּי בְּיַד צוֹרְרַי,
כִּי הִכְעַסְתִּי לְיוֹצְרִי וְגַם מָרַדְתִּי בְצוּרִי,

My assailant found me out, I fell into
the hands of my enemies, because I
angered my Creator and rebelled

לֹא מָשַׁלְתִּי בְיִצְרִי לָכֵן מָשַׁל בִּי צָרִי.
אֵין עָוֹן כַּעֲוֹנִי וְאֵין יֶקֶשׁ כְּיַקְשִׁי
כִּי עֲוֹנוֹתַי עָבְרוּ רֹאשִׁי.

against my Rock. I did not curb my
passion; now my enemy curbs me.
There is no guilt like mine, no trap like
the trap set for me; *for my sins have
swept over my head.*

מִי הָאִישׁ הֶחָפֵץ לְהָמִית נַפְשׁוֹ בְּיָדוֹ —
נִהְיֶה לּוֹ אֲנִי וַעֲוֹנִי, וְלֹא יִהְיֶה הוּא לְבַדּוֹ;
סוֹף וָרֹאשׁ לֹא יִרְצֶה בָזֶה לֹא אִישׁ וְלֹא עַבְדּוֹ,
אֲנִי שָׂחִתִי בְּמֵי פִשְׁעִי, מִי יִדְלֵנִי מֵרַפְשִׁי?
כִּי עֲוֹנוֹתַי עָבְרוּ רֹאשִׁי.

If any man should wish to die by his
own hands, my sin and I shall join him,
and he will not be alone. No man, not
even a slave, would desire to live from
such a beginning to such an end. I
swim in a sea of crime; who will lift me
up out of my filth? *For my sins have
swept over my head.*

עֲשׁוּקִים הֵם בְּנֵי אִמִּי, חֲמָסָם וְדִינָם עָלַי,
פָּטוֹר לֹא יִפָּטְרֵנִי דַּם טַפַּי וְעוֹלָלַי,
צוּרִי, כִּי אֲנִי הֲרַגְתִּים בְּחַטֹּאתַי וּמַעֲלָלַי,
וְיָדִי הִיא פְצָעַתְנִי וַחֲמָסִי עֲלֵי נַפְשִׁי
כִּי עֲוֹנוֹתַי עָבְרוּ רֹאשִׁי.

My mother's sons are oppressed; I
must answer for the violence done to
them. O my Lord, I shall never be
purged of the blood of my children and
infants, for I killed them with my sins
and misdeeds. My own hand wounded
me, my own self did me wrong; *for my
sins have swept over my head.*

קָמוּ בִי עֲוֹנוֹתַי וְלֹא מָצָאתִי תְקוּמָה,
רָמָה יָדָם עָלַי וּבָאוּנִי בְּיָד רָמָה.
שָׁמַיִם וָאָרֶץ אָז רָאוּ בִי נְקָמָה.
אֲנִי אֶבְכֶּה בְּלֵילֵי שָׁנָה, בְּשַׁבַּתִּי וּבְחָדְשִׁי
כִּי עֲוֹנוֹתַי עָבְרוּ רֹאשִׁי.

My iniquities stood up against me, I
could not stand my ground. They
raised their hand high over me, charged
at me defiantly. Then heaven and earth
saw their vengeance upon me. Now I
weep every night, all year long, and on
Sabbaths too, and on New Moons; *for
my sins have swept over my head.*

תְּעֵבוּנִי מְתֵי תַחַת, שִׁנְּאוּנִי צָבָא מְגֻעָל,
יָדְעוּ כִּי אֲנִי נִתְעָב, רָאוּ כִּי אֲנִי נִגְעָל.
צוּרִי, מָה אֲשֶׁר אֶעֱשֶׂה, מָה אֲשֶׁר אֶפְעָל?
שְׁעֵה שׁוּעִי וּפִלּוּלִי וְהַט אָזְנְךָ לְמוֹ רַחֲשִׁי
כִּי עֲוֹנוֹתַי עָבְרוּ רֹאשִׁי.

The dwellers of the underworld detest
me, even the host of the impure abhor
me. They sense that I am loathsome,
they see that I am soiled. My Lord,
what shall I do, what can I do? Oh,
turn to my cry and my plea, listen to
my prayer; *for my sins have swept over
my head.*

חֵפֶץ מָה לִי בַחַיִּים, הֲנָאָה אֵין לִי בְמוֹתִי,
חֶטְאִי עָלַי בְּחַיַּי, וּבְמוֹתִי אַשְׁמָתִי.

I have no pleasure in life, I have no
enjoyment in death. My sin afflicts me
in life, my guilt in death. Hasten to me

חוּשָׁה לִי וְעָזְרֵנִי, אֵל יוֹצֵר נִשְׁמָתִי,
סְלַח פְּשָׁעִי וְחִישׁ יִשְׁעִי, מַלְכִּי גּוֹאֲלִי וּקְדוֹשִׁי
כִּי עֲוֹנוֹתַי עָבְרוּ רֹאשִׁי.

and help me, O God, maker of my
soul. Forgive my crime, speed my
salvation, O my King, my Redeemer,
my Holy One; *for my sins have swept
over my head.*

יִצְחָק אִבְּן־כַּ׳לְפוּן   *Isaac ibn Khalfun*

בְּעֵת חֵשֶׁק יְעִירֵנִי   THE RETREAT

בְּעֵת חֵשֶׁק יְעִירֵנִי, אֲדַלֵּג
כְּאַיָּל לַחֲזוֹת עֵינֵי כְבוּדָּה.
וְאָבוֹאָה, וְהֵן אִמָּהּ לְנֶגְדָּהּ –
וְאָבִיהָ וְאָחִיהָ וְדוֹדָהּ!
אֲשׁוּרֶנָּה, וְאֶפְנֶה לַאֲחוֹרַי,
כְּאִלּוּ לֹא אֲנִי רֵעַהּ־יְדִידָהּ.
יְרֵא מֵהֶם, וְעָלֶיהָ לְבָבִי
כְּלֵב אִשָּׁה מְשֻׁכֶּלֶת יְחִידָהּ.

When desire arouses me, I leap like a
deer to see my lady's eyes. But when I
come, I find her mother there – and her
father and her brother and her uncle![1]
I look at her, then quickly turn away,
as though I were not her beloved. I am
afraid of them, and my heart mourns
for her like the heart of a woman bereft
of her only son.

פְּנֵי תֵבֵל   THE WORLD AND HER
CHILDREN

פְּנֵי תֵבֵל כְּצַוַּאר הַמְצֹרָע –
לָכֵן הָרֹק בְּפָנֶיהָ צְדָקָה;
וְהַגְעַל בְּעֹרֶף אוֹהֲבֶיהָ,
וְגַלּוּי מַעֲרָם – חֻקָּה חֲקוּקָה.
לָכֵן רַוֵּם לְלַעֲנָה, אִם תְּהָכִיל,
וְהַרְאֵם כִּי תְרַוֵּמוֹ מְתִיקָה,
וְרַוֵּה חַרְבְּךָ מִדַּם בְּנֵי אִישׁ,
וְלֹא תִשְׁמַע אֲלֵיהֶם קוֹל נְאָקָה.

The World's face is like a leper's neck.
Therefore, it is only right to spit in her
face; it is fitting and proper to cast
one's sandals at the nape of her lovers
and to strip them bare. So, if you can,
make them drink deep of wormwood,
but pretend to satisfy them with sweet
drinks. Then make your sword drink
deep of men's blood, and do not heed
their groans. Show no mercy to high or

1. Or 'betrothed'.

283

וְלֹא תַחְמֹל עֲלֵי קָטֹן וְגָדוֹל,
וְתֹאמַר: 'כִּי בָזֶה יֶשׁ לִי חֲשִׁיקָה.'
נְחָשִׁים הֵם וְעַקְרַבִּים, וְלוּ תַ־
עֲנִיק לָהֶם יְחִידָתָךְ עֲנִיקָה,
בְּנֵי חֶבֶל לְעוֹלָם יִבְגְּדוּ כַּ־
אֲשֶׁר תִּבְגֹּד בְּעֵת צָרָה וְצוּקָה.
אֱמֶת, הֵמָּה כְאִמָּם, כֵּן הֲבִיאֵם
בְּרֶחֶם הָרְחָבָה, הָעֲמֻקָּה.
הֲרֹג אוֹתָם בְּמוֹ סֵתֶר וְגָלוּי,
וְאֵל עָרֵב לְלֹא תֵרֵד עֲלוּקָה.

low, but say outright: 'This is what I
wish to do'. They are snakes and
scorpions, these children of the World,
and even if you offer them your
precious life as a gift, they will always
betray you, as does the World herself
in time of anguish and distress. Yes,
they are just like their mother – so put
them back into her deep, wide womb;
kill them, either secretly or in the open.
God is your pledge that you will not go
down to hell.

אֲרַדֵּף מַחֲנֶה גָדוֹל

THE POET'S BOAST

[...] אֲרַדֵּף מַחֲנֶה גָדוֹל לְבַדִּי
וְאָנִיס, וַאֲנִי אֶחָד, רְבָבָה.
רֹכֵב עַל בָּמֳתֵי עָב קַל רְצוֹנִי,
וְאֶבְעַט בַּמְּלָכִים לָרְכִיבָה.
אֲנִי עוֹלֵב לְכָל מַמְרֶה אֲמָרַי,
וְנִשְׁמָתִי בְּכַף רֵעַי עֲלוּבָה.
יְדִידְבְּנִי כְּמוֹ דוֹנַג לְשׁוֹן רַךְ,
וְרוּחַ פִּי לְכָל בַּרְזֶל מְדִיבָה.
נְהָרוֹת יִמְחֲאוּ הַכַּף בְּעָבְרִי,
וְלִפְעָמַי מְצוּלֹת יָם חֲרֵבָה.
אֲנִי אוֹהֵב וְגַם חוֹשֵׁק לְכָל בָּר,
וְכֵן נַפְשִׁי לְכָל נָבָר אֲהוּבָה.
וְלֹא מִרְמָה לְכָל אָדָם עֲלֵי פִי,
וְחַיָּתִי לְכָל עָצֵב עֲצֵבָה.
וְאִלּוּ יֻלְּדוּ מֵאֵין נְקֵבוֹת
גְּבָרִים – לֹא יְלָדַתְנִי נְקֵבָה. [...]

I can hunt down great armies by
myself and, single-handed, rout ten
thousand. Whenever I want, I ride
upon swift cloud-banks, kicking the
kings as I ride by. I humble all those
who disobey me, but I humble my soul
and submit to my friends. A soft
tongue melts me like wax, though the
breath of my mouth eats away iron.
Rivers clap their hands as I pass by;
deep waters dry up under my feet. I
have great love for the pure of heart
and am myself beloved by the innocent.
I speak no word of treachery to any
man; I am heartbroken for all the
brokenhearted. If a man could be born
not of a woman, I would be that man!

שְׁמוּאֵל הַנָּגִיד   *Samuel Hanagid*

אָמְרָה: שְׂמַח   THE MOMENT

אָמְרָה: 'שְׂמַח, בַּעֲבוּר הִגִּיעֲךָ אֵל אֱלֵי
שָׁנִים חֲמִשִּׁים בְּעוֹלָמְךָ!' – וְלֹא יָדְעָה
כִּי אֵין חֲלֻקָּה בְּעֵינַי בֵּין יְמוֹתַי אֲשֶׁר
עָבְרוּ וּבֵינוֹת יְמֵי נֹחַ אֲשֶׁר אִשְׁמְעָה.
אֵין לִי בָעוֹלָם לְבַד שָׁעָה אֲנִי בָהּ, וְהִיא
תַּעֲמֹד כְּרֶגַע – וְאַחַר כֵּן כְּעָב נָסְעָה.

She said: 'Rejoice, for God has brought
you to your fiftieth year in the world!'
But she had no inkling that, for my
part, there is no difference at all
between my own days which have gone
by and the distant days of Noah in the
rumoured past. I have nothing in the
world but the hour in which I am: it
pauses for a moment, and then, like a
cloud, moves on.

הֲלִינוֹתִי גְּדוּד כָּבֵד   IN THE RUINED CITADEL

הֲלִינוֹתִי גְּדוּד כָּבֵד בְּבִירָה
הֲרַסוּהָ יְמֵי קֶדֶם קְצִינִים.
וְיָשַׁנּוּ עֲלֵי גַבָּהּ וְצִדָּהּ –
וְתַחְתֵּינוּ בְּעָלֶיהָ יְשֵׁנִים.
וְדִבַּרְתִּי לְלִבִּי: אֵי קְהָלִים
וְעַמִּים שֶׁשָּׁכְנוּ בָזֹאת לְפָנִים?
וְאֵי בוֹנִים וּמַחְרִיבִים, וְשָׂרִים
וְדַלִּים, וַעֲבָדִים וַאֲדוֹנִים,
וּמוֹלִידִים וּשְׁכוּלִים, וְאָבוֹת
וּבָנִים, וַאֲבֵלִים וַחֲתָנִים?
וְעַם רַב נוֹלְדוּ אַחַר אֲחֵרִים,
בְּיָמִים אַחֲרֵי יָמִים וְשָׁנִים,
וְהָיוּ עַל פְּנֵי אֶרֶץ שְׁכֵנִים –
וְהֵם הַיּוֹם בְּלֵב אֶרֶץ שְׁכוּנִים,
וְקֶבֶר חָלְפוּ מֵאַרְמְנוֹתָם,
וְעָפָר – מֵחֲצֵרִים נַעֲמָנִים.

I billeted a strong force overnight in a
citadel laid waste in former days by
other generals. There we slept upon its
back and flanks, while under us its
landlords slept. And I said to my heart:
Where are the many people who once
lived here? Where are the builders and
vandals, the rulers and paupers, the
slaves and masters? Where are the
begetters and the bereaved, the fathers
and the sons, the mourners and the
bridegrooms? And where are the many
people born after the others had died,
in days gone by, after other days and
years? Once they lodged upon the
earth; now they are lodged within it.
They passed from their palaces to the
grave, from pleasant courts to dust.

וְאִלּוּ הֶעֱלוּ רֹאשָׁם וְיָצָאוּ –

שְׁלָלוּנוּ נְפָשִׁים וַעֲדָנִים.

אֱמֶת, נַפְשִׁי, אֱמֶת, כָּהֵם לְמָחָר

אֱהִי אָנִי, וְאֵלֶּה הַהֲמוֹנִים !

Were they now to raise their heads and
emerge, they would rob us of our lives
and pleasures. Oh, it is true, my soul,
most true: tomorrow I shall be like
them, and all these troops as well!

וַיֵּצֵא אָב   THE BATTLE OF ALFUENTE

...וכאשר הצילו האל אמר שירה זאת...והתרחש
הנצחון הנכבד הזה ביום הששי, יום ראשון באלול,
שנת שבע מאות ותשעים ושמונה.

*. . . When God came to his rescue he
spoke this song . . . The great victory took
place on Friday, the first of Elul, in the
year 4798 [4 August 1038].*

[. . .] וַיֵּצֵא אָב בְּרָעָה הַקְּדוּמָה,

וּבָא אֱלוּל בְּטוֹבָה לֹא אֲחוּרָה.

וְתָקַע אָהֳלוֹ בָּהָר בְּעֵבֶר,

וְתָקַעְנוּ בְּדֶרֶךְ הָעֲבָרָה,

וְלֹא שַׁתְנוּ לְבָבֵנוּ לְחֵילוֹ,

חֲשַׁבְנוּהוּ כְּאִלּוּ הוּא שְׁיָרָה.

וְהִרְבָּה, כַּאֲשֶׁר בָּא, הַדְּבָרִים,

וְשִׁסָּה בִי אֲנָשֵׁינוּ וְגֵרָה.

וּבִרְאוֹת צוֹרְרִי כִּי עַל לְשׁוֹנִי,

בְּפֶה אֶחָד, תְּדַבֵּר הַחֲבוּרָה –

אֲזַי הֵרִיק חֲנִית, רֹמַח וְחֶרֶב,

וְגַם סָגַר לְהִלָּחֵם סְגִירָה.

Then Av – the month of ancient woe[1] –
departed, and Elul arrived, speeding
good fortune. Ibn Abbas pitched his
tents on the mountain side, and we
pitched ours in the pass, taking no heed
of his army, as though it were a passing
caravan. Then he drew near and, with
many words, tried to incite my men
against me. But when my adversary
saw that my company spoke with my
voice, as one man, he uncovered spears,
swords, and lances, and prepared his
weapons for battle.

וְקָם הַצָּר – וְקָם הַצּוּר לְנֶגְדּוֹ ;

וְאֵיךְ תָּקוּם, בְּקוּם צוּר, הַיְצִירָה ?

וְעָמְדוּ הַחֲיָלוֹת מַעֲרָכָה

לְעֻמַּת מַעֲרֶכֶת צָר בְּשׁוּרָה.

אֲנָשִׁים יַחְשְׁבוּ, יוֹם אַף וְחֵמָה

My enemy rose – and the Rock rose
against him. How can any creature rise
up against his Creator? Now my
troops and the enemy's drew up their
ranks opposite each other. On such a
day of anger, jealousy, and rage, men

---

1. The first and second Temples were both destroyed on the ninth of Av.

וְקִנְאָה, אֶת בְּכוֹר מָוֶת – בְּכוֹרָה,
וְכָל אֶחָד יְבַקֵּשׁ לוֹ קְנוֹת שֵׁם,
וְנַפְשׁוֹ, בַּאֲשֶׁר יִקְנֶה, מְכוּרָה.
וְנֵעָה הָאֲדָמָה מִיסוֹדָהּ
וְנֶהְפְּכָה כְּמַהְפֶּכֶת עֲמֹרָה,
וּפָנִים קֻבְּצוּ פָארוּר וְהָדָר,
וְנֶהְפְּכוּ אֱלֵי שׁוּלֵי קְדֵרָה.
וְהַיּוֹם – יוֹם עֲרָפֶל וַחֲשֵׁכָה,
וְהַשֶּׁמֶשׁ, כְּמוֹ לִבִּי, שְׁחֹרָה,
וְקוֹל הָמוֹן – כְּקוֹל שַׁדַּי, כְּקוֹל יָם
וּמִשְׁבָּרָיו בְּעֵת יִסְעַר סְעִירָה.
וְהָאָרֶץ, בְּצֵאת שֶׁמֶשׁ, נְמוֹגָה
בְּעַמְדֶיהָ, כְּאִלּוּ הִיא שְׁכוּרָה,
וְהַסּוּסִים יְרוּצוּן גַּם יְשׁוּבוּן
כְּצִפְעוֹנִים נְטוּשִׁים מִמְּאוּרָה,
כְּאִלּוּ הָרְמָחִים הַשְּׁלוּחִים –
בְּרָקִים מִלְאוּ אֲוִיר בְּאוֹרָה,
וְהַחִצִּים כְּמוֹ נִטְפֵי גְשָׁמִים,
וְהַגַּבּוֹת כְּאִלּוּ הֵם כְּבָרָה,
וְקַשְׁתוֹתָם בְּכַפָּם כַּנְּחָשִׁים,
וְכָל נָחָשׁ בְּפִיו יָקִיא דְבוֹרָה,
וְהַחֶרֶב עֲלֵי רֹאשָׁם כְּלַפִּיד,
בְּנָפְלוֹ כָּהֲתָה בוֹ הַנֶּהָרָה.
וְדַם אִישִׁים עֲלֵי אֶרֶץ מְהַלֵּךְ
כְּדַם אֵילִים בְּצַדֵּי הָעֲזָרָה,
וְקָצוּ הַגְּבָרִים הַגְּבִירִים
בְּחַיֵּיהֶם, וְהַמִּיתָה בְחוּרָה.
כְּפִירִים יֶחֱזוּ מַכָּה טְרִיָּה
עֲלֵי רֹאשָׁם כְּאִלּוּ הִיא עֲטָרָה,
וְהַמִּיתָה בְדָתֵיהֶם יְשָׁרָה,
וְחַיָּתָם בְּעֵינֵיהֶם אֲסוּרָה.

deem the Prince of Death a princely prize; and each man seeks to win renown, though he must lose his life for it. The earth's foundations, overthrown like Gomorrah, reeled to and fro. Every face turned red, or black as the bottom of a pot. It was a day of darkness and thick fog. The sun was as black as my heart. The tumult was like that of a cloudburst, like the roar of breakers when the sea is swept by a storm. As the sun came out, the earth rocked on its pillars as if it were drunk. The horses lunged back and forth like vipers darting out of their nests. The hurled spears were like bolts of lightning, filling the air with light. Arrows pelted us like raindrops, as if our shields were sieves. Their strung bows were like serpents, each serpent spewing forth a stinging bee. Their swords above their heads were like glowing torches which darken as they fall. The blood of men flowed upon the ground like the blood of rams on the corners of the altar. Still, my gallant men scorned their lives, preferring death. These young lions welcomed each raw wound upon their heads as though it were a garland. To die – they believed – was to keep the faith; to live – they thought – was forbidden.

וּמָה אֶעֱשֶׂה ? וְאֵין מָנוֹס וּמִשְׁעָן
וּמַשְׁעֵנָה, וְהַתִּקְוָה עֲקוּרָה !
מְשַׂנְאִים יִשְׁפְּכוּ דָמִים כְּמַיִם
בְּיוֹם צַר – וַאֲנִי אֶשְׁפֹּךְ עֲתָרָה
לְאֵל מַשְׁפִּיל וּמַפִּיל כָּל מְעַוֵּל
בְּגֵעָצוֹ אֲשֶׁר חָפַר וְכָרָה,
וּמֵשִׁיב, יוֹם קְרָב, חֶרֶב וְחִצִּים
בְּלֵב אוֹיֵב אֲשֶׁר הֵכִין וְיָרָה. [...]

(1038)

רְאֵה הַיּוֹם בְּצָרָתִי	SHORT PRAYER IN TIME OF BATTLE

And what was I to do with no escape,
no prop or stay, and all hope gone?
While my foes, on this bitter day,
poured out blood like water, I poured
out my prayer to God, who degrades
all evildoers and makes them fall into
the pit which they have dug; to God,
who on the day of battle will make the
enemy's drawn swords and darting
arrows pierce his own heart!

...והמלחמה [בין צבאות הנגיד ובין צבאות אסמעיל
אבן עבאד] התלקחה ביניהם בקרבת הנחל ג׳ניל. אז
אמר את הבתים האלה ושמם במקום תפילת המנחה
ליום ההוא.

*... The battle [between the forces of
the Nagid and the army of Seville
under Isma'il ibn Abbad] flared up near
the Sengil river. It was then that he
composed these verses, which he recited
instead of the afternoon service on that
day.*

רְאֵה הַיּוֹם בְּצָרָתִי, שְׁמַע וּשְׁעֵה עֲתָרָתִי,
זְכָר־דָּבָר לְעַבְדְּךָ וְאַל אֵבוֹשׁ בְּשִׂבְרָתִי.
הֲתַגִּיעַ לְרַע לִי יָד וְאַתְּ יָדִי וְסִתְרָתִי ?
יְעַדְתַּנִי וְהֵיטַבְתָּ בְּיַד צִירִים בְּשׂוֹרָתִי.
אֲנִי עוֹבֵר בְּתוֹךְ מַיִם – דְּלֵנִי מִמְּגוּרָתִי,
אֲנִי הוֹלֵךְ בְּמוֹקֵד אֵשׁ – פְּצֵנִי מִבְּעֵרָתִי.
וְאִם יֶשׁ לִי מְרוֹרוֹת, מָה אֲנִי אוֹ מַה מְּרוֹרָתִי ?
אֲנִי בְצָר וְלֹא אוּכַל לְהַרְבּוֹת אֶת אֲמִירָתִי.
עֲשֵׂה לִי תַּאֲוַת לִבִּי וְחוּשָׁה נָא לְעֶזְרָתִי,
וְאִם אֵינִי כְדַאי אֶצְלָךְ, עֲשֵׂה לִבְנִי וְתוֹרָתִי !

(1039)

See my distress today; listen to my
prayer, and answer it. Remember Your
promise[1] to Your servant; do not
disappoint my hope. Can any hand do
me violence, when You are my hand
and my shelter? You once made me a
pledge and sent me good tidings with
Your angels. Now I am passing through
deep waters – lift me out of my terrors.
I am walking through searing fire –
snatch me from the flames. If I have
sinned – what am I, what are my sins?
I am in danger, and cannot pray at
length. Give me my heart's desire; oh,
hasten to my aid. If I am not deserving
in Your eyes – do it for the sake of my
son and my sacred learning.

1. In his childhood the Nagid had a vision, in which the archangels Michael and Gabriel brought him
God's promise of protection.

288

מְבַשֵּׂר טוֹב, הֲבִינֵנִי

ON LEARNING OF HIS ENEMY'S DEATH

והיה הרופא אבו מדין לן אצלו ויעוררו והודיעו על מה שראה בחלום ולא פקפק עוד בקצו של אבן אבי מוסי. ואכן נהרג הלה כעבור ימים מועטים. ויאמר הנגיד כשנתבשר במותו, והיה זה בשנת ת"ת, ויקרא לשירו בשם 'בשורה'.

One night, when the doctor Abu Medin was sleeping in his house, the Nagid woke him up and told him what he had dreamt; he was now certain that Ibn Abi Musa's death was imminent. And, indeed, the latter was killed a few days later. When the Nagid was informed of his death – this was in the year 4800 [1040] – he composed the following verses, which he entitled 'The Tidings'.

[...] 'מְבַשֵּׂר טוֹב, הֲבִינֵנִי וְהָרֵם קוֹל בְּחַסְדֶּךָ,
וְצַפְצֵף לִי כְּסוּס עָגוּר וְאַל תַּמְעִיט אֲמָרֶיךָ :
הֲצֶדֶק הוּא אֲשֶׁר אֶשְׁמָע, וְאֵיךְ הָיָה וְאֵיכָכָה ?
הֲבִינֵנִי, הֲגוּיַת בֶּן־אֲבִי־מוּסִי מְחֻתָּכָה ?
וְנִבְלָתוֹ – הֲנִסְחֲבָה עֲלֵי חוּצוֹת וְהֻשְׁלָכָה ?'

'Good herald, now tell me and, if you please, speak up. Twitter at me like a swallow, do not spare your words. Is what I hear true indeed? And how, how did it happen? Tell me, was the corpse of Ibn Abi Musa mangled? Was his carcass dragged through the streets, then flung away?'

הֱשִׁיבַנִי : 'חֲדֵה וּשְׂמַח וְיַעֲלֹץ לְבָבֶךָ,
וְקוּם וּרְקַע עֲלֵי רֶגֶל וְשׁוּב וּמְחָא בְכַפֶּךָ !
וְהִרָפֵד בְּתַפּוּחִים וְהִסָּמֵךְ בְּיֵינֶךָ,
וְגַדֵּל שֵׁם אֱלֹהֶיךָ וּמַלֵּא מִשְׂחוֹק פִּיךָ !
וְקוּם וּקְרָא בְּ"שִׁיר שִׁירִים"
וְאַל תִּקְרַב אֱלֵי "אֵיכָה".
וְתֵן לִי בַבְּשׂוֹרָה אֶת חֲלִיצָתְךָ וּמַדֶּיךָ –
לְמַעַן בֶּן־אֲבִי־מוּסִי כְּבָר נָפַל בְּמַהְפֵּכָה,
כְּמוֹ נִכְסַף לְבֶן־עַבָּאס אֲשֶׁר בִּקֵּשׁ לְהָרְגֶךָ,
וְהָלַךְ לַחֲזוֹת פָּנָיו בְּצַלְמָוֶת וּבַחֲשֵׁכָה.
וְהָעִיר מִמְּשֹׂשׂ קָמָיו מְשַׂמַּחַת כְּמוֹתֶךָ,
וּמִשּׁוֹאַת בְּנֵי בֵיתוֹ מְבֹהָלָה וְנָבוּכָה.'

He answered: 'Rejoice and let your heart exult! Arise and stamp your feet, then clap your hands! Indulge yourself in apricots, refresh yourself with wine, glorify the name of your God, fill your mouth with laughter, go and read the Song of Songs, and stay away from Lamentations. And, for my news, give me your belt and clothes. Know that Ibn Abi Musa has already fallen into the pit, as though he were longing for Ibn Abbas – who tried to kill you[1] – and went to see his face in darkness, dark as death. The city, full of his rivals' joy, is as elated as you are, but stunned and dazed as well by his kinsmen's ruin.'

---

1. Ibn Abbas, another enemy of the Nagid, was captured and executed the previous year, after the battle of Alfuente (p. 286).

הֲשִׁיבוֹתִיו: 'דְּבַשׁ מָתוֹק וְחָלָב עַל לְשׁוֹנֶךָ,
וְתִתְבַּשֵּׂר מְהֵרָה כִּי כְּמוֹ זֹאת בָּא לְצָרֶיךָ!
קְחָה מַדַּי וּמַלְבּוּשַׁי וְשִׂים נִזְרִי בְּרֹאשֶׁךָ,
וְלֵךְ אֶל כָּל מְיֻדָּעַי וְהַשְׂמִיחֵם בְּמִלֶּיךָ —
וְיֵדְעוּ כִּי יְחִידָתוֹ לְגֵיהִנֹּם מְמֻשָּׁכָה
וְכִי מֶלֶךְ הֲרָגָהוּ וְרָאָה בוֹ אֲשֶׁר חָכָה'.

I said to him: 'Sweet syrup and milk
are on your tongue! May you quickly
learn that a like fate has struck down
your enemies! Now take my clothes,
my robes, put my diadem on your head,
go to all my friends and gladden them
with your words. Let them know that
his soul has been dragged down to hell,
that he was killed by a king[1] who is
now gloating over him, as he had
hoped.'

בְּנוּ עַבָּאס, שְׂמַח כִּי בָא לְשַׁחֲרֶךָ חֲבֵרֶךָ!
שְׁבוּ יַחַד, וְהַכֵּהוּ בְּצַלְמָוֶת — וְיַכֶּכָה.
וְאִם תַּחְפֹּץ, קְשֹׁר חֶבֶל עֲלֵי רֹאשׁוֹ וְרֹאשֶׁךָ,
וְיָנוּד עַל אֲשֶׁר הָיָה — וְתָשִׁיב לוֹ בְּקִינֶיךָ,
וְיִהְיֶה לָךְ כְּמוֹ פֶסֶל — וְתִהְיֶה לוֹ כְּמוֹ מִיכָה.
וְחִרְשׁוּ עַל בְּנֵי שַׁחַת שְׁנֵיכֶם רַע וְתַהְפּוּכָה.
וְיִרְקַב בֶּן־אֲבִי־מוּסִי כְּמוֹתֶךָ בְּקִבְרֶךָ,
וְיִשָּׁכַח, כְּמוֹ נִשְׁכַּח שְׁמָךְ הָרַע וְזִכְרֶךָ.
כְּבָר בָּאתֶם אֱלֵי צַוָּאר בְּפַח יָקוּשׁ וּבִשְׂבָכָה,
וְנָחָה הַמְּלוּכָה מִן מְשׁוֹאַתְכֶם וְשָׁכָכָה,
וְאֵין בָּכֶם אֲשֶׁר יִצְלַח לְמוֹעֵצוֹת וְלִמְלוּכָה.

Ibn Abbas, be happy that your friend
has come to visit you! Sit together in
the gloom of death, hit him and he will
hit you back. Or, if you wish to mourn,
wind ropes around his head and yours.
He will lament what is past, and you
will answer him with your dirges. He
will be for you a graven image, and you
will be like a father[2] to him. Now the
pair of you can plot your evil and
subversion against the progeny of the
pit. Ibn Abi Musa will rot, as you did
in your grave; he will be forgotten, as
your evil name and memory have been
forgotten. Now that you are up to your
necks in nets and snares, the kingdom
will at last be rid of your havoc and
find peace, for none of you is fit for the
councils of kings.

וְאַתְּ, חוֹפֵר, אֲשֶׁר תַּחְפֹּר קְבוּרָתוֹ בְּיָדֶיךָ —
כְּרֵה לוֹ כַּאֲשֶׁר כָּרָה, בְּדִינָךְ וֵאלֹהֶיךָ,
וְהַעֲמִיק עַד תְּהוֹם לוֹ — וַאֲנִי אֶתֵּן שְׂכָרֶךָ,
וְהַךְ בָּאת לְכָל עַיִן אֲשֶׁר עָלָיו תְּהִי בוֹכָה!

And you, O gravedigger, whose hands
will dig his grave, I charge you by your
God and by your creed: make a pit for
him, as he made for others. Dig down
to the very abyss – I will pay you for it
myself – and with your mattock strike
any eye that sheds a tear for him!

---

1. Nega, king of the Slavs.
2. Lit. 'Micah' (Judges 17.4 ff.), who made an idol and installed a young Levite in his house as priest.

לְזֹאת אֶלְבַּשׁ וְאֶתְעַטֵּף וְאֶתְבַּשֵּׂם וְאֶסּוּכָה
וְאֶתְנַהֵג בְּטוּב לֵבָב וְאָשׁוּבָה וְאֵלֵכָה
וְאֶדָּמֶה אֱלֵי יוֹנִים עֲלֵי מִלֵּאת וּבְבֵרֵכָה,
וְאֶתְאַמֵּץ כְּשִׁמְשׁוֹן עַל יְתַד אֹהֶל וּמַסֵּכָה,
וְאָגִילָה בְּמוֹת צָרַי בְּבֵיתָם אוֹ בְמַעְרָכָה.

As for me, I will put on festive clothing,
I will perfume and anoint myself. I will
move about with a glad heart, coming
and going, as happy as a dove beside a
brook or splashing in a pool. I will
become as strong as Samson, who
pulled away the tent pin and the warp.[1]
I will make merry when my enemies
die, whether it be in their homes or in
battle!

וְאֹמֵר: 'מִי אֲשֶׁר עָשָׂה לְךָ אֶת זֹאת כְּנַפְשֶׁךָ?
עֲנִיתִיהוּ: 'הֲלֹא תֵדַע, אֱלֹהִים יַעֲשֶׂה כָּבָה!
שְׁתֹק, וּכְתֹב לְךָ טוּרִים לְזִכָּרוֹן בְּסִפְרֶךָ,
וְתִקְרָאֵם קְרִיאָתָךְ בְּיוֹם שַׁבָּת בְּדָתֶךָ,
וִיהְיוּ עַל לְבָבֶךָ וְהוֹדַעְתָּם לְבָנֶיךָ.

(1040)

If anyone should ask me, 'Who was it
that made your wish come true?', I will
answer, 'Don't you know? It was God
who did all this! Now be quiet, and
write down these verses! Read them
aloud, as the portion of the Law is read
on Sabbath. Keep them in your heart
and teach them to your sons.'

הֲלָעַד אֲנִי שׁוֹכֵן   COMPLAINT

הֲלָעַד אֲנִי שׁוֹכֵן בְּאֹהֶל, כְּמוֹ עֲרָב,
וְתַחַת יְרִיעָה כָּל יְמוֹתַי מְדוֹרִי?
כְּבָר שְׁכָחוּנִי הָעֲרָבָה וְהַזְּמָן
חֲצֵרַי בְּעִירִי – אָן יְדִידֵי חֲצֵרִי?

Shall I forever live in a tent, like a
Bedouin? Must all my days be passed
beneath tent-curtains? Time and the
desert have already made me forget my
court back in town. Oh, where are my
courtier friends?

קְרָב   WAR

קְרָב דּוֹמֶה בְּרֹאשׁוֹ אֶל יְפֵיפָה
אֲשֶׁר כָּל אִישׁ לְשַׂחֵק בָּהּ יְאַוֶּה,
וְסוֹפוֹ כַּזְּקֵנָה הַמָּאוּסָה
אֲשֶׁר כָּל שׁוֹחֲרָהּ יִבְכֶּה וְיִדְוֶה.

War is at first like a beautiful girl with
whom all men long to play, but in the
end like a repulsive hag whose suitors
all weep and ache.

1. Judges 16.4.

לֹא יַעֲבִידְךָ   THE MASTER

לֹא יַעֲבִידְךָ מוֹשְׁלָךְ עַד יְקַוֶּה כִּי
יִשְׁקֹט וְאַתְּ תִּיגַע וְתִיצַף בְּמַעְבָּדָיו.
אַתָּה כְּמֶלְקָחָיו : בְּיָדוֹ יְבִיאָךְ תּוֹךְ
הָאוּר – וְיִשָּׁמֹר מִשְּׂרֵפָה בְּךָ יָדָיו !

No master will hire you, unless he can
expect to be idle while you tire and
become weary in his service. You are
for him like tongs: with his hands he
pushes you into the fire, but he takes
great care not to burn himself on you.

אֶרֶץ לְאָדָם   THE PRISON

אֶרֶץ לְאָדָם בֵּית כְּלוּא כָּל יָמָיו,
לָכֵן אֲנִי אוֹמֵר אֱמֶת לַסָּכָל :
תָּרוּץ – וְשָׁמַיִם סְבִיבוֹתֶיךָ
מִכָּל עֲבָרִים ; קוּם וְצֵא אִם תּוּכָל.

The earth is a prison to man all his life.
Therefore I say this truth to the fool:
though you rush about, the sky
surrounds you on all sides. Try to get
out, if you can.

אוֹהֲבֵי יָמִים   THE ROOT

אוֹהֲבֵי יָמִים עַל גַּב אָרֶץ,
הַיְדַעְתֶּם כִּי חַיֵּיכֶם שָׁוְא ?
אַתֶּם מִשֹּׁרֶשׁ מָוֶת : כָּל
עָנָף יָשׁוּב אֶל שָׁרָשָׁיו !

Oh, you merry-makers on earth's back,
do you know that your life is nothing?
You grew from the root of death – and
every branch to its own root returns!

שִׁית לִבְּךָ   THE TWO CRIES

שִׁית לִבְּךָ, תָּבִין קְלוֹן שִׂמְחַת
לֵב בֵּין שְׁתֵּי בְכִיּוֹת לְךָ נִמְצָאת:
תִּבְכֶּה בְּעֵת בּוֹאֲךָ אֱלֵי עוֹלָם
אַתָּה, וְאַחַר יִבְכְּךָ עֵת צֵאת.

Reflect, and you will realize how
shameful is your heart's delight, which
comes between two cries: you cry when
you come into the world, and others
cry for you when you leave it.

הַיָּם בֵּינִי וּבֵינֶךְ   LAMENT FOR HIS BROTHER

וְנִסַּע עד שהתקרב למקום קברו והפסיק את
נסיעתו ופנה אליו ואמר בענין זה:

*On one of his journeys, he passed by his
brother's burial-place. There he paused
and addressed him as follows:*

הַיָּם בֵּינִי וּבֵינֶךְ וְלֹא אֶטֶּה לַחֲלוֹתֶךְ
וְלֹא אָרוּץ בְּלֵב חָרֵד וְאֵשֵׁב עַל קְבוּרָתֶךְ?
אֱמֶת, אִם אֶעֱשֶׂה כָזֹאת אֱהִי בוֹגֵד בְּאַחְוָתֶךְ,
אֲהָהּ, אָחִי, אֲנִי יוֹשֵׁב עֲלֵי קִבְרָךְ לְעֻמָּתֶךְ,
לָךְ מַכְאוֹב בְּתוֹךְ לִבִּי כְּמַכְאוֹבִי בְמִיתָתֶךְ.
וְאִם אֶתֵּן לָךְ שָׁלוֹם – וְלֹא אֶשְׁמַע תְּשׁוּבָתֶךְ,
וְלֹא תֵצֵא לְפָגְשֵׁנִי בְּיוֹם בּוֹאִי לְאַדְמָתֶךְ,
וְלֹא תִשְׂחַק בְּקִרְבָתִי וְלֹא אֶשְׂחַק בְּקִרְבָתֶךְ,
וְלֹא תִרְאֶה תְמוּנָתִי וְלֹא אֶרְאֶה תְמוּנָתֶךְ,
לְמַעַן כִּי שְׁאוֹל בֵּיתֶךְ וּבַקֶּבֶר מְעוֹנָתֶךְ.
בְּכוֹר אָבִי וּבֶן אִמִּי, שְׁלוֹמִים לָךְ בְּאַחֲרִיתֶךְ,
וְרוּחַ אֵל תְּהִי נָחָה עֲלֵי רוּחָךְ וְנִשְׁמָתֶךְ!
אֲנִי הוֹלֵךְ לְאַרְצִי, כִּי בְאֶרֶץ סָגְרוּ אוֹתֶךְ.
וְאָנוּם עֵת וְאִיקַץ עֵת – וְאַתְּ לָעַד בְּנוּמָתֶךְ,
וְעַד בּוֹא יוֹם חֲלִיפָתִי בְּלִבִּי אֵשׁ פְּרִידָתֶךְ!

Is there a sea between me and you, that
I should not turn aside to be with you,
that I should not run with a troubled
heart to sit at your grave-side? Truly,
if I did not do so, I would be a traitor
to our brotherly love. O my brother,
here I am, facing you, sitting by your
grave, and the grief in my heart is as
great as on the day you died. If I
greeted you, I would hear no reply.
You do not come out to meet me when
I visit your grounds. You will not
laugh in my company, nor I in yours.
You cannot see my face, nor I yours,
for the pit is your home, the grave
your dwelling-place! First-born of my
father, son of my mother, may you
have peace in your final rest, and may
the spirit of God rest upon your spirit
and your soul! I am returning to my
own soil, for you have been locked
under the soil. Sometimes I shall sleep,
sometimes wake – while you lie in your
sleep forever. But until my last day,
the fire of your loss will remain in my
heart!

רֵעִי, הֲתִישַׁן   THE TWO ECLIPSES

וּבְסוֹף כסלו של שנת תת"ה שׁר שירה וסיפר בה
שתי הלקיות, השמשי והירחי...

*At the end of the year 1044, the Nagid
composed this song, in which he described
the two eclipses, the solar and the lunar.*

רֵעִי, הֲתִישַׁן? קוּם וְהָעִירָה
שַׁחַר, וּבִשְׁמֵי מַעֲלָה שׁוּרָה:

Are you asleep, my friend? Rise and
awake the dawn, look up to heaven.

תִּרְאֶם כְּעוֹר נָמֵר אֲשֶׁר אֵין בּוֹ
מָקוֹם אֲשֶׁר אֵין בּוֹ חֲבַרְבּוּרָה;
וּרְאֵה חֲצִי סַהַר בְּלֵיל תֻּמּוֹ
קוֹדֵר כְּפִי כִבְשָׁן וְכִקְדֵרָה,
כִּדְמוּת פְּנֵי עַלְמָה אֲשֶׁר חֶצְיָם
אָדְמוּ וְעַל חֶצְיָם שְׁקַעְרוּרָה.

See, it is like a leopard's skin, all
covered with spots. And see how the
half-moon – which should be full on
this night – is as black as the mouth of
an oven or the rim of a pot; like the
face of a girl, half flushed and half in
shadow.

שׁוּב וַחֲזֵה שֶׁמֶשׁ אֲשֶׁר רֻבָּהּ
הוּבָא בְּסוֹף חֹדֶשׁ בְּשַׁעֲרוּרָה,
וּדְמוּת מְעַט אוֹרָהּ עֲלֵי חָשְׁכָּהּ
נֵזֶר בְּרֹאשׁ לוּדִית שְׁחַרְחָרָה,
וּדְמוּת אֲדָמָה, עַל אֲשֶׁר בָּא עַל
שִׁמְשָׁהּ, כְּבוֹכִיָּה חֲמַרְמָרָה.

Now look again, at this month's end,
and see the sun, almost engulfed by
gloom. What little light remains upon
its darkness is like a diadem on the
head of a Negress. And the earth, as if
in mourning for its sun, is like a woman
disfigured by tears.

הִכָּה שְׁנֵי אוֹרָיו בְּתוֹךְ חֹדֶשׁ
אֶחָד אֲשֶׁר לוֹ עֹז וְתִפְאָרָה:
כִּסָּה פְּנֵי סַהַר בְּחוּג אַרְצוֹ,
וּבְסַהֲרוֹ שִׁמְשׁוֹ מְסַתָּרָה.
כָּל זֹאת פְּעֻלַּת אֵל, וְהוּא יַעַשׂ
חֶפְצוֹ בְּמִפְעָלָיו אֲשֶׁר בָּרָא.

He who is master of might and beauty,
He struck both His luminaries in the
very same month. He covered the face
of the moon with His terrestrial globe
and blocked off the sun with His moon.
All this was done by God, who does as
He wishes with His works.

נִבְרָא בְּתוֹךְ סַהַר מְעַט אֹפֶל
מֵרֹאשׁ, וְחַמָּה נִבְרְאָה בָרָה;
לָכֵן אֲדַמֵּם, בְּהִקָּדְרָם
עַתָּה בְּחֹשֶׁךְ זֶה אֲשֶׁר קָרָה,
לִשְׁתֵּי שְׁכוּלוֹת: זֹאת בְּפָנֶיהָ
פֶּצַע, וְזֹאת פֶּצַע וְחַבּוּרָה.

From the very beginning He put some
shadow in the moon, but the sun He
created pure. Therefore – as they now
dim, in this darkness that has come to
pass – I compare them to two bereaved
women: the one with bruises on her
face, the other with bruises and sores.

אוֹר יוֹם בְּיוֹם הַקְדַּר, וְאוֹר לַיְל
הִקְדִּיר בְּעֶרֶב יוֹם וְאַשְׁמוּרָה –
כְּגִבִּיר אֲשֶׁר קָצַף וְהֵבִיא כָּל

He darkened the light of day in mid-
morning, and the light of night at
midnight, like a raging king who

294

שָׁרָיו בְּאַרְצוֹתָם בְּתוֹךְ צָרָה.
הִכָּה מְאוֹר לַיְל תְּחִלָּה, אַךְ
מַכַּת מְאוֹר הַיּוֹם מְאָחָרָה –
כִּגְבִיר אֲשֶׁר יַשְׁקֶה לְאָמָה כּוֹס
רַעַל, וְאַחַר יַשְׁקְ לִגְבִירָה. [...]

harasses all his lords in their own
domains. First He struck the night-
light, and only later did He strike the
light of day, like a king who gives a
stupefying drink first to his maid-
servant and afterwards to his queen.

אֲצַפֶּה אֱלֵי שַׁחַק

HEAVEN AND EARTH

אֲצַפֶּה אֱלֵי שַׁחַק וְכוֹכָבָיו
וְאַבִּיט בְּאֶרֶץ אֶת רְמָשֶׂיהָ,
וְאָבִין בְּלִבִּי כִּי יְצִירָתָם
יְצִירָה מְחֻכָּמָה בְּמַעֲשֶׂיהָ.
רְאוּ אֶת שְׁמֵי מָרוֹם כְּמוֹ קֻבָּה,
תְּפוּרִים בְּלוּלָאוֹת קְרָסֶיהָ.
וְסַהַר וְכוֹכָבָיו כְּמוֹ רוֹעָה,
תְּשַׁלַּח בְּתוֹךְ אָחוּ כְּבָשֶׂיהָ.
כְּאִלּוּ לְבָנָה בֵּין נְשִׂיאֵי עָב
סְפִינָה מְהַלֶּכֶת בְּנִסֶּיהָ.
וְעָנָן כְּעַלְמָה עַל פְּנֵי גִנָּה
תְּהַלֵּךְ וְתַשְׁקֶה אֶת הֲדַסֶּיהָ.
וְעָב טַל כְּמוֹ נַעֲרָה, תְּנַעֵר מִן
שְׂעָרָהּ עֲלֵי אֶרֶץ רְסִיסֶיהָ.
וְשׁוֹכְנִים כְּמוֹ חַיָּה אֲשֶׁר נָטְתָה
לְלִינָה, וְחַצְרוֹתָם אֲבוּסֶיהָ –
וְכֻלָּם יְנוּסוּן מֵחֲמַת מָוֶת
כְּיוֹנָה אֲשֶׁר הַנֵּץ יְנִיסֶהָ,
וְסוֹפָם לְהִדַּמּוֹת לְצַלַּחַת
אֲשֶׁר שֻׁבְּרוּ כָתִית חֲרָסֶיהָ.

I survey the heavens and the stars; I
look at the earth with its creeping
creatures; and I understand in my
heart that they were all intricately
fashioned. Look up at the sky – like a
tent, whose clasps[1] are joined to it by
loops; the moon and its stars – like a
shepherdess grazing her flock in a
pasture; the moon among the sweeping
clouds – like a ship sailing with raised
pennants; a cloud – like a girl walking
through a garden, watering the myrtles;
a cloud of dew – like a maiden shaking
the drops from her hair onto the
ground. But the earth's inhabitants are
like an army pitching its tents for a
night, looting the local granaries.[2] And
all flee before the terror of death – like
a dove chased by a hawk. All are
doomed to be like an earthenware plate
which has been smashed to bits.

---

1. The gold fasteners in the Tabernacle hangings (Exodus 26.6) were traditionally compared to the stars.
2. Lit. 'the dwellings [of the inhabitants] are the food-stores [of the army]'. This may also mean 'their
dwellings are as temporary and transient as an army's stores or mess'.

בְּעֵתוֹת עָצְבְּךָ   TAKE HEART

בְּעֵתוֹת עָצְבְּךָ חַזֵּק לְבָבְךָ,
וְאִם תַּעֲמֹד עֲלֵי שַׁעַר הֲרֵגָה:
לְנֵר – מָאוֹר בְּטֶרֶם הַדְעִיכָה,
וְלִכְפִירִים מְדֻקָּרִים – שְׁאָגָה.

In times of sorrow, take heart, even
though you stand at death's door: the
candle flares up before it dies, and
wounded lions roar.

עֲלֵיכֶם לְפוֹעַלְכֶם   THE REWARD

עֲלֵיכֶם לְפוֹעַלְכֶם לְיַשֵּׁר פְּעָלֵיכֶם –
וְלָכֶם יְהִי עָלָיו לְשַׁלֵּם גְּמוּלֵיכֶם.
וְאַל בַּעֲבֹדָתוֹ תְּבַלּוּ יְמוֹתֵיכֶם,
אֲבָל עֵת עֲשׂוּ לָאֵל, וְעִתִּים עֲשׂוּ לָכֶם.
תְּנוּ לוֹ חֲצִי הַיּוֹם, וְחֶצְיוֹ לְמַעֲשֵׂיכֶם –
וְאַל תִּתְּנוּ פוּגַת לְיַיִן בְּלֵילֵיכֶם!
וְכַבּוּ מְאוֹר הַנֵּר וְאוֹרוּ בְכוֹסֵיכֶם,
וְקוּצוּ בְּקוֹל שָׁרִים וְשִׁירוּ בְנִבְלֵיכֶם.
וְאִם אֵין בְּקֶבֶר שִׁיר וְחֶמֶר וְחָבֵר – הוֹי
פְּתָאיִם, יְהִי זֶה חֶלְקְכֶם מֵעֲמָלֵיכֶם!

You owe it to your Maker to pursue a
righteous course, and He must give you
your just deserts. But do not pass all
your days in His service: set aside a
time for God and times for yourselves.
Give half the day to Him, half to your
own needs – and then give wine no
respite all night long! Put out the candle
light – let your goblets shine instead.
Scorn the voice of singers – let your
jugs sing for you. Since you will not
find wine, song, or company in the
grave – let this, O fools, be your reward
for all your labours!

מֵת אָב   WINTER WINE SONG

מֵת אָב וּמֵת אֱלוּל וּמֵת חֻמָּם,
גַּם נֶאֱסַף תִּשְׁרֵי וּמֵת עִמָּם.
בָּאוּ יְמֵי הַקֹּר, וְהַתִּירוֹשׁ
אָדַם, וְקוֹלוֹ בַכְּלִי דָמָם.
לָכֵן, יְדִידִי, סֹב אֱלֵי רֵעִים,
כָּל אִישׁ וְאִישׁ יַעַשׂ אֲשֶׁר זָמָם.

Av[1] has died and Elul has died, and so
has their warmth. Tishri, too, has died
and been gathered to them. The cold
days have come, the must has grown
red and is now silent in its barrel.[2]
Therefore, my friend, go find companions – and let each man fulfil his
own desire! They said: 'Behold the

---

1. Av, Elul and Tishri are the autumn months.   2. After fermentation is complete.

אָמְרוּ: 'חֲזֵה עָבִים בְּהִגָּשְׁימָם
וּשְׁמַע שְׁמֵי מָרוֹם בְּהַרְעִימָם
וּרְאֵה כְפוֹר וּלְשׁוֹן מְדוּרָה – זֶה
יֵרֵד וְזֶה יַעַל וְיִתְרוֹמָם.
קוּמָה שְׁתֵה בַכּוֹס, וְשׁוּב וּשְׁתֵה
בַּכַּד, וּבַלַּיְל וְגַם יוֹמָם.'

clouds pouring down, listen to the
heavens thundering. See the frost and
the tongues of fire: one falls down as
the others rise and swirl. Arise, drink
from the cup, and then again out of the
jug; drink night and day!'

מֵאָדָם בְּמַרְאֵהוּ

WINE

מֵאָדָם בְּמַרְאֵהוּ וְעָרֵב לְשׁוֹתֵהוּ
וּמָזוּג בְּאִסְפַּמְיָא – וְזִכְרוֹ אֱלֵי הֹדּוּ.
וְחַלָּשׁ בְּאַגָּנָיו, אֲבָל בַּעֲלוֹתוֹ אֶל
רָאשִׁים – אֲזַי יִרְדֶּה בְרָאשִׁים אֲשֶׁר יֵרְדוּ.
וְשָׁכוּל אֲשֶׁר דָּמָיו מְסוּכִים בְּדִמְעוֹתָיו –
יְגוֹנָיו בְּדַם אֶשְׁכּוֹל יְנוּסוּן וְיִדֹּדוּ.
כְּאִלּוּ יְדִידִים, עֵת יְסַבּוּם אֲשִׁישׁוֹתָיו
מִיָּד לְיָד, גּוֹרָל עֲלֵי יַהֲלֹם יַדּוּ.

Red to the eye, sweet to the drinker, it
is poured out in Spain but its bouquet
reaches India. When it is in the bowls,
it is feeble; but once it goes to the head,
it holds sway over swaying heads.[1] The
wretch whose heart's blood is mixed
with his tears banishes his sorrows with
the grape's blood. As the goblets make
the rounds, passing from hand to hand,
it seems as if the friends are casting lots
for a diamond.

רְאֵה יַסְמִין

THE JASMINE

רְאֵה יַסְמִין אֲשֶׁר בַּדָּיו יְרָקִים
כְּמוֹ פִטְדָה וְעָלָיו וַאֲגַפָּיו,
וְצִצָּיו כַּבְּדֹלָחִים לְבָנִים,
וְכָאֹדֶם מְאָדָּמִים סְעִפָּיו –
כְּמוֹ עֶלֶם לְבֶן פָּנִים וְשׁוֹפֵךְ
דְּמֵי אִישִׁים נְקִיֵּי כַף בְּכַפָּיו.

Look at the jasmine, whose branches,
leaves, and stems are green as chrysolite, whose flowers are white as rock
crystal, whose tendrils are red as
carnelian – like a white-faced youth
whose hands are shedding the blood of
innocent men.

---

1. Or, according to another reading, 'it rules the heads of states'.

אֱהִי כֹּפֶר לְעֹפֶר

INVITATION

אֱהִי כֹּפֶר לְעֹפֶר קָם בְּלֵיל
לְקוֹל כִּנּוֹר וְעוּגָבִים מְטִיבִים,
אֲשֶׁר רָאָה בְּיָדִי כוֹס וְאָמַר:
'שְׁתֵה מִבֵּין שְׂפָתַי דַּם עֲנָבִים!'
וְיָרֵחַ כְּמוֹ יוֹד נִכְתְּבָה עַל
כְּסוּת שַׁחַר בְּמֵימֵי הַזָּהָבִים.

I would lay down my life for the fawn
who, rising at night to the sound of
melodious harp and flute, saw a cup in
my hand and said: 'Drink your grape's
blood from between my lips.' And the
moon was like a C[1] inscribed in golden
ink upon the robes of night.

אֱהִי כֹּפֶר צְבִי

THE BEAUTIFUL BOY

אֱהִי כֹּפֶר צְבִי הֵפֶר בְּרִיתִי,
וְאַהֲבָתוֹ בְּתוֹךְ לִבִּי שְׁמוּרָה,
אֲשֶׁר אָמַר לְסַהַר בַּעֲלוֹתוֹ:
'הֲתִרְאֶה אֶת מְאוֹר פָּנַי, וְתֵרָא?'
וּמַרְאֵה הַלְּבָנָה בָּאֲפֵלָה
כְּבָרֶקֶת בְּכַף עַלְמָה שְׁחֹרָה.

I would lay down my life for that
gazelle (even though he betrayed me,
my heart still keeps his love) who said
to the rising moon: 'You see my
radiant face, and yet you dare to show
yourself?' And in the dark the moon
looked like an emerald in the palm of a
black girl.

הֲנִמְצָא בְרֵעַי

THE FEAR OF DEATH

וּמְצָאַהוּ – יוֹקִירֵהוּ הָאֵל! – חֲלִישׁוּת הַכֹּחַ וְהַגּוּף
מִדֶּרֶךְ הַזִּקְנָה בַּמִּלְחָמָה אֲשֶׁר הָיְתָה בַּקַּיִץ שֶׁל שְׁנַת
תתי״ד וְאָמַר בָּזֶה שִׁיר כִּמְתְאוֹנֵן:

*He – may God cherish him – was suddenly
beset by the weakness of old age during
a battle which took place in the summer
of 1054. Then he composed this complaint:*

הֲנִמְצָא בְרֵעַי מַר לְבָבוֹ לְמָרוּתִי,
וְאִם אֶמְצָאָה בַּעֲלַת נְהִי רַב בְּגָרוֹתִי?
וְאִם יַחֲלִיף רַגְלָיו צְבִי לִי, וְאָרוּץ בָּם
לְתַנִּים וְיוֹרוּנִי סְפֹד עַל בְּחוּרוֹתִי?

Is there anyone among my friends
whose heart hurts for my hurt? Can I
find, among my neighbours, a woman
skilled in keening? Will the deer lend
me his feet, so that I may run to the
jackals and learn from them how to

---

1. In Hebrew, the letter *yod*.

הֲיֵשׁ – אַחֲרֵי אַחַת וְשִׁשִּׁים עֲבָרְתִּימוֹ –
בְּנַפְשִׁי מָקוֹם חֵפֶץ כְּשַׂעֲרָה בְשָׁרוֹתַי?
וְאַחַר עֲצֹר שַׁחַק עֲנַן אוֹר עֲלוּמַי – טַל
עֲלוּמִים זְמַן יוֹרִיד וְיַשְׁכִּיב בְּאוֹרוֹתַי?
וְאַחַר כְּהוֹת גֵּרוֹת בְּחוּרַי – הֲיֵשׁ לִיצֹק
כְּמֵאָז מְאוֹר שֶׁמֶן בְּחוּרִים בְּגֵרוֹתַי?

bewail my youth? Now that I have
passed my sixty-first year, is there any
room in my heart – even a hair's
breadth – for the delights of singing-
women? Now that heaven has locked
up the rain-clouds of my youth, will
time bring down the dew of youth
upon my blossoms? Now that the light
of my manhood has dimmed, is there
an oil of manhood that can be poured
again into my lamps?

קְבוּרוֹת חֲבֵרַי דִּבְּרוּ כִּי אֲנִי בָהֶם
לְמָחָר, וְעִמָּם אָהֳלִי אַט בְּגֵרוּתַי.
וְאִם אֵין אֲנִי שָׁב אֶל נְעוּרַי אֲחוֹרַנִּית –
קְחוּ אֵת וְהַחֵלּוּ לְהָכִין קְבוּרוֹתַי!
יְגוֹנֵי זְקוּנִים הֶעֱלוּ עַל לְבָבִי אֵשׁ
יְקֹדִים, לְשׁוֹנוֹתָם מְאִירוֹת בְּשַׂעֲרוֹתַי,
וְצִירֵי חֲלוּשָׁה עוֹרְרוּ מַחֲלֵי בְרִכַּי,
וְהִנֵּה אֲנִי כוֹשֵׁל בְּמִישׁוֹר בְּחַצְרוֹתַי!
אֲנִי אֶבְךְּ נַפְשִׁי, כִּי יְקָרָה מְאֹד נַפְשִׁי,
וְלִי נָאֲוֶה לִסְפֹּד וְלִבְכּוֹת יְקָרוֹתַי.
וְאֶרְאֶה, בְּהִתְלַבֵּן זְקָנִי, בְּמוֹרָשִׁי
מְקוֹם שַׁחֲרוּת זֵקֶן כְּפִיחַ בְּסִירוֹתַי.
וְלוּ אֶרֶךְ בּוֹ – כִּמְעַט אֲסַרְתִּיו בְּמֵיתָר, עַד
אֲשֶׁר לֹא יְנוֹפֵף יָד לְהַלְבִּין שְׁחוֹרוֹתַי.
וְלוּ אֵשׁ יְגוֹנִים לְהַטָּה קָדְקֳדִי, הָיוּ
צְרִי אֵשׁ יְגוֹנִים – מֵי עֲנָבִים בְּפוּרוֹתַי.
וְאוּלָם בְּזִקְנָה נִגְעֲרוּ מֵי נְעוּרַי מִן
זְקָנִי, וְזִקְנָה נִאַצְתַּנִי לְנַעֲרוֹתַי!

I have heard the graves of my companions say that I shall be in them
tomorrow, that in this alien land I shall
pitch my tent with my companions.
And indeed if I cannot go backwards to
my youth, take a mattock and begin to
prepare my grave! The sorrows of age
set my heart aflame, and the tongues of
fire brighten my hair. Pangs of weakness plague my knees. I stumble even
on level ground, in my own courtyard.
I shall grieve for my soul – it is so
precious! – and it befits me to grieve
and lament my treasures. As my beard
turns white, I see in my heart a spot
black with age, like soot on a pot. Oh,
if I had power over old age, I would
quickly bind him with a rope, till he no
longer raised his hand to shame my
beard with grey. If it were only the fire
of sorrow that scorched my head,
grape-water from my wine press would
be the cure for this fire. But old age has
shaken all the water of youth out of my
beard and made me loathsome to
women!

וּמִי יִתְּנֵנִי כֵאלֹהִים וְאֶתְבּוֹנָן:
הַקָּרוֹב וְאִם רָחוֹק יְהִי יוֹם מְגוּרוֹתַי,

If only I were like God and knew: is
my day of dread near or far; how long

299

וְכַמָּה אֱהִי עָפָר בְּקִבְרִי בְּלִי רוּחַ,
וּמָתַי תְּחִי רוּחִי וְתוּפַח בְּעַפְרוֹתַי.
וְיֹאמַר לְבָבִי כִּי אֱחִי עוֹד, וְאִם יִכְאַב
בְּשָׂרִי – יְרַפֵּא אֵל אֱלֹהִים חַבּוּרוֹתַי,
וְיִתֵּן אֱיָל חֵלֶף לְחַלְשִׁי, וְיִתֵּן לִי
כְּכֹחַ בְּאֶבְרוֹת הַנְּשָׁרִים בְּאֶבְרוֹתַי.
וְכֵן יַעֲשֶׂה לִי אֵל בְּטוּבוֹ וְחַסְדּוֹ, כִּי
בְאֵל מַחֲסִי שַׂמְתִּי בְעוֹדִי, וְשִׂבְרוֹתַי.

וְיֹאמְרוּ אֲנָשִׁים כִּי מְנוּחָה בְקֶבֶר יֵשׁ –
וְאֶדְאַג אֲנִי פֶּן אֶפְגְּעָה בּוֹ בְּסָרוֹתַי.
וְהֵם יִקְרְאוּ מָוֶת 'הֲלִיכָה אֱלֵי אָבוֹת' –
וְצָדְקוּ, לְמַעַן שָׁם אֲבוֹתַי וְהוֹרוֹתַי.
עֲלֵי מַה בְּיוֹם מוֹתִי תְּחִישׁוּן בְּגוּפָתִי
אֱלֵי צֵל שְׁאוֹל מִצֵּל מְעוֹנִי וְקוֹרוֹתַי?
וְלָמָּה תְצוּרוּן עַל בְּשָׂרִי בְּתַכְרִיכֵי
קְבוּרָה – וְשָׁם אֶבְלֶה אֲנִי עִם צְרוֹרוֹתַי?
וְלָמָּה בְמַיִם תִּטְבְּלוּנִי לְהִטָּהֵר –
וּמָחָר תְּטַנֵּף צַחֲנָתִי חֲגוֹרוֹתַי?

אֱלֹהִים, כְּבָר עָבְרוּ זְמַנִּים וְדוֹרוֹת עַל
אֲדָמָה, וְהָיִיתִי כְאַיִן בְּדוֹרוֹתַי.
וְאַחַר פְּקַדְתַּנִי לְרָצוֹן וְיָצָאתִי
– לְבַל אֶשְׁאָלָה צֵאת מִמְּךָ – אֶל מְכוּרוֹתַי,
וְאַחַר יְצִיאָתִי לְהֹוּוֹת נְתַתָּנִי
וּמְקוֹר לְמִקְרוֹתַי וְכִצְרוֹר לְצָרוֹתַי.
וְאַתָּה יְצַרְתַּנִי בְעוֹלָם יְפֵה מַרְאֶה –
וְאַתָּה בְּאַחֲרִיתִי תְּשַׁגֶּה יְצִירוֹתַי.
וְאוּלָם צְדָקָה מַעֲשֶׂיךָ, וְאִמְרָתְךָ
אֱמוּנָה, וְרוּחַ פִּי מְעֻקָּל, וְאִמְרוֹתַי.

am I to rest in my grave, dust without
spirit, and when will my spirit be
breathed into my dust? Still, my heart
tells me that I shall go on living, and
when my flesh is in pain, the God of
Gods will heal my wounds. He will
replace my weakness with strength;
He will give my limbs the power of
eagle's wings. In His goodness and His
love He will do all this for me, because
all my life I made Him my refuge and
my hope.

People say that the grave is a quiet
place, but I fear that I may encounter
my sins there. They call death 'joining
one's forefathers', and that is true
enough: all my fathers and mothers are
there. But why, when I am dead, will
you hurry my body from under the
shelter of my roof into the shadows of
the underworld? Why wrap my body
in winding-sheets, when both I and my
wrapping will rot in the grave? Why
bathe me with water to purify me, when
on the very next day my stench will
foul my sashes?

O God, so many ages and generations
passed over the earth, and I was
nothing in all these ages. Then You
remembered me with kindness, and
without my asking to come I came
forth into my family. And then You
handed me over to adversity, made me
the root of my disasters, a stone to be
slung by my calamities. And though
You made me handsome at my birth,
in the end You will misshape my limbs.
But Your acts are just and Your word
is true; only my spirit and my words
are crooked.

קְחוּ לִי מְגִלָּה וַעֲשׂוּ לִי דְּיוֹ וָעֵט
לְיָדִי, וְאַשְׁחִירָה פְּהַיּוֹם בְּקוֹרוֹתַי.
וְאֶקְרָא וְתִזַּלְנָה כְעֵינֵי מְאוֹרוֹתַי,
לְמַעַן בְּקֶבֶר לֹא אֲדַמַּע מְאוּרוֹתַי.
וְאֶבְכֶּה עֲלֵי צוּרָה יְפֵיפָה, יָאִיצוּן בָּהּ
לְמוֹעֵד בְּנֵי אָדָם חֲבֵרַי וְחַבְרוֹתַי;
וְיִפְעָה כְבוּדָּהּ – כָּל כְּבוֹדָהּ בְּכַסּוֹתָהּ
בְּעָפָר וּבִסְתָם פִּי וְעַצֵּם שְׁמוּרוֹתַי;
וְכִי אָז יְהִי דוּמָם בָּאָרוֹן, כְּמוֹ אֶבֶן
בְּלֶב יָם, לְשׁוֹנִי הַמְסַפֵּר גְּבוּרוֹתַי;
וְעֵינַי אֲשֶׁר חָזְתָה פְלָאִים אֲזַי תֵּעַשׁ
בְּחֹרָהּ בְּרִקְבוֹן וְתִמַּק בְּנִקְרוֹתַי;
וְכִי אֵין בְּחֵךְ טַעַם וְשִׂיחַ, וְאֵין שֵׁמַע
לְאָזְנַי, וּבָטְלָה יָד וּבָטְלוּ מְהַרְרוֹתַי.
וְרָעָה אֲשֶׁר רָעָה וּמָרָה עֲלֵי כָל זֹאת –
עֲלוֹתִי לְמִשְׁפָּט מִן רִגְבֵי וְקִבְרוֹתַי,
וְכִי כָל פְּעֻלּוֹתַי שְׁקוּלוֹת בְּמֹאזְנָיִם:
בְּכַף זֹאת זְכִיּוֹתַי, וּבָזֹאת מְרוֹרוֹתַי.

Bring me a scroll, get me ink and a quill, and I shall blacken it today with my tale of woe. When I read it, my eyes will flow like fountains, for in the grave I shall not shed any tears. I shall bewail this lovely form, which my friends, both men and women, will rush to the charnel house; and shall bewail this glorious beauty, which can expect no glory but to be covered with dust, mouth stopped and eye-lids shut. For then my tongue, which once told my exploits, will lie still in the coffin, like a stone in the depths of the sea. And my eyes, which once beheld wonders, will rot in their sockets and decay in the pit. For then taste and speech will be gone from my palate, my ears will have no hearing, my hands will be idle, my swift feet idle. And worst of all, most bitter fate of all: I shall have to rise from my dusty grave to stand in judgement, while all my deeds are weighed in a balance, my merits on this scale and my sins on the other.

וְאוּלַי יְהִי מַלְאָךְ וּמֵלִיץ בְּדָבָר טוֹב
לְהָרִים עֲווֹנוֹתַי וְהַשְׁפֵּל יְשָׁרוֹתַי,
וְיַזְכִּיר בְּהִשָּׁפְטִי לְצוּרִי חֲקִירוֹתַי
בְּדָתִי תְעוּדוֹתַי וְדָרְשִׁי בְתוֹרוֹתַי,
וְאֶשְׁמַע: 'כְּבָר רָצָה אֱלֹהִים פְּעָלֶיךָ' –
וְתֵרֵד בְּזֹאת מֵעֶבְרִי כְּשׁוּרוֹתַי.
וְאֶשְׂמַח בְּצֵאתִי אֶל כְּבוֹד אֵל לְאָסְפֵנִי,
וְאֶשְׂמַח בְּהֵאָסֵף יְרֵחִי וְאוֹרוֹתַי.

But perhaps an angel will speak up in my favour to lighten my sins and add weight to my virtues. He will remind my Rock, as I am being judged, that I pored over the Scriptures and expounded the Law. And I shall then hear: 'God has already approved what you have done!' Thus shall the scales be tipped, and my good deeds will outweigh my crimes. Dying, I shall rejoice that I am being taken by the glory of God. And I shall rejoice as my moon and my sun are taken away.

(1054)

301

יוֹסֵף אִבְּן־חִסְדַּאי   *Joseph ibn Ḥisdai*

שִׁירָה יְתוֹמָה   HOMAGE TO SAMUEL THE
PRINCE

הַלַּצְבִי חֵן גְּבוּרַת אוֹן וְעָצְמָה   How did the lovely gazelle find such
לְהִתְעַטֵּף רְדִיד אֹפֶל כְּשַׁלְמָה,   courage and strength to wrap himself
וְלִרְעוֹת כּוֹכְבֵי נֶשֶׁף, וְלִתְעוֹת   in a veil of darkness as in a robe; to
בְּעִי מִדְבָּר, מְעוֹן פַּחַד וְאֵימָה,   tend the flocks of the stars; to wander
וְלָצֵאת מֵחֲדָרִים אֶל חֲרָדָה,   amid desert ruins, haunts of fear and
וּמֵהֲמִיַת נְבָלִים אֶל מְהוּמָה ? —   terror; to abandon his home for
עֲדֵי נִלְכַּד בְּחַבְלֵי הַחֲלוֹמוֹת,   horrors, the music of lutes for turmoil –
וְנִצְטַיַּד בְּפַחֵי הַתְּנוּמָה.   till he was caught in the net of dreams,
    and trapped in the snares of slumber?
וְאָרִיתִי — וְהוּא נִרְדָּם — בִּרְצוֹן   And as he slept I plucked, with his
אֲשֶׁר יִמְנַע — וְהוּא מֵקִיץ — בְּחֵמָה,   consent, that which he angrily refuses
וְהִשְׁקַנִי, בְּיַד שֵׁנָה עֲרֵבָה,   me when awake. With the hand of
עָסִיס פִּיהוּ בְּכוֹסֵי אַחְלָמָה.   sweet sleep, he gave me the nectar of
    his mouth to drink in ruby bowls. I lay
וְשָׁכַבְתִּי — וּבֵין שָׁדַי קְוֻצּוֹת   down, and on my breast were locks
מְרִיקוֹת מֹר עֲלֵי רַקָּה אֲדֻמָּה,   flowing with myrrh over blushing
וְהַיָּמִין מְחַבֶּקֶת לְבָנָה,   cheeks. My right hand embraced the
וְהַשָּׂפָה מְנַשֶּׁקֶת לְחַמָּה,   white moon, my lips kissed the warm
וְהַמִּטָּה מְקֻטֶּרֶת לְבוֹנָה,   sun. Our bed was perfumed with
וְהָעֶרֶשׂ בְּכָל בֹּשֶׂם פְּטוּמָה.   frankincense, our couch fragrant with
    many spices. Oh, I revelled in my
וְנֶעֱצַמְתִּי בְחֶזְיוֹנִי, עֲדֵי כִי   vision until I awoke to find nothing but
הֱקִיצֹתִי — וְהִנֵּה אֵין מְאוּמָה   an aroma that delights the spirit and a
אֲבָל רֵיחַ יְשׁוֹבֵב הַנְּפָשׁוֹת   trace of liquid myrrh that revives the
וּמֹר עוֹבֵר יְחַיֶּה הַנְּשָׁמָה —   soul – like the name of Rabbi Samuel,
כְּשֵׁם נָגִיד וְיָחִיד רַב שְׁמוּאֵל,   the one and only, the Prince, whose
אֲשֶׁר מִלֵּא פְּנֵי כָל הָאֲדָמָה ! [...]   fragrance fills the whole earth!

הַאיִי גָּאוֹן   *Haya Gaon*

אָכֵן סָר מַר הַמָּוֶת   SWEET DEATH

אָכֵן סָר מַר הַמָּוֶת, נִמְתַּק מִדְּבַשׁ הֵיטֵב —
בַּל לְכָל הָעַמִּים וְלֹא לְכָל הַלְּשׁוֹנוֹת.
גּוֹי אֶחָד עָרֵב לוֹ — אֵלֶּה הֵם עַם אֲדֹנָי,
דִּגְלֵי שְׁלֹשֶׁת אָבוֹת, אַבְרָהָם, יִצְחָק וְיַעֲקֹב,
הַמְחַכִּים לַמָּוֶת וְאֵינֶנּוּ, פֶּן יִמְצְאוּ חֶפְצָם.
וּלְבַל יֶעֱדַר בָּם יָגוֹן הִנְחִלוּ אֹרֶךְ יָמִים.

Yes, the bitterness of death is past, and
death is far sweeter than honey, but not
for all nations, not for all races. There
is only one people to whom death is
pleasant – the people of God, the
offspring of the three patriarchs,
Abraham, Isaac, and Jacob, who wait
for death but it does not come. Not
even this wish is granted them. They
have been allotted a long life, so that no
sorrow shall escape them.

זֶה הָעָם לֹא הָיָה. אֲכָלֻתְהוּ כָל פֶּה,
חִלְּקוּהוּ פַּאֲתֵי אֶרֶץ, שְׁלָלוּהוּ כָל הַגּוֹיִים.
טֶרֶם תַּדְרִיחֶנּוּ מָדַי, כִּלַּתְהוּ בָבֶל.
יָוָן הִיא בְלָעַתּוּ וְיִשְׁמָעֵאל לֹא הֱקִיאַתּוּ.
כִּי תוֹסִיף עַל עֻלּוֹ, כִּי תַכְבִּיל עָנְיוֹ?
לֹא חַיִל וְלֹא כֹחַ, מַה יּוּכַל שְׂאֵת.

This is the people that is as though it
had never been. Every mouth devoured
it; it was scattered to the corners of the
earth, plundered by all nations. Before
Media toppled it, Babylon consumed
it; Greece swallowed it up, Ishmael did
not spew it out. Why do You make its
yoke heavier; why do You multiply its
misery? It has neither weapons nor
strength; it can no longer bear the
burden.

מַהֲרוּ וַעֲלוּ אֶל אָבִי וַאֲמַרְתֶּם אֵלָיו:
'נֶפֶשׁ בִּנְךָ קָרְבָה לָצֵאת, הֲלֹא תָבוֹא וּתְבַקְּרֶנּוּ?
שִׂיחַ לָאָרֶץ וְתַרְדְּ אֵיךְ נָד לַאֲפָסֶיהָ.
עֲפָרָהּ גַּם הוּא יוֹדִיעֲךָ אֵיךְ נִגְבַּל מִדָּמָיו.
פְּנֵיךָ בְּאֶרֶץ עֲרָבָה אֵיךְ רֻוְּתָה מִדִּמְעָתוֹ.
צִיָּה הוֹצִיאָה זֶרַע מִדַּם חַלְלֵי עַמּוֹ.'

Make haste, go up to my Father and
say to Him: 'Your son is about to die.
Will You not come to visit him? Speak
to the earth and it will tell You how he
has wandered to its limits. Its dust
will inform you how it was kneaded
with his blood. Go to the wilderness
and see how it was drenched with his
tears. The blood of Your murdered
people has made the desert bring forth
grain.'

קוּם קְרָא אֶל אֱלֹהֶיךָ, קַבֵּץ הֲרוּגֶיךָ וֶאֱמָר־לוֹ:
'רַחוּם וְחַנּוּן אֲדֹנָי, הַעַל אֵלֶּה תִּתְאַפָּק?
שְׁכַּלְתָּם גַּם שְׂבַּלְתָּם, וְלֹא הַשְׁבַּלְתָּ אֲלֵיהֶם.
מִתָּם כְּצֹאן מַאֲכָל, וְעַד הֵנָּה לֹא חֲנַנְתָּם.
הֲגַם עַל הָאַלְמָנָה, אֲשֶׁר הָיְתָה רַבָּתִי עָם,
יִקְשֶׁה בְעֵינֶיךָ לְרַחֵם? יְמָאֵנוּ חֲסָדֶיךָ לְבוֹאָהּ?'

Get up, call on your God, gather all
your dead and say to Him: 'O Lord,
You are compassionate and gracious;
after all this, will You hold back? You
have ravaged them, You have ridiculed
them, You have paid them no heed.
You have given them up to be butchered
like sheep and till now You have shown
them no pity. Is it so hard for You to
have mercy even on the widowed city
which was once so full of people?[1]
Will You refuse to comfort her with
Your love?'

אַבְרָהָם הַכֹּהֵן   *Abraham Hakohen*

יְפֵה תֹאַר   THE NARCISSUS

יְפֵה תֹאַר וְטוֹב רֹאִי
כְּרֻקּוּחִים וְרֹאשׁ סַמִּים,
כְּכוֹס זָהָב בְּכוֹס כֶּסֶף,
כְּמִזְרָקוֹת מְרֻקָּמִים,
אֲשֶׁר אֶחָד כְּמוֹ שֶׁלֶג,
וְהַשֵּׁנִי כְּכַרְכַּמִּים
וְשֵׁשׁ עָלִים סְבוּבִים לוֹ,
כְּמוֹ שַׁבָּת בְּתוֹךְ יָמִים. [...]

Lovely and fair, like blended perfumes
and choicest spices; like richly coloured
jugs; or like a bowl of gold in a bowl of
silver: the one is like snow, and the
other is like saffron and is encircled by
six petals, as the Sabbath is by the
week-days.

שְׁלֹמֹה אִבְּן־גַּבִּירוֹל   *Solomon ibn Gabirol*

אֲנִי הָאִישׁ   NIGHT STORM

אֲנִי הָאִישׁ אֲשֶׁר שִׁנֵּס אֲשֶׁר אֲזוֹרוֹ
וְלֹא יֶרֶף עֲדֵי יָקִים אֲסָרוֹ,

I am the man who braced himself and
will not desist until he fulfils his vow –

---

1. Jerusalem; see Lamentations 1.1.

אֲשֶׁר נִבְהַל לְבָבוֹ מִלְּבָבוֹ
וְנַפְשׁוֹ מָאֲסָה לִשְׁכֹּן בְּשָׂרוֹ,
וּבָחַר בַּתְּבוּנָה מִנְּעוּרָיו –
וְאִם כּוּר הַזְּמָן שֶׁבַע בְּחָרוֹ
וְיַהֲרֹס כָּל אֲשֶׁר יִבְנֶה, וְיִתֹּשׁ
אֲשֶׁר יִטַּע, וְיִפְרֹץ אֶת גְּדֵרוֹ. [...]

whose heart recoiled from his heart,
whose spirit scorned to dwell in his
flesh, who chose wisdom even as a
youth – though he be tested seven
times in the crucible of Time, though
it pull down whatever he has built,
though it uproot whatever he has
planted and breach all his barriers.

בְּעֵת לוּנִי, וְהַשַּׁחַק נְקִי־כָף,
וְהַסַּהַר טְהָר־לֵבָב וּבָרוֹ,
נְהָגַנִי עֲלֵי אָרְחֵי תְבוּנוֹת
וְהוֹרַנִי בְּאוֹר נָהֹג וְהוֹרוֹ.
וְחָמַלְתִּי, בְּפַחְדִּי מִתְּלָאוֹת,
עֲלֵי אוֹרוֹ כְּאָב עַל בֶּן בְּכוֹרוֹ.

As I slept – and the skies were spotless
– the radiant, pure-hearted moon led
me over the paths of wisdom and, as he
led me, instructed me in his light. And
I, fearing some misfortune, was filled
with pity for his light, as a father for
his first-born son.

וְרוּחַ שָׁלְחָה בּוֹ מִפְרְשֵׂי עָב,
וּפָרַשׂ עַל פְּנֵי סַהַר אֲפֵרוֹ,
כְּאִלּוּ אִוְּתָה זֶרֶם גְּשָׁמִים,
וַתִּשְׁעַן לְעָב עַד כִּי תְקֵרוֹ.
וְשַׁחַק הֶעֱטָה קַדְרוּת, וְסָהַר
כְּאִלּוּ מֵת, וְהֶעָנָן קְבָרוֹ,
וּבָכוּ אַחֲרָיו עָבֵי שְׁחָקִים
בָּכוֹת, כִּבְכוֹת אֲרָם עַל בֶּן־בְּעוֹרוֹ.

Then the wind assailed the moon with
sailing clouds, and they covered his
face with a mask. It was as if the wind
craved for streams of rain and pressed
upon the clouds to make them flow.
The skies robed themselves in darkness. It seemed as if the moon had
died, and the cloud had buried him.
And all the other clouds of heaven
wept for him, as the people of Aram
wept for the son of Beor.[1]

וְלָבַשׁ לַיְלָה שִׁרְיוֹן אֲפֵלָה,
וְרַעַם בַּחֲנִית בָּרָק דְּקָרוֹ,
וְהַבָּרָק עֲלֵי שַׁחַק מְעוֹפֵף
כְּאִלּוּ הוּא מְשַׂחֵק עַל דְּבָרוֹ,
אֲשֶׁר פָּרַשׂ כְּנָפָיו כַּעֲטַלֵּף

Then the night put on an armour-
plate of darkness; thunder, with a
spear of lightning, pierced it; and the
lightning flew about the skies, as if it
were jousting with the night, spreading
its wings like a bat; the ravens of the

---

1. Balaam; Numbers 22.5 ff.

וְעָפוּ עוֹרְבֵי חֹשֶׁךְ בְּשׁוּרוֹ.
וְסָגַר מַחְשְׁבוֹתַי אֵל, וְחֵפֶץ
לְבָבִי מִשְּׁנֵי פָנִים אֲסָרוֹ,
וְאָסַר בַּעֲבוֹת חֹשֶׁךְ לְבָבִי —
וְהִתְעוֹרֵר כְּגִבּוֹר מִמְּצוּרוֹ.

dark fled when they saw it. And God
closed in my thoughts. He barred my
heart's desire from all sides. He bound
my heart with ropes of darkness. Yet it
arose like a warrior breaking out of a
siege.

וּבַל אוֹחִיל, יְדִידִי, וַאֲקַוֶּה
לְאוֹר סַהַר, אֲשׁוּן חֹשֶׁךְ הֱמִירוֹ,
כְּאִלּוּ קִנְאוּ עָבִים לְנַפְשִׁי,
וְעַל כֵּן מָנְעוּ מִנִּי מְאוֹרוֹ.
וְאַשְׁקִיף עֵת יְגַל פָּנָיו, וְאָגִיל
כְּגִיל עֶבֶד אֲשֶׁר אֲדוֹן זְכָרוֹ.
בְּהִלָּחֵם אֱנוֹשׁ יֻכַּת חֲנִיתוֹ,
וְעֵת יָרוּץ אֲזַי יִמְעַד אֲשׁוּרוֹ.
וְכֵן אִישׁ — יַדְבִּקוּ אוֹתוֹ תְּלָאוֹת,
וְלוּ יָשִׂים בְּבֵית נֹגַהּ דְּבִירוֹ!

But I dare not hope, my friends, for the
light of the moon, which has turned
into pitch-black darkness, as though
the clouds were jealous of my soul and
therefore deprived me of his light. And
when I chance to see his face revealed,
I rejoice like a slave who sees that his
master remembers him. When a mortal
wages war, his spear is beaten down;
and when he tries to run, his steps
falter. And even the man whose spirit
dwells in the shining heavens –
misfortune overtakes him.

רְאֵה שֶׁמֶשׁ

LAMENT

רְאֵה שֶׁמֶשׁ לְעֵת עֶרֶב אֲדֻמָּה,
כְּאִלּוּ לָבְשָׁה תוֹלָע לְמִכְסֶה.
תְּפַשֵּׁט פַּאֲתֵי צָפוֹן וְיָמִין,
וְרוּחַ יָם בְּאַרְגָּמָן תְּכַסֶּה.
וְאֶרֶץ — עָזְבָה אוֹתָהּ עֲרֻמָּה —
בְּצֵל הַלַּיְלָה תָּלִין וְתֶחֱסֶה.
וְהַשַּׁחַק אֲזַי קָדַר, כְּאִלּוּ
בְּשַׂק עַל מוֹת יְקוּתִיאֵל מְכֻסֶּה.

See the sun at evening time: red, as
though it clothed itself in scarlet. It
disrobes the north and the south, it
covers the west with purple. And the
earth, now left naked, seeks refuge in
the shadow of the night, and sleeps.
Then the skies darken, as if covered
with sackcloth, mourning the death of
Jekuthiel.

רְבִיבֵי דִמְעֵךְ   THE POET'S ILLNESS

'רְבִיבֵי דִמְעֵךְ הָיוּ רְסִיסִים
וְהָיוּ הַבְּקָעוֹת כָּרְכָסִים.
וְאֵיכָה לֹא תְזַמֵּר הַזְּמוֹרָה
וְלָמָּה לֹא תְהַלֵּל הָעֲסִיסִים,
אֲשֶׁר רָדְפוּ יְגוֹנֶיךָ, וְנָסוּ
מְנוּסַת בֶּן־נְבָט אֶל תַּחְפְּנֵסִים ?'

'Your showers of tears, like a torrent,
have made the plains rise like mountain
ranges. Why not celebrate the grape-
vine, why not sing the praises of wine,
which could pursue your sorrows and
make them flee as Jeroboam son of
Nebat fled to Egypt[1]?'

עֲנִיתִיו : 'הַלְּבָבוֹת שָׁכְחוּ רִישׁ
וְשָׂמְחוּ בָם כְּשִׂמְחָה בַגְּבָסִים. [...]
וְהִנֵּה הֶחֱלִי בִּלָּה בְשָׂרִי
וְשָׂם בִּשְׁאָר שְׁאֵרִי אֵשׁ הֲמָסִים,
עֲדִי הָיוּ נְזָמֵינוּ עֲטָרוֹת
וְהָיוּ טַבְּעוֹתֵינוּ עֲכָסִים.
וּבְעֵר הַקְּרָבִים עַל יְקוֹד אֵשׁ
וְדִמִּינוּ עֲצָמֵינוּ נְמַסִּים.
קְרָבִים שֶׁלְּחוּ בָהֶם חֲלָיִים
וּמִצְוַת הַזְּמַן שׁוֹמְרִים וְעוֹשִׂים.
וְאֵיךְ לֹא יִהְיוּ אֶפֶס וָתֹהוּ
עֲצָמוֹת בַּתְּלָאוֹת הֵם אֲבוּסִים ?
חֲמָסִי עַל חֲלִי כִּלָּה שְׁאֵרִי
וְשָׁם אַלּוֹן בְּעֵינַי עֵץ הֲדַסִּים,
וְעַל הַלַּיְלָה אָשִׁית חֲמָסִי
אֲשֶׁר שָׁת שֶׁת אָהֳלֵי חֹשֶׁךְ פְּרוּשִׂים.' [...]

I answered him: 'Yes, the heart forgets
its trouble and rejoices in wine as does
a man in riches. But disease has consumed my flesh and set the shreds of
my body ablaze like brushwood.
[I have grown so thin] that a nose-ring
could serve me as a crown and a ringlet
as an ankle-band. Sickness burned my
innards with a fever like fire, till I
thought my bones would melt. Sores
infested my innards and carried out
Time's orders faithfully. Bones that are
filled with suffering – how should they
not disintegrate? I rage against the
disease that has wasted away my body.
[It has made me so weak] that a myrtle
looks to me like an oak. And I rage
against the night that spreads out its
tents of gloom.'

בְּאָמְרִי : 'מַה לְּבוּשׁ קָדִים ?' יְשִׁיבוּן :
'תְּכֵלֶת וַעֲלוֹת שַׁחַר מְכַסִּים.'
וְעֵת כִּי הֶעֱלָה שַׁחַר דְּגָלָיו

Then when I asked: 'How is the East
robed?', they answered: 'Covered with
blue and dawning light.' And at last,
when the dawn lifted its flags and raised

1. 1 Kings 11.40.

וְהָרִים כּוֹכְבֵי בֹקֶר כְּנִסִּים —
קְרָבַי שָׁקְטוּ כִּי נִמְלְאוּ טָל,
וְעָלַי נִגְּרוּ נִטְפֵי רְסִיסִים.

its morning stars like banners, my
innards were soothed, for they were
filled with dew, and drops of water
flowed upon me.

נִחַר בְּקָרְאִי גְרוֹנִי

ON LEAVING SARAGOSSA

נִחַר בְּקָרְאִי גְרוֹנִי, דָּבַק לְחִכִּי לְשׁוֹנִי,
הָיָה לְבָבִי סְחַרְחַר מֵרֹב כְּאֵבִי וְאוֹנִי,
גָּדַל יְגוֹנִי, וְחָדַל מִתֵּת תְּנוּמָה לְעֵינִי.
כַּמָּה אֲיַחֵל, וְכַמָּה יִבְעַר כְּמוֹ אֵשׁ חֲרוֹנִי ?
אֶל מִי אֲדַבֵּר וְאָעִיד וּלְמִי אֲסַפֵּר יְגוֹנִי ?

My throat is parched with crying, my
tongue clings to my palate. My heart
reels from so much pain and suffering.
My grief has become so great that it
will not let sleep close my eyes. How
much longer must I wait? How long
will my fury burn like a fire? To whom
can I speak and complain? To whom
can I tell my sorrow?

לוּ יֵשׁ מְנַחֵם, מְרַחֵם עָלַי וְיֹאחֵז יְמִינִי,
אֶשְׁפֹּךְ לְבָבִי לְפָנָיו, אַגִּיד קְצֵה עִצְבוֹנִי :
אוּלַי, בְּזָכְרִי יְגוֹנִי, אֶשְׁקֹט מְעַט מִשְׁאוֹנִי.

If only there were someone to comfort
me, someone to pity me and hold my
right hand. I would pour out my heart
to him, I would tell him a small part of
my woes. Perhaps by giving vent to my
sorrow, I would find some relief from
the turmoil inside me.

שׁוֹאֵל שְׁלוֹמִי, קְרַב־נָא וּשְׁמַע כְּמוֹ יָם הֲמוֹנִי !
אִם יֵשׁ לְבָבְךָ כַּשָּׁמִיר — יֵרַךְ לְרֹב דְּרָאוֹנִי.
אֵיךְ תַּחֲשֹׁב כִּי אֲנִי חַי עַל דַּעְתְּךָ דַּאֲבוֹנִי ?
הַמְעַט הֱיוֹתִי בְּתוֹךְ עָם יַחְשֹׁב שְׂמֹאלוֹ יְמִינִי ?
נִקְבָּר — אֲבָל לֹא בְמִדְבָּר, כִּי אִם בְּבֵיתִי אֲרוֹנִי !
נִכְאָב, בְּלִי אֵם וְלֹא אָב, צָעִיר וְיָחִיד וְעָנִי,
נִפְרָד בְּלִי אָח, וְאֵין לִי רֵעַ לְבַד רַעְיוֹנִי.
אֶמְסֹךְ בְּדָמִי דְּמָעַי, אֶמְסֹךְ דְּמָעַי בְּיֵינִי,

O you who wish me well, come closer
and listen to my tumult, which is like
the sea. Though your heart be
adamant, it will soften at the tale of my
debasement. How will you believe that
I am alive once you have learnt of my
distress? Is it a small thing to live among
boors who cannot tell their right hand
from their left? I am buried, but not in
a graveyard: my house is my coffin!
I am full of pain. I am motherless and
fatherless, young and lonely and
oppressed. I am alone, I have no
brother, and I have no friend except
my thoughts. I mix my tears with my
blood, and my wine with my tears.

אֶצְמָא לְרֵעַ – וְאֶכְלֶה טֶרֶם כְּלוֹת צְמָאוֹנִי,
כְּאִלוּ שְׁחָקִים וְחֵילָם בֵּין מַאֲוַתִי וּבֵינִי !
נֶחְשָׁב כְּמוֹ גֵר וְתוֹשָׁב, יוֹשֵׁב בְּשֶׁבֶת יְעֵנִי,
בֵּין כָּל פְּתַלְתֹּל וְסָכָל – לִבּוֹ כְּלֵב תַּחְכְּמוֹנִי.
זֶה יַשְׁקְךָ רֹאשׁ פְּתָנִים, זֶה יַחֲלִיק רֹאשׁ וְעֵנִי,
יָשִׂים אָרְבּוֹ בְקִרְבּוֹ, יֹאמַר לְךָ: 'בִּי אֲדוֹנִי'.
עָם – נִמְאֲסוּ לִי אֲבוֹתָם מִהְיוֹת כְּלָבִים לְצֹאנִי.
לֹא יַאֲדִימוּ פְּנֵיהֶם – כִּי אִם צְבָעוּם בְּשָׁנִי.
הֵם כַּעֲנָקִים בְּעֵינָם – הֵם כַּחֲגָבִים בְּעֵינִי !
בִּשְׂאֵת מְשָׁלַי, יְרִיבוּן עִמִּי כְּמוֹ עִם יְוָנִי :
'דַּבֵּר שְׂפַת עָם וְנִשְׁמָע, כִּי זֶה לְשׁוֹן אֶשְׁקְלוֹנִי !'
עַתָּה אֲדַרְכֵם כְּמוֹ טִיט, כִּי קִלְשׁוֹנִי לְשׁוֹנִי.
אִם אָזְנְכֶם הִיא עֲרֵלָה, מַה יַּעֲשֶׂה פַעֲמוֹנִי ?
לֹא יוּכְלוּ צַוָּארֵיכֶם לָשֵׂאת זָהָב שַׂהֲרוֹנִי.
לוּ פָעֲרוּ הַפְּתָיִים פִּיהֶם לְמַלְקוֹשׁ עֲנָנִי –
נָטַף בְּשָׂמַי עֲלֵיהֶם, בְּשֵׂם עֲנַן קִנְּמוֹנִי.
אוֹי לַתְּבוּנָה וְאוֹי לִי, כִּי גֹו כְּמוֹ זֶה שְׁכֵנִי !
דַּעַת אֱלֹהִים יְשִׂימוּן כָּאוֹב וְכַיִּדְעוֹנִי. [...]

נַפְשִׁי בְמוֹתִי תְרַנֵּן, לוּ מָצְאָה צוּר מְעוֹנִי.
אָקוּץ בְּחַיַּי וְאֶמְאַס לִהְיוֹת בְּשָׂרִי מְכוֹנִי,
כִּי יוֹם שְׂשׂוֹנִי – אֲסוֹנִי, וּבְיוֹם אֲסוֹנִי – שְׂשׂוֹנִי.
אִיגַע לְהָבִין וְאֵדַע, כִּכְלוֹת בְּשָׂרִי וְאוֹנִי,

I thirst for a friend and am quenched
before my thirst is quenched, as though
the heavens and their host stood
between me and my desire. I am
considered an alien or a stranger. I live
among cruel ostriches, among the
crooked and the foolish, who think that
their hearts are the seat of wisdom.
One man gives you asps' poison to
drink; another, fawning, pats your
head. In his heart he sets a trap for
you, but out loud he says: 'If you
please, my lord.' These people – I
would disdain to make their fathers the
dogs of my flock. Their faces never
blush, except if they paint them scarlet.
They are like giants in their own eyes,
but like grasshoppers in mine. When I
utter my sayings, they chide me as if I
were a Greek.[1] 'Speak an intelligible
language, so that we may understand,
for this is gibberish!'[2] Now I shall step
on them like dirt! My tongue will be
my pitchfork! If your ears are uncircumcised, how can my bell be
heard? Your necks are not fit to wear
my golden crescents. If the fools were
to open their mouths to my rainclouds,
my fragrance would fall gently upon
them, the cinnamon fragrance of my
cloud. Woe to wisdom and woe to me,
that I live in the midst of such people!
They think that the knowledge of God
is witchcraft and sorcery.

Oh, my soul would rejoice in death, if
it could find refuge in the Rock. I am
sick of my life, I loathe this house of
flesh. For here all joy is sorrow, but my
final sorrow will be my joy. I struggle
to understand, and I shall learn, when
my flesh and vigour are spent, that the

---

1. Possibly an allusion to the fact that his philosophical views were in part derived from the Greeks.
2. Lit. 'the language of an Ashkelonite'.

כִּי סוֹף אֲנָחָה – הֲנָחָה, עֵקֶב רְזוֹנִי – מְזוֹנִי.
אֶדְרשׁ בְּעוֹדִי, אֲחַפֵּשׂ כְּמִצְוַת שְׁלֹמֹה זְקֵנִי:
אוּלַי מְגַלֶּה עֲמוּקוֹת יִגְלֶה תְבוּנָה לְעֵינִי,
כִּי הִיא מְנָתִי לְבַדָּהּ מִכָּל עֲמָלִי, וְהוֹנִי.

end of all this grief is relief, that my nourishment[1] is the fruit of my leanness. But as long as I live, I shall delve, I shall search, as my forefather Solomon bade me.[2] Perhaps He who uncovers mysteries will reveal wisdom to my eyes; for that is my only wealth and the only reward for all my labours.

כָּתַב סְתָיו — EARTH'S EMBROIDERY

כָּתַב סְתָיו בִּדְיוֹ מְטָרָיו וּבִרְבִיבָיו
וּבְעֵט בְּרָקָיו הַמְּאִירִים וְכַף עָבָיו
מִכְתָּב עֲלֵי גַן מִתְּכֵלֶת וְאַרְגָּמָן,
לֹא נִתְכְּנוּ כָהֶם לְחוֹשֵׁב בְּמַחְשָׁבָיו.
לָכֵן, בְּעֵת חָמְדָה אֲדָמָה פְּנֵי שַׁחַק,
רָקְמָה עֲלֵי בַדֵּי עֲרוּגוֹת כְּכוֹכָבָיו.

With the ink of its showers and rains, with the quill of its lightning, with the hand of its clouds, winter wrote a letter upon the garden, in purple and blue. No artist could ever conceive the like of that. And this is why the earth, grown jealous of the sky, embroidered stars in the folds of the flower-beds.

עָבֵי שְׁחָקִים — TEMPEST AT DAWN

עָבֵי שְׁחָקִים כַּשְּׁוָרִים גָּעוּ,
כִּי הַסְּתָיו זָעַף וּפָנָיו רָעוּ,
וּכְמוֹ תְרָנִים יְרִדְּפֵם סַעַר, כְּמוֹ
סַרְגֵי בְּקַרְנֵי יוֹבְלִים תָּקְעוּ.
וּפְנֵי שְׁחָקִים בַּעֲרָפֶל חָשְׁכוּ,
אַף כּוֹכְבֵי בֹקֶר בְּאוֹרָם לָעוּ.
שֶׁמֶשׁ נְשָׂאָם עַל בְּנָפָיו עַל פְּנֵי

The heavy clouds of heaven lowed like oxen, for the winter was scowling with rage. They were like ship-masts[3] driven on by a tempest, like captains sounding their horns in alarm. Then the face of heaven was darkened by fog, and the morning-stars stammered out their light. The sun bore the clouds on its

---

1. His spiritual food; or, his reward in the world to come.
2. The reference is to King Solomon (Proverbs 2.3-5), whose name the poet bears.
3. Another version has 'like light clouds'.

אֶרֶץ, וְעֵת כִּי נִבְקָעוּ – נִבְקָעוּ.
אֵיךְ עָמְדוּ, אֵיךְ כָּבְדוּ גֶגְדָּהּ, וְעֵת
קַלּוּ – כְּמוֹ נֶשֶׁר אֲזַי נָסָעוּ!
פַּחֵי גְשָׁמִים רִקְּעָה רוּחַ, וְעָב
קָצַץ פְּתִילִים עַד שְׁאוֹל נָגָעוּ.
הוּא בַגְּדוּד נְחַת גְּדוּדֶיהָ וְגַם
הֵכִין תְּלָמֶיהָ עֲדֵי נִזְרָעוּ.
גָּלָה יְבוּל הָרִים אֲשֶׁר נִסְתָּר, כְּמוֹ
סוֹדוֹת יְדָעָם אִישׁ וְלֹא נוֹדָעוּ.
כָּל הַסְּתָיו בָּכוּ עֲנָנָיו, עַד אֲשֶׁר
חָיוּ עֲצֵי שָׂדֶה אֲשֶׁר גָּוָעוּ.

wings over the earth, and when they
burst, the face of the earth burst open.
How still they stood, how heavily they
faced the earth, where once they were
swift and flew like eagles! The wind
beat the plates of rain, cut the cloud
into strips which reached down to the
abyss. The cloud and its battalions
levelled the earth's ridges, prepared its
furrows for sowing. Then the harvest
of the hills, hidden away, like a secret
known to one man but not disclosed to
the many, was revealed. All winter long
its clouds wept until the trees of the
field, which had been dead, lived again.

אָמַר לַפְּתָיִים   TO THE FOOLS

[...] אָמַר לַפְּתָיִים: 'שְׁבוּ, אַל תְּנוּעוּן
לְהָעִיר חֲמַת אִישׁ פְּנוֹעַ כְּכָבְרָה,
אֲשֶׁר שָׁת תְּבוּנָה לְמַקֵּל בְּיָדוֹ
וּמֶזַח מְזִמּוֹת לְמָתְנָיו חֲגוֹרָה.'
וְאַל תַּאֲמֵן בָּם, אֲבָל כִּי בְעֵדוּת
יְעִידוּן לְאִמָּם אֲשֶׁר הִיא עֲקָרָה.
וְאֵיךְ יִפְרְצוּ לַעֲלוֹת אֶל מְקוֹמִי –
וְיָדָם לְהַשִּׂיג לְגֶדֶר קְצָרָה?
וְגֻלַּת שְׁחָקִים עֲצוּרָה בְלִבִּי,
וְתֵבֵל בְּגֻלַּת שְׁחָקִים עֲצוּרָה!
וְאִם הֵם יְקַלּוּ דְבָרַי אֲשֶׁר עַז,
וְחוֹלָה תְחַלֵּל וְאִשָּׁה מְצֹרָה?
וְאִם הֵם כְּשַׁיִת – אֲנִי הַמְּדוּרָה,
וְאִם הֵם כְּרוּחַ – אֲנִי הַסְּעָרָה,

Say to the fools: 'Sit still, do not stir,
lest you rouse the anger of a man who
will shake you to and fro like a sieve, a
man who has taken wisdom for his staff
and has girt his loins with a belt of
knowledge.' Do not believe a word they
say, unless they testify that their
mothers were childless. How can they
hope to force their way up to my station,
when they cannot even reach the fence?
My heart contains the vault of heaven,
and the vault of heaven contains the
wide world. Then how dare they, who
are weak as a sick and wretched
woman, revile and debase my fierce
words? If they are like a thorn-bush,
I am the fire. If they are like a wind,
I am the whirlwind. If they are dogs,

וְאִם הֵם כְּלָבִים – אֲנִי הַמְגָרֶה
וְאִם הֵם כְּשָׁמִיר – אֲנִי הַמְגֵרָה.
וְלוּ יָדְעוּן כָּל יְפִי הַוְּרָדִים –
עֲזָבוּם וְלֹא נִשְׂרְפוּ בְּבַעְרָה.
וְאִם נָשְׁכָה הַדְּבוֹרָה בְּשַׂר אִישׁ –
וְלֹא יָדְעָה אַחֲרִיתָהּ דְּבוֹרָה.

I am he who sets them on. And if they
are like a thistle, I am the scythe. If
the rose's thorns knew its beauty, they
would let it be and thus escape the fire.
The bee which stings a man's flesh
does not know that it has sealed its own
fate.

מַה לַּאֲבִיגַיִל   THE OFFERINGS OF LOVE

מַה לַּאֲבִיגַיִל – אֲשֶׁר לָקְחָה
נַפְשִׁי בְּעֵינֶיהָ וְשָׁם הִנִּיחָה ?
כָּל חוֹשְׁקֶיהָ דִּבְּרוּ לָהּ כִּי שְׂנֵא-
תִיהָ וְשׂנְאָתִי מְאֹד נָצָחָה !
עִם זֹאת וְאִם שָׁכְחָה יְדִידוּתִי, הֲלֹא
אֶשְׁמֹר בְּרִית אַהֲבָה וְלֹא אֶשְׁכָּחָה:
שָׁלַח בְּנוֹ יִשַׁי לְבֵיתָהּ – וַאֲנִי
אֵלֵךְ אֱלֵי בֵיתָהּ, וְלֹא אֶשְׁלָחָה.
אִם אֵין בְּיוֹם גָּלוּת לְאֵל קָרְבָּן – הֲלֹא
עוֹלוֹת וְקָרְבָּנוֹת לְזֹאת אֶזְבָּחָה !

What is the matter with Abigail, that
first she took my soul with her eyes and
then forsook it? All her suitors told her
that I hate her with a most enduring
hatred. Yet despite this slander, and
though she has forgotten my affection,
I shall keep love's pact, I shall not
forget. The son of Jesse sent messengers
to Abigail's house;[1] but I shall go to
her in person, not by proxy. In time of
exile no sacrifices can be offered to God;
then I shall slaughter whole offerings
and sacrifices to this woman!

עֲזָבַתְנִי   THE FAITHLESS WOMAN

עֲזָבַתְנִי וְעָלְתָה לַשְּׁחָקִים,
אֲשֶׁר יָפוּ בְּצַוָּארָהּ עֲנָקִים,
אֲשֶׁר חֵמָר – וְתִמְשֹׁךְ הַלְּבָבוֹת –
וְאִם הָיוּ שְׂפָתֶיהָ מְתוּקִים.

She left me and went up to heaven, she
whose neck is so lovely with its ornaments. But though her lips are sweet,
and she entices men's hearts, yet she is

---

1. To ask for her hand in marriage; see 1 Samuel 25.39.

חָרָבוֹת מִמְּדָנֶיהָ שְׁלוּפוֹת,
רְמָחִים לַהֲרֹג דַּלִּים מְרוּקִים.
תִּרְצֵץ לִי בְּעֵינֶיהָ וְתַעֲרֹג
כְּאַיָּלָה צְמֵאָה אֶל אֲפִיקִים.
אֲשֶׁר תַּזְכִּיר בְּרִית נֹחַ בְּקַשְׁתָּהּ —
וְתִבְרֹק מִלְּחָיֶיהָ בְּרָקִים.
וְעֵת תִּצְמָא — עֲנָנֶיהָ תְצַוֶּה
וְהֵמָּה הַבְּדֹלָחִים מְרִיקִים. [...]

bitter. Swords are unsheathed from the scabbards of her eyes, lances are burnished to kill unlucky men. Her eyes beckon to me; she is as full of longing as a deer thirsting for the running stream. Her arched eyebrow[1] calls to mind the covenant with Noah; she flashes lightning from her cheeks. And when you thirst, she orders her clouds to flood you with crystals.

אִמְרוּ לְמִי חִבֵּק

THE TESTIMONY OF BEAUTY

אִמְרוּ לְמִי חִבֵּק שְׂעָרוֹ לְחָיוֹ:
'אֵיכָה יְחַבֵּק צָהֳרַיִם בֹּקֶר?'
אַל תַּחֲשֹׁב עָוֹן לְאָגוּר בֶּאֱמֹר
כִּי הַיֳּפִי הֶבֶל וְהַחֵן שָׁקֶר.
דַּי כִּי לְחָיֶיךָ יְעִידוּן בֶּאֱמֶת
כִּי אֵין לְמַעֲשֵׂי הָאֱלֹהִים חֵקֶר.

Say to the youth whose hair enfolds his cheeks: 'How can yellow noon enfold the rosy dawn?' Agur said, 'Beauty is vain, and charm a delusion',[2] but do not hold it against him. Clearly, your cheeks bear true witness that the acts of God are unfathomable.

שַׁעַר פְּתַח, דּוֹדִי

TO GOD

שַׁעַר פְּתַח, דּוֹדִי, קוּמָה פְּתַח שַׁעַר,
כִּי נִבְהֲלָה נַפְשִׁי, גַּם נִשְׁעֲרָה שָׂעַר.
לִי לָעֲגָה שִׁפְחַת אִמִּי, וְרָם לִבָּהּ
יַעַן שְׁמֹעַ אֵל קוֹל צַעֲקַת נָעַר.
מִנִּי חֲצוֹת לַיְלָה פֶּרֶא רְדָפַנִי,
אַחֲרֵי אֲשֶׁר רָמַס אוֹתִי חֲזִיר-יַעַר.

Open the gate, my love, arise and open the gate! My soul is dismayed and shaken with terror. Hagar, my mother's slave-girl, laughed me to scorn; she grew haughty because God heard the outcry of her child Ishmael.[3] In this midnight of exile, I was trampled by the wild boar[3] of the thickets, then pursued by the wild ass.[3] When the

1. Lit. 'bow'; also 'rainbow', the sign which God gave Noah that the flood would not recur (Genesis 9.15).
2. Proverbs 31.30.
3. Ishmael (Genesis 21.17) and the wild ass represent Islam; the wild boar, Christianity.

הַקֵּץ אֲשֶׁר נֶחְתַּם הוֹסִיף עֲלֵי מַכְאוֹב
לְבִּי וְאֵין מֵבִין לִי – וַאֲנִי בָעַר.

time of the end was sealed,[1] my agony
redoubled. There is no one to guide
me, and I am like a beast.

שַׁעַר אֲשֶׁר נִסְגַּר

THAT IS MY BELOVED

'שַׁעַר אֲשֶׁר נִסְגַּר – קוּמָה פְּתָחֵהוּ,
וּצְבִי אֲשֶׁר בָּרַח – אֱלַי שְׁלָחֵהוּ !
לְיוֹם בּוֹאֲךָ עָדַי לָלִין בְּבֵין שָׁדַי,
שָׁם רֵיחֲךָ הַטּוֹב עֲלֵי תְּנִיחֵהוּ.'

[Zion:] 'The gate that was shut – oh,
arise and open it! The gazelle[2] that ran
away – oh, send him to me! On the day
You come to me and lie between my
breasts, Your fragrance will rest upon
me.'

'מַה זֶּה דְּמוּת דּוֹדֵךְ, כַּלָּה יְפֵה-פִיָּה,
כִּי תֹאמְרִי אֵלַי: "שִׁלְחָה וְקָחֵהוּ" ?
הַהוּא יְפֵה עַיִן, אָדֹם וְטוֹב רֹאִי ?'

[God:] 'Lovely bride, what shape has
your beloved, that you say to Me:
"Send for him and bring him"? Is he
the bright-eyed one, ruddy and handsome?'

'רֵעִי וְדוֹדִי זֶה – קוּמָה מְשָׁחֵהוּ !'

[Zion:] 'That is my darling, that is my
beloved. Oh, rise and anoint him!'

שׁוֹכֵב עֲלֵי מִטּוֹת

ZION LONGING FOR THE MESSIAH

שׁוֹכֵב עֲלֵי מִטּוֹת זָהָב בְּאַרְמוֹנִי,
מָתַי יְצוּעֵי, יָהּ, תָּכִין לְאַדְמוֹנִי ?
לָמָּה, צְבִי נֶחְמָד, תִּישָׁן – וְהַשַּׁחַר
עָלָה כְּנֵס עַל רֹאשׁ שְׂנִירִי וְחֶרְמוֹנִי ?
מֵעַל פְּרָאִים סוּר, וּנְטֵה לְיַעֲלַת-חֵן.
הִנְנִי לְכָמוֹךְ, וְאַתְּ טוֹב לְכָמוֹנִי.
הַבָּא בְאַרְמוֹנִי יִמְצָא בְמַטְמוֹנִי
עֲסִיס וְרִמּוֹנִי, מוֹרִי וְקִנְּמוֹנִי.

Lord, You who reclined upon couches
of gold in my palace,[3] when will You
prepare my bed for the rosy-cheeked
youth?[2] O lovely Gazelle, why are You
still sleeping? The dawn has already
risen like a banner over the mountains
of Senir and Hermon. Turn away from
the wild asses of Ishmael, come to
Your graceful deer. I am Yours and
You are fit for such as me. He who
enters my palace will find in its treasures
the juice of my pomegranates and my
cinnamon and my myrrh.

1. The end of the period of exile; see Daniel 12.9.　　2. The Messiah.
3. An allusion to the golden cherubim in the Temple.

שְׁחִי לָאֵל   THE SOUL AND ITS MAKER

שְׁחִי לָאֵל, יְחִידָה הַחֲכָמָה,
וְרוּצִי לַעֲבֹד אוֹתוֹ בְּאֵימָה.
לְעוֹלָמֵךְ פְּנִי לֵילֵךְ וְיוֹמֵךְ,
וְלָמָּה תִרְדְּפִי הֶבֶל וְלָמָּה?
מְשׁוּלָה אַתְּ בְּחַיּוּתֵךְ לְאֵל חַי,
אֲשֶׁר נֶעְלָם כְּמוֹ אַתְּ נֶעֱלָמָה.
הֲלֹא אִם יוֹצְרֵךְ טָהוֹר וְנָקִי —
דְּעִי כִּי כֵן טְהוֹרָה אַתְּ וְתַמָּה.
חָסִין יִשָּׂא שְׁחָקִים עַל זְרוֹעוֹ —
כְּמוֹ תִשְׂאִי גְּוִיָּה גֶאֱלָמָה.
זְמִירוֹת קַדְּמִי, נַפְשִׁי, לְצוּרֵךְ
אֲשֶׁר לֹא שָׂם דְּמוּתֵךְ בָּאֲדָמָה.
קְרָבַי, בָּרְכוּ תָמִיד לְצוּרְכֶם,
אֲשֶׁר לִשְׁמוֹ תְּהַלֵּל כֹּל נְשָׁמָה!

Bow down before God, my precious
thinking soul, and make haste to
worship Him with reverence. Night
and day think only of your everlasting
world. Why should you chase after
vanity and emptiness? As long as you
live, you are akin to the living God: just
as He is invisible, so are you. Since
your Creator is pure and flawless, know
that you too are pure and perfect. The
Mighty One upholds the heavens on
His arm, as you uphold the mute body.
My soul, let your songs come before
your Rock, who does not lay your form
in the dust. My innermost heart, bless
your Rock always, whose name is
praised by everything that has breath.

שַׁדַּי אֲשֶׁר יַקְשִׁיב   THE REQUEST

שַׁדַּי אֲשֶׁר יַקְשִׁיב לַדַּל וְיֶעְתַּר —
עַד אָן תְּהֵא רָחוֹק מִנִּי, וְתִסָּתֵר?
לַיִל וְיוֹם אֶעְטֹף, אֶקְרָא בְּלֵב נָכוֹן,
אוֹדֶה לְךָ תָמִיד, כִּי חַסְדְּךָ יָתֵר.
מַלְכִּי, לְךָ אוֹחִיל, לְבִּי בְךָ יִבְטַח,
חוֹלֵם חֲלוֹם סָתוּם יִבְטַח עֲלֵי פוֹתֵר.
הִנֵּה שְׁאֵלָתִי: הַקְשֵׁב תְּחִנָּתִי.
אוֹתָהּ אֲבַקֵּשׁ, לֹא פָחוֹת וְלֹא יוֹתֵר.

God Almighty, You who listen to the
wretched and grant their desire, how
long will You remain far from me and
hidden? Night and day I entreat You,
I cry out with a confident heart. I shall
always praise You, for Your love is
never-ending. My King, I wait for You,
I put my trust in You, like one who has
dreamt an obscure dream and places
his trust in the interpreter. All I ask is
that You listen to my plea. This is my
request, neither more nor less.

שְׁחַרְתִּיךָ　　　IN PRAISE OF GOD

שְׁחַרְתִּיךָ בְּכָל שַׁחְרִי וְנִשְׁפִּי
וּפָרַשְׂתִּי לְךָ כַּפִּי וְאַפִּי.
לְךָ אֶהֱמֶה בְּלֵב צָמֵא, וְאֶדְמֶה
לְדַל שׁוֹאֵל עֲלֵי פִתְחִי וְסִפִּי.
מְרוֹמוֹת לֹא יְכִילוּךָ לְשִׁבְתְּךָ –
וְאוּלָם יֵשׁ מְקוֹמְךָ תּוֹךְ סְעִפִּי !
הֲלֹא אֶצְפֹּן בְּלִבִּי שֵׁם כְּבוֹדְךָ,
וְגָבַר חִשְׁקְךָ עַד יַעֲבָר־פִּי :
אֲנִי עַל כֵּן אֲהוֹדֶה שֵׁם אֲדֹנָי
בְּעוֹד נִשְׁמַת אֱלֹהִים חַי בְּאַפִּי.

Morning and evening I seek You,
spreading out my hands, lifting up my
face in prayer. I sigh for You with a
thirsting heart; I am like the pauper
begging at my doorstep. The heights of
heaven cannot contain Your presence,
yet You have a dwelling in my mind.
I try to conceal Your glorious name in
my heart, but my desire for You grows
till it bursts out of my mouth. Therefore I shall praise the name of the Lord
as long as the breath of the living God
is in my nostrils.

טֶרֶם הֱיוֹתִי　　　BEFORE I WAS

טֶרֶם הֱיוֹתִי חַסְדְּךָ בָאָנִי,
הַשָּׂם לְיֵשׁ אַיִן וְהִמְצִיאָנִי.
מִי הוּא אֲשֶׁר רִקַּם תְּמוּנָתִי ? וּמִי
עָצְמִי בְּכוּר יָצַק וְהִקְפִּיאָנִי ?
מִי הוּא אֲשֶׁר נָפַח נְשָׁמָה בִי ? וּמִי
בֶּטֶן שְׁאוֹל פָּתַח וְהוֹצִיאָנִי ?
מִי נִהֲגַנִי מִנְּעוּרַי עַד הֲלֹם ?
מִי לִמְּדַנִי בִין וְהִפְלִיאָנִי ?
אָמְנָם אֲנִי חֹמֶר בְּקִרְבַּ יָדְךָ.
אַתָּה עֲשִׂיתָנִי, אֱמֶת, לֹא אָנִי.
אוֹדֶה עֲלֵי פִשְׁעִי וְלֹא אֹמַר לְךָ
כִּי הֶעָרִים נָחָשׁ וְהִשִּׁיאָנִי.
אֵיכָה אֲכַחֵד מִמְּךָ חֶטְאִי ? הֲלֹא
טֶרֶם הֱיוֹתִי חַסְדְּךָ בָאָנִי !

Before I was, Your enduring love came
to me, O You who make being out of
nothingness, and You created me. Who
was it that designed my form? Who
cast my body in a crucible and then
made it congeal? Who was it that
breathed into me the breath of life?
Who opened the belly of Sheol[1] and
brought me forth? Who has been my
guide from boyhood to this day? Who
taught me wisdom and showed me
wonders? Yes, I am like clay in Your
hands. Truly, it was You, not I, that
made me. And so I shall confess my
guilt; nor shall I say, 'It was the
serpent[2] who conspired to deceive me.'
How could I ever conceal my sin from
You? Even before I was, Your enduring
love came to me!

1. Here, the womb.　　2. An epithet for the 'evil inclination'.

316

יִצְחָק אִבְּן־גִּיאַת · *Isaac ibn Ghiyyat*

שַׁדַּי, שׁוּבְבָה · THE PROMISE

שַׁדַּי, שׁוּבְבָה חוֹלַת אַהֲבָה,
הוֹמָה לָרְגָעִים עַל דָּת הָכְזְבָה.

O Lord, bring back the one who is faint
with love, who constantly bewails the
broken pledge.

יוֹם רָחַק יְדִידָהּ, נַפְשָׁהּ מֵאֲנָה
הִנָּחֵם, וְיָדָהּ עַל רֹאשׁ נָתְנָה,
וּבְיַד מַעֲבִידָהּ דּוּמָה שָׁכְנָה.
עַל כִּי שׁוֹבְבָה, עֵינָהּ דָּאֲבָה,
וּבְצוּרֵי רְגָעִים בֵּיתָהּ חָצְבָה.

The day her beloved forsook her, she
refused all comfort. She put her hands
on her head and silently submitted to
the hands of her enslaver. She has been
wayward; she has carved her home in
the treacherous cliffs of time. For this
her eyes grow dim with sorrow.

צוֹעֶקֶת וְהוֹמָה מִיַּד לוֹחֲצִים,
כִּי מִשְׁמָע וְדוּמָה אוֹתָהּ קוֹלְסִים,
גַּם גֶּדֶר וְחוֹמָה יַחַד פּוֹרְצִים.
אֵיךְ לֹא־עֲזוּבָה פִּתְאֹם עֲזָבָה,
בֵּין שִׁנֵּי רְשָׁעִים לוֹהֲטִים שָׁכְבָה.

She cries and groans at the hands of
her oppressors; Mishma and Dumah[1]
gloat over her and breach all her
barriers and walls. She who had never
been forlorn – how she was suddenly
abandoned, to lie among the teeth of
ravenous villains!

חֶזְיוֹנֵי כְתָבָהּ הֵן מַה נֶּחְתָּמוּ!
רַעְיוֹנֵי לְבָבָהּ לִמְאֹד נִפְעָמוּ.
כָּל יוֹשְׁבֵי סְבִיבָהּ בָּהּ יִלָּחֵמוּ.
עַל כִּי אוֹהֲבָהּ פִּתְאֹם עֲזָבָה,
בֵּין זֶרַע מְרֵעִים בָּדָד יָשְׁבָה.

Her book of visions was sealed. Oh,
how this troubled her heart's thoughts!
Now those on every side of her attack
her. Because she had betrayed her
beloved, she now sits alone among a
race of evil men.

'קוֹרֵאָה מִמִּצְרַיִם, לָמָּה תִירָאִי?
עַל כַּנְפֵי נְשָׁרִים עוֹד תִּנָּשְׂאִי.
הֵן אֵשֶׁת נְעוּרִים לִי עוֹד תִּקָּרְאִי,
רַעְיָה נֶעֶצָבָה – אוֹתָהּ אוֹהֲבָה,
כִּי עַל כָּל פְּשָׁעִים תְּכַסֶּה אַהֲבָה!'

[God:] 'O you who call out in distress,
why should you fear? You will again be
carried on eagles' wings. I shall again
call you "My youthful bride".[2] My sad
beloved, it is you I love, for love overlooks all offences!'

---

1. The sons of Ishmael (Genesis 25.4), i.e. the Muslims.   2. Isaiah 54.6.

הֲיְדַעְתֶּם, יְדִידִי ?   ZION'S PLEA FOR PARDON

הֲיְדַעְתֶּם, יְדִידִי ? הַצְּבִי בָּרַח מִמְּלוֹנִי !
מָתַי יָשׁוּב מְעוֹנִי ?

Have you heard, my friends? The
Gazelle has fled from my dwelling.
When will He come home to me?

יַגִּיד לָכֶם כְּרוּבִי :
אַחֲרֵי נָשָׂא לְבָבִי
אֵיךְ אֶשָּׂא מַעֲצְבִי ?
לֹא יָדַע, בְּעֵת שֶׁהֶעֱלָה עִמּוֹ כָּל שְׂשׂוֹנִי,
עַל מִי נָטֵשׁ יְגוֹנִי.

If only my Cherub would tell you how
I am to bear my sorrow after He bore
away my heart! When He flew away
with all my joys, He did not know
whose hands I would fall into, grief-
stricken.

צַר לִי צַר עַל נְדוּדוֹ :
סָר מֵעָלַי כְּבוֹדוֹ,
אוֹר יִפְעָתוֹ וְהוֹדוֹ.
אֵי יָמִים שְׂפָתָיו יִטְּפוּ נֹפֶת עַל לְשׁוֹנִי,
וַעֲנָקָיו עַל גְּרוֹנִי ?

I am in anguish because He is gone.
His glory has left me, and the glow of
His beauty and splendour. Where are
the days when His lips dropped sweetness on my tongue like the honeycomb
and His necklaces hung on my throat?

חַנּוֹתִי אֵיךְ שְׁכֵחָם ?
שַׁעֲשׁוּעַי אֵיךְ זְנָחָם ?
וִידִידוּת, בֵּין בְּנֵי חָם
הֶרְאָה לִי בְּאָמוֹן, עֵת אֲשֶׁר מוֹפְתָיו שָׁם בְּמוֹנִי
וַיּוֹצֵא אֶת הֲמוֹנִי ?

How could He forget His favours to
me? How could He forsake my delights
and the love He showed me in Egypt,
among the sons of Ham, when He sent
His portents against my enemies and
led my people out?

קָרַע יַם סוּף לְפָנַי,
הֶרְאָה אוֹרוֹ לְעֵינַי,
דִּבֶּר דּוֹדָיו בְּאָזְנַי,
וּלְחַדְרוֹ אֲהוּבִי סָר, אֱלֵי חִין קוֹל פַּעֲמוֹנִי
וּלְרֵיחַ קִנְּמוֹנִי.

He split the Red Sea before me; He
revealed His light to my eyes; He spoke
words of love in my ear and He came –
my Beloved – into His room,[1] to the
lovely sound of my bells and the
fragrance of my cinnamon.

---

1. The Tabernacle.

עָבְרוּ חֻקִּים וְעֵדוֹת,
הֶעְבִיר מִנִּי יְדִידוֹת
נִכְבָּדוֹת וַחֲמוּדוֹת.
הָשֵׁב לִי שְׂשׂוֹן יִשְׁעֶךָ, וְאִם עָבַר רֹאשׁ זְדוֹנִי –
נָא הַעֲבֶר אֶת עֲוֹנִי!

Because I did not keep His statutes and commands, He did not keep His precious love for me. Oh, restore to me the joy of Your deliverance; and though my insolence has swept over my head – I pray You, sweep away my guilt!

לֵוִי אִבְּן־אַלְטַבָּאן
Levi ibn Altabban

לִקְרַאת מְקוֹר חַיַּי
THE AWAKENING

לִקְרַאת מְקוֹר חַיַּי אֲחֵן מְנַחֲמָתִי,
טֶרֶם יְשִׁיבוּנִי יָמִים לְאַדְמָתִי.
לוּ חָכְמָה נֶפֶשׁ, רוּחַ מְרֻדֶּפֶת,
כִּי הִיא לְבַדָּהּ מַתֵּבֵל תְּרוּמָתִי!
וִיהִי לְבָבִי עֵר מֵבִין לְאַחֲרִיתִי
כִּי יוֹם תְּנוּמָתִי תִּהְיֶה תְקוּמָתִי –
יוֹם יַעֲמִיד מַעֲשֵׂה יָדַי לְעֻמָּתִי,
יוֹם יֶאֱסֹף אֵלָיו רוּחִי וְנִשְׁמָתִי.

I shall turn to the fountain of my life, before time returns me to the earth. If only my soul, which is bent on folly, had the wisdom to know that it alone is my treasure in this world! If only my heart would rouse itself and under-stand my end: that the very day on which I sleep will be my awakening – the day He summons all my deeds to face me, the day He recalls my spirit and my soul to Himself.

יְיָ, לְבָבוֹת נִמְהָרוּ
PRAYER IN TIME OF DROUGHT

יְיָ, לְבָבוֹת נִמְהָרוּ וּנְפָשׁוֹת קָדָרוּ,
כִּי שָׁמַיִם נֶעֶצְרוּ וַיַּחְסְרוּ הַמָּיִם.
וְכִסְּתָה כְלִמָּה פָנֵינוּ, כִּי רַבּוּ עֲוֹנֵינוּ,
וַתֵּרַדְנָה עֵינֵינוּ דִּמְעָה וְעַפְעַפֵּינוּ יִזְּלוּ מָיִם.
בְּהֵעָצֵר עֲנָנִים בָּאנוּ בְּבֹשֶׁת פָּנִים,
הָעֲנִיִּים וְהָאֶבְיוֹנִים, מְבַקְשִׁים מָיִם.

Lord, our hearts are filled with fear and our souls with gloom, for the sky is locked *and there is no water.* Shame covers our faces, so great is our guilt; *our eyes run with tears, our eyelids are moist with water.* Now that the clouds are stopped up, we come shamefacedly, *paupers and wretches, to beg for water.*

רְעֵבִים גַּם צְמֵאִים הִתְעַטְּפוּ כִפְרָאִים,
עָמְדוּ עַל שְׁפָיִים וַיֹּאמְרוּ: 'תְּנוּ לָנוּ מָיִם!'
עָבְשׁוּ פְרֻדוֹת, וְעַל כָּל יָדַיִם גְּדֵדוֹת,
וּנְפָשׁוֹת מְאֹד חֲרֵדוֹת, כִּי קֻלּוּ הַמָּיִם.
קוֹל רַעַמְךָ בַּגַּלְגַּל צַוֵּה, וְחַסְדְּךָ יִגָּל
לְהָנִיף בְּקָצִיר מַגָּל, לְקוֹל תִּתּוֹ הֲמוֹן מָיִם.
בְּרָנָּה יִקְצְרוּ וּבִתְרוּעָה הַזּוֹרְעִים בְּדִמְעָה
וְקוֹל רָנָּה וִישׁוּעָה, כִּי נִבְקְעוּ בַמִּדְבָּר מָיִם.
חֶרְפַּת רָעָב הָסֵר, וְאַל תּוֹסֶף לְיַסֵּר,
וְעַל עַם דַּל וְאֶבְיוֹן בַּשֵּׂר:
'אַשְׁרֵיכֶם זוֹרְעֵי עַל כָּל מָיִם!'

The hungry and the thirsty faint like
wild asses [in a drought]. They stand
on the bare heights *and say: 'Give us
water!'* The soil is parched and all our
hands are gashed in mourning; our
hearts are in anguish *because they are
gone, the waters.* Order Your thunder to
resound in the whirlwind; let Your
steadfast love reveal itself, so that we
may lift our sickles at harvest-time, as
Your love *gives us the sound of tumultuous waters.* Those who sow in tears will
reap with songs of joy and triumph;
there will be shouts of deliverance
when the wilderness gushes with water.
Oh remove the reproach of hunger, and
torment us no more; declare to Your
poor and helpless people: *'Happy shall
you be who sow beside all waters!'*

בִּנְיָמִין בֶּן־זֶרַח

Benjamin ben Zerah

בְּלוּלֵי אֵשׁ וּמֵימוֹת

PRAISE IN HEAVEN AND
ON EARTH

בְּלוּלֵי אֵשׁ וּמֵימוֹת,
גִּבּוֹרֵי עִיר מְרוֹמוֹת,
נִצָּבִים כְּחוֹמוֹת.
בְּרָתָחִים וְאֵימוֹת
מַרְבִּים תַּעֲצוּמוֹת
לָאֵל יוֹסֵד הַדְּמוֹת –
וַאֲנִי, אֹם מְאֻמּוֹת,
בְּחֵךְ וְגָרוֹן רוֹמֵמוֹת.

Fashioned of fire and water, warriors of
the lofty city – they stand before Him
like walls. With trembling and dread,
again and again, they celebrate the
power of God, who built the earth.
And I, chosen of all people – His high
praises are in my throat.

נוֹהֵם מִיכָאֵל
וְגוֹעֶה גַּבְרִיאֵל,

Michael roars and Gabriel clamours.

זוֹעֵק אוּרִיאֵל
וְגוֹעֵשׁ רְפָאֵל,
וּמְהַדֵּר הַדַרְנִיאֵל
הוֹד לְיָהּ אַכְתְּרִיאֵל –
וַאֲנִי, כְּנֶסֶת יִשְׂרָאֵל,
מְעִידָה כִּי אֵין כָּאֵל.

Uriel shouts and Raphael bellows.
Hadarniel extols and Akhteriel acclaims
God's majesty. And I, the assembly of
Israel, declare: there is none like God!

יְרוֹצְצוּ כִּבְרָקִים
חַיִל זְעוֹת וְזִקִּים,
לַפִּידִים דּוֹלְקִים
וְכַבְזָק בּוֹזְקִים,
תִּשְׁבָּחוֹת מְפִיקִים
וְשִׁעוּר רָן מְדַקְדְּקִים –
וַאֲנִי, שׁוֹשַׁנַּת הָעֲמָקִים,
עֲשׂוּקָה בְּמִצְווֹת וְחֻקִּים.

Quivering hosts of firebrands streak
like lightning, flaming torches dart like
rays of light, uttering songs of praise,
keeping the rhythm with care. And I,
the lily of the valley, devote myself to
His precepts and statutes.

מֵאָה וְאַלְפֵי רְבָבוֹת,
מַרְכְּבוֹת אֵשׁ וְשַׁלְהָבוֹת
מַקִּיפוֹת וְסוֹבְבוֹת
עֲלוּי כֵּס עֲרָבוֹת.
שָׁלוֹשׁ קְדֻשּׁוֹת דּוֹבְבוֹת,
וְקוֹל דְּמָמָה מַקְשִׁיבוֹת –
וַאֲנִי, בַּת שְׁלֹשֶׁת אָבוֹת,
תָּמִיד תְּפִלּוֹתַי עֲרֵבוֹת.

Thousands and myriads of angels,
chariots of flame and bolts of fire circle
and whirl around the throne, raised
upon the seventh heaven. Three times
they say 'Holy!', and they listen to the
low murmuring sound. And I, daughter
of the three patriarchs – my prayers
always please Him.

נַהֲרֵי אֵימָה וְחִילָה
זֵעַת חַיּוֹת מַגְדִּילָה,
וְעַל אַרְבַּעְתָּן מִלְמַעְלָה
חַיָּה חֲמִישִׁית גְּדוֹלָה,

The sweat of the four Heavenly Beasts
swells the rushing river of terror,[1] and
above them stands a fifth gigantic
Beast. He begins to chant God's glory,

---

1. The fiery Rigyon; see p. 239.

לְסַלְסֵל הִיא מַתְחִילָה
וְאַחֲרֶיהָ פָּמַלְיָא כֻלָּהּ –
וַאֲנִי בְּבֵית הַתְּפִלָּה
תַּבַּעְנָה שְׂפָתַי תְּהִלָּה.

and all the attendants join in. And I, in the house of prayer – my lips pour forth Your praise.

יוֹסֵף אִבְּן־סַהְל   *Joseph ibn Sahl*

וּפַרְעוֹשִׁים כְּפָרָשִׁים   THE FLEAS

וּפַרְעוֹשִׁים כְּפָרָשִׁים יְרוּצוּן,
וְכָעוֹף לֶאֱכֹל עוֹרִי יָאוּצוּן,
וְכִשְׂעִירִים יְרַקְּדוּן סְבִיבִי,
וְאוֹתִי מִתְּנוּמָתִי יְקִיצוּן.
וְנִלְאֵיתִי הֲרֹג קָטֹן וְגָדוֹל
לְהַכְנִיעָם – וְהֵם לֹא יַעֲרוֹצוּן.
כְּגִבּוֹרִים בְּמִלְחַמְתָּם קְשֵׁי לֵב,
אֲשֶׁר בִּנְפֹל אֲחֵיהֶם יַאֲמִיצוּן.
וְאִם יִהְיוּ מְעַט בַּיּוֹם עֲצֵלִים,
בְּבוֹא לַיִל כְּגַנָּב יְחָרְצוּן.
וְהֵן נַפְשִׁי בְּכָל יוֹם קָצְרָה בָּם,
וְיָדַי מֵהֲרֹג אוֹתָם יְקוּצוּן –
וְהָפַךְ מִגּוּשִׁיכָתָם בְּשָׂרִי
חֲבַרְבּוּרוֹת, כְּמוֹ רִמּוֹן יָנֵצוּן.
אֱלֹהִים, הַחֲרִימֵם, כִּי בְלִי נוּם
אֲנִי, דָּוֶה – וְהֵמָּה יַעֲלֹצוּן!

And the fleas charge like war-horses; they swoop down like birds to devour my skin. They caper around me like he-goats, and rouse me out of my sleep. I have become weary of killing both young and old to rout them; yet they know no fear. They are stout-hearted like warriors in battle who pluck up their courage when their comrades fall. Though they are a bit lazy during the day, when night comes they are as nimble as thieves. Day after day I loathe them, and my hands are sick of killing them; but their bites have covered my flesh with sores that blossom like pomegranates. O God, wipe them out, for I am in anguish and cannot sleep – while they exult!

322

מֹשֶׁה אִבְּן־עֶזְרָא   *Moses ibn Ezra*

כָּתְנוֹת פַּסִים לָבַשׁ הַגַּן   THE ROSE[1]

כָּתְנוֹת פַּסִים לָבַשׁ הַגַּן, וּכְסוּת רִקְמָה מַדֵּי דְשָׁאוֹ,
וּמְעִיל תַּשְׁבֵּץ עָטָה כָל עֵץ, וּלְכָל עַיִן הֶרְאָה פִלְאוֹ.
כָּל צִיץ חָדָשׁ לִזְמַן חָדָשׁ יָצָא, שׂוֹחֵק לִקְרַאת בּוֹאוֹ –
אַךְ לִפְנֵיהֶם שׁוֹשָׁן עָבַר, מֶלֶךְ, כִּי עַל הוּרַם כִּסְאוֹ.
יָצָא מִבֵּין מִשְׁמָר עָלָיו, וַיְשַׁנֶּה אֶת בִּגְדֵי כִלְאוֹ.
מִי לֹא יִשְׁתֶּה יֵינוֹ עָלָיו – הָאִישׁ הַהוּא יִשָּׂא חֶטְאוֹ!

The garden put on a coat of many colours, and its grass garments were like robes of brocade. All the trees dressed in chequered tunics and showed their wonders to every eye. The new blossoms all came forth in honour of Time renewed, came gaily to welcome him. But at their head advanced the rose, king of them all, for his throne was set on high. He came out from among the guard of leaves and cast aside his prison-clothes. Whoever does not drink his wine upon the rose-bed – that man will surely bear his guilt!

זְמַן הַקֹּר   WINE SONG FOR SPRING

זְמַן הַקֹּר כְּצֵל בָּרַח, וְגִשְׁמוֹ
כְּבָר חָלַף, וּפָרָשָׁיו וְרִכְבּוֹ,
וְחַל שֶׁמֶשׁ בְּרֹאשׁ טָלֶה, עֲלֵי חֹק
תְּקוּפָתוֹ, כְּמֶלֶךְ עַל מְסִבּוֹ.
וְחָבְשׁוּ מִגְבָּעוֹת צִיצִים גְּבָעוֹת,
וּמִישׁוֹר – כָּתְנוֹת דְּשָׁאוֹ וְעֶשְׂבּוֹ,
יִשְׁלַח אֶל נְחִירֵינוּ קְטֹרֶת,
יְמוֹתֵי הַסְּתָיו טָמַן בְּחֵבּוֹ.

The cold season has slipped away like a shadow. Its rains are already gone, its chariots and its horsemen.[2] Now the sun, in its ordained circuit, is at the sign of the Ram, like a king reclining on his couch. The hills have put on turbans of flowers, and the plain has robed itself in tunics of grass and herbs; it greets our nostrils with the incense hidden in its bosom all winter long.

תְּנָה הַכּוֹס, אֲשֶׁר יָשִׁיר מְשׂוֹשִׂי
וְיָסִיר מִלְּבָבִי מַעֲצָבוֹ,
וְכַבֵּה אֶת יְקוֹד אִשּׁוֹ בְּדִמְעִי,
לְמַעַן כִּי חֲמָתוֹ בְּצָרָה בוֹ.

Give me the cup that will enthrone my joy and banish sorrow from my heart. The wine is hot with anger; temper its fierce fire with my tears. Beware of

---

1. Or 'The Lily'.   2. The storms of winter.

וְגוּר מֵהַזְּמָן, כִּי מַתְּנוֹתָיו
כְּראֹש פֶּתֶן מְעַט נֹפֶת בְּקִרְבּוֹ,
וְהַשֵּׁא נַפְשְׁךָ בֹּקֶר בְּטוּבוֹ –
וְיַחֵל תַּהֲפוּכוֹתָיו בְּעַרְבּוֹ!

Fortune: her favours are like the
venom of serpents, spiced with honey.
But let your soul deceive itself and
accept her goodness in the morning,
even though you know that she will be
treacherous at night.

שְׁתֵה בַיּוֹם – עֲדֵי יִפֶן, וְשֶׁמֶשׁ
עֲלֵי כַסְפּוֹ יְצַפֶּה אֶת זְהָבוֹ,
וּבַלַּיְלָה – עֲדֵי יִבְרַח כְּשָׁחֹר,
וְיַד שַׁחַר מְאַחֵז אֶת עֲקֵבוֹ.

Drink all day long, until the day wanes
and the sun coats its silver with gold;
and all night long, until the night flees
like a Moor, while the hand of dawn
grips its heel.

דַּדֵּי יְפַת תֹּאַר   YOUR RIGHTFUL PORTION

דַּדֵּי יְפַת תֹּאַר לַיְל חֲבֹק,
וּשְׂפַת יְפַת מַרְאֶה יוֹמָם נְשֹׁק!

Caress the breasts of the lovely girl at
night, and kiss the lips of the beautiful
girl all day long!

וּגְעַר בְּכָל מֵרִיב, יוֹעֵץ לְפִי
דַרְכּוֹ, וְקַח יֹשֶׁר נִמְצָא בְּפִי:
אֵין הַחַיּוּת רַק עִם יַלְדֵי יָפִי
כִּי גֻנְּבוּ מֵעֵדֶן לַעֲשֹׁק
חַיִּים – וְאֵין אִישׁ חַי לֹא יַחְשֹׁק!

Spurn those who chide you for loving,
who counsel you to their own advantage; and heed my words of truth:
there is no life but in the company of
beauty's daughters, who stole out of
Eden to torture the living, and there is
no man living who is not full of desire.

נַסֵּךְ לְבָבְךָ בִּשְׂמָחוֹת, וְשִׂישׂ,
וּשְׁתֵה עֲלֵי יֶבֶל גְּבֶל עָסִיס־
יַיִן, לְקוֹל גֶּבֶל עִם תּוֹר וָסִיס,
וּרְקֹד וְגִיל, גַּם כַּף עַל כַּף סְפֹק,
וּשְׁכָר, וְדֶלֶת יַעֲלַת חֵן דְּפֹק.

Plunge your heart into pleasures, make
merry, drink out of wine-skins by the
riverside to the sound of lyres, doves,
and swifts; dance and rejoice, clap your
hands, get drunk, and knock on the
door of the lovely girl!

זֶה הוּא נְעִים תֵּבֵל – קַח חֶלְקְךָ
מֶנּוּ כְּאֵיל מִלּוּאִים, חֻקְּךָ
שִׂימָה מְנָת רָאשֵׁי עַם צִדְקְךָ :
אַל תֶּחֱשֶׂה לִמְצֹץ שָׂפָה וְרֹק,
עַד תֶּאֱחֹז חָזֶךָ – חָזֶה וְשׁוֹק !

These are the delights of the world;
take your part as [did the priests] from
the ram of installation. Always allot
yourself the very portion that was your
leaders'[1] due; do not stop sipping the
moist lips until you hold your rightful
portion – the breast and the thigh!

תַּאֲוַת לְבָבִי — THE TREACHEROUS FAWN

תַּאֲוַת לְבָבִי וּמַחְמַד עֵינִי –
עֹפֶר לְצִדִּי וְכוֹס בִּימִינִי !

My heart's desire and my eyes' delight:
the hart beside me and a cup in my
right hand!

רַבּוּ מְרִיבַי – וְלֹא אֶשְׁמָעֵם.
בּוֹא, הַצְּבִי, וַאֲנִי אַכְנִיעֵם,
וּזְמָן יְכַלֵּם וּמָוֶת יִרְעֵם.
בּוֹא, הַצְּבִי, קוּם וְהַבְרִיאֵנִי
מִצּוּף שְׂפָתֶךָ וְהַשְׂבִּיעֵנִי !

Many denounce me for loving, but I
pay no heed. Come to me, fawn, and I
shall vanquish them. Time will consume them and death will shepherd
them away. Oh come to me, fawn, let
me feast on the nectar of your lips until
I am satisfied.

לָמָּה יְנִיאוּן לְבָבִי, לָמָּה ?
אִם בַּעֲבוּר חֵטְא וּבִגְלַל אַשְׁמָה
אֶשְׁגֶּה בְּיָפְיֶךָ – אֲדֹנָי שָׁמָּה !
אַל יֵט לְבָבְךָ בְּנִיב מַעֲנִי,
אִישׁ מַעֲקָשִׁים, וּבוֹא נַסֵּנִי.

Why, why would they discourage me?
If there be any sin or guilt in being
ravished by your beauty – let the Lord
be my judge![2] Do not let your heart be
swayed by the words of my tormentor,
that obstinate man. Oh, come put me
to the test!

נִפְתָּה – וְקַמְנוּ אֱלֵי בֵית אִמּוֹ,
וַיֵּט לְעֹל סָבְלִי אֶת שִׁכְמוֹ,
לַיְלָה וְיוֹמָם אֲנִי רַק עִמּוֹ.
אֶפְשֹׁט בְּגָדָיו – וַיַּפְשִׁיטֵנִי,
אִינַק שְׂפָתָיו – וַיֵּינִיקֵנִי.

He was lured and we went to his
mother's house. There he bent his
back to my heavy yoke. Night and day
I alone was with him. I took off his
clothes and he took off mine, I sucked
at his lips and he suckled me.

---

1. Lit. 'the heads of the righteous people'; the breast and the leg of the ram of installation were the perquisite of Aaron and his descendants the priests (Exodus 26.27-28).
2. Lit. 'the Lord is there'.

בַּאֲשֶׁר לְבָבִי בְּעֵינָיו נִפְקַד,
גַּם עַל פְּשָׁעַי בְּיָדוֹ נִשְׁקַד –
דָּרַשׁ תְּנוּאוֹת וְאַפּוֹ פָּקַד,
צָעַק בְּאַף: 'רַב לְךָ, עָזְבֵנִי,
אַל תֶּהְדְּפֵנִי וְאַל תַּתְעֵנִי!'

But once his eyes had done away with
my heart, his hand fastened the yoke of
my sin, and he looked for grievances
against me. He raged and shouted in
fury: 'Enough! Leave me alone! Do
not drive me to crime, do not lead me
astray!'

אַל מֵאֲנַף בִּי, צְבִי, עַד כַּלֵּה.
הַפְלֵא רְצוֹנֶךָ, יְדִידִי, הַפְלֵא,
וּנְשַׁק יְדִידָךְ וְחֶפְצוֹ מַלֵּא.
אִם יֵשׁ בְּנַפְשָׁךָ חַיּוֹת – חַיֵּנִי,
אוֹ חֶפְצְךָ לַהֲרֹג – הָרְגֵנִי!

Oh, do not be unrelenting in your
anger, fawn. Show me the wonders of
your love, my friend; kiss your friend
and fulfil his desire. If you wish to let
me live – give me life; but if you would
kill – then kill me!

וְתַפּוּחַ

THE APPLE

וְתַפּוּחַ, אֱמֶת, אַל לֹא בְרָאוֹ
לְבַד עֹנֶג לְמֵרִיחַ וְנוֹשֵׁק:
חֲשַׁבְתִּיהוּ – בְּשׁוּר יָרֹק וְאָדֹם
קְבוּצִים בּוֹ – פְּנֵי חָשׁוּק וְחוֹשֵׁק.

Truly, God created the apple only to
delight those who smell and fondle it.
Seeing how green and red are joined in
it, I imagine it to be the faces of the
wan lover and the blushing beloved.

חוֹלַת אֲהָבִים

RIDDLE

חוֹלַת אֲהָבִים לַיְלָה בָּכֹה
תִּבְכֶּה, וְדִמְעָתָהּ עֲלֵי לֶחְיָהּ.
תִּשְׂחַק פְּנֵי הַיּוֹשְׁבִים לָרְנִין
אוֹתָם – וְאֵשׁ יֹאכַל שְׁאָר גּוּיָהּ.
תִּתְחַל, וְאִם יָגֹז אֱנוֹשׁ רֹאשָׁהּ,
פָּעִיד – הֲכִי מֵחָלְיָהּ חִיָּהּ!

Love-sick, she weeps bitterly in the
night, tears running down her cheeks.
She laughs before the company to make
them merry, while fire eats away her
flesh. Then she looks ill; but should a
man shave her head, she would clearly
show that he has cured her of her
illness.

יִזְכֹּר גֶּבֶר   THE JOURNEY

יִזְכֹּר גֶּבֶר בִּימֵי חַיָּיו
כִּי לַמָּוֶת הוּא לָקוּחַ.
וּלְאַט יִסַּע כָּל יוֹם מַסָּע,
אָכֵן יַחְשֹׁב כִּי יָנוּחַ:
דּוֹמֶה אֶל אִישׁ שׁוֹקֵט עַל צִי —
אַךְ יֵדֶא עַל כַּנְפֵי רוּחַ.

Let man remember all the days of his
life that he is being led to death.
Stealthily he journeys on, day after
day; he thinks he is at rest, like a man
who is motionless on board ship, while
the ship is flying on the wings of the
wind.

פְּנֵי הָאֵל לְבַד   THE TWO SONS

פְּנֵי הָאֵל לְבַד תָּמִיד אֲחַלֶּה,
וְסוֹד לִבִּי לְאָדָם לֹא אֲגַלֶּה.
וּמַה בֶּצַע בְּיַד גֶּבֶר לְגֶבֶר?
וּמַה הוֹעִיל בְּשִׂפְתֵי רָשׁ לְנִקְלֶה?
מְאַס תֵּבֵל, אֲשֶׁר תַּשְׁפִּיל גְּאוֹנָהּ
בְּיָדֶיהָ, וְקִנְיָנָהּ תְּבַלֶּה,
וּבָנִים יָלְדָה הֵמָּה שְׁנַיִם:
בְּבִטְנָהּ — מֵת, וְעַל גַּבָּהּ — מְחַלֶּה.

I shall always seek God's favour, His
alone; I shall never reveal the secret of
my heart to any mortal. Can any man
help his fellow-man? What use are the
words of a wretch to a pauper? Scorn
the World, who with her hands debases
her own glory and wears out her
treasures. She has given birth to two
sons: the one in her belly is dead, and
the one on her back is dying.

הֱקִיצוּנִי שְׂעִפָּי   IN THE GRAVEYARD

הֱקִיצוּנִי שְׂעִפַּי לַעֲבֹר עַל
מְלוֹן הוֹרַי וְכָל אַנְשֵׁי שְׁלוֹמִי.
שְׁאַלְתִּימוֹ — וְאֵין מַקְשִׁיב וּמֵשִׁיב —
הֲבָגְדוּ בִי צֲדֵי אָבִי וְאִמִּי?
בְּלִי לָשׁוֹן קְרָאוּנִי אֲלֵיהֶם
וְהֶרְאוּנִי לְצִדֵּיהֶם מְקוֹמִי.

My thoughts roused me to stop by the
resting-place of my parents and my
friends. I asked them, though none
could listen or reply: have you all
betrayed me, even my father and my
mother? Mouthlessly they summoned
me to them, and showed me my place
at their side.

הֲדָמִי תִדְרְשׁוּ — A NIGHT OF GRIEF

הֲדָמִי תִדְרְשׁוּ מִפִּי לְבָאִים,
וְנוּמִי תִשְׁאֲלוּ מִידֵי צְבָאִים ?
וְדַם חוֹשֵׁק, הֲיִגָּאֵל ? וְשֵׁנָה,
הֲתֶעֱרַב לוֹ ? וּמַכְאוֹבָיו מְנִיאִים !
כְּאִלּוּ כָחֲלוּ עֵינָיו בְּרֶשֶׁף,
וְאִישׁוֹנָיו בְּקוֹץ מַכְאִיב מְלָאִים,
וְעַפְעַפָּיו לְהִתְקָרֵב רְחוֹקִים,
כְּאִלּוּ הֵם בְּגַבּוֹתָם תְּלוּאִים.
וְהַלַּיְל בְּיָם אָפֵלוּ מְגֻדָּח
בְּלִי רַעַשׁ, וְגַלָּיו לֹא נְשׂוּאִים.
וּמִיָּם רָחֲבוּ יָדָיו בְּעֵינִי,
וְאֵין לוֹ חוֹף וְלֹא עֵבֶר לְבָאִים.
וְסַהַר יַהֲלֹךְ יָקָר כְּרוֹעֶה,
יְנַהֵל אַט בְּכַר נִרְחַב טְלָאִים ;
וְאִם שֶׁמֶשׁ שְׁלָחָהוּ מְאַסֵּף
לְמַחֲנוֹתָיו וְשָׂמוֹ שַׂר צְבָאִים.
וְלֹא אָבִין הֲיֶאֱרַךְ אוֹ הֲיִקְצַר ;
וְאֵיךְ יָבִין אֱנוֹשׁ, יִשָּׂא חֲלָאִים ? [...]

Who will take revenge upon the lions[1]
for my blood? Who will demand my
sleep from the gazelles? Is there
vengeance for a lover's blood? Can he
ever savour sleep? His pain will not
allow it! It is as if his eyes were painted
with burning embers and his pupils
filled with painful briars. His eyelids
cannot come together; it is as if they
were tied to their brows. My night is
plunged into a silent sea of darkness,
where no waves rise – a sea that is to
me far wider than the sea; for it has no
coast, no shore for those who voyage.
The moon, in his glory, moves like a
shepherd, slowly grazing his lambs in
broad pastures; or like a general,
commissioned by the sun, to be the
rearguard of his armies. And I do not
know if this night is long or short: how
can a man who is oppressed with grief
know such a thing?

וְנָהָר, נָהֲרוּ — TO MY DISTANT FRIEND

וְנָהָר, נָהֲרוּ מֵימֵי פְלָגָיו
לְמוּל עֵינַי וְאֶל עֻמַּת עֲמִיתִי,
וְיָנוּעַ עֲלֵי יָמִין וְלִשְׂמֹאל,
כְּמוֹ שִׁכּוֹר וְיִתְרוֹגֵן כְּדָתִי.
וְעֵת רוּחַ עֲלֵי פָנָיו תְּרַחֵף,
אֲדַמֶּה כִּי יִשְׂחַק לַהֲמוֹתִי.

The runnels of this river flow before
my eyes and towards my friend. It
reels right and left like a drunken man,
and moans just as I do. When the
wind sweeps over its face, it seems to
be mocking my sighs. The tumult of

---

1. Lit. 'the mouth of the lions'; the 'lions' and 'gazelles' are the cruel friends who deserted the poet.

שְׁאוֹן מֵימָיו – שְׁאוֹן לִבִּי לְרֵעִי,
וּמֵי דְמָעִי לְאַנְשֵׁי אַחֲוָתִי.
מְיַדְּעִי, הֲכִי רוּחַ תְּרַגֵּל ?
וְהַנָּהָר מְשַׂחֵק מִבְּכוֹתִי ?

its waters is the tumult of my heart for
my comrade; its waves are my tears for
my dear companions. O my friend, will
not the wind inform [on me and tell
you of my longing]? Is the river really
laughing at my tears?

בִּי, הַמְנַגֵּן

TO THE MINSTREL

[...] בִּי, הַמְנַגֵּן הַמְמַגֵּן מַחְשְׁבוֹת
עָצְבִּי וְתוּגָתִי – כְּצֵל יִבְרָחוּ !
כִּנּוֹר – דְּמוּת פַּעַם לְיַד פַּחַד בְּלִי
שׁוֹק, דְּבֵקוּ יַחַד וְלֹא נִתָּחוּ –
יִתַּר לְבָבִי אֶל יְתָרָיו, עֵת אֲשֶׁר
נָעוּ וְלִקְרָאתָם אֲחֵרִים נָחוּ.
אֶתְמַהּ לְהוֹד יָדַיִם אֲשֶׁר הָדוּ וְעַל
קַו קָפְצוּ בְסֵפֶר וְגַם שָׁלָחוּ :
הַקּוֹל וְהַפֹּעַל בְּמוֹ מִשְׁקָל וְעַל
מִסְפָּר בְּמוֹפֵת הָאֱמֶת הֻנָּחוּ.
גִּיל הַנְּשָׁמוֹת הַנְּשַׁמּוֹת וַעֲלֵי
אִישִׁים אֲנוּשִׁים מִנֶּגֶף פָּסָחוּ.
יִסָּגְרוּ דַלְתֵי אֲפֵל, אַךְ מִשְׁכְּנֵי
עֶלְיוֹן לְעֵינֵי יוֹדְעִים נִפְתָּחוּ,
יַעֲלוּ לְעוֹלָם הַנְּפָשִׁים מִבְּלִי
מַעֲלוֹת וְנַחְלֵי הַיְקָר יִצְלָחוּ,
זַכּוּ שְׁעִפֵּיהֶם וְכִמְעַט יֹאמְרוּ :
רוּחוֹת מְשָׁרְתֵי אֵל עֲלֵיהֶם נָחוּ.
עִם תּוֹפְשֵׂי כִנּוֹר וְעוּגָב יִצְהֲלוּ
אוֹנִים, וְלָהֶם מִבְּכִי יְרַוָּחוּ –
בִּלְתִּי כְאֵבִי עַל בְּנֵי אָבִי אֲשֶׁר
סָפוּ וּמוֹדָעַי אֲשֶׁר הֻדָּחוּ. [...]

Play for me, minstrel, for you vanquish
my thoughts of grief and sorrow, and
they disappear like a shadow. Your lute
is like a leg joined to a hip, without a
thigh to divide them. My heart leaps
out to the lute's strings – now some of
them are in motion and some are at
rest. I marvel at the grace of the
plectrums which roam the lute and,
keeping time, pounce upon the strings,
then set them free. The melody and
the gestures accord in measure and in
number and have been established by
veritable proof; they are the joy of
desolate souls and they hover over[1] the
afflicted to shield them from torment.
Now the doors of darkness are closed,
and the heavenly dwellings open before
the initiates. They ascend, without
stairs, to the realm of souls, and cross
the rivers of delight. Their thoughts
become so pure that people almost say:
the spirit of the Lord's angels is resting
upon them. The wretched rejoice with
those who play the lute and pipe,
finding relief from their tears. And only
my pain persists: for my father's sons
who have perished and for my friends
who have gone far away.

---

1. Lit. 'they pass over'; an allusion to Exodus 12.13.

יְעִירוּנִי שְׂעַפַּי

THE GATES OF COMPASSION

יְעִירוּנִי שְׂעַפַּי לַחֲזוֹתֶךָ,
וְיַרְאוּנִי בְּעֵין לֵב נוֹרְאוֹתֶיךָ,
וְיוֹרוּנִי לְהַגִּיד נִפְלְאוֹתֶיךָ –
כִּי אֶרְאֶה שָׁמֶיךָ, מַעֲשֵׂה אֶצְבְּעוֹתֶיךָ.

My thoughts rouse me to behold You;
they show Your fearsome deeds to my
heart's eye; they teach me to recite
Your wonders – when I look up at Your
heavens, the work of Your fingers.

מִתְהַלֵּךְ עֲלֵי קַו חוּג שָׁמַיִם,
וּמְסַבֵּב מְסִבָּתוֹ כְּאָבְנַיִם,
וּמְסַפֵּר כְּבוֹדְךָ בְּלִי שְׂפָתַיִם.
וְהָאָרֶץ עוֹמֶדֶת בְּנֶתַיִם,
וְהִיא תְלוּיָה בְּחַבְלֵי אַהֲבָתֶךָ.

The heavenly spheres move in their
course, turning like a potter's wheel,
telling Your glory without lips. And
the earth is fixed in the centre,
suspended from the cords of Your love.

שָׁם שׁוֹאֵף הַשֶּׁמֶשׁ וְזוֹרֵחַ,
וְהוּא אֹצֵל מְאוֹרוֹ לַיָּרֵחַ,
וְהַגַּלְגַּל כְּמוֹ אֹהֶל מוֹתָח,
וְכוֹכָבִים עָלָיו כְּגַן פּוֹרֵחַ –
לְהוֹדִיעַ עֹמֶק מַחְשְׁבוֹתֶיךָ.

The sun hastens to its place to rise
again; it bestows some of its light on
the moon; the dome of heaven is
spread out like a tent, with stars upon
it like a flowering garden – all to display
Your fathomless thoughts.

הֶאָפֵס חֶסֶד אֵל לַעֲדֵי עַד?
וְאִם גָּבַהּ דְּבַר נִחוּמִים וּמִסְעָד?
אִם רוֹפֵא אוֹ הַצֳּרִי אֵין בְּגִלְעָד?
יְהִי מַחֲזִיק לֵב יֶלֶד יִמְעָד,
וְהוּא דוֹפֵק שַׁעֲרֵי חֶמְלָתֶךָ?

Is God's love gone for ever? Is the
word of comfort and support so far
from us? Is there no healer, no balm in
Gilead, to strengthen the heart of a
faltering child who knocks at the gates
of Your compassion?

נַפְשִׁי אִוִּיתִיךָ בַּלַּיְלָה

THE SOUL

נַפְשִׁי אִוִּיתִיךָ בַּלַּיְלָה!

*With all my soul I long for You in the
night.*

אִוְּתָה נַפְשִׁי אֶל מְקוֹם נַפְשָׁהּ
וְכָלְתָה אֶל מְקוֹר שָׁרְשָׁהּ
וְנִכְסְפָה לִנְוֵה קָדְשָׁהּ –
לָלֶכֶת יוֹמָם וָלַיְלָה!

My soul longs for the home of her
soul,[1] she yearns for her fountainhead,
she pines for her holy dwelling – *she
would travel there day and night.*

נֹעַם הַכָּבוֹד בְּעֵין הַדַּעַת תִּרְאֶה
וּמִבְּלִי אֵבֶר אֵלָיו תִּדְאֶה
וְתִשְׁאַף עָדָיו וְתִשְׁתָּאֶה –
בְּנֶשֶׁף, בְּעֶרֶב יוֹם, בְּאִישׁוֹן לַיְלָה.

There, with her mind's eye, she would
look on the delights of His glory; she
would fly to Him without wings; she
would hasten to Him and marvel –
*at twilight, as the day fades, and in the
dark of night.*

יְקָרוֹ תָשׁוּר עַל יְדֵי פְעָלָיו
וְתִתְאָו לָגֶשֶׁת אֵלָיו,
יוֹם לְיוֹם תַּבִּיעַ אֹמֶר מַהֲלָלָיו
וְלַיְלָה לְּלַיְלָה.

She would see His splendour in His
handiwork; she would long to approach
Him; day after day she would speak
His praises, *and night after night.*

מֵעוֹדִי עָלַי דֶּגֶל חַסְדְּךָ נוֹדַע,
וְאֹהֶל יִרְאָתְךָ מִלִּבִּי בַּל נִגְדַּע.
אֲדֹנָי, חֲקַרְתַּנִי וַתֵּדַע,
בָּחַנְתָּ לִבִּי פָּקַדְתָּ לַיְלָה!

You have always kept the banner of
Your love over me; Your awe is never
absent from my heart.[2] O Lord, You
have examined me and known me,
*You have tested my heart and watched
me by night.*

שָׂבַעְתִּי נְדוּדִים עַל עַרְשׂוֹת אֲנוּשִׁים,
הֱרִיצוּנִי פְעָמַי לִמְעוֹנוֹת קְדוֹשִׁים,
בִּנְפֹל תַּרְדֵּמָה עַל אֲנָשִׁים
בִּשְׂעִפִּים מֵחֶזְיוֹנוֹת לַיְלָה.

I have had my fill of sleepless nights,
tossing on my sick-bed. My feet have
hurried me to the holy houses of
worship even *when deep sleep falls upon
men and they have visions in the night.*

---

1. I.e. God, the all-encompassing soul.
2. Lit. 'the tent of Your awe has never been cut off from my heart'.

הִסְכַּלְתִּי וָאֶשְׁגֶּה כָּל יְמֵי שַׁחֲרוּתִי
וְנִכְלַמְתִּי כִּי הָבַלְתִּי זְמַן יַלְדוּתִי.
לְזֹאת הָיְתָה לִּי דִמְעָתִי
לֶחֶם יוֹמָם וָלָיְלָה !

I was a fool, I blundered all the days of
my childhood; I am ashamed that I
wasted my youth; that is why *tears are
now my food, day and night.*

בָּרָה, בִּכְלוּא הַגּוּף עֲצֶרֶת,
הִתְבּוֹנֲנִי כִּי הָעוֹלָם מַעְבֶּרֶת,
עוּרִי, עוּרִי לְרֹאשׁ אַשְׁמֶרֶת,
קוּמִי, רֹנִּי בַלָּיְלָה !

O pure one, held in the body's prison,
observe that this world is nothing but a
passageway. Then rouse, rouse yourself
at the beginning of every watch, *rise
and cry aloud in the night.*

חָלְפוּ כְצֵל יְמֵי עֲלוּמוֹתַי,
וְקַלּוּ מִנְּשָׁרִים שְׁנוֹתַי,
וְלֹא אֶזְכֹּר מִזְּמַן שְׂמָחוֹתַי
לֹא יוֹם וְלֹא לָיְלָה !

My youthful days vanished like a
shadow, my years flew away more
swiftly than eagles. Of all my joys I
cannot remember *a single day or night.*

זֵדִים הֲצִיקוּנִי וְהִגְדִּילוּ עָלַי בְּפִיהֶם,
דּוֹבְרִים שָׁלוֹם וְנוֹשְׁכִים בְּשִׁנֵּיהֶם.
נָא יִזָּכֵר רֹעַ מַעַלְלֵיהֶם
לְפָנֶיךָ הַיּוֹם, יוֹמָם וָלָיְלָה !

Proud men oppress me and gloat over
me; they speak words of peace as their
teeth bite into me. Let their evil doings
be remembered *before You day and
night!*

קַדְּשׁוּ עֲצָרָה וְרַחֲצוּ וְהִתְקַדְּשׁוּ,
הָבֵרוּ סִיג לְכָבוֹת וְהִתְאֹשָׁשׁוּ,
הַמַּזְכִּירִים אֶת אֲדֹנָי, אַל תֶּחֱשׁוּ
כָּל הַיּוֹם וְכָל הַלָּיְלָה.

You who invoke the Lord's name – call
a solemn assembly, wash yourselves,
hallow yourselves, purge your hearts of
dross, stand fast, do not be silent *day
or night.*

'הִתְבַּשְּׂרִי, בִּתִּי, כִּי עוֹד אַנְחִילֵךְ חִנִּי
וּלְאַט אַנְחֵךְ וְאַנִּיחֵךְ בִּמְעוֹנִי,
כִּי אֵין גּוֹאֵל קָרוֹב קָרוֹב מִמֶּנִּי :
לִינִי הַלַּיְלָה !'

[God:] 'My daughter, know that I shall
yet endow you with My grace; I shall
gently lead you to My dwelling and
instal you there. You have no kinsman[1]
closer than I: *now go and sleep through
the night.*'

---

1. Also, 'saviour'.

332

הֱקִיצוֹתִי תְּנוּמַת רַעְיוֹנִי　　IN OLD AGE

הֱקִיצוֹתִי תְּנוּמַת רַעְיוֹנִי,
לְיַשֵּׁן מַאֲוַת נַפְשִׁי וְעֵינִי,
וְחוֹלְפוֹת הַזְּמַן תַּרְתִּי בְלִבִּי,
לְהַשְׁמִיעַ עֲתִידוֹתָיו לְאָזְנִי.
וּפִי דֵעִי יְחַוְּנִי גְדוֹלוֹת,
וַיַּצִּיב מִפְלָאוֹת צוּרִי לְפָנַי,
וַיַּגֶּד לִי צְפוּנֵי תַעֲלוּמוֹת,
עֲדֵי אֶחְשֹׁב בְּנֵי עֶלְיוֹן שְׁכֵנַי.
וְאָחַז מַחֲזֵה שַׁדַּי בְּשִׂכְלִי,
וְאָבִין כִּי בְּקִרְבִּי יֵשׁ אֲדֹנָי,
אֲשֶׁר נִסְתַּר יְקַר עַצְמוֹ, וְנִגְלָה
בְמִפְעָלָיו לְעֵינֵי רַעְיוֹנִי.
בִּפְגָרִי הֶעֱלָה נֵר מִכְּבוֹדוֹ,
יְשִׂיחֵנִי שְׁבִילֵי חַתְחַמּוֹנַי,
וְהוּא הָאוֹר, אֲשֶׁר יֵלֵךְ וְיֵאוֹר
יְמֵי נֹעַר, וְיוֹסִיף עֵת זְקוּנַי. [. . .]

I rouse my slumbering thoughts to lull
the cravings of my heart and eyes.
I delve into the past to tell my ears
what the future will be. Then my
mind's lips tell me of great things, and
set the marvels of my Rock before me.
They disclose to me deep mysteries,
until I believe that I dwell among the
angels. My intellect beholds visions
from the Almighty and I understand
that the Lord is within me; that His
Precious Self is hidden, but His works
reveal Him to the eye of thought. He
kindled a lamp, lit with His glory, in
my body; it shows me the ways of the
ancient sages. And this is the light that
grew brighter in youth, and shines even
more now that I am old.

יְהוּדָה הַלֵּוִי　　*Judah Halevi*

מֵאָז מְעוֹן הָאַהֲבָה　　THE HOME OF LOVE

מֵאָז מְעוֹן הָאַהֲבָה הָיִיתָ —
חָנוּ אֲהָבַי בַּאֲשֶׁר חָנִיתָ.
תּוֹכְחוֹת מְרִיבֵי עָרְבוּ לִי עַל שְׁמָךְ;
עָזְבֵם — יְעַנּוּ אֵת אֲשֶׁר עִנִּיתָ.
לָמְדוּ חֲרוֹנְךָ אוֹיְבַי — וָאֹהֲבֵם,
כִּי רָדְפוּ חָלָל אֲשֶׁר הִכִּיתָ.

Ever since You were the home of love
for me, my love has lived where You
have lived. Because of You, I have
delighted in the wrath of my enemies;
let them be, let them torment the one
whom You tormented. It was from You
that they learned their wrath, and I
love them, for they hound the wounded
one whom You struck down. Ever

מִיּוֹם בְּזִיתַנִי בְּזִיתִינִי אֲנִי,
כִּי לֹא אֲכַבֵּד אֶת אֲשֶׁר בָּזִיתָ.
עַד יַעֲבָר־זַעַם, וְתִשְׁלַח עוֹד פְּדוּת
אֶל נַחֲלָתְךָ זֹאת אֲשֶׁר פָּדִיתָ.

since You despised me, I have despised myself, for I will not honour what You despise. So be it, until Your anger has passed, and again You will redeem Your own possession, which You once redeemed.[1]

יְדִידִי, הֲשָׁכַחְתָּ

ZION COMPLAINS TO GOD

יְדִידִי, הֲשָׁכַחְתָּ חֲנוֹתְךָ בְּבֵין שָׁדַי —
וְלָמָּה מְכַרְתַּנִי צְמִיתוּת לְמַעֲבִידַי ?
הֲלֹא אָז בְּאֶרֶץ לֹא זְרוּעָה רְדַפְתִּיךְ ?
וְשֵׂעִיר וְהַר פָּארָן וְסִינַי וְסִין עֵדַי !
וְהָיוּ לְךָ דוֹדַי, וְהָיָה רְצוֹנְךָ בִּי —
וְאֵיךְ מְחַלֵּק עַתָּה כְּבוֹדִי לְבִלְעָדַי ?
דְּחוּיָה אֱלֵי שֵׂעִיר, הַדּוּפָה עֲדֵי קֵדָר,
בְּחוּנָה בְּכוּר יָוָן, מְעֻצָּה בְּעֹל מָדַי :
הֲיֵשׁ בִּלְתְּךָ גּוֹאֵל, וּבִלְתִּי — אֲסִיר־תִּקְוָה ?
תְּנָה עֻזְּךָ לִי, כִּי לְךָ אֶתְּנָה דוֹדַי !

My love, have you forgotten how you lay between my breasts? Then why have you sold me forever to my enslavers? Did I not follow you[2] through a barren land? Let Mount Seir and Mount Paran, Sinai and Sin be my witnesses! There my love was yours, and I was your delight. Then how can you now bestow my glory upon others? I am thrust into Seir,[3] driven towards Kedar,[4] tested in the furnace of Greece, crushed under the yoke of Media. Is there any saviour but you? any prisoner of hope but I? Give me your strength, for I shall give you my love!

יָשֵׁן – וְלִבּוֹ עֵר

TO ISRAEL, IN EXILE

יָשֵׁן – וְלִבּוֹ עֵר, בּוֹעֵר וּמִשְׁתָּעֵר –
צֵא נָא וְהִנָּעֵר וּלְכָה בְּאוֹר פָּנַי.
קוּמָה, צְלַח וּרְכַב ! דָּרַךְ לְךָ כּוֹכָב,
וַאֲשֶׁר בְּבוֹר שָׁכַב עָלָה לְרֹאשׁ סִינַי.
אַל תַּעֲלֹז נֶפֶשׁ, הָאוֹמְרִים 'מֵאָשָׁם

O sleeper, whose heart is awake, burning and raging, now wake and go forth, and walk in the light of My presence. Rise, and ride on! A star has come forth for you, and he who has lain in the pit will go up to the top of Sinai. Let them not exult, those who

---

1. From the bondage of Egypt.   2. After the exodus from Egypt.
3. The Christian nations.   4. The Muslim nations.

צִיּוֹן !' וְהִנֵּה שָׁם לִבִּי וְשָׁם עֵינָי.
אֶגָּל וְאֶסָּתֵר, אֶקְצֹף וְאֶעָתֵר –
מִי יַחְמֹל יוֹתֵר מִנִּי עֲלֵי בָנַי ?

say, 'Zion is desolate!' – for My heart
is in Zion and My eyes are there. I
reveal Myself and I conceal Myself,
now I rage, now I consent – but who
has more compassion than I have for
My children?

יַעֲלַת־חֵן   TO THE RIVALS

יַעֲלַת חֵן, מִמְּעוֹנָהּ רָחֲקָה,
אוֹהֲבָהּ כּוֹעֵס – וְלָמָּה צָחֲקָה ?
צָחֲקָה עַל בַּת אֱדוֹם וּבְנוֹת עֲרָב
הַמְבַקְּשׁוֹת לַחֲשֹׁק דּוֹד חָשְׁקָה.
הֵן פְּרָאִים הֵם – וְאֵיךְ יִדְמוּ אֱלֵי
יַעֲלָה עַל הַצְּבִי הִתְרַפְּקָה ?
אֵי נְבוּאָה, אֵי מְנוֹרָה, אֵי אֲרוֹן
הַבְּרִית, אֵי הַשְּׁכִינָה דָּבְקָה ?
אַל, מְשַׂנְאַי, אַל תְּכַבּוּ אַהֲבָה,
כִּי תְכַבּוּהָ – וְהִיא אֵשׁ נִשָּׂקָה !

The lovely doe, far from her home,
whose lover is angry – why did she
laugh? She laughed at the daughter of
Edom and the daughter of Arabia who
covet her beloved. Why, they are
nothing but wild asses, and how can
they compare to the doe who nestled
against her gazelle? Where is the spirit
of prophecy found, where the lampstand, the Ark of the Covenant, the
ever-present Shekinah? No, my rivals,
do not try to quench love, for if you do,
it will blaze up like fire!

יְשֵׁנָה בְּחֵיק יַלְדוּת   TO THE SOUL

יְשֵׁנָה בְּחֵיק יַלְדוּת, לְמָתַי תִּשְׁכְּבִי ?
דְּעִי כִּי נְעוּרִים כַּנְעֹרֶת נִנְעָרוּ.
הֲלַעַד יְמֵי הַשַּׁחֲרוּת ? קוּמִי צְאִי,
רְאִי מַלְאֲכֵי שֵׂיבָה בְּמוּסָר שִׁחֲרוּ.
וְהִתְנַעֲרִי מִן הַזְּמָן, כַּצִּפֳּרִים
אֲשֶׁר מֵרְסִיסֵי לַיְלָה יִתְנַעָרוּ.
דְּאִי כַדְּרוֹר לִמְצֹא דְרוֹר מִמַּעֲלֵךְ
וּמִתּוֹלְדוֹת יָמִים כְּיַמִּים יִסְעָרוּ.
הֲיִי אַחֲרֵי מַלְכֵּךְ מְרֻדֶּפֶת, בְּסוֹד
נְשָׁמוֹת אֲשֶׁר אֶל טוּב יְיָ נָהָרוּ.

Oh, you that sleep in the bosom of
childhood, how long will you rest there?
Know that youth is shaken off like
straw! Do you think boyhood lasts for
ever? Get up, go out and see the grey
heralds, who have come to rebuke you.
Shake off Time as birds shake off the
dew-drops of the night. Soar like a
swallow to find freedom from your sins
and from the vagaries of Fortune, that
rage like a sea. Pursue your King, at
one with the souls who flock towards
the bounty of God.

אֲדֹנָי, נֶגְדְּךָ כָּל תַּאֲוָתִי

FOR THE DAY OF ATONEMENT

אֲדֹנָי, נֶגְדְּךָ כָּל תַּאֲוָתִי,
וְאִם לֹא אַעֲלֶנָּה עַל שְׂפָתִי.
רְצוֹנְךָ אֶשְׁאֲלָה רֶגַע – וְאֶגְוַע,
וּמִי יִתֵּן וְתָבוֹא שְׁאֶלָתִי,
וְאַפְקִיד אֶת שְׁאָר רוּחִי בְּיָדֶךָ,
וְיָשַׁנְתִּי, וְעָרְבָה לִי שְׁנָתִי!
בְּרָחְקִי מִמְּךָ – מוֹתִי בְחַיַּי,
וְאִם אֶדְבַּק בְּךָ – חַיַּי בְּמוֹתִי.
אֲבָל לֹא אֵדְעָה בַּמֶּה אֲקַדֵּם,
וּמַה תִּהְיֶה עֲבֹדָתִי וְדָתִי.

Lord, all my longing is before You,
even though it does not pass my lips.
Grant me Your favour for even a
moment, and I will die. If only You
would grant my wish! I will commit
my spirit into Your keeping, I will
sleep, and my sleep will be pleasant.
When I am far from You my life is
death; but if I cling to You, my death
is life. But I do not know what to offer
You, what my service and my worship
should be.

דְּרָכֶיךָ, אֲדֹנָי, לַמְּדֵנִי,
וְשׁוּב מִמַּאֲסַר סִכְלוּת שְׁבוּתִי.
וְהוֹרֵנִי בְּעוֹד יֶשׁ בִּי יְכֹלֶת
לְהִתְעַצּוֹת, וְאַל תִּבְזֶה עֱנוּתִי,
בְּטֶרֶם יוֹם אֱהִי עָלַי לְמַשָּׂא,
וְיוֹם יִכְבַּד קְצָתִי עַל קְצָתִי,
וְאֶכָּנַע בְּעַל-כָּרְחִי, וְיֹאכַל
עֲצָמַי עָשׁ וְנִלְאוּ מִשְּׂאֵתִי,
וְאֶסַּע אֶל מְקוֹם נָסְעוּ אֲבוֹתַי
וּבִמְקוֹם תַּחֲנוֹתָם תַּחֲנוּתִי.
כְּגֵר תּוֹשָׁב אֲנִי עַל גַּב אֲדָמָה,
וְאוּלָם כִּי בְבִטְנָהּ נַחֲלָתִי.

Show me Your ways, O Lord, restore
me from the bondage of folly. Teach
me while I still have the strength to
endure – do not scorn my plight! –
before I become a burden to myself and
my limbs weigh heavy on each other;
before I yield unwillingly, and my
bones wither and are unable to bear
me; before I journey to where my
fathers have gone, and come to rest
where they are resting. I am like a
stranger upon the earth, but my true
home is in her womb.

נְעוּרַי עַד הֲלֹם עָשׂוּ לְנַפְשָׁם,
וּמָתַי גַּם אֲנִי אֶעֱשֶׂה לְבֵיתִי?
וְהָעוֹלָם אֲשֶׁר נָתַן בְּלִבִּי
מְנָעַנִי לְבַקֵּשׁ אַחֲרִיתִי.

My youth has thus far had its pleasure,
but when shall I, too, provide for my
household? The world and its delights,
which He put in my heart, have kept

וְאֵיכָה אֶעֱבֹד יוֹצְרִי – בְּעוֹדִי
אֲסִיר יִצְרִי וְעֶבֶד מַאֲוָתִי?
וְאֵיכָה מַעֲלָה רָמָה אֲבַקֵּשׁ –
וּמָחָר תִּהְיֶה רִמָּה אֲחוֹתִי?
וְאֵיךְ יִיטַב בְּיוֹם טוֹבָה לְבָבִי,
וְלֹא אֵדַע – הֲיִיטַב מָחֳרָתִי?
וְהַיָּמִים וְהַלֵּילוֹת עֲרֵבִים
לְכַלּוֹת אֶת שְׁאֵרִי עַד כְּלוֹתִי,
וְלָרוּחַ יְזָרוּן מַחֲצִיתִי,
וְלֶעָפָר יְשִׁיבוּן מַחֲצִיתִי.

me from seeking my aim. And how can I worship my Maker while I am still captive to my lust, slave to my desire? How can I aspire to a high rank, when tomorrow the worm will be my sister? How can I be cheerful on a happy day, when I do not know if there will be happiness tomorrow? The days and nights have pledged to consume my flesh, to scatter half of me to the winds and return the other half to the dust.

וּמָה אֹמַר – וְיִצְרִי יִרְדְּפֵנִי
כְּאוֹיֵב מִנְּעוּרַי עַד בְּלוֹתִי?
וּמָה לִי בַּזְּמָן – אִם לֹא רְצוֹנָךְ?
וְאִם אֵינָךְ מְנָתִי – מָה מְנָתִי?
אֲנִי מִמַּעֲשִׂים שׁוֹלָל וְעָרֹם,
וְצִדְקָתָךְ לְבַדָּהּ הִיא כְסוּתִי,
וְעוֹד מָה אַאֲרִיךְ לָשׁוֹן וְאֶשְׁאַל?
אֲדֹנָי, נֶגְדְּךָ כָל תַּאֲוָתִי!

What more can I say? My passions hound me like an enemy from youth to withered old age. Does Time hold anything for me except Your favour? And if You are not my lot, what other lot do I have? I am stripped naked, devoid of good works, and only Your righteousness is my covering. Then why do I go on wagging my tongue and pleading? O Lord, all my longing is before You!

לִקְרַאת מְקוֹר חַיֵּי אֱמֶת

THE TRUE VISION

לִקְרַאת מְקוֹר חַיֵּי אֱמֶת אֲרוּצָה –
עַל כֵּן בְּחַיֵּי שָׁוְא וְרִיק אָקוּצָה.
לִרְאוֹת פְּנֵי מַלְכִּי מְגַמָּתִי לְבָד,
לֹא אֶעֱרָץ בִּלְתּוֹ וְלֹא אַעֲרִיצָה.
מִי יִתְּנֵנִי לַחֲזוֹתוֹ בַחֲלוֹם!
אִישַׁן שְׁנַת עוֹלָם וְלֹא אָקִיצָה.
לוּ אֶחֱזֶה פָנָיו בְּלִבִּי בָיְתָה,
לֹא שָׁאֲלוּ עֵינַי לְהַבִּיט חוּצָה.

I am running towards the fountain of true life; therefore, I spurn the life of lies and trifles. To look at the face of my King – that is my only wish. None but Him do I fear and venerate. If only I could see Him in a dream! Oh, I would sleep forever and never wake up. If I could see His face inside my heart, my eyes would no more wish to look outside.

יָהּ, אָנָה אֶמְצָאֲךָ ?   LORD, WHERE SHALL I FIND YOU ?

יָהּ, אָנָה אֶמְצָאֲךָ ? מְקוֹמְךָ נַעֲלָה וְנֶעְלָם !
וְאָנָה לֹא אֶמְצָאֲךָ ? כְּבוֹדְךָ מָלֵא עוֹלָם !

Lord, where shall I find You? Your place is lofty and secret. And where shall I not find you? The whole earth is full of Your glory!

הַנִּמְצָא בַּקְּרָבִים, אַפְסֵי אֶרֶץ הֵקִים.
הַמִּשְׂגָּב לַקְּרוֹבִים, הַמִּבְטָח לָרְחוֹקִים.
אַתָּה יוֹשֵׁב כְּרוּבִים, אַתָּה שׁוֹכֵן שְׁחָקִים.
תִּתְהַלֵּל בִּצְבָאָךְ – וְאַתָּ עַל רֹאשׁ מַהֲלָלָם.
גַּלְגַּל לֹא יִשָּׂאָךְ – אַף כִּי חַדְרֵי אוּלָם !

You are found in man's innermost heart, yet You fixed earth's boundaries. You are a strong tower for those who are near, and the trust of those who are far. You are enthroned on the cherubim,[1] yet You dwell in the heights of heaven. You are praised by Your hosts, but even their praise is not worthy of You. The sphere of heaven cannot contain You; how much less the chambers of the Temple!

וּבְהִנָּשְׂאָךְ עֲלֵיהֶם עַל כֵּס נִשָּׂא וָרָם,
אַתָּה קָרוֹב אֲלֵיהֶם מֵרוּחָם וּמִבְּשָׂרָם.
פִּיהֶם יָעִיד בָּהֶם, כִּי אֵין בִּלְתְּךָ יוֹצְרָם.
מִי זֶה לֹא יִירָאָךְ – וְעֹל מַלְכוּתְךָ עֻלָּם ?
אוֹ מִי לֹא יִקְרָאָךְ – וְאַתָּה נוֹתֵן אָכְלָם ?

Even when You rise above Your hosts on a throne, high and exalted, You are nearer to them than their own bodies and souls. Their mouths attest that they have no Maker except You. Who shall not fear You? All bear the yoke of Your kingdom. And who shall not call to You? It is You who give them their food.

דָּרַשְׁתִּי קֻרְבָתְךָ, בְּכָל לִבִּי קְרָאתִיךָ,
וּבְצֵאתִי לִקְרָאתְךָ – לִקְרָאתִי מְצָאתִיךָ,
וּבְפִלְאֵי גְבוּרָתְךָ בַּקֹּדֶשׁ חֲזִיתִיךָ.
מִי יֹאמַר לֹא רָאָךְ ? הֵן שָׁמַיִם וְחֵילָם
יַגִּידוּ מוֹרָאָךְ בְּלִי נִשְׁמָע קוֹלָם !

I have sought to come near You, I have called to You with all my heart; and when I went out towards You, I found You coming towards me. I look upon Your wondrous power with awe. Who can say that he has not seen You? The heavens and their legions proclaim Your dread – without a sound.

1. Above the Ark.

הַאֻמְנָם כִּי יֵשֵׁב אֱלֹהִים אֶת הָאָדָם?
וּמַה יַחְשֹׁב כָּל חוֹשֵׁב, אֲשֶׁר בֶּעָפָר יְסוֹדָם –
וְאַתָּה, קָדוֹשׁ, יוֹשֵׁב תְּהִלוֹתָם וּכְבוֹדָם!
חַיּוֹת יְדֵי פֹלְאָךְ, הָעוֹמְדוֹת בְּרוּם עוֹלָם.
עַל רָאשֵׁיהֶם כִּסְאָךְ – וְאַתָּה נוֹשֵׂא כֻלָם!

But can God really dwell among men?
Their foundations are dust – what can
they conceive of Him? Yet You, O
Holy One, make Your home where
they sing Your praises and Your glory.
The living creatures, standing on the
summit of the world, praise Your
wonders. Your throne is above their
heads, yet it is You who carry them all!

הֲיֵדְעוּ הַדְּמָעוֹת

TOMBSTONE INSCRIPTION

הֲיֵדְעוּ הַדְּמָעוֹת מִי שְׁפָכָם,
וְיֵדְעוּ הַלְּבָבוֹת מִי הֲפָכָם?
הֲפָכָם בּוֹא מְאוֹרָם תּוֹךְ רְגָבִים,
וְלֹא יֵדְעוּ רְגָבִים מַה בְּתוֹכָם.
בְּתוֹכָם שַׂר וְגָדוֹל, תָּם וְיָשָׁר,
יְרֵא הָאֵל וְאִישׁ נָבוֹן וְחָכָם.

Do these tears know who made them
fall? Do these hearts know who made
them recoil? Oh, they recoiled because
their sun sank into the dust, and the
dust does not know what it holds. It
holds a princely man, blameless and
upright, a God-fearing man, discreet
and wise.

הָהּ, בִּתִּי

A MOTHER'S LAMENT

'הָהּ, בִּתִּי, הֲשָׁכַחַתְּ מִשְׁכָּנֵךְ?
כִּי לִשְׁאוֹל נָסְעוּ נוֹשְׂאֵי אֲרוֹנֵךְ,
וְאֵין חֶלְקִי מִמֵּךְ רַק זִכְרוֹנֵךְ.
וַאֲחוֹנֵן אֶת עַפְרוֹת צִיּוּנֵךְ
עֵת אָסוּר לִשְׁאוֹל שְׁלוֹמֵךְ – וְאֵינֵךְ:
כִּי הַמָּוֶת יַפְרִיד בֵּינִי וּבֵינֵךְ.

'Alas, my daughter, have you forgotten
your home? The coffin bearers have
taken you to the grave, and I have
nothing left of you but your memory.
When I come to greet you, and do not
find you, I take pity on the dust of your
tomb; for death has parted us.

בַּת מוּצֵאת מֵחֶדֶר הוֹרָתָהּ –
אֵיךְ אֶחְיֶה וּמְנַפְשִׁי גְזָרָתָהּ?
צוּר אֲבַקַּע עֵת אֶרְאֶה צוּרָתָהּ.
אֵיךְ תִּשְׁגֶּה לְבָנָה מֵהֲדָרָתָהּ!

'O the daughter is taken from her
mother's room! How can I live? Her
limbs were part of me. My tears cleave
rocks when I remember her. How the
lustre of the moon has been tarnished!

שָׁם בִּשְׁאוֹל אֶרְאֶה אֶת חֲתֻנָּתָהּ,
אֵיךְ מָשִׂים גּוּשׁ עָפָר חֻפָּתָהּ,
אֵיךְ מָתְקוּ לָהּ רִגְבֵי קְבוּרָתָהּ.
מַר לִי מָר, בִּתִּי, עַל חֶסְרוֹנֵךְ:
כִּי הַמָּוֶת יַפְרִיד בֵּינִי וּבֵינֵךְ. [...]

There, in the grave, I see her being
wed: clods of earth are her canopy, and
the dust of the pit is sweet to her. O my
daughter, your loss is bitter to me; for
death has parted us.

הָהּ, בִּתִּי, הַכְרֵעַ הִכְרַעְתִּנִי!'
'אוֹי, אִמִּי, אוֹי לִי כִּי יְלָדְתִּנִי.
אַךְ הַיּוֹם אֵיךְ מָאוֹס מְאַסְתִּנִי?
כִּי לִבְכוֹר מָוֶת גִּדַּלְתִּנִי.
בְּהַגִּיעַ תּוֹר, לְנַפְשִׁי שְׁלַחְתִּנִי,
וּבַעֲטֶרֶת עָפָר עִטַּרְתִּנִי,
וּבְחֶפַּת אֲבַדּוֹן הוֹשַׁבְתִּנִי.
בְּעַל־כָּרְחֵךְ, אִמִּי, לֹא בִרְצוֹנֵךְ:
כִּי הַמָּוֶת יַפְרִיד בֵּינִי וּבֵינֵךְ.' [...]

'Alas, my daughter, what sorrow you
have brought me!' 'Alas, alas, my
mother, that you ever gave me birth.
How, on this day, how could you cast
me off? Oh, you brought me up to be
Death's bride! When my turn came,
you sent me away alone; you crowned
me with a garland of dust; you set me
down in the bridal-bower of destruction. O my mother, it was against your
will, it was not of your doing, for death
has parted us.'

THE MURDER OF ZECHARIAH

יוֹם אַכְפִּי הִכְבַּדְתִּי

יוֹם אַכְפִּי הִכְבַּדְתִּי וַיִּכְפְּלוּ עֲווֹנַי,
בְּשָׁלְחִי יָד בְּדַם נָבִיא בַּחֲצַר מִקְדַּשׁ אֲדֹנָי.
וְלֹא כִסָּתְהוּ אֲדָמָה עַד בּוֹא חֶרֶב מוֹנַי,
וְלֹא שָׁקַט עֲדֵי הֻקַּם וְעַד הִפְלִיא פְּלִילָיָה —
וַיֶּרֶב בְּבַת יְהוּדָה תַּאֲנִיָּה וַאֲנִיָּה.

On that day I made my burden heavier
and multiplied my crimes when I shed
the prophet's blood in the court of the
Lord's temple. The earth would not
cover it until my enemies[1] came with
the sword; it would not rest until it was
avenged, wreaking terrible judgements.
Oh, He brought sorrow upon sorrow to
the daughter of Judah.

הָיָה הוֹלֵךְ וְסוֹעֵר עַד בּוֹא רַב טַבָּחִים,
וּבָא אֶל מִקְדַּשׁ אֲדֹנָי וְרָאָה דָמִים רוֹתְחִים.
וַיִּשְׁאַל בַּעֲבוּר זֹאת לַפֹּהֲנִים הַזּוֹבְחִים,

The blood grew more and more
tempestuous until Nebuzaradan, the
commander of the guard, arrived. When
he entered the Lord's temple, he
discovered the seething blood. He
asked the priests who were offering

1. The Babylonian armies, under the command of Nebuzaradan (2 Kings 25.8).

וַיַּעֲנוּהוּ: 'אֵין זֶה כִּי אִם דַּם הַזְּבָחִים'.
גַּם הוּא זָבַח לַחֲקֹר מַה זֶּה וְעַל מֶה הָיָה —
וָאֹמַר לְנַפְשִׁי: זֹאת חַטָּאתֵךְ וְזֶה פִּרְיָהּ!

sacrifices, what it signified; and they
replied: 'It is nothing but the blood of
the sacrifices.' Then he, too, slaughtered
a beast to see if this was so and how it
came about; and I said to myself: 'This
is your sin, and this is its fruit.'

וּבְכָל זֹאת לֹא שָׁקַט וְעוֹדוֹ כַּיָּם נִגְרָשׁ.
וַיְבֻקַּשׁ הַדָּבָר וַיִּמָּצֵא מְפֹרָשׁ,
כִּי דַם אִישׁ הָאֱלֹהִים עַל לֹא חָמָס שֹׁרָשׁ.
וַיֹּאמֶר נְבוּזַרְאֲדָן: 'וְגַם דָּמוֹ הִנֵּה נִדְרָשׁ!
אִסְפוּ לִי הַכֹּהֲנִים וְהוֹצִיאוּם מִבֵּית יָהּ,
וְלֹא אֶשְׁקֹט עַד יִשְׁקֹט דַּם הַנָּבִיא זְכַרְיָה'.

Still, the blood would not rest; it
surged like the sea. Then, after
questioning, the truth came to light:
this was the blood of the man of God,
cut down though he had done no
wrong. Nebuzaradan said: 'The time
has come to pay for his blood. Gather
all the priests, take them out of the
house of God. I shall not rest until the
blood of the prophet Zechariah finds
rest.'

דָּקַר יְשִׁישִׁים לְמֵאוֹת וּבַחוּרִים לִרְבָבוֹת,
וַיּוֹרֶד לַטֶּבַח כֹּהֲנֵי אֲדֹנָי צְבָאוֹת.
וְתִינוֹקוֹת שֶׁל בֵּית רַב, וְעֵינֵי אָבוֹת רוֹאוֹת.
וְאֵין שֶׁקֶט לְדַם נָבִיא, וַיְהִי לְמוֹפֵת וּלְאוֹת!
וְחֶרֶב צָר נֹקֶמֶת וְהַקִּרְיָה הוֹמִיָּה —
בְּכָל זֹאת לֹא שָׁב אַפּוֹ וְעוֹד יָדוֹ נְטוּיָה.

He murdered old men by the hundreds,
and young men by the tens of thousands. He slaughtered the priests of the
Lord of hosts, and school-children
before the very eyes of their fathers.
Still the blood of the prophet would
not rest. This was a sign and a portent.
The enemy's sword wreaked vengeance,
the city was filled with uproar – yet His
anger was not turned back and His
hand was stretched out still!

הוֹסִיף לַהֲרֹג נָשִׁים עִם יוֹנְקֵי שָׁדַיִם,
וְדָם עוֹלֶה בֵּינֵיהֶם כַּיָּם וִיאֹר מִצְרָיִם,
עֲדֵי נָשָׂא נְבוּזַרְאֲדָן עֵינָיו לַשָּׁמַיִם
וַיֹּאמֶר: 'הַאֵין דַּי לְדָם בִּבְנוֹת יְרוּשָׁלַיִם?
הֲכָלָה אַתָּה עוֹשֶׂה אֶת שְׁאֵרִית הַשִּׁבְיָה?'
וְאָז שָׁקַט דָּם נָקִי, וְחֶרֶב נָקָם רְוָיָה.

Then he killed women as well as babes
at the breast, and the blood rose among
them like a sea, like the river of Egypt,
until Nebuzaradan raised his eyes to
heaven and said: 'Will this blood not be
content with the blood of Jerusalem's
daughters? Are You going to wipe out
the remnant of Israel?' Only then did
the innocent blood come to rest; the
sword of vengeance had drunk its fill.

יַעֲלַת־חֵן, רַחְמִי לְבָב

THE SENSITIVE DOE

יַעֲלַת חֵן, רַחְמִי לְבָב שְׁכַנְתִּיו מְעוֹדֵךְ.
תֵּדְעִי כִּי יוֹם תָּנוּדִי – אֲסוֹנִי בִּנְדוֹדֵךְ.
גַּם בְּעֵת יֶהֶרְסוּ עֵינַי לְהַבִּיט אֶל הוֹדֵךְ,
מִלְּחָיַיִךְ פָּגְעוּ בִי נְחָשִׁים יַפְרִישׁוּ,
כִּי חֲמָתָם בָּאֵשׁ יַחְתּוּ, וְאוֹתִי יְגָרְשׁוּ.

O graceful doe, pity this heart in which
you have dwelled all your life. Know
that the day you leave me, your going
will be my ruin. And even now, when
my eyes dare to glance at your splendour, I am stung by the serpents that
guard your cheeks, for their poison
burns like fire and they drive me out.

שָׁלֲלָה לִבִּי בַדַּדִּים עֲלֵי לֵב מֻנָּחִים :
לֵב כְּמוֹ אֶבֶן וְרַק יִגְמֹל שְׁנֵי תַפּוּחִים!
נִצְּבוּ וַיִּהְיוּ לִשְׂמֹאל וְיָמִין כִּרְמָחִים.
מוֹקְדֵיהֶם הֵם בְּלִבָּבִי – וְהֵם לֹא נִגָּשׁוּ,
גַּם בְּפִיהֶם דָּמִי שָׁתוּ – וְלֹא הִתְבּוֹשָׁשׁוּ!

She ensnared my heart with the breasts
that lie upon her heart - a heart of
stone, and yet it put forth two apples!
They stand guard, to the left and to the
right, like lances. Their fiery [nipples
burn] in my heart, though they have
never come near me. Their mouths
have drunk my blood, they felt no
shame at all!

יַעֲלָה חֻקֵּי דָת הָאֵל בְּעֵינֶיהָ חָפֵר,
כִּי תְמִיתֵנִי בִּצְדִיָּה אֲבָל אֵין לִי כֹפֵר.
הַרְאִיתֶם עוֹד לֵב אַרְיֵה וְעַפְעַפֵּי עֹפֶר?
לָמְדוּ לִטְרֹף בַּלָּבִיא, וְחִצִּים יִלְטֹשׁוּ,
דַּם לְבָבִי יִמְצוּ יִשְׁתּוּ, וְנַפְשִׁי בְּקֵשׁוּ.

This doe violates the laws of God with
her eyes: she kills me with malice
aforethought, yet no one avenges me.
Have you ever seen the heart of a lion
joined to the eyelids of a gazelle? Her
eyelids have learned to tear like a lion,
they hurl sharpened arrows at me, they
drain my heart's blood to the dregs.
They are out for my life.

יוֹם אֲנִי מֵיֵּין דּוֹדֶיהָ כְּשִׁכּוֹר מִתְרוֹגֵן,
כִּי שְׁלוֹמֶיהָ תַפְגִּיעַ וְעָלַי תִּתְלוֹנֵן
עַל יְדֵי צִירִים ; וּבְבוֹאָם, אֲלֵיהֶם תִּתְחַנַּן :
'מַלְאֲכֵי שָׁלוֹם, פִּגְעוּ בִי, שְׁנוּ גַּם שַׁלֵּשׁוּ !'
מַאֲמָרָם לִבִּי פִתּוּ וְרוּחִי חִדֵּשׁוּ.

One day, when I was reeling like a
drunkard, longing for the wine of her
love, she dispatched envoys to me
bearing greetings and complaints; and
when they returned to her, she begged
them: 'O messengers of peace, come
again and yet again!' These tidings
seduced my heart and revived my spirit.

יוֹם בְּגַנָּהּ רָעוּ יָדַי וְדַדֶּיהָ עָשׂוּ,

אָמְרָה: 'הֶרֶף יָדֶיךָ – הֲכִי עוֹד לֹא נָסוּ !'

וַאֲמָרִים לִי הֶחֱלִיקָה לְבָבִי הֵמַסּוּ:

'גן מתא נקש, יא חביבי, פאנכר דנאשו

אלגלאלה רכיצה בשתאת הפרמשו.'

But one day when my hands were grazing in her garden and fondling her breasts, she said: 'Now take away your hands – they are not skilful enough.'[1] And her words were so seductive that they melted my heart: 'Do not touch me, friend, I do not like those who hurt me. My breasts are soft and sensitive. Enough! I shall refuse one and all!'[2]

עָפְרָה תְכַבֵּס   THE LAUNDRESS

עָפְרָה תְכַבֵּס אֶת בְּגָדֶיהָ בְּמֵי

דְמָעִי וְתִשְׁטָחֵם לְשֶׁמֶשׁ זָהֳרָהּ:

לֹא שָׁאֲלָה מֵי הָעֲיָנוֹת – עִם שְׁתֵּי

עֵינַי, וְלֹא שֶׁמֶשׁ – לִיפִי תָאֳרָהּ.

My love washes her clothes in the water of my tears and spreads them out in the sun of her beauty. She has no need of spring-water – she has my two eyes; nor of the sun – she has her own radiance.

מַה לָּךְ, צְבִיָּה   SONG OF FAREWELL

מַה לָּךְ, צְבִיָּה, תִּמְנְעִי צִירַיִךְ

מְדּוֹד, צְלָעָיו מָלְאוּ צִירַיִךְ ?

לֹא תֵדְעִי כִּי אֵין לְדוֹדֵךְ מִזְמַן

בִּלְתִּי שְׁמֹעַ קוֹל שְׁלוֹמוֹתַיִךְ ?

אִם הַפְּרִידָה עַל שְׁנֵינוּ נִגְזָרָה –

עִמְדִי מְעַט עַד אֶחֱזֶה פָנָיִךְ.

לֹא אֵדְעָה אִם בֵּין צְלָעַי נֶעֱצַר

לִבִּי, וְאִם יֵלֵךְ לְמַסָּעַיִךְ.

Why, O fair one, do you withhold your envoys from the lover whose heart is filled with pain of you? Do you not know that Time means nothing to your beloved, unless he hear your welcoming voice? If we two are doomed to parting, stay a while and let me look at your face. I do not know if my heart has come to a stop between my ribs, or else has wandered off with you. Oh,

---

1. Or, 'they [my breasts] have not yet experienced such things'.
2. The last two lines are in mixed Arabic and Romance. The meaning is uncertain.

343

חֵי אַהֲבָה, זְכָרִי יְמֵי חִשְׁקֵךְ כְּמוֹ
אֶזְכֹּר אֲנִי לֵילוֹת תְּשׁוּקוֹתַיִךְ.
כַּאֲשֶׁר דְּמוּתֵךְ בַּחֲלוֹמִי יַעֲבֹר,
כֵּן אֶעְבְּרָה־נָּא בַחֲלוֹמוֹתַיִךְ.
בֵּינִי וּבֵינֵךְ יָם דְּמָעוֹת יֶהֱמוּ
גַּלָּיו, וְלֹא אוּכַל עֲבֹר עָבַר אֵלָיִךְ.
אַךְ לוּ פְעָמַיִךְ לְעָבְרוֹ קָרְבוּ,
אָז נִבְקְעוּ מֵימָיו לְכַף רַגְלָיִךְ.
לוּ אַחֲרֵי מוֹתִי בְּאָזְנִי יַעֲלֶה
קוֹל פַּעֲמוֹן זָהָב עֲלֵי שׁוּלָיִךְ!
אוֹ תִשְׁאֲלִי לִשְׁלוֹם יְדִידֵךְ, מִשְּׁאוֹל
אֶשְׁאַל בְּדוֹדַיִךְ וּבִשְׁלוֹמַיִךְ! [...]

for the life of love, remember the days of your desire, as I remember the nights of your passion. And just as your image moves through my dreams, let mine move through yours. A sea of tears roars between us, and I cannot cross its waves to reach you. But if your steps approached to cross them, the waters would divide before your feet. Oh, after my death, let me still hear the sound of the golden bells on the hem of your skirt. And if you then ask how your beloved is, I, from the grave, will send you my love and my blessings!

מִי יִתְּנֵנִי אֶחְיֶה עַד אֶאֱרֶה
בֹּשֶׂם וּמֹר מִבֵּין הֲלִיכוֹתַיִךְ.
לֹא אֶשְׁמְעָה קוֹלֵךְ, אֲבָל אֶשְׁמַע עֲלֵי
סִתְרֵי לְבָבִי קוֹל צְעָדוֹתַיִךְ. [...]

If only I could live until I gather myrrh and spices from among your footprints! I cannot hear your voice, but in the covert of my heart I hear the sound of your steps.

בִּי הַצְּבִי, בִּי אֲדוֹנִי

THE CRUEL LOVER

בִּי הַצְּבִי, בִּי אֲדוֹנִי,
יֵקַר בְּעֵינֶךְ יְגוֹנִי,
פֶּן יְקָרֵנִי אֲסוֹנִי.
אַט, אַט, אַט בְּדָמִי,
כִּי רַק בְּיָדְךָ שְׁלוֹמִי!

O my fair youth, my lord, take my grief to heart, lest disaster overtake me. Oh, gently, deal gently with my blood, for my fate is in your hands alone.

יֵרֶךְ לְבָבְךָ לְנִדְכֶּה
יָצוּם לְזַעְמְךָ וְיִבְכֶּה
וּלְמָן רְצוֹנְךָ יְחַכֶּה.
מָן, מָן מִן לְצוּמִי,
וּתְנָה שְׂכָרִי בְּיוֹמִי.

Pity the forlorn one, fasting and
weeping because of your anger, waiting
for the manna of your favour. Oh, give
me manna, manna for my hunger and
pay me my wages every day.

אִם תַּעֲלֹז עַל חֲלָיַי —
אֶשְׁטַח לְךָ אֶת לְחָיַי,
וַתַּעֲנֵנִי: 'וְחַיַּי!
אֵין, אֵין, אֵין בְּחֶרְמִי
רַק הַהֲרוּגִים לְתֻמִּי'.

When you laugh at my suffering, I
show you my tear-stained cheeks. But
you answer: 'Truly, there are none in
my trap, none but those whom I
captured unwittingly.'

אָרִיב בְּנַפְשִׁי לְכִילַי:
לוּ יִפְחֲדֵנִי וְאֵלַי
יָשִׁיב שְׁנָתִי, וְאוּלַי
עָף, עָף, עָף בְּנוּמִי,
יָבוֹא בְּכֶפֶל חֲלוֹמִי!

I reproach myself because of this
miserly youth: if he were to fear me, he
might give me back my slumber; he
might fly, Oh fly to me in my sleep,
and be caught in the mesh of my
dreams.

אִם אֶשְׁאָלָה צוּף שְׂפָתוֹ,
יַאְדִּים כְּשֶׁמֶשׁ בְּצֵאתוֹ —
עַד אֶחֱזֶה מִדְּמוּתוֹ
אֵיךְ, אֵיךְ, אֵיךְ אֲרַמִּי
יַהֲפֹךְ דְּמוּתוֹ אֲדוֹמִי!

When I ask for the nectar of his lips, he
blushes like the rising sun, until I see
in his face how, Oh how the Aramean
turns into an Edomite![1]

שִׁירוֹ יְפַלַּח כְּבֵדִי.
יָשִׁיר לְעוֹרֵר יְקוֹדִי:
'שַׁק פִּי וְרַב לָךְ, יְדִידִי,
בַּס, בַּס, בַּס בְּפֻמִּי
וְדַע סוּאַדַךְ, יָא עַמִּי!'

His song pierces my heart. He sings to
fan my flames: 'Kiss my mouth, and
no more, my friend. Kiss me on the
mouth, kiss me, and forget your
melancholy, love.'[2]

---

1. A play on words: i.e. how Laban (*lavan*, 'white') the Aramean turns into an Edomite (*adom*, 'red').
2. The last couplet is in Arabic.

אַט לִי, חֲזַק לֵבָב — THE PURE LOVER

אַט לִי, חֲזַק לֵבָב, רְפֵה מָתְנַיִם,
אַט לִי עֲדֵי אֶשְׁתַּחֲוֶה אַפַּיִם!
שָׁגוּ בָךְ עֵינַי לְבַדָּם, וַאֲנִי
אָמְנָם טְהָר-לֵב, לֹא טְהוֹר עֵינַיִם.
הֶרֶף לְצִיִּין תְּאָרֶה מִתְּאָרֶךְ
וֶרֶד וְשׁוֹשָׁן נִזְרְעוּ כִּלְאַיִם.
אֵשׁ לֶחָיֶךְ אֶחְתֶּה לְכַבּוֹת אֵשׁ בְּאֵשׁ,
עֵת אֶצְמָאָה כִּי אֶמְצָאָה בוֹ מָיִם.
מָצָה שְׂפַת אֹדֶם אֲשֶׁר תִּיקַד כְּמוֹ
רִצְפָּה, וּמַלְקוֹחַי כְּמַלְקָחַיִם.
חַיַּי תְּלוּאִים בֵּין שְׁנֵי חוּטֵי שָׁנִי
תוֹלָע, אֲבָל מוֹתִי בְּבֵין עַרְבַּיִם.
לֹא אֶמְצָאָה עַתָּה לְלֵילוֹת קֵץ, וְאָז
לֹא בָא אֱשׁוּן לַיְל בְּתוֹךְ יוֹמָיִם —
בִּהְיוֹת זְמַנִּי בֵּין יְדֵי חֶפְצִי כְּמוֹ
חֹמֶר, וְהַגַּלְגַּל כְּמוֹ אָבְנָיִם.

Gently, my hard-hearted, soft-hipped one, deal gently with me and let me bow down before you. It is only my eyes that were ravished by you; my heart is pure, yes, but my eyes are not. Oh, let my eyes pluck the roses and lilies that were sown together in your face![1] I rake the fire of your cheeks, to put out fire with fire: and when I am thirsty, it is there that I look for water. Oh, I would suck your red lips that flame like glowing coals, and my jaws would be like tongs. My life hangs upon the two scarlet threads [of your lips], but my death lurks in the twilight [of your hair]. Now the nights are endless, though once no darkness came between the days; Time was like clay in my hands, and the zodiac turned like a potter's wheel.

מַה תַּאֲמִין בַּזְּמָן — THE EXCUSE

מַה תַּאֲמִין בַּזְּמָן אֲשֶׁר אֵין בּוֹ אֱמֶת?
הָהּ, כִּי עֲמָלִי רַב וְיוֹמִי קָצֵר!
כָּל אִישׁ יְצַו אָחִיו לְבִלְתִּי יֶחֱטָא,
לֵאמֹר: 'שְׁמָר-לָךְ פֶּן יְסִיתְךָ יֵצֶר.'
וּבְעֵת חֲטֹא, שָׂח: 'מַה בְּיַד אִישׁ לַעֲשׂוֹת?
הַיְצוּר וְהַיֵּצֶר בְּיַד הַיּוֹצֵר!'

Why put your trust in Time, which has no truth in it? Alas, my labours are so great and my day is so short. Each man urges his neighbour not to sin, saying: 'Don't let your passions lead you astray.' But when he himself sins, he says: 'What can a man do? All creatures and their passions are in the hands of the Creator'.

---

1. A playful allusion to the scriptural prohibition: 'You shall not plant your field with two kinds of seed' (Leviticus 19.19).

עַבְדֵי זְמָן

THE LORD IS MY PORTION

עַבְדֵי זְמָן עַבְדֵי עֲבָדִים הֵם –
עֶבֶד אֲדֹנָי הוּא לְבַד חָפְשִׁי.
עַל כֵּן, בְּבַקֵּשׁ כָּל אֱנוֹשׁ חֶלְקוֹ,
'חֶלְקִי אֲדֹנָי!' אָמְרָה נַפְשִׁי.

The slaves of Time are the slaves of a
slave; only the slave of the Lord is
free. Therefore, while other men seek
their portion, 'The Lord is my portion,'
says my soul.

לִבִּי בְמִזְרָח

MY HEART IS IN THE EAST

לִבִּי בְמִזְרָח, וְאָנֹכִי בְּסוֹף מַעֲרָב –
אֵיךְ אֶטְעֲמָה אֵת אֲשֶׁר אֹכַל וְאֵיךְ יֶעֱרָב?
אֵיכָה אֲשַׁלֵּם נְדָרַי וֶאֱסָרַי, בְּעוֹד
צִיּוֹן בְּחֶבֶל אֱדוֹם וַאֲנִי בְּכֶבֶל עֲרָב?
יֵקַל בְּעֵינַי עֲזֹב כָּל טוּב סְפָרַד, כְּמוֹ
יֵקַר בְּעֵינַי רְאוֹת עַפְרוֹת דְּבִיר נֶחֱרָב.

My heart is in the East and I am at the
edge of the West. Then how can I taste
what I eat, how can I enjoy it? How
can I fulfil my vows and pledges[1]
while Zion is in the domain of Edom,
and I am in the bonds of Arabia? It
would be easy for me to leave behind
all the good things of Spain; it would
be glorious to see the dust of the
ruined Shrine.

צִיּוֹן, הֲלֹא תִשְׁאֲלִי

ODE TO ZION

צִיּוֹן, הֲלֹא תִשְׁאֲלִי לִשְׁלוֹם אֲסִירַיִךְ,
דּוֹרְשֵׁי שְׁלוֹמֵךְ, וְהֵם יֶתֶר עֲדָרָיִךְ?
מִיָּם וּמִזְרָח וּמִצָּפוֹן וְתֵימָן שְׁלוֹם
רָחוֹק וְקָרוֹב שְׂאִי מִכֹּל עֲבָרָיִךְ,
וּשְׁלוֹם אֲסִיר תַּאֲוָה, נוֹתֵן דְּמָעָיו כְּטַל-
חֶרְמוֹן וְנִכְסָף לְרִדְתָּם עַל הֲרָרָיִךְ!
לִבְכּוֹת עֱנוּתֵךְ – אֲנִי תַנִּים, וְעֵת אֶחֱלֹם
שִׁיבַת שְׁבוּתֵךְ – אֲנִי כִנּוֹר לְשִׁירָיִךְ.

O Zion, will you not ask how your
captives are – the exiles who seek your
welfare, who are the remnant of your
flocks? From west and east, north and
south, from every side, accept the
greetings of those near and far, and the
blessings of this captive of desire, who
sheds his tears like the dew of Hermon
and longs to have them fall upon your
hills. I am like a jackal when I weep for
your affliction; but when I dream of
your exiles' return, I am a lute for your
songs.

---

1. The poet had made a vow to leave Spain for Zion.

לִבִּי לְבֵית־אֵל וְלִפְנִיאֵל מְאֹד יֶהֱמֶה
וּלְמַחֲנַיִם וְכָל פִּגְעֵי טְהוֹרַיִךְ.
שָׁם הַשְּׁכִינָה שְׁכֵנָה לָךְ, וְהַיּוֹצְרֵךְ
פָּתַח לְמוּל שַׁעֲרֵי שַׁחַק שְׁעָרַיִךְ,
וּכְבוֹד אֲדֹנָי לְבַד הָיָה מְאוֹרֵךְ, וְאֵין
שֶׁמֶשׁ וְסַהַר וְכוֹכָבִים מְאִירַיִךְ.
אֶבְחַר לְנַפְשִׁי לְהִשְׁתַּפֵּךְ בְּמָקוֹם אֲשֶׁר
רוּחַ אֱלֹהִים שְׁפוּכָה עַל בְּחִירַיִךְ.
אַתְּ בֵּית מְלוּכָה וְאַתְּ כִּסֵּא אֲדֹנָי, וְאִם
יָשְׁבוּ עֲבָדִים עֲלֵי כִסְאוֹת גְּבִירַיִךְ!

My heart longs for Bethel and Penuel,
for Mahanaim[1] and for all the shrines
of your pure ones. There the Shekinah
dwelled within you, and your Maker
opened your gates to face the gates of
heaven. There the glory of the Lord
was your only light; it was not the sun,
moon, or stars that shone over you. Oh,
I would pour out my life in the very
place where once the spirit of God was
poured out upon your chosen ones.
You are the seat of royalty, you are the
throne of the Lord – though slaves now
sit upon your princes' thrones!

מִי יִתְּנֵנִי מְשׁוֹטֵט בַּמְּקוֹמוֹת אֲשֶׁר
נִגְלוּ אֱלֹהִים לְחוֹזַיִךְ וְצִירַיִךְ.
מִי יַעֲשֶׂה לִּי כְנָפַיִם וְאַרְחִיק נְדֹד,
אָנִיד לְבִתְרֵי לְבָבִי בֵּין בְּתָרַיִךְ.
אֶפֹּל לְאַפַּי עֲלֵי אַרְצֵךְ וְאֶרְצֶה אֲבָ־
נַיִךְ מְאֹד וַאֲחוֹנֵן אֶת עֲפָרַיִךְ.
אֶבְכֶּה בְּעָמְדִי עֲלֵי קִבְרוֹת אֲבוֹתַי וְאֶשְׁ־
תּוֹמֵם בְּחֶבְרוֹן עֲלֵי מִבְחַר קְבָרַיִךְ.
אֶעֱבֹר בְּיַעְרֵךְ וְכַרְמְלֵךְ וְאֶעֱמֹד בְּגִל־
עָדֵךְ וְאֶשְׁתּוֹמֵמָה אֶל הַר עֲבָרַיִךְ –
הַר הָעֲבָרִים וְהֹר הָהָר, אֲשֶׁר שָׁם שְׁנֵי
אוֹרִים גְּדוֹלִים, מְאִירַיִךְ וּמוֹרַיִךְ.
חַיֵּי נְשָׁמוֹת – אֲוִיר אַרְצֵךְ, וּמִמָּר־דְּרוֹר
אַבְקַת עֲפָרֵךְ, וְנֹפֶת צוּף – נְהָרַיִךְ!
יִנְעַם לְנַפְשִׁי הֲלֹךְ עָרֹם וְיָחֵף עֲלֵי
חָרְבוֹת שְׁמָמָה אֲשֶׁר הָיוּ דְבִירַיִךְ,

If only I could roam through those
places where God was revealed to your
prophets and heralds! Who will give
me wings, so that I may wander far
away? I would carry the pieces of my
broken heart over your rugged mountains.[2] I would bow down, my face on
your ground; I would love your stones;
your dust would move me to pity. I
would weep, as I stood by my ancestors'
graves, I would grieve, in Hebron, over
the choicest of burial places![3] I would
walk in your forests and meadows, stop
in Gilead, marvel at Mount Abarim;
Mount Abarim and Mount Hor, where
the two great luminaries [Moses and
Aaron] rest, those who guided you and
gave you light. The air of your land is
the very life of the soul, the grains of
your dust are flowing myrrh, your
rivers are honey from the comb. It
would delight my heart to walk naked
and barefoot among the desolate ruins
where your shrines once stood; where

---

1. All sites figuring in the life of Jacob.
2. The hills of Bether (Song of Songs 2.17), in the vicinity of Jerusalem.
3. The burial cave of the Patriarchs (Genesis 23.17).

בִּמְקוֹם אֲרוֹנֵךְ אֲשֶׁר נִגְנַז, וּבִמְקוֹם כְּרוּ־
בַיִךְ אֲשֶׁר שָׁכְנוּ מַדְרֵי חֲדָרָיִךְ.
אָגֹז וְאַשְׁלִיךְ פְּאֵר נִזְרִי וְאֶקֹּב זְמַן,
חִלֵּל בְּאֶרֶץ טְמֵאָה אֶת נְזִירָיִךְ. [...]

your Ark was hidden away,[1] where your
cherubim once dwelled in the innermost chamber. I shall cut off my
glorious hair and throw it away, I shall
curse Time that has defiled your pure
ones in the polluted lands [of exile].

אַשְׁרֵי מְחַכֶּה וְיַגִּיעַ וְיִרְאֶה עֲלוֹת
אוֹרֵךְ וְיִבָּקְעוּ עָלָיו שְׁחָרָיִךְ,
לִרְאוֹת בְּטוֹבַת בְּחִירָיִךְ, וְלַעֲלֹז בְּשִׂמְ־
חָתֵךְ בְּשׁוּבֵךְ אֱלֵי קַדְמַת נְעוּרָיִךְ!

Happy is he who waits and lives to see
your light rising, your dawn breaking
forth over him! He shall see your
chosen people prospering, he shall
rejoice in your joy when you regain the
days of your youth.

וְאַל יִמּוֹט

THE POET IMAGINES HIS VOYAGE

[...] וְאַל יִמּוֹט בְּלֵב יַמִּים לְבָבֶךְ
וְהָרִים תֶּחֱזֶה מָטִים וּמָשִׁים,
וּמַלָּחִים יְדֵיהֶם כַּמְּלָחִים,
וְחַכְמֵי הַחֲרָשִׁים מַחֲרִישִׁים. –
שְׂמֵחִים הַהוֹלְכִים נֹכַח פְּנֵיהֶם –
וְשָׁבִים אֶל אֲחוֹרֵיהֶם וּבוֹשִׁים. –
וְאָקְיָנוֹס לְפָנֶיךָ לְמָנוֹס –
וְאֵין מִבְרָח לְךָ כִּי אִם יְקוּשִׁים!
וְיָמוּטוּ וְיָנוּטוּ קְלָעִים,
וְיָנוּעוּ וְיִזוּעוּ קְרָשִׁים,
וְיַד רוּחַ מְצַחֶקֶת בְּמַיִם,
כְּנוֹשְׂאֵי הָעֳמָרִים בַּדְּלָשִׁים,
וּפַעַם תַּעֲשֶׂה מֵהֶם גְּרָנוֹת,
וּפַעַם תַּעֲשֶׂה מֵהֶם גְּדִישִׁים.
בְּעֵת הִתְגַּבְּרָם דָּמוּ אֲרָיוֹת,
וְעֵת הֵחָלְשָׁם דָּמוּ נְחָשִׁים,

Let not your heart tremble in the heart
of the sea, when you see mountains
trembling and heaving, and sailors'
hands as limp as rags, and soothsayers
struck dumb. When they set their
course, they were full of joy, but now
they are beaten back in shame. The
whole ocean is yours to escape in, but
your only refuge is the snare of the
deep. The sails quiver and quake, the
beams creak and shudder. The hand of
the wind toys with the waves, like
reapers at the threshing: now it flattens
them out, now it stacks them up. When
the waves gather strength, they are like
lions; when they weaken, they are like

1. According to Talmudic legend,
King Josiah hid the holy Ark from the enemy.

349

וְרִאשׁוֹנִים דְּלָקוּם אַחֲרוֹנִים
כְּצִפְעוֹנִים וְאֵין לָהֶם לְחָשִׁים. [...]

snakes, who then pursue the lions –
like vipers that cannot be charmed.

וְרֶגַע יִשְׁתְּקוּ גַלִּים, וְיִדְמוּ
עֲדָרִים עַל פְּנֵי אֶרֶץ נְטוּשִׁים.
וְהַלַּיְל – כְּבוֹא שֶׁמֶשׁ בְּמַעֲלוֹת
צְבָא מָרוֹם, וְעָלָיו שַׂר חֲמִשִּׁים –
כְּכוּשִׁית מִשְׁבְּצוֹת זָהָב לְבוּשָׁהּ,
וְכִתְכֵלֶת בְּמִלּוּאַת גְּבִישִׁים.
וְכוֹכָבִים בְּלֵב הַיָּם נְבוּכִים
כְּגֵרִים מִמְּעוֹנֵיהֶם גְּרוּשִׁים,
וְכִדְמוּתָם בְּצַלְמָם יַעֲשׂוּ אוֹר
בְּלֵב הַיָּם כְּלֶהָבוֹת וְאִשִּׁים.
פְּנֵי מַיִם וְשָׁמַיִם עֲדָיִים
עֲלֵי לַיְל מְטֹהָרִים לְטוּשִׁים.
וְיָם דּוֹמֶה לְרָקִיעַ בְּעֵינוּ,
שְׁנֵיהֶם אָז שְׁנֵי יַמִּים חֲבוּשִׁים –
וּבֵינוֹתָם לְבָבִי יָם שְׁלִישִׁי,
בִּשׂוֹא גַּלֵּי שְׁבָחַי הַחֲדָשִׁים!

Suddenly, the waves calm down, and
are like flocks spread out over the fields.
And the night – once the sun has gone
down the stairway of the heavenly
hosts, who are commanded by the
moon[1] – is like a Negress dressed in
gold embroidery, or like a violet robe
spangled with crystal. The stars are
astray in the heart of the sea, like
strangers expelled from their homes.
And in the heart of the sea they cast
a light, in their image and likeness,
that glows like fire. Now the sea and
the sky are pure, glittering ornaments
upon the night. The sea is the colour of
the sky – they are two seas bound
together. And between these two, my
heart is a third sea, as the new waves of
my praise surge on high!

זֶה רוּחֲךָ, צַד מַעֲרָב

TO THE WESTERN WIND

זֶה רוּחֲךָ, צַד מַעֲרָב, רָקוּחַ:
הַנֵּרְדְּ בִּכְנָפָיו וְהַתַּפּוּחַ.
מֵאוֹצְרוֹת הָרוֹכְלִים מוֹצָאֲךָ,
כִּי אֵינְךָ מֵאוֹצְרוֹת הָרוּחַ!
כַּנְפֵי דְּרוֹר תָּנִיף, וְתִקְרָא לִי דְרוֹר,
וּכְמָר-דְּרוֹר מִן הַצְּרוֹר לָקוּחַ.

This wind of yours, O West, is all
perfume – it has the scent of spikenard
and apple in its wings. Wind, you come
from the storehouse of spice-merchants,
and not from the common storehouse
of winds. You lift up the swallow's
wings, you set me free, you are like the
purest perfume, fresh from a bunch of

1. Lit. 'commander over unit of fifty'.

מַה גִּכְסְפוּ לָךְ עָם, אֲשֶׁר בִּגְלָלָךְ
רָכְבוּ בְּגַב הַיָּם עֲלֵי גַב לוּחַ !
אַל נָא תְרַפֶּה יָדְךָ מִן הָאֳנִי,
כִּי יַחֲנֶה הַיּוֹם וְכִי יָפוּחַ.
וּרְקַע תְּהוֹם וּקְרַע לְבַב יַמִּים, וְגַע
אֶל הַרְרֵי קֹדֶשׁ וְשָׁם תָּנוּחַ.
וּגְעַר בְּקָדִים הַמְסָעֵר יָם, עֲדֵי
יָשִׂים לְבַב הַיָּם כְּסִיר נָפוּחַ.

מַה יַּעֲשֶׂה אָסוּר בְּיַד הַצּוּר, אֲשֶׁר
פַּעַם יְהִי עָצוּר, וְעֵת שָׁלוּחַ ?
אַךְ סוֹד שְׁאֵלָתִי בְּיַד מָרוֹם – וְהוּא
יוֹצֵר מְרוֹם הָרִים וּבוֹרֵא רוּחַ !

קִרְאוּ עֲלֵי בָנוֹת

קִרְאוּ עֲלֵי בָנוֹת וּמִשְׁפָּחוֹת
שָׁלוֹם, וְעַל אַחִים וְעַל אֲחוֹת,
מֵאֵת אֲסִיר תִּקְוָה אֲשֶׁר נִקְנָה
לַיָּם, וְשָׁם רוּחוֹ בְּיַד רוּחוֹת.
דְּחוּי בְּיַד מַעֲרָב לְיַד מִזְרָח,
זֶה יַעֲבֹר לַנְחוֹת, וְזֶה – לִדְחוֹת.
בֵּינוֹ וּבֵין מָוֶת כְּפֶשַׂע, אַךְ
בֵּינוֹ וּבֵינָיו מַעֲבֶה לוּחוֹת.
קָבוּר בְּחַיָּיו בְּאָרוֹן עֵץ – לֹא
קַרְקַע, וְלֹא אַרְבַּע, וְלֹא פָחוֹת !
יוֹשֵׁב – וְאֵין לַעֲמֹד עֲלֵי רַגְלָיו,
שׁוֹכֵב – וְאֵין רַגְלָיו מְשֻׁלָּחוֹת,
חוֹלֶה וְיָרֵא מִפְּנֵי גוֹיִים,

myrrh. Everyone here longs for you; by
your good graces, they ride over the sea
upon a mere plank. Oh, do not abandon
the ship, when the day draws to its end
or when it begins. Smooth out the
ocean, break a path through the sea
until you reach the holy mountains, and
there subside. Rebuke the east wind
that whips up the sea and turns it into
a boiling cauldron.

But how can the wind help, for it is a
prisoner of the Rock – sometimes held
back and sometimes let loose? Only
God can grant my deepest wish: for He
is the maker of high mountains and
the creator of winds!

SONG AT SEA

Greetings to the kinsfolk, to brothers
and sisters, from this prisoner of hope
who was ransomed by the sea and
committed his spirit into the hands of
the winds. Now they push him back
and forth: the west wind guides his
ship, while the east wind thrusts it
back. Between him and death there is
nothing but a step; between them only
the thickness of the planks. He is
buried alive in a wooden coffin, but
without any earth: not even four cubits,[1]
not even a handful. He sits, for there
is no room for him to stand; he lies
down, and he cannot stretch out his
legs. He is ill, he is afraid of the

---

1. The minimum required for a grave.

גַּם מִפְּנֵי לִסְטִים וּמְרוּחוֹת.

חוֹבֵל וּמַלָּח, כָּל בְּנֵי פְרָחָח,

הֵם הַסְּגָנִים שָׁם וְהַפַּחוֹת.

לֹא לַחֲכָמִים שָׁם וְגַם לֹא חֵן

לַיִּדְעִים – רַק יוֹדְעִים לְשֹׁחוֹת !

יִתְעַצְּבוּ רֶגַע לְזֹאת פָּנַי –

אֵיךְ יַעֲלֹז הַלֵּב וְהַטּוּחוֹת –

עַד אֶשְׁפְּכָה נַפְשִׁי בְּחֵיק הָאֵל,

נֹכַח מְקוֹם אָרוֹן וּמִזְבְּחוֹת.

אֶגְמֹל לָאֵל, גּוֹמֵל לְחַיָּבִים

טוֹבוֹת, בְּטוּב שִׁירוֹת וְתִשְׁבָּחוֹת.

Gentile passengers, as well as of pirates and ghosts. The helmsman and the sailors – all of them riffraff – are the viceroys and governors here! Honour does not belong to the wise nor success to the skilful – only to those who know how to swim! Because of this my face is downcast – how could my heart rejoice? – but only for a moment: until I come to pour out my soul in the bosom of God, at the site of the Ark and the Altar. Then I shall render to God, who renders favours to the undeserving,[1] my choicest songs and praises.

הַבָּא מַבּוּל   ON THE HIGH SEAS

הַבָּא מַבּוּל וְשָׂם תֵּבֵל חֲרָבָה ?

וְאֵין לִרְאוֹת פְּנֵי אֶרֶץ חֲרֵבָה,

וְאֵין אָדָם וְאֵין חַיָּה וְאֵין עוֹף –

הֲסָף הַכֹּל וְשָׁכְבוּ מַעֲצֵבָה ?

וּבִרְאוֹת הַר וְשׁוּחָה לִי מְנוּחָה,

וְאֶרֶץ הָעֲרָבָה לִי עֲרֵבָה.

וְאַשְׁגִּיחַ לְכָל עֵבֶר – וְאֵין כֹּל,

אֲבָל מַיִם וְשָׁמַיִם וְתֵבָה,

וְלִוְיָתָן בְּהַרְתִּיחוֹ מְצוּלָה,

וְאֶחְשֹׁב כִּי תְהוֹם יַחְשֹׁב לְשֵׂיבָה.

וְלֵב הַיָּם יְכַחֵשׁ בָּאֳנִיָּה,

כְּאִלּוּ הִיא בְּיַד הַיָּם גְּנֵבָה !

וְיָם יִזְעַף – וְנַפְשִׁי תַעֲלֹז, כִּי

אֱלֵי מִקְדַּשׁ אֱלֹהֶיהָ קְרֵבָה.

Has a flood come and laid the world waste? For dry land is nowhere to be seen. There is neither man, nor beast, nor bird. Have they all perished, all lain down in torment and died? If only I could see a hill or valley, I would be comforted; even a desert would delight me. I look in every direction, and there is nothing but sea and sky and ship,[2] and leviathan churning the deep, until it seems that the abyss is white with age! Deceitfully, the sea covers the ship, as though it had taken it by theft. The sea is in turmoil, but my soul is full of joy, for she is drawing near to the temple of her God.

---

1. An allusion to the Benediction on Deliverance, recited by those who come safely through danger.
2. The word here is the one used for Noah's ark.

אַבְרָהָם אִבְּן־עֶזְרָא   *Abraham ibn Ezra*

אַשְׁכִּים לְבֵית הַשַּׂר   THE PATRON

אַשְׁכִּים לְבֵית הַשַּׂר – אוֹמְרִים : 'כְּבָר רָכַב'.
אָבוֹא לְעֵת עֶרֶב – אוֹמְרִים : 'כְּבָר שָׁכַב'.
אוֹ יַעֲלֶה מֶרְכָּב אוֹ יַעֲלֶה מִשְׁכָּב –
אוֹיָה לְאִישׁ עָנִי נוֹלַד בְּלִי כוֹכָב!

When I come to the patron's house
early in the morning, they say: 'He has
already ridden away.' When I come in
the evening, they say: 'He has already
gone to sleep.' He either climbs into his
carriage or climbs into bed – woe to the
poor man, born to misfortune![1]

בְּלִי מַזָּל   OUT OF LUCK

א   *1*

גַּלְגַּל וּמַזָּלוֹת בְּמַעֲמָדָם
נָטוּ בְּמַהְלָכָם לְמוֹלַדְתִּי :
לוּ יִהְיוּ נֵרוֹת סְחוֹרָתִי –
לֹא יֶחֱשַׁךְ שֶׁמֶשׁ עֲדֵי מוֹתִי !

The heavenly sphere and the constellations strayed from their path when I
was born. If my business were in
candles, the sun would not set until I
died!

ב   *2*

אִינַע לְהַצְלִיחַ וְלֹא אוּכַל,
כִּי עִוְּתוּנִי כּוֹכְבֵי שָׁמָי :
לוּ אֶהְיֶה סוֹחֵר בְּתַכְרִיכִין –
לֹא יִגְוְעוּן אִישִׁים בְּכָל יָמָי !

However I struggle, I cannot succeed,
for my stars have ruined me: If I were
a dealer in shrouds, no one would die
as long as I lived.

מְעִיל יֵשׁ לִי   THE OLD CLOAK

מְעִיל יֵשׁ לִי וְהוּא כִּדְמוּת כְּבָרָה
לְחִטָּה לַהֲנָפָה אוֹ שְׂעוֹרָה.
כְּאֹהֶל אֶפְרְשֶׁנּוּ לֵיל בְּאִישׁוֹן,

I have a cloak that is like a sieve to sift
wheat or barley. I spread it out like a
tent in the dark of night, and the stars

---

1. Lit. 'without a star'.

353

וְכוֹכְבֵי רוֹם יְשִׁימוּן בּוֹ מְאוֹרָה.
בְּתוֹכוֹ אֶחֱזֶה סַהַר וְכִימָה,
וְיוֹפִיעַ כְּסִיל עָלָיו נְהָרָה.
וְאֵלֶּה מִסְפֹּר אֶת כָּל נְקָבָיו
אֲשֶׁר דּוֹמִים לְשִׁנֵּי הַמְּגֵרָה.
וְתִקְוַת חוּט תְּפִירַת כָּל קְרוּצָיו –
עֲלֵי שְׁתִי וָעֵרֶב – הִיא יְתֵרָה.
וְאִם יִפֹּל זְבוּב עָלָיו בְּחָזְקָה,
כְּמוֹ פֶתִי יְהִי נִמְלָךְ מְהֵרָה.
אֱלוֹהַי, הַחֲלִיפֵהוּ בְּמַעֲטֶה
תְהִלָּה לִי – וְתֵיטִיב הַתְּפִירָה !

shine through it; through it I see the moon and the Pleiades, and Orion, flashing his light. I am tired of counting all its holes, which are shaped like the teeth of a saw. No thread can hope to mend its gaps with warp and woof. If a fly landed on it with its full weight, it would quickly regret its foolishness. O God, give me a robe of glory in exchange – this would be properly tailored!

אֶשְׁתַּחֲוֶה אַפַּיִם אַרְצָה

PENITENTIAL PRAYER

אֶשְׁתַּחֲוֶה אַפַּיִם אַרְצָה,
כִּי אֵין לְמַטָּה מִמֶּנָּה.
אֶתְנַפֵּל לִפְנֵי עֶלְיוֹן,
גָּבֹהַּ עַל כָּל גְּבֹהִים.
בַּמָּה אֲקַדֵּם פָּנָיו, כִּי אִם בְּרוּחִי ?
הֲלֹא הִיא מֵאִתּוֹ,
בְּמִבְחַר גּוּפָתִי הוּא יְחַיֶּה –
וְאֵין לְאִישׁ נִכְבָּד מִנַּפְשׁוֹ.
רֹאשׁ נָסוֹף אֵין לִגְדֻלָּתוֹ,
וּלְשׁוֹנִי אֵיךְ תְּגַדְּלֶנּוּ ?
רָחוֹק רָחוֹק מִשְּׁמֵי הַשָּׁמַיִם,
וְקָרוֹב קָרוֹב מֵעַצְמִי וּבְשָׂרִי !
הִנֵּה בָאתִי לָךְ, אֱלוֹהַי,
כִּי אֵין מוֹעִיל זוּלָתֶךָ.
הֲלֹא כָּל צְבָא הַשָּׁמַיִם וְהָאָרֶץ

I bow down with my face to the ground, for there is nothing lower than it. I throw myself down before the Supreme One, highest of the high. What but my spirit shall I bring when I approach Him? It comes from Him, He gives it life in the choicest part of my body, and a man has nothing dearer than his soul. There is no end and no beginning to His glory – how then can my tongue glorify Him? He is farther from me than the farthest heaven, and closer than my flesh and bone! I come to You now, my God, because none but You can be of help. The earth and all the

heavens are, like me, Your creations;
how then could I ask them to save me,
when salvation by any creature is a
vain hope! A slave can find no refuge
but in his master. What more can I
hope to know, knowing that You
created me for my good? Your acts of
love are beyond number, but my sins
outnumber the sand of the sea-shore.
How shall I lift up my eyes to You?
They, too, are sinful. What more can
my lips say? They, too, have done
wrong. My wanton heart has done to
me what no enemy could have done.
Gusts of anger sieze me as I think of it
– woe is me, I have disobeyed. My evil
passions led me astray; I had no wish
to anger You. My wrongs have wronged
no one but me, and none but You will
keep faith with me. Show me the right
path for it is You who have taught me
all I know. I have heard myself speak
the words of my heart; may You hear
them in heaven!

כֻּלָּם נִבְרָאִים כָּמוֹנִי;

מֵהֶם אֵיךְ אֶדְרֹשׁ תְּשׁוּעָה,

וּתְשׁוּעַת כָּל יָצוּר כָּזָב!

מָנוֹס אֵין לְעֶבֶד

בִּלְתִּי לַאֲשֶׁר קָנָהוּ.

מַה אֲחַשְׁבָה לָדַעַת?

וְיָדַעְתִּי כִּי לְהֵיטִיב לִי בְּרָאתַנִי.

מִסְפָּר עָצְמוּ חֲסָדֶיךָ,

וּמֵחוֹל הַיָּם חַטָּאתִי.

עַיִן אֵיךְ אֶשָּׂא אֵלֶיךָ?

וְהִיא גַם הִיא חָטָאָה.

עוֹד מַה יַּעֲנוּ שְׂפָתַי?

גַּם הֵמָּה הִרְשִׁיעוּ.

זְדוֹן לִבִּי עָשָׂה לְנַפְשִׁי

אֲשֶׁר אוֹיֵב לֹא יוּכַל עֲשׂוֹהוּ;

זַלְעָפָה אֲחָזַתְנִי מִמֶּנּוּ –

אוֹי לִי כִּי מָרִיתִי!

רֹעַ יִצְרִי הִתְעַנִי,

כִּי לֹא הָיָה רְצוֹנִי לְהַכְעִיסֶךָ.

רָעוֹתַי לִי לְבַדִּי הֵרֵעוּ,

וְאַתָּה לְבַדְּךָ תַּעֲשֶׂה חֶסֶד.

הוֹדִיעֵנִי דֶּרֶךְ יוֹעִילֵנִי,

כִּי כָל יָדַעְתִּי – אַתָּה הוֹדַעְתָּנִי.

הִשְׁמַעְתִּי דִבְרֵי לִבִּי לְאָזְנִי –

וְאַתָּה תִּשְׁמַע הַשָּׁמַיִם!

יִצְחָק אִבְּן־עֶזְרָא   *Isaac ibn Ezra*

בְּכִי תִשָּׂאוּ   THE DIRTY OLD MAN

בְּכִי תִשָּׂאוּ עֲלֵי כָּל הַר,
וְאֶשָּׂא עַל נְאוֹת מִדְבָּר,
וּמִסְפֵּד מַר אֲנִי אַעַשׂ,
כְּמוֹ תַנִּים, בְּכָל מַעְבָּר.
אֲדַבְּרָה בְּצַר רוּחַ
וְרַב יָגוֹן וְלֵב נִשְׁבָּר
עֲלֵי רֵעַ אֲשֶׁר נִתְרַע
לְכָל אִישׁ רָע וְנִתְחַבָּר [...]
אֲנִי הוֹלֵךְ, וְהֵן שִׁפְחָה
פְּגָשַׁתְנִי לְאִישׁ גּוּבָר.
קְרָאַתְנִי וְהִיא תִשְׂחָק:
'הֲשָׁמַעְתָּ אֲשֶׁר דִּבַּר
זְקַנְכֶם זֶה, אֲשֶׁר שָׁכַן
עֲלִיַּת קִיר כְּמוֹ מִכְבָּר,
אֲשֶׁר פָּנָיו וְצוּרָתוֹ
פְּנֵי שָׁחֹר כְּפַת קִבָּר?
רְאִינוּהוּ עֲלֵי נַעֲרוֹ,
וְשִׂפְתוֹתָיו בְּפִיו יִצְבָּר,
וְהוּא יִדְמֶה – וּפִיו עַל פִּיו –
כְּמוֹ עוֹרֵב, בְּפִיו עַכְבָּר!'

Go and weep upon every mountain,
and I shall wail in the desert pastures
and howl bitterly like a wolf at every
turn of the road. With anguish in my
soul, grief-stricken and broken-hearted,
I shall speak of a friend who made
friends with evil men and kept company
with them. One day, as I was walking,
I met the maid-servant of some
notable. Laughing, she called to me:
'Have you heard the talk about your
old friend, who lives in the latticed
attic and has a face like a loaf of black
bread? We saw him bent over his
boyfriend, gathering the boy's lips in
his mouth; and, lying there, mouth to
mouth, he looked like a crow with a
mouse in its beak!'

יְהוּדָה אִבְּן־עַבָּאס   *Judah Samuel Abbas*

עֵת שַׁעֲרֵי רָצוֹן   AT THE HOUR OF MERCY

עֵת שַׁעֲרֵי רָצוֹן לְהִפָּתֵחַ,
יוֹם אֶהְיֶה כַפִּי לְאֵל שׁוֹטֵחַ,
אֹמַר: 'זְכָר־נָא לִי בְּיוֹם הוֹכֵחַ
עוֹקֵד וְהַנֶּעְקָד וְהַמִּזְבֵּחַ!'

When the gates of mercy are about to
open, on this day, as I spread out my
hands to You, I shall say: 'Oh,
remember in my behalf, on this day
of judgement, the one who bound, the
one who was bound, and the altar!'

בָּאַחֲרִית נִסָּה בְּסוֹף הָעֶשָׂרָה:
'הַבֵּן אֲשֶׁר נוֹלַד לְךָ מִשָּׂרָה,
אִם נַפְשְׁךָ בּוֹ עַד מְאֹד נִקְשָׁרָה,
קוּם, הַעֲלֵהוּ לִי לְעוֹלָה בָרָה
אֶל הַר אֲשֶׁר כָּבוֹד לְךָ זוֹרֵחַ.'

This was the last of Abraham's ten
trials: 'The son that was born to you of
Sarah – though you love him dearly,
now go and offer him to Me as a
perfect sacrifice on the mountain where
you will see My glory shining.'

אָמַר לְשָׂרָה: 'כִּי חֲמוּדֵךְ יִצְחָק
גָּדַל וְלֹא לָמַד עֲבוֹדַת שַׁחַק,
אֵלְכָה וְאוֹרֵהוּ אֲשֶׁר לוֹ אֵל חָק.'
אָמְרָה: 'לְכָה אָדוֹן, אֲבָל אַל תִּרְחַק.'
עָנָה: 'יְהִי לִבֵּךְ בָּאֵל בּוֹטֵחַ.'

Then Abraham said to Sarah: 'Your
beloved Isaac has grown up, but he has
not yet studied the worship of God.
Let me go and teach him what God
has ordained for him.' 'Go, my lord,'
she said, 'but do not go too far.' He
answered: 'Let your heart trust in God.'

שִׁחַר, וְהִשְׁכִּים לַהֲלֹךְ בַּבֹּקֶר,
וּשְׁנֵי נְעָרָיו מִפְּתֵי הַשֶּׁקֶר.
יוֹם הַשְּׁלִישִׁי נָגְעוּ אֶל חֵקֶר,
וַיַּרְא דְּמוּת כָּבוֹד וְהוֹד וַיֶּקֶר.
עָמַד וְהִתְבּוֹנֵן לְהִמָּשֵׁחַ.

So he rose at dawn to start on his
journey, and with him two of his
heathen servants. On the third day they
reached their destination, and he saw a
shape of glory and resplendent majesty.
There he paused to consider how he
should perform his priestly office.

יָדַע נְעָרָיו כִּי קָרְעָם לֵאמֹר:
'אוֹר הַרְאִיתֶם צָץ בְּרֹאשׁ הַר הַמּוֹר?'
וַיֹּאמְרוּ: 'לֹא נֶחֱזֶה רַק מַהְמוֹר.'

He told his servants that they would
have to stay behind: 'Do you see a light
flowering on top of Mount Moriah?'
They said: 'We can see nothing but
valleys.' To which he replied: 'Then

עֲנֵה : 'שְׁבוּ פֹה, עַם מְשׁוּלִים לַחֲמוֹר,
וַאֲנִי וְהַנַּעַר לְהִשְׁתַּחֲוֹת.'

stay here – since you are [as dull-eyed]
as donkeys – while the boy and I go
there to worship.'

הָלְכוּ שְׁנֵיהֶם לַעֲסֹק בִּמְלָאכָה.
וַיַּעֲנֶה יִצְחָק לְאָבִיו כָּכָה :
'אָבִי, הֲלֹא אֵשׁ וַעֲצֵי מַעֲרָכָה.
אַיֵּה, אֲדוֹנִי, שֶׂה אֲשֶׁר בַּהֲלָכָה ?
הַאַתְּ בְּיוֹם זֶה דָּתְךָ שׁוֹכֵחַ ?

Then the two of them went to perform
their task. And this is what Isaac said
to his father: 'Father, we have the fire
and the wood, but where, my lord, is
the lamb prescribed for the sacrifice?
Could you, on such a day, forget the
Law?'

וַיַּעֲנֶה אָבִיו : 'בְּאֵל חַי מַחְסֶה,
כִּי הוּא אֲשֶׁר יִרְאֶה לְעוֹלָה הַשֶּׂה.
דַּע, כִּי אֲשֶׁר יַחְפֹּץ אֱלֹהִים – יַעֲשֶׂה.
נִבְנֶה, בְּנִי, הַיּוֹם לְפָנָיו כִּסֵּא,
אָז יַאֲמִיר זֶבַח וְהַזּוֹבֵחַ.

His father replied: 'The living God is
our refuge. It is He who will provide
the lamb for a sacrifice. Know that He
does what He pleases. Now, my son,
let us build an altar[1] before Him. Then
He will exalt the sacrifice and the one
who sacrifices.'

דָּפְקוּ בְּשַׁעֲרֵי רַחֲמִים לִפְתֹּחַ,
הַבֵּן לְהִזָּבַח וְאָב לִזְבֹּחַ,
קֹוִים לְאֵל וּבְרַחֲמָיו לִבְטֹחַ.
קֹוֵי יְיָ יַחֲלִיפוּ כֹחַ.
דָּרְשׁוּ בְּנַחֲלַת אֵל לְהִסְפַּפֵּחַ.

And so the son, ready to be sacrificed,
and the father, ready to sacrifice – both
hoping for the Lord and trusting in His
mercy – knocked at the Gates of Mercy,
to open the Gates. For those who look
to the Lord will renew their strength.
Thus they sought to win their share in
the Lord's inheritance.

הֵכִין עֲצֵי עוֹלָה בְּאֹן נַחֲיִל,
וַיַּעֲקֹד יִצְחָק כְּעָקְדוּ אַיִל,
וַהֲמוֹן דְּמָעָיו נוֹזְלִים בַּחֲיִל.
וַיְהִי מְאוֹר יוֹמָם כְּעֶצֶם לַיְל –
עַיִן בְּמַר בּוֹכָה וְלֵב שָׂמֵחַ.

With unflagging strength, Abraham
arranged the wood upon the altar, and
bound Isaac as one binds a ram. The
tears ran down his cheeks. The light of
day was like the very dark of night to
them – their eyes wept bitterly, but
their hearts rejoiced.

שׁוּרוּ לְאִמִּי כִּי שְׂשׂוֹנָהּ פָּנָה.
הַבֵּן אֲשֶׁר יָלְדָה לְתִשְׁעִים שָׁנָה
הָיָה לְאֵשׁ וּלְמַאֲכֶלֶת מָנָה.

'See how my mother's joy is gone; the
son she bore when she was ninety years
old has fallen prey to the slaughtering
knife and the fire. Where shall I find

1. Lit. 'chair' or 'throne'.

אָנָה אֲבַקֵּשׁ לָהּ מְנַחֵם, אָנָה?
צַר לִי לְאֵם תִּבְכֶּה וְתִתְיַפַּח!

someone to bring her comfort? I am
sorry for the mother who must weep
and sob.

מְמַאֲכֶלֶת יֶהֱמֶה מִדְבָּרִי.
נָא חַדְּדָהּ, אָבִי, וְאֶת מַאֲסָרִי
חַזֵּק, בְּעֵת יֵקַד יִקֹּד בִּבְשָׂרִי.
קַח עִמְּךָ הַנִּשְׁאָר מֵאֶפְרִי,
וֶאֱמֹר לְשָׂרָה: "זֶה לְיִצְחָק רֵיחַ".'

'The knife makes me cry out. Oh,
father, sharpen it, and bind me securely
as the fire consumes my flesh. Then
gather the remains of my ashes and
say to Sarah: "This is the sweet savour
of Isaac"!'

וַיֶּהֱמוּ כָּל מַלְאֲכֵי מֶרְכָּבָה,
אוֹפָן וְשָׂרָף שׁוֹאֲלִים בִּנְדָבָה,
וּמַחֲנָנִים לָאֵל בְּעַד שַׂר צָבָא:
'אָנָּא, תְּנָה פִדְיוֹם וְכֹפֶר הָבָה,
אַל נָא יְהִי עוֹלָם בְּלֹא יָרֵחַ.'

All the angels of the Chariot cried out:
Ofanim and Seraphim begged for
charity and implored God to spare this
prince: 'Oh, redeem him, appoint a
ransom for him! Do not let the world
be left without its moon!'

אָמַר לְאַבְרָהָם אֲדוֹן שָׁמַיִם:
'אַל תִּשְׁלְחָה יָד אֶל שְׁלִישׁ אוּרַיִם!
שׁוּבוּ לְשָׁלוֹם, מַלְאֲכֵי מַחֲנַיִם.
יוֹם זֶה זְכוּת לִבְנֵי יְרוּשָׁלַיִם —
בּוֹ חֵטְא בְּנֵי יַעֲקֹב אֲנִי סוֹלֵחַ.'

Then the Lord of Heaven spoke to
Abraham: 'Do not raise your hand
against this luminary.[1] And you, angels,
go in peace. The merit of this day will
protect the children of Jerusalem; for
its sake, I shall pardon the sins of
Jacob's sons.'

לִבְרִיתְךָ, שׁוֹכֵן זְבוּלִים שִׁבְעָה,
זָכְרָה לְעֵדָה סֹעֲרָה וּנְגוּעָה,
וּשְׁמַע תְּקִיעָה תּוֹקְעָה וּתְרוּעָה,
וֶאֱמֹר לְצִיּוֹן: 'בָּא זְמַן הַיְשׁוּעָה,
יִנּוֹן וְאֵלִיָּה אֲנִי שׁוֹלֵחַ!'

Oh, dweller of the seven heavens,
remember Your covenant with this
storm-tossed and tormented people.
Hear the sound of the ram's horn, and
proclaim to Zion: 'The time of salvation has come. I shall send you Yinon
(the Messiah) and the prophet Elijah!'

---

1. Lit. 'one of the three lights', i.e. 'one of the three Patriarchs'.

מֹשֶׁה דַרְעִי   *Moses Dar'i*

לַחֲבַצֶּלֶת שָׁרוֹן   THE SPY'S PROMISE

לַחֲבַצֶּלֶת שָׁרוֹן נָמַתִּי:

'סִגְרִי עֵינֵךְ גַּם הָעֲצִימִי.

נִכְלַמְתִּי לִנְשֹׁק דּוֹד, כִּי עֵי־

נֵךְ מִמֶּנִּי לֹא תַעֲלִימִי.

דּוֹד יָשַׁב רֶגַע נֶגְדִּי וַ־

יִּישָׁן, אַךְ אַתְּ לֹא תָנוּמִי!'

וַתַּעֲנֵנִי: 'שִׁמְעָה, חוֹשֵׁק,

נֹעַם מִלִּים מִטּוּב טַעֲמִי –

חֲבוֹק וּנְשֹׁק דּוֹד־חֶפְצֵךְ,

כִּי סוֹד חוֹשְׁקִים צָפוּן עִמִּי.' [...]

I said to the spying lady:[1] 'Can't you
shut your eyes? I am ashamed to kiss
my beloved because you never take
your eyes off me! My beloved and I
sat face to face, and in an instant he was
asleep; but you never slumber!' To
which she replied: 'Listen, love, to the
gracious words of my wisdom: you
may hug and kiss the youth you long
for, for lovers' secrets are safe with me!'

עֲלוּמֵי־שֵׁם   *Anonymous*

וּפֶה עָגֹל כְּטַבַּעַת   THE IDEAL WOMAN

[...] וּפֶה עָגֹל כְּטַבַּעַת וְחוֹתָם,

כְּאִלּוּ הִיא בְּיַד מֶלֶךְ לְחָתְמָהּ.

וְשִׁנַּיִם כְּאִלּוּ הֵם בְּדֹלַח,

וְכַבָּרָד בְּרִדְתּוֹ עַל אֲדָמָה.

וְגַם צַוָּאר כְּצַוְּאר הַצְּבִי, עֵת

יְהִי צָמֵא וְעֵינָיו אֶל מְרוֹמָא.

וְשָׁדַיִם כְּתַפּוּחֵי כְפָרִים,

עֲלֵי רֹאשָׁם נְקֻדַּת מֹר חֲתוּמָה.

A mouth as round as a signet-ring, fit
for a royal hand to seal with; teeth that
are like crystals, or like pellets of hail as
they fall to earth; also, a neck like the
neck of a gazelle when it thirsts and
lifts up its eyes to heaven; breasts like
apples of henna,[2] studded at their tips
with a bit of myrrh; a belly like white

1. Lit. 'to the rose of Sharon'.
2. Presumably, round boxes for storing henna.

וְגַם בֶּטֶן כְּמוֹ עֲשָׂה לְבָנָה,
וְגַם יַדְמֶה כְּחָטִים בַּעֲרֵמָה.
וְגַם שָׁרְרָה בְתוֹךְ בִּטְנָה כְּמוֹ בוֹר,
כְּאִלּוּ הִיא בְאֵר אֵין בָּהּ מְאוּמָה.
וּמָתְנַיִם מְאֹד דַּקִּים כְּמָתְנֵי
דְּבוֹרָה, עֵת תְּהִי עָפָה בְּכַרְמָהּ.
וְשׁוֹקַיִם כְּעַמּוּדִים, עֲלֵיהֶם
יְרֵכַים, וְגַם אַלְיָה עֲצוּמָה.
וְיָדַיִם וְרַגְלַיִם קְטַנִּים
וְגַם לַחִים, כְּמוֹ רַגְלֵי עֲלִימָה.
וּמֵרֹאשָׁהּ עֲדֵי רַגְלָהּ שְׁלֵמָה
כְּמוֹ יָפְיָהּ, וּמוּם אֵין בָּהּ, תְּמִימָה.
וְאִשָּׁה בַּעֲלַת חַיִל וְשֵׂכֶל,
כְּמוֹתָהּ אֵין אֱנוֹשׁ מוֹצֵא בְּעוֹלָמָהּ.
וְעֵת עוֹנָה כְּמוֹ [ ]וֹמָה [ ]
בְּמִשְׁכָּבָהּ, וְתוֹךְ בֵּיתָהּ חֲכָמָה.
וְלֹא נִמְצָא כְּמוֹ יָפְיָהּ וְשִׂכְלָהּ,
כְּאִלּוּ הִיא בְעוֹלָמָהּ יְתוֹמָה.
וּמִי יִשְׁגֶּה בְּאַהֲבַת זֹאת – הֲיִמְצָא
בְּעַפְעַפָּיו, בְּעֵת יִשְׁכַּב, תְּנוּמָה? [...]

dough, or like a heap of wheat; a navel in her belly like a cistern, as though she were an empty well; very narrow hips, like the hips of a bee as it flits through the vineyard; legs like pillars, on which the thighs can rest, as well as ample buttocks; hands and feet that are both small and fresh, the feet like those of a young girl; wholly beautiful from head to foot, flawless, perfect; a woman resourceful and intelligent, whose equal cannot be found in the whole world; who during intercourse . . .[1] on her bed; wise in the ways of the household; whose beauty and good sense are unrivalled; unique in the world – whoever falls in love with such a woman, how can he ever fall asleep at night?

עֹפֶר אֲשֶׁר לִבִּי — THE ENTHRALLED LOVER

עֹפֶר אֲשֶׁר לִבִּי לְעֶבֶד לוֹ
נִרְצַע, וְכֵן נַפְשִׁי כְּמוֹ שִׁפְחָה –
אַבִּיט חֲנִית עֵינָיו – וְלִי אֵימָה,
אֶרְאֶה יְפִי לֶחְיוֹ – וְלִי בִטְחָה.
שָׂם הַזְּמָן לִבִּי בְּבֵית אֵבֶל
תָּמִיד, אֲבָל עֵינִי בְּבֵית שִׂמְחָה.

This gazelle – to whom my heart surrendered itself like a slave, and my soul like a handmaid – when I look at the spears of his eyes, I am all fear; when I see the beauty of his cheeks, I am all faith. Time has put my heart in a house of mourning forever, but my eyes are in a house of joy.

---

1. The manuscript is defective at this point.

תְּנָה כּוֹסִי TO THE CUP-BEARER

תְּנָה כּוֹסִי בְּמוֹ יָדִי,
יְדִידִי, אַל תְּהִי פוֹתֶה —
הֲלֹא תִרְאָה פְּנוֹת חֹשֶׁךְ
וְהָלֹכוּ, וְאוֹר יֵאתֶה,
וְהַחַמָּה כְּמוֹ הַכּוֹס
בְּיַד יָדִיד וְהוּא חוֹתֶה.
וְהַמִּזְרָח כְּמוֹ מַשְׁקֶה,
וְהַמַּעֲרָב כְּמוֹ שׁוֹתֶה.

Put my cup in my hand, friend; do not
be foolish. Can't you see that the
darkness is leaving, and the light is
coming? The sun is like a cup in the
hand of a friend who stirs its flame –
as though the East were pouring out the
drink, and the West were drinking.

לְאַט מִשְׁכָה TO THE CAMEL DRIVER

לְאַט מִשְׁכָה גְּמַלֶּיךָ, עֲרָבִי —
הֲלֹא עִמָּךְ כְּבָר נִמְשַׁךְ לְבָבִי
לְפֵרוּד רַב אֲשֶׁר אֶחְיֶה בְּצִלּוֹ,
גְּבִיר קָדוֹשׁ כְּמַלְאַךְ־אֵל וְנָבִיא.
הֲכִי לוֹ נִכְסְפָה נַפְשִׁי וְכָלְתָה,
וְסָר אוֹנִי וְתָעָה מַחְשָׁבִי
לְעֵת אֶזְכֹּר דְּבָרָיו הָעֲרֵבִים,
אֲשֶׁר לִי נֶחְמְדוּ מִכָּל זְהָבִי. [...]

Lead your camels slowly, Arab; you
are leading my heart away with you.
For I am being parted from the teacher
who is the refuge of my life, from the
master who is as holy as an angel of
God or a prophet. Oh, I already pine,
I faint with longing for him, my
strength leaves me, my mind reels,
when I recall his sweet words, dearer
to me than all my gold.

צְבִי – יֵין הָרֶקַח THE FIFTEEN-YEAR-OLD BOY

צְבִי – יֵין הָרֶקַח בְּעֵינָיו יַשְׁקֵנִי, לוּ בְּפִיו יִשָּׁקֵנִי!

The fawn gives me spiced wine to
drink with his eyes; if only he would
kiss me with his mouth!

בְּנַפְשִׁי! צְבִי עִנָּה לְבָבִי וְחִלַּנִי
בְּרַקָּה כְּשׁוֹשַׁנָּה וְשָׂפָה כְּחוּט שָׁנִי.
בְּפִתְחוֹ בַנְגִינָה בְּשִׁיר עַל הַשְּׁמִינִי,
בְּשִׁירָתוֹ לְקַח אֲשֶׁר יַשְׁמִיעֵנִי, לוּ בְחַסְדּוֹ יְחַיֵּנִי!

Upon my life! This fawn has tormented
my heart and made me ill, with his
lily cheeks and lips like scarlet thread.
When he sings to the accompaniment
of his lyre, there are words of wisdom
for me in his song. If only he would
give me life by giving me his favours!

לְבָבִי כְּיָם יֶהֱמֶה, יְדִידַי, לְפֵרוּדוֹ
וְלַתַּנִּים אֲדַמֶּה בְּבֶכִי לְיוֹם נֻדּוֹ.
וְעַל מָה אֱנוֹשׁ, עַל מָה, יְחִי עוֹד, וְאֵין דּוֹדוֹ?
וּמִיּוֹם כִּי לֻקַּח, בְּפֵרוּד יְמִיתֵנִי, בַּגֶּדוֹד יַצְמִיתֵנִי.

Friends, my heart moans like the sea
because of his absence. I wail like a
jackal over his departure. Why should
a man go on living when his beloved is
gone? Ever since he was taken away,
his absence is my death, his going my
destruction.

עֲדֵי מָתַי אוֹחִיל כְּעוֹמֵד עֲלֵי מִצְפֶּה?
וְאָנֹכִי אָחִיל וְלֹא אֶמְצָא מַרְפֶּה.
וּמִי יִתֵּן אַתְחִיל וְאָשִׂים פֶּה אֶל פֶּה. —
וּבִרְצוֹנוֹ אֶרְקַח עֲסִיסִי וְשׁוֹשַׁנִּי, פַּעֲמוֹנִי וְרִמּוֹנִי.

How much longer must I wait, like a
look-out on a watch-tower? I am torn
with anguish, I can find no relief. If
only he would let me put my mouth to
his and blend our nectar and our lips,
O my bell, my pomegranate!

מְטִיבִים וּמְלִיצִים עֲלֵי עֹפֶר יָדִינוּ,
אֲשֶׁר עֵינָיו חִצִּים לְהָרְגִי הֱכִינוּ —
וּבִלְחָיָיו צִצִּים נְעִימִים, לֹא יִשְׁנוּ,
וְכָל־פַּעַם אֶפְקַח בְּפָנָיו אִישׁוֹנִי, אוֹר לְחָיָיו יְכַסֵּנִי

My eloquent friends condemn this
gazelle who armed his eyes with arrows
to kill me. But his cheeks are full of
sweet blossoms that never wilt. Every
time I open my eyes to look into his
face, the light of his cheeks engulfs me.

מְבֹרָךְ צְבִי, אַעֲלִים שְׁמוֹ מִפְּנֵי מוֹנִים.
אֲבָל הוּא אֲשֶׁר הַכְּלִים מְאוֹרִים בָּמְעוֹנִים —
צְבִי חֵן אֲשֶׁר הַשְׁלִים חֲמֵשׁ עֶשְׂרֵה שָׁנִים:
נהייד במא ילקח כגצן מן אלבאני
עאד אליי אצלאן.

Blessed be this fawn, whose name I
conceal from my spying rivals, though
he is the one who puts the lights of
heaven to shame; this graceful fawn,
now in his fifteenth year. Oh, we shall
set in motion that which impregnates.
He, who is like a willow branch, has
come back to me entirely.[1]

---

1. The last line is in Arabic. The meaning is unclear.

אָמְרוּ לְרֹאשׁ פֶּתֶן   SONG OF HOPE

אָמְרוּ לְרֹאשׁ פֶּתֶן : 'הָבָה צֳרִי' —
וּלְשׁוֹן דְּוֵה לֵבָב : 'שִׁיר דַּבְּרִי' !

You might as well say to the poisonous
asp: 'Give me balm,' as say to the man
who is sick at heart: 'Sing!'

שׁוֹכֵב בְּלֵב יַמִּים, אֵלֵךְ בְּלִי
חוֹבֵל, וְרֹאשׁ חֶבֶל הוּא אָהֳלִי.
עֵינַי לְמֵרָחוֹק אֶל פּוֹעֲלִי :
לֹא יָם סְעָרָה, אַךְ מַשְׂאַת מְרִי,
אַף עָב — עֲווֹנִי יַטְרִיחַ בְּרִי.

I am tossing out at sea, sailing without
a captain; the top of the rigging is my
tent; my eyes scan the distance for my
Maker. It is not the stormy sea [that I
fear], but my sinful defiance. It is my
crimes that make the clouds so heavy.

שֵׁבֶט לְגַו נוֹאָל — נֹפֶת וּמָן,
מַכַּת אֲהָבִים — פֶּצַע נֶאֱמָן.
לֹא דִכְּאָה נֶפֶשׁ יַד רַחֲמָן.
מִקְטַר קְטֹרֶת הוּא יַעְצֹר חֲרִי,
מוּסַר שְׁלוֹמִים הוּא יַעֲשֶׂה פְּרִי.

A rod to a fool's back is like honey and
manna. Blows given out of love leave
beneficial wounds. The hand of the
Compassionate One never crushes the
soul. The offering of prayer can placate
His wrath. His chastisement, meant to
bring us peace, bears fruit.

תִּקְוָה לְמַפֶּלֶת נוֹפֵל בְּבוֹר
עֵת בַּחֲמַת רוּחוֹ יִשְׁאַף דְּרוֹר,
וּבְמַאֲסַר חָשְׁכּוֹ יוֹחִיל מָאוֹר.
קַוֵּה לְשָׁלוֹם — אִם יִשְׁאַג אֲרִי,
קַוֵּה בְּיוֹם סַגְרִיר אוֹר שַׁחֲרִי.

There is hope for the man who has
fallen into a pit if, even in his anguish,
he longs for freedom; if, in his dark
prison, he waits for light. Though the
lion roar, hope for peace; though the
day be bleak, look for the glow of dawn.

שִׁלְטִי וּמָגִנִּי, שַׁלִּיט, בָּךְ.
אֵיךְ אַחֲרַי יִדְלַק צוּר חַרְבְּךָ,
וַאֲנִי בְּךָ צוֹפֶה וּלְטוּבְךָ ?
הִתְעוֹרְרִי, נַפְשִׁי, הִטָּהֲרִי,
וּלְטוּב אֲדוֹנָיִךְ אָז תִּנְהֲרִי.

O King, You are my shield and my
buckler. Why should Your sharp sword
pursue me, when it is You I am looking
to, and Your goodness? Arise, my soul,
cleanse yourself. Then, in the bounty
of the Lord, you will shine with joy.

יְקוֹדֵי אֵשׁ   THE HOSTS OF HEAVEN

יְקוֹדֵי אֵשׁ, כְּיִדּוֹדֵי אֵשׁ, יְצוּרֵי צוּר כְּרוּבִים דָּר.
עֵינֵיהֶם וּמַרְאֵיהֶם כְּעֵין סֹחֶרֶת וּכְעֵין דָּר.
קוֹל יְנוֹפְפוּן, וְיִתְעוֹפְפוּן עָשׂוֹת חֵפֶץ אֵל נֶאְדָּר.
בְּטוּב שִׁירָה, בְּרָן זִמְרָה יְשׁוֹרְרוּן – אִישׁ בְּלִי נֶעְדָּר.
קוֹל יְיָ בַּכֹּחַ, קוֹל יְיָ בֶּהָדָר.

Creatures of flame and sparks, made by
the Rock whose throne is on the
cherubim: They are the colour of
mother-of-pearl and turquoise. They
raise their voices, darting to and fro to
do the bidding of the majestic Lord.
Not one is missing as they sing their
choice songs and celebrate with joy:
*The voice of the Lord is power; the voice
of the Lord is majesty.*

עָצְמָתָם וְקוֹמָתָם כְּקוֹמַת תָּמָר.
לֵיל וָיוֹם, לְמוּל אָיֹם, מְטִיבִים שֶׁבַח וּזְמָר.
הֲמֻלּוֹת, מְחִילּוֹת, וּמַחֲנוֹת כְּיֶלֶק סָמָר.
מַצָּבָם וּמוֹשָׁבָם – מִשְׁמָר לְעֻמַּת מִשְׁמָר,
כִּי קוֹנָם הִתְקִינָם וּמַעַרְכוֹתָם סָדַר.
קוֹל יְיָ בַּכֹּחַ, קוֹל יְיָ בֶּהָדָר.

They are stately and strong as palm
trees; night and day, before the Dread
One, they sing their songs of praise.
There are hosts of them, armies and
camps like a dark swarm of locusts.
They stand and they sit, guard
corresponding to guard, for thus their
Maker arranged them and fixed their
formations. *The voice of the Lord is
power; the voice of the Lord is majesty.*

קוֹל יְרִימוּן וְיַעֲצִימוּן לְאֵל גַּבִּיר מִמְּקֹמוֹ.
וְעַל מְעוֹנוֹ וְחֶבְיוֹנוֹ זֶה יִשְׁאַל כְּנֶאֱמוֹ.
וְהֵם עוֹמְדִים וַחֲרֵדִים מִפַּחְדוֹ וּמֵאֵימוֹ.
יַעֲרִיצוּן וְיַקְדִּישׁוּן כְּבוֹד יְיָ מִמְּקֹמוֹ.
כִּי סָכוּ, מִכֹּה וּמִכֹּה, בְּסוּפָה וָסַעַר לְגָדָר.
קוֹל יְיָ בַּכֹּחַ, קוֹל יְיָ בֶּהָדָר.

They cry aloud, they roar to the Mighty
Lord in His heavens. When He speaks,
they ask each other: where is His home,
His hiding-place? Trembling, overcome by fear and awe, they revere and
sanctify the Glory of the Lord in His
abode. He is shielded on either side,
and set apart, by whirlwind and storm.
*The voice of the Lord is power; the voice
of the Lord is majesty.*

וְנֶשֶׁר וְיִצִּיר וְשׁוֹר וּכְפִיר מוּכָנִים בְּמֶרְכַּבְתּוֹ.
וְתַחֲנוֹתָם וּמַחֲנוֹתָם סְבִיבוֹת תְּכוּנוֹת שִׁבְתּוֹ.
לִפְנֵיהֶם – אוֹפַנִּים, סוֹבְלֵי כֵּס תִּפְאַרְתּוֹ
לְשָׁרֵת פְּנֵי הַמַּחֲנֶה וְהַסֶּדֶר הַנֻּסְדָּר.
קוֹל יְיָ בַּכֹּחַ, קוֹל יְיָ בֶּהָדָר.

[And the faces of] an eagle and a man,
an ox and a lion are set in His Chariot-
Throne, encamped around His
dwelling-place. Next to them are the
Ofanim, who carry His Throne of
Glory, and minister to the hosts, in the
order He prescribed. *The voice of the
Lord is power; the voice of the Lord is
majesty.*

בִּימִינוּ, עַל שְׁכְנוֹ, שָׁת מַחֲנֵה מִיכָאֵל.
וְלִשְׂמֹאלוֹ וּמִמּוּלוֹ – גַּבְרִיאֵל וְאוּרִיאֵל.
וּמֵאַחֲרָיו, בְּמִשְׁמָרָיו, הֵכִין מַחֲנֵה רְפָאֵל.
יַקְדִּישׁוּן וִישַׁלְּשׁוּן קָדְשָׁה בְּעִתּוֹת הָאֵל.
לְדָר חֲבִיוֹן, לְאֵל עֶלְיוֹן, שְׁמוֹ מְרוֹמָם וּמְהֻדָּר.
קוֹל יְיָ בַּכֹּחַ, קוֹל יְיָ בֶּהָדָר.

To the right of His throne, He put the
camp of Michael; to the left and in
front – the camps of Gabriel and Uriel;
and behind Him He arrayed the camp
of Raphael. They acclaim Him 'holy,
holy, holy' at the hours He ordained,
singing to the One who dwells in secret,
to the God supreme, whose name is
exalted and glorious. *The voice of the
Lord is power; the voice of the Lord is
majesty.*

אֱנוֹשׁ רוֹצֶה

THE USES OF REASON

[...] אֱנוֹשׁ רוֹצֶה לְהַכְרִיחַ טִבְעָיו,
לְהַכִּיר בַּאֲשֶׁר אֵין בּוֹ וְיוֹתֵר –
פְּרָעֵהוּ, וְאַל נָא מַעֲבָר־בּוֹ,
שְׁטֵה מֶנְהוּ וּמֵעָלָיו תְּנַתֵּר:
כִּיוֹצֵא מִמְסִלָּה הַיְשָׁרָה
וְתַחַת דֶּרֶךְ בְּמַלָמִישׁ יַחְתֵּר.

Shun the man who tries to force his
nature, to see in it more than is there.
Do not go near him, turn aside, skip
out of his way. For he is like one who
leaves a highway to burrow through
granite cliffs.

הֱיֵה מַשְׂכִּיל זְמָן הַבָּא, לְהַכִּיר
בְּשֶׁעָבַר, וּבִין אֶת אַחֲרִיתוֹ.
וְתַשִּׂיג אֶת אֲשֶׁר לֹא בָא לְיָדְךָ
בְּמַה שֶּׁבָּא לְיָדְךָ וַעֲבַרְתּוֹ:
כְּאִישׁ צָד צִפֳּרִים עָפוֹת בְּצִפּוֹר
אֲשֶׁר צָד מִתְּמוֹל שִׁלְשׁוֹם בְּרִשְׁתּוֹ.

Learn the ways of time to come. Know
the past, and you will understand the
end. Thus you will grasp what has not
yet come your way by what you have
already grasped, like a man who lures
flying birds with the bird that he
caught in his net the day before.

וְהַכֵּר בַּדְּבָרִים עַד אֲשֶׁר לֹא
עֲשִׂיתָם, אִם בְּמַעֲשׂ אוֹ בְמִבְטָא.
וּמַה בֶּצַע בְּהַכֵּר אַחֲרֵי כִי
כְּבָר נַעֲשָׂה, וּמַה תּוֹעִיל חֲרָטָה?
הֲתָשׁוּב עוֹד וְתָשׁוּר לַחֲזוֹת עַיִן
אֱנוֹשׁ אַחַר תְּנֻקַּר בַּעֲלָטָה?

Comprehend your actions before you
commit them, whether in deed or in
word. What good is comprehension
after the fact? What use is regret? Can
a man's eye, after it has been gouged
out, ever see again in that darkness?

אֲשֶׁר יִרְאֶה וְיַכִּיר בָּאֲחֵרִים,
וְאִם נִמְצָא פְּתִיל שֵׂעָר בְּעֵינָם,
וְלֹא יַכִּיר בְּעַצְמוֹ אֶת אֲשֶׁר בּוֹ,
עֲלֵי מַה נִּפְקְחוּ עֵינָיו ? וְאֵינָם !
הֲלֹא טוֹב עָצְמוּ עֵינָיו, וְיֵקַל
בְּעֹל זָרִים, אֲשֶׁר נוֹשֵׂא לְחִנָּם.

The man who can discern a mere mote
in the eyes of others, but cannot discern
what is in himself – why were his eyes
ever opened? He has no eyes. It would
be better for his eyes to be shut; then
he would no longer have to bear the
yoke of strangers' faults, a yoke he
bears in vain.

כִּי הִנֵּה כַּחֹמֶר

THE COVENANT

כִּי הִנֵּה כַּחֹמֶר בְּיַד הַיּוֹצֵר,
בִּרְצוֹתוֹ מַרְחִיב וּבִרְצוֹתוֹ מְקַצֵּר,
כֵּן אֲנַחְנוּ בְיָדְךָ, חֶסֶד נוֹצֵר.
לַבְּרִית הַבֵּט וְאַל תֵּפֶן לַיֵּצֶר.

Like clay in the hands of a potter, who
expands or contracts it, as he wishes, so
are we in Your hands, God of constant
love. Oh, look to the covenant,[1] do not
heed the Accuser.

כִּי הִנֵּה כָאֶבֶן בְּיַד הַמְסַתֵּת,
בִּרְצוֹתוֹ בּוֹדֵל וּבִרְצוֹתוֹ מְכַתֵּת,
כֵּן אֲנַחְנוּ בְיָדְךָ, מְחַיֶּה וּמְמוֹתֵת.
לַבְּרִית הַבֵּט וְאַל תֵּפֶן לַיֵּצֶר.

Like a stone in the hands of a mason,
who splits it in two or shatters it, as he
wishes, so are we in Your hands, God
of life and death. Oh, look to the
covenant, do not heed the Accuser.

כִּי הִנֵּה כַּגַּרְזֶן בְּיַד הֶחָרָשׁ,
בִּרְצוֹתוֹ דִּבֵּק לָאוּר וּבִרְצוֹתוֹ פֵּרַשׁ,
כֵּן אֲנַחְנוּ בְיָדְךָ, תּוֹמֵךְ עָנִי וָרָשׁ.
לַבְּרִית הַבֵּט וְאַל תֵּפֶן לַיֵּצֶר.

Like an axe in the hands of a blacksmith, who forges it or cools it, as he
wishes, so are we in Your hands,
champion of the poor and suffering.
Oh, look to the covenant, do not heed
the Accuser.

כִּי הִנֵּה כַּהֶגֶה בְּיַד הַמַּלָּח,
בִּרְצוֹתוֹ אוֹחֵז וּבִרְצוֹתוֹ שִׁלַּח,
כֵּן אֲנַחְנוּ בְיָדְךָ, אֵל טוֹב וְסַלָּח.
לַבְּרִית הַבֵּט וְאַל תֵּפֶן לַיֵּצֶר.

Like a helm in the hands of a sailor,
who holds or releases it, as he wishes,
so are we in Your hands, God of
kindness and mercy. Oh, look to the
covenant, do not heed the Accuser.

---

1. The 'covenant of the thirteen divine attributes' pronounced in Exodus 34.7.

כִּי הִנֵּה כַּזְּכוּכִית בְּיַד הַמְזַגֵּג,
בִּרְצוֹתוֹ חוֹגֵג וּבִרְצוֹתוֹ מְמוֹגֵג,
כֵּן אֲנַחְנוּ בְיָדְךָ, מוֹחֵל זָדוֹן וְשָׁגַג.
לַבְּרִית הַבֵּט וְאַל תֵּפֶן לַיֵּצֶר.

Like glass in the hands of a blower,
who lines it or melts it, as he wishes, so
are we in Your hands, Pardoner of
malice and error. Oh, look to the
covenant, do not heed the Accuser.

כִּי הִנֵּה כַּיְרִיעָה בְּיַד הָרוֹקֵם,
בִּרְצוֹתוֹ מְיַשֵּׁר וּבִרְצוֹתוֹ מְעַקֵּם,
כֵּן אֲנַחְנוּ בְיָדְךָ, אֵל קַנּוֹא וְנוֹקֵם.
לַבְּרִית הַבֵּט וְאַל תֵּפֶן לַיֵּצֶר.

Like cloth in the hands of a draper,
who smooths it or twists it, as he wishes,
so are we in Your hands, God of
jealous vengeance. Oh, look to the
covenant, do not heed the Accuser.

כִּי הִנֵּה כַּכֶּסֶף בְּיַד הַצּוֹרֵף,
בִּרְצוֹתוֹ מְסַגְסֵג וּבִרְצוֹתוֹ מְצָרֵף,
כֵּן אֲנַחְנוּ בְיָדְךָ, מַמְצִיא לְמָזוֹר תֶּרֶף.
לַבְּרִית הַבֵּט וְאַל תֵּפֶן לַיֵּצֶר.

Like silver in the hands of a smith, who
alloys or refines it, as he wishes, so are
we in Your hands, Healer of wounds.
Oh, look to the covenant, do not heed
the Accuser.

קוּמִי, לְכִי　　THE CRUSADERS

'קוּמִי לְכִי,' אוֹמְרִים, 'מֻכַּת לְחָיַיִם,'
עָרֵל וְטָמֵא וְצָר, כָּל אִישׁ שְׂפָתַיִם:
'הִנֵּה הֲלֹא נוֹסְעִים אָנוּ אֶל מְקוֹם
אֶרֶץ צְפִירַת צְבִי, מְאוֹר לְעֵינָיִם —
נַעֲלֶה וְנָבֹז שְׁלַל עָרִים בְּצוּרוֹת, וְשָׁם
נַחְלִק צְבָעִים, לְרֹאשׁ אִישׁ רִקְמָתָיִם.'

'Come with us, you of the smitten
cheeks,' say the uncircumcised and the
unclean, my smooth-tongued enemies.
'We are on our way to the land of the
lovely diadem, the radiant land. We
shall attack and plunder the spoil of the
fortified cities. There we shall take our
shares, to each man two lengths of dyed
cloth!'

חֶרֶב לְשׁוֹנָם וְחֵץ שָׁחוּט בְּלִבִּי, וְאֵשׁ
תּוּקַד בְּקִרְבִּי וְגַם כֹּשֶׁל לְבִרְכַּיִם,
כִּי אֵיךְ אֲנִי אֶעֱלֶה עִם הַפְּסִילִים וְעִם
עִוְרִים וְחֵרְשִׁים וְלֹא עַיִן וְאָזְנָיִם,

Their tongues, sharp as swords and
deadly arrows, pierce my heart. Fire
rages within me, my knees wobble. For
how could I join forces with the idols,
the blind and the deaf, eyeless and
earless; or with a log of wood, named

אוֹ עִם יְבוּל עֵץ, וְשָׁם בֶּן הַזְּנוּנִים, וְעִם
נִסְבָּל בְּכָתֵף – וְלוֹ יָרֵךְ וְשׁוֹקַיִם,
אוֹ עִם רְשָׁעִים אֲשֶׁר גּוֹזְלִים וְחוֹמְסִים וְשׁוֹפְ־
כִים דַּם נְקִיִּים וְאוֹרְבִים בֵּין שְׁפַתַּיִם. [...]

after the child of harlotry, that is
hoisted shoulder-high though it has
legs and thighs; or with the wicked
who rob and injure, who shed the
blood of the innocent and lie in wait
among the sheepfolds?

אֶזְכֹּר וְאֶבְכֶּה עֲלֵי מַסַּע דְּגָלִים אֲשֶׁר
חָנוּ סָבִיב מִשְׁכָּן אֶל אַרְבַּעְתַּיִם:
דֶּגֶל יְהוּדָה, אֲשֶׁר חָנָה בְּרֹאשׁ מַחֲנוֹת,
עָלָיו מְרֻקָּם פְּנֵי אַרְיֵה בְּשַׁחֲלַיִם.
דֶּגֶל רְאוּבֵן, אֲשֶׁר חָנָה לְתֵימָן, וּבוֹ
טוֹבִים לְרֵיחַ, וְהֵם זֵכֶר לְדוּדָאִים.
דֶּגֶל שְׁלִישִׁי לְיָם חָנָה, עָלָיו דְּמוּת
דָּגָה לְדָגִינוּ כְּבִרְכַּת אָב לְאֶפְרָיִם.
דֶּגֶל רְבִיעִי לְדָן, אוֹסֵף לְכָל מַחֲנוֹת,
עָלָיו שְׁפִיפוֹן אֲשֶׁר מַפִּיל לְאָחוֹרַיִם.
מַחֲנֵה שְׁכִינָה בְּתוֹךְ מַחֲנוֹת לְהָאִיר בְּאוֹר
עָנָן לְפָנַי, וְשָׁם כֹּהֲנִים וְהַלְוִיִּים. [...]

I weep as I recall the troops [of Israel]
on the march, and how they once
encamped to the four sides of the
Lord's Tabernacle. The division of
Judah was the first to march, with a
mighty lion embroidered upon its
standard. Second was the division of
Reuben, stationed to the south, with
fragrant mandrakes[1] upon its standard.
The third division was stationed to the
west, upon its standard the image of
fish, so that Ephraim's tribe should
multiply, as Jacob had promised in his
blessing.[2] The division of Dan was the
last to march, upon its standard a viper,
which makes the rider tumble from his
horse. And in the midst of these troops
was the division of the Shekinah, where
the priests and Levites were stationed,
lighting my way with a pillar of cloud.

אֶקְרַע בְּגָדַי בְּעֵת אֶזְכֹּר כֻּתֹּנֶת, מְעִיל,
פַּעֲמוֹן וְרִמּוֹן אֲשֶׁר הָיוּ בַּשּׁוּלַיִם.
אֵשֵׁב בְּמַחְשַׁךְ מְאֹד בְּזָכְרִי מְנוֹרָה וְעַד
פִּרְחָהּ יְרֵכָהּ, וְגַם הַמֶּלְקָחַיִם.
שֻׁלְחָן בְּזָכְרִי – הֲלֹא אֵשֵׁב וְאֶסְעַד בְּתוֹךְ
עָפָר וָאֵפֶר, לְבֵין תַּנּוּר וְכִירַיִם.
אֶשָּׂא בְכִי מַר עֲלֵי מִזְבַּח נְחֹשֶׁת אֲשֶׁר
פִּשְׁעִי מְכַפֵּר בְּדַם אַרְבַּע קְרָנָיִם.

I tear my clothes as I recall the [high
priest's] chequered tunic and his robe,
with the bells and pomegranates all
around its hem. I sit in deep darkness
when I recall the lampstand [in the
Tabernacle], with its stem and petals
all of one piece, and its tongs. When I
recall the Table of the Presence, I
crouch in a corner[3] and eat among
ashes and dust. I weep bitterly over the
bronze altar, which once atoned for my
sins with the blood on its four horns.

---

1. Lit. 'the sweet-smelling in remembrance of the mandrake'; a reference to Genesis 30.14.
2. Genesis 48.16.
3. Lit. 'between the oven and the stove'.

מָה אֲחָשְׁבָה ? שִׁבְרִי עָצוּם וְגָדוֹל כְּיָם.
מִי יִרְפָּא, בִּלְתְּךָ, רוֹפֵא לְחוֹלָיִים ?
יוֹם אֶשְׁמַע קוֹל מְבַשֵּׂר טוֹב לְפָנַי, וְאָז
אֶקֹּד וְאֶשְׁתַּחֲוֶה אַרְצָה לְאַפָּיִם.
אָגִיל וְאֶשְׂמַח בְּעֵת גּוֹאֵל אַבִּיר יַעֲקֹב
יֹאמַר בְּקוֹל 'נַחֲמוּ נַחֲמוּ' בְּכִפְלַיִם.

What can I hope for? My wound is as
huge as the sea. Who but You can ease
my pain, O Healer of all suffering? On
the day when I hear the voice that
bears good tidings, I shall bow down
and prostrate myself. I shall rejoice
greatly when my ransomer, the Mighty
One of Jacob, cries aloud: 'Comfort ye,
comfort ye my people!'

אֶחֱדֶה לָאֵל   SONG AT DAYBREAK

אֶחֱדֶה לָאֵל, לְבַב חוֹקֵר,
בְּרָן־יַחַד כּוֹכְבֵי בֹקֶר.

I shall give thanks to the Lord, who
tests the heart, when the morning stars
sing together.

שִׂימוּ לֵב אֶל הַנְּשָׁמָה,
לֶשֶׁם, שְׁבוֹ וְאַחְלָמָה,
וְאוֹרָהּ כְּאוֹר הַחַמָּה —
שִׁבְעָתַיִם כְּאוֹר הַבֹּקֶר.

Take care of the soul: she is turquoise,
agate, and jasper. Her light is like the
light of the sun, like the light of seven
mornings at once.

מִכִּסֵּא כָבוֹד חֻצָּבָה,
לָגוּר בְּאֶרֶץ עֲרָבָה,
לְהַצִּילָהּ מִלֶּהָבָה,
וּלְהַאִירָהּ לִפְנוֹת בֹּקֶר.

She was hewn from the Throne of
Glory, sent to live in a desert land, to
deliver it from fire, to shine upon it in
the early morning.

עוּרוּ נָא, כִּי בְּכָל לַיְלָה
נִשְׁמַתְכֶם עוֹלָה לְמַעְלָה,
לָתֵת דִּין וְחֶשְׁבּוֹן מִפְעָלָהּ
לְיוֹצֵר עֶרֶב וָבֹקֶר.

Rouse yourselves, for every night your
soul goes to heaven to account for its
actions before the Maker of evening
and morning.

יִמְצָאָהּ מְקֻשֶּׁטֶת
בְּטַלִּית וְטוֹטֶפֶת,
כְּמוֹ כַּלָּה מְקֻשֶּׁטֶת –
תָּמִיד בַּבֹּקֶר בַּבֹּקֶר.

May He find her wrapped in prayer-shawl and frontlets, always dressed like a bride, morning after morning.

הַנֶּאֱמָן בְּפִקְדוֹנוֹ
יַחֲזִירֶנָּה לוֹ כִּרְצוֹנוֹ:
אִישׁ לֹא נָגַע בַּעֲווֹנוֹ –
וַיְהִי עֶרֶב וַיְהִי בֹקֶר.

He who keeps all souls in trust will return her to you if He wishes. No man died through His error – and there was evening, and there was morning.

וְהַחֲיֵה הָעֲנִיָּה,
יְחִידָה, תַּמָּה וּנְקִיָּה.
וַאֲשֶׁר נַפְשׁוֹ לֹא חִיָּה –
אֵיךְ יִזְכֶּה לְאוֹר הַבֹּקֶר?

Gladden the afflicted one, the only one, perfect and pure. If a man does not keep his soul alive, how will he be worthy of the light of morning?

אָנָּא, בְּכֹח

INVOCATION

אָנָּא, בְּכֹחַ גְּדֻלַּת יְמִינְךָ תַּתִּיר צְרוּרָה.
קַבֵּל רִנַּת עַמְּךָ, שַׂגְּבֵנוּ, טַהֲרֵנוּ, נוֹרָא.
נָא, גִּבּוֹר, דּוֹרְשֵׁי יִחוּדְךָ כְּבָבַת שָׁמְרֵם.
בָּרְכֵם, טַהֲרֵם, רַחֲמֵם, צִדְקָתְךָ תָּמִיד גָּמְלֵם.
חֲסִין קָדוֹשׁ, בְּרֹב טוּבְךָ נַהֵל עֲדָתֶךָ.
יָחִיד גֵּאֶה, לְעַמְּךָ פְּנֵה, זוֹכְרֵי קְדֻשָּׁתֶךָ.
שַׁוְעָתֵנוּ קַבֵּל וּשְׁמַע צַעֲקָתֵנוּ, יוֹדֵעַ תַּעֲלוּמוֹת.

We pray You: with the strength of Your great right hand, set the captive free. Accept Your people's prayer, lift us up, make us pure, O Dread God! God of Might, guard as the apple of Your eye those who seek Your oneness. Bless them, purify them, pity them, reward them always with Your charity. O mighty and Holy One, with Your endless grace guide Your flock. Unique and Exalted One, turn to Your people, who remember Your holiness. Accept our plea, hear our cry, You who know the secrets of the heart!

THE MARTYRS OF MAINZ

אֲדַבְּרָה בְּצַר רוּחִי

אֲדַבְּרָה בְּצַר רוּחִי בִּפְנֵי מְעוּט קְהָלִי,
אֶקֹונֵן וְאֶתְאַבֵּל כִּי שַׁדַּי הֵמַר לִי.
הַחֲרִישׁוּ, וְהָבִינוּ מִלּוּלִי וּפִלּוּלִי —
מִי יִתֶּן־לִי שׁוֹמֵעַ לִי! [...]

I shall speak out in the grief of my
spirit before my small congregation. I
shall wail and lament, for the Almighty
has dealt bitterly with me. Be silent,
hear my words and my prayer. If only
He would hear me!

טוֹעִים בַּשַּׁעַר נֶאֶסְפוּ יַחַד
לְהַכְרִית שֵׁם שְׁאֵרִית הַמְיָחָד.
יְלָדִים רַכִּים כְּנֶגְדּוֹ עָנוּ קוֹל אֶחָד;
'שְׁמַע יִשְׂרָאֵל יְיָ אֱלֹהֵינוּ יְיָ אֶחָד'.

The Crusaders[1] massed at the gateway
to blot out the name of His remnants.
Small children cried out to Him with
one voice: 'Hear, O Israel, the Lord is
our God, the Lord is One!'

יָצְאוּ בַּחוּרִים אִישׁ מֵחֲדָרָיו
לְקַדֵּשׁ הַשֵּׁם הַגָּדוֹל, כִּי הַיּוֹם מְנַסֶּה אֶת בְּחִירָיו.
קִבְּלוּ דִין מִשָּׁמַיִם בִּגְזֵרַת אֲמָרָיו.
קָפַץ קָלוֹנִימוֹס וְכֻלָּם אַחֲרָיו.

Young men left [the shelter of] their
rooms to sanctify the Great Name, for
on that day He was putting His chosen
ones to the test. He had decreed this in
heaven, and they submitted. Kalonymus
leaped [into battle] and all the others
followed.

נִגְזְרָה גְּזֵרָה בִּשְׁמֵי שְׁמֵי שַׁחַק,
וְרָפְתָה יָדָם וְגֻבַּר הַדֹּחַק,
'הִנְנִי בָרֹאשׁ וְלֹא אֶרְחַק!' —
פָּשַׁט צַוָּארוֹ וְנֶהֱרַג תְּחִלָּה רַבִּי יִצְחָק.

But the decree had been passed in the
heaven of heavens: their hands hung
limp, they were crushed together. 'Let
me take the lead, I shall not retreat!'
Rabbi Isaac bared his neck and was the
first to be slaughtered.

נִתְקַבְּצוּ מִסָּבִיב מִכָּל הֶעָרִים
בַּחֲרָבוֹת וּבְחִצִּים לְהִלָּחֵם בַּחֲדָרִים,
וְלִמְאֹד תָּקְפָה יַד אַכְזָרִים,
וַחֲסִידִים מִבְּפָנִים בְּצוֹם וּבְכִי וּבְתַמְרוּרִים.

They gathered from all the nearby
towns, armed with swords and arrows,
to attack the rooms. The cruel ones
charged in force while, within, the
pious ones fasted and wept bitterly.

---

1. Lit. 'the [misguided] wanderers' or 'vagabonds'.

צַעֲקַת יְלָדִים אֵיךְ גָּדְלָה !
רוֹאִים אֲחֵיהֶם נִשְׁחָטִים בְּמַחְלָחָלָה,
הָאֵם קוֹשֶׁרֶת בְּנָהּ פֶּן בְּפִרְכּוּס יְחַלְּלָהּ,
וְהָאָב מְבָרֵךְ עַל הַשְּׁחִיטָה לְכַלְּלָהּ.

Oh, how the children cried aloud!
Trembling, they see their brothers
slaughtered; the mother binding her
son, lest he profane the sacrifice by
shuddering;[1] the father making the
ritual blessing to sanctify the slaughter.

נָשִׁים רַחֲמָנִיּוֹת בְּנֵיהֶן חוֹנְקוֹת,
בְּתוּלוֹת טְהוֹרוֹת בְּמֶרֶד זוֹעֲקוֹת,
כַּלָּה מִן חֲתָנָהּ נִפְטָרוֹת וְנוֹשְׁקוֹת,
וְאֵצֶל הַשְּׁחִיטָה דוֹבְקוֹת וְדוֹחֲקוֹת. [...]

Compassionate women strangle their
own children; pure virgins shriek
bitterly; brides kiss their bridegrooms
farewell – and all rush eagerly to be
slaughtered.

חֲסִין יָהּ, שׁוֹכֵן מְעָלִים !
מִקֶּדֶם עַל עֲקֵדָה אַחַת צָעֲקוּ לְפָנֶיךָ אֶרְאֶלִּים,
וְעַתָּה כַּמָּה גֶעֱקָדִים וְנִכְלָלִים –
וּמַדּוּעַ לֹא הִרְעִישׁוּ עַל בָּנַי עוֹלָלִים ?

Almighty Lord, dwelling on high, in
days of old the angels cried out to You
to put a halt to one sacrifice.[2] And now,
so many are bound and slaughtered –
why do they not clamour over my
infants?

וְאָנוּ אֵין לְהַרְהֵר עַל הָרְדוּמִים,
כִּי הֵם לְחַיֵּי עַד עֲרוּכִים וּמְחֻתָּמִים ;
אֲבָל עָלֵינוּ, כִּי לְמֹאד חַיַּבְנוּ אֲשֵׁמִים
אֲשֶׁר עָבַרְנוּ מִצְווֹת תְּמִימִים.

But we must not question the fate of
the dead, for they have been destined
for eternal life. We must question
ourselves, for we have been found very
guilty; we have transgressed the
precepts of right.

חַי עוֹלָמִים, בְּצֵל כְּנָפֶיךָ אָנוּ בוֹרְחִים,
כִּי נִשְׁאַרְנוּ עֲגוּנִים וַאֲנוּחִים
מִבְּלִי לְהִשְׁתַּחֵף לְתָלוּי שׁוֹחֲחִים –
פֶּגֶר מוּבָס, יֵבוֹשׁוּ כֹּל אֵלָיו בּוֹטְחִים !

O everlasting God, we seek refuge in
the shadow of Your wings. We have
been abandoned, alone and suffering,
because we refused to bow our heads
before the crucified one, a corpse
trampled underfoot. Let all who put
their trust in him be put to shame!

לְיַחֶדְךָ, נוֹרָא וּמְהֻלָּל, שׁוֹכֵן מְרוֹמִים,
נַעֲבָדְךָ בְּיִרְאָה, לֵילוֹת וְיָמִים.
וּנְקֹם נִקְמָתֵנוּ, דּוֹרֵשׁ דָּמִים,
רָם עַל רָמִים, יוֹשֵׁב עַל כִּסֵּא רַחֲמִים !

To unify Your Name – O fearful God,
dwelling in heaven, worthy of all praise
– we worship You in dread, night and
day. Now avenge us, O Avenger of the
blood, Highest of the high, who sit upon
the throne of compassion!

---

1. According to the laws of ritual slaughter, a blemish disqualifies the offering.
2. The binding of Isaac.

דָּוִד בַּר־מְשֻׁלָּם · *David bar Meshullam of Speyer*

אֱלֹהִים, אַל דֳּמִי · THE SACRIFICES

אֱלֹהִים, אַל דֳּמִי לְדָמִי!
אַל תֶּחֱרַשׁ וְאַל תִּשְׁקֹט לְמִתְקוֹמְמִי!
בַּקְּשֵׁהוּ, דָּרְשֵׁהוּ מִיַּד מַחֲרִימִי,
בַּל תְּכַסֶּה אֶרֶץ בְּכָל מְקוֹמִי.

O God, do not let my blood rest in
peace! Do not be silent. Give my
enemy no respite. Avenge my blood,
require it at the hand of my destroyer.
Let not the earth cover it, wherever it
is shed.

גַּל יִגָּלֶה וּלְפָנֶיךָ יִשָּׁפֵךְ וְיִזָּלֵף,
גַּם בְּפַרְפִּירְךָ מָלֵא גְוִיּוֹת יִצָּלֵף.
דּוֹן יָדוֹן שׁוֹפְכֶךָ, חֲלֹף בְּחֵלֶף,
דְּמֵי עֲנִיֶּיךָ הַנִּשְׁפָּכִים כְּשִׂגְרֵי אָלֶף. [...]

Let it be revealed, pouring forth before
Your eyes. Let the blood of all the
corpses be inscribed in Your royal
purple. Punish them, pay them back
in kind, for shedding the blood of Your
helpless people as though they were
cattle.

טַף וְנָשִׁים הִשְׁלִימוּ יַחַד לְעֶקֶד,
טְלָאִים הַמְבֻקָּרִים בְּלִשְׁכַּת בֵּית הַמּוֹקֵד.
יָחִיד וְנִשָּׂא, עָלֶיךָ גֹהֳרַג וְנִשְׁקֵד,
יְחוּם הַזִּמָּה אֵלָיו רֹאשׁ מְלִַּקֵּד.

Tender children and women gave
themselves up to the binding, like
choice lambs in the Chamber of the
Hearth.[1] O Only One, Lofty One, we
are pierced and murdered for Your
sake, for refusing to bow our heads
before the child of wantonness.

כְּבָשִׂים בְּנֵי שָׁנָה לְעוֹלָה תְּמִימִים
כֻּבְּשׁוּ עוֹלוֹת כְּזִבְחֵי אֱמוּרֵי שְׁלָמִים.
לְאִמּוֹתָם אוֹמְרִים: 'לֹא תִכְמְרוּ רַחֲמִים,
לְקָרְבָּן אִשֶּׁה לַיְיָ נִתְבַּקַּשְׁנוּ מְרוֹמִים.

Yearling lambs without blemish were
slaughtered like whole offerings,
trapped and burnt like the sacrificial
portions of shared offerings.[2] They
said to their mothers: 'Do not be
moved by pity. Heaven has summoned
us to be an offering by fire to the Lord.'

---

1. One of the Chambers of the Temple.
2. Leviticus 4.8–10; the ritual terms are derived from the book of Leviticus and from the Mishnah *Yoma*.

מְפַרְפְּרִים הַיְלָדִים זֶה עַל זֶה מְפַרְכָּסִים.
מְמַהֲרִים שָׁחֵט אֲחֵרִים וּבְדָמֵיהֶם מִתְבּוֹסְסִים.
נָתוּן עַל רֹבֶד הֵיכָלְךָ וְאַף לְמָרְסִים,
נֶגֶד עֵינֶיךָ לָעַד יְהוּ תוֹסְסִים. [...]

The young struggle in agony, heaped
on top of one another. [The old],
writhing in their own blood, hasten to
sacrifice their fellows.[1] Let this blood
be stirred on the terrace of Your
Sanctuary.[2] Let it boil before Your
eyes forever, [like the blood of
Zechariah].

דְּמָעוֹת מִפֹּה וּמִפֹּה נוֹבְעִים וּמְקַלְּחִים,
וְשׁוֹחֲטִים וְנִשְׁחָטִים אֵלּוּ עַל אֵלּוּ גּוֹנְחִים,
דְּמֵי אָבוֹת וּבָנִים נוֹגְעִים וְטוֹפְחִים,
בִּרְכַּת הַזֶּבַח 'שְׁמַע יִשְׂרָאֵל' צוֹרְחִים.

The tears well up and stream from
every side. Those who slaughter and
those who are slaughtered all groan
upon one another. The blood of fathers
laps against the blood of sons, as they
howl their benediction over slaughter:
'Hear, O Israel!'

יִרְאֶה יֵרָאֶה פְּצַעַת בָּנוֹת בּוֹטְחוֹת,
בְּחֹם הַיּוֹם עֲרֻמּוֹת לַשֶּׁמֶשׁ נִשְׁטָחוֹת.
יָפָה בַנָּשִׁים מְבֻקְּעֵי כָרֵס וּמְפֻלָּחוֹת,
מִבֵּין רַגְלֶיהָ שִׁלְיָה וָלָד מַפְרִיחוֹת.

Let this sight come before You: young
women, who put their trust in You,
slaughtered naked in broad daylight;
the fairest of women – their wombs
slashed open and the afterbirth forced
out from between their legs.

שָׁמוֹעַ הֲנִשְׁמַע אוֹ אִם נִרְאָה ?
לְהַאֲמִין מִי יַאֲמִין גְּדוֹלָה פְּלִיאָה :
מוֹלִיכִין בְּנֵיהֶם לַטֶּבַח כְּלַחֻפָּה נָאָה.
הַעַל אֵלֶּה תִתְאַפַּק, רָם גֵּאֹה גֵּאָה ?

[Has the like of this] ever been seen or
heard? Could anyone believe such a
stupefying sight? They lead their
children to the slaughter as if to a
beautiful bridal canopy. After this,
O Exalted and Triumphant Lord, will
You hold back?

קֶדֶם שֶׁעֲנָנוּ וַתַּעֲמֹד עֲקֵדַת הַר-מֹר,
טָמוּן לְיֶשַׁע בְּכָל דּוֹר וָדוֹר לְשָׁמֹר.
נִתּוֹסְפוּ אֵלֶּה וְכָאֵלֶּה עַד בִּלְתִּי לֵאמֹר.
חַי, זְכוּתָם קוּם תִּשְׁמָר-לָנוּ וְצָרוֹתֵינוּ תִּגְמֹר.

Once, long ago, we could rely upon the
merit of Abraham's sacrifice at Mount
Moriah, that it would safeguard us and
bring salvation age after age. But now
one sacrifice follows another, they can
no longer be counted. O Living God,
may the merit of their righteousness
protect us and call a halt to our miseries!

1. To prevent their being seized by the enemy and forcibly converted.
2. The blood of sacrifices was stirred up so that it should not congeal (*Yoma* 4.6).

אֶפְרַיִם מֵרֶגֶנְשְׁבּוּרק   *Ephraim of Regensburg*

רָמֵה הַגָּלוּת   TO GOD IN EXILE

[...] רָמֵה הַגָּלוּת בְּתַעֲלוּמָה,
הָאִירָה עֵינֵי אֲיֻמָּה,
כִּי אֲפֵלוֹת הֵמָּה.

Lord, thrust Exile into oblivion,
brighten the eyes of the terrible one,[1]
for they are full of darkness.

יִשְׁעֲךָ מֵעַתָּה וָהָלְאָה,
לְנַחֲלָתְךָ נִלְאָה וְנִכְאָה,
בַּאֲשֶׁר אָהַבְתִּי, הָבִיאָה.

Your salvation is my heart's desire.
Oh, bring it now to Your weary and
languishing people.

אֵלִי, אֵלִי, לָמָה
אֲנָחָתִי מִמְּךָ נֶעֱלָמָה,
וַאֲנִי כְּיוֹנָה נֶאֱלָמָה ?

My God, my God, why are my sighs
hidden from You? I am nothing but a
helpless dove.

מִיַּד שְׁאוֹל, מִמָּוֶת —
גְּאָלָה נַפְשִׁי, מִשֶּׁבֶת
אֶרֶץ חֹשֶׁךְ וְצַלְמָוֶת.

Ransom my soul from Sheol, from
death. Let me not dwell in a land of
gloom and deep darkness.

חֵרוּת לְבַקֵּשׁ יָאַשְׁתִּי,
לְהַחֲיוֹת נַפְשִׁי בַּקַּשְׁתִּי,
אֶת יְיָ דָּרַשְׁתִּי.

I have despaired of finding freedom;
my only wish is to keep my soul alive.
I seek the Lord's help.

אֵלִי, אֵלִי, לָמָה
אֲנָחָתִי מִמְּךָ נֶעֱלָמָה,
וַאֲנִי כְּיוֹנָה נֶאֱלָמָה ?

My God, my God, why are my sighs
hidden from You? I am nothing but a
helpless dove.

---

1. A conventional epithet for Zion based on Song of Songs 6.4: 'terrible as an army with banners'.

זַמּוֹתִי : דְּרוֹר מָה אֶשְׁאַל,
וְאַתָּה עִמִּי נִשְׁאָל.
אִם תִּגְאַל – גְּאַל.

I thought: what right have I to ask for liberty when You, too, are in exile with me? But if You so desire, redeem me.

קוֹל צוֹפִי קְרָאַנִי.
קוּי, נַפְשִׁי – הֶלְאָנִי.
אֹמֵר לְנַפְשִׁי : 'יְשׁוּעָתֵךְ אָנִי'.

The voice of my watchman calls out to me. Do not lose hope, my soul, though He has wearied you. And You, O Lord, say to my soul: 'I am your salvation.'

אֵלִי, אֵלִי, לָמָה
אַנְחָתִי מִמְּךָ נֶעֱלָמָה,
וַאֲנִי כְּיוֹנָה גֶאֱלָמָה ?

My God, my God, why are my sighs hidden from You? I am nothing but a helpless dove.

אֱלֹהַי בְּךָ אֶחָבֵק   BE NOT FAR FROM ME

אֱלֹהַי, בְּךָ אֶחָבֵק
כְּטוֹבֵע לְגָמֵל יֵאָבֵק.
אוֹמֵר טוֹב לַדְּבֵק.
בְּשִׁמְךָ תָּמִיד חֻתַּלְתִּי,
אַף כִּי עָלֶיךָ נִקְטַלְתִּי,
נַפְתּוּלֵי אֱלֹהִים נִפְתַּלְתִּי.
אַל תִּרְחַק מִמֶּנִּי. [...]

My God, I cling to You, like a drowning man struggling to reach land. How good to be joined to You! I have always wrapped myself in Your Name, even though because of You I have been slaughtered. I have fought God's fight. *Be not far from me!*

הִרְחַקְתִּי נְדוֹד מִמְּךָ,
וְלִבִּי קָרוֹב לְשִׁמְךָ.
וּרְאֵה כִּי עַמְּךָ
וְצֹאן יָדְךָ גְּמוֹנָה
וְאָחוֹר לֹא נָסוֹנָה.
רְעֵה אֶת צֹאן הַהֲרֵגָה.
אַל תִּרְחַק מִמֶּנִּי.

I have wandered far from You, but my heart has always been near to Your Name. Look: Your people, Your sheep, were carried away and still they did not turn their backs on You. Oh, tend the doomed flock. *Be not far from me!*

זְכֹר הֶרֶג רַב
עָלֶיךָ נַפְשִׁי נִקְרַב
וְנָפַל מִמֶּנִּי רָב.
חֲסִידֶיךָ וּמְיַחֲדֶיךָ מְקֶרֶב,
בֹּקֶר וְצָהֳרַיִם וָעֶרֶב,
עַם שְׂרִידֵי חָרֶב.
אַל תִּרְחַק מִמֶּנִּי.

Remember the massacre I suffered for
Your sake. So many of us perished. Yet
morning and evening and at noon Your
loyal servants acclaim Your Oneness
with all their hearts. This is the people
that survived the sword. *Be not far
from me!*

טָחֵי תָפֵל וּמַדּוּחִים
אֱלֵי גִיל הַשְּׂמֵחִים
וּבְמִשְׁכְּנוֹת מִבְטַחִים.
יְרֵאֶיךָ נִסְקָלִים וְנֶחֱנָקִים,
וְאִלּוּ הֵן הַלּוֹקִים —
בְּיָי הַדְּבֵקִים.
אַל תִּרְחַק מִמֶּנִּי.

The men of deceit[1] and sham rejoice in
houses full of ease while those who
revere You are stoned and strangled.
Only those who hold fast to the Lord
are scourged. *Be not far from me!*

כּוֹרֵעַ לְתָלוּי בְּמַגּוֹד
יְעַצֵּנִי בְּךָ לִבְגֹּד,
לִבוּל עֵץ יִסְגֹּד.
לֹא אַצַּתִּי לְרֵעוֹת אַחֲרָיו.
נַמְתִּי : "יֵבוֹשׁוּ כָּל חֲבֵרָיו.'
רַע יֵרוֹעַ כִּי עָרַב.
אַל תִּרְחַק מִמֶּנִּי.

They urge me to betray You, those who
fall down before an image hanging on a
rack, who worship a block of wood. But
I did not join its ranks. I said: 'All its
votaries will be put to shame.' They
pledged themselves to it and they will
know no peace. *Be not far from me!*

מֵחֲמַת עָפָר זוֹחֵל
יַרְחִי-שָׁוְא אֲנִי נוֹחֵל.
וּמַה כֹּחִי כִּי אֲיַחֵל ?
נַפְשִׁי בְּךָ דָבְקָה
כְּיוֹנֵק נִכְנָס לִרְבָקָה :

The venom of creeping things fills my
mouth with despair. Do I have the
strength to wait? My soul clings to You
like a calf yoked to a team.[2]

---

1. Lit. 'those who slap on plaster', or 'those who daub with whitewash'.
2. A Talmudic expression : the calf is taken into the threshing team so that it may suck its mother's milk.

הַשְׂבַּע נֶפֶשׁ שׁוֹקֵקָה.
אַל תִּרְחַק מִמֶּנִּי. [...]

Oh, satisfy the thirsty. *Be not far from me!*

אֵלִי גּוֹאֲלִי, דָּמִי דוֹרֵשׁ,
לֹא יַעֲזֹב לָהֶם שֹׁרֶשׁ,
כָּלָה גֵּרֵשׁ יְגָרֵשׁ.
פַּגֵּה חַיַּת קָנֶה
מַלְכוּתָהּ תְּקֵל מְנֵא מְנֵא,
תּוֹצִיא אוֹתָהּ אֶל מִחוּץ לַמַּחֲנֶה.
אַל תִּרְחַק מִמֶּנִּי.

My God is my redeemer, the avenger of my blood. He will cut away their roots, He will drive them out, one and all. Tell the wild beast of the reeds[1] that its kingdom has been weighed in the balance and found wanting, that its days are numbered.[2] Banish it from the company of man. *Be not far from me!*

רוּמָה, יַחַד מַצִּיתֶנָּה,
לְיַרְכְּתֵי בוֹר תִּשְׁפְּתֶנָּה,
עַוֵּה עַוֵּה תְּשִׁיתֶנָּה,
יַעַן מְשָׁכַנְתִּי בְּעַבְדוּת,
נִשְׁפַּטְתִּי בְּכָל מִינֵי מַרְדוּת.
הֲקָצוֹר קָצְרָה יָדְךָ מִפְּדוּת?
אַל תִּרְחַק מִמֶּנִּי. [...]

Lift up Your hand, set the beast on fire, hurl it into the depths of the abyss, destroy it. It has lured me into servitude, and thus subjected me to every kind of punishment. Is Your arm too short to redeem? *Be not far from me!*

אֶפְרַיִם מִבּוֹנָא

Ephraim of Bonn

אֶת אֲבוֹתַי אֲנִי מַזְכִּיר

THE SLAUGHTER OF ISAAC AND HIS REVIVAL

אֶת אֲבוֹתַי אֲנִי מַזְכִּיר
הַיּוֹם לְפָנֶיךָ, בּוֹחֵן וּמַכִּיר.
פָּחָן זְכוּת אָבוֹת לַבָּנִים,
אָב זָקֵן וְיֶלֶד זְקֻנִים.

Lord, who test and know [man's heart], today I shall invoke before You the memory of my Fathers. Oh, favour the sons for the sake of the Fathers – for the sake of *the aged father* [Abraham] *and the child of his old age.*

---

1. An expression from Psalms (68.31) which was interpreted by the Midrash as a reference to the Christian nations.
2. Lit. '*Tekel, mene, mene*'; Daniel 5.25.

זָרִיז הֵשִׂים עַל בְּנוֹ
עֲצֵי הָעוֹלָה, עֲשׂוֹת קָרְבָּנוּ.
עָנָה הַבֵּן וּפָץ לְשַׁאֲלָה:
'הִנֵּה הָאֵשׁ וְהָעֵצִים וְאַיֵּה הַשֶּׂה לְעוֹלָה ?'

You told Your beloved to sacrifice his favoured one on one of the mountains, where You would consecrate him [as a priest]: 'Offer as a sacrifice to Me the soul of him you love; *get her* [the soul] *for Me, because she pleases Me.*'

חָסִיד דִּבֶּר נְכוֹנָה בְּמִלּוּלוֹ:
'יֵדַע יְיָ אֶת אֲשֶׁר לוֹ.
סָקַר הַשֶּׂה, בְּנִי, בְּעָלָיו,
וְאֶת הַקָּדוֹשׁ וְהִקְרִיב אֵלָיו.'

You called upon him to endure the trial, as a king [at war] appeals to his seasoned warrior: 'This will put you to the test and prove that you always triumph.' *The Lord tests the righteous.*

טָהוֹר הֶרְאָהוּ מִזְבַּח הָרִאשׁוֹנִים:
'זָכַר תָּמִים מַקְרִיב לִרְצוֹנִים !'
נָמָה יוֹנַת אֵלֶם: 'מְאַסְּרֵנִי לַזֶּבַח
בַּעֲבֹתִים עַד קַרְנוֹת הַמִּזְבֵּחַ.

[Ishmael], the wild ass, boasted of his blood and brayed: 'My blood was drained when I was thirteen!'[1] The beloved [Isaac] whispered: 'If God wishes to take me, *let Him take all of me.*'

יָדַי וְרַגְלַי לִי תֶאֱסֹר,
פֶּן אֲחַלֵּל הַזֶּבַח וְאֶחְסַר.
מִדְאֶגֶת בְּעֵתוּת חַסְתִּי לִכְבוֹדֶךָ,
אָמַרְתִּי כַּבֵּד אֲכַבְּדֶךָ.'

The zealous [father] hurried to fulfil the commandment. [He rose at dawn] to saddle his ass with his very own hands; for the love of God, he put aside his dignity. *O Lord, You know all this!*

כְּשָׁמֹעַ קָשׁוּר בְּנַפְשׁוֹ כְּצָמִיד,
צָעֲדוּ יָד וְרֶגֶל כְּתָמִיד.
לַעֲרֹךְ אֵשׁ וְעֵצִים הֶעֱלָה,
וַיַּעַל עָלָיו אֶת הָעוֹלָה.

Then Satan came and stationed himself among them, saying: 'May one venture a word with you?' But the blameless one cried out: 'I shall walk on without reproach, *for this is what the King ordained.*'

אֲזַי אָב וּבֵן חָבָקוּ,
נִפְגָּשׁוּ, אֱמֶת וְשָׁלוֹם נָשָׁקוּ.
'פִּיךָ תִּפְתַּח, אָבִי, בְּשֶׁבַח,
כִּי הוּא יְבָרֵךְ הַזֶּבַח.

On the third day they reached Mount Scopus, and there they saw the presence of their Maker: the pillar of cloud shone gloriously *like a devouring fire, on the mountain-top.*

---

1. 'Ishmael said to Isaac: "I am more pious than you. You were only eight days old when you were circumcised, but I was thirteen years old [and felt all the pain]"' (*T.B. Sanhedrin* 89b).

380

אָמַרְתָּ לִידִידְךָ לְהַעֲלוֹת יְחִידוֹ
לְאַחַד הֶהָרִים, לְמַלֵּא יָדוֹ :
'תַּעֲלֶה נֶפֶשׁ אֲהַבְתָּ לְקָרְבָּנִי,
אוֹתָהּ קַח לִי כִּי הִיא יָשָׁרָה בְּעֵינָי !'

The zealous one laid the firewood for
the sacrifice on his son's shoulder.
Then the son opened his mouth and
said: *Here are the fire and the wood,
but where is the sheep for the burnt
offering?*

בְּקַשְׁתָּ מֵאִתּוֹ בְּנִסָּיוֹן לַעֲמֹד,
כְּמֶלֶךְ מִגִּבּוֹר לָנֶצַח יִתְמֹד :
'שֶׁבָּזֹאת תִּבָּחֵן וְתִמָּצֵא נֶאֱמָן !'
יְיָ צַדִּיק יִבְחָן.

The loyal one answered and he spoke
the truth: 'The Lord will make known
who is to be His. The Master will see
to the sheep, my son. *He will draw the
holy one to Himself.*'

גָּאָה בְדָמוֹ וְנָהַק פֶּרֶא :
'מָצִיתִי דָמִי לִשְׁלוֹשׁ־עֶשְׂרֵה !'
רָחַשׁ אָהוּב : 'אִם לָאֵל אֶלָּקַח,
גַּם אֶת הַכֹּל יָקַח.'

Then the Pure One showed him the
altar of the ancients:[1] 'Here offer a
male without blemish, of your own free
will.' The soft-spoken dove whispered:
'Bind me for the sacrifice *with cords to
the horns of the altar.*

דִּין זָרִיז לְהַקְדִּים לַמִּצְוָה,
לַחֲבשׁ חֲמוֹרוֹ בְּעַצְמוֹ אָוָּה.
קָשַׁר אַהֲבָה בְּטָלָה גְדֵלָה.
הֵן יְיָ יָדַעְתָּ כֻלָּהּ.

'Bind my hands and my feet lest I
render myself unfit [by trembling] and
profane the sacrifice. I fear that out of
panic I may violate your honour,[2] and
I desire to honour you greatly.'

הַשָּׂטָן בְּתוֹכָם בָּא לְהִתְיַצָּבָה,
'הֲנִסָּה דָבָר אֵלֶיךָ ?' לְנוּבְבָה.
צָרַח תָּם : 'בְּחַטְמִי אֵלֵךְ
כִּי כֵן יִסַּד הַמֶּלֶךְ.'

When he heard this, [Abraham], whose
soul was linked to the boy's like a
bracelet, bound him hand and foot as
if he were a whole offering. He put fire
on the altar, wood on the fire,[3] *and on it
offered the burnt offering.*

וּבַיּוֹם הַשְּׁלִישִׁי לַצּוֹפִים הִגִּיעוּ,
אֲזַי אֶל עוֹשֵׂיהֶם שָׁעוּ :
פְּאֵר עַמּוּד הֶעָנָן מָצָהָר
כְּאֵשׁ אוֹכֶלֶת בְּרֹאשׁ הָהָר.

Then the father and the son embraced;
Faithfulness and Peace met and kissed
each other. 'My father, fill your mouth
with praise, *for He will bless the offering.*

---

1. The altar on which Adam, Cain, Abel, and Noah had made their offerings.
2. He might kick Abraham, thus transgressing the commandment to honour one's father.
3. In keeping with the precise ritual of Leviticus 1.7.

רְצוֹנִי פָּתֹחַ פִּי לְזַמֵּן :
בָּרוּךְ יְיָ לְעוֹלָם אָמֵן.
יֵאָסֵף אֶפְרִי וְיוּבָא הָעִירָה,
הָאֹהֱלָה אֶל שָׂרָה.'

'And I too wish to open my mouth in
benediction: "Blessed be the Lord
forever. Amen." Let my ashes be
gathered and taken to the village *to
Sarah in her tent.*'

מִהַר וְנָתַן עָלָיו אַרְכֻּבּוֹתָיו,
וּכְגִבּוֹר אִמֵּץ שְׁתֵּי זְרוֹעוֹתָיו.
בְּיָדָיו אֱמוּנָה שְׁחָטוֹ בְּתֹכֶן
וּטְבֹחַ טֶבַח וְהָכֵן.

Quickly he pinned him down with his
knees, straining his arms greatly. Then
he slaughtered him, with steady hands,
as prescribed by law. *The slaughter had
been duly prepared.*

רַד טַל חֶחִי עָלָיו וַיְחָיֶה.
תְּפָשׂוֹ לְשָׁחֲטוֹ פַּעַם שְׁנִיָּה.
יָעִיד הַמִּקְרָא וְלַדָּבָר רַגְלַיִם :
'וַיִּקְרָא יְיָ אֶל אַבְרָהָם שֵׁנִית מִן הַשָּׁמַיִם.'

Now the dew of Resurrection fell down
upon him, and he revived. The father
seized him, to slaughter him once more.
Scripture itself bears witness that this
was so: '*And the Lord called from
heaven a second time to Abraham.*'

עָנוּ מַלְאֲכֵי הַשָּׁרֵת בְּמַהוּמָה :
'שְׁתֵּי שְׁחִיטוֹת הֲיֵשְׁנָן בַּבְּהֵמָה ?'
קוֹל בָּרָמָה הִשְׁמִיעוּ בִּנְחִיצָה,
הֵן אֶרְאֶלָּם צָעֲקוּ חֻצָה.

The ministering angels cried out in
terror: 'Even an animal is never
slaughtered twice!' They filled the
heavens with their urgent cries. *The
angelic order shrieked above the earth.*

'בְּבַקָּשָׁה מִלְּפָנֶיךָ, עָלָיו רַחֵם,
בְּבֵית אָבִיו אָכַלְנוּ לָחֶם !'
חָתְפוּ נַחַל דִּמְעוֹת גְּבוֹהִים
בְּעֵדֶן גַּן אֱלֹהִים.

'We beg of You, have pity on him. We
once broke bread in his father's house.'
At once a river of heavenly tears swept
Isaac *into Eden, the garden of God.*

זַךְ חָשַׁב : הַיֶּלֶד אֵינֶנּוּ בְּחוֹבָה,
וַאֲנִי – אָנָה אֲנִי בָא ?
קָשַׁב : 'בִּנְךָ נִרְצָה לְקָרְבָּנִי,
כִּי נִשְׁבַּעְתִּי נְאֻם יְיָ.'

Pure-hearted [Abraham] thought: The
child is guiltless, but I, what am I to
do?[1] Then he heard: 'I have accepted
the sacrifice of your son; *this is the
word of the Lord – by My own self I
swear it!*'

---

1. Abraham thought that some sin of his had caused Isaac to vanish.

בְּסָבְךְ אָדֹן אֶצְלוֹ הֵשִׁית
אַיִל שֶׁכָּלוּ לְמִצְוָה מִבְּרֵאשִׁית.
תַּחְתָּיו פָּשַׁט יָדוֹ בְּטַלִּיתוֹ,
וְהִנּוּ נִצָּב עַל עֹלָתוֹ.

Nearby, in a thicket, the Master put a ram, which had been destined for this holy act ever since Creation.[1] The ram, in place of Isaac, clutched at Abraham's cloak with his foreleg – *and behold, he stood beside his burnt offering.*

וַיִּקַּח אֶת הָאַיִל כִּרְצוֹנוֹ
וַיַּעֲלֵהוּ לְעוֹלָה תַּחַת בְּנוֹ.
רָאָה וְשָׂמַח בְּכֹפֶר יְחִידוֹ
וְהָאֱלֹהִים אִנָּה לְיָדוֹ.

And thus he fulfilled his desire: he took the ram and offered it as a sacrifice instead of his son. He rejoiced as he looked at the ransom of his favoured son *which had come his way by an act of God.*

הַמָּקוֹם קָרְאוֹ 'יְיָ יִרְאֶה',
לְמָקוֹם אוֹרָה וְהוֹרָאָה יֵרָאֶה.
וְנִשְׁבַּע לְבָרְכוֹ בִּמְקוֹם הַמַּעֲרָכָה,
כִּי שָׁם צִוָּה יְיָ אֶת הַבְּרָכָה.

He named that place *Adonai-yireh*,[2] the place from which light and learning would be revealed. And He swore to bless him at the very site of the altar,[3] *for there the Lord bestowed His blessing.*

בְּכֵן עוֹקֵד וְנֶעֱקָד הִתְפַּלְּלוּ,
בְּעֵת בְּנֵיהֶם מַעֲלֵיהֶם יַצְוִּילוּ
מִפְעֲלוֹתָם לְהַזְכִּיר, לְחַלְּצָם מֵרְעוֹתָם,
וּמִפִּשְׁעֵיהֶם לְכָל חַטֹּאתָם.

[Now Isaac came back from Eden.] He who made the sacrifice and he who was the sacrifice both prayed together that when their descendants do evil, this act would be recalled to save them from disaster and [to atone for] *their sins and transgressions.*

צַדִּיק, טוֹבָה עֲשֵׂה עִמָּנוּ,
חֶסֶד לְאַבְרָהָם נִשְׁבַּעְתָּ לַאֲבֹתֵינוּ,
וְעָנְתָה בָּם צִדְקָתָם לְהֵיטִיבֵנוּ,
וְסָלַחְתָּ לַעֲוֹנֵנוּ וּלְחַטָּאתֵנוּ וּנְחַלְתָּנוּ.

O Righteous One, deal kindly with us. You promised our father steadfast love, Your love for Abraham. Let their merit answer for us and make us prosper. *Forgive our iniquity and our sin and take us for Your own.*

---

1. The proxy-ram was made at twilight on the Sabbath eve of the week of creation.
2. I.e. 'The Lord will see', 'the Lord will provide'.
3. According to the tradition that Solomon's Temple was built on Mount Moriah (2 Chronicles 3.1).

תִּזְכָּר־לָנוּ כַּמָּה עֲקֵדוֹת,
הַנֶּהֱרָגִים עָלֶיךָ, חֲסִידִים וַחֲסִידוֹת.
הָעֲקֻדִים לְצֶדֶק לִיהוּדָה נֶקֶב,
וְהַקְּשֻׁרִים לְיַעֲקֹב.

Remember, in our favour, how many have been slaughtered – pious men and women murdered for Your sake. Oh, reward the martyrs[1] of Judah, slain in righteousness, *and the bound*[1] *[victims] of Jacob.*

וְתִרְעֶה אֶת הַצֹּאן הַנּוֹתָרוֹת,
בֵּין הָעַמִּים מְפֹרָדוֹת וּמְפֻזָּרוֹת.
וְשַׁבֵּר מוֹטוֹת וְנַתֵּק מוֹסֵרוֹת,
בְּכָל יַחֵם הַצֹּאן הַמְקֻשָּׁרוֹת.

Tend the sheep that still remain, dispersed among the nations. Break their yoke and snap their cords. *In every way, increase the bound flocks.*

אוֹי לִי אִם אֹמְרָה

LAMENT FOR THE MASSACRE AT BLOIS

[...] אוֹי לִי אִם אֹמְרָה וַאֲהַרְהֵר עַל חוֹצְבִי,
אוֹי לִי אִם לֹא אֹמְרָה מֵהָשִׂיחַ דַּאֲגַת לִבִּי.
אוֹי לִי כִּי פָנָה יוֹם טוּבִי,
כִּי רָחַק מִמֶּנִּי מְנַחֲמִי וּקְרוֹבִי.

Woe is me if I speak and cast doubt on my Maker; woe is me if I do not speak, venting my sorrow. Woe is me, my day of goodness has declined. All my comforters and near ones are far away.

אֶל מִי תְדַמְּיוּנִי וְאֶשְׁוֶה בְּדַאֲבִי ?
כִּי מִי גוֹי מִכָּל שְׁכֵנַי סְבִיבִי
אֲשֶׁר חָטָא וְנִפְרַץ בּוֹ כַּאֲשֶׁר בִּי ?
עָלַי עָבְרוּ חֲרוֹנֶיךָ, נַפְשִׁי לְהַדְאִיבִי:

To whom can you liken me, who is my equal in suffering? Is there a nation, of all those around me, that has been broken for its sins as I have been? Your wrath has swept over me and made me writhe in pain.

אֲנִי נִסְקָל, אֲנִי נִתְקָל לְהַצְלִיבִי.
אֲנִי נִשְׂרָף, אֲנִי נֶעֱרָף לְהַלְעִיבִי.

I am stoned, I am struck down and crucified. I am burned, my neck is snapped in shame. I am beheaded and

---

1. A play on words which figure in the story of Jacob (Genesis 30.39); *akudim* means both 'sacrificed, bound for slaughter' and 'striped sheep'.

אֲנִי נֶהֱרָג, אֲנִי נִדְרָג בְּחוֹבִי.
אֲנִי נֶחֱנָק, אֲנִי נִשְׁנָק לִמְרִיבִי.
אֲנִי מֻכֶּה, אֲנִי לֻקֶּה בְּגֵוִי.
אֲנִי מוּמָת, אֲנִי מָצְמָת לְלָבִיא.
אֲנִי מְאֻבָּד בְּבֵית הַבַּד, דָּמִי לַהֲזִיבִי.
אֲנִי נִתְלֶה, אֲנִי נִקְלֶה וְגוֹלֶה לְהַכְאִיבִי.
אֲנִי נִדְרָס, אֲנִי נֶהֱרָס לַהֲדִיבִי.
דָּמִי נִשְׁפָּךְ, עוֹרִי נֶהְפָּךְ, וְנָוִי.
אֲנִי נִרְדָּף, אֲנִי נֶהְדָּף לְאִישׁ רִיבִי.
אֲנִי נֶאֱנָס, אֲנִי נִקְנָס לְאוֹיְבִי.
אֲנִי חָבוּי, אֲנִי שָׁבוּי בְּשִׁבְיִי.

trampled on for my guilt. I am strangled and choked by my enemy. I am beaten, my body is scourged. I am killed, I am at the mercy of a lion. I am crushed [as if] in an oil press, my blood is squeezed out. I am hung, despised, exiled in pain. I am stamped on, ruined, made to pine away. My blood is shed, my skin turned inside out, my home overturned. I am pursued, thrust back by my opponent. I am raped, I am damned by my enemy. I am driven into hiding and led into captivity.

שָׁבוּ לְאֵיתָנָם כָּל גּוֹי מַחֲרִיבִי,
וַאֲנִי עַד מָתַי אֲצַפֶּה לַהֲשִׁיבִי
בְּיַד בֶּן־נִפְלִי וְאֵלִיָּהוּ הַנָּבִיא ?
הוֹי עַל כָּל שְׁכֵנֵי הָרָעִים רָעָה לְהָבִיא !
אוֹי לָנַפְשָׁם, כִּי גָמְלוּ לָהֶם רָעָה לְהַחֲרִיבִי !
הֵן לֹא קָצְרָה יָדְךָ מִלְהֵיטִיבִי.
יָבוֹא דְּבָרְךָ וְכִבַּדְנוּךְ בְּעִיר מוֹשָׁבִי.

All the peoples that laid me waste have regained their strength. But I, how long must I wait until the Messiah and the prophet Elijah restore my fortunes? May disaster strike all my evil neighbours! Woe upon them! They have earned their own disaster by destroying me. Is the Lord's arm so short that it cannot change my lot? Let Your words come true and we will pay homage to You in my city, Jerusalem.

אַעֲלֶה פָרִים עַל מִזְבַּחֲךָ לְהַתְמִידָה.
בִּרְצוֹנְךָ יְרוּשָׁלַיִם עִירְךָ קַשֵּׁט בִּכְבוֹדָהּ,
וְהַתָּמִיד אָזַי פַּתְמִיד נֶצַח לְהַתְמִידָה.
וְזֹאת תּוֹרַת הָעוֹלָה, הִיא הָעוֹלָה עַל מוֹקְדָה.

There I shall offer young bulls daily on Your altar. Oh, let it be Your pleasure to adorn Your city Jerusalem with all its glory and to preserve the daily offering forever. *This is the law of the burnt offering on the altar hearth.*

385

בָּרוּךְ מִמָּגֶנְצָא

Barukh of Magenza

אֵש אוֹכְלָה אֵש

THE MARTYRS OF BLOIS

אֵש אוֹכְלָה אֵש, בְּסַרְפִּירָתוֹ מְאָדָּם,
אָסַף לוֹ חֲסִידָיו, הַבָּשָׂר וְהַדָּם.
אִיש בִּבְנוֹ וּבְאָחִיו מָלְאוּ יָדָם.
אֲלֵיכֶם אִישִׁים אֶקְרָא וְקוֹלִי אֶל בְּנֵי אָדָם.

[Dressed in] His purple cloak, gleaming red, He – a fire that devours fire – gathered to Himself His loyal servants, their flesh and their blood. They consecrated themselves to Him, each man killing his own son and his own brother. *O sons of men, it is to you I call, I appeal to every man.*

דֹּמּוּ לְשֹׁבֵי אִי, נְצוּרֵי אֱמוּנִי,
דִין שָׁמַיִם קַבְּלוּ לְרֵיחַ שְׁמָנִי.
דַּם חַטַּאת הַכִּפּוּרִים כֹּהֲנַי וּזְקֵנַי,
דֹּעֲכוּ כְּאֵש קוֹצִים בְּשֵׁם אֲדֹנָי.

Be still, my abandoned people,[1] my survivors, my loyal ones. Submit to the decree of Heaven, be like the sweet-smelling incense. The blood of my priests and my elders [was spattered] like blood from the sin-offering of expiation.[2] *They blazed like a fire of thorns, in the name of the Lord.*

וְהֵם הֵבִיאוּ קָרְבָּנָם אִשֶּׁה לְיוֹצְרָם,
וַחֲטָאתָם לִפְנֵי יְיָ בְּנֶפֶש צְרוֹרָם.
וְצוּרָם מְכָרָם וְהִסְגִּירָם בְּיַד צוֹרְרָם,
וְשָׂרְפוּ בָאֵש אֶת עוֹרְתָם וְאֶת בְּשָׂרָם.

They brought their offering, an offering by fire, to their Maker. They gathered their lives into a bundle and presented them as a sin-offering to the Lord. But their Rock sold them and handed them over to the enemies *who destroyed them by fire – skin and flesh.*

זִכְרוּ זֹאת וְהִתְאוֹשָׁשׁוּ – בְּטֶרֶף מַתָּנָם!
זְמִירוֹת הָיוּ חֻקָּם בְּקוֹל הֲמוֹנָם.
זֹאת חֲשַׁבְתָּ לְמִשְׁפָּט, עֶזְרָם וּמָגִנָּם ?
זֶה יִהְיֶה לְךָ מִקְדֵּש הַקֳּדָשִׁים, מִן הָאֵש, כָּל קָרְבָּנָם.

Remember this and abandon hope: they were given away and devoured, though they sang Your praises daily in their multitudes. Did You, their helper and their shield, think this just? *You took for Your own the most holy sacrifices, the offerings by fire, all they had to offer.*

---

1. Lit. 'island inhabitants'.
2. Exodus 30.10.

מִיכָאֵל הַשַּׂר הַגָּדוֹל לַמִּזְבֵּחַ מְעוֹנָה
מַקְטִיר נַפְשׁוֹת נְקִיִּים, צַדִּיקִים בֶּאֱמוּנָה.
מַדּוּעַ רְשָׁעִים עָזַבְתָּ בְּעוֹלוֹתֶיךָ לְדַשְּׁנָה ?
מִמָּרוֹם שָׁלַח אֵשׁ בְּעַצְמֹתַי וַיִּרְדֶּנָּה.

Michael, prince of angels, sacrifices the
souls of the pure and the devout upon
the heavenly altar.[1] But why did You
allow the wicked to fatten on Your
burnt sacrifices? *He sent down fire from
heaven, it ran through my bones.*

עָרֵל בָּשָׂר צִוִּיתָ מֵהַקְרִיבְךָ אֵילִים.
עַל מַה פָּנֶיךָ הִסְתַּרְתָּ בְּהִתְעוֹלֵל הָעֲרֵלִים
עַם קָדוֹשׁ סְמוּכִים, הַיְּהוּדִים הָאֲמֵלָלִים ?
עָלָה עָשָׁן בְּאַפּוֹ וְאֵשׁ מִפִּיו תֹּאכֵל גֶּחָלִים.

You forbade the uncircumcised to offer
You even rams. Then why did You
hide Your face when they ravaged the
holy people, the feeble Jews, who put
their trust in You? *Smoke rose from His
nostrils, devouring fire came out of His
mouth, and glowing coals.*

יָשִׂימוּ קְטוֹרָה בְּמִזְבֵּחַ זָהָב מְעֻבָּה.
עוֹרֵנוּ אֵל יֶחְסַר בֶּאֱמוּנָה רַבָּה.
קְנוּיִים בְּדִבְרֵי אֵשׁ, אֵיךְ נִתְלַבָּה
בֵּית־יַעֲקֹב אֵשׁ וּבֵית־יוֹסֵף לֶהָבָה ?

We offer You thick clouds of incense
[as if] on a golden altar.[2] Our skin is
always ready for the sacrifice, so great
is our faith in You. You made us Your
own with words of fire; how could You
let us be seized by fire? [You promised
that] *the house of Jacob would be fire, the
house of Joseph flame [and the house of
Esau chaff].*[3]

אֱלִיעֶזֶר בַּר־יְהוּדָה

Eliezer bar Judah of Worms

אֲסַפֵּר מַעֲשֵׂה בֶּלֶּט

THE MURDER OF BELLET
AND HANNAH

[...] אֲסַפֵּר מַעֲשֵׂה בֶּלֶּט, בִּתִּי הַגְּדוֹלָה :
בַּת שְׁלוֹשׁ־עֶשְׂרֵה שָׁנָה הָיְתָה, צְנוּעָה כַּכַּלָּה.
לָמְדָה כָּל הַתְּפִלּוֹת וְהַזְּמִירוֹת מֵאִמָּהּ,
צְנוּעָה וַחֲסִידָה וּנְעִימָה וַחֲכָמָה.
עָשְׂתָה מַעֲשֵׂה אִמָּהּ יָפָה הַבְּתוּלָה,

Let me tell the story of my eldest
daughter, Bellet: She was thirteen
years old, and as chaste as a bride. She
had learnt all the prayers and songs
from her mother, who was modest and
kind, sweet[4] and wise. The girl took
after her beautiful mother and every

---

1. In the Temple of the Celestial Jerusalem.
2. Exodus 40.5   3. Obadiah 18.   4. The mother's name was Dolce ('sweet').

מַצַּעַת מִטָּתִי וְחוֹלֶצֶת מִנְעָלַי בְּכָל לַיְלָה.

זְרִיזָה בַּבַּיִת בֶּלֶט, וּמְדַבֶּרֶת רַק אֱמֶת,

עוֹבֶדֶת בּוֹרְאָהּ וְטוֹוָה וְתוֹפֶרֶת וּמְרַקֶּמֶת.

רְצוּפָה בְּיִרְאָה, בְּאַהֲבַת יוֹצְרָהּ בְּלִי דֹפִי,

כַּוָּנָתָהּ לַשָּׁמַיִם וְיָשְׁבָה לִשְׁמֹעַ תּוֹרָה מִפִּי.

וְנֶהֶרְגָה עִם אִמָּהּ וְעִם אֲחוֹתָהּ בְּלֵיל כָּף בֵּית בְּסְלֵו,

בִּהְיוֹתִי יוֹשֵׁב עַל שֻׁלְחָנִי שָׁלֵו.

בָּאוּ שְׁנַיִם מְתוֹעָבִים וַהֲרָגוּם לְעֵינַי,

וּפְצָעוּנִי, וְתַלְמִידַי וְגַם בְּנִי.

night she would make my bed and take off my shoes. She did her housework quickly, and always spoke the truth. She worshipped her Maker, she weaved and sewed and embroidered [in His Honour], she was filled with reverence and pure love for her Creator. For the sake of Heaven, she sat down by me to hear my teaching. And that is when she and her mother and her sister were killed, on the night of the twenty-second of *Kislev*, as I was sitting peacefully at my table. Two wicked men broke in and killed them before my eyes; they also wounded me, and my students, and my son.

אֲסַפֵּר מַעֲשֵׂה בִּתִּי הַקְּטַנָּה:

קָרְאָה קְרִיאַת־שְׁמַע בְּכָל יוֹם פָּרָשָׁה רִאשׁוֹנָה.

בַּת שָׁנִים שֵׁשׁ הָיְתָה, וְטוֹוָה וְתוֹפֶרֶת

וּמְרַקֶּמֶת וּמְשַׁעֲשַׁעַת אוֹתִי וּמְזַמֶּרֶת. [...]

Now let me tell the story of my younger daughter [Hannah]: every day she would recite the first portion of the *Shema*.[1] She was six years old, and she knew to weave and sew and embroider, and to delight me with her singing.

אוֹי לִי עַל אִשְׁתִּי הַחֲסוּדָה,

אוֹי לִי עַל בָּנַי וּבְנוֹתַי, אֶנוּדָה!

נֶאֱמָן עָלַי הַדַּיָּן אֲשֶׁר דַּנַּנִי,

בְּחַטָּאתִי וּבְפִשְׁעִי הִכְנִיעַנִי.

לְךָ יְיָ הַצְּדָקָה וְלִי בֹּשֶׁת הַפָּנִים,

יְיָ הַצַּדִּיק וְלִי הָעֲווֹנוֹת וְהַזְּדוֹנִים.

לְךָ אֲבָרֵךְ בְּכָל מִדָּה, שִׁיר אֲחַוֶּה,

לְךָ אֶכְרַע וְאֶשְׁתַּחֲוֶה.

O my lovely wife! O my sons and daughters! I weep for them. I put my trust in the Judge who decreed my sentence; He has crushed me for my crimes. O Lord, the right is on Your side, the shame belongs to me. No matter how You treat me, I shall bless You and sing in Your honour; and I shall bow down before You.

---

1. A morning and evening prayer, composed of three biblical portions.

יְהוּדָה אַלְחֲרִיזִי   *Judah Al-Ḥarizi*

וְהַבָּרָק   THE LIGHTNING

וְהַבָּרָק מְשַׂחֵק עַל עֲנָנִים
כְּגִבּוֹר רָץ וְלֹא יִיעַף וְיִיגַע.
כְּשׁוֹמֵר לֵיל אֲשֶׁר נִרְדַּם וְיִפְקַח
קְצָת עֵינוֹ וְתִסָּגֵר כְּרָגַע.

And the lightning laughs at the clouds,
like a warrior who runs without growing
weary or faint. Or like a night watchman who dozes off, then opens one eye
for an instant, and shuts it.

רְאוּ שֶׁמֶשׁ   THE SUN

רְאוּ שֶׁמֶשׁ אֲשֶׁר יִפְרֹשׂ כְּנָפָיו
עֲלֵי אֶרֶץ לְהָאִיר אֶת נְשָׁפָיו.
כְּעֵץ רַעֲנָן אֲשֶׁר צָמַח בְּשַׁחַק
וְהִגִּיעוּ עֲדֵי אֶרֶץ עֲנָפָיו.

Look: the sun has spread its wings over
the earth to dispel the darkness. Like a
great tree, with its roots in heaven, and
its branches reaching down to the earth.

רְאוּ כִּנּוֹר   THE LUTE

רְאוּ כִּנּוֹר בְּחֵיק צַלְמָה יְרַגֵּן
וְיִמְשֹׁךְ לֵב בְּהוֹד קוֹלוֹ וְצִבְיוֹ.
כְּמוֹ יוֹנֵק בְּחֵיק אִמּוֹ מְבַכֶּה
וְהִיא תָשִׁיר וְצוֹחֶקֶת לְבִכְיוֹ.

Look: the lute sounds in the girl's arms,
delighting the heart with its beautiful
voice. Like a baby crying in his mother's
arms, while she sings and laughs as he
cries.

לְהַכְנִיס אוֹרְחִים   THE YOKEL'S SPEECH OF
WELCOME

לְהַכְנִיס אוֹרְחִים יִמְתַּק לְחִכִּי
כְּמִיץ חָלָב בְּחֶמְאַת הַבְּקָרִים

Hospitality is as sweet to my taste as
milk wrung out of cattle-curds; or as

וְכַפְּתִּים בְּתוֹךְ חֶמְאָה שְׁרוּיִים
בְּעֵת כִּי יִצָּבְרוּ אוֹתָם חֲמָרִים.
וְעֵת קוֹל אוֹרְחִים אֶשְׁמַע חֲצוֹת לֵיל,
לְבָנַי אֶקְרָאָה 'פִּתְחוּ שְׁעָרִים!'
וְשָׂמַחְתִּי בְאוֹרֵחַ כְּשִׂמְחַת
זְאֵב גָּנַב גְּדִי מִן הָעֲדָרִים.
וְכָל יוֹם אֶחֱרֹשׁ אַדְמַת נְדָבוֹת
כְּחוֹרֵשׁ הָאֲדָמָה בַּבְּקָרִים.
וְיִיטַב לִי עֲשׂוֹת חֶסֶד, כְּרָעֵב
בְּמָצְאוֹ פַת יְבֵשָׁה עִם חֲצִירִים.
וְעֵינַי לַחֲזוֹת אוֹרְחִים תְּקַוֶּה
כְּעֵינֵי הַחֲמוֹרִים לַשְּׂעוֹרִים!

breadcrumbs soaked in cream, piled up
in countless heaps. When I hear the
voices of guests at midnight, I call out
to my sons: 'Throw open the gates!'
Guests make me as happy as a wolf that
has filched a kid from the flock. And
every day, like a ploughman with his
oxen, I turn over the clods of my
bounty. I delight in doing favours, as a
hungry man delights in finding a dry
crust and a clump of grass. My eyes
long to see guests, as the eyes of asses
long for barley.

מְיֻדָּעַי וְרֵעַי

THE COCK'S ORATION

מְיֻדָּעַי וְרֵעַי, רַחֲמוּנִי
וְעַל גֹּדֶל יְגוֹנִי נַחֲמוּנִי!
הֲכָזֶה יִהְיֶה תַּגְמוּל אֱמוּנִים,
אֲשֶׁר עַל טוֹב בְּרָעָה יִגְמְלוּנִי?
יְדִידִים שָׁכְחוּ חֶסֶד גְּמַלְתִּים,
וְהֵם תָּמִיד לְהָרְגִי יִדְרְשׁוּנִי.
אֲנִי אֶרְדֹּף שְׁלוֹמוֹתָם וְטוּבָם
וְתַחַת אַהֲבָתִי יִשְׂטְנוּנִי,
וְתָמִיד אֶשְׁמְעָה עָלַי עֲצָתָם
וְכָל הַיּוֹם כְּלוֹחֵם יִלְחָצוּנִי.
וְקִדַּמְתִּים בְּבָנִים גַּם בְּבָנוֹת —
וְהֵם בַּמַּאֲכָלוֹת קִדְּמוּנִי,
וְהֶאֱכַלְתִּים בְּשַׂר בָּנַי — וְהֵמָּה
מְבַקְשִׁים תֹּאֲנָה עַד יֹאכְלוּנִי.

Friends, companions, pity me! Comfort
me in my great misery! Shall this be
the reward of loyalty? Will they repay
good with evil? My loved ones have
forgotten all my acts of kindness. They
look continually for ways to kill me. I
seek their peace and well-being, but
they give me hatred for my love.
Constantly I hear them plot against
me; all day long my assailants harass
me. I came to meet them with sons as
well as daughters; they come to meet
me with slaughtering-knives. I fed them
the flesh of my children, but they seek
an occasion to feed upon me. I am old,

אֲנִי זָקֵן וְאֵין בָּשָׂר בְּגוּפִי,
וְלָמָּה־זֶּה לְאָכְלִי יַחְמְדוּנִי ?
רְדָפוּנִי בְּרִשְׁעוּתָם, וְאִלּוּ
אֲחָזוּנִי – כְּרֶגַע אִבְּדוּנִי !
אֲבָל הָאֵל עֲזָרַנִי בְּחַסְדּוֹ,
וְנִמְלַטְתִּי בְּעֵת כִּי בִקְּשׁוּנִי.
וְלוּלֵא צוּר כְּתָבַנִי לְחַיִּים,
לְהָרְגִי נִקְבְּצוּ וַיִּשְׁחַטוּנִי,
וְנָשַׁי גֵּרְשׁוּ מִבֵּין זְרוֹעַי,
וּמֵעַל תַּרְנְגוֹלַי רִחֲקוּנִי.

there is hardly any flesh on my body –
why then do they long to eat me? They
hunted me with malice; if they had
caught me, they would have wiped me
out in a flash. But the Lord, in His
never-failing love, came to my aid, and
I escaped when they were chasing me.
If the Rock had not inscribed me in the
book of life, they would have gathered
together to slaughter me. They would
have torn my wives out of my arms and
driven me far from my chicks.

הַמִּשֵּׁדִים וְזִקִים

TO HIS BEDMATE

הַמִּשֵּׁדִים וְזִקִים אַתְּ גְּזוּרָה ?
יִשְׁלַח בָּךְ אֱלֹהִים הַמְּאֵרָה !
כְּאִלּוּ מַלְאֲכֵי זַעַם וּמַשְׁחִית
לְאַחִים לָךְ – אֲבָל לָךְ הַבְּכוֹרָה.
כְּאִלּוּ תָאֲרֵךְ כִּשְׂעִיר עֲזָאזֵל –
וְאֵיךְ נִמְלַטְתְּ מֵאֶרֶץ גְּזֵרָה ?
כְּאִלּוּ הַזְּמָן חָשַׁק בְּלִילִית
וּמֵאַהֲבָה שְׁלָחֵךְ לָהּ תְּשׁוּרָה.
וְיוֹצְרֵךְ לֹא יְצָרֵךְ רַק לְמַעַן
תְּהִי אֶל מַלְאֲכֵי מָוֶת לְעֶזְרָה.
וְאַשְׁרֵי יוֹלַדְךָ לוּ מֵת בְּלֵדְתֵּךְ –
וּמִי יִתֵּן תְּהִי אִמֵּךְ עֲקָרָה !
שְׂפָתַיִךְ כְּמוֹ שִׂפְתֵי שְׁוָרִים,
וּפִיךְ – קֶבֶר, אֲבָל בִּטְנֵךְ – מְעָרָה.
וְשִׁנַּיִךְ כְּשִׁנֵּי דֹב זְהוּמוֹת
וּבָם צוֹאָה וְרִיר כִּמְלוֹא קְעָרָה,

Were you compounded of demons and
fiends? May the Lord lay a curse upon
you! Angels of rage and destruction
seem to have been your brothers, but
you were the first born. Your face is
like that of the desert-demon's goat;[1]
how, then, did you escape from the
barren waste? Time, it would seem,
lusted for Lilith and sent you to her as
a token of love. It is as if your Maker
manufactured you only to be a help-
mate for the angels of death. Your
father would have counted it a blessing
had he died at your birth. If only your
mother had been barren! Your lips are
like the lips of oxen; your maw is a
tomb; and, what is more, your belly is
a cave. Your teeth are as evil-smelling
as the teeth of a bear, as full of filth and
spittle as a bowl. Your eyes are as

---

1. The 'goat for Azazel', the scape-goat (Leviticus 16.8 ff).

וְעֵינֶיךָ כְּמוֹ כִירָה עֲשֵׁנִים,
וּפָנֶיךָ כְּמוֹ שׁוּלֵי קְדֵרָה,
וְקוֹמָתֶךָ כְּעֵץ הָמָן גְּבֹהָה –
וּמִי יִתֵּן וְאֶרְאֶךָ בּוֹ מְהֵרָה! [...]

smoky as a stove and your face as black
as the bottom of a pot. You are as tall
as a gallows – if only I could see you
swinging from it soon!

אֱלֹהִים יַהֲפֹךְ רֹאשְׁךָ בְּשַׁחַת
כְּמַהְפֵּכַת סְדֹמָה וַעֲמֹרָה,
וְתַכְרִיכֶךָ יְשַׁו בְּטְנֵי אֲרָיוֹת
וְיָשִׂים לָךְ בְּתוֹךְ קִרְבָּם קְבוּרָה!

May God turn you upside down –
overturned like Sodom and Gomorrah –
with your head in hell. May He give
you the stomachs of lions for shrouds
and their entrails for a resting-place!

שְׁאֵלוּנִי עַל הַנְּדָבָה

THE GENEROUS MAN

שְׁאֵלוּנִי עַל הַנְּדָבָה וּשְׁלֹמֹה.
עֲנִיתִים: הִיא וָהוּא כְּאֵשׁ עִם נוֹזְלֵי עָב.
לְשׁוֹן כּוֹסוֹ דָבַק לְחִכּוֹ בַצָּמָא,
וְשִׂפְתֵי שֻׁלְחָנוֹ עֲטוּפִים בָּרָעָב.
לְהָסֵךְ מֵי רַגְלָיו מְפַחֵד פֶּן יִצְמָא,
וְכֵן יִרָא לִבְדֹּק נְקָבָיו פֶּן יִרְעָב.

I was asked for my opinion of Solomon's
generosity. And this was my answer:
He and it are like fire with rain-water.
The tongue of his goblet is dumb with
thirst,[1] and the lips of his table are
faint with hunger. He is afraid to pass
water, lest he should thirst; and he
dares not relieve himself, lest he should
hunger.

מֵאִיר הַלֵּוִי אַבּוּלְעָאפִיָּה

Meir Halevi Abulafia

שְׂאוּ עָבִים

A LETTER FROM THE GRAVE

ולו כשמחתה אחותו, האל ירצה אותה, ביום השבת
י"ד בכסלו שנת ד' תקע"ג, וכתב אל אביו
להודיע אותו ולנחמו על לשונה:

*He wrote this when his sister – may God
delight in her – died on the Sabbath of
10 November 1212; he wrote to his
father, in the name of his sister, to inform
him and to bring him comfort.*

---

1. Lit. 'clings to the roof of its mouth'.

שְׂאוּ, עָבִים, שְׁלוֹם קִבְרִי לְאָבִי,
וְלֹא מִפִּי, אֲבָל מִפִּי כְתָבִי,
וְקִרְאוּ לוֹ בְּשִׂפְתֵי קוֹרְאוֹתַי
אֲשֶׁר קָרְאוּ לְשִׂפְתוֹתַי וְנִיבִי.
וְגוּרוּ, פֶּן יְצִיקוּהוּ מְצוּקַי,
וְיִתְעַצֵּב לְגֹדֶל מַעֲצָבִי.
וּמַה בֶּצַע בְּמַעְצָבוֹ לְעָצְבִּי,
וּבִכְאֵבוֹ – הֲיַחְשֹׁךְ כְּאֵבִי?
הֲטוֹב כִּי תִקְרְעוּ בַעֲדִי כְּרֶגַע
סְגוֹר לִבּוֹ? וְחָטָאתִי לְאָבִי,
אֲשֶׁר כַּנְפֵי חֲסָדָיו שָׁת יְצוּעִי
וְנָתַן צַוְּארֵי רַחֲמָיו רְכוּבִי.
וְזָרַחְתִּי כְּשֶׁמֶשׁ מִמְּעוֹנָיו,
וְהִנֵּה בָאֲבַדּוֹן מַעֲרָבִי. [...]

O clouds, bear these greetings to my father from my grave, in words not spoken but written. Tell him, with the dumb lips of my disaster, what has become of my lips and my voice. But take care that my distress should not overwhelm him, that my great sorrow should not oppress him. What good would it do to oppress him with my sorrow? Would his pain spare me mine? Would it be right to tear open his heart because of me? No, I would be wronging my father, whose loving wings were my bed, whose compassionate shoulders were my chariot. Once I shone like a sun in his house, but now I have set in the abyss.

שְׁעוּ מִנִּי, עֲדֵי מָה תִּקְרְאוּ לִי?
דְּעוּ כִּי יַד אֱלוֹהַּ נָגְעָה בִּי,
וּמָוֶת מֵחֲדַר אַלּוּף נְעוּרַי
כְּרֶגַע הֵן טְרָפַנִי כְּלָבִיא.
וְסָר מֶנְהוּ עֲדֵי עַד בִּטְחוֹנִי,
וְהִשְׁלַכְתִּי עֲלֵי קִבְרִי יְהָבִי.
וְכִסּוּ קוֹבְרַי פָּנַי בְּעָפָר
אֲשֶׁר הָיָה תְמוֹל מִדְרַךְ עֲקֵבִי.
וְאֶמְשֹׁךְ כָּל אֱנוֹשׁ אַחְרַי, וְיַחַד
יְבוֹאוּנִי מְתֵי חִשְׁקִי וְרִיבִי:
וְאֵל קָרָא לְבֵית מוֹעֵד לְכָל חַי,
וְיַחַד יִגְוְעוּ חוֹטֵא וְנָבִיא,
עֲדֵי יָשִׁיב נְשָׁמוֹת לַפְּגָרִים –
וְאָז אֶרְאֶה פְּנֵיכֶם עוֹד בְּשׁוּבִי.

Turn away from me [my friends]! How much longer will you call to me? Know that the hand of God has touched me. Death, like a ravening lion, tore me out of the room of my beloved. No longer can I cast my fortunes on the dear friend of my youth; now I must commit my fortunes to the grave. They buried me, covering my face with the very dust which only yesterday I trampled underfoot. But I shall draw all men after me; both my loved ones and my rivals will join me. God summons all mortals to the house of the dead. Sinner and prophet perish alike. Until [the day of resurrection, when] He restores all souls to their bodies. Then shall I come into your presence again.

וְאִם הִכְאִיב בְּמַכְאוּבֵי לְבַבְכֶם,
אֲשֶׁר הָיָה בְּאָמְנָה עִם לְבָבִי,
וְהֵצִיף יָם דְּמָעוֹת עַל פְּנֵיכֶם
וּמַבּוּל הַבְּכִי אָמַר לְהָבִיא —
יָרוּ קִבְרִי בְּטַל אוֹרוֹת, וְעֵת
לְצוּלַת דִּמְעֲכֶם יֹאמַר: 'חֲרָבִי!'

(1212)

Though He has made your heart – my
heart's guardian – share my grief,
though He has made a sea of tears flow
over you and almost flooded you with
weeping, He will now fill my grave
with His dew of sparkling light, He
will say to your welling tears: 'Subside
and dry!'

מֹשֶׁה בֶּן-נַחְמָן

Nahmanides

מֵרֹאשׁ מִקַּדְמֵי עוֹלָמִים

HYMN ON THE FATE OF
THE SOUL

מֵרֹאשׁ מִקַּדְמֵי עוֹלָמִים
נִמְצֵאתִי בְּמִכְמַנָּיו הַחֲתוּמִים.
מֵאַיִן הִמְצִיאַנִי, וּלְקֵץ יָמִים
נִשְׁאַלְתִּי מִן הַמֶּלֶךְ.

[The Soul:] From the very beginning,
before times long past, I was stored
among His hidden treasures. He had
brought me forth from Nothing, but at
the end of time *I shall be summoned
back before the King.*

שַׁלְשֶׁלֶת חַיַּי מִיסּוֹד הַמַּעֲרָכָה,
לִמְשֹׁךְ תַּבְנִית בְּתַמוּנָה עֲרוּכָה,
לְשִׁקֵל עַל יְדֵי עוֹשֵׂי הַמְּלָאכָה,
לְהָבִיא אֶל גִּנְזֵי הַמֶּלֶךְ.

My life flowed out of the depth of the
spheres which gave me form and order.
Divine forces shaped me *to be treasured
in the chambers of the King.*

הוֹפִיעַ לְגַלּוֹת אֲשֶׁר הִטְמִין.
הֵן מִשְּׂמֹאל הֶגְלָה וּמֵהַיָּמִין
מִמַּעֲלוֹת הַיּוֹרְדוֹת מִן
בְּרֵכַת הַשֶּׁלַח לְגַן הַמֶּלֶךְ.

Then He appeared to bring me out of
hiding. He drove me out, from all sides,
made me descend the steps leading
down from *the Pool of Shelah to the
garden of the King.*[1]

---

1. I.e. from heaven to earth. The stanza may also be understood as follows: 'Then he shined His light
to bring her [the soul] forth in hidden well-springs, on the left and on the right. He made her descend, etc.'

בְּעָצָר רַקְמְתִּי, וְאִם רוּחַךְ בִּי נָשׁוּב.
בַּנֹּפַ לְרֵעִי, כְּגֵר בָּאָרֶץ אֶהְיֶה חָשׁוּב.
'עַד מָתַי יִהְיֶה מַהֲלָכְךָ וּמָתַי תָּשׁוּב
וַיִּיטַב לִפְנֵי הַמֶּלֶךְ ?'

[Man:] I was moulded in dust, though
Your spirit breathes in me. How well
You know me. I am no more than a
stranger in this land. 'How long will
your journey last? When will you turn
back *and merit the approval of your
King?*'

גֵּר לְרַגְלִי שַׂמְתְּ וְלִנְתִיבָתִי,
תְּחַפֵּשׂ כָּל חַדְרֵי בֶטֶן בְּרוּחַ נְדִיבָתִי,
וּבְצֵאתִי מִלְּפָנֶיךָ הִזְהַרְתָּ אוֹתִי :
יְרָא אֶת יְיָ, בְּנִי, וָמֶלֶךְ !

You gave her to me as a lamp to light
my way. With my willing soul You
search out my inmost being. When I
took my leave of You, You warned me:
'Child, fear the Lord your King!'

נָתַתָּ בְּיָדִי לֵב מֹאזְנֵי מִשְׁפָּט וָפֶלֶס.
אִם לְחֶסֶד יַמְצִיאֵנִי – בּוֹ אֶתְעַלֵּס,
וְאִם לְרָעָה – יִהְיֶה לַעַג וָקֶלֶס,
כִּי לֹא הָיְתָה מֵהַמֶּלֶךְ.

You armed my heart with balances and
scales. If it moves me to goodness I
delight in it, but if it moves me to evil
I earn contempt and scorn. *This
[choice] is not determined by the King.*

חָגוּר חֲרָדוֹת לְהוֹדוֹת פְּשָׁעַי אָחִישׁ
בְּטֶרֶם לְבֵית מוֹעֵד כְּבוֹדִי גֵז חִישׁ.
שָׁם פִּי בְּפָנַי יַעֲנֶה – וּמִי יַכְחִישׁ
אֶת אִגְּרוֹת הַמֶּלֶךְ ? [...]

Covered with trembling, I rush to
confess my sins before I and my honour
vanish into the grave. There my own
signature will testify against me, for
who can deny *the indictment in the
hands of the King?*

נִסְמַכְתִּי עָלֶיךָ וְלֹא לְמַעֲשַׂי אֶפְנֶה,
כִּי אָמַרְתִּי : עוֹלָם חֶסֶד יִבָּנֶה.
בְּטֶרֶם אֶקְרָא הֲלֹא תַעֲנֶה,
כִּי בֹשְׁתִּי לִשְׁאֹל מִן הַמֶּלֶךְ.

I put my trust in You, not in my own
deeds, for I know that Your world is
built on charity. Before I call to You,
*will You not answer? I am ashamed to
entreat the King.*

דְּרָכֶיךָ יְנַחֲמוּנִי, כִּי שְׁמַעְתִּי עֲווֹנוֹת תִּכְבַּשׁ.
וּבְךָ חָסָיָה נַפְשִׁי וְלֹא תֵבוֹשׁ,
כִּי הַגּוּף בַּמַּסְגֵּר תִּכְבַּשׁ,
וְהִיא – בְּהֵיכְלֵי מֶלֶךְ !

Your ways are my comfort. I know You
will tread my guilt underfoot. My soul
takes refuge in You; she shall not be
shamed. For You press the body into
the grave's prison, *but she dwells on in
the palaces of the King.*

יוֹדַעַת אָז : בַּשַּׁחַת אוֹתִי תִטְבֹּל,
הֲלֹא אִם שַׂלְמָתָהּ חָבֹל תַּחְבֹּל —
תְּשִׁיבֶנּוּ לָהּ אַחֲרֵי תִסְבֹּל
הַמִּשְׁפָּט אֲשֶׁר שָׁפַט הַמֶּלֶךְ.

And she knows: though You plunge
me into the pit, though You take her
cloak [the body] as a pledge, You will
clothe her again once she has suffered
the sentence decreed by the King.

חַזֵּק יַד חַלּוּשָׁה וְתֵשֵׁב לָהּ בְּאֵיתָן.
וּבְעֵת יָשׁוּבוּ הַדְּבָרִים לַהֲוָיָתָן
תְּשַׁנֶּה לְטוֹב מִגְּנַת הַבִּיתָן
הַפַּרְדֵּס אֲשֶׁר לַמֶּלֶךְ.

Strengthen the feeble one, let her stand
firm. And when all things return to
their primal state, make her pure, as
she rejoins the royal pavilion in the
orchard of the King.

דָּוִיד הַכֹּהֵן   *David Hakohen*

הִשְׁתַּחֲוִי וּבָרְכִי   SILENCE AND PRAISE

הִשְׁתַּחֲוִי וּבָרְכִי לִפְנֵי צוּר מָעֻזִּי,
וּתְהַלְלִי וּבָרְכִי, נַפְשִׁי, אֶת אֲדֹנָי!

Bow down, my soul, and kneel before
my rock of refuge; praise the Lord and
bless Him!

דַּלּוּ מְאֹד שְׂפָתַי מִדֵּי מַהֲלָלָיו,
לֹא רַב סְפָר שְׁנוֹתַי מִמִּסְפַּר חֲיָלָיו,
אֵין דַּי בְּרֹב יְמוֹתַי סַפֵּר הוֹד פְּעָלָיו —
אָמְנָם בְּרָן וּבְבֶכִי — מְמַסַּךְ רַעְיוֹנִי —
צוּר שַׁחֲרִי, וְחֵלְכִי לִדְרֹשׁ אֶת אֲדֹנָי.

My lips are too low to sing His high
praises. My years are too few to recite
His glorious works. All my days would
not suffice to tell His mighty deeds.
Therefore, with song and tears, my
mind's libation, seek the Rock, look
eagerly for the Lord.

וּבְעֵת תְּהוֹם אֲרָחָיו יֵרֵד רַעְיוֹנִי,
וּבַחֲגוֹג שְׁמֵי שְׁבָחָיו יִתְהַלֵּךְ לְשׁוֹנִי,
מְלַהֲטֵי שְׁלָחָיו סַגְרִירִים בְּעֵינִי.
מִתְהַפְּכִים בְּהָפְכִי אֶל אַחֲרֵי תְבוּנִי,
בַּל אֶמְצָאָה, בְּעָרְכִי, דֵּעָה אֶת אֲדֹנָי.

When my mind tries to fathom the
abyss of His ways and my words move
on the vault of His heavenly praise, I
am struck blind by His flashing swords.
They turn over and over as I turn
beyond the limits of my reason. My
thoughts cannot attain the knowledge
of the Lord.

יַעֲמֹד – וְרֹדְפִים לֹא יַשִׂיגוּ כְבֹדוֹ,
כִּי יַחֲשִׁיךְ בְּהִלּוֹ מֵהַבִּיט בְּהוֹדוֹ.
כָּל הוֹד וְכָל יָקָר לוֹ, יִתְבָּרֵךְ בְּיָדוֹ:
מִי הוּא אֲנִי וּמִי, כִּי אַרְבֶּה־לּוֹ רְנָנִי?
אֶחְשֹׁךְ, הֲכִי בְחָשְׁכִי אוֹדֶה אֶת אֲדֹנָי.

Though He stand still, no pursuer can
overtake His glory. His light casts
darkness: you cannot see His splendour. All majesty, all precious things
are His, and blessed in His hands.
Then who am I and what am I to
burden Him with innumerable songs?
I shall be silent, and by my silence shall
thank the Lord.

דּוּמָם אֲנִי מְחַוֶּה כִּי לוֹ הַגְּדֻלָּה.
כִּי אַחֲרִישׁ מְקַוֶּה – וְאֶהְיֶה לְמָלָה,
אוֹחִיל עֲדֵי יְצַוֶּה עָלַי צוּר גְּאֻלָּה.
אֶתְפָּאֲרָה בְּמָשְׁכִי עֹל חֻקֵּי אֱמוּנִי
עִם עֹל עַל שִׁבְיִי, בְּתָמְכִי אֶת אַהֲבַת אֲדֹנָי.

Mutely, I proclaim that greatness is
His. I have become a byword for
hoping in dumb silence; yet I shall
wait until the Rock decrees my
redemption. I shall glory in wearing
both the yoke of His statutes[1] and the
yoke of exile, as I uphold the love of
the Lord.

כָּל מַחֲנוֹת כְּרוּבָיו בָּרְכוּ אֵל, וְלִשְׁמוֹ
הוֹדוּ בְּסוֹד אֲהוּבָיו, כָּל עֶצֶם לְעַצְמוֹ.
נוֹרָא בְּכָל סְבִיבָיו, אִישׁ לוֹ מִמְּקוֹמוֹ
הִשְׁתַּחֲווּ, בְּשָׁפְכִי שִׂיחִי תַחֲנוּנִי;
וּמְשָׁרְתָיו, בְּבָרְכִי נַפְשִׁי אֶת אֲדֹנָי,
[בָּרְכוּ אֶת אֲדֹנָי הַמְבֹרָךְ.]

Now bless God, all His hosts of
cherubs; let each one praise His name,
in the company of His loved ones. He
is terrible above the hosts who stand
about Him. Let each one, at his
station, bow down as I pour forth my
supplications. And when my soul
blesses the Lord, let His ministers too,
['bless the Lord who is blessed'].

יִצְחָק הַגָּרְנִי   *Isaac Hagorni*

לְחַשְׁקִי הִנְנִי   THE FATE OF THE
ADULTERER

לְחַשְׁקִי הִנְנִי הוֹלֵךְ לְתַנּוֹת,
וְקוֹל תֻּפִּי כְּבָר שָׁבַת לְעַנּוֹת.
פְּשָׁעַי מָנְעוּ הַטּוֹב, מְלִיצִי, –

I shall now lament my desires, the
silenced beat of my drum. Friends, my
own sins deprived me of favours, so

---

1. Lit. 'the yoke of the statutes of the loyal ones [of Israel]'.

וְכַמָּה לִי חֲטָאִים וַעֲוֹונוֹת!
לְאֵבְלִי נֶהֱפַךְ כִּנּוֹר מְחוֹלִי,
וְעוּגָבִי – לְקוֹל בּוֹכִים וְקִינוֹת,
כְּתֹם חִשְׁקִי וְאֶפֶס מַאֲוַיֵּי
וְיִכְלוּ מַתְּנוֹת הַחֵן וּמְנוֹת.

great were my offences. My merry harp was tuned to mourning and my flute to the sound of weeping and lament, when my desire died and my passion vanished, when the gracious gifts of love came to an end.

וְהַיּוֹם רַד וְנָסוּ הַצְּלָלִים
וְאֵין רוּחַ מְרַחֶפֶת בְּגַנּוֹת,
וְאֵימָתָה בְּלִבִּי מִתְּמוּתָה –
וּמַה שִּׂבְרִי כְּצָעִיר בֶּן אֲתוֹנוֹת?
וְחִשְׁקִי מוֹסָדוֹת תֵּבֵל יְלַהֵט,
וְתִשְׁכְּנָה עֲלֵי קִבְרִי עֲנָנוֹת.
וְאִם אָמוּת וְעוֹדֶנִּי בְּעַלְמוּת,
וְאִתִּי יֵרְדוּ לִשְׁאוֹל תְּלֻנּוֹת.

The day was far gone, the shadows had fled, no wind stirred in the gardens. And my heart was filled with a sudden dread of death – what hope is there for an ass like me? Oh, my passion will set fire to the earth's foundations, clouds will hover above my grave. And if I should die while still young, my complaints will accompany me down into Sheol.

לְפָנִים אֶהְיֶה רוֹדֵף חֲשָׁקִים
וְנִמְשַׁלְתִּי כְּתֹפֶת בַּמְּדִינוֹת –
וְעַתָּה נֶהֶפְכוּ עָלַי לְמַשְׁחִית
אֲהָבִים נֶעֶדְרוּ בָהֶם אֱמוּנוֹת.
וּמֵרָחָק, לְכָל רוֹכֵל יְבִיאוּן
עֲפַר קִבְרִי לְתַמְרוּקֵי עֲדִינוֹת,
וּמִקַּרְשֵׁי אֲרוֹנִי לַעֲקָרוֹת –
אֲזַי תֵּלַדְנָה בָנִים וּבָנוֹת.
וְרִמָּתִי לְעָלֶג יְרַקְחוּנָה
וְאִלֵּם – לַהֲגוֹת שִׁבְעִים לְשׁוֹנוֹת.
וְשַׂעֲרוֹתַי – יְחֻדִּים עַל כְּלֵי שִׁיר –
וְיֵיטִיבוּ בְּאֵין נוֹגֵן נְגִינוֹת.
וְאַבְנֵטִי לְמַחְגֹּרֶת מְנָאֵף,
לְמַעַן יֶחְדַּל לִנְאֹף וְלִזְנוֹת.
וְכָל כְּלֵי כְּלֵי קֹדֶשׁ יְשִׂימוּן,

In days gone by I was a hunter, hot in pursuit of desires. In all the provinces, [my lust] was likened to [the fires of] hell. But all those loves that had no virtue to them have now turned against me and fearfully disfigured me. The dust of my grave will be sent to foreign merchants, to be blended in cosmetics for pleasure-loving girls. From the boards of my coffin [they will concoct powders] for barren women, to have them bring forth sons and daughters. Of my maggots they will compound ointments for stammerers and mutes, to make them speak seventy tongues. My hair will serve as strings in musical instruments, which will then play sweetly even without a player. My sash will be made into a loincloth for the adulterer, to put a stop to his fornicating and whoring. And all my belongings will be declared holy relics,

וְשַׂלְמוֹתַי לְמִשְׁמֶרֶת צְפוּנוֹת.
וּמִי יָדֵק לְעָפָר אֶת עֲצָמַי
בְּטֶרֶם יַעֲשׂוּן אוֹתָם תְּמוּנוֹת?

and my clothes will be treasured as
keepsakes. Oh, who will grind my bones
as fine as dust before they are turned
into icons?

אֲמָרַי יִתְּנוּ חָכְמָה לְפָתִי,
וְלַנַּעַר וְלַנָּבֹן – תְּבוּנוֹת!

May my words endow the fool with
wisdom, and the young and wise with
understanding!

עִיר אַרְלְדִי   GORNI PLEADS HIS CAUSE

עִיר אַרְלְדִי – עִיר עֹז לְמִיּוֹם נוֹסָדָה,
וּבְמִשְׁפָּחוֹת אַנְשֵׁי מְלוּכָה נִכְבְּדָה,
עִיר אֵם בְּיִשְׂרָאֵל, בְּצָרוֹת נִקְרָאָה
מִשְׂגָּב לְעִתּוֹת, בַּפְּרָצִים עָמְדָה!
בַּצֵּר לְגָרְנִי יוֹשְׁבֶיהָ קָדְשׁוּ
צוֹמוֹת, כְּיוֹם הָעִיר אַרִיאֵל נִלְכְּדָה –
אוּלָם מְצַעֵק עַל קְצִינֶיהָ אֲנִי,
הָאוֹמְרִים: נַפְשִׁי עֲדִינוֹת חָמְדָה!
וַאֲנִי מְאַסְתִּין, אַף גְּעַלְתִּין מֵרְאוֹת:
אִם בַּחֲלוֹם אֶרְאֵם – שְׁנָתִי נָדְדָה,
אִם בַּדְּרָכִים אֶפְגְּשֵׁם – קַל אֶעֱבֹר,
לוּ אַחֲרַי אַבִּיט – לְגַל אֶתְעַתְּדָה.
קִרְאוּ שְׁמִי פֶלֶג – בְּיָמַי נִפְלְגָה
חֶבְרַת בְּנוֹת עַמִּים וּמִנִּי נִפְרָדָה.

From its very first day, the city of
Arles was known as a city of strength
and was honoured as the seat of
[David's] royal kin. A mother city[1] in
Israel, it was famed as a stronghold in
times of need; it stood in the breach.
And when Gorni found himself in
distress, its citizens proclaimed a
solemn fast, as if for the fall of the city
of Ariel [Jerusalem]. But the rulers of
Arles – against them I shall cry out, for
they claim that my soul lusts for the
lovely ladies! And in truth, I spurn
them, I abhor the very sight of them.
If I see them in my dream, sleep
deserts me. If I meet them in the
street, I quickly step aside. If ever I
did look behind me [at a woman], may
I be turned into a heap of rubble![2]
Call me Peleg [Division], for in my
time womankind was divided and all

---

1. Arles was formerly the capital of Provence.
2. Like Lot's wife, who was turned into a pillar of salt (Genesis 19.26).

הֲלֹא יְמֵי דוֹדִים נְדוּדִים נֶהְפָּכוּ,
חִנָּם עֲלָמוֹת עוֹד וּבָנוֹת צָעֲדָה.
הַחֵן וְהַיֹּפִי כְּבָר הִתְנַכְּרוּ
עָלַי, וְתָמִיד בָּאֲהָבִים אֶמְרָדָה.
קֵרַח, בְּחֹם חִשְׁקִי בְּלֵילוֹת, יֶחֱשֹׁף
בִּגְדִי, וְשֶׁלֶג עַל עֲצָמַי יֵרָדָה.
לִבִּי כְּבָר נִשְׁבַּר, וְאֶתְחַבֵּר לְבַר
עִם זַךְ וְעִם חָסִיד וּבָם אֶתְחַסָּדָה.

withdrew from me. For days of loving
have turned into days of wandering. In
vain do the girls still parade [before
me]; I have estranged myself from
beauty and charm. I am in constant
revolt against love. In the heat of my
passion, at night, ice strips off my
clothes [and bares my shame], snow
comes down and covers my bones. My
heart has already been broken. I now
lead a pure life in the company of the
pure, the blameless, and the loyal; to
them I give my loyalty.

אַל תִּתְּנֵנִי, יָהּ, בְּיַד מִתְקוֹמֲמָי!
לָמָּה בְּיוֹם אָבְדִי מְלִיצָה אָבְדָה?
כִּי הִיא – בְּעוֹדִי חַי, וְאִתִּי אַחֲרֵי
בִּשְׁאוֹל וּבַחֹשֶׁךְ יְצוּעָהּ רִפֵּדָה.
אִם לָךְ לְבַדְּךָ הֶעֱוֵיתִי, מַחֲמַל
עַל מַחֲמַד שִׁירִי, וְלֹא אַשְׁמָדָה. [...]

Lord, do not hand me over to my
enemies! Why should Poetry perish on
the day I perish? For as long as I live,
she lives too. But once I have died, she
will follow me down to Sheol and there
spread her couch in the darkness. If I
have sinned against You only, have
mercy on my precious song; do not let
them destroy me!

מֹשֶׁה בֶּן-יוֹסֵף

Moses ben Joseph

אָזְנוּ יְצוּרַי אֵלַי

BODY AND SOUL DISPUTE

אָזְנוּ יְצוּרַי אֵלַי,
רְפוּ, הוֹדוּ רִשְׁעַתְכֶם.
אֲחַלֶּה פְּנֵי אֵל, אוּלַי
אֲכַפְּרָה בְּעַד חַטַּאתְכֶם,

Listen to me, my limbs. Leave off your
wickedness, confess it. Perhaps *I may
win forgiveness for your sin,*

בְּטֶרֶם תִּתַּךְ בָּכֶם
חֲמָתוֹ כְּאֵשׁ בּוֹעֶרֶת
וּבְטֶרֶם יַשְׁלִיכְכֶם
אֶל אֶרֶץ אַחֶרֶת.

before He pours out His wrath upon you like fire, before He casts you *into another region*.

גַּרְתִּי מְאֹד מִמַּעֲלָי,
וָאֹמַר: אָשׁוּבָה-לִי.
וְיִצְרִי קָם לְשָׂטָן לִי
וְהוּא יֹשֵׁב מִמֵּלִי.

I was terrified by my treachery, and I said: 'Let me now repent'. But my lust barred my way, *and still it camps before me*.

דָּמִי תּוֹךְ גְּוִיָּתִי
הָלוֹךְ וְחָסוֹר יֵלֵךְ
בַּיּוֹם אֲשֶׁר נִקְרֵאתִי
לָבוֹא אֶל הַמֶּלֶךְ.

The blood in my body will slowly recede on the day that I am summoned *to come before the King*.

הָהּ, שִׁחַתִּי דַרְכִּי,
וַעֲווֹנִי אֹהַבְנוּ.
וּמָה אֶעֱשֶׂה בְּקוּם אֵל, וְכִי
יִפְקֹד, מָה אֲשִׁיבֶנּוּ?

Oh, my ways are corrupt, and I love my crimes. What shall I do when God appears? *When He questions me, what shall I answer?*

וְאָנָה אֲנִי בָא, זְקֵנִי,
וּלְמִי אָנוּס לְעֶזְרָה
לִפְנֵי בּוֹא יוֹם יְיָ
הַגָּדוֹל וְהַנּוֹרָא.

And where, my old limbs, can I go? To whom can I flee for help *before the great and terrible day when the Lord comes?*

זֹאת יִזְכֹּר יְמֵי עֲלוּמָיו,
לְבִלְתִּי יָרוּם לִבּוֹ:
אֱנוֹשׁ כְּחָצִיר יָמָיו
כִּי רוּחַ עָבְרָה בּוֹ.

To overcome his pride, let man remember in his youth that his days are like the grass; *a wind passes over it [and it is gone]*.

חֲבֵרָיו יוֹצִיאוּהוּ
מְחוּץ לָעִיר מְהֵרָה,
וּבְבוֹר יַשְׁלִיכוּהוּ
שָׁם אֶל אֶרֶץ גְּזֵרָה.

His friends rush him out of the city,
and cast him into a pit, *there in the
wilderness.*

טָמַן הַגּוּף וְנֶעְלָם,
רַגְלוֹ תְּעֻנֶּה בְכֶבֶל,
וְיָשַׁב שָׁם עַד עוֹלָם.
לֹא יֵצֵא בַּיּוֹבֵל.

The body is buried and disappears from
sight, a prisoner with fetters on his
feet. It will stay there always; *not even
the jubilee can set it free.*[1]

יוֹאֵל עוֹד וִיסַפַּח
בְּתָרִים, אֱלֹהִים חַיִּים,
וְיָשׁוּב בְּגָדְלוֹ וְיִפַּח
בְּאַפָּיו נִשְׁמַת חַיִּים.

May it please the living God to bind
the body's limbs together and, once
again, in His greatness, *to breathe into
its nostrils the breath of life.*

כֹּה יַעַן רָם בְּעָצְמָה:
'מַמְרִים, אֶת דְּבָרְתִי
מַה זֶּה בְזִיתֶם, וְלָמָּה
לֹא קִדַּשְׁתֶּם אוֹתִי?

The High One, the Mighty One will
say: 'Rebels, how have you dared to
flout My word, *why have you not
upheld My sanctity?*

לֹא דַי חֲרַשְׁתֶּם לֶאֱמֹר
לֶאֱהֹב אֶת תּוֹעֲבוֹתַי,
עוֹד מֵאַנְתֶּם לִשְׁמֹר
מִצְוֹתַי וְתוֹרֹתַי?'

'Not only have you conspired to love
what I loathe, but you have also
refused to obey *My commandments and
My teachings.*'

מֵשִׁיב הַגּוּף בְּאֵימָה:
'אֲנִי, צוּר, מֶה עָשִׂיתִי?
זַךְ אֲנִי מִפֶּשַׁע. מַה
פִּשְׁעִי וּמַה חַטָּאתִי?

Then the body, terrified, answers: 'My
Rock, what have I done? I am blameless.
What crime is mine and what offence?

---

1. Unlike the Hebrew slave, who is released in the period of the jubilee (*T.B. Kiddushin* 15a).

נְשָׁמָה אֲשֶׁר נָתַתָּה
עִמָּדִי – הִיא תְשַׁבֵּשׁ.
וּמֵאָז מֶנִּי לְקַחְתָּהּ
הֵן אֲנִי עֵץ יָבֵשׁ.

'It is the soul whom You assigned to me – she is the depraver. Look: ever since You took her from me *I am [as harmless as] a dried-up tree.*

סָתַתְנִי כְּאִוֶּלֶת
סֶמֶל לַעֲבֹד וְחֶרֶף.
שֵׁם קָדְשֶׁךָ מְחַלֶּלֶת –
הִיא בָּאֵשׁ תִּשָּׂרֵף !

'She wickedly enticed me to worship carved images and idols. It is she who desecrates Your holy name. *She should be destroyed by fire!'*

עוֹנָה נֶפֶשׁ אַחַר :
'הַגּוּף עוֹנֶה שָׂרָה.
אָנָּא, אַל נָא יִחַר
לַאדֹנָי וַאֲדַבֵּרָה.

To which the soul replies: 'The body bears false witness. *Do not be angry, Lord, if I speak:*

פֶּה אֶפְתַּח, וּמִלּוּלִי
בָּרוּר כִּי לֹא אֲכַנֶּה.
אֲדַבְּרָה וְיִרְוַח לִי,
אֶפְתַּח שְׂפָתַי וְאֶעֱנֶה.

'I am ready to answer. My words are sincere, I never use flattery. Let me speak to find relief, *I must open my mouth and answer.*

צֶדֶק אֶתֵּן לְקוֹנִי.
זְדוֹנוֹת הַגּוּף מַבְאִישׁ.
לֹא אֲכַחֵד מֵאֲדֹנִי,
אַל נָא אֶשָּׂא פְּנֵי אִישׁ.

'I shall tell the truth to my Maker: it is the body in its insolence that has made the stink. I shall conceal nothing from my Lord. *I shall show no favour to anyone.*

קְלוֹנוֹ אַגִּידֶנּוּ
וְתָבוֹא בְלִבּוֹ חַרְבּוֹ.
לָמָה אִירָאֶנּוּ ?
פֶּה אֶל פֶּה אֲדַבֶּר בּוֹ !

'Let me tell him his disgrace outright and his sword will pierce his own heart. Why should I fear him? *I shall tell him to his face.*

403

רָדַף בְּכֹחַ וְלָאֵל
עָבַר מִצְוָתְךָ, קְדוֹשִׁי.
בְּאָמְרִי: "נֵלְכָה בֵית אֵל,"
יֹאמַר: "אוֹי לִי רֹאשִׁי."

'Zealously, persistently, he searched for ways, my Holy One, to violate Your commands. When I would say to him, "Let us go to the house of God," he would evade me, *saying: "O my head, my head!"*

שׁוֹאֵל אוֹב וּמְעוֹנֵן,
כָּל תּוֹעֵבָה בְּלִבּוֹ.
לָכֵן, צוּר, כִּי יְחַנֵּן
קוֹלוֹ, אַל תַּאֲמֶן בּוֹ.

'He traffics with ghosts and soothsayers. Abominations fill his heart. Therefore, O Rock, *when he speaks graciously, do not trust him.*

"תִּירָא מֵאֵל וְחֶבְלוֹ",
יְעַצְתִּיו יוֹמִי וְלֵילִי.
לְעַנֵּנִי, לֵאמֹר: "לֹא,
כִּי שָׁלוֹם יִהְיֶה לִי."

'"Fear God and His punishment" – thus I counselled him day and night. But he mocked me: "Never you mind, *all will be well with me."*

מֵאָז בּוֹ כְלָאתַנִי
תַּמּוּ כָּל מַאֲוַיָּי.
שׁוֹכֵב זֶה טִמְּאַנִי,
צֻמְּתוּ בַבּוֹר חַיָּי.

'Ever since You locked me up inside him, all my heart's desires have been thwarted. This apostate defiled me and *I was thrust alive into the pit.*

הָשֵׁב גְּמוּלוֹ, וְאַיֵּה
תּוֹעֲבוֹתָיו? יִתְמְכוּ בוֹ!
בִּי, חָיוֹ לֹא יִחְיֶה,
מוֹת יוּמָת, דָּמָיו בּוֹ.' [...]

'Give him his deserts. Then let him look to his abominations to save him. I beg of You, do not let him live. *He should die; let his blood lie on his own head.'*

עִמָּנוּאֵל בֶּן־שְׁלֹמֹה מִן הָאֲדֻמִּים

Immanuel dei Rossi

אֱנוֹשׁ אָנוּשׁ

MAN

אֱנוֹשׁ אָנוּשׁ הֶבֶל יַפְצֶה,
נָהַר אֲשָׁמָיו עַד צַוָּאר יֶחֱצֶה,
בְּנַפּוֹ יָבֹא בְּנַפּוֹ יֵצֵא.

Doomed, man gives vent to empty talk.
The torrent of his guilt rises neck-high.
He comes alone and will go away alone.

בְּמִסְבּוֹת הַזְּמָן יָרוּץ וְיִרְכַּב,
וְהָאֲדָמָה אֲשֶׁר מִמֶּנָּה הָרְכַּב
הִיא שִׂמְלָתוֹ לְעֹרוֹ. בַּמֶּה יִשְׁכָּב ?

He rides headlong through the winding
course of Time, but the earth of which
he was compounded, *that will be the
cloak which will wrap his body; in what
else can he sleep?*

גּוּף נָגוּף וְאַשְׁמָתוֹ נוֹבַעַת
בְּנֶפֶשׁ נִגְאֶלֶת גַּם בְּלֹא דַעַת
כִּי תֹאכְלֶנּוּ הַתֹּלַעַת.

His body is infested; its guilt ferments
in the polluted soul, all unaware that
the worm will eat him.

יָגוֹן לֵילוֹ וַאֲנָחָה יוֹמוֹ,
וּבִמְלֹאת קִצּוֹ יִכָּרֵת שְׁמוֹ
מֵעַם אֶחָיו וּמִשַּׁעַר מְקוֹמוֹ.

His night is agony and his day despair.
When his time is up, his name is cut off
*from among his brethren and from the
gate of his native place.*

יָשֹׁם עַל עֵקֶב בָּשְׁתּוֹ
וַעֲדֵי אֹבֵד אַחֲרִיתוֹ,
וְעָלָה בָאְשׁוֹ וְתַעַל צַחֲנָתוֹ.

He is aghast with shame, fated to perish
forever. *The stench will rise from his
rotting corpse.*

בְּפֶתַע יֵצֵא מִכַּנּוֹ
וְיָשִׂים בַּסֶּלַע קִנּוֹ
וְיֵבוֹשׁ מְקוֹרוֹ וְיֶחֱרַב מַעְיָנוֹ.

Suddenly, he is torn from his base and
his home is set among the rocks. *His
spring fails and his fountain runs dry.*

אֵיךְ יָרוּם לִבּוֹ וְעַפְעַפָּיו יִנָּשֵׂאוּ —
וּמְהָרְסָיו וּמַחֲרִיבָיו מִמֶּנּוּ יֵצֵאוּ,

How can his heart be proud and his
eyes haughty? His own despoilers come

עַל פִּיו יֵצְאוּ וְעַל פִּיו יָבֹאוּ.

from within himself. *They come out of his mouth and go back into it.*[1]

מַה יִּתְרוֹן הָעוֹשֶׂה בַּאֲשֶׁר יִצְבֹּר —
וְעָרֹם יְרִיצוּהוּ אֶל הַבּוֹר,
אַל יָנוּס הַקַּל וְאַל יְמַלֵּט הַגִּבּוֹר.

What does a man gain by heaping up riches? Naked, he is hurried off to the grave. *The swift cannot escape, the warrior cannot save himself.*

זָכְרָה זֹאת, אֱנוֹשׁ, וְהַעֲלֵה עַל לְבָבֶךְ:
פְּקֻדַּת כָּל הָאָדָם תִּפָּקֵד וּמָוֶת תְּשִׁיבֶךְ,
הָאָרֶץ יִהְיֶה מוֹשָׁבֶךְ.

Remember this, O man, and take it to heart: the lot of all mankind awaits you, to surrender you to death. *Then the earth will be your home.*

דָּמִיתָ כְּמַר מִדְּלִי וּכְשַׁחַק מֹאזְנָיִם,
וַעֲפַר אֶרֶץ אֲשֶׁר בְּפֶתַח עֵינַיִם
הִנֵּה הוּא לָךְ כְּסוּת עֵינָיִם.

You were no more than a drop from a bucket, a speck of dust on the scales; and the soil of the earth in the doorway of your eyes, *this will be the covering for your eyes.*

בְּשָׂרְךָ יִלְבַּשׁ גּוּשׁ עָפָר וְרִמָּה,
וְכַחוֹל אֲשֶׁר עַל שְׂפַת יָם הָעֲצוּמָה
יַאֲרִכוּן יָמֶיךָ עַל הָאֲדָמָה. [...]

Your body will be clothed with worms and scabs. And, like the grains of sand on the endless sea-shore, *you will long endure in the land.*

מְשֻׁלָּם דַּאפִּיאֶרָה

Meshullam da Piera

שְׁאָלוּנִי: חֲכַם לֵבָב

THE POET

שְׁאָלוּנִי: 'חֲכַם לֵבָב, וּמִי זֶה
אֲשֶׁר בֵּין טוֹב וּבֵין רַע לֹא יְבַקֵּר,
וְיָשִׁיר אֶל מְתֵי הַדּוֹר בִּכְבוֹד —
וְלִבּוֹ הָאֱמֶת אָז וְחִקֵּר?'
הֲשִׁיבוֹתִים: 'מְיֻדָּעַי, אֲנִי הוּא,
אֲנִי הוּא הַמְשׁוֹרֵר הַמְשַׁקֵּר!'

They asked me: 'Tell us, wise of heart, who is it that makes no distinction between good and bad and sings the praises of the men of his time, though his heart has weighed the truth and pondered it?' I answered them: 'Why, that is I, my friends, I, the lying poet!'

---

1. A play on the literal meaning of Numbers 27.21 which, in context, reads: 'At his [the priest's] word they [the people] shall go out and shall come home.'

בְּרָן־יַחַד   SONG AT DAWN

בְּרָן־יַחַד, בְּרָן כּוֹכְבֵי שְׁחָרַי,
כְּתָם־לַיְל וְאוֹר מִכָּל עֲבָרַי;
כְּתָם־לַיְל וְהָאֹפֶל מְנֻדָּח,
וְעָלוּ מִפְּאַת מִזְרָח מְאוֹרַי;
בְּהִנָּעֵר שְׂעִפַּי מִתְּנוּמָה,
בְּהָקִיץ מִשְּׁנַת לַיְל יְצוּרַי –
אֲשַׁחֵר הַשְּׁחָרִים בַּנְּגִינָה,
וְהַבֹּקֶר אֲבַקֵּר עִם זְמִירַי.
וְיָדַי תָּמְכָה כִּנּוֹר וְעוּגָב,
וְתִרְגַּלְתִּי שְׂמֹאלִי עַל יְתָרַי.
אֲקַשֵּׁר מַעֲדַנּוֹת תֹּף וְחָלִיל –
וְעֵת אֲמַשֵּׁךְ, וְעֵת אַתִּיר קְשָׁרַי.
וְאֶפְצַח רָן וּמְשַׁכְתִּי בְשֵׁבֶט,
לְדֵעָה אִם יְשִׁיבוּן לִי אֲמָרַי,
לְדֵעָה אִם יְנַחֲמוּנִי בְנוּדִי
בְּאֶרֶץ הַגְּדוּד, אֶרֶץ מְגוּרַי.
אֲזַמֵּר – לֹא יְשִׁיבֵנִי חֲלִילִי,
וְעוֹד לֹא צָהֲלוּ קוֹלָם זְמִירַי!
יְדוּעֵי סוֹד, יְדַעְתֶּם עַל כְּלֵי שִׁיר
אֲשֶׁר לֹא יִפְצָחוּ רִנָּה לְשִׁירַי,
וְאֵין קוֹל צִפֳּרִים מִבֵּין עֲפָיִים
וְלֹא שִׁיר הַדְּרוֹר מִבֵּין דְּבִירַי?
אֲלֵיהֶם רַב שְׁלוֹמִי, כִּי בְאֵין פֶּה
יְשִׂיחוּנִי לְהַצְנִיעַ סְפָרַי,
לְהַצְנִיעַ מְשָׁלַי מִבְּנֵי אִישׁ,
וְיוֹתֵר מֵאֱנוֹשׁ הַסְתֵּר סְתָרַי. [...]

When they sang together, when my morning stars sang as the night was ending and light came up from all sides; when the night was ending, the darkness expelled, and my sun rose in the East; when my thoughts shook off slumber and my limbs woke from their sleep of night – then I sought to greet the dawn with music and to worship the morning with song. In my hands I held the lyre and the pipe, and my left hand moved skilfully over the strings. I tied the timbrel and the flute to my side and adjusted their loops, now tightening, now loosening them. Then I began to sing and improvise, to see if my instruments would answer my words, to see if they would comfort me in my wandering, in this land of exile which is my home. But though I sang, my flute did not answer, and even the birds did not raise their voices in mirth. O masters of mysteries, have you ever known a musical instrument that would not strike up when I sing – and the birds voiceless among the branches, the swallow songless in my house? Yet I wish them well, for with their silence they counsel me to hide my works, to hide my words from men, to conceal my secrets from all men with even greater care.

לָנוּ עֲלָמוֹת   OF LOVE AND LIES

[...] לָנוּ עֲלָמוֹת לֹא יְדָעָן אִישׁ, וְהֵן
רֵאשִׁית אֲהָבֵינוּ וְקִנְיָנֵינוּ,
וּמְשַׂקְּרוֹת עַיִן לְשֵׁמַע פַּעֲמֹן
שׁוּלֵי מְעִילֵנוּ וְרִמּוֹנֵינוּ.
וּכְסוֹחֲרֵי רִקְמָה – רִקְמוֹת יִשְׂאֲלוּ
לָהֶן שְׁלוּחֵינוּ וְנֶאֱמָנֵינוּ;
אָז דִּבְּרוּ לֹא עַל דְּבַר מְמְכָּר וְלֹא
לִמְכֹּר סְחָרֵינוּ וְעִזְבוֹנֵינוּ.
יָגֵל מְבַשֵּׂר בְּאָמֵר כִּי לָקְחוּ
אֶשְׁכּוֹל כְּפָרֵינוּ וְשׁוֹשַׁנֵּינוּ –
כֶּתֶם חֲלִי הֵם שָׁלְחוּ לָנוּ, וְהוּא
תּוֹרֵי זְהָבֵינוּ וְשַׂהֲרוֹנֵינוּ;
שָׁם תֶּחֱזֶה צוּרוֹת כְּתַבְנִית חוֹשְׁקִים,
צוּרוֹת מְחֻשָּׁבוֹת בְּדִמְיוֹנֵנוּ –
דְּמִיוֹן יְפַת תֹּאַר יְשֵׁנָה בֵּין שְׁדֵי
אוֹהֵב, וּפָנֶיהָ עֲלֵי פָנֵינוּ. [...]

I have a maiden[1] whom no man has
ever known; she is my chief love and
treasure. Her eyes brighten when she
hears the bells and pomegranates on
the hem of my cloak. My faithful
envoys, as if they were clothing-
merchants, brought her embroideries,
but they made no mention of payment,
demanded no return for my wares.
How joyfully the messenger then
informed me that she had accepted my
garland of henna blossoms and lilies,
and had sent me a necklace of Nubian
gold. It is as dear to me as braided
plaits of gold and crescents. In it I can
see the carved figures of lovers, like the
very figures that are engraved in my
imagination: a beautiful woman
sleeping on the breast of her lover, and
her face upon mine.

מַה יָּקְרוּ יָמִים אֲשֶׁר בָּהֶם לְקוֹל
מַזְכִּיר בְּנוֹת חֵן צָלְלוּ אָזְנֵינוּ!
חָלְפוּ יְמֵי נֹעַר – וְכַמָּה נַּעֲלֹז
בִּכְבוֹד יְמֵי שֵׂיבָה וּבִזְקֵנֵינוּ.
חָבוּשׁ לְרֹאשֵׁנוּ פְּאֵר, כִּי עָלְתָה
שֵׂיבָה בְּרֹאשֵׁנוּ וּבִזְקֵנֵנוּ.
הוּסַר חֲלִי יַלְדוּת, וְיִרְאַת חֵטְא – עֲנָק
עַל גַּרְגְּרוֹתֵינוּ וּבְגְרוֹנֵנוּ.
אִם תִּמְצְאוּ שֶׁבַח בְּכָזָב הֶאֱרִיךְ –

How precious were those days when
the voices of graceful girls rang in our
ears! Those youthful days are gone, yet
we greatly rejoice in the honour of old
age. My head is covered with a
glorious turban of grey hairs, my beard
is white. Youth's ornament has been
removed; now the fear of sin hangs like
a jewel from my neck. If you find that
my tributes are wordy with falsehood,

1. In Hebrew 'we have maidens'.

408

מִתּוֹךְ שְׂחוֹק נִכְתַּב וְעַל יֵין גֵּנוּ.
אַל תִּשְׁמְעוּ עֵדוּת יְדוּעִים מֵאֲשֶׁר
עַל פִּי חֲלִילִים יֹאמְרוּ נוֹגְנֵינוּ:
זֹאת הַמְּלָאכָה מֶאֱהָב כַּחַשׁ, וְהוּא
הַשָּׁוְא אֲשֶׁר בַּשִּׁיר וּבִלְשׁוֹנֵינוּ.
כִּמְשַׂחֲקִים נָשִׁיר מְתֵי הַדּוֹר, וְלֹא
לָתֵת בְּעֵין הַשּׁוֹמְעִים חִנֵּנוּ.
נֶאֱהַב אֲשֶׁר פָּנָיו מְעִידוֹת אַהֲבָה,
יַכִּיר בְּרִית אַהֲבָה בְּאִישׁוֹנֵינוּ.
וּשְׁנֵי לְבָבוֹת עַל חֲשׁוּדֵי תַאֲנָה
לָנוּ, וְיִמָּצֵא הַחֲשָׁד מֹאזְנֵינוּ. [...]

[know that] they were written in jest and over wine. When we poets extol the virtues of famous men to the sound of pipes, pay no heed: ours is a labour of lies, and that is why my verses and my mouth are full of deceit. It is in play that we celebrate the men of our time, and not to win the favour of our listeners. In truth, I love only that man whose face bespeaks his love for me, and he too will see love's pledge in my eyes. As for those whose love is suspect, for them I have a double heart; and I can weigh the suspicion in the balance.

הָרוּג בְּיַד

TO A FATHER IN MOURNING

[...] הָרוּג בְּיַד יַלְדֵי תְמוּתָה, לֹא בְיַד
נִרְצָח; וְלֹא שָׁפַךְ אֱנוֹשׁ דָּמֶךָ:
רְפָאוֹת תְּעָלָה אֵין בְּיָדֵנוּ, אֲבָל
נַזְכִּיר יְגוֹן רַבִּים לְהַחֲלִימֶךָ:
מִשֹּׁד מְרִירֵי יוֹם וּמֵאַנְקַת מְתֵי
מַכְאוֹב אֲשֶׁר הָיוּ בְעוֹלָמֶךָ,
מִיֹּדְעֵי שֶׁבֶר וְעֹצֶם הֶחֱלִי –
נִשָּׂא מְשָׁלֵינוּ לְהַעֲצִימֶךָ.
נַזְכִּיר יְמֵי רָעָה וְתַלְאוּבוֹת בְּנֵי
אָדָם – וְאוּלַי יַעֲבֹר זַעְמֶךָ.
אוֹי לָהּ לְנֶחָמָה לְקוּחָה מִכְּאָב
אַחִים וְכָל עֶצֶב לְתַנְחוּמֶיךָ!

You have been felled by death's messenger, not by a murderous hand: no human being shed your blood.[1] We have no cure to offer you, but we can invoke the sorrows of others to help you recover. To fortify you, we shall make our song out of the havoc of embittered men, the groans of the tormented whom you have known, the victims of disaster and harsh sickness. We shall recall evil days and the searing pain of men: perhaps your fury will abate. Woe to the comfort that must feed on the pain and sorrow of brethren for your consolation!

---

1. Presumably, addressed to the father, whose blood is one with the blood of his son.

יוֹשֵׁב וּמִשְׁתּוֹמֵם, הֲלֹא תֵדַע סְפֹד?
נִכְוֶה, וְאֵיךְ עָמַד בְּךָ טַעְמֶךְ?
הַאַתְּ לְגֹדֶל שִׁבְרְךָ נִבְהָל, וְאִם
הָיוּ כְּאַכְזָרִי הֲמֹן רַחֲמֶיךָ?
לֹא תֵבְךְּ וְלֹא תָנֹד לְבֵן וּלְאָח אֲשֶׁר
מֵעִמְּךָ לֻקַּח בְּסוֹף יָמֶיךָ.
מֵעִמְּךָ לֻקַּח – וְלָנוּ בַּבְּכִי
נְמַן שֶׁכֶם אַחַד עֲלֵי שִׁכְמֶךָ.
כּוֹאֵב, גְּעַר בִּמְנַחֲמִים וּזְעַק, עֲדֵי
מִצַּעֲרָתְךָ יִתְמְהוּ שָׁמֶיךָ,
וּרְעַשׁ בְּמִסְתָּרִים, עֲדֵי כִי יִרְעֲשׁוּ
סִפִּים וְהַגַּלְגַּל לְקוֹל רַעְמֶךָ.
אַל תַּחֲשֹׁב, עָצֵב, לְהִתְנַחֵם כְּתֹם
שִׁבְעַת יְמֵי אֵבֶל וְכַהַתְמֶךָ;
נַחְנוּ נְגַלֶּה סוֹד מְהוּמָתְךָ לְכָל
יָבוֹא. וּמַה בֶּצַע בְּהַעֲלִימֶךָ?
אִם תֶּחֱשֶׁה, הִנְנִי לְעוֹרֵר הַבְּכִי
וּבְתוֹכְחוֹת מוּסָר לְהַכְלִימֶךָ.
הֵא לְךָ יְדִיד נֶאֱמָן אֲשֶׁר עַל הַדֲּמִי
יָרִיב בְּךָ תָמִיד וְיִלָּחֲמֶךָ.
יֵחַם לְבַב עַצְבִּי לְהָעִיר דִּמְעָךָ,
עֵת אַהֲבָה אוֹסִיף וְאֶרְחָמֶךָ. [...]

O you who sit dumbfounded, do you not know how to lament? Scorched [by grief], how can you be as you were? Are you stunned by your great disaster? Or has your tender love turned into cruelty? You do not weep or moan for the son and companion taken from you in your old age. He was taken from you, but our share of tears is greater than yours. Sufferer, rebuke your comforters, cry out until the heavens are aghast at your rebuke; clamour in the secret [chambers], until the thresholds and the spheres quake at the sound of your thunder. Sorrower, do not think to find comfort when the seven days of mourning come to an end. We shall reveal your secret terror to all comers; why try to hide it? If you keep silent, I shall call for weeping, I shall shame you with my sharp reproaches. You have in me a true friend who will always contest your silence and dispute with you. It grieves my heart to stir up your tears, for all the while I love you dearly.

טָדְרוֹס אַבּוּלְעָאפִיָּה   *Todros Abulafia*

בָּאַהֲבָה חָלִיתִי   OH, TO BE A WOMAN!

וְעַל בַּת עֲרָב עָרְבָה לִי אהבתה, ובתוך עלמות ראיתי אותה, משיקות אשה אל אחותה.

Upon seeing an Arab girl whom I loved in the company of other girls, kissing one another.

בְּאַהֲבָה חַלְתִּי וְלֹא יָלַדְתִּי,
וּבְפַח צְבִיָּה בַּת עֲרָב נִלְכַּדְתִּי.
לִנְשֹׁק בְּפִיהָ אוֹתָהּ נַפְשִׁי, עֲדֵי
לִהְיוֹת נְקֵבָה בַעֲדָהּ חָמַדְתִּי –
כִּי הַנְּקֵבוֹת הִיא מְנַשֶּׁקֶת, וּבְשֶׁ־
בִיל שֶׁאֲנִי זָכָר, אֲנִי הִפְסַדְתִּי !

I have laboured in love but have not
given birth, caught in the toils of this
daughter of Arabia. So great is my
desire to kiss her on the mouth that, for
her sake, I wish I were a woman. For
it is women that she kisses and I, being
a male, am the loser.

אָמְרָה – הֲכִי נֹד רָצְתָה

THE OLD POET AND THE GIRL

אָמְרָה – הֲכִי נֹד רָצְתָה, עֵת רָאֲתָה
בִּי זָקְנָה שֵׂיבָה וְהִלְבִּין שְׂעָרִי :
'שַׁחַר כְּבָר עָלָה בְּרֹאשְׁךָ, וַאֲנִי
סַהַר – וְהַשַּׁחַר יְגָרֵשׁ זָהֳרִי !'
וָאֶעֱנֶה : 'לֹא כֵן, אֲבָל שֶׁמֶשׁ, וְזֶה
חֻקֵּךְ בְּעוֹד יוֹמָם לְבַל תִּסְתַּתְּרִי.'
אָמְרָה : 'כְּבָר לִרְדֹּף אֲהָבִים אֵין בְּךָ
כֹּחַ, וּמַה יִּסְכָּן־לָךְ הִשָּׁאֲרִי ?'
'גִּבּוֹר כְּאַרְיֵה לַעֲשׂוֹת חֶפְצֵךְ אֲנִי',
שַׂחְתִּי, 'וּבִי לֹא נֶחֱלַף רַק מַאֲרִי.'
עָנְתָה : 'אֲרִי אַף, וַאֲנִי עָפְרָה – לְזֹאת
אָגוּר לְהִתְגּוֹרֵר אֲנִי עִם גּוּר אֲרִי.'

Wishing to leave me, when she saw
that I was growing old and grey, she
said: 'Dawn has already risen upon
your head. I am the moon, and dawn
drives away my splendour!' I answered:
'Ah no, you are the sun, and it is in
your nature not to hide all day long.'
Said she: 'You are no longer strong
enough for the pursuit of love. What
good will it do you if I stay on?' 'I am
as bold as a lion to do your will,' I
answered. 'Nothing in me has changed
except for my outward appearance.'
Said she: 'You are indeed a lion. But I
am a gazelle, and that is why I am
afraid to live with a lion-whelp.'

מַה מַּר וְנוֹרָא

A REMEMBRANCE

מַה מַּר וְנוֹרָא יוֹם נְדֹדֵךְ, יַעֲלַת
הַחֵן, לְזִכְרוֹ אֵין מְתֹם בִּבְשָׂרִי.
אַךְ מַה מְּאֹד יָפוּ פְעָמַיִךְ, בְּעֵת
הִשְׂתָּרְגוּ עָלוּ עֲלֵי צַוָּארִי.

How terrible, how bitter was the day of
your parting, my graceful girl. When I
remember it, no part of my body is left
unscarred. But how very beautiful
were your feet when they twined and
climbed my neck.

וְשָׁמַעְתִּי בְּרָאשֵׁי הַבְּכָאִים

THE NECKLACE

וְשָׁמַעְתִּי בְּרָאשֵׁי הַבְּכָאִים
כְּקוֹל יוֹנָה, בְּעֵת בָּאתִי לְגַנִּי.
וְהִבַּטְתִּי גְרוֹנֶיהָ, וְהִנֵּה
עֲנָק מָלֵא – כְּשִׁירַי בַּאֲדוֹנִי.
כְּאַלְמָנָה מְבַכָּה לַדּוֹד, אַךְ
כְּכַלָּה בַּעֲנָק נִרְאֵית לְעֵינִי.
שְׁאַלְתִּיהָ: 'הֲבִנְדֹד אוֹהֲבָיִךְ
תְּשִׂימִין לָךְ עֲנָק?' וַתַּעֲנֵנִי:
'פְּנִינֵי הַבְּכִי קָפְאוּ בְּרִדְתָּם
וְהָיוּ לַעֲנָק עַל צַוְּרוֹנִי.'

When I came into my garden, I heard the voice of a dove from the top of the poplars. I looked at her throat and there I saw a necklace full [of gems] – as full as my songs are with my lord's praise. She moaned like a widow lamenting her loss, but she seemed to me a bride wearing her necklace. I asked her: 'Would you put on a necklace when your beloved is gone?' And she answered: 'My coral tears froze as they came down and turned into this necklace around my throat.'

אֵשׁ מִלְּבָבִי

THE DAUGHTER OF ARABIA

אֵשׁ מִלְּבָבִי, וּמֵעֵינַי זְרָמִים.
תֹּפֶת בְּלִבִּי, אֲבָל עֵינַי כְּיַמִּים.
צָחוּ דְמָעַי, וְהֵם כַּדָּם אֲדֻמִּים.
שָׁלַח נְדֹד אֵשׁ בְּעַצְמַי, מָסַךְ דְּמָעַי בְּדָמִי,
זֻקְּקוּ בַּעֲלִיל חִיל, דְּזָעֲכוּ בִי בְּחֻמִּי.

הַשּׁוֹמְעִים נִפְלְאוֹת עֹז אַהֲבָתִי
אוֹתִי תְּמוֹל שָׁאֲלוּ מִי יַעֲלָתִי.
וָאֶעֱנֶם: 'בַּת־עֲרָב הִיא רַעֲיָתִי –
אַךְ לֶחֱיָהּ הוּא אֲדוֹמִי חֶצְיוֹ, וְחֶצְיוֹ אֲרָמִי.
זָהֲרוּ עָשׁ, כְּסִיל מַחְפִּיר וְכוֹכְבֵי מְרוֹמִי.'

Fire flows from my heart and a river from my eyes; there is a hell in my heart, but my eyes are like seas. My tears are pure, yet red as blood. Parting has set my bones on fire and mixed my tears with my heart's blood. They were purified in the crucible of anguish and leaped to my eyes as my heat rose.

Those who had heard of the wonders of my fierce love asked me yesterday who my gazelle was. And I told them: 'My dearest is a daughter of Arabia; yet her cheeks are half Edomite, half Aramean.[1] Their radiance puts the Great Bear to shame, as well as Orion and all the stars of heaven.'

---

1. That is, half red and half white; see note on p. 345.

נָמְתִּי, וְלִי אָמְרָה יָפָה וְתַמָּה:
'חוֹשֵׁק הֲיָנוּם?' עֲנִיתִיהָ: 'אֲיֻמָּה,
חֵי אַהֲבָה, אֵין הֲנָחָה לִי בְּנוּמָה!
אָכֵן שְׁנָתִי וְנוּמִי אוּלֵי יִצֹדֵךְ חֲלוֹמִי.
וָאֶסָּלֵד בְּחִיל נֹדֵךְ בְּשִׁבְתִּי וְקוּמִי.'

I slept, and she, lovely and perfect,
said to me: 'How can a lover sleep?'
I answered her: 'O majesty, I swear by
Love that I can find no rest in slumber.
I am sleeping only in the hope that my
dream may trap you. [Awake,] sitting
or standing, I am shaken with the
anguish of your parting.'

שָׂרְפָה לְבָבִי, וְאֵין עוֹזֵר וְסוֹמֵךְ.
וָאֹמְרָה: 'אֵיךְ בְּאֵשׁ קִצְפֵּךְ וְזַעְמֵךְ
תִּשְׂרֹף לְבָבִי, וְהוּא מֵאָז הֲדוֹמֵךְ?'
וַתַּעֲנֶה: 'מִי-לָךְ מִי, אִם אֶשְׂרְפָה אֶת הֲדוֹמִי?
רֹן לְבָבִי וְגִיל, עֵת אֶשְׂרְפֶנּוּ בְּזַעְמִי!'

She burnt my heart, and there was no
one who could help me. I said: 'How
can you, in the fire of your fury, burn
my heart that has always been your
foot-stool?' To which she answered:
'What concern is it of yours if I burn
my own foot-stool? Sing out, my heart;
rejoice as I burn it in my rage!'

בֹּאִי, וְלוּ בַחֲלוֹם, עָפְרַת אֲהָבִים,
הִתְנַדְּבִי, לוּ בְמִדְבָּרִים עֲרֵבִים.
נְאֻמֵךְ מְעַט קָט יְכַב מוֹקְדֵי קְרָבִים.
זרני ולו פי אלמנאם וגד ולו באלסלאם
פקאל אלקליל בך צמא אלמסתהאם.

Oh come, my lovely doe, if only in a
dream. Give yourself to me, if only in
sweet speech. Even a few words would
put out the flaming furnace within me.
Oh come to me, if only in my dream;
favour me, if only with your greeting.
For your words, however few, can
quench the thirst of the one who is
yearning.[1]

אִם הַזְּמָן   THE MERRY DEBTOR

אִם הַזְּמָן מוּל זָהֳרִי נוֹבֵחַ,
הוּא כְּכֶלֶב, וַאֲנִי יָרֵחַ!
אֶשְׂחַק לְקוֹרוֹתָיו וְאֵלָיו אֶלְעָגָה,
אֵעָשׁ כְּעִוֵּר, וַאֲנִי פִּקֵּחַ.
אַרְאֶה, לְהַכְעִיס אוֹיְבִים, כֹּחַ וְאוֹן.
לֹא לַזְּמָן אַכַּף וְאֶשְׁתּוֹחֵחַ.

If Time barks at my brilliance, he is a
dog and I am the moon. I laugh him
and his accidents to scorn. I play the
blind man, but I am clear-sighted. To
spite my enemies, I make a show of
prowess. I will not bow or stoop before

---

1. The last two verses are in Arabic, probably from a popular song.

אֵצֵא בְּפָנִים נַעֲלָסִים לַיְקוּם,
וַאֲנִי בְּתוֹךְ לִבִּי בְּמַר צוֹרֵחַ.
אֶלְבַּשׁ וְאֶרְכַּב, אֹכְלָה, אֶשְׁתֶּה עֲדֵי
אֶשְׁכַּר, וְרֵישִׁי אֶהְיֶה שׁוֹכֵחַ.
אִיגַע לְהִתְנַהֵג כְּרֵעַי, וַאֲנִי
כְּמַחֲתָרֵה סוּסִים וְהוּא פִּסֵּחַ.
אֶלְוֶה בְּעֵת לֹא יִהְיֶה לִי, אֶתְּנָה
לָזֶה אֲשֶׁר מִזֶּה אֲנִי לוֹקֵחַ.
כָּזֹאת וְכָזֹאת מִפְעָלוֹתַי עַד הֲלוֹם,
חַי אֵל, וְאָנֹכִי בְּרָן פּוֹצֵחַ!

Time. I put on a merry face when I go
out into the world, though deep in my
heart I am crying bitterly. I dress up
and go out riding, I dine and drink
myself drunk until I forget my poverty.
I slave to keep up with my companions;
I am like a lame man competing with
horses. I borrow money when I have
none, and what I take from the one I
give to the other. Such are my doings
to this very day and, so help me God,
I still shout for joy!

יְדַעְתִּיךְ נְדִיב־לֵב   FIGS

לבן שושן, בבקשו ממנו כי ישלח לו תאנים:

*To Ibn Shoshan, after I had requested
him to send me figs:*

יְדַעְתִּיךְ נְדִיב־לֵב בַּתְּאֵנִים,
וּמָאֵחַ אֵינְךָ נוֹצֵר תְּאֵנָה.
וְאֵיךְ שַׁבְתָּ כְּהַיּוֹם לִי לְכִילַי
וְנֶהְפַּךְ לָךְ לְרַע לִבָּא וְעֵינָא?
וְקָרֵאתָ לְסוּסָתִי חֲמוֹרָה —
וְעֵינֶיךָ, אֱמֶת, לֹא תֶחֱזֶינָה.
אֱמֶת, רוֹאֶה אֲנִי דַּיָּן עֲמֹרָה
בְּשׁוּרְךָ הֵן בְּכָל רֶגַע וְעוֹנָה.
וְיָדַעְתִּי לְךָ בַּגּוֹ דְּבָרִים
דְּפָסִילְנָא בְּדִינָא לָךְ לְדִינָא.
וְנִסְתָּרוֹת אֲנִי עוֹד לֹא אֲגַלֶּה,

I have known you to be generous with
figs; you never withheld your figs from
your fellows. Then how did it happen,
today, that you turned into a skinflint?
What made you become tight-fisted
and flint-hearted? And how could you
call my mare an ass when, in fact, you
are blind? In truth, whenever I look at
you, I see that you are fit to be a judge
in Gomorrah.[1] The things I know
about you would disqualify you by law
from trying my case. But, as yet, I shall
not reveal your secrets. Instead, let me

---

1. The judges of Sodom and Gomorrah were notorious for their injustices.

אֲבָל אִיעָצְךָ עֵצָה נְכוֹנָה:
תְּאֵנָה חָנְטָה שְׁלַח, וְחֵלֶק
לְשִׁבְעָה בָם תְּנָה, גַּם אֶל שְׁמוֹנָה.
וְהִנֵּה לָךְ זְמוֹרָתִי שְׁמוּרָה,
הֲכִי הֵן לֹא לְזָר עוֹד אֶתְּנֶנָּה.
וְעִם גִּבּוֹר קְטָטָה אַל תְּבַקֵּשׁ,
וְאַל תָּבוֹא בְיָם מֵאֵין סְפִינָה.

give you some sound advice: send me
figs in plenty, enough for seven or even
eight mouths. And in return, here is
my flatus,[1] henceforth reserved for you
alone, not to be given to any stranger.
In short, never pick a fight with a man
of might, nor put to sea without a boat!

שְׁלֹשָׁה שִׁירִים מִבֵּית־הַסֹּהַר

THREE POEMS FROM PRISON

א

I

טַבְּעוֹתַי אִם נָפְלוּ – אֶצְבְּעוֹתַי
נִשְׁאָרוּ. אֵין הוֹדִי בְּרֹב טַבְּעוֹתַי!
דָּת וּמִשְׂרָה עוֹד לִי, וְנֶפֶשׁ יְקָרָה,
זֹאת יְרֶשֶׁת הוֹרַי וְנַחֲלַת אֲבוֹתַי.
רַב פְּעָלִים לִבִּי וְטוֹב מַעֲלָלִים,
אַךְ בְּחֶסְרוֹן כִּיס חָסְרוּ מִפְעָלוֹתַי.
וַאֲקַו יָהּ שֶׁהוּא, וְיִהְיֶה, וְהָיָה,
כִּי יְהִי עוֹד זְמַן וְיָמִים מְשָׁרְתַי.
סָמְכֵנִי, יָהּ, כִּי רְצוֹנְךָ רְצוֹנִי.
עַד לְמָתַי יִגְבַּר כְּסִיל? עַד לְמָתַי?

My rings have fallen off, but I still have
my fingers; my glory is not in my
wealth of rings. I still have my faith,
my dignity, and my precious soul, the
legacy of my parents, the patrimony of
my ancestors. My heart harbours
exploits and good deeds, but having
lost all my money, I am at a loss to act.
Yet I hope in the Lord, Who is, was,
and shall be, that Time and its days
will once again be in my service.
Uphold me, Lord, for Your will is
mine. How much longer shall the fool
prevail? How much longer?

ב

2

וכאשר שם המלך אותי בבור ואת השרים
האחרים... שמעתי כקול סיסים ותורים:

*When I was in prison, by order of the
king, together with some other noblemen,
I heard voices like those of swallows and
doves:*

חֵי אַהֲבָה, צִפֳּרִים, עוּפוּ אֱלֵי אוֹהֲבִים
וּשְׂאוּ שָׁלוֹם כּוֹאֲבִים תּוֹךְ בּוֹר כְּלוּא יוֹשְׁבִים.

I adjure you, birds, in the name of
Love: fly to the lovers and bear them
greetings from those who are tormented

---

1. *Zmora*, which also means a vine-twig.

בִּי, תֹּאמְרוּ כִּי רְעֵבִים הֵם, צְמֵאִים, אֲבָל
לֶחֶם דְּמָעוֹת דָם לֵב אוֹכְלִים שׁוֹאֲבִים.
יוֹשְׁבִים בְּבוֹר מַאֲפֵל שָׁפֵל כְּנֵפֶל, וּבֵין
פַּרְעֹשׁ וְיַתּוּשׁ וְכִנִּים לוֹהֲטִים שׁוֹכְבִים.
חַיּוֹת קְטַנּוֹת אֲשֶׁר לֹא נִקְרְאוּ עוֹד בְּשֵׁם
מִשְׁתַּקְשְׁקִין שָׁם כְּמוֹ חוֹשְׁקִים בְּעֵת עוֹגְבִים.
יִשְׁרַק זְבוּב לַדְּבוֹרָה שָׁם, וְשֵׁן יַחֲרַק
עַכְבָּר, וְיֶחְדְּוּ עֲלֵי נֶפֶשׁ וְגוּף אוֹרְבִים.
הַנּוֹגְשִׂים צוֹרְרִים, אָצִים, וְהַשּׁוֹטְרִים
צֻוּוּ לְבַל יִתְּנוּ לֶחֶם – וְהָעוֹרְבִים.

in prison. Tell them, I pray you, that
they hunger and thirst, though they
feed on the bread of tears and drink
their heart's blood. They sit in a dark,
vile dungeon, [hidden away] like an
untimely birth. They lie among fleas,
gnats, and man-eating lice. Tiny
beasts, who haven't yet been named,
jostle one another there like lovers in
their lust. There the fly whistles for the
bee, the rat grinds his teeth, and all lie
in ambush for their body and soul. The
overseers assail them and harass them;
the guards are under orders not to give
them food, and the ravens are too.[1]

ג

3

טִיט יְגָרְשׁוּ מֵי יָם וְרֶפֶשׁ יַעֲלוּ,
אַךְ הַפְּנִינִים בַּמְּצוֹלוֹת צָלֲלוּ.
דֶּרֶךְ זְמָן כֵּן הוּא, לְהַעֲלוֹת זוֹלֲלִים,
וּבְכֵן כְּרֻם זֵלוּת – יְקָרִים יֻשְׁפֲּלוּ.
רָעוֹת וְטוֹבוֹת הַזְּמָן מִתְהַפְּכוֹת:
הַחוֹשְׁבִים כִּי הֵם תְּמִידוֹת – סָכְלוּ;
וַאֲשֶׁר תְּבוּנָה בוֹ יְהַתֵּל בַּזְּמָן
וִישַׁעֲשַׁע נַפְשׁוֹ בְּ'אוּלַי' אוֹ בְּ'לוּ'.
סוֹף סוֹף בְּשַׁחַק מֹאזְנַיִם יֵשׁ, וּבָם
יֵרְדוּ תְמִימִים, וַחֲסֵרִים יַעֲלוּ!

The seawater casts up mud and filth,
but corals sink into their depths. This
is the way of Time: he lifts up the
dissolute, and as the base are raised the
noble are debased. Time reverses the
good and the bad. Only a fool could
imagine that his state is constant. The
man of sense laughs at Time, and
cheers himself with 'perhaps' or 'if'.
After all, there is a Balance in heaven[2]
in which the flawless go down while
the faulty rise up.

---

1. Unlike the ravens who brought bread and meat to Elijah (1 Kings 17.6).
2. Shahak means both 'heaven' and 'dust'; the pun is on Isaiah 40.15: '. . . the nations . . . are accounted as the dust on the scales [or balance]'.

אַבְרָהָם אַבּוּלְעָאפְיָה   *Abraham Abulafia*

הֵן הָעָם הַמָּךְ   ZECHARIAH, THE MESSIAH

הֵן הָעָם הַמָּךְ,
אֲשֶׁר כָּל גּוֹי שׁוֹסֵהוּ
וְכָל עַם בּוֹזֵהוּ,
הֵן הַיּוֹם הַזֶּה
יוֹם בְּשׁוֹרָה הוּא לוֹ:
וּזְכַרְיָהוּ הַמְבַשֵּׂר
רוֹכֵב עַל עֲנַן עָב,
וְהָעָב עַב טַל,
וְהַטַּל דַּק קַל,
וְהֶעָנָן כָּבֵד מְאֹד.
הֵן רִכְבּוֹ רֶכֶב אֵשׁ,
וְסוּסָיו סוּסֵי רוּחַ,
וּמְשָׁרְתָיו חַיּוֹת אֵשׁ מְמַלְּלוֹת.
אֵשׁ וְעָנָן סָבִיב
הָרֵי הֲרָרִים סוֹבְבִים,
וְרוּחַ הַמְבַשֵּׂר
מַרְעִישׁ כָּל הָאָרֶץ בְּרַחֲפוֹ.
דִּינִים וּדְבָרִים
מְחַדֵּשׁ לְבּוֹ בְּקִרְבּוֹ,
וּבְמִכְתַּב אֵשׁ יִכְתְּבֵם
בְּעֵט שַׁלְהֶבֶת.
נוֹרָא וְאָיֹם כֹּחַ הָעֵט,
וְהִדְרִיו דָּם שָׂמוֹ בְּקִרְבּוֹ.
וְטִפֵּי טַלּוֹ מַשְׁקִים הָאָרֶץ
וּמְלַחְלְחִים הַיַּבָּשָׁה,
וַיַבֶּשֶׁת מָצוּי מִמָּצוּי.

This poor people, plundered by all nations, abused by all peoples – this is the day that shall bring it good tidings. For Zechariah the Herald is riding upon a thick cloud, a cloud thick with dew, dew that is flaky and swift, and the cloud is heavy and full. His chariot is a chariot of fire, his horses horses of wind, his servants murmuring fiery creatures. Fire and cloud surround the whirling towering mountains, and the breath of the Herald shakes the earth as he hovers over it. His heart moves him to new revelations, which he writes in a script of fire with a pen of flame. Fearful and awesome is the power of the pen, for he has filled it with blood for ink. His dew-drops water the earth and freshen the dry land, the stone-dry land.[1] And his bow

1. The line is obscure.

417

וְהַקֶּשֶׁת חִצִּים שְׁנוּנִים תּוֹרֶה
עַד אֲשֶׁר יַבְקִיעַ חַלּוֹנֵי הָרָקִיעַ
בְּחֵצִי חִצָּיו.
רוּחַ הַחִצִּים מְרַחֶפֶת בַּלְּבָבוֹת
וְשׂוֹרֶפֶת הַכְּלָיוֹת
וּמְפַזֶּרֶת כָּל הָרוּחוֹת,
וְאֵין מַרְפֵּא לַגְּוִיּוֹת.
וְהָרוּחַ הֶחָזָק
הַמְּנִיעַ לֵב הַמְבַשֵּׂר
נוֹפֵחַ נִשְׁמַת חַיִּים
בְּאַפֵּי כָּל חַי.

shoots pointed arrows, until he splits
the windows of the firmament with his
multitude of arrows. The wind of the
arrows quivers in the hearts, it burns
men's vitals and scatters their spirits,
and there is no remedy for the bodies.
Then the mighty spirit, that moves the
heart of the Herald, breathes the breath
of life into the nostrils of every living
creature.

וַיְדַבֵּר ידוד אֵלַי

THE BATTLE OF BLOOD AND INK

וַיְדַבֵּר ידוד אֵלַי
בְּעֵת רְאוֹתִי שְׁמוֹ
מְפֹרָשׁ בָּדָם וּמְיֻחָד בְּלִבִּי,
מַבְדִּיל בֵּין דָּם לִדְיוֹ,
וּבֵין דְּיוֹ לְדָם.
וַיֹּאמֶר אֵלַי ידוד:
'הִנֵּה נַפְשְׁךָ דָּם שְׁמָהּ
וּדְיוֹ שֵׁם רוּחֶךָ,
וְהִנֵּה אָבִיךָ וְאִמְּךָ כָּלִים
לִשְׁמִי זֶה וּלְזִכְרִי זֶה.
וָאֶשְׁמַע הַהֶבְדֵּל הַגָּדוֹל
אֲשֶׁר בֵּין נַפְשִׁי וְרוּחִי,

Then YDWD[1] spoke to me when I saw
His Name spelled out in blood and
designated in my heart, separating the
blood from the ink and the ink from
the blood. And YDWD said to me:
'Know that your soul's name is blood,
and ink is the name of your spirit. Your
father and mother long with all their
hearts for this Name of mine and for
my Title.'[2] When I heard the great
difference between my soul and my

---

1. A variation on the Tetragrammaton YHWH.
2. An allusion to Exodus 3.15: 'This is my name forever, this is my title in every generation'.

וָאֶשְׂמְחָה בּוֹ שִׂמְחָה גְדוֹלָה מְאֹד.

וָאֵדַע כִּי נַפְשִׁי

שֶׁכְנָה עַל צִבְעָהּ

בַּמַּרְאָה הָאֲדֻמָּה כְּדָם,

וְרוּחִי שֶׁכְנָה עַל צִבְעָהּ

בַּמַּרְאָה הַשְּׁחֹרָה כְּדְיוֹ.

וְהַמִּלְחָמָה הָיְתָה חֲזָקָה מְאֹד בְּלֵב

בֵּין הַדָּם וּבֵין הַדְּיוֹ,

וְהַדָּם הָיָה מִן הָרוּחַ

וְהַדְּיוֹ מִן הֶעָפָר –

וְנִצַּח הַדְּיוֹ לַדָּם,

וְהַשַּׁבָּת גָּבְרָה עַל כָּל יְמֵי הַחֹל.

spirit, I was filled with great joy. Then
I knew that my soul was encamped
under its own colour, in the mirror that
is red as blood, and that my spirit was
encamped under its own colour, in the
mirror that is black as ink. And there
was bitter warfare in my heart between
the blood and the ink – the blood was
from the air, the ink from the earth –
and the ink triumphed over the blood,
and the Sabbath overcame all the days
of the week!

אַבְרָהָם בֶּן־שְׁמוּאֵל

Abraham ben Samuel

אֶל מִי מִגּוֹאֲלֵי דָם

CONFESSION

אֶל מִי מִגּוֹאֲלֵי דָם אֶצְעַק,

וְיָדַי שָׁפְכוּ דָמִי?

בָּחַנְתִּי לְבוֹת מְשַׂנְאִים,

וְאֵין שׂוֹנֵא אוֹתִי כִּלְבָבִי.

רַבִּים פִּצְעֵי אוֹיְבִים וּמַכּוֹתָם,

וְאֵין מַכֶּה וּפוֹצֵעַ כְּנַפְשִׁי.

הִדִּיחוּנִי מַשְׁחִיתִים לְחַבֵּל,

וְאֵין מֵסִית וּמַדִּיחַ כְּעֵינָי.

מִגַּחַל אֶל גַּחַל הִתְהַלַּכְתִּי,

וְלֹא שְׂרָפַתְנִי אֵשׁ כְּחֹם מַאֲוָתִי.

בְּפַחִים נִלְכַּדְתִּי וּבִמְצוּדוֹת,

וְלֹא לְכָדַנִי מוֹקֵשׁ כִּלְשׁוֹנִי.

To whom, among the avengers of blood,
can I cry out, when my own hands have
shed my blood? I have tested the hearts
of those who hate me, but no one hates
me as my own heart does. Many are
the blows and wounds inflicted by my
enemies, but no one batters me and
wounds me as my soul does. Men of
havoc have seduced me to do evil, but
none incites me and seduces me as my
eyes do. I have walked from fire to fire,
but no flame has scorched me as the
heat of my lust has. I have been caught
in snares and nets, but no snare has
caught me as my tongue has. Scorpion

נְשָׁכוּנִי נָחָשׁ וְעַקְרָב,
וְאֵין נוֹשֵׁךְ בְּשָׂרִי כְּשִׁנָּי.
שָׂרִים עַל קַל רָדָפוּנִי,
וְאֵין רוֹדֵף אוֹתִי כְּרַגְלִי.
מַכְאוֹבַי עָצְמוּ וְאָמְצוּ מִמֶּנִּי,
וְאֵין מַכְאוֹב כְּמִרְיִי.
וַיִּרְבּוּ מַדְוֵי לְבָבִי,
וַעֲוֹנִי יוֹתֵר מִכֻּלָּם.
אֶל מִי אֶצְעַק וְעַל מִי?
וּמַחֲרִיבַי מִמֶּנִּי יֵצְאוּ.
לֹא מָצָאתִי לִי טוֹב כִּי אִם לָבוֹא בְּסֵתֶר רַחֲמֶיךָ.
רַחֲמֶיךָ הַפְלֵה עַל לֵב נִדְהָמִים,
אֵל מֶלֶךְ יוֹשֵׁב עַל כִּסֵּא רַחֲמִים!

and snake have bitten me, but none
bites my flesh as my teeth do. Swift-
riding princes have pursued me, but
none pursues me as my feet do. My
torments are past counting, past
endurance, but there is no torment like
my own rebelliousness. Great are the
sorrows of my heart, yet my sins outnumber them. To whom can I cry out,
whom can I condemn, when those who
are destroying me come from within
myself? I have found nothing better
than to seek refuge in Your mercy. Oh,
shower Your excellent mercies upon
our dumbstruck hearts – Lord, King,
who sit upon the Throne of Mercy!

נחוּם *Nahum*

הַסְּתָיו אָרַח SPRING SONG

הַסְּתָיו אָרַח, אָרַח מֵעֲצָבִי.
עֵץ פְּרִי פָּרַח, פָּרַח גִּיל לְבָבִי.

Winter is gone, gone is my sorrow. The
fruit-tree is in flower, and my heart
flowers with joy.

נָתְנוּ רֵיחַ יַחְדָּו הַנְּרָדִים,
צָץ וְצָמַח פַּרְדֵּס הַמְּגָדִים,
שָׂשׂ וְשָׂמֵחַ בָּהֶם לֵב יְדִידִים.
שׁוּב, צְבִי מָדָּח בָּרַח מִפְּלוּבִי,
בֹּא, שְׁתֵה רֶקַח יֵינִי עִם חֲלָבִי!

The spikenards, as one, give forth their
scent; the orchard of rare fruits is in
full blossom. The hearts of friends are
filled with merriment. O hunted
gazelle[1] who escaped far from my hut,
come back, come drink my mulled
wine and my milk!

1. An allegorical figure of God.

420

חָלְפוּ תוּגוֹת יוֹם חָלְפוּ עֲרוּגוֹת
בַּהֲדַס סוּגוֹת, בְּרִקְמוֹת אֲרוּגוֹת.
מִבְּלִי פוּגוֹת נָסוּ הַדְּאָגוֹת.
מִגְדְּלוֹת מֶרְקָח נוֹטְפוֹת מוֹר סְבִיבִי,
הָאֱגוֹז סָרַח דָּלְיוֹ עַל מְסִבִּי.

Sorrows fled the day the flower-beds
revived, fenced in by myrtles, braided
with embroideries. Swiftly, then, all
cares took flight. I am surrounded by
coffers full of perfumes, dripping liquid
myrrh. The boughs of the nut-tree
trail low along my couch.

וַעֲצֵי חֶמְדָּה נָטוּ בֵּין צְלָלִים –
מִשְּׂמֹאל קִדָּה, מִיָּמִין אֲהָלִים.
כּוֹס כְּעֵין פִּטְדָה וּכְמַעֲשֵׂה גְלִילִים,
יַיִן כְּעֵין אֶקְדָּח מָסוּךְ מֵרְבִיבִי –
רִישׁ וְאוֹן אֶשְׁכַּח, הַטָּמוּן בְּחֻבִּי.

Trees of delight sway among the
shadows: cassia on the left, aloes on the
right. With an emerald-coloured cup,
ringed [with gold], and garnet-
coloured wine, mixed with dew, I shall
forget the misery and grief hidden deep
in my heart.

מַה לְּדוֹד הָיָה רוֹעֶה בֵּין עֳפָרִים
לַעֲזֹב קִרְיָה, לִשְׁכֹּן בֵּין יְעָרִים?
בֹּא לְחֵיק רַעְיָה מְעַטְּפָה־לָךְ בְּשִׁירִים.
הַעֲלֵה, דּוֹד צַח, לִי נֵר מַעֲרָבִי,
בָּךְ כְּרוּב מִמְשָׁח יִגַּהּ אוֹר שְׁבִיבִי!

What made my beloved, who used to
graze between my fawn [-like breasts],
leave me[1] and take to the woods?
Come to the arms of your dearest, who
sings of her longing for you. O, my fair
love, light the western lamp[2] for me. In
you, towering cherub, my flame will
burn anew.

עִמָּנוּאֵל הָרוֹמִי

Immanuel of Rome

נַפְשִׁי בְּקִרְבִּי

EDEN AND HELL

נַפְשִׁי בְּקִרְבִּי פִּתְּחָשֹׁב מַחְשֶׁבֶת
לָקוּץ בְּעֵדֶן גַּן וְלִרְצוֹת תֹּפֶת,
כִּי אֶמְצָאָה שָׁם שׁוּף דְּבַשׁ עִם נֹפֶת,
שָׁם כָּל צְבִיַּת חֵן וְכָל עוֹגֶבֶת.

Deep in my heart I have resolved to
spurn the garden of Eden in favour of
Hell, for there I shall find dripping
honey and nectar: all the graceful does
and lustful ladies.

---

1. Lit. 'the [faithful] city', that is, Jerusalem.
2. The brightest light on the candlestick in the Temple.

מַה לִּי בְּעֵדֶן גַּן – וְאֵין אוֹהֶבֶת
שָׁם, רַק שְׁחֹרוֹת מִשָּׁחוֹר אוֹ זֶפֶת,
שָׁמָּה זְקֵנוֹת בַּעֲלוֹת יַלֶּפֶת –
נַפְשִׁי בְּחֶבְרָתָן תִּהְי נֶעֱצֶבֶת.

What is there for me in Eden? There
are no loves there, only women blacker
than soot or pitch, and crones covered
with lichen. My spirit would droop in
their company.

מַה לִּי וְלָךְ, עֵדֶן! וְאַתְּ אָסַפְתָּ
כָּל בַּעֲלוֹת מוּמִים וְכָל אִישׁ בֹּשֶׁת;
עַל כֵּן חֲשַׁבְתִּיךְ בְּעֵינַי אָיִן.

Eden, what are you to me? You
assemble all the maimed women and
infamous men. That is why I think of
you with contempt.

תֹּפֶת! בְּעֵינַי חֵן וְהוֹד יָסַפְתָּ;
בָּךְ כָּל צְבִיָּה הַיָּקָר לוֹבֶשֶׁת,
וַתֶּאֱסֹף כָּל מַחֲמַדֵּי עָיִן!

Hell, I consider you excellent in charm
and grandeur, for you house all the
girls in their elegant dresses. It is you
who have assembled all the delights of
our eyes.

שֵׂכֶל מְצַיֵּר   THE ODIOUS GIRL

שֵׂכֶל מְצַיֵּר! יוֹם אֲשֶׁר צִיַּרְתָּ
בַּת גֵּרְשֹׁם – כָּל הַיְקוּם הִכְלַמְתָּ;
יַעַן בְּגִשְׁמָהּ כָּל גְּנוּת הִשְׁלַמְתָּ,
כִּי בָא חֲלוֹם הַבּוּז, וְאַתְּ פָּתַרְתָּ.[1]

O creative Intelligence! The day you
created Gershom's daughter, you
shamed the universe, for in her body
you brought odium to perfection. It
seems you had a vile dream and
made it come true.[1]

אוּלַי לְקַבֵּץ כָּל גְּנוּת נָדַרְתָּ,
אוֹ לַעֲשׂוֹת יַנְשׁוּף וְקוֹף זָמַמְתָּ?
מָה הַחֲלוֹם הַזֶּה אֲשֶׁר חָלַמְתָּ?
אִם רוּחֲךָ סָרָה וְאִם שָׁכַרְתָּ?

Perhaps you vowed to lump all loathsome things together? Or else proposed
to fashion an owl and a monkey? How
did you ever dream up such a dream?
Were you soul-sick or were you drunk?

הַגֵּד, כְּרוּב מְמֻשָּׁח! הַאִם הַשֶּׂרֶד
אוֹ הַמְּחוּגָה מִמְּךָ גֻּנְּבוּ,
וַתַּעֲשֶׂה בַּת גֵּרְשֹׁם בָּרַחַת?

Tell me, Angel of delineation: were
your scribers or callipers stolen from
you, so that you had to use a winnowing
shovel in making Gershom's daughter?

---

1. Lit. 'you interpreted' [the dream by materializing it].

אוֹ פָּעֲלוּ בָה כּוֹכְבֵי רוֹם מֶרֶד –
סַרְטָן וְעַקְרָב אִם אֲזַי נִצָּבוּ
בְּזָנָב תְּלִי בַּמַּעֲלָה צוֹמַחַת !

Or did the stars rise up against her?
Did the Crab and the Scorpion then
station themselves at the tail end of the
Serpent, as it ascended the heavens?[1]

מִי הֶאֱמִין, עָפְרָה   IN PRAISE OF YOUR EYES

מִי הֶאֱמִין, עָפְרָה, אֲשֶׁר עֵינַיִךְ
הֵם יַעֲלוּ בַסַּעֲרָה שָׁמַיִם !
כִּי אֶחֱזֶה שַׁחַק בְּבֵין עַרְבַּיִם,
וְאֶחֱזֶה יוֹמָם בְּאוֹר פָּנָיִךְ.

Love, who would believe that your eyes
are carried up in a whirlwind to
heaven? But it is a fact: I see them in
the skies at twilight, and in your
shining face by day.

חַיַּי תְּלוּיִים בַּעֲגִיל אָזְנַיִךְ,
כִּי אֶחֱזֶה בּוֹ מַעֲשֵׂה מִצְרָיִם.
עוֹד אֶחֱזֶה בָךְ, מַאֲוַת עֵינַיִם,
עַל כּוֹכְבֵי שַׁחֲרֵךְ, בְּרַד שִׁנַּיִךְ.

My life hangs upon the earrings in
your ears, for they bewitch me with
Egyptian sorcery. Delight of my eyes, I
shall always behold your dawn-star
[eyes] and your hail [white] teeth.

אֶשְׁאַל, צְבִיַּת חֵן : הַאִם עֵינַיִךְ
הֵם כּוֹכְבֵי שַׁחַק, וְתִקְחִים בְּשִׁבְיִ
יוֹמָם, וְלַיְלָה יַעֲלוּ בַשָּׁחַק ?

Tell me, lovely gazelle: do you take the
stars of heaven for your eyes, holding
them captive by day, and when night
comes let them go back to heaven?

אוֹ הֵם דְּמוּת כּוֹכָב, וְאוֹר פָּנַיִךְ
דְּמִיּוֹן גְּלִילֵי רוֹם ? אֲשֶׁר כָּל הַצְּבָ-
יוֹת לָךְ כְּמוֹ מַר מִדְּלִי וּכְשַׁחַק !

Or are your eyes the likeness of the
stars, and is the light of your face the
image of the heavenly spheres? For, in
fact, all the other gazelles, compared to
you, are no more than drops from a
bucket, or specks of dust on the scales.

---

1. A configuration that would result in the birth of an ugly girl.

שָׁדַי נְכוֹנִים   THE VIRGIN'S COMPLAINT

שָׁדַי נְכוֹנִים, שְׂעָרַי צָמֵחַ,
וָאֵשְׁבָה עֵירֹם וְעֶרְיָה בֹשֶׁת.
דֹּדִים לְעָנְיִי רָאוּ מָגֵּשֶׁת,
וָאֵשְׁבָה בָרֹאשׁ בְּבֵית מַרְזֵחַ.

My breasts are firm and my hair is long,
yet I still sit in nakedness and shame.
My poverty has frightened away all the
suitors, and I sit [as if] at the head of
the table in a house of mourning.[1]

אֵיךְ יִהְיֶה עוֹד הַלֵּבָב שָׂמֵחַ?
אָפְסוּ כְסָפַי, אֵין זָהָב וּנְחֹשֶׁת.
אֵיךְ אֶמְצָאָה בַעַל אֲנִי – וּשְׁלֹשֶׁת
אֲחָיוֹת גְּדוֹלוֹת לִי, וְלֵב גּוֹנֵחַ.

How can my heart ever rejoice when
all my silver is gone and I have no gold
or bronze? How will I ever find a
husband, when all I have are three
older [impoverished] sisters and a
groaning heart?

מָה אָמְרָה, דּוֹדַי: עֲצָמַי חָרוּ,
אוֹ עִם זְמַן בּוֹגֵד בְּרִית אֶכְרָתָה?
עָפוּ שְׁנוֹתַי, פָּשְׂטוּ כַיֶּלֶק.

How can I tell, suitors, if my bones
will be scorched [by desire] or if I will
be able to strike a bargain with
treacherous Time? My years are flying
away, spreading their wings like locusts!

גַּם יָשְׁבוּ שָׂרִים וּבִי נִדְבָּרוּ:
אִשָּׁה אֲשֶׁר תָּמוּת בְּתוּלָה – נִכְרָתָה,
אֵין לָהּ בְּעוֹלָם הַנְּשָׁמוֹת חֵלֶק!

And what is more, the wise men sit and
scheme together against me: 'She that
dies a virgin is cut off; she will have no
share in the world to come!'

זֶה לִי שְׁנָתַיִם   THE WIFE'S COMPLAINT

זֶה לִי שְׁנָתַיִם אֲשֶׁר נָשָׂאתִי
בַּעַל – וְעוֹדוֹ חַי, וְאֵין לִי נֹעַם.
יָמוּת בְּחֵץ בָּרָק וּמִקּוֹל רַעַם,
אָז בֵּין בְּנוֹת הַחֵן אֱהִי שָׂרָתִי.

Two years have already passed since I
took a husband, but he is still alive, and
I can have no pleasure. If only he
would die of lightning's dart or
thunder's roar, I would be queen
among the charming ladies.

---

1. The chief mourner customarily presided over the mourning feast.

הַמָּוְתָה יוֹם יוֹם אֲנִי קָרָאתִי,
כִּי נִכְסְפָה נַפְשִׁי לְשַׁנּוֹת טָעַם.
לֹא אֵדְעָה מָה אַחֲרִית הַזַּעַם,
יוּאַר וְיֹאבַד יוֹם בְּבֵיתוֹ בָּאתִי !

Day after day I call for Death to come,
for my soul longs for a change of fare.
I do not know how this outrage will
end. Oh, perish the day when I came
into his house!

אֶרְאֶה שְׁכָנְתִּי : בֵּין שְׁלוֹשִׁים חֹדֶשׁ
שָׁלוֹשׁ פְּעָמִים בְּעָלִים קָבָרָה.
כָּל הַשְּׁכֵנוֹת אוֹמְרוֹת : אַשְׁרֶיהָ !

I see that my neighbour, within the
span of thirty months, has three times
buried a husband. All the neighbourhood wives exclaim: 'How happy she
must be!'

הִיא חִלְּלָה אֵלִים וְשָׂרֵי קֹדֶשׁ.
הִיא כַּלְּבִיָּא בֵּין אֲרָיוֹת גָּרָה
וּבְתוֹךְ כְּפִירִים רִבְּתָה גּוּרֶיהָ.

She spurned heroes and princes [for
the sake of lovers]. Like a lioness, she
made her lair among young lions, and
she lay in their midst, bearing her cubs.

רְאוּ נָבָל   THE MISER

וְזֶה הַשִּׁיר אֲשֶׁר חִבַּרְתִּי עַל הָאִישׁ
אֲשֶׁר בַּסֵּתֶר יֵחַם [אֶת בִּגְדִי] :

*And this is the poem I wrote about the
man who secretly wore my clothes:*

רְאוּ נָבָל, יְהִי רַע אַחֲרִיתוֹ
וְשָׁמַיִם יְגַלּוּ אֶת עֲווֹנוֹ !
אֲשֶׁר לוֹ צֹאן – וְכִבְשַׂת רָשׁ יְאַוֶּה
לְקַחְתָּהּ לוֹ, בְּחֶמְלָתוֹ לְצֹאנוֹ ;
וְלוֹ עָרְלָה, וּמִיִּרְאַת בְּלוֹתָהּ –
יְאַו לִבְעֹל בְּמוֹ עָרְלַת שְׁכֵנוֹ.

Behold this scoundrel – may his end be
bitter, may the heavens lay bare his
guilt! He has flocks of his own, but
rather than deplete them he prefers to
take the poor man's lamb. He has a
foreskin, but for fear of wearing it out
he would rather use his neighbour's
when he copulates.

דּוֹד, יוֹם קְרָאתִיהוּ   THE EGOIST

דּוֹד, יוֹם קְרָאתִיהוּ לְעֶזְרָתוֹ,
גָּז חִישׁ כְּצִפּוֹר מִמְּרוֹם קִנּוֹ.
אַךְ יוֹם לְעֶזְרָתִי קְרָאתִיהוּ,
הֶחֱרִישׁ כְּפֶתֶן יַאְטֵם אָזְנוֹ.
נִדְמֶה לְכֶלֶב אִישׁ חֲרַשׁ בַּרְזֶל,
בֵּית הוֹלְמִים שִׁבְתּוֹ וּמִשְׁכָּנוֹ :
יִישַׁן לְקוֹל פַּטִּישׁ וְיֵרָדֵם,
יִיקַץ לְעֵת אֹכֶל לְקוֹל שִׁנּוֹ.

This friend – when I summoned him, to come to his aid, he swooped to my side like a bird from its high nest. But when I summoned him, to come to my aid, he turned as deaf as an asp that stops its ears. He is like a blacksmith's dog, living in a forge: he dozes off and sleeps to the sound of the hammers, but wakes up for meals to the sound of teeth.

חוּשָׁה, מְשִׁיחַ אֵל   ADVICE TO THE MESSIAH

חוּשָׁה, מְשִׁיחַ אֵל, וְלָמָּה תַעֲמֹד ?
הִנֵּה מְחַכִּים לָךְ דְּמָעוֹת נוֹטְפִים.
הָיוּ דְמֵי דִמְעָם נְחָלִים שׁוֹטְפִים,
כָּל לֵב וְכָל לָשׁוֹן לְךָ, שַׂר, יַחֲמֹד.

Make haste, Lord's anointed, why are you lingering? They are waiting for you, weeping bitterly. Their tears, mixed with their heart's blood, have swelled to a torrent. O Prince, every heart and every tongue longs for you.

וּקְחָה פְּתִיל פִּשְׁתִּים בְּיָדֶיךָ, וּמֹד
צִיּוֹן כְּלִיל יֹפִי, וּבָנֶיהָ – עוֹדְפִים
יִהְיוּ בְּכָל חֵן טוֹב, וְצָרִים שׁוֹאֲפִים
יִגְלוּ בְרֹאשׁ גּוֹלִים, וְאַתָּה פֹה עֲמֹד.

Now take a cord of linen thread in your hands,[1] and measure Zion, perfect in beauty. Then her children will surpass all others in grace and goodness. The oppressive enemies will be the first to go into exile, and you will stand fast [in Zion].

עוּרָה, מְשִׁיחֵנוּ, צְלַח כַּיּוֹם רְכַב
עַל סוּס אֲשֶׁר דּוֹהֵר, וּמֶרְכָּבָה רְתֹם,
כִּי כָל עֲצָמַי נִפְזְרוּ, אֵין בָּם מְתֹם !

Arise, Messiah, ride forth today victoriously upon a charging horse, harness the steeds to the chariot – for all my bones have been scattered, and not one is intact.

1. As did the bronze-like man in Ezekiel's vision (40.3).

426

אִם עַל חֲמוֹר תִּרְכַּב, אֲדוֹנִי – שׁוּב שְׁכָב !
אִיעָצְךָ, הַשַּׂר מְשִׁיחֵנוּ, בְּתֹם
לִבִּי : סְתֹם הַקֵּץ וְהֶחָזוֹן חֲתֹם !

But if you mean to ride on an ass,[1] my
lord, go back to sleep! If so, prince and
Messiah, allow me, in good faith, to
give you this advice: You had best keep
the end secret and seal up the vision!

יִצְחָק אַלְחָדִיב   *Isaac Alḥadib*

אִישׁ מָהִיר   ISAAC-OF-ALL-TRADES

אִישׁ מָהִיר אֲנִי בַּמְּהִירִים,
וּמְלָאכוֹת רַבּוֹת לָמַדְתִּי.
לִטְווֹת גַּם לֶאֱרֹג יָדַעְתִּי,
וּלְהָכִין לִי בָּתֵּי־נִירִים.

I am the most skilful of men and I have
mastered many trades. I know how to
spin as well as to weave, and how to
prepare the meshes.

בִּימֵי חָרְפִּי חָשְׁקָה נַפְשִׁי
לִהְיוֹת פָּרָשׁ אִישׁ מִלְחָמָה,
לָשׂוּם לִי כּוֹבַע עַל רֹאשִׁי,
לִרְכֹּב עַל סוּס נַחֲרוֹ אֵימָה.
שִׁרְיוֹן קַשְׂקַשִּׂים מַלְבּוּשִׁי,
רוֹבֶה קַשָּׁת, מַפִּיל חוֹמָה.
אַךְ בִּרְאוֹתִי כִּי בַמְּהוּמָה
עִם הָרוֹדְפִים יָשׁוּב נִרְדָּף,
יִבְרַח מִקּוֹל עָלֶה נִדָּף –
שַׁבְתִּי לִמְלֶאכֶת אִכָּרִים.

In my youth I longed to be a horseman
and a warrior; to wear a helmet on my
head, and ride a horse whose neighing
strikes terror; to put on a coat of mail;
to be an archer, and batter down the
fortress walls. But when I saw that in
this tumult the pursuer becomes the
pursued, taking flight at the sound of a
driven leaf, I turned back to the
peasant's toil.

---

1. As prophesied in Zechariah 9.9: 'Lo, your king comes to you . . . humble and riding on an ass . . .'

טָעַמְתִּי מִמְּסַּר הַיַּיִן,
כַּמָּה נָעִים, כַּמָּה יָפֶה !
שׁוֹתֶה יִתֵּן בְּכוֹס עַיִן,
מוֹכֵר אֶל כִּיס שׁוֹתֶה צוֹפֶה.
כָּל זֶה הָיָה נֶגְדִּי אַיִן.
עוֹד לָמַדְתִּי לִהְיוֹת רוֹפֵא :
מֵעוֹת חִנָּם עַל דִּבְרֵי פֶה,
בְּקּוּר חוֹלִים, בְּקּוּר חוֹלוֹת,
מְשׁוּשׁ בַּנָּשִׁים וּבְתוּלוֹת,
חָזֶה וּזְרוֹעַ נִסְתָּרִים.

I tasted the wine trade: what a pleasure, what a delight! The drinker eyes his cup while the merchant eyes *his* pocket ... But this was child's play for me, so I learned to be a doctor: pocketing undeserved fees for idle talk, making the rounds of bed-ridden men and women, fingering women and girls down to their hidden breasts and thighs.

קָלִי, כַּרְמֶל אֵדַע לַחֲרֹךְ,
לְצְלוֹת בָּשָׂר תּוֹךְ הַכְּבְשָׁן.
יַיִן חָדָשׁ בַּגַּת אֶדְרֹךְ,
אַךְ לִשְׁתּוֹת אֶבְחַר הַיָּשָׁן.
לִפְנֵי שׁוֹפְטִים טַעֲנוֹת אֶעֱרֹךְ,
לִפְנֵי קָהָל אֶהְיֶה דַרְשָׁן.
מִבַּלְתִּי אֵשׁ – אַעֲלֶה עָשָׁן,
אֲחַזְתִּי בַּלָּט עֵינַיִם,
אִתִּי כָּל חָכְמַת מִצְרַיִם :
חַרְטֹם, אַשָּׁף, רֹאשׁ הַהוֹבְרִים.

I know how to parch ripe grain, and to roast meat in the oven. I tread young wine in the press but for my drink I take the old. I can argue a case before the bench and deliver a sermon in public. I can raise smoke, without fire. Stealthily I hoodwink one and all, for I possess all the wisdom of Egypt: magician, exorcist, and astrologer-in-chief!

זֶה כַּמָּה שָׁנִים חָשַׁבְתִּי
בִּמְלֶאכֶת כִּימְיָא מַחְשָׁבוֹת;
כַּמָּה כֵלִים לִי תִקַּנְתִּי
מֵעֲפַר אֶרֶץ־מַלְאוּבוֹת;
לוּלֵי מִין אֶחָד חָסַרְתִּי –
הָיוּ קוֹרוֹתַי מְזֻהָבוֹת!
עַתָּה בִּרְקִיקִים וּלְבִיבוֹת
וּמְלֶאכֶת־בֹּרִית עָסַקְתִּי
– כִּי בָהֶם יוֹתֵר הִרְוַחְתִּי –
וּבַמֶּרְחָץ לִרְחֹץ לַאֲחֵרִים.

For several years I pondered over the art of alchemy. I fashioned a few vessels out of scorched earth. Had I not lacked one single element, my rafters would now be covered with gold! So then I dealt in wafers and pancakes; I manufactured soap and scrubbed down people in the bath house. In these callings, I raked in a bigger profit.

חָקַרְתִּי כָּל אַרְצוֹת מַעֲרָב,
אֶל הַמִּזְרָח שַׂמְתִּי פָנַי,
קוֹרֵא : מִי זֶה לְבּוֹ עָרֵב –
יָבוֹא יָשִׁיב עַל הִגְיוֹנַי !
בִּגְלִילוֹת צָרְפַת וּבַעֲרָב
לֹא עָמַד אִישׁ עַל עִנְיָנַי.
נִלְאֵיתִי עוֹד, אֶשָּׂא פָנַי
אַשּׁוּר, בָּבֶל, גַּם תּוֹגַרְמָה :
אָז נוֹדַע כִּי בִלְתִּי – מִרְמָה,
בִּלְעָדַי אִישׁ יָד לֹא יָרִים !

I explored all the lands of the West,
then made my way through the East.
Everywhere I announced: 'If anyone
dare, let him step forth and discredit
me!' In all the provinces of France and
Arabia, no one saw through my game.
Tiring of them, I turned and made for
Assyria, Babylon, and Turkey. There it
became clear, at last, that except for me
all was fraud, and without me no man
could lift a finger!

דּוֹן וִידָאל בֶּנְבְנִשְׂתְּ *Don Vidal Benveniste*

נֹחַם לְנַפְשָׁהּ ## DINAH REJECTS THE OLD SUITOR

נֹחַם לְנַפְשָׁהּ מֵאֲנָה לָקַחַת
דִּינָה בְּקָרַחַת וְגַם גַּבַּחַת:
כִּי רָאֲתָה שֵׂיבָה בְּדֶגֶל אַהֲבָה
עַל קִיר לְבָבָהּ הוּא כְּמוֹ מִסְפַּחַת.
לֹא יַעֲלֹז רוּחָהּ בְּחֶמְדַּת אוֹצְרוֹת
כֶּסֶף, וְלֹא מָצְאָה לְנַפְשָׁהּ נַחַת.
יֶעֱרַב מְשׁוֹשׁ גִּילָהּ בְּבֶן גִּילָהּ, וְתוֹךְ
חֶבְרַת צְבִי־עֹפֶר זְמִיר פּוֹצַחַת.
מֵאֵין מְחִיר דּוֹד נֶאֱהָב נֶחְשַׁב זָהָב
אוֹפִיר, וּפָנָיו – מִגְדְּלוֹת מִרְקַחַת.
אָכֵן מְלֵא יָמִים בְּפָנִים זוֹעֲפִים
– עִם רֹב זָהָבוֹ – נֶחְשַׁב אַמְתַּחַת !

Dinah refuses to take comfort in a bald
pate and a bare forehead. She knows
that such a hoary love[1] will cover the
walls of her heart with scurf. Her spirit
cannot rejoice in precious stores of
silver; her soul would find no rest. She
can savour delight only with a youth of
her own age; in the company of a
young lover she would break into song.
Though penniless, the true love is as
dear as the gold of Ophir. His cheeks
are like chests full of perfumes. But the
greybeard with the glowering face, for
all his gold, he is nothing but a bag!

1. Lit. 'old age with a banner of love'.

יְדִידוּת יְפַת תֹּאַר | BITTER AND SWEET

יְדִידוּת יְפַת תֹּאַר חֲזָקָה וְאַדֶּרֶת,
חֲלָקָה כְּחֶמְאָה, אַךְ שְׂעִירָה כְּאַדֶּרֶת.
וְרַכּוּ דְבָרֶיהָ, וְעוֹדָהּ מְדַבֶּרֶת –
בְּחִנָּהּ חֲנִיתוֹת עַל לְבָבִי מְעוֹרֶרֶת.
דְּבַשׁ עַל שְׂפָתֶיהָ, וְרוֹשׁ מַאֲכִילֵנִי,
וְנֹפֶת בְּתוֹךְ חִכָּהּ, וְחַיַּי מְמָרֶרֶת.
וְחָלְקוּ אֲמָרֶיהָ, וְטוּחוֹת מְחַלֶּקֶת,
וְעֵת מַעֲנֶה רַכּוֹת, עֲצָמוֹת מְשַׁבֶּרֶת. [...]
לְשָׁרֵת יְדִידוּתָהּ אֲנִי הוּא וְלֹא אַחֵר,
אֲנִי הוּא – וְלֹא אָמִיר כְּבוֹדָהּ בְּאַחֶרֶת.

The love of this graceful girl is strong
and formidable. It is as smooth as
butter and as prickly as a hairy mantle.
Her words are soft, but even as she
speaks, she brandishes her charm like
spears over my heart. There is honey
on her lips, but she feeds me poison;
her tongue drips sweetness, yet she
makes my life bitter. Her speech is
smooth, but it pierces my bowels; and
when she answers softly, she breaks my
bones. Still, I, and none but I, shall
wait upon her love. I am the only one,
and I would not exchange her glory for
any other.

שְׁלֹמֹה בּוֹנָפִיד | *Solomon Bonafed*

רְאֵה סוּסִים | TOPSY-TURVY WORLD

רְאֵה סוּסִים בְּלֵב יָם כַּבְּרָקִים
יְרוֹצְצוּ, וָאֳנִיּוֹת – בַּשְּׁוָקִים,
וְחוּט פִּשְׁתִּים מָטִיל בַּרְזֶל יְפוֹצֵץ,
וּמַיִם בּוֹעֲרִים כָּעֵץ וְדוֹלְקִים,
וּבוֹרְחִים הַנְּמֵרִים מִגְּדָיִים,
וְשׁוּעָלִים אֲרֵי רוֹדְפִים וְדוֹלְקִים.
וְאַל תִּתְמַהּ בְּשׁוּב עוֹלָם הֲסַכְפַּךְ
וְעִתִּים מִנְּתִיב טִבְעָם רְחוֹקִים,
וְהַאֲמֵן זֶה בְּשׁוּרְךָ מַעֲגְּלֵי אִישׁ
נְלוֹזִים: יוֹם וְיוֹם נַעֲשׂוּ עֲשׁוּקִים,
וְהַחָכְמָה כְּמֵת מָלֵב זְנוּחָה,

See how horses streak through the sea
like lightning bolts, and ships sail
through the market-place. A thread of
linen splinters a bar of iron, and water
blazes like wood. Leopards flee before
kids and foxes give chase to lions. Nor
should you marvel that the world is
turned topsy-turvy and the times have
strayed from their natural course.
Believe all this when you behold how
man perverts his ways. Oppression
grows from day to day. Wisdom, like a
dead man, is put out of mind; it is the

וּבָהּ יִתְעַלְלוּ עוֹלְלִים וְיוֹנְקִים.
וְעֵת יִתְחַתְּנוּ לֹא יִשְׁאֲלוּ, אִם
חֲכָמִים הֵם – אֲבָל אִם הוֹן מְרִיקִים!
וְהַחַיָּט, בְּעֵת יוֹצֵא בְמַחְטוֹ,
יָדַם לַנְפִּיל יְלִידֵי הָעֲנָקִים;
פְּתִילֵי בַד לְצַוָּארוֹ עֲנָקִים,
וְחוּטָיו מִדְּבַשׁ אֶל פִּיו מְתוּקִים.
וְהַצּוֹרֵף בְּכוּר יְשֹׁרַף זְקָנוֹ,
וְעֵינָיו יַאְדִּים עִם אֵשׁ וְזִקִים;
חֲמָדוּהוּ בְּכַסְפּוֹ אוֹ זְהָבוֹ –
וְאוּלַי אֵין בְּכַסְפּוֹ לוֹ חֲלָקִים.
וְאוֹרֵג יַחֲשֹׁב מָנוֹר כְּכִנּוֹר,
וּמַסֶּכֶת – כְּמַסֶּכֶת נְזִיקִים.
וְרַצְעָן – נוֹשְׁקוֹת נָשִׁים שְׂפָתָיו,
וְשִׁנָּיו מוֹשְׁכִים עוֹרוֹת וְנוֹשְׁקִים.
וְנָבָל יַעֲנֶה עַזּוּת בְּעָשְׁרוֹ,
וְגַאֲוָתוֹ וְעֻזּוֹ בַּשְּׁחָקִים.

לְכָה, דּוֹד צַח, וְנֵלְכָה עַל פְּנֵי חוּץ
לְמֶרְחַקִּים בְּבֵין שִׂיחִים מְשַׂחֲקִים,
בְּבֵין שִׂיחִים וּבֵין אַחִים כְּאַחִים,
בְּתוֹךְ גַּנִּים, וְלֹא בֵּינוֹת נְקִיקִים,
וְנַקִּיף אָהֳלֵנוּ מַעֲרוּגוֹת
חֲבַצֶּלֶת וְשׁוֹשַׁנַּת עֲמָקִים,
וְרֵעֵינוּ יְהוּ כָּל צִפֳּרֵי חֵן
וְזִיו שַׂדַּי וְיוֹנִים עַל אֲפִיקִים.
וְלֹא נִרְאֶה בְּתַהְפּוּכוֹת זְמַנִּים
וְלֹא נָבִין בְּסָרָה מַעֲמִיקִים,

sport of babes and infants. And when
they marry off their daughters they do
not ask if the bridegroom is wise, but
how much money pours out of him!
The tailor, stepping forth with his
needle in hand, deems himself a giant-
killer. The cords of cloth, hung round
his neck, he takes for necklaces, and his
threads are sweeter to his tongue than
honey. The goldsmith's beard is singed
in the crucible and his eyes bloodshot
from fire and sparks, and still he is
prized for his silver or gold – though
none of it may be his! The weaver
thinks his loom is a lyre, and his warp
a harp.[1] The cobbler – women kiss his
lips, while his teeth are tugging hides
and kissing them. The churl, secure in
his riches, makes harsh replies; his
pride and his might as high as heaven!

Oh, let us go, my fair companion, let us
walk far afield, and amuse ourselves
among the thickets. Let us sport like
brothers in thicket and meadows, in
soft gardens, not in rocky crevices. We
shall surround our tents with beds of
lilies and roses. All birds of grace, the
teeming life of the fields, doves beside
brooks of water – these shall be our
playmates. And there we shall not see
the vagaries of time nor pay heed to
wicked betrayers. Now we shall laugh

---

1. Lit. 'thinks his web (*masekhet*) is a tractate (*masekhet*) from the Talmudic division of *Nezikin*
("Damages")'.

וּפַעַם נִלְעֲגָה עַל הַזְּמַנִּים,
וּפַעַם נִדְרְשָׁה סוֹדוֹת עֲמֻקִּים,
עֲסִיס חָכְמָה לְאַט נִשְׁתֶּה בְּצָמָא,
וּמִסֹּלֶת זְמִיר נֹאכַל רְקִיקִים.
עֲדֵי יָשׁוּב זְמַן עָוֶל לְתַקֵּן
אֲשֶׁר עִוֵּת, הֲרִיסוֹתָיו לְהָקִים,
וְיַבְדִּיל בֵּין בְּדִיל אֶל פָּז וְיַחְפֹּץ
לְהַפְרִישׁ בֵּין חֲגָבִים לַעֲנָקִים.

time to scorn and now we shall delve
into deep mysteries. Slowly, eagerly,
we shall drink the wine of wisdom and
feed on wafers of choice[1] melodies –
until time mend again what it had
twisted and restore all it has ruined;
until time set apart the lead from the
gold, and the grasshoppers from the
giants.

קְרַב, דּוֹד צַח, וְאֶפְצַח רָן, וְתָרֹן
לְשׁוֹן אִלֵּם וְנָסוּ כָּל מְצוּקִים.
קְרַב, פֶּן יַדְרְכוּ קַשְׁתָּם מְקַנְּאִים
וְחוֹשְׁקִים לִהְיוֹת לָבוּז חֲשׁוּקִים.
בְּעֵת תִּקְרַב וְעֵת תִּרְחַק, כְּרוּבִי,
לְשֵׁם חֶבְרָתְךָ יָמַי עֲסוּקִים.
וְאִם תִּרְאֶה בְּדוֹד אַחֵר אֲמִירְךָ –
רְאֵה סוּסִים בְּלֵב יָם כַּבְּרָקִים!

Draw near, my fair companion, and I
shall break into song, and the mouths
of the dumb will shout for joy, and all
distress will vanish. Draw near, lest the
jealous ones, who love to put lovers to
scorn,[2] string their bows against us.
But whether you draw near or go afar,
my cherub, all my days are given over
to your friendship. And should you
ever see me exchanging you for another
love – you will also see horses streaking
through the sea like lightning bolts!

מֹשֶׁה רִיאָטִי

Moses da Rieti

פֶּלֶא עָצוּם רָאִיתִי

IN THE PALACE OF HEAVEN

פֶּלֶא עָצוּם רָאִיתִי בַּהֵיכָל:
נְשָׁמוֹת נְשָׂאוֹת בָּאֲוִירוֹ,
לְסַפֵּר יְקָרָם אִישׁ לֹא יוּכָל.

Then I saw a great marvel in the palace:
souls hovering in the air. No one could
describe their splendour.

1. A play on *solet* which also means 'flour'.
2. Or, 'who desire to be loved by vileness'.

הֵם כָּל מַפְלִיג לְאֱהֹב יוֹצְרוֹ,
מוֹסֵר עַצְמוֹ עַל קְדֻשַּׁת הַשֵּׁם,
מַזְכִּיר 'אֶחָד' וּפוֹשֵׁט צַוָּארוֹ.

The souls of those who loved their
Creator passionately, who sanctified
the Holy Name with their lives, baring
their necks to the knife as they proclaimed 'The [Lord is] One.'

אֶל מַלְאֲכֵי שָׁרֵת הֵן אֲקִישֵׁם,
בְּהוֹדָם וּבְהָדָר אֶל הַחַיּוֹת.
וְצִיץ עֲלֵי רֹאשָׁם וּבוֹ רוֹשֵׁם:

I would compare them to the ministering angels; in majesty and glory, to the
living creatures. There is a rosette on
their forehead, and on it is engraved
[as on a seal]:

'הוּא קֹדֶשׁ לַיְיָ' בָּאוֹתִיּוֹת.
וּכְנָפַיִם לָהֶם וּמְעוֹפְפִים
לְהַשִּׂיג הָרִאשׁוֹן לְכָל הֱיוֹת.

'Holy to the Lord.'[1] They have wings
and they soar to approach the Primal
Being.

הַנִּשְׂרָפִים מַרְאֵיהֶם כִּשְׂרָפִים,
הַנִּשְׁחָטִים רוֹחֲצִים בֶּחָלָב,
וְהַנִּתְלִים, כֵּן, עֵינֵיהֶם יָפִים.

Those who died by fire look like the
fiery seraphim; those who were
slaughtered bathe in milk; and those
who were hung, their eyes are sparkling.

וְכָל נִדְחָק – כְּפִי מַה שֶּׁנֶּעֱלַב
שָׁם יִשָּׂא הוֹד, וּמַטֵּהוּ יִפְרַח,
בִּבְנֵי אֵלִים מִתְרַפֵּק וְנִשְׁלָב.

And all those who were oppressed – the
greater their humiliation, the greater
now their glory. Their staffs blossom
forth; they lean on the sons of God and
join in their ranks.

סַנְהֶדְרִין גְּדוֹלָה בְּצַד מִזְרָח,
וּדְמוּת פְּנֵי כֻלָּם צַח וְאָדֹם,
וּבָם אוֹר הַדַּעַת רִאשׁוֹן יִזְרַח.

The Great Sanhedrin[2] is assembled in
the east; their faces glow, ruddy and
pure. The light of divine wisdom shines
first upon them.

יְלָדִים בְּלִי מוּם עַל כָּל הֲדוֹם. [...]

[And at their feet,] upon every foot-
stool, there sits a perfect child.

---

1. Exodus 28.36.
2. The supreme judicial council.

הַיּוֹם פָּנָה — THE ENCOUNTER

הַיּוֹם פָּנָה וְנָטָה לַעֲרָב,
וְהַזָּקֵן, תָּמִים, אַב הַחָכְמָה,
יָעַד פָּנָיו נֶגְדִּי וּמִקָּרוֹב.

The day was declining and drawing to
its close, when the righteous old man,
this father of wisdom, drew his face
close to mine.

וְעֵת נִרְאוּ מְכוֹכְבֵי רוֹמָה
שָׁלוֹשׁ הַכּוֹכָבִים הַמַּבְדִּילִים
הָאוֹר וְהַחֹשֶׁךְ כְּמְלוֹא נִימָא –

And when the three stars which
separate light from dark by a hair's
breadth appeared high up in heaven,

כְּגֶבֶר שׁוֹתֵק לְזְמִירוֹת אֵלִים,
אוֹ לְקָרִיאַת מָרוֹם אֹמֶר גָּמַר,
לָבַשׁ מַלְאָכוּת וְעָצַר מִלִּים.

then, like a man who falls silent when
the angels sing, or like one who is
speechless, obeying a summons from
heaven, he clothed himself in the shape
of an angel and said no more.

וּכְאִישׁ, עַל פֵּרוּד בֵּן לִבּוֹ נִכְמָר,
צוּרַת נַפְשׁוֹ בְּרַחֲמִים סוּגָה,
בְּעַיִן מָלֵא חֶמְלָה 'בְּנִי,' אָמַר,

But then, like a man whose heart is
moved, whose soul is flooded with
compassion as he bids his son farewell,
his eyes filled with pity and he said,
'My son,

'כְּבָר נִשְׁלַם הֶקֵּף הַהַשָּׂגָה.
אֵלְכָה לִּי אֶל הַר שָׁם אָהֳלִי,
שֶׁמָּא אֲחוּרִי עוֹד הוּא כִּשְׁגָגָה.'

'The [light of] intelligence has run its
course; let me return to my home on
the mountain. My delay may still be
taken as an oversight.'

'אֲדוֹנִי,' אָמַרְתִּי, 'כִּמְדֻמֶּה לִי
רְאִיתִיךָ כְּבָר בִּימֵי נַעֲרוּת,
וּתְמוּנָתְךָ לֹא תִתְבָּאֵר אֶצְלִי.

'My lord,' I said, 'it seems to me that I
have seen you in my youth, but I
cannot place your image.

אַחַר אִם לֶכְתְּךָ מִשְׁפָּט חָרוּת,
שֵׁם כְּבוֹדְךָ אֶשְׁאַל נָא בְּדֶמַע,
שֵׁם מִדְרָשְׁךָ וְכֵן בֵּית הַסְּפָרוּת.

'If, indeed, you are compelled to leave,
let me tearfully inquire what your
honour's name is, and the name and
place of your house of study.

וְאִם מֵי חָכְמָתְךָ עוֹד לֹא אֶגְמַע,
בָּרְכֵנִי עֵת אֲשַׁאֵר בִּלְתָּךְ!'
'נָשָׂאתִי פָנֶיךָ,' הֵשִׁיב, 'וּשְׁמַע –

'And if I can no longer drink from the waters of your wisdom, bless me, now that you are leaving me behind.' 'I shall grant your request,' he answered. 'Now listen –

אִם אֹרֶךְ הַזְּמַן אוֹ צוּק עִתְּךָ
צָרוּ לַזִּכָּרוֹן וַיִּמָּחֵק,
אוֹ עֹצֶם מַרְאָה זוֹ מְבַעֶתְךָ –

'If the passage of time or your hardships have conspired to erase this memory, or if the power of this vision stuns you with fear,

יָמִים רַבִּים נְשָׂאתִיךָ עַל חֵיק,
וּבַתּוֹרָה שֶׁבִּכְתָב מִלְּשׁוֹנִי
הֵן בְּתֵבֵל הָיִיתָ מְשַׂחֵק.

'[know that] for many days I carried you in my arms, and it was from my lips that you learned the Written Law, in which you rejoiced on earth.

אָבִיךָ זֶה יְלָדְךָ אֲנִי!
נַעַר הָיִיתָ עֵת אֲשֶׁר כָּלָה
עֲנַן חַיַּי וְסָלַק לִמְעוֹנִי.'

'I am your father, who gave you life! You were but a child when my life's cloud faded and was banished to the zone I now inhabit.'

אֲזַי מָתְנַי אָחֲזוּ חַלְחָלָה,
וָאֶקֹּד לְפָנָיו מֵאֵין אוֹנִים.
וְנֶעֱלַם מֵעֵינַי שָׁם, וְעָלָה –

At this, my limbs writhed in anguish; all my strength fled, I bowed down before him. And he vanished before my eyes, he flew up,

לָקַח דַּרְכּוֹ פְּנֵי שַׂר הַפָּנִים.
וְקוֹל יוֹרֵד אָז מִפֶּתַח שָׁמָיו,
רֶגַע אֲשֶׁר נִכְנַס לִפְנַי לִפְנִים:

making his way towards the Angel of the Presence.[1] And just as he entered the Innermost Chamber, a voice came down from the gate of heaven:

'וְאֵל שַׁדַּי יִתֵּן לְךָ רַחֲמָיו.'

'May God Almighty grant you His mercy!'

---

1. Lit. 'the Prince of the Face'.

מֹשֶׁה גַבַּאי *Moses Gabbai*

אַשְׁרֵי עַיִן INVOCATION OF RAIN

אַשְׁרֵי עַיִן רָאֲתָה כָּל אֵלֶּה !
הֲלֹא לְמִשְׁמַע אֹזֶן צָהֲלָה נַפְשֵׁנוּ.

Happy the eye that saw all this! We
hear of it and our soul rejoices.

אַשְׁרֵי עַיִן רָאֲתָה מַיִם יוֹרְדִים מִשְּׁחָקִים,
וְהָרוּחַ מְרַחֵף עַל פְּנֵי אֲרָקִים,
וְהַצַּדִּיק מְרַחֵשׁ לָאֵל עוֹשֵׂה בְרָקִים,
לְמוּל כָּל הָעָם אוֹמְרִים דְּבָרִים מְתוּקִים.
הֲלֹא לְמִשְׁמַע אֹזֶן צָהֲלָה נַפְשֵׁנוּ.

Happy the eye that saw water pouring
down from heaven, and the wind
sweeping over the earth, as the
righteous man whispers to God, Maker
of lightning, and all the people stand
before him, murmuring sweet words.
We hear of this and our soul rejoices.

אַשְׁרֵי עַיִן רָאֲתָה שַׁחֲרוּת עָבִים נִצָּבוֹת,
וְהָרוּחַ מְרַחֵף בְּמֵי גֶשֶׁם נְדָבוֹת,
וְהַצַּדִּיק מְרַחֵשׁ לָאֵל רוֹכֵב עֲרָבוֹת:
'הִתְחַזְּקוּ, אֱמוּנִים, כִּי זֹרְמוּ מַיִם עָבוֹת!'
הֲלֹא לְמִשְׁמַע אֹזֶן צָהֲלָה נַפְשֵׁנוּ.

Happy the eye that saw the blackness
of massed clouds, and the wind sweeping through with a downpour of
blessings, as the righteous man whispers
to God, who rides over the desert
plains. 'Courage, my faithful ones, the
clouds are pouring down water!' We
hear of this and our soul rejoices.

אַשְׁרֵי עַיִן רָאֲתָה הֲדַר בָּרָק וּרְעָמִים נוֹהִים,
וְהָרוּחַ מְרַחֵף וְכָל הַלְּבָבוֹת רוֹהִים,
וְהַצַּדִּיק מְרַחֵשׁ לָאֵל צוּר דָּר גְּבֹהִים,
וּלְמוּל כָּל הָעָם כַּאֲרִי עַל טַרְפּוֹ מֵהִים:
'הִתְחַזְּקוּ, אֱמוּנִים, גֶּשֶׁם נְדָבוֹת הֵנִיף אֱלֹהִים!'
הֲלֹא לְמִשְׁמַע אֹזֶן צָהֲלָה נַפְשֵׁנוּ.

Happy the eye that saw the glory of
lightning, and thunders in hot pursuit,
with the wind sweeping over, and all
hearts struck with fear, as the righteous
man whispers to God, the Rock, who
dwells on high, and before him stand
the people, roaring like a lion over its
prey. 'Courage, my faithful ones, God
is raining a downpour of blessings.'
We hear of this and our soul rejoices.

אַשְׁרֵי עַיִן רָאֲתָה מַיִם בְּחוּצוֹת וּשְׁבִילִים,
וְהָרוּחַ מְרַחֵף לְדַשֵּׁן כָּל יְבוּלִים,
וְהַצַּדִּיק עַל רֹאשׁוֹ מַיִם יוֹרְדִים וְעוֹלִים,
וְזֹרְקִים אֶת אֶפְרוֹ וְשַׂעֲרוֹתָיו טְבוּלִים —

Happy the eye that saw water in the
streets and in the pathways, and the
wind sweeping over to make the
harvests great as the righteous man
stands there, with water streaming,
ever stronger, down his head, washing

מֵרֹב הַגְּשָׁמִים קְוֻצּוֹתָיו תַּלְתַּלִּים.
הֲלֹא לְמִשְׁמַע אֹזֶן צָהֲלָה נַפְשֵׁנוּ.

away the wood-ashes, drenching his hair – such a torrent of rain that his locks curl into waves! We hear of this and our soul rejoices.

מֹשֶׁה רֵימוֹס

Moses Remos

מִי הֶאֱמִין

THE DIRGE OF MOSES REMOS

קוננתי אותה יום א׳ כי אמרו לי כי היום הבא אחריו היו עתידים להרגני. אוי לי! יהי רצון שתהיה מיתתי כפרה לעונותי. ובבכי תמרורים בבלתי מחשבה והסתכלות לקחתי הקולמוס, והייתי צועק וכותב. אשביע בה׳ אלהי ישראל שכל מי שתגיע לידו יעתיקנה ויקראנה וישלחנה לאחרים עד שתבא ליד קרובי העלובים. ורשום בה שמי משה רימוס. אוי לי!

I composed this dirge the day I was told that I would be executed on the morrow. Woe is me! May it be His will that my death atone for my sins. Weeping bitterly, without thought or reflection, I took my pen in hand, and I wrote, screaming all the while. By the Lord God of Israel, I charge all those who will come into possession of this lament that they copy it, read it and pass it on to others until it reach the hands of my unfortunate relatives. In it, I have indicated my name, Moses Remos.[1] Woe is me!

מִי הֶאֱמִין כִּי כְּמוֹת נָבָל
יָמוּת מַשְׂכִּיל דּוֹרֵשׁ אֱלֹהִים?
וּכְאַלּוּף לַטֶּבַח יוּבָל,
הוּבַל מֹשֶׁה אִישׁ הָאֱלֹהִים?

Who could have believed that a wise man, a man who sought out God, would die so base a death; that, like a sheep led obedient to the slaughter, Moses, the man of God, would be led to his death?

מְקַטְרֶגֶת מִדַּת הַדִּין, בִּי נֶחֱרִים
זְעֵיר אַפִּין עִם בַּעַל הַחֹטֶם.
אָסְפוּ נָגְהָם פָּנִים מְאִירִים,
וְעַתִּיק יוֹמִין אָזְנוֹ אוֹטֵם.

Divine judgement denounces me; the Impatient One and the Forbearing One[2] both rage against me; the Shining Face has withdrawn His light and the Ancient of Days has stopped His ears.

---

1. In the acrostic.
2. Lit. 'the Short Face and the One with the Nose'; Kabbalistic epithets derived from the doctrine of the *Sefirot*.

מְחֻיַּב הַמְּצִיאוּת, אֶחָד, בְּלִי גַשְׁמוּת,
פּוֹעֵל וְצוּרָה, תַּכְלִית, קַדְמוֹנִי,
חָכָם, יָכוֹל, רוֹצֶה, בְּלִי שִׁנּוּי וּדְמוּת –
אֵלִי, אֵלִי, לָמָה עֲזַבְתָּנִי! [...]

O Necessary Being, One, Incorporeal,
Efficient, Formal and Final Cause,
Eternal, Wise, Potent, Supreme Will,
Changeless, Shapeless – my God, my
God, why have You forsaken me?

שָׁמַיִם לָבְשׁוּ קַדְרוּת, וְשַׂק
שָׂמוּ כְּסוּתָם הַגַּלְגַּלִּים.
יוֹם מוֹתִי, עֲרָבוֹת נָח, לֹא חָשַׁק
כְּמִשְׁפָּטוֹ לְהַשִּׂיג בְּנֵי אֵלִים.

The skies clothe themselves in mourning, and the spheres put on a sackcloth.
On the day I die, *Aravot*[1] will come to
a standstill; it will lose all desire to
contemplate the sons of God.

שַׂמּוּ שָׁמַיִם לְאַכְזָרִיּוּת מוֹתִי!
גַּלְגַּל הַמַּזָּלוֹת מֶרְכָּב נָטָה:
כְּכֶבֶשׂ, כְּאַלּוּף, יוֹבִילוּ אוֹתִי,
יָדַי וְרַגְלַי תְּאוֹמִים מִלְמַטָּה.

Stand aghast at my cruel death, you
heavens! The zodiac is out of joint: I
am led away like a Ram or a Bull; my
hands and my feet are tied to each
other like Twins.

הֵן אֲחוֹרַנִּית כַּהֲלֹךְ סַרְטָן
יָדַי אֲסוּרוֹת וְצַוָּרִי יַעֲרֹף,
וּמְשׁוֹפְטִי עַל יְמִינִי כְּשָׂטָן,
דְּמִינוּ כְּאַרְיֵה יִכְסוֹף לִטְרֹף.

I am forced to walk backwards like a
Crab, hands shackled, neck broken. At
my right side stands the accuser, like
Satan, a Lion eager for prey.

הֵן צַעֲקַת בְּתוּלָה צוֹעֵק קוֹבֵל,
מֹאזְנֵי מִשְׁפָּט שׁוֹאֵל, וְאֵין עוֹנֶה.
מְיֻסָּר בְּעַקְרָב, נֶחְבָּל בְּחֶבֶל,
קֶשֶׁת דְּרוּכָה נִכְחוֹ פוֹנֶה.

I shout my complaints like a Virgin; I
ask for the Scales of justice, but no one
answers; I am chastised by a Scorpion,[2]
whipped with a rope. The Archer
bends his bow at me.

הֵן כְּשֶׂשַׂע הַגְּדִי יְשַׂסְּעוּנִי.
אוֹי לָעֵינַיִם כֵּן רוֹאוֹת הֵן!
אֶדְלֶה בְּדֶלִי דִּמְעוֹת עֵינִי,
עַד כִּי דָגִים יִדְגּוּ בָהֶן. [...]

They will tear me in pieces as if I were
a Goat. Pity the eyes that witness this!
[Like a Water-Bearer,] I draw my tears
in buckets; Oh, Fish could swarm in
these waters!

---

1. Here, the ninth, and uppermost, heavenly sphere; or, a term for the twelve signs of the Zodiac (*A Dictionary of Angels*, 1967, p. 269).   2. Also, 'leash' (1 Kings 12.11).

סַעֲרַת מָוֶת, שָׁבָץ אֲחָזָנִי.
לֹא אוּכַל לָנוּד עוֹד, כִּי שָׁלְחוּ לֵאמֹר:
'מָחָר תָּמוּת' – אוֹי לִי, עָנִי –
'סָחוֹב וְהַשְׁלֵךְ, קְבוּרַת חֲמוֹר'.

The whirlwind of death, the throes of death have seized me. I cannot hope to flee for they have sent a message, saying: 'Tomorrow you shall die' – ah, wretched me – 'You shall be buried like a dead ass, dragged along and flung away.'

סֹעֲרָה וַעֲנִיָּה, אִמִּי, מַה תַּעֲשִׂי
עֵת אֲשֶׁר תַּגִּיעַ לָךְ הַשְּׁמוּעָה?
'מַחְמַד עֵינִי, עֲטֶרֶת רֹאשִׁי,' –
תִּסְפְּדִי עָלַי בִּמְקוֹר דִּמְעָה.

O my mother, storm-tossed and distressed, what will you do when the word reaches you? 'Delight of my eyes, crown of my head,' you will mourn for me with flowing tears.

סֻכָּתְךָ נָפְלָה, מַה תַּעֲשֶׂה, אָבִי?
מַה מְּאֹד רָעָה תְּהִי זִקְנָתֶךָ!
אַחֲלַי, תִּמְחַל לִי פְּשָׁעַי וְחוֹבִי,
אִם לֹא כָרָאוּי כִּבַּדְתִּיךָ.

Your house has fallen, my father, and what will you do? What a sad old age awaits you! I pray you, pardon my offences, if ever I failed to show you due honour.

סְאוֹן סוֹאֵן בְּרַעַשׁ, שָׂטָן מְקַטְרֵג –
מָצָא בַּעַל חוֹב לִגְבּוֹת חוֹבוֹ.
דְּעוּ, מְיֻדָּעַי, כִּי לֹא אֵהָרֵג
עַל עָוֹן גָּדוֹל עָוִיתִי בוֹ.

Bellowing, clamouring, Satan accuses me; the Creditor has found occasion to collect his bill. But know, my friends, that I am not being killed for having committed a terrible crime.

סַם הַמָּוֶת, אָמְרוּ, כִּי יָעַצְתִּי
לְהִנָּתֵן קֻבַּעַת כּוֹס הַתַּרְעֵלָה
לַעֲרֵלִים מֵתוּ – לֹא פָשַׁעְתִּי!
הִצְמִיתוּ חַיַּי בְּזֹאת הָעֲלִילָה.

They claim that I prescribed a deadly poison which was administered in a bowl of drunkenness to the gentiles who died; but it was none of my doing. With this false charge, they are silencing my life.

סוֹד הַשֵּׁם לִירֵאָיו! לוּלֵי רַבִּי עֲקִיבָא
וַחֲבֵרָיו, כִּמְעַט נָטָיו רַגְלָי
בִּרְאוֹתִי מוֹתִי עַל לֹא סִבָּה.
אַךְ יְיָ הַצַּדִּיק עַל כָּל הַבָּא עָלָי.

The Lord confides in those who fear Him. If I had not [called to mind the martyrdom of] Rabbi Akiva and his companions,[1] my feet would almost have slipped, seeing that I was doomed to die for no reason at all. But the Lord is just in all that has befallen me.

---

1. The ten martyrs executed in the reign of Hadrian.

שָׂח שַׂר הַצּוֹרֵר לְהַצִּיל רֹאשִׁי,
אִם כָּבוֹד אָמִיר לַעֲבֹד אֵלוֹ.
עֲנִיתִיו: 'טוֹב מוֹת גּוּפִי מִמּוֹת נַפְשִׁי.'
חֶלְקִי – הַצּוּר הַחַי, וְהַמֵּת יִהְיֶה לּוֹ!

The arch-enemy offered to save my
head if I would exchange my Glory for
the worship of his god. I answered
him: 'It is better for my body to die
than my soul.' My portion is the living
God; let the dead one[1] be his!

סָחִי וּמָאוֹס הוּשַׂם, כָּל רַגְלָם תִּרְמֹס,
כִּי מוֹת אַכְזָרִיּוּת אָז זַמּוּנִי.
מִי הֶאֱמִין זֹאת עַל מֹשֶׁה רֵימוֹס!
אֲנִי הַגֶּבֶר רָאָה עֳנִי.

I am treated as offscouring and refuse,
trampled under every foot. They have
plotted a cruel death for me. Oh, who
would have believed that such would be
the fate of Moses Remos? I am the
man who has known affliction!

שַׂר מַר הַמָּוֶת – אָמְנָם אוֹי לִי
עַל שִׁבְרִי! הָיִיתִי בְּמִבְחַר חַיַּי,
אַרְבָּעָה וְעֶשְׂרִים שָׁנָה יֶשׁ לִי,
גַּבְרָא בְּכֹלָּא וְכָל מַאֲוַיַּי.

Death's bitterness is at my side – oh,
the pain of my wounds! I was in the
prime of my life; I am twenty-four
years old, in the fullness of manhood
and desire.

סוֹף דָּבָר: הַדִּין עָלַי אַצְדִּיק,
אֶתְוַדֶּה וְאֹמַר: 'אֲבָל חָטָאתִי!'
רָשַׁעְתִּי, כִּי יְיָ הַצַּדִּיק.
אָנָּא אֵל נָא, מְחַל אַשְׁמָתִי.

The end of the matter: I hereby justify
the Divine decree. I confess and say:
Truly, I have sinned![2] I have acted
wickedly, and the Lord is in the right.
O God, I pray You, pardon my guilt.

סְעָדֵנִי, צוּרִי, וּתְהִי כַפָּרָה
מִיתָתִי עַל עֲווֹנִי, וּכְנֶפֶשׁ מַאֲמִין
בִּצְרוֹר הַחַיִּים תִּהְיֶה צְרוּרָה
נַפְשִׁי אִתְּךָ לְקֵץ הַיָּמִין.

Sustain me, my Rock, and may my
death atone for my sins; and, like the
souls of all believers, may mine be kept
forever alive in Your care, until the end
of days.

---

1. I.e. Jesus; the phrase is taken from Exodus 21.34.
2. 'Truly, we have sinned' is the Talmudic formula of the Confession on the Day of Atonement.

רְפָאֵל בֶּן־יִצְחָק *Raphael da Faenza*

רַעְיָתִי, לִי אָזְנֵךְ הַטִּי־נָא SONG WITH GALANTINA

רַעְיָתִי, לִי אָזְנֵךְ הַטִּי־נָא :
בַּמֶּה מִנֹּפֶת נָעַמְתְּ
מִמֶּתֶק חִשְׁקִי טָעַמְתְּ !
אֲמָרַי וְקוֹלִי תִּשְׁמְעִי־נָא,
אִי גָלַנְטִינָה.

Hear my words, my dearest: you were
far more delicious than honey when
you tasted my sweet desire. Now listen
to my voice, O Galantina!

פְּלוּלֵי אַהֲבָה תְּקַבְּלִי,
כּוֹכָב צַח, מִמֶּנִּי דְרוּשָׁה.
שִׂפְתוֹתַיִךְ מִצּוּף מָתְקוּ לִי
בָּהֶם תִּשְׁקִי פִּי, וְהַגִּישָׁה
לְשׁוֹנֵךְ אֶל חִכִּי, וּתְכַלְכְּלִי,
יוֹנָתִי, לְדוֹדֵךְ בְּלִי בוּשָׁה.
וְנָשִׁירָה בְּשִׁירָה חֲדָשָׁה
וְנָגִילָה בְּמַקְהֵלוֹת,
אֲיֻמָּה כַּנִּדְגָּלוֹת.

Bright star, I am in need of you; accept
my love's entreaties. Your lips, which
kiss my mouth, are sweeter to me than
nectar. Put your tongue to mine, my
dove, and feed your beloved without
shame. Then we shall sing new songs
and rejoice in unison, my fairest,
majestic as flying banners.

זְמִירוֹת אֲהָבִים רָנִּי־נָא,
אִי גָלַנְטִינָה.

Loud sing your serenades, O Galantina!

אַתְּ שֶׁאָהֲבָה נַפְשִׁי,
יַעֲלָה בָּרָה וּמְתֹאָרֶת,
נֹעַם חִשְׁקֵךְ אַשְׁשִׁי,
עֶנֶק צַוְּרוֹנִי לְתִפְאָרֶת,
וּלְעוֹלָם תְּהִי לִי גְּבָרֶת.
וְאָשִׂימָה עָלַיִךְ כַּפִּי,
תְּהִי עִם פִּי וְתִתְיַפִּי.

You are my true love, my pure and
beautiful gazelle. Redouble your sweet
passion, hang round my neck like a
precious jewel, and forever be my
mistress. I shall put my hand upon
you. Mouth to mouth, your loveliness
will grow.

הוֹד פָּנַיִךְ מְאִירִים לִי תַּרְאִי־נָא,
אֵי גָלַנְטִינָה.

Let me see the splendour of your
shining face, O Galantina!

זְכַרְתִּיךְ בַּלַּיְלָה עַל מִשְׁכָּבִי,
תֻּמָּתִי, וְיָפִי מַכְלוּלַיִךְ.
יוֹמָם וָלַיִל, עֵינַי וְלִבִּי,
לְסַפֵּר בְּרָן מַהֲלָלַיִךְ
וּלְהַנִּיחַ רֹאשִׁי בֵּין שָׁדַיִךְ
שָׁם בְּחַדְרֵי מַשְׂכִּיּוֹת.
מִמִּגְדָּל בָּנוּי לְתַלְפִּיּוֹת,

Night after night on my bed I think of
you, my perfect one, and of your
charming robes. O my eyes, my heart –
I long to sing your praises day and
night, to rest my head between your
breasts, there, within the ornamented
shrine. Out of the lofty tower,[1]

צְבִיָּה, לְדוֹדֵךְ תִּקְרְאִי־נָא,
אֵי גָלַנְטִינָה.

summon your lover, gazelle.
O Galantina!

ועתה שמע תשובת החשוקה לדודה:

*Now listen to the reply of the maiden to
her beloved:*

גַּם אֲנִי לִמְאֹד אִוִּיתִיךָ,
דּוֹד אוֹהֵב, נָאֶה וְנָעִים.
וּמֵאָז מִקֶּדֶם רְאִיתִיךָ
כָּל קְרָבַי לְךָ הָיוּ נִשְׁמָעִים.
נִשְׁתָּעֶה־נָא בְּשַׁעֲשׁוּעִים
בְּעַרְשֵׂנוּ רַעֲנָנָה,
בָּהּ לִשְׂמֹחַ בְּרִנָּה

I, too, have deeply yearned for you, my
handsome one, my pleasant love. Ever
since I first saw you, long ago, my
heart has been yours to command. Let
us give ourselves over to delights in our
bed that is shaded with branches.
There I shall dally with you,

עִמְּךָ, צְבִי חֵן, וְלָלִינָה,
אֵי גָלַנְטִינָה.

my fair love, singing, lying at your side.
O Galantina!

יָפְיָפִיתָ מִכָּל דּוֹדִים,
הוּצַק חֵן בְּשִׂפְתוֹתֶיךָ.
נִכְבַּדְתָּ עַל כָּל דּוֹדִים,

You surpass all lovers in beauty. Your
lips are moulded in grace. You rank
higher than all lovers in honour. Noble

---

1. 'Your neck is like David's tower, girt with battlements' (Song of Songs 4.4).

עֲלָמוֹת בְּיִקְרוֹתֶיךָ.
כִּי תִשְׁמֹר מְדַבְּרוֹתֶיךָ
וּפְרָשׁ־נָא כְּנָפְךָ עָלַי,
כִּי תְמַשֵּׁשׁ כָּל כֵּלַי

maidens wait upon you. If you keep
your pledge and spread your wing over
me, you will yet finger all my
possessions

וְתָבוֹא אֵלַי, הַאֲמִינָה,
אִי גָלַנְטִינָה.

and lie with me – rest assured!
O Galantina!

חִזְקוּ־נָא, חוֹשְׁקִים, וְאִמְצוּ
וּתְעוֹרְרוּ הַבָּנוֹת.
חוּשׁוּ, רֵעִים, וְהָאִיצוּ,
כִּי כָאן מְזֻמָּנוֹת
לְמַלֹּאת חֶפְצְכֶם נְכוֹנוֹת,
לִהְיוֹת לְבָשָׂר אֶחָד.
וְאַתָּה, הַדּוֹד, בְּרָן־יַחַד –

Take courage, you lovers, take heart,
go and rouse the girls. Hurry, friends,
there is no time to lose, for they are all
at hand, prepared to fulfil your desires,
to cling to you and to become one
flesh. And you, my love, when they all
sing together,

שְׁמַע רַעְיָתְךָ וּלְכָה לִינָה,
אִי גָלַנְטִינָה.

listen to your darling and come to lie
with her. O Galantina!

עֲלוּמֵי־שֵׁם

Anonymous

יָהּ, לְמָתַי פֵּרוּד

SONG FOR PASSOVER

"יָהּ, לְמָתַי פֵּרוּד יְנִדֵּנִי מִבְּלִי מִשְׁכָּן?
אֵשׁ נְדֹד תּוּקַד, וְהִנְנִי לַיְקוֹד מוּכָן.

[Zion:] Lord, how much longer will
this separation make me a homeless
fugitive? The fires of wandering are
ablaze, and I am ready for the stake.

"שׁוֹחֲרַי, אַט!" – פֶּן לַהֲטֵי לִבִּי יֹאחֲזוּ בָהֶם,
וּמְאַהֲבַי – פֶּן גַּחֲלֵי קִרְבִּי יִשְׂרְפוּ אֶתְהֶם,

'My friends, beware!' [I say to them,]
lest the flames of my heart ignite them;
[and I warn] those who love me, lest
the embers of my soul consume them.

443

ANONYMOUS

כִּי יְדִידִי רָחַק וְהִבְעִיר בִּי אֶת שְׁבִיבֵיהֶם.
אָמְרוּ אוֹיְבַי כִּי עֲזַבְנִי וַאֲנִי אַלְמָן
מֵאֱלֹהַי, גַּם רָחַקוּ מִגִּי נָתְנוּ סִימָן.

For my Beloved, by going far away, has
kindled these sparks in me. My enemies
say that I have been abandoned, left
widowed by my God. He is far from
me and that, they say, is proof enough.

מִנְּדוּדִים אֶשְׂבַּע עֲדֵי נֶשֶׁף, אֶת כְּסִיל רוֹעֶה,
כִּי כְמוֹ שֶׂה אוֹבֵד בְּהַר נֶשֶׁף אֵלְכָה תוֹעֶה.
מִפְּרִידָה אֶהֱמֶה, וּמֵרֶשֶׁף אֶשְׁאָפָה, אֶפְעֶה.
צוּר, הֲלַעַד עַל עַם מְאֹד עָנִי אַפְּךָ יֶעְשָׁן ?
רַחֲמֶיךָ אָנָּא יְבוֹאוּנִי, וַעֲזוֹב עָשָׁן.

All night I toss and turn, in company
with Orion. I stray like a lost sheep on
the twilit hill-side. The parting makes
me moan and the fires make me cry
and gasp. Lord, will You forever be
incensed against this destitute people?
Oh, extend Your compassion to me,
have done with wrath.

וַאֲנִי, אִם חֹשֶׁךְ יְשׁוּפֵנִי, בָּךְ אָשׂוּ מַחְסִי,
אוֹ פְּרִידָתָךְ תַּאֲדִיבֵנִי, אַךְ מְנָת כּוֹסִי.
רַחֲמֶיךָ סִתְרִי וּמְגִנִּי מֵחֲמַס שׁוֹסִי.
אִם תְּדַכֵּא אוֹ תַחֲלִיאֵנִי מַחֲלָה גָאָמָן,
יֶשְׁעֲךָ תִשְׁלַח יַחֲלִימֵנִי, אָב לְבֵן – רַחֲמָן.'

And I, though darkness cover me, shall
make You my refuge; though Your
parting grieve me, You are all I have.
Only Your mercy can shield me from
my violent enemies. Even if You beat
me down or plague me with persistent
sickness, You will send Your deliverance and restore me, for a father has
mercy on his child.

'אֲהַבְתִּי לָךְ, בַּת יְפֵה-פִיָּה, רְחָבָה מִיָּם.
שׁוּב אֲשִׁיבֵךְ אֵלַי, וְעַם נִהְיָה יִשְׁכְּחוּ עָנְיָם.
אוֹהֲבַי אַנְחִיל דָּת וְתוּשִׁיָּה, אֶאֱסוֹף שְׁבָיָם.
אוֹמְרָה לַצָּפוֹן : "תְּנִי, תְּנִי שׁוֹכְבֵי אַשְׁמָן !"
כִּי מְקוֹם שַׂק עוֹד יִלְבְּשׁוּ שָׁנִי, שֵׁשׁ וְאַרְגָּמָן.'

[God:] My love for you, O my beautiful
daughter, is broader than the sea. I
shall take you back to Me, and the
people, who were overcome, will forget
their misery. I shall endow those who
love Me with laws and wisdom. I shall
assemble their captives. I shall say to
the North: 'Give them up, give up all
those who sleep in the ghostly underworld!' For instead of sackcloth they
will yet dress themselves in fine linen,
in purple and scarlet.

'לוֹעֲגִים לִי אֶתְמוֹל בְּיוֹם אֵידִי גַם בְּיוֹם צַר לִי :
הֵן הֱשִׁיבַנִי בֶּאֱמֶת דּוֹדִי לוֹ, וְסָר מָחֳלִי.

[Zion:] All of you who mocked me
yesterday in the hour of my peril, in
the day of my distress – my Beloved
has truly taken me back and my illness

444

עַל מְשַׂנְאַי אָבוּס וְעַל רוֹזִי אַשְׁלִיךְ נַעֲלִי !
וַאֲבַשֵּׂר אוֹמְרִים שְׁנֵאַנִי עוֹבְדֵי חַמָּן —
כִּי כְבָר אִישִׁי יֶאֱהָבַנִי לְכָל זְמָן.'

has disappeared. I shall stamp on my enemies and fling my shoes at my adversaries. And to the idol-worshippers, who had said that He hates me, I shall proudly declare: 'My husband loves me now, and for all time.'

לִבִּי לְיוֹכֶבֶד — JOKHEBED'S CRY

לִבִּי לְיוֹכֶבֶד ! 'מֹשֶׁה בְּנִי,'
תִּצְעַק וְתֹאמַר, 'הֵהּ מֵתָה אָנִי !

My heart goes out to Jokhebed! 'O, Moses, my son,' she moans, 'Oh, I am dying!'

שַׁאֲלוּ לְהַר סִינַי, שַׁאֲלוּ מְבוֹא
שֶׁמֶשׁ וּמִזְרָח, אָן לֶשֶׁם־שְׁבוֹ ?
מִיּוֹם אֲשֶׁר עָלָה אֶל הַר נְבוֹ
לֹא שָׁב, וְלִבִּי עָלָיו כָּאֳנִי
סוֹעֵר, צֲדֵי נֶהְפַּךְ אוֹנִי עָנִי.

[Jokhebed:] 'Go and ask Mount Sinai, ask the West and the East, where is [Moses, precious as] turquoise and agate? Since the day he went up Mount Nebo, there has been no trace of him. My heart trembles for him like a ship caught up in a storm. My strength is gone, drained by misery.

מוֹאָב, הֱיֵה סֵתֶר עַל בֶּן דְּרוֹר
לָקַח וְלֹא נָתַן לוֹ אֶל דְּרוֹר.
מִבַּלְעֲדֵי מֹשֶׁה אֵין לִי מָר־דְּרוֹר.
עָלָיו, עֲדַת יַעֲקֹב, אֶבֶל עֲנִי,
כָּל עוֹד בְּרוּם שַׁחַק כּוֹכַב מְנִי.'

'Moab,[1] shelter the son of freedom! The Lord has taken him and refused to let him go. Without Moses, I cannot savour flowing myrrh. And you, Jacob's flock, mourn for him so long as the Pleiades shine in the high heavens.'

וַיֶּחֱרַד סִינַי וּנְבוֹ וְהוֹר
עַל צַעֲקַת יוֹכֶבֶד מָמְרוֹר.
תִּצְעַק וּפָנֶיהָ אֶל מוּל פְּעוֹר :
'הֵהּ עַל זְרוֹעִי, הֵהּ עַל בְּהֶנִי,
הֵהּ עַל לְוִיִּי, הֵהּ עַל כֹּהֲנִי.'

Then Sinai and Nebo and Hor all trembled at Jokhebed's bitter lament, as she faced Peor[1] and wailed: 'O my [right] arm, my [precious] thumb, O my Levite, my Priest!'

---

1. Mount Nebo is located in the land of Moab. Moses 'was buried in a valley in Moab opposite Bethpeor' (Deuteronomy 34.6).

'אִמִּי, חֲכִי, אַל תָּרִימִי בְקוֹל,
כִּי לֹא יְכַסֵּנִי עָפָר וְחוֹל
הָאֵל, וְהִבְדִּיל בֵּין קֹדֶשׁ לְחֹל.
בֵּין מַחֲנוֹת מַלְאָכִים מַחֲנִי,
גַּם מָחֳרָת אַתְּ אַף תִּצְעֲנִי׳.

[Moses:] 'O my mother, take heart, do
not raise your voice, for the Lord has
not covered me with dust and sand;
He sets apart the sacred from the
common. My resting-place is among
the hosts of angels and tomorrow you
too will join me.'

'לֵךְ נָא בְשָׁלוֹם, נוֹטֵה אָהֳלִי!
מַר לִי לְנִדְךָ, מַר מִכָּל חֳלִי.
שָׁלוֹם יְהִי מֵאֵל גַּם לָךְ וְלִי,
יַקְשִׁיב לְמַר שִׂיחִי וּלְמַעֲנִי,
יֵיטִיב לְמַעֲנֵךְ וּלְמַעֲנִי׳.

[Jokhebed:] 'Go then in peace, O you
who pitched my tent! Your parting is
a bitter thing for me, more bitter than
any illness. May the Lord bestow His
peace upon you and also upon me. May
He listen to my bitter lament, and
show His favour for your sake and for
mine.'

הַיּוֹם בְּשִׂמְחַת תּוֹרָה תַּעֲלֹזוּ,
עֵין בְּצִיּוֹן כָּבוֹד תֶּחֱזוּ.
יוֹם יַעֲנֶה שַׁדַּי, אַל תִּרְגָּזוּ,
יֹאמַר לְצָפוֹן וּלְתֵימָן 'תְּנִי',
יוֹצִיא שְׁאָר עַמּוֹ מִבּוֹר עֳנִי.

Make merry today, rejoice in the Law.
With your own eyes, you will behold
the Glory. And on the day the Lord
answers, do not tremble with fear. He
will say to the North and the South,
'Give them up.' He will bring His
people out of the pit of affliction.

בִּרְאוֹתִי כִּי עָבַר סַגְרִיר

THE DOVE AND THE HART

בִּרְאוֹתִי כִּי עָבַר סַגְרִיר
וּפְרִי כָל עֵץ צוֹמֵחַ,
וּבְהַגִּיעַ עֵת הַזָּמִיר
וּגְפָנִים נָתְנוּ רֵיחַ,
וּזְמַן רוּחַ אַהֲבָה יָעִיר
אֵלַי שׁוֹאֵף זוֹרֵחַ –
אָז יֵיטִיב נַגֵּן, אָז יָשִׁיר
לִבִּי לְקִרְאַת עֹפֶר וּבְחִיר:

[She:] 'When I see that the rains are
past and the fruit of every tree is in
blossom; when the time of singing
birds has come and the vines give forth
their fragrance; when Time stirs the
winds of love, which seek me out, and
rise all around me – then my heart
makes sweet melody, singing to my
hart, my chosen one. [He is as wise as]

יוֹסֵף צָפְנַת פַּעְנֵחַ,
הַבֵּן יַקִּיר.

Joseph, master of mysteries,[1] and as dear as a son.'

יוֹנָה, בָּךְ חָשַׁקְתִּי וּבְקִרְךְ
בִּי אֵשׁ חִשְׁקֵךְ נוֹפֵחַ.
אָמְנָם זָחַלְתִּי וָאַסְתִּיר
חִשְׁקֵךְ הַמִּתְלַקֵּחַ
וָאֹמַר: הַס, כִּי לֹא אַזְכִּיר
בִּשְׁמֵךְ, לֹא יִפְתַּח
פִּי, פֶּן מְקַנְאִאַנִי יַכִּיר,
יָנִיעַ רֹאשׁוֹ, וּלְהָפִיר
אַהֲבָה – כָּזָב יָפִיחַ,
שָׂפָה יַפְטִיר.

[He:] 'O dove, it is you I desire, and deep in my heart I fan these passionate flames. But out of fear, I have concealed my fiery passion, saying: Hush, I must not mention your name, my mouth must remain dumb, lest my rival find you out and wag his head. He will tell a pack of lies, he will make mouths at me to undo our love.'

עֹפֶר, לִבִּי הוֹמֶה כִּכְפִיר,
לְפָרִידָתָךְ צוֹרֵחַ
וּבְיָד תַּאֲוָה רוּחוֹ הִסְגִּיר
וּבְכַנְפֵי נוֹד פּוֹרֵחַ.
בִּי חִשְׁקֵךְ בִּכְסָלַי מָאִיר
וּבְכִלְיוֹתַי פּוֹלֵחַ.
לִירוֹת יֶתֶר קַשְׁתּוֹ הִתִּיר,
וַיִּז מִדָּמִי אֶל הַקִּיר,
כָּל עַצְמוֹתַי פִּצֵּחַ,
חִצָּיו הִשְׁכִּיר.

[She:] 'O hart, my heart roars with pain, like a lion, because you are gone. It has surrendered itself to desire and flies after you on wings of exile. This passion pierces my loins and cuts deep into my vitals. It strung its bow to shoot at me, and my blood splashed onto the wall. It splintered all my bones, made its arrows drunk [with my blood].'

יוֹנָה, שִׁמְעִי אֶנְקַת אָסִיר
לִנְדֻדֵךְ מִתְיַפֵּחַ.
כָּלוּ חַיַּי, כִּי כֶּחָצִיר
יָמַי וּכְצִיץ פּוֹרֵחַ.

[He:] 'O dove, listen to the groaning of this prisoner, bewailing your absence. My life has worn away: my days are like the grass, like a vanishing flower.

1. *Żaphenath-paneah*, Joseph's Egyptian name (Genesis 41.45), was taken to mean 'he who reveals secrets'.

אֶשְׁאַל לָמוּת כִּי חֲשָׁקֵךְ צִיר
נֶאֱמָן אַךְ בִּי שׁוּלַח.
וּבְכּוֹר מָוֶת בַּיּוֹם אַבִּיר,
וַהֲרוּגֵי הַחֵשֶׁק אוֹקִיר.
הַמֵּתִים אֲנִי שַׁבֵּחַ
מִפַּז אוֹפִיר.

I pray for death to come, so fierce are
the pangs[1] that passion hurls at me.
Today, I hold death most dear, and I
prize the victims of Desire. I count the
dead more precious than the fine gold
of Ophir.

יוֹנַת חֵן, יֵין זִכְרֵךְ אַזְכִּיר
רֹקַח מַעֲשֵׂה רוֹקֵחַ,
וּבְחַשְׁקֵךְ אֶשָּׂא קוֹל בְּזָמִיר
מִתְגַּבֵּר וּמְנַצֵּחַ,
וּלְנֶגֶד יְפָעָתֵךְ אַעְתִּיר
אַכַּף וְאֶשְׁתּוֹחֵחַ.
כִּי צוּרֵךְ נָתַן אוֹר בָּהִיר
אֶל עֵבֶר פָּנַיִךְ הֵאִיר,
לְחָיֵךְ עָשָׂה יָרֵחַ,
כּוֹכָב מַזְהִיר.

'Fair dove, I shall celebrate the wine of
your fame, this perfume so expertly
blended. And, moved by desire, I shall
raise my voice in song, in swelling
songs of praise. I shall pay homage to
your beauty, and bow down before it.
For your Lord has shed a bright light
over your face. He has made your
cheek a moon, a shining star!'

תְּנָה לִי כוֹס

THE DRUNKARD'S TESTAMENT

תְּנָה לִי כוֹס אֲשֶׁר יָנִיס יְגוֹנִים
וְתֵן חֶלְקִי בְּנַחַל הָעֲדָנִים.
קְחָה אֶלֶף תְּמוּרָתוֹ, וְאוֹסִיף
לָךְ מֵאָה וְעֶשְׂרִים, גַּם שְׁמוֹנִים.
וְעֵת אָמוּת לְפָנֶיךָ, יְדִידִי,
חֲצֹב קִבְרִי בְּשָׁרְשֵׁי הַגְּפָנִים.

Give me the cup that puts sorrow to
flight, and let me have my share in the
river of delights. Take a thousand in
payment, and I shall add another
hundred and twenty, and eighty more.[2]
And when I die before your very eyes,
my friend, dig my grave among the
roots of vines. Do not scatter dust upon

---

1. A play on words. The phrase 'fierce pangs' also means 'a trusty messenger' (Proverbs 25.13).
2. The rate is based on Song of Songs 8.12: 'But my vineyard is mine to give; the thousand pieces are yours, O Solomon, and the guardians of the fruit shall have two hundred.'

וְאַל תָּשִׂים עֲלֵי קִבְרִי עֲפָרִים,
אֲבָל כַּדִּים תְּמוּרַת הָאֲבָנִים.
וְאַל תִּבְכּוּ וְתָנוּדוּ בְּמוֹתִי,
עֲשׂוּ כִנּוֹר וְעוּגָבִים וּמִנִּים.
וְסִיר רַחֲצִי בְּמֵימֵי הָעֲנָבִים,
וְחָנְטוּנִי בְּזַגִּים הַיְשָׁנִים.
וְאַבְשַׁי הוּא אֲבִי כָּל הַשְּׂמָחוֹת –
שְׁמוֹ זִכְרוּ לְדוֹר דּוֹרִים וְשָׁנִים.

my grave; cover it with jugs instead of
stones. And do not cry and mourn
when I die; but make music with harp,
lute and pipe. Fill my wash basin with
grape-water, and embalm me in old
grape husks. For Avshay is the father
of all merriment. Remember his name
through all generations.

הַזָּן אֶת הָעוֹלָם

THE GENEROUS BRIDEGROOM

הַזָּן אֶת הָעוֹלָם כֻּלּוֹ,
בָּרוּךְ שֶׁאָכַלְנוּ מִשֶּׁלּוֹ.

He sustains the whole world – blessed
be He Whose food we have eaten.

יוֹצֵר הַכֹּל יִתְבָּרַךְ,
כִּי שֻׁלְחָן לָנוּ עָרַךְ,
נוֹדֶה לִשְׁמוֹ בְּלָשׁוֹן רַךְ.
צֹאן וּבָקָר
לְאֵין מֶחְקָר,
הַפַּת עִקָּר
וְהַשְּׁאָר טְפֵלָה לוֹ.

Blessed be the Creator of all things, for
He spread a table for us. Let us praise
His name with gentle words. He fed us
with sheep and cattle beyond reckoning; bread is the main dish, and all the
rest is complementary.[1]

הֶחָתָן אֲשֶׁר קָבַע
סְעוּדָּתוֹ לָשֹׂבַע,
זָכָה לְבִרְכוֹת שֶׁבַע –
יִזְכֶּה לְבָנִים שֶׁבַע.
נָתַן יַיִן

The bridegroom who set out such a
lavish banquet was favoured with the
Seven Blessings[2]; may he now be
favoured with seven sons. He poured

---

1. And therefore may be eaten without an additional benediction. The phrase is derived from a Talmudic
regulation.
2. Which are recited at weddings.

בְּטוֹב עַיִן.
עֲלֵי עַיִן
יִפְרַח בְּכַרְמִלּוֹ.

out wine with a generous flourish; may
he flourish in his meadow, by a spring.

הֶאֱכִילָנוּ בְּשַׂר פָּרָה –
כַּלָּתוֹ תִּהְיֶה פּוֹרָה
כְּמוֹ רָחֵל וְצִפֹּרָה.
עוּגוֹת סֹלֶת
לַגֻּלְגֹּלֶת,
וְתַרְנְגֹלֶת
נָתַן לְאִישׁ כְּפִי אָכְלוֹ.

He fed us with beef and we ate our fill;
may his bride be as fertile as Zipporah
and Rachel! Each guest could take the
choicest cake, and chicken meat – each
as much as he could eat.

הֶאֱכִילָנוּ בְּשַׂר הַצֹּאן –
כַּלָּתוֹ אֵשֶׁת רָצוֹן
כְּמוֹ רָחֵל רוֹעָה בַּצֹּאן.

He fed us lamb without measure; his
bride is surely a treasure, like Rachel
who tended her flocks.

הֶאֱכִילָנוּ בְּשַׂר אַיִל –
כַּלָּתוֹ אֵשֶׁת חַיִל
כְּמוֹ רָחֵל וַאֲבִיגַיִל.

He fed us ram's meat; his bride is a
sweet helpmeet, like Rachel and
Abigail.

הֶאֱכִילָנוּ בְּשַׂר דָּגָה –
כַּלָּתוֹ תִּהְיֶה מְעֻנָּגָה
כְּמוֹ יוֹנָה בִּמְעֵי הַדָּגָה.
עוּגוֹת סֹלֶת
לַגֻּלְגֹּלֶת,
וְתַרְנְגֹלֶת,
נָתַן לְאִישׁ כְּפִי אָכְלוֹ.

He fed us fish and jelly; may his bride
luxuriate like Jonah in the fish's belly.
Each guest could take the choicest cake,
and chicken meat – each as much as he
could eat!

450

שִׁיר יְדִידִים   SONG OF THE NEWBORN ON THE EVE OF HIS CIRCUMCISION

שִׁיר יְדִידִים אָעִירָה,
אֶתֵּן תּוֹדָה וַאֲזַמֵּר
לָאֵל כֻּלּוֹ כָּבוֹד אוֹמֵר,
וּבְשֵׁם יְיָ אֶקְרָא.

I shall awake a song of love. I shall give
praise and sing to God, in whose temple
all cry, 'Glory.' I shall invoke the Lord
by name.

פָּדָה נַפְשִׁי מִכָּל צָרָה
— הָיִיתִי הוֹלֵךְ קֹדֵר
בִּמְעֵי אִמִּי, בְּתוֹךְ חֶדֶר —
וּמֵאֲפֵלָה לְאוֹרָה.

He has delivered me from all my
troubles. I was going about downcast
in the chamber, in my mother's womb,
[when He brought me] out from
darkness to light.

שְׁמַע מִלִּין וְאָשִׁירָה
יוֹם בְּרִיתִי מְלֵיל שׁוֹמֵר.
מָחָר יַאְדִּים תּוֹלָע צֶמֶר.
יְיָ לִי וְלֹא אִירָא.

Listen to my words: I shall celebrate
the day of my circumcision,[1] for which
I now keep this all-night vigil. Tomorrow the wool will be red like
crimson. The Lord is on my side; I
have no fear.

הַמְשַׂחֵק בְּקֻבְיָא   THE GAMBLER'S FATE

הַמְשַׂחֵק בְּקֻבְיָא
מַכָּתוֹ טְרִיָּה
וְאַחֲרִיתוֹ שְׁאִיָּה,
יֻקַּל בַּשְּׁעָרִים.

The dice-player is always covered with
raw wounds. His end is utter ruin; he
is cursed in every city gate.

---

1. Also, 'the day of my covenant'.

יְפַזֵּר מָמוֹנוֹ
וְיוֹסִיף עֲווֹנוֹ
וּמוֹרֵד בְּקוֹנוֹ
בִּשְׁבוּעוֹת שְׁקָרִים.

He spends his money freely and piles up sins. He flouts his Maker with false oaths.

יַחֲשֹׁב כִּי יַרְוִיחַ
וּלְעוֹלָם לֹא יַצְלִיחַ,
וְגַם כִּי יוֹנֶה אָח.
וְיָמָיו מְרוֹרִים.

He hopes to make money but though he deceive his own brother, he will never succeed. All his days are a diet of bitter herbs.

יֹאכַל בְּחִפָּזוֹן
בְּלִי בִרְכַּת מָזוֹן,
וְלֹא יִמְצָא רָזוֹן
בְּעִנּוּי כִּפּוּרִים.

He gobbles down his food without saying Grace. He doesn't lose a pound on the Fast of Atonement.

יֵלֵךְ מֵעִיר לְעִיר,
מְקוֹמוֹ לֹא יַכִּיר,
וְהוּא עָנִי וְצָעִיר
מְדַלֵּג עַל הֶהָרִים.

He rushes from one town to another and can call no place his own. He is poor and despised, bounding from mountain to mountain.

רֹאשׁוֹ פָרוּעַ
וּבִגְדוֹ קָרוּעַ
כִּי רַע יֵרוֹעַ
לְעַצְמוֹ וְלָאֲחֵרִים.

His hair is dishevelled, his clothes are in tatters. He hurts himself as he hurts other people.

כָּל אַנְשֵׁי בֵיתוֹ
שׂוֹנְאִים אוֹתוֹ,
וְיַעֲשׂוּ יוֹם מוֹתוֹ
בְּשִׂמְחָה וּבְשִׁירִים.

All the members of his household hold him in contempt. They celebrate his death with song and merriment.

ANONYMOUS

יוֹם מִצָּרְפַת יָצָאתִי   A TRIP TO GERMANY

יוֹם מִצָּרְפַת יָצָאתִי
אֶל אֶרֶץ אַשְׁכְּנַז יָרַדְתִּי
וְעַם אַכְזָר מָצָאתִי
כַּיְעֵנִים בַּמִּדְבָּר.
כִּי לֹא אַלְמָן יִשְׂרָאֵל.
מַה לַתֶּבֶן אֶת הַבָּר ?

When I left France and journeyed down
to Germany, I found a people there as
cruel as ostriches in the desert. *Oh,
Israel is not forsaken!*[1] *What has chaff to
do with grain?*

צִפִּיתִי לִי לִישׁוּעָה
יוֹם נֹפֶשׁ וּמַרְגּוֹעַ,
וּמִנְחָתָם בְּלִי שָׁעָה
לְבָבִי הָיָה נִשְׁבָּר.
כִּי לֹא אַלְמָן יִשְׂרָאֵל.
מַה לַתֶּבֶן אֶת הַבָּר ?

I had hoped for deliverance, for a day
of peace and repose, but my heart was
broken by their worthless gifts. *Oh,
Israel is not forsaken! What has chaff to
do with grain?*

חִפַּשְׂתִּי אֶלְזוּשׁ אָרְכָּהּ
וְלֹא יָדַע אֱנוֹשׁ עֶרְכָּהּ,
לוּלֵא שֶׁלֹא כְדַרְכָּהּ
הָאִשָּׁה עַל אִישׁ תִּגְבָּר.
כִּי לֹא אַלְמָן יִשְׂרָאֵל.
מַה לַתֶּבֶן אֶת הַבָּר ?

I searched up and down Alsace but
could find nothing of note, except that
– Oh, perversity! – there the women
ride over the men. *Oh, Israel is not forsaken! What has chaff to do with grain?*

קַצְתִּי מְאֹד בְּאַשְׁכְּנַזִּים
כִּי הֵם כֻּלָּם פָּנִים עַזִּים
אַף זְקָנָם כְּמוֹ עִזִּים.
אַל תַּאֲמֵן לָהֶם דָּבָר !
כִּי לֹא אַלְמָן יִשְׂרָאֵל.
מַה לַתֶּבֶן אֶת הַבָּר ?

I am heartily sick of these *Ashkenazim.*
They are all grim-faced and have
beards like goats. Don't believe a word
they breathe. *Oh, Israel is not forsaken!
What has chaff to do with grain?*

---

1. Hebrew *alman* ('forsaken, widowed') echoes the French *allemand* ('German') so that the phrase
(Jeremiah 51.15) can be read: 'A [French] Israelite is not a German [Jew].'

כָּלֵב אֲפֶנְדוֹפּוֹלוֹ *Caleb Afendopolo*

צְבִיָּה גָּעֲלָה A COLD COMFORT

'צְבִיָּה גָּעֲלָה חִשְׁקִי וְאוֹתִי
וְשָׁכְחָה אַהֲבָתִי הַקְּדוּמָה.
לְבִלְתִּי אֶחֱזֶה – הִיא כִּרְאוֹתִי
אֲזַי תִּבְרַח, בְּלִי עָוֹן וְאַשְׁמָה.
וְלֹא דֵי לָהּ, אֲבָל גַּזְלָה שְׁנָתִי
לְבִלְתִּי אֶחֱזֶנָּה בַּחֲלוֹמָה.'

'יְדִיד נַפְשִׁי, אֲמַלֵּא אֶת שְׁנָתָךְ
לְמַעַן כִּי רְאוֹתִי בַחֲלוֹמָךְ.
בְּעֵת תִּישַׁן, בְּצֵל חָרְשִׁי תְּהִי נָח,
וְתֶחֱזֵנִי בְּהָקִיצְךָ לְמוּלָךְ.'

[He:] This gazelle spurns my passion and me. She has forgotten my long-standing love. To keep me from seeing her, she runs away – though I am utterly blameless – as soon as she catches sight of me. Nor will this content her: she has also robbed me of sleep, so that I cannot even see her in my dreams.

[She:] Dear love, I shall fill your sleep until you see me in your dreams. Lie in the shade of my bower when you sleep, and you will see me in your daydream when you awaken.

יוֹסֵף צָרְפָתִי *Joseph Tsarfati*

יְשֵׁנָה אַתְּ TO HIS SLEEPING MISTRESS

יְשֵׁנָה אַתְּ, אֲנִי עֵעוֹר וְנוֹדֵד
וּמִתְנַמְגֵּם סָבִיב בֵּיתֵךְ, עֲדִינָה.
יְשֵׁנָה אַתְּ, אֲנִי צוּרִים אֲעוֹדֵד
בְּמַכְאוֹבִי וְאַחְשִׁיךְ הַלְּבָנָה.
יְשֵׁנָה אַתְּ, וְזִיו מַרְאֵךְ יְשׁוֹדֵד
תְּנוּמָה מִבְּנוֹת עֵינִי וְשֵׁנָה.
בְּצַלְמֵךְ כָּל מְזִמּוֹתַי כְּנוּסִים,
וְכַדּוֹנַג בְּתוֹךְ אִשֵּׁךְ נְמַסִּים.

You are asleep, my gentle love, but I am awake, wandering about, drowsily walking around your house. You are asleep, but I summon cliffs to witness my pain, and I blacken the moon. You are asleep, but your splendour robs my eyes of all slumber. All my thoughts are gathered in your body, and all of them melt like wax in your flame.

זְמַן, הַחֵן אֲשֶׁר זָרַע — THE JUDGEMENT OF TIME

זְמַן, הַחֵן אֲשֶׁר זָרַע בְּמִצְחֲךָ —
יַאַסְפֵהוּ וְלֹא יוֹסִיף לְתִתּוֹ.
וְכֵס גָּבְהֶךָ אֲשֶׁר חָשַׁבְתָּ לְנִצְחֶךָ —
שְׁאוֹל יוּרַד בְּבוֹא יוֹמוֹ וְעִתּוֹ.
וְחֶבֶל בּוֹ קְשַׁרְתַּנִי בְּנִצְחֶךָ —
זְמַן יִכְרֹת בְּמַזְמֵרָתוֹ וְאֵתוֹ.
זְמַן מַשְׁפִּיל, זְמַן מֵרִים וּמֵקִים,
וְעוֹשֶׂה דִין וּמִשְׁפָּט לַעֲשׁוּקִים.

That grace which Time has sown in
your forehead, Time will harvest and
never give back. And your high throne,
which you believed would be yours
forever – when the hour comes, it will
be lowered into the pit. And those
bonds with which you tied me in your
triumph, Time will cut them with its
knife and mattock. Time throws down,
Time raises up, Time deals out justice
to the oppressed.

וְאִם רָחַקְתָּ, צְבִיָּה — THE CAPTIVE

וְאִם רָחַקְתָּ, צְבִיָּה, מִמְּגוּרַי,
קְרוֹבָה אַתְּ לַעֲצָמִי מִבְּשָׂרִי.
וְאִם חָפְשִׁי אֲנִי נֶחְשָׁב לְשׁוּרַי,
גְּבִירִי נִיב שְׂפָתַיִךְ, וְשָׂרִי.
וְאִם אַרְחִיב לְעֵין רוֹאַי אֲשׁוּרַי,
תְּאַסְרִי חִישׁ כְּרֶגַע מַאֲסָרִי.
לְבַדֵּךְ אַתְּ לְמִיתָתִי אֲשֵׁמָה,
וְתָשִׁיבִי, בְּחֶפְצֵךְ, בִּי נְשָׁמָה.

And though you are far from where I
live, gazelle, you are closer to my bones
than my own flesh. And though people
look at me and take me[1] for a freeman,
your every word is my lord and master.
And though I walk along briskly, in full
view, in an instant you could make me
your prisoner. You alone are guilty of
my death, and only you, if you wish,
can restore my soul to me.

אֲהָהּ, כַּמָּה מְצָא חִנֵּךְ — THE OBSTINATE MISTRESS

אֲהָהּ, כַּמָּה מְצָא חִנֵּךְ אֲשַׁבֵּר,
וּבַמָּה אֶת פְּנֵי חַסְדֵּךְ אֲכַבֵּר?
וְכָל עֵת שִׁיר בְּמַהְלָלֵךְ אֲחַבֵּר,

How I long to win your favour! What
expiation must I make to be in your
good graces? At all times, I compose a
song in your praise, telling your virtues

1. Or, 'And though my enemies take me . . .'

וְגָדְלֵךְ בּוֹ לְכֹל יָבֹא אֲסַפֵּר.
וְלֵב כֶּלֶב נְהִי בִכְיִי יְשַׁבֵּר,
וְכִלְיוֹתָיו לְאָבָק דַּק יְצַעֵר!
וְאַתְּ שָׁמִיר לְבָבֵךְ שַׂמְתְּ וְעָרְפֵּךְ,
וְאָזְנֵךְ אֶל תְּחִנּוֹתַי כְּמַשְׁפֵּךְ.

to one and all. My tearful lament would break a dog's heart and grind his innards to fine dust. But you have made your heart and neck like adamant, and turned your ear like a funnel to my plea.

יוֹסֵף הַכֹּהֵן

Joseph Hakohen

עוּרָה, כְּבוֹדִי

THE CONDITIONS OF BEAUTY

עוּרָה, כְּבוֹדִי, וַאֲסַפֵּר לָךְ בְּשִׁיר
יְפִי הֲדַר נָשִׁים, וּבְמִצְלְתַּיִם:
אֶרֶךְ בְּחַר בְּשֵׂעָר וְלֹא תֵבוֹשׁ, וְגַם
אֶרֶךְ בְּיָדַיִם וְגַם שׁוֹקַיִם.
שָׁלוֹשׁ קְצָרִים הֵם נְתוּנִים לָהּ לְחֵן:
אֹזֶן וְשָׁדַיִם וְגַם שִׁנַּיִם.
מֵצַח יְהִי רָחָב, וְהֶחָזֶה, וְגַם
יִהְיוּ כְסָלִים רַחֲבֵי יָדַיִם.
צָרָה בְּעֶנְיָנָהּ בְּחַר, צוֹפֶה, וְגַם
צָרָה בְּמוֹ יָרֵךְ וְגַם מָתְנַיִם.
עָבָה בְּצִיצִית רֹאשׁ תְּהִי אִשָּׁה, וְגַם
בִּשְׁתֵּי זְרוֹעֶיהָ וְיַרְכָתַיִם.
דַּקִּים שְׁלוֹשָׁה הֵם: שְׂעַר רֹאשָׁהּ, וְגַם
כָּל אֶצְבְּעוֹתֶיהָ וְהַשְּׂפָתַיִם.
צַוָּאר בְּחַר עָגֹל, עֲגֻבוֹת גַּם זְרוֹ-
עַ, אָז לְיָפְיָהּ יֶהֱמוּ מֵעַיִם.
פִּיהָ תְהִי קָטָן, בְּלִי שָׂטָן, בְּלִי
מוּם רַע, וְהַחֹטֶם וְהָרַגְלַיִם.

Awake, my spirit, and I shall tell you in song, to the sound of cymbals, of woman's beauty and splendour. Choose hair that is long and you will not be put to shame; also prefer length in hands and legs. These three should be short to give her grace: ears, breasts, and teeth. Her forehead should be broad; so, too, her chest; her loins should also be spacious. Spectator, choose the woman whose thing is narrow, who has narrow thighs and hips. She should have thick forelocks, thick arms and buttocks. These three should be fine: the hair of her head, her fingers and her lips. Choose a neck that is round, a round behind and forearm, and your vitals will thrill to her beauty. Her mouth should be small, discreet,[1] flawless; this goes for her nose and

---

1. Lit. 'without Satan'; an allusion to a saying that one should not invite misfortune by ominous words.

תַּלְבִּין בְּשִׁנֶּיהָ, וּבִשְׁתַּיִם אֲשֶׁר
אֹמַר: וְהֵם גָּרוֹן וְהַיָּדַיִם.
אֹדֶם בְּפָנֶיהָ לְחֵן חֵן לָהּ בְּחַר,
וּשְׁתֵּי שְׂפָתֶיהָ וְצִפָּרְנַיִם.
שַׁחֲרוּת בְּגַבּוֹת לָהּ לְיֹפִי נֶהֱדָר,
גַּם בִּשְׂעַר יָפָה וְהָעֵינַיִם.
אִשָּׁה אֲשֶׁר אֵלֶּה תְּנָאֵי יָפְיָהּ –
לֹא יַעֲרִיכֶנָּה זְהַב פַּרְוָיִם.

feet, too. Her teeth must be white and
so should these two: her throat and her
hands. Choose the one who is graced
with red on her cheeks, lips, and
fingernails. Her eyebrows black, to
enhance her loveliness; black, also, her
hair and eyes. The woman who fulfils
these conditions of beauty – not even
the gold of Parvaim can measure her
worth.

אָמְנָם אֲשֶׁר חֶפְצָהּ בְּתוֹרַת אֵל, וְגַם
כָּל מַחְשְׁבוֹת לִבָּהּ לְאֵל כַּפַּיִם,
אִשָּׁה לְזֹאת תִּקָּרֵא וְאֵלֶיהָ קְרַב,
אַל נָא לְזָרָה תִּפְרְשָׂה כַפַּיִם.
שֶׁקֶר לְחֵן תֹּאמַר וְהֶבֶל אֶל יְפִי
נָשִׁים, וְהַלֵּל יִרְאַת שָׁמַיִם.
קַח לָךְ, בְּנִי, עֵצָה אֲשֶׁר נָתַן לְךָ
יוֹסֵף וְגַם כֹּהֵן לְאֵל שָׁמַיִם.

Of course, she who delights in the Law
of the Lord, whose every thought goes
out to Him in prayer – she alone merits
the name of woman. Go seek her
company, and do not spread out your
hands to an adulteress. Call charm a
delusion and woman's beauty a bubble,
and give all honour to the fear of God.
My son, accept this advice given to you
by Joseph, who is also a priest[1] of God
in Heaven.

שִׁמְעוֹן לָבִיא   *Simeon Labi*

בַּר יוֹחַאי   HYMN TO BAR YOḤAI[2]

בַּר-יוֹחַאי, נִמְשַׁחְתָּ – אַשְׁרֶיךָ! –
שֶׁמֶן שָׂשׂוֹן מֵחֲבֵרֶיךָ.

Happy are you, Bar Yoḥai! He anointed
you above your fellows with oil, the
token of joy.

1. Hebrew *cohen*, a reference to the author's lineage.
2. The hymn refers to the ten *Sefirot* in the following order: Stanza 1 – *Malkhut* ('kingdom'); 2 – *Yesod Olam* ('foundation of the world'); 3 – *Netsah* ('lasting endurance') and *Hod* ('majesty'); 4 – *Tiferet* ('beauty'); 5 – *Gevura* ('power'); 6 – *Ḥesed* ('love'); 7 – *Bina* ('intelligence'), which is the source of freedom, redemption and temporal order; 8 – *Ḥokhma* ('wisdom') the ideal thought of creation, which is represented by the letter *yod*, the first letter in the name of God; 9 – *Keter Elyon* ('supreme crown') and, above it, *Ayin* ('absolute nothingness') from which all the *Sefirot* emanate. (See G. Scholem's *Kabbalah*, 1974, p. 96 ff.)

בַּר־יוֹחַאי, שֶׁמֶן מִשְׁחַת קֹדֶשׁ
נִמְשַׁחְתָּ מִמִּדַּת הַקֹּדֶשׁ.
נָשָׂאתָ צִיץ גֵזֶר־הַקֹּדֶשׁ,
חָבוּשׁ עַל רֹאשְׁךָ פְּאֵרֶךָ.

Bar Yoḥai, you were anointed with the holy oil, drawn from the quality of holiness. You wore the rosette of the holy diadem, your turban was bound on your head.[1]

בַּר־יוֹחַאי, מוֹשָׁב טוֹב יָשַׁבְתָּ
יוֹם נַסְתָּ, יוֹם אֲשֶׁר בָּרַחְתָּ.
בִּמְעָרַת צוּרִים שֶׁעָמַדְתָּ,
קָנִיתָ הוֹדְךָ וַהֲדָרֶךָ.

Bar Yoḥai, you chose an excellent retreat on the day you fled [from the Romans]. There, in that cave in the rocks, you attained glory and majesty.

בַּר־יוֹחַאי, עֲצֵי שִׁטִּים עוֹמְדִים,
לְמוּדֵּי יְיָ הֵם לוֹמְדִים.
אוֹר מֻפְלָא, אוֹר הַיְקוֹד הֵם יוֹקְדִים,
הֲלֹא הֵמָּה יוֹרוּךָ מוֹרֶיךָ.

Bar Yoḥai, the seraphim[2] stood about you, the Lord's disciples, deep in study. They burnt with a flaming light of mystery. These were the teachers who instructed you.

בַּר־יוֹחַאי, וְלִשְׂדֵה תַפּוּחִים
עָלִיתָ לִלְקָט־בּוֹ מֶרְקָחִים,
סוֹד תּוֹרָה כְּצִיצִים וּפְרָחִים.
'נַעֲשֶׂה אָדָם,' נֶאֱמַר בַּעֲבוּרֶךָ.

Bar Yoḥai, you ascended to the Field of Apple Trees[3] to gather fragrances: the mysteries of the Torah, which are like blossoms and flowers. 'Let us make man'[4] was pronounced for your sake.

בַּר־יוֹחַאי, נֶאֱזַרְתָּ בִּגְבוּרָה,
וּבְמִלְחֶמֶת אֵשׁ דָּת הַשַּׁעֲרָה,
וְחֶרֶב הוֹצֵאתָ מִתַּעְרָהּ,
שָׁלַפְתָּ נֶגֶד צוֹרְרֶיךָ.

Bar Yoḥai, girded with strength, you repelled them at the gate with the flaming Law. You drew your sword from the scabbard and wielded it against your enemies.

1. The High Priest wore a 'golden frontlet' (Exodus 39.20) as a symbol of his dedication and was anointed with oil (Exodus 30.30).
2. Lit. '[planks of] acacia wood, upright' of which the Tabernacle was built.
3. The mystical garden of Eden; this also symbolizes the Divine Presence.
4. Genesis 1.26.

בַּר־יוֹחַאי, לִמְקוֹם אַבְנֵי שַׁיִשׁ
הִגַּעְתָּ, לִפְנֵי אַרְיֵה לַיִשׁ.
גַּם גֻּלַּת כּוֹתֶרֶת עַל עַיִשׁ
תָּשׁוּר, וּמִי יְשׁוּרֶךָ.

Bar Yoḥai, you reached the Palace of the stones of pure marble[1] and came into the presence of the Lion [engraved in the Chariot-Throne]. You saw the orb of the crown set upon the Pleiades, but no one could see you.

בַּר־יוֹחַאי, בְּקֹדֶשׁ הַקֳּדָשִׁים
– קַו יָרֹק מְחַדֵּשׁ חֳדָשִׁים,
שֶׁבַע שַׁבָּתוֹת, סוֹד חֲמִשִּׁים –
קָשַׁרְתָּ קִשְׁרֵי שִׁי"ן קְשָׁרֶיךָ.

Bar Yoḥai, when you entered the Holy of Holies, the green zone which is the source of time, the palace of the seven Sabbaths, the mystery [of the fifty gates and] of the Jubilee – you bound together the three supreme Sefirot.[2]

בַּר־יוֹחַאי, יו"ד חָכְמָה קְדוּמָה
הִשְׁקַקְפָּתָ לִכְבוֹדוֹ פְּנִימָה,
ל"ב נְתִיבוֹת, רֵאשִׁית, תְּרוּמָה.
אַתָּ כְּרוּב מְמְשַׁח, זִיו דוֹרֶךָ.

Bar Yoḥai, you gazed into the depths of His Glory, into the primordial point of Wisdom – the Beginning, [the first word of creation] – which flows forth into the thirty-two paths [of hidden lore]. You were the towering cherub, the splendour of your generation.

בַּר־יוֹחַאי, אוֹר מֻפְלָא, רוֹם־מַעְלָה –
יָרֵאתָ מִלְּהַבִּיט, כִּי רַב לָהּ.
תַּעֲלוּמָה, וְאַיִן קְרָא לָהּ.
נָמְתָּ: 'עַיִן לֹא תְשׁוּרֶךָ.'

Bar Yoḥai, you were afraid to look at the wondrous light, the Supreme Crown, for its fullness is overwhelming. This is the mystery, named Ayin. You said: 'No eye will catch sight of You.'

בַּר־יוֹחַאי, אַשְׁרֵי יוֹלַדְתֶּךָ,
אַשְׁרֵי הָעָם הֵם לוֹמְדֶיךָ,
אַשְׁרֵי הָעוֹמְדִים עַל סוֹדֶיךָ,
לוֹבְשֵׁי חֹשֶׁן תֻּמֶּיךָ וְאוּרֶיךָ.

Bar Yoḥai, happy is your mother! Happy are the people who study your doctrines, who penetrate into your secrets, as they wear your breastpiece[3] over their hearts.

---

1. 'When you come to the place of the shining marble plates, then do not say: Water, water! For it is written: "He that telleth lies shall not tarry in my sight"' (*T.B. Ḥagigah* 14b).

2. Represented by the three crowns of the letter *shin*, שׁ.

3. Lit. 'the breastpiece of your Urim and Thummim'; the 'symbols of judgement' worn by Aaron whenever he entered the presence of the Lord (Exodus 28.30).

459

סְעַדְיָה לוֹנְגוֹ   *Sa'adiah Longo*

סִבָּה וְעָלָה וּמַעֲמִיד   THE PARADOX

סִבָּה וְעָלָה וּמַעֲמִיד, אֵל חַי לְכָל יֵשׁ מְצָאתִיו.
נֶעְלָם וְנִסְתָּר וְנִגְלָה, עִם עֵין לְבָבִי רְאִיתִיו.
פּוֹעֵל הֲפָכִים וְאֶחָד, יָחִיד וּמְיָחָד קְרָאתִיו.
אֵל שׁוֹאֲלִי: 'אֵיךְ?' עֲנִיתִיו: 'אִלּוּ יְדַעְתִּיו, הָיִיתִיו!'

I have found the Living God to be the
cause and support of all Being. Concealed and yet revealed, I have seen
Him with my mind's eye. Maker of
opposites and yet One, I have called
Him the Single and Unique. When
asked: 'How can this be?', I answer: 'If
I knew, I would be He!'

שְׂפָתַיִם יִשָּׁק   THE SCOUNDREL'S SONG

'שְׂפָתַיִם יִשָּׁק מֵשִׁיב דְּבָרֵי חֵן,' אָמַר נָבָל.
נַפְשׁוֹ עָלָיו תֶּאֱבָל !

'Pleasing words,' said the scoundrel,
'are like a kiss on the lips.' May he
mourn his own loss!

'לָבְשׁוּ פְּנֵי תֵבֵל רִקְמָה,
עֵץ הַשָּׂדֶה סוּת עֶלְצוֹן,
וְדֶרֶךְ גֶּבֶר בְּעַלְמָה
חָמְדוּ כָּל אַנְשֵׁי לָצוֹן.
לָבְשׁוּ כָרִים הַצֹּאן' —
אָמַר נָבָל.
נַפְשׁוֹ עָלָיו תֶּאֱבָל !

'The earth put on robes of brocade;
and the trees of the country-side,
mantles of joy. Then all the insolent
youths avidly pursued the way of a
man with a girl. Oh, the meadows
clothed themselves with sheep,' said
the scoundrel. May he mourn his own
loss!

'כְּסוּס עָגוּר כֵּן יְצַפְצֵף
נוֹאֵף עִם יַעֲלַת מַלְכָּדְתּוֹ,
וְשִׁיר עֲנָבִים יְרַצֵּף,
שָׂשׂ לְעָמַת מַחְבַּרְתּוֹ,
אִישׁ אִישׁ כִּי תִשְׂטֶה אִשְׁתּוֹ' —

'The adulterer twitters like a swallow,
together with the paramour whom he
has snared. And every man whose wife
has gone astray rejoices over his
mistress,[1] multiplying songs of lust,'

---

1. Lit. 'seam, juncture'.

אָמַר נָבָל.
נַפְשׁוֹ עָלָיו תֶּאֱבָל !

said the scoundrel. May he mourn his
own loss!

'יַעֲלָה מִנְּתִיב אֲהָבִים
מְשָׁרֶכֶת דְּרָכֶיהָ.
סַלּוֹנִים הֵם וְסָרְבִים
צְבָא חוֹשְׁקִים לְצִדֶּיהָ.
נָאֲפוּפֶיהָ בֵּין שָׁדֶיהָ –'
אָמַר נָבָל.
נַפְשׁוֹ עָלָיו תֶּאֱבָל !

'The lady twisted and turned, leaving
the path of [true] love. Like briars and
thorns, a host of suitors beset her.
Adultery nests between her breasts,'
said the scoundrel. May he mourn his
own loss!

'בְּעַד הַחַלּוֹן נִשְׁקָפָה,
כְּמוֹ הַשַּׁחַר עָלָה.
לִרְאוֹת בְּבָנִים שָׁאָפָה
מַשְׂאַת הַחֵשֶׁק עָלָה.
הִנֵּה זוֹ רָעָה חוֹלָה !'
אָמַר נָבָל.
נַפְשׁוֹ עָלָיו תֶּאֱבָל !

'At the crack of dawn, she peered
through her lattice, panting to see the
smoke of desire rising amongst the
boys. Oh, this is a singular evil,' said
the scoundrel. May he mourn his own
loss!

'שִׁפְעַת הָרוֹעֶה רָאָתָה
וְחֵץ חִשְׁקָהּ שָׂמָה עַל קֶשֶׁת,
פָּרְשָׂה עָלָיו מְצוֹדָתָהּ
וַתִּקְרָא לוֹ אֶל הָרֶשֶׁת,
הַרְחֵק כְּמִטַחֲוֵי קֶשֶׁת –'
אָמַר נָבָל.
נַפְשׁוֹ עָלָיו תֶּאֱבָל !

'Seeing the shepherd, in all his fulness,
she strung her bow with the arrow of
desire, from a distance, like an archer.
She threw her net over him and
tempted him into its meshes,' said the
scoundrel. May he mourn his own loss!

'קְרָאַתְהוּ לְסוֹד נִכְמָס,
וְחִשְׁקָהּ בְּעֵינָיו חָלָךְ.
צוּף לְשׁוֹנָהּ הֲמֵס יָמֵס

'She invited him to share a deep secret.
He made light of her desire. But her
honeyed words could melt the heart of

461

לֵב קָצִין וְשַׂר וּמֶלֶךְ.
"לֹא, כִּי בִּשְׁרִירוּת לִבִּי אֵלֵךְ.'"
אָמַר נָבָל.
נַפְשׁוֹ עָלָיו תֶּאֱבָל !

any lord, prince, or king. "No, [thought the shepherd] I shall follow my wilful heart",' said the scoundrel. May he mourn his own loss!

'"סוּרָה, שְׁבָה פֹּה לִימִינִי,
הָרוֹעֶה, וְהַט אָזְנֶךָ.
חֵשֶׁק בְּסֵתֶר מְלָשְׁנִי,
פִּתַּנִי וָאֹהֲבֶךָ.
קְרָא נָא, הֲיֵשׁ עוֹנֶךָ ?'"
אָמַר נָבָל.
נַפְשׁוֹ עָלָיו תֶּאֱבָל !

'"'Come, shepherd, sit at my right hand, and bend down your ear to me. Desire secretly informed on you, seduced me and now I love you. Call, if you wish – will anyone answer you?''' said the scoundrel. May he mourn his own loss!

דָּוִד עוֹנְקִינֵירָה   *David Onkinerah*

קוֹלֵךְ, צְבִיָּה   WOUNDS OF LOVE

קוֹלֵךְ, צְבִיָּה, שָׁמְעָה אָזְנִי –
חָרְדוּ מְאֹד חוּשַׁי וְנַפְשִׁי נִבְהֲלָה,
קָדַר מְאוֹר פָּנַי וְשִׁמְשִׁי אָפְלָה,
וּכְמוֹ נְחָלִים נִגְּרָה עֵינִי.

I heard your voice, my love, and all my senses throbbed and my soul quivered in dismay. The light of my face darkened, my sun was covered with shadows, and my eyes streamed like rivers.

חִצֵּי בְרָקֶיךָ בְּתוֹךְ בִּטְנִי.
אֶתְקַע בְּכַף יָדְךָ, וְהִגָּה עָפְלָה.
יִפְעַת דְּמוּת צַלְמְךָ כְּבֵדִי חִלְלָה,
תָּחִישׁ בְּלֵיל חִשְׁקִי לְהַלְמֵנִי.

The arrows of your lightning are deep within my belly. I put my hand in yours and it swells with pain. The pride of your figure has pierced my heart. In the night of my desire, it swiftly strikes me down.

לֹא יִשְׁכְּבוּן עוֹרְקַי עֲלֵי מִשְׁכָּב
אַף כִּי בְּעֵדֶן גַּן מְעוֹנִי אֶתְּנָה,
כִּי גַחֲלֵי חִשְׁקֵךְ בְּלִבִּי בוֹעֲרִים.

Though I make my home in Paradise,
my veins will wildly beat with pain
when I lie down, for the embers of
desire burn in my heart.

לֹא אֶמְצָאָה מָנוֹס וְאִם אֶרְכַּב
עַל הַכְּרוּב אוֹ בַתְּהוֹמוֹת אֶשְׁכְּנָה,
כִּי מֵי נְהַר זַעְפֵּךְ בְּפָנַי סוֹעֲרִים.

Whether I soar on a cherub or descend
into the depths, I can find no escape,
for your raging waters surge over my
face.

נִחְיֶה בְּצֵל

BLISS

[. . .] נִחְיֶה בְּצֵל יַעֲלַת־חֵן,
נִחְיֶה וְנִהְיֶה סְעוּדִים.
גֵלֵךְ לְאוֹרָהּ חֲשֵׁכִים,
נִהְיֶה בְּשִׂמְחָה תְּמִידִים.
תִּשְׂחַק – וְנִפְצַח בְּרִנָּה,
תִּזְעַף – וְנִלְבַּשׁ פְּחָדִים.
תָּצִיף בְּאוֹרָהּ וְנָשׁוּב
לִהְיוֹת גְּאוּלִים וְנִפְדִּים.

We shall live in the shade of the
graceful doe and, living there, shall be
sustained. We shall walk through
darkness by her light, with never-
ending joy. When she laughs, we will
burst into song; when she frowns, we
shall clothe ourselves in fear. And when
she looks with radiant eyes, we shall
once again be ransomed and redeemed.

דְּמוּת צַלְמֵךְ, צְבִיָּה

THE VOW

דְּמוּת צַלְמֵךְ, צְבִיָּה, בַּחֲלוֹמִי
הֲכִי נִרְאָה וְהִבְרִיק כַּבְּרָקִים
וְהֵאִיר מַחֲשַׁךְ עֵינַי, וְרָאוּ
בְּפָנַיִךְ כְּמוֹ תַבְנִית שְׁחָקִים,
וּבָם שֶׁמֶשׁ וְיָרֵחַ נְתוּנִים
וְכוֹכָבִים וּמַזָּלוֹת אֲדוּקִים,
וּבָם חִצִּים שְׁנוּנִים וַחֲנִיתוֹת

I saw your figure in my dream, gazelle,
flashing like lightning. It gave light to
my darkened eyes, and I saw that your
face was a model of the heavens. The
sun and moon are set in it, the stars
and planets are fixed there. And it holds
sharp arrows and spears, burnished to

לְפַלֵּחַ הַלְּבָבוֹת הֵם בְּרוּקִים. [...]
הֵאִירוּנִי בְּלֵיל חָשְׁכִּי וְאָפְלִי
וְנָטְלוּ מֵעֲלֵי עֵינַי פְּקָקִים,
וְהֵנִיסוּ יְגוֹנוֹת וַאֲנָחוֹת,
וְנִשְׁמַע קוֹל שְׂמָחוֹת בַּשְּׁוָקִים.

pierce all hearts. It lit up my pitch-black night and pulled the stoppers from my eyes. It put sorrows and sighing to flight, and the sound of rejoicing was heard in the market-places.

אֲנִי, עָנִי, בְּהַבִּיטִי בְּעֵינִי
הֲדַר יָפְיָהּ, וְחוּשַׁי בָּהּ דְּבֵקִים —
צְבִיָּה נֶעֱלָמָה, עָלְתָה וְנָסְעָה
וְגָבְהָה עַל עֲנָנִים מֵאֲרָקִים.
וְנִשְׁאַרְתִּי בְּתוֹךְ חֹשֶׁךְ אֲפֵלָה,
כְּמוֹ עַכְבָּר מְהַלֵּךְ בַּסְּדָקִים;
כְּמוֹ בָרָק אֲשֶׁר יִזְרַח אֱלֵי אִישׁ
בְּעוֹד לַיְלָה, וְעֵינָיו בּוֹ בְּהוּקִים,
וְכַאֲשֶׁר יַעֲבֹר אוֹרוֹ וְנָגְהוֹ
יְהִי נִשְׁאָר בְּאָפְלוֹ בָּעֲמָקִים;
כְּאִישׁ מְסָכֵּן וְחוֹזֵר עַל פְּתָחִים
אֲשֶׁר עֵינָיו בְּתוֹךְ חֹרָיו נְמַקִּים. [...]

O wretched me! As I gazed upon her radiant beauty, with all my senses clinging to her, she suddenly rose from the earth, flew high above the clouds and disappeared. And I was left behind in pitch darkness, like a mouse crawling through a crack; like a man whose eyes glow when lightning flashes before him in the night, and then the glow is gone, leaving him in his valley of darkness; or like a wretch who goes begging from door to door, his eyes rotting in their sockets.

לְכָל אֵלֶּה אֲנִי אֲדַמֶּה וְאֶשְׁוֶה,
וְרַעְיוֹנַי כְּמוֹהֶם נֶאֱנָקִים.
וְהֵן אַרְחִיק נְדֹד, אָלִין בְּמִדְבָּר,
וְאֶשְׁכֹּן בַּסְּלָעִים עַל נְקִיקִים,
וְאֶקְרַע אֶת לְבוּשֵׁי מַחֲמַדַּי,
וְאֶתְחַפֵּשׂ וְגַם אָלִין בְּשַׂקִּים —
עֲדֵי אָשׁוּב לְהַבִּיט הוֹד צְבִיָּה
וְתָשִׁיב אֶת שְׁבוּתִי כַּאֲפִיקִים,
וַדַדֶּיהָ יְרַוּוּנִי בְּכָל עֵת
וּבְשָׂעֲרָהּ יְמֵי חַיַּי עֲנוּקִים.

Such is my lot, as grievous as theirs and, like them, my thoughts groan and lament. I will go far away and find a refuge in the wilderness, I will make my home among the crags, I will tear up my precious garments, I will cover them with mud and lie in sackcloth all night long – until I once more behold her splendour; until she turns my fortune around as streams return in the desert, and I am bathed in her love at all times, and the days of my life are entwined in her tresses.

JUDAH ZARCO

בַּסִּי, כְּלִילַת־חֵן HER HAIR

[...] בַּסִּי, כְּלִילַת־חֵן, שְׂעַר רֹאשֵׁךְ,
כִּי תִקְטְלִי הַיְקוּם בְּלִי יָדַיִם!
טִבְעָם בְּכָל תֵּבֵל הֲכִי יָצָא,
עַל כֵּן לְשִׁמְעָם צָלְלוּ אָזְנַיִם.
חָלוּשׁ וְרַךְ מִשַּׂעֲרוֹת רֹאשֵׁךְ
יָכוֹל עֲקֹר הָרִים וְיַרְכָּתַיִם —
מַה יַּעֲשֶׂה אִישׁ רָשׁ בְּעֵת כֻּלָּם
מִתְחַזְּקִים נֶגְדּוֹ בְּרִבּוֹתַיִם?
בִּי, יַעֲלַת הַחֵן, עֲלֵי נַפְשִׁי
חוּסִי, לְבַל אָמוּת בְּלִי יוֹמַיִם,
וּתְשַׁלְּמִי דָמִי אֲשֶׁר יֻקַּם
מִמֵּךְ כְּדַם קַיִן לְשִׁבְעָתַיִם.

O peerless beauty, veil your hair, lest
you play havoc with the world, without
lifting a finger! They are famous
throughout the world, they ring in the
ears of all who hear of them. The
weakest, softest strand on your head
can pull out a mountain by its roots.
What, then, can a poor man do, when
they fall upon him in their myriads? I
pray you, graceful deer, have pity on
my life, don't make me die so young;
you would have to pay for my blood
which, like Cain's, would be exacted
seven times over.

עֶבֶד אֲנִי, נִרְצָע וְנִמְכָּר לָךְ,
וּלְנֹעֲמֵךְ מִשְׁתַּחֲוֶה אַפַּיִם.
אֶת פִּי לְמַלְקוֹשֵׁךְ אֲנִי פוֹעֵר —
בֹּקֶר אֲקַו חַסְדֵּךְ עֲדֵי עַרְבַּיִם.

I am, for life, your abject slave and
chattel. I prostrate myself before your
delights. I open my mouth wide,
hoping for your spring showers. From
dawn to dusk I await your favour.

יְהוּדָה זַרְקוֹ *Judah Zarco*

אִם תֶּחֱזוּ THE CELESTIAL RACE

אִם תֶּחֱזוּ כִּי בְשַׁחַק יְסוֹבֵב
גַּלְגַּל וְאוֹפַן בְּכָל עֵת וְשָׁעָה,
אַל תַּחְשְׁבוּ כִּי לְהַרְאוֹת גְּבוּרָה
רוּצָם מְהֵרָה, כְּאִישׁ רָץ בְּבִקְעָה.

When you see the planets and constellations circling heaven at all hours,
do not imagine that they are speeding,
like a runner in a valley, to show off
their prowess. No, it is a sublime cause

רַק הֵם יְרוּצוּן לְסַבָּה גְדוֹלָה,
חוֹזְרִים חֲלִילָה בְּלִי שׁוּם יְגִיעָה:
כִּי עַל חֲגוֹרַת מְזָרִים תְּסוֹבֵב
יַעֲלָה בְתוּלָה וְאִישׁ לֹא יְדָעָהּ.
לָכֵן יְרוּצוּן לְהַשִּׂיג הֲדָרָהּ,
לִשְׁכַּב בְּחֵיקָהּ בְּסוֹף הַתְּנוּעָה.

that makes them run, over and over
again, unflaggingly. For there, on the
celestial sphere, revolves a lovely virgin,
whom no man has ever known. That is
why they are racing: to attain her glory,
to lie in her bosom at the end of the
circuit.

אֵיךְ אֶחֱצֹב שִׁיר   AFTER THE VISION

אֵיךְ אֶחֱצֹב שִׁיר – וְהִנֵּה בְּפַטִּישׁ
חוּשַׁי הֲלֹא יַעֲלָה בּוֹ חֲלֻדָּה?
אוֹ מָה אֲנַגֵּן בְּגֵבֶל – וְיָדִי
עִם סַח פְּחָדִים וּמוֹרָא לְכוּדָה?
כִּי בָא לְלִבִּי בְּרִצְפַת צְבִיָּה,
אַבְנֵי יְסוֹדָהּ כְּאֹדֶם וּפִטְדָה,
מַלְאָךְ וְשָׂרָף בְּתוֹכוֹ יְעוֹפֵף,
חוֹפֵף וּמַחֲוֶי כְּרִיעָה וְקִדָּה.
רָאָה לְלִבִּי דְּמוּת מַלְאֲכֵי אֵל –
אֵיכָה יְחִי עוֹד בְּקָהָל וְעֵדָה?

How can I hew out a song when the
hammer of my senses is coated with
rust? How can I play the lute when my
hand is ensnared in fetters of fear? For
my heart has entered the gazelle's
paved [palace]; its fountain-stones are
as sardin and chrysolite. Angels and
seraphs hover within it, bending low,
kneeling before her. Having seen the
image of God's angels, how can my
heart live on in the company of mortals?

שָׁבוּי בְּעִיר מִקְלָט   THE PRISONER OF DESIRE

שָׁבוּי בְּעִיר מִקְלָט – וּמֵת כֹּהֵן – וְלֹא
נִגְאָל, וְעִם שֵׂבֶר לְפִדְיוֹנוֹ יְחִי;
תָּפוּשׂ בְּשַׁלְשֶׁלֶת וְחַבְלֵי אַהֲבָה
תָּמִיד, וְהֻכָּה שָׁם בְּשֵׁבֶט עַל לְחִי –

Caged in a city of refuge, unredeemed,
though the High Priest is already
dead;[1] kept alive by the hope of being
ransomed; at all times manacled in the
chains and bonds of love; struck on the
cheek with a rod – oh, make haste,

---

1. The homicide may leave the city of refuge and go back to his property after the death of the High
Priest (Numbers 35.28).

חוּשִׁי צְבִיָּה כִּי כְּבָר עָבַר זְמַן
יוֹבֵל וְצֵאת חָפְשִׁי, וְכִלְאוֹ תִּפְתְּחִי.
פִּתְחִי כְּלוֹב חָשְׁכּוֹ בְּלִי מָמוֹן וְהוֹן,
אַף כִּי בְּחֶרֶב צוּר גְּרוֹנוֹ תִּטְבָּחִי.

gazelle, for the year of the jubilee, the
time of his freedom, is long past.
Release him, without ransom, from his
cage of darkness, though you then cut
his throat with a sharp sword.

יִסְלַח עֲווֹנַיִךְ – וְאוֹתוֹ תִּסְחָבִי
עַל אַשְׁפּוֹת הַשֶּׁלֶךְ וּמָאוֹס גַּם סְחִי.
אַף תִּקְבְּרִי אוֹתוֹ בְּקִיר לִבֵּךְ, אֲשֶׁר
דָּמוֹ יְהִי מֹהַל וְעוֹרוֹ תִּמְלְחִי.
אוֹ עִם עֲבוֹת שַׂעְרֵךְ תְּלִי אוֹתוֹ עֲלֵי
דַּדַּיִךְ וְנִבְלָתוֹ עֲלֵי עֵץ תִּשְׁכָּחִי.
חֵץ אַהֲבָה שִׂימִי בְּקֶשֶׁת גַּב, וְהוּא
יִהְיֶה לְמַטָּרָא לְחֵץ בּוֹ תִּשְׁלְחִי.

He forgives you your crimes, and yet
you drag him along and fling him on
dung hills, amidst offscouring and
refuse. You bury him in the walls of
your heart; you take his blood for juice
and you salt his skin.[1] Or else, you use
your long curls to hang him upon your
breasts, and then abandon his corpse
on the gibbet. You string your eyebrow's bow with love's arrow, and
make him the target for your whistling
darts.

יִשְׁלַח אֲנִי־עֵינוֹ, בְּיָם יָפְיֵךְ יְהִי
שׁוֹטֵט, וְגַבּוֹתָיו לְמָשׁוֹטִים קְחִי.
כָּל יוֹם מְיַחֵל עֵת יְשׁוּעָתֵךְ – וְנָא
חִישׁ גֹּאֲלִי אוֹתוֹ וְדִמְעָתוֹ מְחִי.

Oh, let him send forth the fleet of his
eyes, let him sail your beauty's sea, as
you take his eyebrows for oars. Each
day he waits for you to be his saviour.
Pray redeem him quickly and wipe
away his tears.

אֵל חַי וְנוֹרָא

THE PLEA

אֵל חַי וְנוֹרָא, חְּצוּ לַהֲפֹךְ בֵּית
כֶּלֶא וְסֹהַר בְּסַהַר וְאַגָּן.
אֹפֶל שְׁאוֹלִי הָפָךְ־נָא לְהִלִּי,
מִשְׁכַּן עֲלָטָה לְפַרְדֵּס וְנִיר גָּן.
אֶקְרָא לְךָ, אֵל, בְּחֹר מַחְשָׁבִי,
אֶצְעַק כְּתָם, לֹא כְּרָכִיל וְנִרְגָּן.

O living and terrible God, replace my
prison, this round pit,[2] by a full moon[2]
and a goblet. Pray, turn the darkness of
my hell into a shining light, and this
dwelling-place of dusk into an orchard,
a blossoming garden. I call to You, O
God, out of the depths of my thoughts.
I cry out in innocence, not as a rebel or

---

1. As the hides of animal offerings were salted (*Mishnah Middoth* 5.3).
2. A play on *sohar*, 'prison', and *sahar*, 'moon'.

הוֹצֵא אֲנִי מַאֲנַיִ כְּחֶפְצִי,
כִּי הוּא בְּלֵב יָם־תְּלָאוֹת מְעֻגָּן.
תָּמִיר שְׁמִירִי בְּשׁוֹשַׁן שְׂשׂוֹנִי,
לַעֲנָה וּמֵי רֹאשׁ בְּתִירֹשׁ וְדָגָן.

a slanderer. Grant me my wish, set
loose my ship of desire, for it is now
anchored deep in a sea of troubles.
Exchange my briars for lilies of joy, my
wormwood and gall for wine and grain.

יוֹסֵף בִּיבַּאס   *Joseph Bibas*

בֹּא יָבוֹא   THE LATE-COMER

בֹּא יָבוֹא נוֹשֵׂא בְרִנָּה
הַיֶּלֶד בְּמַקְהֵלוֹת.
קְהָלָתִי, פֹּה הַמְתִּינָה
חֲתַן דָּמִים לַמּוּלוֹת.

He will surely come with songs of joy,
carrying the child, in the full assembly.
My friends, wait here for the bridegroom of blood.[1]

מַדּוּעַ בּוֹשֵׁשׁ עַד הֵנָּה,
יֶלֶד יָבוֹא בַּמְסִלּוֹת?
לָכֵן צְאֶינָה וּרְאֶינָה,
הַנָּשִׁים הַמְחַתִּלוֹת —

He should be coming down the road.
Why is the child so late? You ladies,
who are charged with swaddling the
child, go forth and see

אִם שׁוֹשְׁבִינוֹת תֵּעָגֵנָה,
לְאַטָּן מִתְנַהֲלוֹת,
אוֹ אִם הַמּוֹהֵל הָלַךְ לוֹ
אֶל גִּבְעַת הָעֲרָלוֹת.

whether his kinswomen have lingered
and are moving at a slow pace, or
whether the circumciser has gone off to
the Hill of the Foreskins?[2]

הִנֵּה, אֲדוֹנִי, סוּרוּ נָא,
אַל תָּהִינוּ לַעֲלוֹת —
יֶלֶד רַךְ, עָנֹג, בְּאָמְנָה,
בְּבִגְדֵי מֹר וַאֲהָלוֹת!

I pray you, my lords, stay with us, do
not presume to leave. Truly, here he
comes – the soft-skinned delicate child,
wrapped in robes of myrrh and aloes!

---

1. 'Blood-bridegroom by circumcision' (Exodus 4.26) is the conventional epithet for the child who is circumcised.
2. Where Joshua circumcised the Israelites (Joshua 5.3).

שַׁחֲרִית אֲנָסַתּוּ שֵׁנָה
כִּי בָכָה כָּל הַלֵּילוֹת.
אַחַרְתֶּם – כִּי עֵת לְחֶנְנָהּ
תִּמְחֲלוּ לוֹ מְחִילוֹת.

When morning came he was overcome by sleep, for he had been crying all these nights. Sirs, you have been made to wait, but this is an hour of mercy. Forgive him with all your heart.

יְשַׁלֵּם שׁוֹכֵן מְעוֹנָה
לְפָם צַעֲרָא תַּגְמוּלוֹת.
הִנֵּה בָא, נוֹשֵׂא בְרָנָּה,
בָּרְכוּ אֵל בְּמַקְהֵלוֹת.

May He who dwells on high make the reward match the pain. Now, here he comes, carrying the child with songs of joy. Bless God in the full assembly!

יֶלֶד יֻלַּד נִכְנַס בִּבְרִית עֲדִינָה,
הָסֵר, צוּר, מִצִּיר מַחֲלוֹת.
אָנָּא רְפָא, אֵל נָא,
חֲתַן דָּמִים לַמּוּלוֹת.

This new-born child has been introduced into the covenant of Israel. O Rock, let not sickness touch his pain. Heal him, O God, I beseech You, heal the bridegroom of blood!

שְׁמוּאֵל אַרְקֵוולְטִי

Samuel Archevolti

שִׁיר שְׁמוֹלֵל הַחֲמוֹר

THE ASS'S COMPLAINT

לָמָה עֲלֵי שִׁכְמִי יְבִיאוּן סֹלֶת,
וּבְפִי יְהִי תֶבֶן, וְלֶחֶם אַיִן?
אֶשְׁתֶּה בְּמֵי בוֹרוֹת, וְאֶשָּׂא יַיִן.
מַקֵּל יְשִׂימֵנִי רְצוּץ גֻּלְגָּלֶת.

Why is my back loaded with fine flour, while in my mouth there is no bread at all, but only straw? I drink well-water, though I carry wine. And the stick goes on fracturing my skull!

אֶשְׁכֹּן בְּמוֹ חָרְבָּה וּבַמַּפֹּלֶת,
כַּצַּר בְּעִיר מִבְצָר, וּפֶתַח אַיִן.
אֶשָּׂא בְּכוֹרוֹת צֹאן וּמִנְחַת קַיִן,
הוֹי הוֹי, לְבַד דַּרְדַּר לְפִי מַפֹּלֶת!

I live in rubble and ruins, barred like an enemy in a fortified town, with no way out. I carry the first-born of the flocks and the finest produce of the soil,[1] but, oy!, my only food is thistles.

1. Lit. 'Cain's gift'; see Genesis 4.3.

גַּם אַחֲרֵי מוֹתִי אֱנוֹשׁ יַכֵּנִי:
אֶצְרַח בְּקוֹל גָּדוֹל, וְלִי יָרוּצוּ
כָּל יוֹצְאֵי צָבָא וְרֹאשׁ וָמֶלֶךְ.

Even after my death, Man goes on
beating me: then my voice rolls, and
the troops and officers and kings rush
to my call.[1]

אֶל צוּר יְשׁוּעוֹת אֹמְרָה: זַכֵּנִי
לָשֵׂאת מְשִׁיחָךְ חִישׁ, וְלֹא יָפוּצוּ
בָּנִים בְּכָל פִּנָּה כְּדַל נָחֵלֶךְ.

To the Rock of Salvation I say: Make
haste, grant me the privilege of carrying
Your Messiah, so that Your children
should no longer be scattered in every
corner like paupers and vagabonds.

מָרְדְּכַי דָּאטוֹ

Mordecai Dato

אַל תִּלְעֲגוּ עָלַי

THE OLD MAN AND THE GIRL

אַל תִּלְעֲגוּ עָלַי כִּי כַיּוֹם אָשִׁירָה
בְּפִי שִׁיר עֲגָבִים – וַאֲנִי זָקַנְתִּי.
תַּחַת רֶשֶׁף גַּחֶלֶת הֲלֹא בוֹעֵרָה,
כֵּן בְּקִרְבִּי לֵב עֵר גַּם עֵת כִּי יָשַׁנְתִּי.
אֶל זוּגָתִי אֲהַב וְהוּא בְּתַבְעֵרָה
כִּי אֲהַבְתִּיהָ כְּנַפְשִׁי בָּהּ נִשְׁעַנְתִּי.
נִשְׁתַּפָּה שְׂעָרִי לְגַוֶן סַהֲרָא;
תְּכוּנָתִי לֹא כֵן, וּבָהּ הִתְבּוֹנַנְתִּי.
אַךְ לְלַמֵּד דַּעַת אֶל זֹאת הַצְּעִירָה,
עֲצוּרָה לִי עַתָּה, וְאֶל זֶה כִּוַּנְתִּי.

Do not mock me for singing songs of
lust now that I have grown old. Does
not the ember glow beneath the ashes?
So is my heart awake within me even
when I sleep. It is on fire for love of
my partner; I love her as dearly as my
own soul, my mainstay. My hair has
taken on the colour of the moon, but
my mettle is the same, and that is all
that matters. I am saying all this to
open the eyes of the young girl who,
so far, will not give herself to me.

1. When the ass's hide is used as a drumskin.

470

יִצְחָק לוּרְיָא · *Isaac Luria*

מַה לְּךָ, יִצְרִי · TO HIS SELF

מַה לְּךָ, יִצְרִי, תָּמִיד תִּרְדְּפֵנִי
וּלְאוֹיֵב לָךְ כָּל יוֹם תַּחְשְׁבֵנִי?
יוֹם לְיוֹם תִּטְמֹן חִנָּם פַּח יְקוּשִׁים,
עַד אֲשֶׁר תּוֹךְ פַּח מוֹקְשֵׁי תִּלְכְּדֵנִי.
צַר וְאוֹיֵב לִי אַתָּה מִנְּעוּרַי,
תַּחֲרֹק עָלַי שֵׁן וַתִּשְׂטְמֵנִי.
חָשְׁבָה נַפְשִׁי לִנְטוֹת אַחֲרֶיךָ,
כִּי בְצֵל יָדָךְ מִצַּר תִּצְּרֵנִי.
קִדְּמוּ עֵינַי לִבְכּוֹת בָּאַשְׁמוּרוֹת,
כִּי בְעֶצֶב סָכוֹתָ וַתִּרְדְּפֵנִי.
אִם אֲדַמֶּה כִּי תִהְיֶה לִי לְעֶזְרָה,
וּבְיוֹם צָרָה אֶקְרָא, וְתַעֲנֵנִי:
'צוּף דְּבַשׁ אִמְרֵי נֹעַם חִכְּךָ לִי' –
הֵן בְּחַכָּה עַד דַּכָּא תִּמְשְׁכֵנִי!

What is the matter, my nature, why do you always pursue me and treat me every day as your enemy? Day after day, for no reason, you set hidden traps for me, until you finally catch me in my own snare. You have been my arch-enemy since childhood, you have gnashed your teeth at me in hatred. My soul had hoped to follow you; that, under the shadow of your hand, you would shield me from distress. But my eyes awoke to weep before the midnight watch, because you hid away in darkness and persecuted me. When I imagine that you will come to my aid; that, in time of distress, I will cry out and you will answer: 'Your kind words are like dripping honey to me' – you pull me out with a fishhook to my doom.

אֱלִיעֶזֶר אַזִכְּרִי · *Eliezer Azikri*

יְדִיד נֶפֶשׁ · BELOVED OF MY SOUL

יְדִיד נֶפֶשׁ, אָב הָרַחֲמָן,
מְשֹׁךְ עַבְדְּךָ אֶל רְצוֹנָךְ.
יָרוּץ עַבְדְּךָ כְּמוֹ אַיָּל,
יִשְׁתַּחֲוֶה מוּל הֲדָרָךְ,
כִּי יֶעֱרַב לוֹ יְדִידוּתָךְ
מִנֹּפֶת צוּף וְכָל טָעַם.

Beloved of my soul, merciful Father, draw Your servant after You to do Your will. He would run, swift as a deer, to kneel before Your majesty, for Your love is sweeter to him than honey from the comb, than any pleasing savour.

471

הָדוּר, נָאֶה, זִיו הָעוֹלָם,
נַפְשִׁי חוֹלַת אַהֲבָתָךְ.
אָנָּא, אֵל נָא, רְפָא נָא לָהּ
בְּהַרְאוֹת לָהּ נֹעַם זִיוָךְ.
אָז תִּתְחַזַּק וְתִתְרַפֵּא
וְהָיְתָה לָךְ שִׁפְחַת עוֹלָם.

Glorious, beautiful, Light of the world
– my soul is faint with love for You.
Heal her, O God, I beg You, by letting
her gaze upon Your splendour. Then
she will be healed and grow strong and
be Your slave forever.

נָתִיק, יֶהֱמוּ רַחֲמֶיךָ
וְחוּס נָא עַל בֵּן אוֹהֲבָךְ,
כִּי זֶה כַּמֶּה נִכְסֹף נִכְסַף
לִרְאוֹת בְּתִפְאֶרֶת עֻזָּךְ.
אָנָּא, אֵלִי, מַחְמַד לִבִּי,
חוּשָׁה נָּא, וְאַל תִּתְעַלָּם.

Faithful One, let your heart be moved
with tenderness, spare the son of Your
beloved friend, [Abraham,] for he has
longed these many years to behold
Your mighty splendour. My God, my
heart's delight, oh come quickly, do not
forsake me.

הִגָּלֶה נָא וּפְרֹשׂ, חָבִיב,
עָלַי אֶת סֻכַּת שְׁלוֹמָךְ.
תָּאִיר אֶרֶץ מִכְּבוֹדָךְ,
נָגִילָה וְנִשְׂמְחָה בָּךְ.
מַהֵר, אָהוּב, כִּי בָא מוֹעֵד,
וְחָנֵּנִי כִּימֵי עוֹלָם.

Reveal Yourself, my Dearest, and
spread over me Your canopy of peace.
Let the earth shine with Your glory,
let us rejoice in You. Make haste, my
Love, for the time has come; show me
Your favour as in the days of old.

יִשְׂרָאֵל נַגְ'אָרָה

Israel Najara

נְהִי נִהְיָה אֲעוֹרֵר

THE FAMINE IN
JERUSALEM

[...] נְהִי נִהְיָה אֲעוֹרֵר
וְלִבִּי בְּרוּחַ סוֹעָה מַסְעִיר
בְּזָכְרִי צַר חָשַׁף מַצְפּוּנִי
וּבְהֵיכָלִי אֵשׁ לְהָבוֹת הִבְעִיר.

Now I shall raise a bitter lament, and
my heart will heave in a raging storm
as I recall the enemy who ransacked
my treasure and set fire to my Temple.

הֵבִיא בְמָצוֹר עִירִי
וְכָל חֲמָתוֹ הֵעִיר,
וַיֶּחֱזַק הָרָעָב בָּעִיר.

He laid siege to my city, all his wrath was stirred up. *And the famine was severe in the city.*

יָרְדוּ חִצֵּי רָעָב לְכַלּוֹת הֲמוֹנִי,
כִּי קָרַב יוֹם אֵידָם.
פָּרִיצֵי עַמִּי סָבְבוּ בָעִיר
לְבַקֵּשׁ מִחְיָה בְּכָל מְאֹדָם.
כְּעָלוּ וּבָאוּ בְּבֵית אֵם
עוֹלֵל טִפּוּחִים, בְּעֹז יָדָם
וַיִּקְחוּ הָאֲנָשִׁים מְצֵידָם.

The arrows of famine poured down to wipe out my people, when the day of their doom was at hand. Men of violence among my own people made the rounds of the city, searching for food at any price. They went up into the mother's house – there she was with the child of her tender care – and violently *took away the provisions.*

יַחַד הָאִשָּׁה וּבְנָהּ
נִשְׁאֲרוּ רֵיקָם בְּרֹב מַלְחָלָה,
עֲטוּפִים בְּרָעָב,
נוֹהִים וְצוֹעֲקִים בְּקוֹל יְלָלָה.
לֵאמֹר: ׳מָה אֶעֱשֶׂה לִבְנִי
אֲשֶׁר טִפַּחְתִּי בְּרֹב חֶמְלָה,
וּבְבֵיתִי אֵין לֶחֶם וְאֵין שִׂמְלָה ?׳

The woman and her child were left empty-handed, writhing in anguish, faint with hunger, howling and wailing aloud. 'What shall I do,' she said, 'with my son whom I reared with such tenderness? *There is neither food nor clothing in my house.*'

שָׁאַל הַנַּעַר לְאִמּוֹ בְּקוֹל מַר:
׳פַּת לֶחֶם יְזוּנֶנּוּ ?׳
עָנְתָה אִמּוֹ: ׳כָּמוֹנִי כָמוֹךָ,
שְׁנֵינוּ בְרָעָב קָצָה נַפְשֵׁנוּ.
מֵאַיִן אוֹשִׁיעֶךָ, מַחְמַד עֵינִי,
וְתוֹחֶלֶת אֵינֶנָּה,
כִּי הַלֶּחֶם אָזַל מִכֵּלֵינוּ.׳

Bitterly, the child asked his mother: 'Is there not even a crumb of bread to keep us alive?' His mother answered: 'What is mine is yours. We are both of us sick with hunger. Where can I find any help for you, delight of my eyes? All hope is gone, *for there is no food left in our sacks.*'

׳רָעֵב לַלֶּחֶם וְצָמֵא לַמַּיִם –
נֶהְפְּכוּ מַעֲדַנֶּיךָ.

'Hungry for bread and thirsty for water, your delights have wasted away.

473

אָמוּתָה הַפַּעַם אַחֲרֵי רְאוֹתִי
אֲשֶׁר קֻבְּצוּ פָארוּר פָּנָיִךְ.
עַתָּה יַחַד נָמוּת
וְלֹא יוֹעִיל הוֹנִי וְרֹב פְּנִינָיִךְ,
כִּי הַמָּוֶת יַפְרִיד בֵּינִי וּבֵינָיִךְ.'

Oh, let me die now that I have seen
your face turn ashen. Now we shall die
together. My wealth is worthless, all
your corals are useless, *for death shall
divide us.*'

'אַךְ אִם אַתָּה לוּ שְׁמָעֵנִי –
וְרוּחִי לָךְ אַבִּיעָה –
תְּנָה אֶת בְּשָׂרֵךְ לִי לְאָכְלָה
וְיַחַד לֹא נִגְוָעָה.
טוֹב שׁוּבֵךְ אֶל תּוֹךְ מֵעַי,
וְלֹא לִכְלָבִים לְאָכְלָה לְשָׂבְעָה.
וְאֵיכָכָה אוּכַל וְרָאִיתִי בָּרָעָה !'

'But hear me, if you will, and I shall
give you my advice: let me eat your
flesh, and we shall not both perish. It
would be better for you to return to my
womb than to let the dogs devour you.
How could I bear to see such an outrage?'

לָחַשׁ יֶלֶד שַׁעֲשׁוּעִים לְאִמּוֹ
בְּאַף וְקֶצֶף וָמֶרִי :
'אִמִּי, אֵיךְ בְּדַם פְּרִי בִטְנֵךְ
תִּשְׁכְּרִי וְתִתְעָרִי ?
עֲשִׂי הַטּוֹב בְּעֵינָיִךְ !
גַּם אֲנִי אֶבְחַר בַּאֲשֶׁר תִּבְחָרִי,
וּתְהִי לִי אִמִּי קִבְרִי.'

Then the darling child, full of fury and
venom, whispered to his mother:
'Mother, how could you get drunk on
the blood of your child, the fruit of
your body, and expose yourself to
shame? But do what you think best.
I will accept whatever you choose. *Let
my mother become my grave!*'

בָּנְתָה לְשַׁחֲטוֹ
וּבְיָדֶיהָ תָּמְכָה שְׁלָחִים.
גַּם הִיא גֶאֶנְחָה וַתָּשָׁב אָחוֹר
מֵרְאוֹת בְּרַע עוֹלֵל טִפּוּחִים.
וַתִּשְׁחָטֵהוּ וַתַּפְשֵׁט עוֹרוֹ
וּבְשָׂרוֹ עָשְׂתָה כִּבְשַׂר זְבָחִים –
לַעֲצָמֶיהָ לִשְׁנֵים עָשָׂר נְתָחִים.

She built [an altar on which] to
slaughter him. She grasped the knife in
her hand. She too groaned and turned
away; she could not look upon the
suffering of the child whom she had
tenderly reared. Then she slaughtered
him and stripped off his skin and
prepared his flesh like the flesh of an
offering. [She cut him up] *limb by limb
into twelve pieces.*[1]

1. As the Levite had cut up his dead concubine (Judges 19.29).

474

רָעֵב בְּטְנָהּ הֶצִיקָהּ
לָשׁוּם בְּשִׁפּוֹד בְּשַׂר לֶשֶׁם שְׁבוֹ.
אַכְזְרִיּוּת לָבְשָׁה וְאֵשׁ הִצִּיתָה,
כִּסְּתָה פָּנָיו בְּחֶלְבּוֹ.
נָאֲצָה לְאָכְלוֹ מְבֻשָּׁל
בַּעֲבוּר הִתְעַכְּבוֹ,
כִּי אִם צְלִי אֵשׁ רֹאשׁוֹ עַל כְּרָעָיו וְעַל קִרְבּוֹ.

Hunger gripped her bowels. She clothed herself in cruelty to put him – flesh of turquoise and agate – on the spit. She kindled a fire; she covered his face with his fat. She chose not to boil him, for that would prolong the matter. And so she ate him *roasted – head, shins and entrails – over the fire.*[1]

מִהֲרָה לְמַלֵּא רָעֵב בְּטְנָהּ
וְלִבָּהּ יֶחֱרַד וְיִתַּר.
חֶדֶר בְּחֶדֶר הִתְחַבָּאָה
לֶאֱכֹל עָנִי בַּמִּסְתָּר,
וּבְשַׂר בְּנָהּ עָרְכָה לְפָנֶיהָ
מְמֻלָּח וּמְבֻתָּר
וַתֹּאכַל וַתִּשְׂבַּע וַתּוֹתַר.

Quickly she ate her fill, her heart beating wildly, leaping up. She hid in an inner room to devour the victim in secret. She arranged her son's flesh, salted and cut up, before her. *She ate until she was satisfied and still had some left over.*

שׁוֹמְרִים לַבֹּקֶר הַסּוֹבְכִים בָּעִיר,
שְׁלֹשֶׁת הַפָּרִיצִים,
דֶּרֶךְ בֵּיתָהּ צָעֲדוּ,
הֵרִיחוּ צְלִי בְּשַׂר פְּטוּרֵי צִצִים.
בָּאוּ בֵיתָהּ וְאָמְרוּ:
'הִנֵּה לְאוֹת טֶרֶף בֵּיתֵנוּ אֲשֶׁר אָנוּ חֲפֵצִים,
הִנֵּה הָאֵשׁ וְהָעֵצִים!'

In the morning, the guards, those three men of violence, going the rounds of the city, passed by her house. They smelled the young roast,[2] came into her house and said: 'This is a sign that you have what we seek: meat for our household. *Here are the fire and the wood!'*

הֶגֶה מִפִּיהֶם יָצָא
וְדָרְשׁוּ מִמֶּנָּה בְּלֵב זָעֵף וָסָר:
'תְּנִי לָנוּ בָשָׂר וְנֹאכְלָה,
הָבִיאִי לִבֵּךְ לַמּוּסָר.'

With rumbling voices, sullen and angry, they demanded: 'Give us meat to eat! Let virtue rule your heart!' She

---

1. Like the Paschal sacrifice (Exodus 12.9).
2. Lit. 'the meat roast of the open flowers'.

עָנְתָה לָהֶם:
'לֶחֶם צַר מֵהָעִיר חָסוֹר חָסֵר
וּמֵאַיִן לִי בָשָׂר?

answered them: 'There is hardly a
morsel of food in all the city. *Where am
I to find meat?*

חַוֶּה אֲחַוֶּה דְעִי לָכֶם
וּמִקְרֵה קְרָאַנִי לָכֶם אַגִּידֶנּוּ:
הַסִּיר וְהַבָּשָׂר אֲשֶׁר הֲרִיחוֹתֶם,
לִפְנֵיכֶם אַצִּיגֶנּוּ.
הַיְדַעְתֶּם? יְדִיד נַפְשִׁי,
אֲשֶׁר עֲטָרוֹת אֶעֶנְדֶנּוּ,
אָכַלְתִּי בְאוֹנִי מִמֶּנּוּ.

'But I will let you in on the secret, I
will tell you what happened to me. The
stewpot and the meat which you
smelled – I shall now set them before
you. Could you have imagined this? It
is my dearly beloved, whom I once
wore like a crown on my head. *I have
eaten him in despair.*

זֶבֶד טוֹב וְבוֹדָה לָכֶם
אִתִּי, שׁוּבוּ, סוּרוּ נָא.
הִנֵּה חֶלְקִי מִכָּל עֲמָלִי
אָכַלְתִּי בְרֹב מְגִנָּה.
אִכְלוּ, רֵעִים,
הִנֵּה לָכֶם חֶלְקְכֶם צְפוּנָה:
שׁוֹק הַיָּמִין לְמָנָה.'

'I have kept a choice gift for you. Come
back, I pray you, stay with me. Here,
this was my reward for all my labour.
I ate it, overcome with grief. Eat,
friends, this is the portion reserved for
you: *the offering of the right hind leg.'*

קָמוּ כֻלָּם בַּחֲרָדָה
וְעֵינֵיהֶם לַשָּׁמַיִם הִגְבִּיהוּ.
פַּחַד קְרָאָם וּרְעָדָה,
הֵמָּה רָאוּ כֵּן תָּמָהוּ.
אָמְרוּ: 'לֹא נִרְאֲתָה כָּזֹאת
וְלֹא שָׁמְעָה אֹזֶן שֶׁמֶץ מֶנְהוּ.'
וַיִּתְמְהוּ הָאֲנָשִׁים אִישׁ אֶל רֵעֵהוּ.

They all stood up in terror, lifting their
eyes to heaven, shuddering with dread.
Staring at her, amazed, they said: 'The
like of this has never been seen. No ear
has ever heard the whisper of it.'
Dumbstruck they looked at one another.

נָא יִכָּמְרוּ רַחֲמֶיךָ
עַל עַם עָבַר בָּם מָוֶת וְרָעָב וְכִלָּיוֹן.

Let Your heart be moved with love for
this people, who have been tried by
death, famine, and destruction. Fulfil

476

קַיֵּם מַאֲמַר חוֹזֶיךָ
דִּבְּרוּ נֶחָמוֹת בְּטוּב הַצִּיּוֹן.
תִּבְנֶה חוֹמוֹת יְרוּשָׁלַיִם
וְתוֹשִׁיב בָּהּ עַם אֶבְיוֹן —
אַתָּה תָקוּם תְּרַחֵם צִיּוֹן.

the pledge of Your seers, who spoke
kind words of consolation. Build anew
the walls of Jerusalem and make this
poor people live in them again. *You
will surely arise and have mercy on Zion.*

תְּרַד שְׁנַת עֵינִי

IF I WERE

תְּרַד שְׁנַת עֵינִי וְאֶסְעַר כָּאֳנִי
תּוֹךְ יָם תְּשׁוּקָתָךְ, וְאֵלֶּה אֶזְכְּרָה:
לוּ אֶהְיֶה יוֹנֵק וְאַתָּה אוֹמְנִי,
אִינַק שְׁדֵי יָפְיָךְ, צְמָאִי אֶשְׁבְּרָה.
לוּ אֶהְיֶה שֶׁלַח, וְאַתָּה וַאֲנִי
נֵשֵׁב בְּצֵל גַּנִּי, לְפִרְיָךְ אֶשְׁמְרָה.
לוּ אֶהְיֶה רֹמַח וְאַתָּה נוֹתְנִי
תּוֹךְ לֵב מְשַׂנְאֶיךָ, בְּדָמָם אֶשְׁכְּרָה.
לוּ אֶהְיֶה אֹהֶל וְאַתָּה שׁוֹכְנִי,
נִתְעַלְּסָה אַהַב, בְּגִיל נִתְאַזְּרָה.
לוּ אֶהְיֶה לָשׁוֹן וְאַתָּה מַעֲנִי,
אַשְׁקִיט יְקֹד חִשְׁקִי בְּשִׁיר וַאֲזַמְּרָה.
לוּ אֶהְיֶה עֶבֶד וְאַתָּה רוֹזְנִי,
אֶשְׁאַף עֲבוֹדָתָךְ, דְּרוֹר לֹא אֶבְחֲרָה.

Sleep deserts my eyes and I toss like a
ship in the sea of my yearning for You
as I imagine these things: If I were an
infant and you were my nurse, I would
suckle your beautiful breasts, and
quench my thirst. If I were a stream
and you and I sat in the shade of my
garden, I would look after your fruit.
If I were a spear and you thrust me
into your enemies' hearts, I would be
drunk with their blood. If I were a tent
and you dwelt in me, we would delight
ourselves with love and clothe ourselves
with joy. If I were a tongue and you
were my words, I would soothe desire's
flame with a song. If I were a slave and
you were my lord, I would long to
serve you, I would never choose
freedom.

יְדִידִים לָאֵל נִבְחֲרוּ

THE MESSIAH

יְדִידִים לָאֵל נִבְחֲרוּ
וּבָהֶם אֵל מִכָּל עַם חָפֵץ —
שׁוֹכְנִים בַּגָּלוּת יְשַׁבְּרוּ

Languishing in exile, God's chosen
companions, in whom He delighted
above all nations, now wait for Him to

לָאֵל יְקַבֵּץ אֲשֶׁר נָפַץ.
רַגְלֵי דוֹד עַל הַר יִנְהָרוּ
וְעַל הַגְּבָעוֹת קָפַץ.
אַל תָּעִירוּ וּתְעוֹרֲרוּ
אֶת הָאַהֲבָה עַד שֶׁתֶּחְפָּץ !

assemble those whom He dispersed;
the feet of the Beloved will come
leaping over the hills and streaming to
the Mountain. But do not stir up or
awaken love until it is ready!

בֶּן דָּוִד בָּא פֶּתַע לָשִׂים
עַל הַר הַקֹּדֶשׁ הַדְרַת דִּגְלוֹ.
מַה לָּכֶם יוֹם יוֹם דּוֹרְשִׁים ?
וּבָזֶה תְּאַחֲרוּ רַגְלוֹ.
שַׂר אֲשֶׁר אַתֶּם מְבַקְשִׁים
פִּתְאֹם יָבוֹא אֶל הֵיכָלוֹ,
הָלוֹךְ וְרוֹכֵב עַל חֲמוֹר,
לֹא בִגְבוּרַת הַסּוּס יֶחְפָּץ.
אַל תָּעִירוּ וּתְעוֹרֲרוּ
אֶת הָאַהֲבָה עַד שֶׁתֶּחְפָּץ !

The son of David will come suddenly
to set his glorious flag upon the holy
Mountain. Why then do you clamour
for him day after day? You are only
delaying his coming. The Prince whom
you seek will, all of a sudden, come to
his Temple; but he will come riding
on an ass; he sets no store by the
strength of a horse. Oh, do not stir up
or awaken love until it is ready!

עֲלוּמֵי שֵׁם

Anonymous

אַהֲבַת בַּת נְדָבָה

GOD'S BELOVED

אַהֲבַת בַּת נְדָבָה
מָתְקָה גַּם עָרְבָה.

The love of the princely daughter [of
Zion] has been most sweet and pleasant
to Me.

שַׁאֲלוּ־נָא, שַׁאֲלוּ:
אוֹהֲבַי מַה פָּעֲלוּ ?
אִם לְשׁוּבִי יְחַלּוּ ?
מָחֳרָת קַל אֶרְכָּבָה
וּלְעַד אֶתְיַצָּבָה.

Oh, ask and ask again: What have My
dear ones [the righteous] been doing?
Have they been longing for My return?
Soon, I shall swiftly fly [to the Temple]
to stand at My post forever.

וַאֲנִי עַד מוֹעֲדֵךְ,
הִנְנִי צֵל בַּעֲדֵךְ
מִשְּׁאוֹן כָּל בּוֹגְדֵךְ.
חַי אֲנִי, לֹא אֶכְזָבָה
לָךְ, וְלֹא שָׁוְא אֶכְתָּבָה.

And until your time comes, I shall shield you from the clamour of those who seek to betray you. By My life, I shall not fail you nor speak in vain.

הֵן אֲהַבְתִּיךְ אַהֲבָה
עַד לְמֵאָז קֵרְבָה,
הַנְּפָשׁוֹת שׁוֹבְבָה,
הַלְּבָבוֹת לִבְּבָה –
אַהֲבָה תּוֹךְ אַהֲבָה!

For I have long loved you with a love that drew us close together, nurtured the soul and gave the heart courage – a love encompassed with love!

לַנְּבִיאִים אָמְרָה:
'הַרְאִיתֶם סְעָרָה
חֹק יְדִידָהּ שָׁמְרָה?'
אָמְרוּ: 'זֹאת אַהֲבָה
נִפְלָאָה מֵאַהֲבָה.'

And I say to the prophets: 'Have you seen how the maiden, though battered by storm, kept her troth to her Friend?' And they answer: 'This love is a wonder surpassing all love.'

שָׁלוֹם, בָּךְ נִשְׁבַּעְתִּי

THE SEDUCTION OF SHALOM

שָׁלוֹם, בָּךְ נִשְׁבַּעְתִּי,
חֵי רֹאשְׁךָ, אָמַרְתִּי,
כִּי אוֹתְךָ תָּאַבְתִּי.
תֵּלֵךְ לְבֵיתִי, שָׁלוֹם.

Shalom, I swear by you; by your life, I say, it is only you I desire. Come to my house, Shalom.

תִּשְׁתֶּה לְכוֹס מֵיֵּינִי,
תֹּאכַל לְפַת שֻׁלְחָנִי,
תָּרַח לְרֵיחַ בּוֹסְמָנִי.
תָּלִין בְּשִׂמְחָה, שָׁלוֹם.

Come drink wine from my cup, eat bread from my dish and breathe in my fragrance. You will sleep in joy, Shalom.

תָּלִין עֲלֵי מִטָּתִי
בְּמָר־דְּרוֹר קִשַּׁרְתִּי.
מִכָּל בְּשָׂמִים נָפַתִּי
מִשְׁכַּב יְדִידִי שָׁלוֹם.

You will sleep upon the bed which I have perfumed with burning sticks of myrrh. I have sprinkled the choicest spices on the bed of my beloved Shalom.

אַל תִּירָאָה מִמֶּנִּי,
כִּי בַּת נְדִיבִים אָנִי.
אָבִי אָצִיל קַדְמוֹנִי.
תָּבִין וְתֵדַע, שָׁלוֹם.

Do not be afraid of me, for I am of noble lineage. My father was a prince in days gone by. Know this and you will understand, Shalom.

חַבֵּק, יְדִידִי, עַלְמָה
תָּאִיר כְּאוֹר הַחַמָּה,
וּגְשָׁה וּמוּשׁ לְפִימָה.
אֶשְׁתַּעְשְׁעָה בָּךְ, שָׁלוֹם.

O my friend, embrace this girl who shines with a brightness like the sun's. Come close and feel her lips. Let me revel in you, Shalom.

הִשְׁתַּעְשְׁעָה תּוֹךְ חֵיקִי
וּדְבַק וְשַׁלֵּם חֻקִּי
וּטְעַם דְּבַשׁ מֵרִיקִי
צָפוּן בְּפִי לָךְ, שָׁלוֹם.

Take pleasure in my bosom, cling to me and give me my due. Taste the flowing honey which awaits you in my mouth, Shalom.

קוּמָה, יְדִיד, הַשְׁקֵנִי,
מִיֵּין עֲסִיס רִמּוֹנִי,
חַיֶּיךָ, אָהוּב, הַחֲיֵנִי.
נַשֵּׁק שְׂפָתַי, שָׁלוֹם.

Come, my friend, give me to drink. Let me have my fill of fresh wine. By your life, my love, revive me. Kiss my lips, Shalom.

אִישִׁי בְּדֶרֶךְ, נֶחְבָּא,
לָקַח בְּיָדוֹ זָהָבוֹ.
אֵינוּ בְּזֶה יוֹם יָבוֹא.
יַאֲמֵן לְבָבְךָ, שָׁלוֹם.

My husband is away, gone on a journey. He has taken his gold with him. He will not be back by tomorrow. You may rest assured, Shalom.

עֵת אֶרְאֵךְ בָּאָרֶץ,
אֶקֹּד וְאֶשְׁחֶה אָרֶץ
אֵין לִי בְּזֶה דּוֹד חֵפֶץ
כִּי אִם יְדִידִי, שָׁלוֹם.

When I lay eyes upon you, I bow low
and prostrate myself. Oh, I have no
love in this world but my beloved
Shalom!

לִקְרַאת שַׁבָּת   SABBATH SONG

לִקְרַאת שַׁבָּת אֵצֵא בְּחֶמְבָּה
מִיוֹם שִׁשִּׁי, זָקֵן וְשֵׂיבָה.
שְׂשׂוֹנִי קָרֵב, יְגוֹנִי נֶחְבָּא,
וְאַעַן וְאֹמַר: 'בָּרוּךְ הַבָּא !'

Old and grey as I am, I hurry forth on
Friday, filled with love, to meet the
Sabbath. My joy approaches, my grief
disappears and I sing out: 'Welcome!'

וּמֵרֹב חִבָּה לַיּוֹם הַהוּא
נַפְשִׁי אֲטַהֵר, יָהּ אֲבָרְכֵהוּ.
אָפֵזָּה, אֲכַרְכֵּר: זֶהוּ, זֶהוּ !
דִּגְמָא מֵעֵין עוֹלָם הַבָּא.

For love of this day, I purify my soul, I
bless the Lord. I leap and dance, 'Yes,
this is it! A foretaste of the world to
come!'

דִּבְרֵי נָבִיא, אֱלֹהַי, תָּבִיא,
תְּמַהֵר בְּמֶלֶךְ, כֹּהֵן וְנָבִיא.
וְנַעֲלֶה לְצִיּוֹן כְּאַרְיֵה וְלָבִיא,
וְנִבְנֶה לְמִקְדָּשׁ בְּהַדְרָא רַבָּא.

Make the words of the seers come true,
my God. Hasten the advent of King,
Priest, and Prophet. Then, rearing up
like lions, we shall go up to Zion and
build the Temple, majestic in
splendour.

כּוֹכָב אֲשֶׁר הִשְׁקִיף   THE STAR[1]

כּוֹכָב אֲשֶׁר הִשְׁקִיף בְּאוֹרוֹ עַל נְוַת
חוֹשֵׁק, לְפִרוּדוֹ בְּמַר צוֹרֵחַ.
כַּמָּה תְקָפוּהוּ יְגוֹנִים ! עַד אֲשֶׁר

The star looked down and shone into
the lover's room, as he was bitterly
lamenting his friend's departure. How
grief-stricken he had been, until this

---

1. The comforting star is sent by the friend who has gone on a voyage.

פָּגַע בְּפָנָיו וַיְהִי שָׂמֵחַ.
יָדַע חֳלִי לִבּוֹ וְשָׁלַח מְצָרִי
חַסְדּוֹ וּמָרַח עַל שְׁחִין צוֹמֵחַ.
יִשְׁלַח אֱלֹהִים לוֹ בְּרָכָה כָּל יְמֵי
חַיָּיו וְאוֹרוֹ יִהְיֶה זוֹרֵחַ.
וִינַהֲלֵהוּ אֶל מְחוֹז חֶפְצוֹ בְּרֹב
שָׁלוֹם וְכַתָּמָר יְהִי פוֹרֵחַ.
וִיסוֹבְבוּהוּ מַלְאֲכֵי חֶסֶד, וְחֵן
יֵט לוֹ אֱלֹהָיו עַד בְּלִי יָרֵחַ.

star-light touched his face and brought
him joy. Knowing that he was sick at
heart, the star sent him this balm of
kindness to soothe the festering sore.
May God send the friend blessings all
the days of his life, and may his light
shine forever. May He guide him, in
abundant peace, to his desired haven,
and may he flourish like a palm-tree.
May angels of grace enfold him and
may he win the favour of his God until
the moon is no more.

יַחְסִין עַלִי אלמחבוב אדי הו סַיִּדְנָא,
יחמיה מן אלאשרראר עדד מא ברק וַלַאח.

May He prosper my beloved master.[1]
May He protect him from all evil, just
as He glittered and shone [upon me].

רָאֲתָ תְּמוּנָה בַּחֲלוֹם   THE RING

רָאֲתָ תְּמוּנָה בַּחֲלוֹם וַתֹּאמְרָה:
'מִי נְשָׁקַנִי, וַאֲנִי נִרְדֶּמֶת?'
עֵת יָדְעָה כִּי הִיא תְּמוּנָתִי, אֲזַי
כִּחֲשָׁה וְנָמָה: 'הֵן אֲנִי חוֹלֶמֶת!'
וָאֹמְרָה: 'אִם הוּא חֲלוֹם – מִי זֶה אֲשֶׁר
נָתַן בְּאֶצְבַּע הַשְּׂמֹאל חוֹתֶמֶת?'
וַתֶּחֱרַשׁ, כִּי יָדְעָה כִּי נָאֲמִי
צֶדֶק, וְכִי הָיוּ דְבָרַי בֶּאֱמֶת.
אָז לָקְחָה מַסְוֶה וּפָנִים כִּסָּתָה,
וָאֵדְעָה כִּי הִיא לְזֹאת נִכְלֶמֶת.
תַּעֲלִים לְחָיֶיהָ – יָאִירוּן בַּעֲדִי
צַפָּה כְּמוֹ חַמָּה בְּעָב נִגְלֶמֶת. [...]

She saw a figure in her dream and said:
'Who kissed me while I was asleep?'
But when she understood that it had
been my form, she denied me, saying:
'Why, I was only dreaming!' To which
I said: 'If it was only a dream, then
who was it that put the ring on your
left finger?' She said nothing, for she
knew that I was right and that my
words were true. Whereupon she took
a veil and covered her face. I understood that she was overcome with
shame. But though she hid her cheeks,
they shone through her veil like the sun
enveloped in a cloud.

1. Lit. 'our master'; the last two lines are in Arabic.

אַתָּה אָדוֹן וַאֲנִי עֶבֶד

YOU AND I

אַתָּה אָדוֹן וַאֲנִי עֶבֶד.
וּמִי יְרַחֵם עַל עֶבֶד,
הֲלֹא אָדוֹן.
אַתָּה בּוֹרֵא וַאֲנִי בּוּלֶה.
וּמִי יְרַחֵם עַל בּוּלֶה,
הֲלֹא בּוֹרֵא.
אַתָּה דַיָּן וַאֲנִי נִדָּן.
וּמִי יְרַחֵם עַל נִדָּן,
הֲלֹא דַיָּן.
אַתָּה וָעֵד וַאֲנִי לְבוּד.
וּמִי יְרַחֵם עַל לְבוּד,
הֲלֹא וָעֵד.
אַתָּה חַי וַאֲנִי מֵת.
וּמִי יְרַחֵם עַל מֵת,
הֲלֹא חַי.
אַתָּה יוֹצֵר וַאֲנִי חֹמֶר.
וּמִי יְרַחֵם עַל חֹמֶר,
הֲלֹא יוֹצֵר.
אַתָּה לַהַב וַאֲנִי קַשׁ.
וּמִי יְרַחֵם עַל קַשׁ,
הֲלֹא לַהַב.
אַתָּה שׁוֹמֵעַ וַאֲנִי קוֹרֵא.
וּמִי יְרַחֵם עַל קוֹרֵא,
הֲלֹא שׁוֹמֵעַ.
אַתָּה תְּחִלָּה וַאֲנִי סוֹף.
וּמִי יְרַחֵם עַל סוֹף,
הֲלֹא תְּחִלָּה.

You are the Lord and I am the servant.
Who should have mercy on the servant
if not the Lord? You create and I
decay. Who should have mercy on the
decayed if not the Creator? You are the
Judge and I am the accused. Who
should have mercy on the accused if
not the Judge? You are All and I am a
fragment. Who should have mercy on
the fragment if not the All? You are
the Living One and I am the dead.
Who should have mercy on the dead if
not the Living One? You are the Potter
and I am clay. Who should have mercy
on clay if not the Potter? You are the
Fire and I am stubble. Who should
have mercy on stubble if not the Fire?
You are the Listener and I am the
pleader. Who should have mercy on the
pleader if not the Listener? You are
the Beginning and I am the end. Who
should have mercy on the end if not the
Beginning?

סְעַדְיָה בֶּן־עַמְרָם   *Sa'adiah ben Amram*

סַפְּרִי, תַּמָּה תְּמִימָה

THE POET, THE DOVE AND THE BELOVED

'סַפְּרִי, תַּמָּה תְּמִימָה,
סַפְּרִי, נָגִיל בְּתֵימָא,
בַּת מְלָכִים הַחֲכָמָה,
אָן מְקוֹמֵךְ, סַפְּרִי לִי.'

[The Poet:] 'Tell me, pure and perfect
one, tell me so that we may rejoice here
in Taima[1] – O wise princess, tell me,
where do you make your home?'

עָנְתָה יוֹנָה: 'סְעַדְיָה,
לִי בְּפַלְטֵרִין עֲלָיָה,
וַאֲנִי תוֹךְ לֵב – אֲנִיָּה,
בְּיָפְי עוֹטָה מְעִילִי.

The dove answered: 'Sa'adiah, there is
a high chamber reserved for me in the
Palace.[2] But though I could robe myself
in beauty, my heart is full of lamentation.

דְלְנִי יָא צָאח הַיַּא,
דְלְנִי פָאנָא גָבִיַּא,
וַאפְהַאם אָפְהַאם לָא תְעַיַּא,
אֵין טְרִיק אטלב כְּלִילִי.'

'Oh, show me the way, my friend,
guide me, for I am at a loss. Pray,
understand, and do not lose patience:
where is the road that will lead me to
my Beloved?'

'יָא מַסְמָא לֵב אלאלבַאב
וַאפְתַחִי יָא צָפָה אלבַאב,
אָן פִי אלבסתַאן אטַיַאב
דָא כְּרוּם דָא שַׂהֵד חַאלִי.

[The Beloved:] 'O heart of hearts, open
the gate to Me. There are beds of
balsam in My garden and vines sweet
with honey.

הָרְשׁוּת בֶּאֱמֶת נְתוּנָה,
לָךְ שְׁלוֹמוֹת הַחֲתֻנָּה,
אַל יְסִיתֵךְ צָר מְמֶנָּה,
בַּת, וְאַל יַסִּיג גְּבוּלִי.

'Truly, I now give you leave [to be
redeemed], to enjoy the peace of
wedlock. Do not let the evil spirit
incite you, My daughter, let him not
encroach on My domain.

---

1. A province in North Arabia.   2. The Land of Israel.

בַּחֲרִי מִבְחַר מְקוֹמוֹת,
הֵיכְלֵי שֵׁן הַפְּנִימוֹת,
וַעֲלִי מִתּוֹךְ תְּהוֹמוֹת,
וּשְׁמְעִי, תַּמָּה, לְקוֹלִי.

'You may choose the choicest land, and the inner chamber of the Palace panelled with ivory. Oh, arise from the depths, My pure one, and heed My words.

נַעֲלֶה הַר הָעֲבָרִים,
נִשְׁכְּבָה יַחַד חֲבֵרִים,
מִבְּלִי מַגַּע בְּשָׂרִים,
שָׁם, וְיִיטַב לָךְ וְגַם לִי.

'Let us go up to Mount Abarim and lie there together in friendship, without flesh touching flesh. You will find contentment there, and so will I.

עֵץ פְּרִי הָדָר בְּגַנִּי,
וַעֲסִיסִי שָׁם וְיֵינִי.
קַבְּלִי מִתּוֹךְ יְמִינִי
כּוֹס, אֲשֶׁר נִמְזַג בְּחַר לִי.

'There will be fruit of goodly trees in My garden, fresh juice and wine. Accept this cup from My right hand – I have filled it with My finest wine.[1]

מִבְּאֵר שֶׁבַע צְאִי לָךְ,
וּזְנַחִי יַנְשׁוּף וְשָׁלָךְ,
וַחֲכְמִי, בִּינִי בְּשֶׁלָּךְ,
מְיַמִּין, אַל מַשְׂמְאִילִי.

'Now leave the pit of exile,[2] spurn the screech owl and the fisher owl.[3] Learn wisdom from your own Law, take the right path, shun the left.

רַחֲצִי טִנּוּף, הָסִירִי,
עֵת עֲלוֹת שַׁעַר חֲצֵרִי.
קַדְּשִׁי אֶת הָעֲשִׂירִי,
גַּם תְּנִי חַלָּה וְאָכְלִי.

'And when you enter the gate of My courts, wash yourself, purge yourself of impurity. Set aside a tithe as holy to the Lord,[4] and give the priest his gift of dough before you eat the bread.[5]

---

1. The allegorical meaning is: the people of Israel ('fruit of goodly trees') will be in My world ('garden') and the ceremony of libation ('juice and wine') will be performed in the Temple.

2. Lit. *Be'er-Sheva*, 'the well (pit) of seven (countries)' into which the world was divided.

3. 'Unclean' birds, representing foreign cultures.

4. Exodus 27.30 ff.

5. Numbers 15.20.

מַעֲדַנִּים הַמְּתוּקִים
נֶחְלְקוּ שָׁלוֹשׁ חֲלָקִים,
זֶה בָּזֶה הֵמָּה אֲדוּקִים –
סוֹד מְכֻסֶּה הוּא וּפֶלִי.'

'The fragrant sacrifices must be shared by three,[1] and these three parts are interlocked. This is a mystery, deep and wondrous.'

סְעַדְיָה

Sa'adiah

לַנֵּר וְלִבְשָׂמִים

SONG FOR HAVDALAH[2]

לַנֵּר וְלִבְשָׂמִים נַפְשִׁי מְיַחֲלָה.
אִם תִּתְּנוּ לִי כּוֹס יַיִן לְהַבְדָּלָה !
סֹלּוּ דְרָכִים לִי, פַּנּוּ לְנָבוֹכָה,
פִּתְחוּ שְׁעָרִים לִי כָּל מַלְאֲכֵי מַעְלָה.
עֵינַי אֲנִי אֶשָּׂא אֶל אֵל בְּלֶב כּוֹסֵף,
מַמְצִיא צְרָכַי לִי בַּיּוֹם וּבַלַּיְלָה.
דֵּי מַחְסוֹר תֵּן לִי מֵאוֹצְרוֹת טוּבֶךָ,
כִּי לַחֲסָדֶיךָ אֵין קֵץ וְאֵין תִּכְלָה.
יִתְחַדְּשָׁה גִילִי, טַרְפִּי וְטוֹבָתִי,
תָּסִיר יְגוֹנוֹתַי, מַכְאוֹב וּמַאְפֵּלָה.
הִנֵּה יְמֵי מַעֲשֶׂה מִתְחַדְּשִׁים תָּמִיד –
יִתְחַדְּשׁוּ בָהֶם שָׁלוֹם וְטוֹב סֶלָה.

My soul longs for the candle and the fragrant spices; won't you pour me a cup of wine for *havdalah*? You angels on high, build a way for me, clear the track for the bewildered daughter [of Zion], open the gates to let me in! I shall lift up my eyes with heartfelt yearning to the Lord who provides for me day and night. Oh, give me as much as I need from the treasure-house of Your goodness, for there is no end or limit to Your unfailing love. Give new life to my joy, renew my bread and my bliss, remove all sorrow, pain, and gloom. Now the days of work return again. May peace and goodness be renewed in them, *selah*.

---

1. God, priest, and Israelite.
2. The ceremony, employing a candle, spices, and wine, which marks the end of the Sabbath.

שָׁלֵם שַׁבְּזִי *Shalem Shabazi*

אַהֲבַת הֲדַסָּה A WEDDING SONG

אַהֲבַת הֲדַסָּה עַל לְבָבִי נִקְשָׁרָה,
וַאֲנִי בְּתוֹךְ גּוֹלָה פְּעָמַי צֹלְלִים.
לוּ יֵשׁ רְשׁוּת לִי אֶעֱלֶה אֶתְחַבְּרָה
תּוֹךְ שַׁעֲרֵי צִיּוֹן אֲשֶׁר הֵם נֶהֱלָלִים.
שַׁחֲרִית וְעַרְבִית בַּת נְדִיבִים אֶזְכְּרָה,
לִבִּי וְרַעְיוֹנִי בְּחֵשֶׁק נִבְהָלִים.
בִּנְעִים זְמִירוֹת מִמְּדַד אֶתְעוֹרְרָה,
וַאֲנִי וְרַעְיָתִי בְּרִנָּה צֹהֲלִים.

My heart is bound to Hadassah[1] in
love, but my feet are sinking in the
depths of exile. When will He give me
leave to go up and make my home
within the extolled gates of Zion?
Morning and evening I call to mind
the Princess.[2] My heart and my mind
reel with desire. With sweet song I
shall shake off the pain of separation,
and then my dearest and I will loudly
rejoice.

בִּינוּ, עֲדַת קֹדֶשׁ, בְּשִׁירָה חֻבְּרָה:
חָתָן וְהַכַּלָּה בְּחֻפָּה נִכְלָלִים,
זֶה יוֹם שְׂמָחוֹת לַאֲיֻמָּה יָקָרָה,
כִּי הִיא וְדוֹדָהּ חֵן וְחֶסֶד גּוֹמְלִים.
יַחְדָּו אֱלֵי שֻׁלְחָן וְכוֹס, דּוֹדִי, קְרָא,
וַמֵּן שְׁרִידֵינוּ וְכָל הַנִּסְגָּלִים.
מִכּוֹס יְשׁוּעוֹת אֶשְׂמְחָה וַאֲזַמְּרָה,
אוֹצִיא לְכָל סוֹדִי וְאָשִׁיב שׁוֹאֲלִים.

Now, my holy flock, fathom this song
I have composed. The bridegroom and
the bride have been crowned in wedlock, and this is a day of joy for the
majestic one, the precious one,[3] for she
and her Beloved now endow each other
with grace and love. O my Beloved,
invite us all together to Your table and
Your cup, summon the remnants of
Your treasured people. And I shall
sing happily over this cup of salvation.
I shall disclose my mystic secret to
those who question me.

שֵׁם טוֹב לְמַשְׂכִּילִים בְּדַעַת יָשָׁרָה,
כִּי הֵם עֲלֵי יִצְרָם בְּוַדַּאי מוֹשְׁלִים.
תַּאֲוַת לְבָבָם לַעֲשׂוֹת טוֹב גָּבְרָה,
יַעֲלוּ לְגַן עֵדֶן וְחַיִּים נוֹחֲלִים.
אַהֲבַת יְחִידָתִי לְטוּב אֵל נֶהֱרָה,
בָּרוּךְ שֶׁהוּא נוֹתֵן שָׂכָר כָּל פּוֹעֲלִים.

The wise and pure of heart are assured
of a good name, for they firmly rule
their passions. Their desire to do good
prevails. They will go up to the Garden
of Eden and inherit everlasting life. All
the love in my soul surges to the goodness of God. Blessed is He who rewards

---

1. The Land of Israel (Esther 2.7).
2. The Shekinah.
3. Or, 'the terrible one', an epithet for Daughter-Zion (Song of Songs 6.10).

שָׁלוֹם כְּנָהָר לַעֲדָתִי יִנְהֲרָה,
זָקֵן וְגַם בָּחוּר וְכָל הָעוֹלְלִים.

each and every workman! May peace
flow over my flock like a river, over old
and young, over all the little children.

מִי נְשָׁקַנִי

THE SEAL

'מִי נְשָׁקַנִי וַאֲנִי נֶעְלָמֶת,
וַיֹּאמְרָה לִי: "אַל תְּהִי נִדְהָמֶת!"
שַׁפְרִיר כְּבוֹד דּוֹדִי בְּהֵיכַל אַהֲבָה,
מִתּוֹךְ נְוֵה חַדְרִי, בְּלֵיל חוֹלָמֶת.
לַנְתִּי בְּחֵיקוֹ מִבְּעוֹד יוֹם נִכְסָפָה,
אֶרְחַץ בְּנִקְיוֹן וּמִתְבַּשָּׂמֶת.'

[The Daughter of Zion:] 'Who kissed
me until I fell into a faint, then said to
me: "Do not be overwhelmed!" That
night I dreamt that I was [back] in the
Temple of Love, [under] the canopy of
my Beloved's Glory, in my own dwelling. Before the time was due, I longed
to sleep in His bosom, to cleanse myself
[with prayer] and perfume myself [with
incense].'

מְדֵי צְלוֹתָהּ עַל יְדֵי צִיר נֶאֱמָן,
דְּגָלִי בְּמַסָּעוֹת בְּאוֹת רוֹשָׁמֶת.
יֵרַד יְדִידִי אֶל נְוֵה גַּנַּת-אֱגוֹז,
זָכַר בְּרִית אָבוֹת שֶׁהִיא קוֹדָמֶת.
וְעַד שְׁבָטַי בַּעֲלֵי חֶסֶד וָחֵן,
וּבְשַׁעֲרֵי צִיּוֹן תְּהֵא מַשְׁכֶּמֶת.

[The Poet:] 'Oh, then [Moses,] the
faithful messenger will lead her [out of
exile], and the emblems [of the tribes]
will be inscribed upon my banners.[1]
My Beloved will come down into the
Garden of Nut Trees,[2] He will
remember His ancient covenant with
the Patriarchs. He will assemble all my
kind and righteous tribes, and Israel
will rise to greet the dawn in Zion's
gates.

סוּרוּ בְּנֵי נֵכָר וְגַם הִתְרַחֲקוּ,
וּלְכוּ לְפִי חֶרֶב נָקָם נוֹקָמֶת.
פִּתְאֹם הֲלֹא יָבוֹא יְדִיד הֵיכָלוֹ,
תִּכּוֹן בְּטוּב כִּסְאוֹ, וּמִתְרוֹמָמֶת.
מַלְאָךְ וְגַלְגַּל שִׁיר וְהַלֵּל פּוֹצְחִים,
עִם בַּת יְפֵהפִיָּה שֶׁבַח נוֹאָמֶת.
שְׂאוּ מְלָכִים רוֹזְנִים מִצַּד שְׂמֹאל,
לָהֶם יְמִין הָאֵל תְּהֵא הוֹלָמֶת.

'Away, you foreigners, leave [my land],
flee before the sword that wreaks
vengeance. For the Beloved will come
suddenly to His Temple; His throne
will rest firmly upon goodness, and [the
Daughter of Zion] will be exalted. The
angels and the chariot wheels will break
into songs of praise as the lovely
Daughter hymns His glories. Kings and
rulers will be devastated by Divine
judgement[3] and smitten by the right
hand of the Lord.

1. As they were when Israel marched through the desert (e.g. Numbers 2.2).
2. An epithet for the Land of Israel.
3. Or, 'the potencies of evil'; lit. 'the left side'.

תִּשָּׂאִי, יְחִידָתִי, שְׁלוֹמוֹת וְסַגֵּלִי
חַיִּים וְרָבִיתֶם, בְּרָן מַנְעֵמֶת.
אֶשַּׁק פְּנֵי חֶבְרַת סְגֻלָּה בַּחֲלוֹם,
בִּכְתָב רְשֹׁם שִׁירִי כְּמוֹ חוֹתֶמֶת.

'May peace be yours, my soul, and a long life of piety, singing psalms of joy. Now, in my dream, I kiss the faces of my elect companions with the letters of my song. These shall be for us like a seal [of friendship].'

שָׁמַעְתִּי מִפַּאֲתֵי תֵימָן　　SONG FOR CIRCUMCISION

שָׁמַעְתִּי מִפַּאֲתֵי תֵימָן
קוֹל יָדִיד קַיַם בְּרִית נֶאֱמָן.

From the far reaches of Yemen I have heard of a friend who fulfilled the steadfast covenant.

לִשְׁכֵנָיו שָׂמַח בְּרֹב גִּילָה,
הִזְמִינָם לִרְאוֹת בְּרִית מִילָה.
רְפָא, צוּרִי, בֵּן זֶה וְהַצִּילָה,
אַתָּה אֵל מֶלֶךְ וְגַם רַחֲמָן.

He gave his neighbours great cause for rejoicing, inviting them to witness the circumcision. My Rock, cure this child and save him; for You are almighty and merciful too.

מִילָתוֹ רֵאשִׁית לְכָל מִצְוָה.
יִתְרַפֵּא, יִזְכֶּה לְרֹב שַׁלְוָה
בְּסוֹד הֶגְיוֹן תּוֹרָה וְגַם חֶדְוָה,
וּמְזוֹנוֹ יָפֶה וְגַם מְשֻׁמָּן.

This circumcision is his first religious duty. May he recover, and enjoy great peace of mind and pleasure in the study of the Torah's mysteries. May his food be choice and succulent.

שָׁלוֹם לָךְ, נִמּוֹל, כְּמוֹ נָהָר,
וְאָבִיךְ יְזֻכֶּה, אֲשֶׁר נִזְהַר
בַּמִּילָה מִיּוֹם עֲלוֹת בָּהָר,
יוֹם קִבֵּל מִצְווֹת וְקִיּוּמָן.

O circumcised child, may peace flow over you like a river, and your father will surely be blessed. For he was charged to perform this act the day he vowed to maintain the holy precepts,[1] when Moses ascended Mount Sinai.

1. According to legend, the souls of those who were not yet born were present at the revelation on Mount Sinai.

489

בְּרִית מִילָה תַּחֲלִישׁ לְיֵצֶר רַע,
וּקְלִפָּה שֵׁנִית אֲשֶׁר יִפָּרַע,
הִיא זֻהֲמַת נָחָשׁ אֲשֶׁר נִגְרַע.
וְהַמִּילָה לַדָּת תְּהֵא סִימָן. [...]

Circumcision makes the evil impulse
wane, and the removal of the foreskin
excises the Serpent's foulness.[1] Circumcision is the sign of our faith.

שֶׁפַע טוֹב יוֹסִיף לְזֶה שְׂמָאל,
וּבְחַיִּים טוֹבִים יְהֵא נִגְמָל.
נָתַן לוֹ מִיּוֹצְרוֹ מַחֲמָל,
וּבְחָרוֹ מִיּוֹם אֲשֶׁר זֻמָּן. [...]

May He shower this child with goodness and reward him with a good life.
His Creator gives him His love; from
the day he is singled out [for circumcision.] He counts him among the
chosen.

יוֹסֵף יְדִידְיָה קַרְמִי   *Joseph Jedidiah Carmi*

אֶהְיֶה אֲשֶׁר אֶהְיֶה   THE MOON-POET

אֶהְיֶה אֲשֶׁר אֶהְיֶה,
הַבֵּט מִשָּׁמַיִם וּרְאֵה:
יָרֵחַ אֲשֶׁר כּוֹנַנְתָּ
וְעַל מְקוֹמוֹ הִתְבּוֹנַנְתָּ –
אֵיךְ חָשַׁךְ מִשְׁחוֹר תָּאֳרוֹ
וַיְהִי לְאֵבֶל כִּנּוֹרוֹ. [...]

Ehyeh-Asher-Ehyeh,[2] look down from
heaven and behold: the moon which
You set in place and then looked kindly
upon – how its face has turned blacker
than soot, and its harp has been tuned
to a dirge.

אֲנִי, אֲנִי הוּא הַיָּרֵחַ
אֲשֶׁר מֵאָז אַתָּה, שִׁמְשִׁי, אֲהַבְתַּנִי
וּבְאוֹר פָּנֶיךָ הֶאֱרַתַּנִי,
וְעַתָּה חֹשֶׁךְ יְשׁוּפֵנִי

It is I who am this moon! Long ago, O
my Sun, You loved me and let Your
face shine upon me. But now darkness

---

1. With which he infected Eve when he mated with her (*T.B. Yebamoth* 103b).
2. A name of God: 'I am that I am', or 'I will Be What I Will Be' (Exodus 3.14).

וְאוֹר לַיְלָה בַּעֲדֵנִי.
וַתֶּרֶב מַשְׂאַת אָפְלָתִי
מֵהַמָּאוֹר הַקָּטֹן אֲשֶׁר לְעֻמָּתִי:
כִּי מִדֵּי חֹדֶשׁ בְּחָדְשׁוֹ
הוֹד וְהָדָר לְבוּשׁוֹ;
אַךְ לִי נָפְלוּ פָנַי,
וְנֹחַם יִסָּתֵר מֵעֵינַי
בְּדִינִים מִדִּינִים שׁוֹנִים
זֶה לִי אֶלֶף וַחֲמֵשׁ מֵאוֹת וְעוֹד שָׁנִים.
וּמָה אֹמַר עוֹד, צוּרִי,
אִם לִי יָרֵחַ נֶהְפַּךְ לָחֳרִי,
סַהַר לְסָרָה, וּלְבָנָה לִנְבֵלָה?
וּלְךָ מִשְׁפַּט הַגְּאֻלָּה.

has stolen over me and night has closed around me. My share of the dark is larger than that of the lesser light, facing me. For month by month, it is newly arrayed in majesty and splendour. But I am always overcast, and compassion is hid from my eyes, scourged by endless punishments, for over one thousand five hundred years! What more can I say, my Rock, since my moon has turned into a moan, my globe into a glob, my crescent to putrescence. But Yours is the right of redemption!

יְהוּדָה אַרְיֵה מוֹדֵנָה

Judah Aryeh Modena

סְלִיחָה לְיוֹם כִּפּוּר קָטָן

SONG FOR THE MINOR DAY OF ATONEMENT

יוֹם זֶה יְהִי מִשְׁקַל כָּל חַטֹּאתַי
בָּטֵל בְּמִעוּטוֹ כִּדְמוּת יָרֵחַ.
הַיּוֹם — לְבַד מִסְפַּר זַכְיוֹתַי
יִרְבֶּה וְיָצִיץ צִיץ וִיהִי פוֹרֵחַ.

On this day, may the weight of all my sins dwindle to nothing like the crescent moon. Today, may the sum of my merits alone grow and bud and blossom.

וַדַּאי, זָדוֹן לִבִּי אֶצְלִי גָּלוּי,
חוּטֵי עֲווֹנוֹתַי עִם דַּק רִשְׁעִי.
דִּינִי, אֲנִי אֵדַע, בְּאֵשׁ קָלוּי
כִּי רַע וּבִישׁ אַרְגַּמְתִּי אֶל פִּשְׁעִי.
הוֹלֵךְ בְּיוֹם וָיוֹם אַחַר בְּצָעִי,
מִבֵּית מְקוֹם סֵפֶר תִּינוֹק בּוֹרֵחַ.

Oh, I am aware of my insolent heart, my threads of wrong and my web of wickedness. My fate, I know, is to burn by fire, for I have woven evil and wrong-doing into my crime. Day after day, I set my heart on dishonest gain and, like a truant child, I fled from the house of learning.

אָכֵן, בְּחַבְלֵי שָׁוְא עֲוֹן עוֹן מוֹשֵׁךְ
אָחוֹר, לְךָ, אֵלִי, בָּאתִי נִצָּב.
רְפָאוֹת לְאֶרֶס מַר נָחָשׁ נוֹשֵׁךְ —
שׁוֹאֵל וּמִתְחַנֵּן, נִכְאָב, נֶעֱצָב.
יוֹשֵׁב בְּעִנּוּיֵי אֶבֶן מַחְצָב,
יָד, פֶּה וְעַיִן – אֵין לִי טַעַם, רֵיחַ.

הֵן רֹאשׁ חֲדָשִׁים לָעָם נָתַתָּ
לִזְמָן לְכַפֵּר עַל כָּל תּוֹלְדוֹתָם.
מֵאֵת אֲהוּבִים שׁוֹטֵן הַשְׁבַּתָּ,
עַל כֵּן אֲקַדֶּמְךָ בִּתְחִנָּתָם.
מִיּוֹם לְפָנָיו בָּא כִּי אָז אִיתָם —
אָשׁוּב לְאִישׁ תּוֹשָׁב, לֹא עוֹד אוֹרֵחַ.

וּבְרֹב חֲסָדֶיךָ אַתָּה, מַלְכִּי,
תָּקוּם־תְּרַחֵם צִיּוֹן קָדְשֵׁנוּ.
דִּירַת מְנוּחָתָךְ שִׂים כָּבוֹד, כִּי
בָּהּ נַעֲלֶה עוֹלוֹת רֹאשׁ חָדְשֵׁנוּ.
נָא, אֵל, שְׁלַח נוֹשֵׂא הוֹד הֲדַר רֹאשֵׁנוּ,
כִּי שָׁם לְבָבֵנוּ שׁוֹאֵף זוֹרֵחַ.

Though iniquity drags me down with cords of falsehood, I have come, my God, to stand before You. Out of my pain and sorrow, I beg a remedy for the bitter venom of the stinging snake.[1] Pent up, tortured, in a cell of hewn rock,[1] hand, mouth, and eye are all deprived of feeling.[2]

You gave the new moon to Your people as a time of atonement through all their generations. [On this day] You rid Your loved ones of the Accuser, and therefore I approach You with their supplications. If I come blameless on the eve of the new moon, I shall dwell in my home again and no longer be a vagrant.

And through Your great love, my King, You will arise and have mercy on our holy Zion. You will restore Your glory to Your dwelling, and there we shall present the burnt-offerings of the new month. O God, pray send [the Messiah,] bearer of our royal honour, for it is there, in Zion, that our hearts yearn to shine.

1. Epithets for the Evil Inclination.   2. Lit. 'I have no taste, smell'.

492

יַעֲקֹב פְּרַאנְשֵׂיס   *Jacob Frances*

קוּם, אַשְׁמְדַאי   TO THE KING OF THE
DEMONS

קוּם, אַשְׁמְדַאי! קוּם לָךְ, דְּחֹף רָצִים
אֶל תָּפְתְּךָ מַהֵר, וּבִמְדִינוֹת
מַלְכוּתְךָ פִּתְגָם שְׁלַח לִקְנוֹת
עִטְרָן וְנֶפְטְ, גָּפְרִית וְרֹב עֵצִים.

Up, Asmodeus! Rise up, dispatch
urgent couriers to your hell, and issue
an edict to all the provinces of your
kingdom, commanding them to buy
tar, kerosene, brimstone, and logs in
plenty.

צַוֵּה עֲלֵיהֶם נוֹגְשִׂים אָצִים
לֶאֱסֹף צְבָא שֵׁדִים וְלִגְיוֹנוֹת,
כִּי יוֹם עֲבָרוֹת זֶה וְעֵת עַנּוֹת
אִישׁ רַע וְשׂוֹנֵא טוֹב, אֲבִי לֵצִים.

Set taskmasters over them who will
press them to muster legions of demons,
for this is the day of wrath, the time to
rack an evil man, an enemy of good, an
arch-villain.

הַצֵּת בְּעֵרָה בּוֹ, וְאַל יֵרַךְ
לְבָּךְ בְּעֵת תִּזְכֹּר אֲשֶׁר אֶתְמוֹל
מִלֵּא נְשָׁמוֹת יַרְכְּתֵי בוֹרֶךָ;

Scorch him with flames, and do not
lose heart when you recall that, only
yesterday, he filled the depth of your
abyss with souls.

עַל צַוְּרוֹנֵי רוֹזְנִים דָּרַךְ
אִישׁ זֶה, וְאִם בּוֹ, אַשְׁמְדַאי, תַּחְמֹל —
מָחָר בְּעַזּוּת יַעֲשֹׁק כִּתְרֶךָ.

This man trod the necks of princes,
and should you show him mercy,
Asmodeus, tomorrow he will im-
pudently rob you of your crown.

מֵבִין עֲפָיִים   THE TRIUMPH OF WINE

מֵבִין עֲפָיִים נִתְּנָה קוֹלוֹת,
רֵעַי, עֲגוּרֵי שִׁיר, דְּרוֹרֵי זֶמֶר,
לִכְבוֹד שְׁנֵי דוֹדִים שְׁכוֹרֵי חֶמֶר,
שֶׁחֻבְּרוּ הַיּוֹם לְרֹב גִּילוֹת.

My friends, all you wrynecks of song
and swallows of melody, let us sing
between the branches, in honour of
these two lovers, drunk with wine, who
were joined today, most joyfully.

אַחַי, שְׁבָחֵינוּ וּמַהֲלָלֵינוּ
יִהְיוּ לְיֵין הַטּוֹב בְּלִי כָּל שֶׁמֶר.
נַלְבִּין פְּנֵי חֶשֶׁק כְּהַלְבִּין צֶמֶר:
לֹא עוֹד יְהִי שׁוֹפֵט וְשַׂר עָלֵינוּ,

Brothers, let our praise and acclaim go
to the choice wine which has no dregs
at all. We shall shame Eros, make him
turn as white as wool. No longer will
he lord it over us,

כִּי לֹא יְמִינוֹ הֶחֱבִירָה אֵלֶּה —
לִשְׁתּוֹת וְלִשְׁכֹּר יַחְדָּו נִקְשָׁרוּ,
חֶשֶׁק לְאֶפֶס חָשְׁבוּ וּלְאַיִן.

for it was not his right hand that paired
them off. They banded together to
drink and to be drunk; and as for Eros,
they held him in contempt.

אִם כֵּן, בְּקוֹל נָשִׁיר: יְחִי הַיַּיִן!
יָדִיו עֲלֵי הָאַהֲבָה גָּבְרוּ —
נוֹרָא תְהִלּוֹת הוּא וְעוֹשֵׂה פֶלֶא.

Then let me sing lustily: Long live
wine! It has triumphed over love. It is
worthy of awe and praise. It works
wonders!

לוּלֵי יְדַעְתִּיךָ, אַהֲבָה

THE DEFEAT OF EROS

לוּלֵי יְדַעְתִּיךָ, אַהֲבָה, מֵאָמֶשׁ,
לוּלֵי בְּיָדִי פָּעֳלֵךְ מִשַּׁשְׁתִּי,
לוּלֵי בְּלִבִּי לַהֲבֵךְ הִרְגַּשְׁתִּי,
וּכְשַׁבְּלוּל אֵלֵךְ לְמֵאָז תֶּמֶס;

Love, had I not known you during
other nights; had I not fingered your
works with my own hands; had I not
felt your flame within my heart; had I
not melted away, after that, like a snail;

לוּלֵי לְמִיּוֹם אָחֱזֶה הַשֶּׁמֶשׁ
תָּקְפֵּךְ וּמֶמְשַׁלְתֵּךְ בְּעֵינֵי חַשְׁתִּי
בַּמַּחֲנֶה הַזֶּה אֲשֶׁר פָּגַשְׁתִּי
מִמִּין אֱנוֹשֵׁי עַד בְּעִיר וָרֶמֶשׂ —

had I not sensed with my own eyes,
ever since I saw the sunlight, what
mastery and power you exercise over
all this company which I have met,
from man to beast to insect —

הָאַהֲבָה, הַיּוֹם חֲשַׁבְתִּיךָ אַיִן,
תֹּהוּ וְאֶפֶס נֶחֱשַׁב לִי חֵשֶׁק,
לָךְ אֶקְרָאָה טָלֶה בְּצוּרַת לַיִשׁ;

Love, I would have considered you
today a mere nothing, I would have
regarded Eros as naught and emptiness;
I would have called you a lamb in lion's
clothing.

כִּי אָזְרָה עָפְרָה לְנֶגְדּוֹ זַיִן,
לְבָּהּ לְבוּשׁ שִׁרְיוֹן לְמוּל כָּל נֶשֶׁק.
חִצָּיו בְּחֵיקָהּ שֶׁעֲנָה עַל שַׁיִשׁ.

For the maiden armed herself and
stood up to Eros, with a heart like a
coat of mail that withstands all
weapons; and his arrows dropped onto
her bosom like wax onto marble.

חַסְדֵי שְׁנָתִי　　THE LOVER RECANTS

חַסְדֵי שְׁנָתִי, אוֹהֲבַי, אַזְכִּירָה
עַל כִּי צְבִיָּה בַּחֲלוֹם הֶרְאַתְנִי.
לֹא אֵדְעָה נַפְשִׁי – וְאֵיךְ שָׂמַתְנִי
נָאוֹר, וְאֵיךְ תּוֹךְ מַאֲפָל הֵאִירָה !

Friends, let me praise the goodness of
my sleep, for in a dream it showed me
my beloved. I still cannot understand
it: how she filled me with light; how
she shone in the darkness!

חַסְדָּהּ גְּבַרְתִּי בֶּאֱמֶת הִגְבִּירָה
עֲלֵי בְּחֶזְיוֹנָהּ אֲשֶׁר חִיַּתְנִי ;
אָמְנָם בְּעֵת הָקִיץ הֲלֹא הֶלְאַתְנִי –
מִי יִתְּנֵנִי אָז וְלֹא אָעִירָה !

Truly, my mistress showered me with
goodness, when, with this vision, she
brought me back to life. But when I am
awake, she does nothing but wear me
out. If only I could sleep and never
wake!

יָשׁוּב חֲלוֹמִי נָא וְיַחֲלִימֵנִי,
אָז לַתְּנוּמָה אֶקְרָאָה ׳שָׂרָתִי׳,
כִּי הִיא תְחַיֵּנִי וְתַחֲלִימֵנִי.

May my dream return and make me
dream again. Then shall I call slumber
'my queen', for it is she who gives me
life and heals me.[1]

אוֹדֶה עֲלֵי פְשָׁעִי אֲשֶׁר חָטָאתִי,
גַּם כָּל תְּבוּנָה נִדְחָה מִמֶּנִּי,
יוֹם לָהּ ׳דְּמוּת הַמָּוְתָה׳ קָרָאתִי.

I confess that I sinned against her and
that all wisdom abandoned me the day
I named her 'death's image'.

---

1. A play on the root _ḥalom_, which means both 'to dream' and 'to heal'.

הַרְפּוּ, מְלִיצִים

FOR HIS BROTHER'S MARRIAGE

הַרְפּוּ, מְלִיצִים, מִזְמִיר הַרְפּוּ!
סָחֹוב, הַשְׁלֵךְ כָּל עֵטֵיכֶם לַזֵּבֶל!
פּוּ, פּוּ עֲלֵיכֶם, פּוּ וְאֶלֶף פּוּ!
רַב שְׁבַּרְתֶּם רֹאשִׁי בִּמְלִיצוֹת הֶבֶל.
עֵת תִּשְׁמְעוּ מִלַּי, אֲשֶׁר צָפוּ
זָהָב, מִקִּנְאָה תִּתְּלוּ בַּחֶבֶל.
אָז תּוֹדוּ, כִּי אֵין לִי וּלְשִׂכְלִי רֵעַ,
גַּם נַעֲלִי מִכֻּלְּכֶם יוֹדֵעַ.

אֹמַר עֲלֵי דוֹד זֶה אֲשֶׁר הוּא גֶבֶר
בַּכֹּל: פָּנָיו חַמָּה בְּלִתִּי לָקוּת.
יֵשׁ לוֹ יְהוּדוּת רַב, וְיַעַל אֵבֶר
לָעוּף לְדָבָר מִצְנָה עַד קָלִיקוּת.
חָכָם מְחַכְמָם הוּא, וְיֵט אֵל עֵבֶר
הַשִּׁיר מֵחוֹ – אָכֵן לֹא מֵרֵיקוּת.
תַּכְלִית דְּבָרִים: הוּא לְכָל בִּין אָב,
אִישׁ טוֹב, אִישׁ תָּם, אִישׁ מִשְׁקָלוֹ זָהָב.

עָפְרָה יְרֵאת אֵל וּכְמַלְאָךְ יָפָה,
טוֹבָה כְּפַת טוֹב, אֵין בְּלִבָּהּ כַּעַשׂ.
הָיוּ סִבְלוֹת הַבַּיִת עַל כְּתֵפָה,
לֹא חֶחֱזֶה דָבָר אֲשֶׁר לֹא תַעַשׂ.
לֹא אֵדַע, אֵיךְ תָּלִין עִם אַלּוּפָהּ –
הִיא מֵאֱנוֹשׁ תִּרְעַשׁ, כְּמִשֵּׁד, רַעַשׁ.
לַחֲסִין רָמִים הִיא גַם דוֹד יֶחֱסוּ,
שָׁוִים כְּאִלּוּ בַּדְּפוּס נִדְפָּסוּ. [...]

Leave off, you poetasters, leave off your singing! All your pens should be dragged along and flung on a dung heap! Pooh, pooh to you, pooh and a thousand poohs! Enough! You have already broken my head with your empty rhetoric. When you hear my words, words coated with gold, you will take a rope and hang yourselves out of envy. Then you will concede that my wit and I are beyond compare. Even my shoe knows more than all of you put together.

Let me now proclaim that this lover is, in all things, a real man: his face is like a sun untouched by eclipse; he is God-fearing and devout, and for the sake of a good deed would grow wings and fly as far as Calicut.[1] He is wise beyond the wisest, and his mind – but, mark you, not out of emptiness – has given itself to poetry. In short: he is the father of all insight, a good man, a mild man, a man worth his weight in gold.

His bride is pious, beautiful as an angel, wholesome as a good loaf of bread, her heart free of vexation. She shoulders all the household cares and never overlooks a chore. I cannot imagine how she manages to sleep with her dear friend, for she quakes at the mere sight of humans as if they were demons. Both she and her beloved are of noble stock, both equal in rank, as if cast from the same mould.

1. A port-town in South West India, on the shores of the Arabian Sea.

נִשְׁאַר הַטּוֹב מִכֹּל – אֹזֶן הַטּוּ:
נִשְׁאַל מְשִׁיחֵנוּ אֲשֶׁר נוֹחִילָה.
הַלְוַאי מַהֵר יָבוֹא, גַּם לֹא יַשְׁטוּ
בָּנוּ לְאֻמִּים עוֹד, וְעֹז נַגְדִּילָה.
עֵת יָבוֹא אֵלִיָּה עִם קוֹל טוּ טוּ.
שִׁירוּ, אֲדוֹנִים, אֵיךְ וְאֵיךְ נָגִילָה !
אָז מִי יְהִי רֹאשׁ, מִי יְרוֹמֵם דֶּגֶל,
מִי עַל סוּס יָרוּץ אֹרַח – מִי בָרֶגֶל ? [...]

Now for the best of all – lend me your
ears: we shall ask for our Messiah, on
whom we fix our hopes. If only he
came quickly, the nations would no
more deride us. We shall grow in
might when Elijah appears to the sound
of 'Toot! Toot!' Sing, gentlemen!
How happy we shall be! Who then will
be the leader, who will raise the flag
aloft, who will gallop on a horse – and
who will go afoot?

לָקֵב זֶה תִּשְׂאוּ קוֹל – אַךְ לַגַּגּוֹת,
כִּי קוֹל חֲמוֹרִים לַזְּבוּל לֹא יַעַל.
תִּרְאוּ רֹב טָעֻיּוֹת בּוֹ וּמִשְׁגָּגוֹת,
אַךְ שִׁירְכֶם לֹא טוֹב לְחַלְצוֹ נַעַל.
מָתַי אַעַשׂ מֶחֱטָמְכֶם עוּגוֹת,
לֵצִים, וְאֶטַּע עַל פְּנֵיכֶם שַׁעַל ?
אָז, אָז בְּשֶׁבַח הַסַּחִי תָּמִירוּ,
לִקְרַאת שִׁירֵי הַכּוֹבָעִים תָּסִירוּ !

You raise your voices to denounce my
song, but they go no higher than the
roof, for the voice of an ass cannot
mount to heaven. You find many a
fault and flaw in my song, but yours is
not fit to wipe its shoes. Buffoons!
When shall I knead your noses into
cakes, and plant my foot on your faces!
Then your words of slander will give
way to praise, and you will take off
your hats to my songs!

(1656)

אַהֲבָה לִתְמוּנָה

LOVE FOR A PORTRAIT

א

A

אֵיךְ אֶעֱשֶׂה, דּוֹד, מִפְּנֵי הַחֵשֶׁק ?
חֵצוֹ, אֲשֶׁר יָדָה בְּיָד מִרְשַׁעַת,
חָלַף לְבָבִי כַּחֲלֹף דַּלַּעַת,
חִנָּם, בְּלִי הִתְעַשְּׂקִי בּוֹ עֵשֶׁק !

What can I do, my friend, in the face of
Eros? The arrow which he let fly with
a malicious hand pierced my heart as if
it were a pumpkin – and all for no
reason, without my having provoked
him!

מִי הֶאֱמִין, כִּי הֶחֱבִיא הַגֶּשֶׁק
בִּדְמוּת צְבָעִים בָּרְחוֹב מֻקַּעַת ?
סוֹף סוֹף, צָעִיר יָמִים וְנֶעְדַּר דַּעַת,
גַּם כִּי בְּבֵית הָאַהֲבָה בֶּן מֶשֶׁק !

Who would have believed that he
would hide his arms in a coloured
figure, hanging on display in the street?
After all, he is no more than a young,
ignorant boy, although he is in charge
of Love's household.

497

עֵת אֹמְרָה אֵלָיו בְּאַף וָזַעַם :
'כִּסְדֹם תְּהִי, חֵשֶׁק, וְכַעֲדַת קֹרַח !
לָמָּה תְּהָתֵל בִּי בְּאַהֲבַת רוּחַ ?'

When I say to him in grim anger:
'Eros, may you be [overturned] like
Sodom and [swallowed up] like Korah's
crowd![1] Why do you mock me with a
futile love?' –

עוֹנֶה לְבָבִי : 'הוֹי מְשֻׁגֶּה טַעַם !
הַמְעַט אֲשֶׁר תִּסְבֹּל בְּכָבְדּוּת טֹרַח
אִשָּׁה מְצֻיָּרָה עֲלֵי הַלּוּחַ ?'

then my heart speaks up: 'O you
lunatic! Isn't it enough for you to bear
the heavy burden of a woman who is
painted on a canvas?'

ב   B

לוּחַ, אֱמֹר, מַה זֶּה אֲשֶׁר עַל לוּחַ
לִבִּי לְפֶתַע אוֹתְךָ חֲקַקְתִּי ?
מֵאָז רְאִיתִיךְ בָּךְ חָשַׁקְתִּי,
לֹא אֶשְׁקֹטָה, אוֹי לִי, וְלֹא אָנוּחַ.

Tell me, tableau, why have I suddenly
engraved you on the tablets of my
heart? I have desired you from the
moment I saw you. Woe is me! I have
had no peace of mind, no rest.

מַה זֶּה וְעַל מַה זֶּה יְהִי קִלּוּחַ
עֵינִי, וְכִמְעַט בַּבְּכִי נֶחֱנַקְתִּי ?
אֵיךְ מִמְּשׁוֹשׁ לִבִּי לָרִיק הוּרַקְתִּי ?
לָךְ אֶשְׁפְּכָה רוּחִי – וְאֵין בָּךְ רוּחַ.

Why, oh why have my eyes been
streaming until I nearly choke on my
tears? How did it come about that my
heart's joy was emptied out in vain? I
pour out my life before you, though
you are lifeless.

בְּשֻׁלַּל צְבָעִים בַּעֲדֵךְ נִשְׁלַלְתִּי
מִיּוֹם אֲשֶׁר מֵעֶפֶק בָּךְ רָאִיתִי
תַּבְנִית יְפִי עַפְרָה, וְאָז הִסְכַּלְתִּי –

With your ravishing colours you carried
me away the day I saw that shape of
girlish beauty traced upon you; it was
then that I turned into a fool

וָאֹמְרָה : 'הַלְוַאי אֲשֶׁר הָיִיתִי
חֹמֶר לְצוּרָה זֹאת, וּבָהּ נִפְתַּלְתִּי,
גַּם כִּי צְנוּעָה הִיא, וּבָהּ חָסִיתִי !'

and said: 'Oh, if only I could serve as
matter to this form, and be enmeshed
in her; though she be chaste, I would
take cover in her!'

---

1. Who were swallowed up by the earth (Numbers 17.31 ff).

עֵת אֶזְכְּרָה יוֹם · DEATH AND THE LOVER

עֵת אֶזְכְּרָה יוֹם, כִּי כְּאֵשׁ בּוֹעֶרֶת
הָיָה לְחִי עָפְרָה וּמַר צָעָקָה;
עֵת אֶזְכְּרָה יוֹם, כַּף לְכַף דָּפָקָה;
פִּיהָ לְפִי מֵת הָיְתָה נִקְשֶׁרֶת,

When I recall the day her cheek was like a blazing fire and she cried out most bitterly; when I recall the day she beat her hands together, and her mouth was clinging to the dead man's mouth,

עֵת כִּי לְהַפְרִידָהּ בְּיָד גּוֹרֶרֶת
רָצוּ בְּנוֹת הַחֵן, וְשֵׁן חָרָקָה;
נֶגֶד רְצוֹן כֹּל בַּעֲלָהּ נָשָׁקָה
עִם צוּף שְׂפָתֶיהָ, וְאֵין עוֹצֶרֶת –

and when the good ladies tried to tear her away by force, she ground her teeth; defying one and all, she kissed her husband with her honeyed lips, and none could stop her –

עַל כָּל תְּשׁוּקוֹתַי אֲנִי תָאַבְתִּי
כִּי יוֹם פְּקֻדָּתִי וְיוֹם צַלְמָוֶת
שֶׁמֶשׁ נְשִׁיקָתָהּ בְּפִי יַזְרִיחַ,

then, with a passion exceeding all my passions, I long for her kiss's sun to shine in my mouth, on my day of reckoning and deep shadows,

וְאֹמְרָה: 'קִרְבִי!' וְאִם חָשַׁבְתִּי
לִטְעֹם שְׂפָתֶיהָ בְּיוֹם הַמָּוֶת,
אוֹחִיל לְיוֹם מוֹתִי כְּמוֹ מָשִׁיחַ.

and I shall say: 'Come close!' And if I thought I might taste her lips the day I die, I should long for the day of my death as if for the Messiah.

דּוֹד, מַרְאָה נוֹרָאָה · ON TURNING GREY IN A DREAM

דּוֹד, מַרְאָה נוֹרָאָה אֶתְמוֹל הָרְאֵיתִי,
וָאֶפֹּל עַל פָּנַי פִּתְאֹם מִפַּחַד.
פָּנַי וִיחִידָתִי נָפְלוּ בִי יַחַד,
וָאֹמַר תּוֹךְ קִרְבִּי: 'אוֹי לִי, נִדְמֵיתִי!'

Friend, yesterday I was shown a terrible vision; terrified, I immediately flung myself to the ground. My face and my soul were both cast down, and I said deep within me: 'Alas, I am lost.'

דּוֹד, בַּמַּרְאָה הַזֹּאת קִצִּי נִבֵּאתִי –
הָהּ, כִּי מָוֶת עָלַי פִּי חַרְבּוֹ יַחַד.

Friend, in this vision my end was prophesied. Death is sharpening the blade of his sword against me. With

אִם עַל שְׁעָרִי שׁוֹקֵד קָרוֹב הַכַּחַד,
אוֹי, אֵיךְ אֶבְרַח אִם בִּשְׂעָרִי הוּבָאתִי ?

doom prowling at my gate,[1] how can I escape when I am being dragged by my hair?

הַעַל שֶׁצָּמָתִי גֵּאוּת לָבַשְׁתִּי
כִּי נִתְלוּ בָהּ חַיַּי כְּתָלוּיֵי חֶבֶל,
וּכְאַבְשָׁלוֹם בְּשַׂעַר רֹאשִׁי נִתְפַּשְׂתִּי ?

Is it because I took pride in my locks that my life now hangs from them as one hangs from a halter and, like Absalom, I am held fast by my hair?

צָחֹר, לֹא עוֹד שָׁחֹר, יִהְיֶה אוֹת אֵבֶל :
עַד כֹּה בַּקַּדְרוּת גִּיל בְּלֵב הִרְגַּשְׁתִּי,
וּבְלֹבֶן זֶה הַיּוֹם אַרְגִּישָׁה חֶבֶל.

White, not black, shall henceforth be the sign of mourning. Before, it was blackness that made my heart rejoice, but now it is this whiteness that makes me feel the noose.

עִמָּנוּאֵל פְרַאנְשֵׁיס

Immanuel Frances

עֵת אֶחֱזֶה חַנָּה

THE DILEMMA

עֵת אֶחֱזֶה חַנָּה בְּאוֹר זוֹרֵחַ,
עֵת נָעֳמִי אַזְכִּיר כְּלִיל תִּפְאֶרֶת –
נַפְשִׁי בְּעַד חַנָּה הֲכִי בוֹעֶרֶת,
וּלְנָעֳמִי רוּחִי כְּאֵשׁ קוֹדֵחַ !

When I see Hannah in full light, when I remember Naomi, perfect in splendour – my soul is aflame for Hannah, my spirit is kindled for Naomi.

תִּשְׁתֵּי סְעִפִּים הִנְנִי פוֹסֵחַ :
חַנָּה כְּהַיּוֹם בִּי תְּהִי לִגְבֶרֶת,
גַּם נָעֳמִי בִּי מִתְּמוֹל שׁוֹרֶרֶת.
אָן, אַהֲבָה, מִמְּךָ אֱהִי בוֹרֵחַ ?

Here I am, sitting on the fence: Hannah, as of today, is my mistress; but Naomi has been reigning over me since yesterday. O Love, whither can I flee from your presence?

1. The author punctuated this word so that it can be read to mean 'my gate' (*sha'ri*) as well as 'my hair' (*sa'ri*).

הָהּ, כִּי כְּמוֹ בַרְזֶל בְּבַרְזֶל יַחַד,
חֵשֶׁק בְּחֵשֶׁק חַדְדוּ כִּפְלַיִם,
עַל כֵּן סְעַפַּי פָּחֲדוּ שָׁם פַּחַד.

Alas, as iron sharpens iron, so has
desire twice sharpened desire. That is
why my thoughts are so alarmed.

לָךְ, אַהֲבָה, אֹמַר פְּרוּשׂ כַּפַּיִם:
אוֹ לִי שְׁנֵי לִבּוֹת תְּנִי גַּם יַחַד,
אוֹ אֶת לְבָבִי בַּתְּרִי לִשְׁנָיִם!

Love, I pray you with outspread hands:
Either give me two hearts together, or
else split my one heart in two!

עֵינֵי צְבִיָּה   HER EYES

עֵינֵי צְבִיָּה הֵם שְׁמֵי הָאַהֲבָה,
בָּם מַעֲטֵה אוֹרָה וְזִיו לוֹבֶשֶׁת.
גַּם אִם עֲלֵיהֶם שָׁם עֲנָנָיו הַבְּכִי –
אַל נָא, יְדִידִים, תִּירְאוּ מִגֶּשֶׁת.
אַל תִּירְאוּ מֵהֶם וּמֵימֵיהֶם, הֲכִי
עַל כֵּן עֲלֵיהֶם נִרְאָתָה הַקֶּשֶׁת.

The girl's eyes are the heavens of love,
a robe of light and splendour in which
she clothes herself. Even when they are
hidden by clouds of tears, lovers, do
not be afraid to come near. Do not fear
them or their torrents, for the bow[1] has
already appeared above them.

שִׁמְעִי, כְּלִילַת הוֹד   THE INNKEEPER'S LOVE SONG

שִׁמְעִי, כְּלִילַת הוֹד וְחֵן בִּמְאֹד,
אֶל צַעֲקַת פַּפּוֹס וְרִנָּתוֹ!
גּוֹעֶה כְּמוֹ שׁוֹר, כַּחֲמוֹר נוֹעֵר
לָךְ, כִּי אֲתוֹנוֹ אַתְּ וּפָרָתוֹ.
לִבּוֹ כְּבָר קָלִי, וְכַצָּלִי
בְּשַׁפּוּד אֲהָבִים הוּא וְלַבָּתוֹ.

O you paragon of glory and grace,
listen to the call of Papos and his cry!
He is bellowing like a bull, braying at
you like a donkey, for you are his cow
and his she-ass. His heart is already
parched like grain, he and his passion
are impaled on love's spit like a roast.

---

1. I.e. the eyebrows. The 'bow in the clouds' is the sign that the flood will never recur (Genesis 9.12 ff).

הַשְׁקְפִי, עָפְרָה, בְּעַד אֶשְׁנָב
וּרְאִי בְּצוּרָתוֹ וְתַבְנִיתוֹ :
כִּי נָפְלוּ פָנָיו וּמַעֲנָיָו,
לֹא פָסְקוּ בִּכְיוֹ וְדִמְעָתוֹ,
קֶרַח בְּקָרְחָתוֹ וְגַבַּחְתּוֹ
הֻשְׁלַךְ, וְטַל נִמְלָא קְוֻצָתוֹ.
דּוֹמֶה אֱלֵי חָתוּל אֲשֶׁר עַל גַּג
בּוֹדֵד וְיִתְמוֹגֵג בְּרָעָתוֹ,
קוֹרֵא נְהִי נִהְיָה בְּקוֹל מָרָה,
יַעַן עֲרָפֶל שָׁם חֲתוּלָּתוֹ.

Look through your lattice, gazelle, and
observe his sorry figure: his face has
fallen and so have his thoughts; no end
to his crying and tears; flecks of ice are
scattered on his bald pate, and his
locks are drenched with dew. He is like
a lonely tomcat on a roof, melting away
in distress, wailing bitter lamentations,
for his mistress[1] is swaddled in mist.

אֵי סוֹחֲרִים

THE OLD WHORE'S LAMENT

אֵי סוֹחֲרִים הַשּׁוֹחֲרִים אוֹתִי
לִקְנוֹת יְדִידוּתִי ? זְמַן שׂוֹנֵא !
כִּי בָחֲלוּ הַיּוֹם בְּחֶבְרָתִי,
כִּי אֶקְרָאָה אוֹתָם, וְאֵין עוֹנֶה !
אֵיךְ הָיְתָה לָבֵז סְחוֹרָתִי,
אֵיךְ אֶמְכְּרֶנָּה, אֵיךְ, וְאֵין קוֹנֶה.
אָז בַּעֲדָהּ לִי יִתְּנוּ הוֹנָם,
הַלְוַאי כְּהַיּוֹם יִלְקְחוּ חִנָּם.

Where are the merchants who used to
chase after me to purchase my favours?
O malevolent Time! Nowadays, they
abhor my company; when I call for
them, there is no answer. How has my
merchandise been brought so low! How
can I possibly sell it, when there is no
buyer? Once they would have given all
their wealth for it. Now I would be
lucky if they took it free of charge.

לְבַד שָׁלוֹשׁ יְצִיאוֹת

TO HIS GADABOUT WIFE

לְבַד שָׁלוֹשׁ יְצִיאוֹת הֵן רָאוּיוֹת
לְכָל אִשָּׁה, קְטַנָּה אוֹ גְדוֹלָה :
וְאַחַת הִיא בְּהִוָּלְדָהּ וְצֵאתָהּ

Only three exits are becoming to every
woman, big or small. The first is when

---

1. A play on ḥatulato which in Job 38.9 means 'his swaddling clothes' but can also mean 'his she-cat'.

מְלֻכְלֶכֶת כְּמוֹ מִיַּן מְצוּלָה;
וְהַשֵּׁנִית בְּצֵאת מִבֵּית נְוָתָהּ
וְהוֹלֶכֶת לְבֵית חָתָן וּבַעְלָהּ;
וְיוֹם תּוּבַל לְקֶבֶר הַשְּׁלִישִׁית —
וּמִכָּל הַיְצִיאוֹת זֹאת מְעֻלָּה.

she exits from the womb, dirtied, as if
from a deep swamp. The second is
when she exits from her woman's tent
and enters the home of her husband
and lord. And the third is the day she
is led to her grave. This is the finest
exit of all.

צִיּוּנֵי־קֶבֶר — EPITAPHS

לאשה — For A Wife

גַּל זֶה לְמַשָּׂא, לֹא לְמַצֵּבָה,
שַׂמְתִּי לְאִשְׁתִּי עַל קְבוּרָתָהּ,
פֶּן, חָס וְשָׁלוֹם, אַחֲרֵי מוֹתָהּ
תָּקוּם וְאֶל בֵּיתִי תְּהִי שָׁבָה.

I have set this stone as a weight, not as
a memorial, over my wife's grave, lest
(God forbid!) she rise from the dead
and come back home.

לננס — For A Dwarf

צִיּוּן זֶה אֶל אָדָם נַס
בָּזֶה הוּבָא לִקְבוּרָתוֹ,
וּבְבַת אַחַת, עֵת פֹּה נִכְנַס,
תּוֹלָע אֶחָד בָּלַע אוֹתוֹ.

This inscription is for a dwarf: he was
buried in this plot, but as soon as he
settled in, a worm gobbled him up.

לגבן ובשמו — For A Hunchback

לֹא דַי לְךָ, מַזָּל, אֲשֶׁר הָיִיתִי
נוֹשֵׂא חֲטוֹטָרָה בְּעוֹד חָיִיתִי,
כִּי אַחֲרֵי מוֹתִי לְאוֹיֵב קַמְתָּ
עָלַי, וְאֶבֶן זֹאת בְּגַבִּי שַׂמְתָּ?

'O Fortune, weren't you content to
make me bear a hump as long as I
lived? Did you have to rise against me
after my death and stick this slab on
my back?'

לאיש כסיל ורגזן

For An Angry Fool

פֹּה אִישׁ חֲסַר דֵּעָה וּמִתְעַבֵּר.
כִּמְטַחֲוֵי קֶשֶׁת רְחַק, עוֹבֵר,
פֶּן, בַּחֲרוֹן אַפּוֹ, בָּאֶבֶן זֹאת
אֶת רֹאשְׁךָ הַיּוֹם יְהִי שׁוֹבֵר.

Here lies a witless and irascible man.
Passerby, keep a safe distance, for in
his fury, with this very stone, he might
now smash your head.

לבעל חטם גדול

For A Big-Nosed Man

לָמָה צִיּוּן הַלָּז בָּנוּ עַל גֶּבֶר
מִכָּל אַנְשֵׁי דוֹרוֹ אֶרֶךְ אַפַּיִם ?
כִּי הָיָה לוֹ צִיּוּן גָּדוֹל כִּפְלַיִם
אִלּוּ נִשְׁאַר חָטְמוֹ מִחוּץ לַקֶּבֶר !

Why have they erected this monument
over a man who was the most long-
suffering[1] of his generation? He would
have had a monument twice as big had
his nose remained outside the tomb!

אֶפְרַיִם לוּצָאטוֹ

Ephraim Luzzato

מִי אָנֹכִי וּמִי בֵיתִי

OF MYSELF

אַרְצִי הַנִּשְׁקָפָה — הִנֵּה נָכוֹנָה
עַל רֹאשׁ גִּבְעָה רָמָה רַבַּת יָדַיִם.
בֵּיתִי בִּרְחוֹבָהּ הוּא כִּדְמוּת הָרְמוֹנָה,
לוּצָאטוֹ מִשְׁפַּחְתִּי וּשְׁמִי אֶפְרַיִם.

My land,[2] spread out before my eyes, is
set securely on a high and spacious
hill. On a street there is my house,
grand as a palace. Luzzato is my
family, and my given name is Ephraim.

שָׁם אָנֹכִי עַל רֹב שָׁלוֹם אֶשְׁכֹּנָה,
שָׁם לִי נָטַעְתִּי גַן עַל עֵין הַמַּיִם,
וּבְנוֹת הַשִּׁיר עַל הַשָּׂפָה תָּרֹנָּה
מִשְׁלֵי דוֹדִים יוֹם יוֹם בֵּין הָעַרְבַּיִם.

There do I dwell in untold peace.
There have I planted my own garden
by a spring. And on its banks, every
day at dusk, the songbirds[3] sing lovers'
tales.

---

1. The Hebrew idiom literally means 'long-nosed'.
2. 'That is, San Daniele, a pleasant land in the duchy of Friuli.' [Author's note]
3. Or, 'daughters of song'.

הִנֵּה, אָמְנָה, אַף כִּי עוֹדֶנִּי יֶלֶד,
אֵין כָּל דָּבָר כִּי עַל רוּחִי אוֹת יַעַשׂ,
קִנְאָה אֵין בְּלְבָבִי, אַף אֵין בִּי כַּעַשׂ.

And so, though I am still a youth,
nothing can mar my peace of mind.
There is no envy in my heart, nor is
there anger.

אַף כִּמְצַחֵק אֶל מוּל קוֹרוֹת הַחֶלֶד,
לֹא עֹשֶׁר אֶתְאַוֶּה, לֹא אִירָא עֹנִי.
מִי זֶה הָאִישׁ, אֵפוֹא, אֲשֶׁר כָּמוֹנִי ?

And what is more, mocking the world's
affairs, I do not desire riches, I am not
afraid of want. Is there any man as
fortunate as I?

עוּרָה, אָדוֹן דָּוֶה   KIDNEY SONNET

דברים נחומים אל החכם הנעלה כמוהר"ר יעקב
חי חפץ מ"ץ בק"ק גוריציאה, בחלותו בכאב
הכליות כי השקט לא יוכל ויגרשו מימיו רפש
וטיט, וכל קהל ישראל עומד בית י"י ביום צום
להפיל תחנה לישועתה לו, ותחל רוח י"י לפעמו
והוציא את האבן הראשה ברב חיל :

*Words of comfort addressed to the
sublime sage, our honoured Master and
Mentor, Jacob Hai Hefetz, Teacher of
Righteousness in the Holy Community of
Gorizia, who contracted a kidney malady.
He was unable to rest, and his troubled
waters cast up mud and filth, and the
whole congregation of Israel gathered in
the House of God to hold a day of fasting
and to beseech Him for help. Then the
spirit of the Lord began to stir him and
he forcibly brought forth the top stone.*

עוּרָה, אָדוֹן דָּוֶה, וּרְאֵה כִּי מַיִם
יִזֶּה הָעָם הַזֶּה הַזֶּה דּוּמָם כָּאֶבֶן,
וּלְשֶׁבֶר אַנְחָתָם נֶעֶרְמוּ מַיִם,
כָּפִיס מֵעֵץ תִּצְעַק, מְקִיר – הָאֶבֶן.

Arise, afflicted master, see how this
people, silent as a stone, is here
shedding water. At their groans of
distress the waters of the sea pile up.
Beams cry out from the woodwork, and
stones from the wall.

אַתָּה עַתָּה, כַּבִּיר, הַשֵּׁף הַמַּיִם,
וּבְנַחַת וּרְוָחָה הוֹצֵא הָאֶבֶן ;
וּלְבַב הַנִּצָּבִים נָמֵס כַּמַּיִם –
אַל נָא יֵרַךְ לְבָּךְ חָזָק מֵאֶבֶן.

Now, mighty one, give forth a torrent
of water and – gently, easily – discharge
the stone. The hearts of those about
you are melting, flowing away like
water. But you, do not lose heart, for
yours is stronger than stone.

הָאֵל חַנּוּן, הַהוּא, כִּי נַחַל מַיִם
אָז בִּישִׁימוֹן מִדְּבָר הִזִּיל מֵאָבֶן,
מִמַּעְיְנֵי יִשְׁעוֹ יָרִיק לְךָ מָיִם.

The merciful God, who once made
streams of water run from a rock in the
wilderness, will now draw out water for
you from His springs of deliverance.

הֵן עוֹד מִפִּי הַבּוֹר תָּסִיר הָאָבֶן,
עוֹד כַּמִּשְׁפָּט רֹאשׁוֹן תַּשְׁקֵנוּ מַיִם –
עַד כִּי בָהָר הַטּוֹב יֻסַּד אָבֶן.

Surely you will yet remove the stone
from the mouth of the well. You will
give us waters [of wisdom] to drink, as
you did in former days – until the
cornerstone is laid on the good
Mountain.

עַל הָרוֹפֵא
הַנּוֹפֵל שָׁדוּד בְּרֶשֶׁת הָאַהֲבָה

THE DOCTOR WHO FELL
PREY TO LOVE

יַלְדָּה יָפָה אַחַת וּמְאֹד אוֹהֶבֶת
בָּאָה בֵּיתָה רוֹפֵא מָזוֹר לָקַחַת,
לֵאמֹר: כִּי זֶה יָמִים נַפְשָׁהּ כּוֹאֶבֶת,
אַף בַּלֵּילוֹת רָחַק מִמֶּנָּה נַחַת.

A beautiful girl, very much in love,
came to the doctor's house, seeking a
cure. These many days, she said, her
soul had been in pain and even at night
peace had eluded her.

עוֹד הַשֵּׁגֶל הַזֹּאת אֶצְלוֹ נִצֶּבֶת,
שָׁלַח יָדוֹ לַחְקֹר אִם יֵשׁ קַדַּחַת;
וַתִּצַּת בְּלִבָּבוֹ פִּתְאֹם שַׁלְהֶבֶת –
אָהַב, נִלְכַּד גַּם הוּא אֶל תּוֹךְ הַפַּחַת.

Now, as this queenly girl stood beside
him, he put his hand out to discover if
she had a fever. And, suddenly, a flame
was kindled in his heart. He, too, fell in
love, and into the pit.

נִדְהָם אַף מִשְׁתָּאֶה הָיָה הַגֶּבֶר,
עַד הַחוֹלָה שֵׁנִית הֵטִיבָה טַעַם:
'בִּי, הָאָדוֹן, הַאֵין מַרְפֵּא לַשֶּׁבֶר?'

The gentleman was overcome and
dumbstruck, until the patient again
spoke up discreetly: 'Please, sir, is
there no cure for my complaint?'

אָז הוּא: 'הָהּ רַעְיָתִי, אַל נָא תַחְשְׁכִי!
חִבְשִׁי אַתְּ אֶת פִּצְעִי, אָמְנָם הַפַּעַם
לֹא הָרוֹפֵא, אַךְ הַחוֹלֶה אָנֹכִי.'

Then he: 'O my dearest, do not hold
back! *You* dress *my* wound, for this
once – I am not the doctor, but the
patient.'

MODERN TIMES

חַיִּים נַחְמָן בְּיַאלִיק | *Ḥayim Naḥman Bialik*

עִם דִּמְדּוּמֵי הַחַמָּה | AT TWILIGHT

עִם דִּמְדּוּמֵי הַחַמָּה אֶל־הַחַלּוֹן נָא־גְשִׁי
וְעָלַי הִתְרַפָּקִי,
לִפְתִי הֵיטֵב צַוָּארִי, שִׂימִי רֹאשֵׁךְ עַל־רֹאשִׁי –
וְכֹה עִמִּי תִדְבָּקִי.

> At twilight, come over to the window
> and lean upon me. Put your arms round
> my neck, rest your head on mine – and
> hold fast to me.

וּמְחֻשָּׁקִים וּדְבֵקִים, אֶל־הַזֹּהַר הַנּוֹרָא
דּוּמָם נִשָּׂא עֵינֵינוּ;
וְשִׁלַּחְנוּ לַחָפְשִׁי עַל־פְּנֵי יַמֵּי הָאוֹרָה
כָּל־הִרְהוּרֵי לִבֵּנוּ.

> Thus joined and fastened, we shall
> silently lift our eyes to the terrible
> splendour. We shall let all our fantasies
> go free, to roam upon the seas of light.

וְהִתְנַשְּׂאוּ לַמָּרוֹם בִּיעָף שׁוֹקֵק כַּיּוֹנִים,
וּבַמֶּרְחָק יַפְלִיגוּ, יֹאבֵדוּ;
וְעַל־פְּנֵי רְכְסֵי אַרְגָּמָן, אִיֵּי־זֹהַר אַדְמוֹנִים,
בִּיעָף דּוּמָם יֵרֵדוּ.

> They will soar to the heights rustling
> like doves, and sail along into the
> distance and vanish. There, upon the
> purple mountain ridges, the roseate
> islands of splendour, they will silently
> flutter to rest.

הֵם הָאִיִּים הָרְחוֹקִים, הָעוֹלָמוֹת הַגְּבֹהִים
זוּ בַּחֲלוֹמוֹת רְאִינוּם;
שֶׁעֲשָׂאוּנוּ לְגֵרִים תַּחַת כָּל־הַשָּׁמַיִם,
וְחַיֵּינוּ – לְגֵיהִנֹּם.

> Those are the distant islands, the lofty
> worlds that we saw in our dreams; that
> made us strangers everywhere under
> heaven, and made our lives a hell.

הֵמָּה אִיֵּי־הַזָּהָב זוּ צָמֵאנוּ אֲלֵיהֶם
כְּאֶל־אֶרֶץ מוֹלֶדֶת;
שֶׁכָּל־כּוֹכְבֵי הַלַּיִל רָמְזוּ לָנוּ עֲלֵיהֶם
בְּאוֹר קֶרֶן רוֹעֶדֶת.

> Those are the golden islands for which
> we longed as one longs for a homeland,
> to which all the nightstars beckoned
> us with the light of a trembling ray.

וַעֲלֵיהֶם נִשְׁאַרְנוּ בְּלִי־רֵעַ וְעָמִית

כִּשְׁנֵי פְרָחִים בַּצִּיָּה;

כִּשְׁנֵי אֹבְדִים הַמְבַקְשִׁים אֲבֵדָה עוֹלָמִית

עַל־פְּנֵי אֶרֶץ נָכְרִיָּה.

(1902)

And we have been left upon them, without friend or companion, like two flowers in the wasteland, like two who are lost, forever seeking something lost in a foreign land.

מִשִּׁירֵי הַחֹרֶף

FROM THE WINTER SONGS

הַצּוּר הוֹרִיד לָנוּ יוֹם חָזָק מִצֹּר,

יוֹם עָז, מוּצָק אֶחָד כְּפוֹר, קֶרַח נָקָר.

The Rock sent down to us a day harder than flint, a fierce day, a cast-iron day of frost, ice, and cold.

רוּם עוֹלָם, כָּל־כַּדּוּר הָאָרֶץ מִתַּחַת,

הָאוֹר וְהָאֲוִיר כְּעֵין מִקְשָׁה אַחַת.

The summit of the world, the whole sphere of the earth below, the light and the air – all are like a single piece of hammered work.

אֵין זֹאת כִּי נִתְרוֹפֵף הָעוֹלָם – וּנְתָנוֹ

הַיּוֹצֵר בַּלַּיְלָה הַזֶּה עַל־גַּב סַדָּנוֹ,

The world must have begun to loosen, and so, last night, the Creator put it on His anvil,

וַיָּנֶף פַּטִּישׁוֹ, וּבְהַלְמוּת עֲנָק

אֵל קָרָא לַכֹּחַ וַיִּשֹּׁם: חֲזָק !

and swung His hammer, and with this mighty blow, God summoned strength and breathed: 'Be firm!'

וְלֵיל תָּמִים בֵּין פַּטִּישׁ וּסְדָן אוֹתוֹ רָקַע,

וּכְאִלּוּ כָל־כֹּחוֹ, כִּבְיָכוֹל, בּוֹ שִׁקַּע.

Then, all night long, he pounded it between the hammer and the anvil, as if He were sinking all His strength into it.

וַיֵּצֵא עִם־שֶׁמֶשׁ יוֹם עַזִּיז וּמִסְמָר

וְכֹחַ עוֹלָמִים בּוֹ חָסוּם וּמְשֻׁמָּר.

And, with the sun, there emerged a bold, hardened day; eternal strength is sealed within it and preserved.

וְעוֹד תְּלוּיִם בָּאֲוִיר צַחְצוּחֵי הַזִּיו

מִנִּשְׁמַת אֱלוֹהַּ, מֵאֵד רוּחַ פִּיו.

And in the air there still hang gleaming drops from the breath of God, from the vapour of His mouth.

וְאוֹר בֹּקֶר מְסֻתָּן עֲלֵיהֶם בִּיקָרוֹ,
וְנִטַּל כָּל־חֻמּוֹ וְנִשְׁאַר זָהֲרוֹ.

The morning light, in all its glory,
filters through them; and all its heat
subsides, only its lustre remains.

וְאֵין סוֹף לַלַּבְנוּנִית וְלַזֹּהַר אֵין קֵץ,
מִתַּחְתִּית עַד־רוֹם וּמִבַּיִת עַד־עֵץ.

There is no end to the whiteness, no
bounds to the splendour, from depth
to height, from house to tree.

וְהַשֶּׁלֶג בִּשְׁלֹשׁ עֶשְׂרֵה נָפָה מְנֻפֶּה,
כַּזְּכוּכִית הַלְּבָנָה עַל־כָּלָּם מְצֻפֶּה.

And the snow, sifted through thirteen
sieves,[1] coats all things like white glass.

וְהַגַּגּוֹת כְּכוֹבְעֵי הַשַּׁיִשׁ מַרְאִיתָם,
מַחֲצִיתָם מַבְהִיקִים וְעֵין תְּכֵלֶת מַחֲצִיתָם,

And the roofs look like alabaster
helmets, one half glistening white, the
other blue,

וּלְעֵינֵי כָל־חַי וְהַשֶּׁמֶשׁ מַזְהִירִים —
הָעוֹרְבִים לְבַדָּם עַל־גַּבָּם מַשְׁחִירִים,

shining in the sight of all the living and
of the sun – only the ravens upon them
are black to the eye,

מַחֲלִיקִים עַל־צִפּוּי הַזְּכוּכִית וְצֹרְחִים,
מְנַקְּרִים וְשׂרְטִים — וּפִתְאֹם הֵם פּרְחִים.

sliding and screeching on the glass
glaze, pecking and scratching. Suddenly
they fly off.

וַעֲשַׁן הָאֲרֻבּוֹת, כִּזְקַן עַתִּיק יוֹמִין,
מִסְתַּלְסֵל בְּהָדָר וְנִשָּׂא לַמְּרוֹמִים.

And the smoke from the chimneys, like
the beard of the Ancient of Days, curls
majestically, and rises to the heights.

וְהַקֶּרַח הַלּהֵט בַּכֹּל מְפַעְפֵּעַ,
וּבְלֶב־כֹּל אֹן אֵיתָן כַּמַּסְמֵר נוֹטֵעַ;

And the flaming ice permeates all, and,
like a nail driven home, drives steadfast
force into the heart of all things.

וּבָהִיר וּמוּצָק הָעוֹלָם! זֶה־כֹּחוֹ —
שֶׁכּוֹבֵשׁ אֶת־עַצְמוֹ וְהוּא חָזָק מִתּוֹכוֹ.

How bright and hard is the world! In
this lies its strength – that it masters
itself, drawing its force from within.

מֵרֹב אַמֵּץ כֹּחַ, מֵרֹב עֹצֶר אוֹנִים
מִתְבַּקְּעִים בַּיַּעַר חֲסִינֵי אַלּוֹנִים.

Their strength is so tensed, their
powers so fiercely restrained, that the
sturdiest oaks split apart in the forest.

---

1. As was the Meal-offering at the Temple.

כְּמוֹ רֻתְּקוּ בַזִּקִּים כָּל־מְצוּקֵי הָאָרֶץ
בְּאוֹתוֹ הָרֶגַע שֶׁחָשְׁבוּ הִתְפָּרֵץ,

As though all the pillars of the earth
had been shackled in irons the moment
they had threatened to break loose –

וְהֵם חוֹתְרִים וְחוֹרְגִים מִמִּסְגְּרוֹתֵיהֶם –
עוֹד מְעַט וְהִתְפּוֹצֵץ הַכַּדּוּר מִפְּנֵיהֶם !

and now they are burrowing, straining
to lunge out of their strongholds. Any
moment now they will break the sphere
asunder !

(1902)

עַל הַשְּׁחִיטָה   ON THE SLAUGHTER

שָׁמַיִם, בַּקְּשׁוּ רַחֲמִים עָלָי !
אִם־יֵשׁ בָּכֶם אֵל וְלָאֵל בָּכֶם נָתִיב –
וַאֲנִי לֹא מְצָאתִיו –
הִתְפַּלְלוּ אַתֶּם עָלָי !
אֲנִי – לִבִּי מֵת וְאֵין עוֹד תְּפִלָּה בִּשְׂפָתָי,
וּכְבָר אָזְלַת יָד אַף־אֵין תִּקְוָה עוֹד –
עַד־מָתַי, עַד־אָנָה, עַד־מָתָי ?

Heaven, beg mercy for me! If there is
a God in you, and a pathway through
you to this God – which I have not
discovered – then pray for me! For my
heart is dead, no longer is there prayer
on my lips; all strength is gone, and
hope is no more. Until when, how
much longer, until when?

הַתַּלְיָן ! הֵא צַוָּאר – קוּם שְׁחָט !
עָרְפֵנִי כַּכֶּלֶב, לְךָ זְרֹעַ עִם־קַרְדֹּם,
וְכָל־הָאָרֶץ לִי גַרְדֹּם –
וַאֲנַחְנוּ – אֲנַחְנוּ הַמְעָט !
דָּמִי מֻתָּר – הַךְ קָדְקֹד, וִיזַנֵּק דַּם רֶצַח,
דַּם יוֹנֵק וָשָׂב עַל־כֻּתָּנְתְּךָ –
וְלֹא יִמַּח לָנֶצַח, לָנֶצַח.

You, executioner! Here's my neck – go
to it, slaughter me! Behead me like a
dog, yours is the mighty arm and the
axe, and the whole earth is my scaffold
– and we, we are the few! My blood is
fair game – strike the skull, and
murder's blood, the blood of nurslings
and old men, will spurt onto your
clothes and will never, never be wiped
off.

וְאִם יֵשׁ־צֶדֶק – יוֹפַע מִיָּד !
אַךְ אִם־אַחֲרֵי הִשָּׁמְדִי מִתַּחַת רָקִיעַ
הַצֶּדֶק יוֹפִיעַ –

And if there is justice – let it show
itself at once! But if justice show itself
after I have been blotted out from

יְמַגֵּר־נָא כִסְאוֹ לָעַד !
וּבְרֶשַׁע עוֹלָמִים שָׁמַיִם יָמָקּוּ ;
אַף־אַתֶּם לְכוּ, זֵדִים, בַּחֲמַסְכֶם זֶה
וּבְדַמְכֶם חֲיוּ וְהִנָּקוּ.

beneath the skies – let its throne be
hurled down forever! Let heaven rot
with eternal evil! And you, the arrogant,
go in this violence of yours, live by
your bloodshed and be cleansed by it.

וְאָרוּר הָאוֹמֵר : נְקֹם !
נְקָמָה כָזֹאת, נִקְמַת דַּם יֶלֶד קָטָן
עוֹד לֹא־בָרָא הַשָּׂטָן –
וְיִקֹּב הַדָּם אֶת־הַתְּהוֹם !
יִקֹּב הַדָּם עַד תְּהֹמוֹת מַחֲשַׁכִּים,
וְאָכַל בַּחֹשֶׁךְ וְחָתַר שָׁם
כָּל־מוֹסְדוֹת הָאָרֶץ הַנְּמַקִּים.

And cursed be the man who says:
Avenge! No such revenge – revenge for
the blood of a little child – has yet been
devised by Satan. Let the blood pierce
through the abyss! Let the blood seep
down to the depths of darkness, and
eat away there, in the dark, and breach
all the rotting foundations of the earth.

(1903)

הָיָה עֶרֶב הַקַּיִץ

IT WAS A SUMMER
EVENING

וּבְנוֹת לִילִיּוֹת זַכּוֹת שׁוֹזְרוֹת מוֹזְרוֹת בַּלְּבָנָה
חוּטֵי כֶסֶף מַזְהִירִים,
וְהֵן אֹרְגוֹת כְּסוּת אַחַת לְכֹהֲנִים גְּדוֹלִים
וְלִמְגַדְּלֵי חֲזִירִים.

And the pure daughters of Lilith are
twining-spinning shiny silver threads
by moonlight, weaving one and the
same garment for high priests and for
swineherds.

הָיָה עֶרֶב הַקַּיִץ. כָּל־הַבָּתִּים נִתְרוֹקְנוּ
וְנִתְמַלְאוּ הַגַּנִּים ;
יָצָא אָדָם, כְּדַרְכּוֹ, בְּמַאֲנָיָיו הַגְּדוֹלִים
לַחֲטָאָיו הַקְּטַנִּים.

It was a summer evening. All the
houses emptied out and the parks filled
up. Then man, in his usual manner,
full of grand aspirations, went forth to
his petty sins.

קָצְרָה רוּחַ הָאָדָם, כָּלוּ עֵינֵי מִיַחֵל –
וּתְפִלָּתוֹ הָאַחַת :
'הַכּוֹכָבִים הַצְּנוּעִים, מַהֲרוּ צֵאתְכֶם מִלְמַעְלָה,
וְהַקְּדֵשׁוֹת מִתָּחַת !'

His patience is at an end, his eyes have
grown dim with waiting – and he has
only one prayer: 'O you chaste stars,
come out quickly above, and you,
harlots, below!'

וּבַגָּן זֶה הֵחֵלָּה נְגִינָה קַלָּה, הוֹלֵלָה —
וְהַגָּן כֻּלּוֹ נִנְעָר,
וּמִבֵּין הָאִילָנוֹת הִנֵּה הַשְׁחִיר זְנַב צָעִיף
וְהִלְבִּינָה כְּנַף סִנָּר.

Now a light, licentious melody starts up
in the park, and the whole park comes
to life; from among the trees the tail of
a black veil is glimpsed and the wing of
a white pinafore.

וּכְסַרְסוּרֵי עֲבֵרָה קוֹרְצִים, רוֹמְזִים כּוֹכָבִים,
וְעֵינֵיהֶם פָּז תִּבְעוֹת;
צָרַר רוּחַ הַזְּנוּנִים גַּם אֶת־עֶשְׂבוֹת הַשָּׂדֶה
וְאֶת־אַבְנֵי הָרְחֹבוֹת.

And the stars, like panders, wink and
beckon, their eyes demanding gold;
the spirit of lechery has swept even the
green growth on the fields and the
cobblestones in the street.

וּמֵאֶמְצַע הַנָּהָר וּמִמְּרוֹמֵי הַגְּזוּזְטְרוֹת
וּמֵאַחֲרֵי הַגְּדֵרוֹת
בָּא הַצְּחוֹק — וּבַחַלּוֹנוֹת מוּרָדִים וִילוֹנוֹת
וְכָבִים הַנֵּרוֹת.

And from the middle of the river, from
the heights of balconies, from behind
fences comes the laughter, and in the
windows, curtains are lowered and
candles go out.

הַס, הַשְּׁאָר נָתַן רֵיחוֹ, זוֹלֵל סוֹבֵא הָעוֹלָם,
יֵין עֲנָבִים עֲבָרוֹ,
וְהוּא יוֹצֵא מִדַּעְתּוֹ וּמִתְגּוֹלֵל בְּקִיאוֹ
וּמִתְבּוֹסֵס בִּבְשָׂרוֹ.

Hush! The flesh has given forth its
scent, the world is glutting, guzzling,
overcome with the wine of lust; it is
going out of its mind, rolling in its
spew, weltering in the flesh.

וּבְנוֹת לִילִיּוֹת זַכּוֹת שׁוֹזְרוֹת מוֹזְרוֹת בַּלְּבָנָה
חוּטֵי כֶסֶף מַזְהִירִים,
וְהֵן אֹרְגוֹת כְּסוּת אַחַת לְכֹהֲנִים גְּדוֹלִים
וְלִמְגַדְּלֵי חֲזִירִים.

And the pure daughters of Lilith are
twining-spinning shiny silver threads
by moonlight, weaving one and the
same garment for high priests and for
swineherds.

(1908)

צָנַח לוֹ זַלְזַל   A TWIG ALIGHTED

צָנַח לוֹ זַלְזַל עַל־גָּדֵר וַיָּנֹם —
כֹּה יָשֵׁן אָנֹכִי:
נָשַׁל הַפְּרִי — וּמַה־לִּי וּלְגִזְעִי,
וּמַה־לִּי וּלְשׂוֹכִי ?

A twig alighted on a fence and dozed;
so do I sleep. The fruit fell – and what
have I to do with my trunk, what with
my branch?

נָשַׁל הַפְּרִי, הַפֶּרַח כְּבָר נִשְׁכָּח —
שָׂרְדוּ הֶעָלִים —
יִרְגַּז יוֹם אֶחָד הַסַּעַר — וְנָפְלוּ
אַרְצָה חֲלָלִים.

The fruit fell, the flower is already
forgotten, the leaves survive. One day
the storm will rage, they will drop to
the ground, dead.

אַחַר — וְנִמְשְׁכוּ לֵילוֹת הַזְּוָעָה,
לֹא מְנוּחָה וּשְׁנָת לִי,
בָּדָד אֶתְחַבֵּט בָּאֹפֶל וַאֲרַצֵּץ
רֹאשִׁי אֶל־כָּתְלִי.

Afterwards the nights of dread go on,
no rest or sleep for me, alone I thrash
about in the dark, smashing my head
against my wall.

וְשׁוּב יִפְרַח אָבִיב, וְאָנֹכִי לְבַדִּי
עַל־גִּזְעִי אֶתָּלֶה —
שַׁרְבִיט קֵרֵחַ, לֹא צִיץ לוֹ וָפֶרַח,
לֹא־פְרִי וְלֹא־עָלֶה.

And again spring blossoms, and alone
I hang from my trunk – a bare shoot,
without bud or flower, without fruit or
leaf.

(1911)

שָׁחָה נַפְשִׁי   MY SOUL HAS SUNK DOWN

שָׁחָה נַפְשִׁי לֶעָפָר
תַּחַת מַשָּׂא אַהֲבַתְכֶם;
אֲלָלַי, כִּי הָיִיתִי
אִסְתְּרָא בִּלְגִינַתְכֶם!

My soul has sunk down to the dust
under the burden of your love. Woe is
me, for I have become a coin rattling
in your empty jug.[1]

---

1. An allusion to a Talmudic maxim: 'A coin in an [empty] vessel makes a loud noise: *kish-kish*.'

וְלָמָּה שַׁתֶּם עַל־נָוִי ?
מַה־חַטָּאתִי, מַה־כֹּחִי ?
לֹא מְשׁוֹרֵר, לֹא נָבִיא —
חוֹטֵב עֵצִים אָנֹכִי.

Why have you beset my home? What is my offence, what is my strength? I am not a poet nor a prophet, but a wood-cutter.

חוֹטֵב עֵצִים, אִישׁ קַרְדֹּם,
עוֹשֶׂה מְלַאכְתִּי לְתֻמִּי ;
וְרַד הַיּוֹם, וְיָדִי רָפָתָה,
וְקֵהָה שׁוֹבֶת קַרְדֻּמִּי.

A woodcutter, a man of the axe, doing my work at random, and the day has waned, and my hand hangs limp, and my blunted axe stands still.

שְׂכִיר יוֹם קָצָר אָנֹכִי,
פּוֹעֵל נָטָה לִגְבוּלְכֶם ;
וְלֹא עֵת־דְּבָרִים לִי עָתָּה,
וְלֹא יוֹם תְּרוּעָה לְכָלְכֶם.

I am a day worker, for a short day, a hireling who has chanced into your grounds. This is not a time of words for me, nor a day of trumpeting for you.

אֵיכָה נִשָּׂא פָנֵינוּ ?
בַּמֶּה נְקַדֵּם יוֹם יָבֹא ? —
אִישׁ לְחֶשְׁבּוֹן עוֹלָמוֹ !
אִישׁ לְסִבְלוֹת לְבָבוֹ !

How, then, shall we raise our faces? With what shall we receive the coming day? Let each take stock of his own world! Let each bear the burden of his own heart!

(1923)

שָׁאוּל טְשֶׁרְנִיחוֹבְסְקִי

Saul Tchernikhovsky

[בְּעָמְדִי בֵּין הַחַי]

[AS I STOOD]

בְּעָמְדִי בֵּין הַחַי וּבֵין הַגּוֹסֵס כְּבָר
(אֻמָּנוּת מַה־נּוֹרָאָה !) וְאִזְמֵל חַד בְּכַפִּי,
יֵשׁ בּוֹכֶה מִתּוֹךְ גִּיל וְיֵשׁ מְקַלֵּל בְּאַפִּי,
סָפַגְתִּי אַחֲרוֹן אוֹר תּוֹךְ אִישׁוֹן גּוֹסֵס זָר.

As I stood between the living and those already dying (oh, what a terrible craft!), with a sharp scalpel in my hand, now weeping for joy, now cursing in anger, I absorbed the last light from the pupil of a dying stranger.

אֶל רַעַם תּוֹתְחֵי־אֹן מִתְגַּלְגְּלִים בַּכַּר,
לְאֵשׁ נוֹצְצָה בְּאֶשׁוּן מִנְהַרְתִּי לִי בְנַפִּי
הִתְוֵיתִי אַחֲרוֹן־קָו, מָחַקְתִּי חַי מְדַּפִּי,
מִסַּף מְשׁתָהֶם כָּךְ תֵּעָקֵר אֶבֶן־יְקָר.

וְאוּלָם בְּאוֹתוֹ זִיק בָּעַיִן הָעוֹמֶמֶת,
בָּאוֹר הַסּוֹפֵג אוֹר וּבְטֶרֶם קָם לָעַד ;
וְאוּלָם בְּאוֹתוֹ בְּרַק אֵשׁ קוֹדְחָה וְצוֹרֶמֶת,

בָּאֵשׁ הַקּוֹרְאָה לְאֵשׁ, הַמְצַוָּה אִיד וּשְׁמָד, —
הָיִיתָ אַתָּה בָם ; זֶה הוֹדְךָ הֲמָמָנִי ; —
הַאִם קַדַּמְתִּי בֹא אוֹ אֵחַר צוּר בְּרָאָנִי ?

To the thunder of mighty cannon
rolling over the plain, by the flame that
flickered in my pitchdark trench for me
alone, I drew the last line, I erased a
living being from my page – as a
precious stone is ripped out of a
jewelled goblet.

Yet in that very spark of the fading eye,
in the light that absorbs light before it
dims forever; yet in that very flash of
scorching, lacerating fire,

in the fire that summons fire, ordering
misery and persecution – You were in
them; Your glory overwhelmed me.
Had I come too soon, or was the Rock,
my creator, late?

עַיִט ! עַיִט עַל הָרַיִךְ

EAGLE! EAGLE OVER YOUR MOUNTAINS

עַיִט ! עַיִט עַל הָרַיִךְ, עַיִט עַל הָרַיִךְ עָף !
אַט נָקֵל, — נִדְמֶה כְּאִלּוּ רֶגַע — אֵינוֹ אֶלָּא צָף,
צָף־מַפְלִיג בְּיָם שֶׁל תְּכֵלֶת, עֵר לְרֶנֶן־גִּיל בְּלֵב
הַשָּׁמַיִם־הָרָקִיעַ, חָג אִלֵּם בְּאוֹר צוֹרֵב.

Eagle! Eagle over your mountains, an
eagle over your mountains in flight!
Slow and easy – for an instant, so it
seems – merely floating, floating-
sailing through a sea of blue, alive to
the song of delight in the heart of the
high heavens, mutely circling in the
searing light.

עַיִט ! עַיִט עַל הָרַיִךְ, עַיִט עַל הָרַיִךְ עָף !
יְשַׁר־גֵּו וְכָבֵד־אֵבֶר, שְׁחוֹר־נוֹצָה וּרְחַב־כָּנָף ;
טָס מָתוּחַ (חֵץ מְקֻשֶּׁת), עַיִט עָג עוּגִיּוֹת חוּגָיו ;
תָּר עִקְּבוֹת טַרְפּוֹ מִמַּעַל בָּאֲפָר וּבְחֶגְוָו.

Eagle! Eagle over your mountains, an
eagle over your mountains in flight!
Body rigid, heavy pinions, black-
plumed, broad of wing; soaring, wings
outspread (swift as an arrow), wheeling
round in circle within circle, tracking
its prey from above in meadow and in
cleft.

עַיִט! עַיִט עַל הָרַיִךְ, עַיִט עַל הָרַיִךְ עָף!
טָס גּוֹלֵשׁ־גּוֹלֵשׁ וּבְמַגַּע פֶּלֶא אֵבֶר לֹא נָקָף.
רֶגַע קַל – קָפָא, מִשֶּׁנֵּהוּ – נִיד־לֹא־נִיד בְּאֵב
רֶטֶט כָּל־שֶׁהוּא לְפֶתַע – וְעוֹלֶה לִקְרַאת הָעָב

Eagle! Eagle over your mountains, an
eagle over your mountains in flight!
Soaring, gliding – miracle of motion –
not a wing has wavered. For a second
frozen, then the barest ruffling of the
pinions, suddenly a slight tremor – and
it rises to the clouds.

עַיִט! עַיִט עַל הָרַיִךְ, עַיִט עַל הָרַיִךְ עָף!
אַט נָקַל, – נִדְמֶה כְּאִלּוּ רֶגַע – אֵינוֹ אֶלָּא צָף
אֶרֶץ, עַיִט עַל הָרַיִךְ, – עַל פָּנַיִךְ מַשְׁרַת צֵל,
מֵאֶבְרוֹת עֲנָק חוֹלֶפֶת, מְלַטֶּפֶת הַרְרֵי־אֵל...

(1936)

Eagle! Eagle over your mountains, an
eagle over your mountains in flight!
Slow and easy – for an instant, so it
seems – merely floating . . . O Land,
there is an eagle over your mountains,
and from its giant wings a massive
shadow moves across your face, caress-
ing the mountains of God.

שָׁלֹשׁ אֲתוֹנוֹת

THREE ASSES

(אגדה)

(A Legend)

שָׁלֹשׁ אֲתוֹנוֹת מִשְׂרְכוֹת אֶת דַּרְכָּן,
שָׁלֹשׁ אֲתוֹנוֹת – מִבְּאֵר־שֶׁבַע לְדָן:
חוּמָה וּשְׁחוֹרָה וּצְחוֹרָה, – לְאַט.

Three asses trudge down the road,
three asses plodding from Beersheba to
Dan:[1] one brown, one black, one white.

עָבְרוּ הַשָּׁלֹשׁ עַל־יַד צְרִיחַ מִסְגָּד,
כָּרְעָה הַשְּׁחוֹרָה, כִּי קָרְאוּ לַמּוֹעֵד.
עָבְרוּ הַשָּׁלֹשׁ עַל־יַד פֶּתַח מִנְזָר,
צָנְחָה הַחוּמָה מוּל אִיקוֹנִין מָשְׁזָר.
עָבְרוּ הַשָּׁלֹשׁ עַל חָרְבָּה קְדוֹשָׁה,
עָמְדָה הַצְּחוֹרָה מַרְכִּינָה אֶת רֹאשָׁהּ.

When the three passed by a mosque's
minaret, the black one knelt, hearing
the summons to prayer. When the three
passed by a monastery gate, the brown
one fell down before a braided icon.
When the three passed by a holy ruin,
the white one halted, and bent its head.

1. The proverbial limits of the Land.

עַל־גַּב הַשְּׁחוֹרָה, עַל גַּבָּהּ, סַיִף רָב;
עַל־גַּב הַחוּמָה, עַל גַּבָּהּ, מְטַל צְלָב;
עַל גַּב הַצְּחוֹרָה אַךְ שְׁטִיחַ זָהָב.

On the back of the black one there is a mighty scimitar; on the back of the brown one there lies a crucifix; on the back of the white one – only a golden rug.

אֵין כְּלוּם עַל גַּבָּהּ בִּלְתִּי אִם־הַשָּׁטִיחַ —
בִּמְהֵרָה בְּיָמֵינוּ יִרְכַּב עָלֶיהָ מָשִׁיחַ.

There is nothing on its back, only the rug – *Soon, in our days, may the Messiah ride upon it.*

(1939)

הַמֵּתִים הָרִאשׁוֹנִים

THE FIRST DEAD[1]

'הוּא בָא! הוּא בָא! הוּא כָאן! הוּא כָאן!
הַמָּוֶת הַשָּׁחוֹר!'
אוֹמֵר מַכְרִיז פַּעֲמוֹן־נַגָּן
בַּצְּרִיחַ הַצָּחוֹר.

'He's come! He's come! He's here! He's here! The Black Death!' – proclaims the chiming bell in the white belfry.

'הוּא בָא! הוּא בָא! הוּא כָאן! הוּא כָאן!
אָים הוּא וְנוֹרָא!
בִּצְרִיף שֶׁל עֵץ, וּבְתוֹךְ מִשְׁכַּן
רַבֵּי דָת וּשְׂרָרָה.

'He's come! He's come! He's here! He's here! Most dread and terrible! In wooden huts and in the abodes of the high and mighty!

הוּא בָא! קוֹצֵר אֶת קְצִירוֹ
בָּעִיר בֵּין הַחוֹמוֹת,
בַּכְּפָר וּבַשָּׂדֶה — נִירוֹ;
אַךְ לֹא בַּגֶּטָאוֹת.

'He's here! He's reaping his harvest between the walls of the city, ploughing his furrow in hamlet and field; but not in the ghettos.

---

1. The bubonic plague, known as the Black Death, which devastated much of Europe in the middle of the fourteenth century, was not widespread in the ghettos. The Jews were accused of having poisoned the waters and some 300 communities were destroyed. In several cities, the Jews set fire to their own houses and died in the flames.

בְּמֶרְחַב כָּרִים וְעֵינוֹת טְרָשִׁים
עוֹמֵד עוֹלָם בְּעֵינוֹ, —
הַמָּוֶת שָׁם ; בְּמַעֲפָשִׁים
בַּגְּטָאוֹת – אֵינוֹ.'

'In the broad pastures and along the
craggy springs, nothing has changed:
Death is there. But among the putrid
of the ghettos – no sign of him.'

מַכְרִיז אוֹמֵר הַפַּעֲמֹן :
מֵאָה בְּמֶעֶת־לְעֵת!'/
חוֹזֵר רוֹטֵן קוֹל הֶהָמוֹן :
'בַּגְּטוֹ – שָׁם אֵין מֵת...'.

The bell proclaims: 'A hundred from
dawn to dawn.' The mob growls again:
'In the ghetto – not a single dead.'

מַה יֶּהְגּוּ הֶבֶל הַנְּזִירִים ?
זוֹעֵף אֲסַפְסוּף רָב ?
בַּגְּטוֹ כָּל פָּנִים קוֹדְרִים
מִקּוֹל עָלֶה נִדָּף.

Why are the monks prattling? Why is
the rabble sullen? In the ghetto, every
face darkens at the sound of a fluttering
leaf.

עַד שֶׁהָיְתָה גַם הָרְוָחָה,
שִׂמְחָה גַם בִּמְעוֹנָם :
הִנֵּה בַּגְּטוֹ מֵת! חָה־חָה!
תּוֹדָה לְאֵל עוֹלָם.

Until relief and joy both came into their
dwelling: Look – a death in the ghetto!
Ha! Thank the everlasting God!

לֹא כְדַרְכָּהּ, לֹא מְחִישָׁה,
עֵינֶיהָ מְאִירוֹת,
חֶבְרָה צוֹעֶדֶת קַדִּישָׁא.
צְאוּ, אֶזְרָחִים, לִרְאוֹת.

Not at the usual pace, not in haste, with
shining eyes, the funeral procession[1]
moves along. O, citizens, come out and
see!

לֹא לְשֵׁם מָכוֹר, לֹא לְשֵׁם סָחוֹר,
נָא בֹּאוּ בִגְדוּדִים :
מֻכֵּי הַמָּוֶת הַשָּׁחוֹר!
מֵתִים – שְׁנֵי יְהוּדִים!

Not for wheeling, not for dealing, come
in hordes: these were smitten by the
Black Death! Dead – two Jews!

---

1. Lit. 'the holy brotherhood', the members of the Jewish burial society.

גַּם בָּנוּ, גַּם בַּחֲשׁוּדִים
נָגַף, נוֹדֶה לָאֵל !
גַּם בַּיְּהוּדִים, גַּם בַּיְּהוּדִים
הוּא אֶת קְצִירוֹ הֵחֵל.

We too, we the suspect, have been struck down by Death – thank God! He has begun his reaping of the Jews too, yes, of the Jews.

חֲבָל, הַצְּרִיחַ הַצָּחוֹר
לֹא לָנוּ, וְאֵין פַּעֲמוֹן,
וְיַכְרִיז – 'הַמָּוֶת הַשָּׁחוֹר
כְּבָר בָּא !' – פַּרְנָס־הֶגְמוֹן !

A pity! The white belfry is not ours, *Judenbischof*,[1] and we have no bell that might proclaim: – 'The Black Death has already come!'

(1942)

יַעֲקֹב פִיכְמַן *Jacob Fichman*

שׁוּלַמִּית THE SHULAMMITE

אַתְּ שׁוּלַמִּית. צִפּוֹר שְׁכוּחָה בַּכֶּרֶם.
אַתְּ לֵב פָּרַח בְּאֶרֶץ עֲזוּבָה.
וּבֵין הָרֵי־בְשָׂמִים, אוֹבֶדֶת דֶּרֶךְ,
אַתְּ לְדוֹדֵךְ שׁוֹאֶלֶת כּוֹאָבָה.

You are the Shulammite. A bird forgotten in a vineyard; a heart that flowered in a desolate land. And, lost among the spicebearing mountains, heartsick, you seek your lover.

הַעַל כִּי הִכְלִימוּךְ אַחַיִךְ אַתְּ נִסְעֶרֶת,
כִּי הָרוֹעִים סָנְטוּ בָךְ אַתְּ דָּוָה –
וְאַתְּ אַחַת בְּתֻם־חִנֵּךְ כְּבַחֶרֶב
גּוֹזֶרֶת לֵב עוֹלָם. אַתְּ אֲהוּבָה.

Are you so overwrought because your brothers shamed you? So hurt because the shepherds sneered at you? You only, with your innocent charm, like a sword, split the heart of the world. You are loved.

הַיּוֹם שָׁזַף לֶחְיֵךְ וְלֵיל בִּכֵּר
בַּצֵּל גְּבִיעֵךְ, כְּפֶרַח מְשַׁכֵּר,
בְּכָל סִתְרֵי גַּנֵּךְ יָצַק חֶמְדָּה.

Day bronzed your cheeks and night ripened your chalice in the shadow, like an intoxicating flower, pouring loveliness into all the coverts of your garden.

1. 'Jews' Bishop', the head of the Jewish community.

אֵיךְ לֹא מָצָא בַּסֶּלַע נְתִיבֶךָ
דּוֹדֵךְ עַד פֹּה – וְרֵיחַ אֲבִיבֵךְ,
כְּמוֹר עוֹבֵר כָּל אֶרֶץ יְהוּדָה !

How is it that your beloved has not yet found your pathway through the rocks – when the fragrance of your spring like myrrh sweeps over the whole land of Judea.

אַבְרָהָם בֶּן־יִצְחָק

Avraham ben Yitshak

אַשְׁרֵי הַזּוֹרְעִים וְלֹא יִקְצֹרוּ

HAPPY ARE THEY WHO SOW

אַשְׁרֵי הַזּוֹרְעִים וְלֹא יִקְצֹרוּ
כִּי יַרְחִיקוּ נְדוֹד.

Happy are they who sow but do not reap, for they wander afar.

אַשְׁרֵי הַנְּדִיבִים אֲשֶׁר תִּפְאֶרֶת נְעוּרֵיהֶם
הוֹסִיפָה עַל אוֹר הַיָּמִים וּפִזְרוֹנָם
וְהֵם אֶת עֶדְיָם הִתְפָּרְקוּ עַל אֵם הַדְּרָכִים.

Happy are the noble of heart whose youthful glories enhanced the days' light and largesse, while they themselves stripped off their ornaments at the parting of the ways.

אַשְׁרֵי הַגֵּאִים אֲשֶׁר גַּאֲוָתָם עָבְרָה גְּבוּלֵי נַפְשָׁם
וַתְּהִי כְּעַנְוַת הַלֹּבֶן
אַחֲרֵי הֵעָלוֹת הַקֶּשֶׁת בֶּעָנָן.

Happy are the proud-of-heart whose pride overflowed the borders of their soul, and came to be the humility of white after the rainbow has risen into the clouds.

אַשְׁרֵי הַיֹּדְעִים אֲשֶׁר יִקְרָא לְבָּם מִמִּדְבָּר
וְעַל שְׂפָתָם תִּפְרַח הַדּוּמִיָּה.

Happy are they who know that their heart cries out from a wilderness, and silence blossoms on their lips.

אַשְׁרֵיהֶם כִּי יֵאָסְפוּ אֶל תּוֹךְ לֵב הָעוֹלָם
לוּטֵי אַדֶּרֶת הַשִּׁכְחָה
וְהָיָה חֶקָּם הַתָּמִיד בְּלִי אֹמֶר.

Happy are they – for they will be gathered into the heart of the world, wrapped in oblivion's robe, and their everlasting lot[1] will be wordless.

---

1. Or, 'their lot will be a constant offering (*tamid*) without words'.

JACOB STEINBERG

[שַׁחַר שֶׁל מִי]   [WHOSE DAWN]

שַׁחַר שֶׁל מִי קָרָא הַגֶּבֶר
וְשָׁבָה הַחַשְׁכָה עַל תְּרוּעָתוֹ הַנֶּחֱרָה
וְיֶדְכֶם הָרְשָׁלָה אֲשֶׁר עַל עֵינֵיכֶם הֶאֱהִילָה
מִפְּנֵי גְבוּרַת שֶׁמֶשׁ וְהֵן לֹא בָּאָה
הֵן פֶּה וְיָד שָׁקָרוּ.

Whose dawn did the cock proclaim?
And the darkness reiterated his
wheezing fanfare; and your feeble hand
that shielded your eyes from the sun's
might – but no sun had come. The
mouth and the hand – both had lied.

יַעֲקֹב שְׁטַינְבֶּרְג   *Jacob Steinberg*

[כְּזוּג טוֹרְפִים]   [LIKE TWO BEASTS OF PREY]

כְּזוּג טוֹרְפִים תּוֹעֵי־לַיְל וּמֻכֵּי־צָמָא, –
מְרוּץ וַעֲרָג לְאֵד יְאוֹרִים מְתוּקִים
כִּי יִפְּלוּ עַל שְׂפַת בְּרֵכָה נֶאֱלָמָה;

Like two beasts of prey, lost in the
night and stricken by thirst, who had
scurried about, panting for the vapour
of sweet waters, then dropped beside
the banks of a soundless pool,

כִּי יִשְׁעוּ לְדָבָר־מָה מִן הָאֲפֵלָה
וּכְאֶחָד הֵם נוֹאָשִׁים וְזוֹמְמִים,
רַק שְׂפֵי קְצֵה הַגַּלִּים הַדּוֹמְמִים
לְשׁוֹנָם תָּלֹק רֶגַע וְחָדֵלָה: –

and, overhearing something in the
darkness, desperate and wary in the
same breath, they only let their tongues
gently lick the edges of the still waves,
for an instant, then stop –

בְּלַהַט מַעֲרֻמֵּינוּ הַנֶּחֱרִים
כֵּן נַחְנוּ אָז, נוֹאָשִׁים וַחֲבוּקִים,
עַל שְׂפַת יְאוֹר עֹנֶג נָם וְגַל לֹא יָרִים.

thus, in the ardour of our parched
nakedness, we paused, despairing and
embraced, on the banks of a slumbering
lake of pleasure, where not one wave
stirred.

[לֹא גַן נָעוּל]

[NOT AN ENCLOSED GARDEN]

לֹא גַן נָעוּל הָעוֹלָם ; בְּיוֹם צַר לְעֵת שֵׂיבָה
שֶׁבַע שְׂמָחוֹת יָצֵרוּ אֶת תּוּגָתְךָ הַשְּׁלֵנָה.

The world is not an enclosed garden;
in time of trouble, when your hair is
grey, seven joys will harass your
tranquil sorrow.

שְׁפִי תִּצְעַד הַזִּקְנָה ; גַּם בִּנְאוֹת הַמַּזְקִינִים
שׁוֹרֵץ שֶׁפֶק אַכְזָרִי עִם עַקְרַבֵּי הַמִּינִים.

Old age steps gingerly. Even the oases
of the aged swarm with cruel doubts
and scorpions of heresy.

דּוּמָם תֵּשֵׁב וּתְהַרְהֵר – שָׁבְתָה דַּרְכִּי הַסְּלוּלָה –
וּמֵעֵבֶר לָהּ יַעַל הֲמוֹן־עָם בַּהֲמֻלָּה.

Silently, you sit and muse: my highway
is deserted, and the clamour of the
mob thunders beyond it.

בַּקֶּר תָּקִיץ וְתָחוּד : תְּקוּפָה אַחַת נָגֹלָה –
וּבְנֵי־עָשׁ בְּשׁוּלֶיהָ כְּבָר נִנְעָרִים שְׁאוֹלָה.

In the morning you wake up and
wonder at the riddle: one era has been
rolled up,[1] and from its rim the stars
are already shaken off into the nether-
world.

אַךְ בְּשֶׁקֶט עֶרֶב בָּהִיר רַנִּים יַחַד מַזָּלוֹת,
וּבֵין מַזָּל לְמַזָּל רַק כִּגְבוּל הַנִּמְשָׁלוֹת.

But in the quiet of a clear evening all
the planets sing in unison, and between
one planet and another there is no
more than a thin boundary-line as in
a parable.

אָז אֵין נִבְדָּל וָשָׁב ; וַאֲשֶׁר נִשְׁפַּט לָרָקָב –
רוֹאֶה קֶבֶר וּמַחֲרִישׁ וּמִתְאַפֵּק אֶל שְׁחָקָיו.

Then none is separate and none turns
back; and he who has been condemned
to decay sees the grave, is silent, and
holds his peace in the face of heaven.

1. 'The heavens shall be rolled up like a scroll' – Isaiah 34.4.

דָּוִד פוֹגֶל   *David Vogel*

[כִּי יִגַּשׁ הַלַּיְל]

[WHEN NIGHT DRAWS NEAR]

כִּי יִגַּשׁ הַלַּיְל אֶל חַלּוֹנֵךְ —
צְאִי אֵלָיו עֲרֻמָּה.

When night draws near your window,
come to him naked.

רַךְ יִזַּל וְיַשְׁחִיר
סְבִיב יָפְיֵךְ הַשּׁוֹקֵט,
וְיִגַּע קְצוֹת שָׁדַיִךְ.

Softly will he ripple and darken round
your still beauty, touching the tips of
your breasts.

אִתּוֹ אֶעֱמֹד אֹבַד־דֶּרֶךְ
וְחֶרֶשׁ נִתְאָו:
בֹּאִי אֶל אֲפֵלֵנוּ.

I shall stand with him there, a stray
wanderer, and silently we shall yearn:
come into our dark.

וְתִסַּעְנָה שְׁתֵּי עֵינַיִךְ
לְפָנֵינוּ
לָאִיר לִי וּלְרֵעִי. —

And let your two eyes travel before us
to light the way for me and my friend.

[בָּעֲלִיָּה]

[IN THE ATTIC]

בָּעֲלִיָּה
נִתְלִים מֵתֵינוּ עֲרֻמִּים
אִישׁ עַל רֵעֵהוּ.

Our dead hang in the attic, naked, one
on top of the other.

לַיְלָה עַל לַיְלָה
הֵם תְּלוּיִים בַּחֲבוּרָה
וְשׁוֹתְקִים.

Night after night they hang banded
together, keeping silent.

כִּי רַבּוּ הַיָּמִים
יִכְחַשׁ בְּשָׂרָם וְיִבָּל.
הַגְּוִיּוֹת תֶּאֱרַכְנָה מְאֹד.

As the days go by, their flesh wastes
away and withers. The corpses become
very long.

הַשּׁוֹמֵר הָעִוֵּר
יוֹשֵׁב לָנֶצַח עֲלֵיהֶם
וִיצַוֶּה הַמְּנוּחָה.

The blind watchman sits over them
forever, ordaining rest.

[אַל תִּירָא, יַלְדִּי]   [DON'T BE AFRAID]

אַל תִּירָא, יַלְדִּי,
רַק שְׁנֵי עַכְבָּרִים הֵם
הַקּוֹפְצִים מִן הַשֻּׁלְחָן אֶל הַכִּסֵּא.
קְטַנִּים הֵם מִמְּךָ
וְלֹא יוּכְלוּ בָּלְעֶךָ.

Don't be afraid, my child, those are
only two mice, jumping down from the
table to the chair. They are smaller
than you and couldn't gobble you up.

אַל תִּירָא, יַלְדִּי,
רַק אֶצְבַּע הַגֶּשֶׁם הִיא,
הַדּוֹפֶקֶת רְטֻבָּה בַּחַלּוֹן —
לֹא נִפְתַּח לוֹ.

Don't be afraid, my child, that's only
the rain's finger tapping wetly on the
window. We won't let it in.

הֵחָבֵא בִּי הֵיטֵב,
אֲנִי אִמֶּךָ.
נִמְשֹׁךְ לַיִל אָפֵל מֵעַל לְרָאשֵׁנוּ
וְאִישׁ לֹא יִמְצָאֵנוּ.

Hide deep inside me, I am your mother.
We'll pull the dark night over our
heads and no one will find us.

[עָרַי נְעוּרַי]   [MY CHILDHOOD CITIES]

עָרַי נְעוּרַי,
עַתָּה אֶת כֻּלָּן כְּבָר שָׁכַחְתִּי
וְאוֹתָךְ בְּאַחַת מֵהֵנָּה.

My childhood cities, by now I've
forgotten them all, and you in one of
them.

תּוֹךְ שְׁלוּלִית מֵי־גֶשֶׁם
יְחֵפָה בִּשְׁבִילִי עוֹד תִּרְקֹדִי —
וְהִנֵּה וַדַּאי כְּבָר מַתְּ.

You still dance on for me in a puddle
of rainwater - but surely you're already
dead.

מִתּוֹךְ יַלְדוּתִי הָרְחוֹקָה
לִדְהֹר אֵיךְ נֶחְפַּזְתִּי,
עַד בּוֹא אֶל הֵיכַל הַזִּקְנָה הַלָּבָן —
וְהוּא רָחָב וָרֵיק.

How quickly I galloped out of my
distant childhood, until I reached the
white palace of old age, and found it
wide and empty.

רֵאשִׁית דַּרְכִּי
שׁוּב לֹא אֶרְאֶה,
וְאוֹתָךְ לֹא אֶרְאֶה,
וְלֹא אוֹתִי מֵאָז.

I can no longer see my road's beginning; I cannot see you or the self that
I was.

אֹרְחַת הַיָּמִים,
מֵרָחוֹק,
לָנוּעַ תּוֹסִיף הָלְאָה,
מֵאַיִן אֶל אָיִן,
בִּלְעָדַי.

The caravan of days, from afar, will
move on its way, from nothingness to
nothingness, without me.

יִשְׂרָאֵל אֶפְרָת · *Israel Efrat*

הָאֲנִי צְעָקָה · THE I, A SCREAM

פְּכְפּוּךְ דָּם חַם אֶל תּוֹךְ מַשְׁפֵּךְ, · The bubbling of warm blood into a funnel, and infinite,
וְאֵינְסוֹפִי,

וְעֹמֶק שִׁכָּרוֹן שֶׁל הֲוָיָה מִבַּעַד סְגוֹר עֵינַיִם — · the deep intoxication of a life behind the eyes' cage –
פִּתְאֹם עוֹלָם,

וְקוֹל צוֹעֵק מִתַּחַת לַסַּכִּין : · and a voice screaming under the knife: 'I!'
אֲנִי ! —

וּלְכָל חַיָּיו שֶׁל הָאָדָם כּוֹאֲבִים צְדָדָיו · And for the rest of man's life, his sides hurt like the sides of the moon.
כְּמוֹ צְדָדָיו שֶׁל הַיָּרֵחַ.

וְאֵין חַוָּה עוֹלָה מֵחֶתֶךְ זֶה, · And no Eve rises out of this gash; there is no reparation.
וְאֵין פִּצּוּי.

אוּרִי צְבִי גְּרִינְבֶּרג · *Uri Zvi Greenberg*

עִם אֵלִי הַנַּפָּח · WITH MY GOD, THE BLACKSMITH

כְּפִרְקֵי נְבוּאָה בּוֹעֲרִים יָמוֹתַי בְּכָל הַגִּלּוּיִים · Like chapters of prophecy, my days burn in all their revelations, and my body, in their midst, is like a melted mass of metal. And over me stands my God, the blacksmith, hammering mightily. Every wound that Time has cut in me, opens its gash and spits forth the pent-up fire in sparks of moments.
וְגוּפִי בֵּינֵיהֶם כְּגוּשׁ הַמַּתֶּכֶת לְהִתּוּךְ.
וְעָלַי עוֹמֵד אֵלִי הַנַּפָּח וּמַכֶּה בִּגְבוּרָה :
כָּל פֶּצַע, שֶׁחָתַךְ הַזְּמַן בִּי, פּוֹתֵחַ לוֹ חִתּוּךְ
וּפוֹלֵט בְּגִצֵּי רְגָעִים הָאֵשׁ הָעֲצוּרָה.

זֶהוּ גּוֹרָלִי־מִשְׁפָּטִי עַד עֶרֶב בַּדֶּרֶךְ.
וּבְשׁוּבִי לְהָטִיל אֶת גּוּשִׁי הַמֻּכֶּה עַל עֶרֶשׂ,
פִּי – פֶּצַע פָּתוּחַ.
וְעֵירֹם אֲדַבֵּר עִם אֵלִי : עָבַדְתָּ בְּפָרֶךְ.
עַתָּה בָּא לַיְלָה ; תֵּן – שְׁנֵינוּ נָנוּחַ.

This is my fate, my daily lot, until evening falls. And when I return to fling my beaten mass upon the bed, my mouth is a gaping wound. Then, naked, I speak to my God: 'You have worked so hard. Now night has come; let us both rest.'

בְּשׁוּלֵי שָׁמַיִם – –

AT THE RIM OF THE HEAVENS

כְּאַבְרָהָם וְשָׂרָה בְּאֵלוֹנֵי מַמְרֵא
לִפְנֵי הַבְּשׂוֹרָה הַיְקָרָה,
וּכְדָוִד וּבַת שֶׁבַע בְּבֵית הַמַּלְכוּת
בְּחִבַּת לַיְלָה רִאשׁוֹן,
עוֹלִים אָבִי וְאִמִּי קְדוֹשִׁים
בְּמַעֲרָב עַל הַיָּם,
וְכָל נְגֹהוֹת־אֱלֹהִים עֲלֵיהֶם –
מִכֹּבֶד יָפְיָם הֵם שׁוֹקְעִים .. לְאַט ;
מֵעַל לְרָאשֵׁיהֶם זוֹרֵם הַיָּם הָאַדִּיר,
תַּחְתָּיו בֵּיתָם הֶעָמֹק –
– –

Like Abraham and Sarah by the terebinths of Mamre[1] before the precious tidings, and like David and Bathsheba, in the king's palace, in the tenderness of their first night – my martyred father and mother rise in the West over the sea with all the aureoles of God upon them. Weighed down by their beauty they sink, slowly. Above their heads flows the mighty ocean, beneath it is their deep home.

קִירוֹת אֵין לַבַּיִת הַזֶּה מִשּׁוּם צַד,
מַיִם־בְּמַיִם בָּנוּי הוּא.
בָּאִים בִּשְׂחִיָּה טְבוּעֵי יִשְׂרָאֵל
מִכָּל עֶבְרֵי יָם
וְכוֹכָב בְּפִיהֶם ..
וַאֲשֶׁר הֵם שָׂחִים שָׁם,
אֵין יוֹדֵעַ הַשִּׁיר ;
יוֹדְעִים הֵם – שֶׁבַּיָּם – –

This home has no walls on any side, it is built of water within water. The drowned of Israel come swimming from all the corners of the sea, each with a star in his mouth. And what they speak of there, the poem does not know; only they know who are in the sea.

---

1. Where the angels announced to Abraham that Sarah would bear him a son (Genesis 18.1 ff).

כְּכִנּוֹר כָּבוּי מִזִּיו נִגּוּן מַקְרִין —
כֵּן אֲנִי, בְּנָם הַטּוֹב,
הָעוֹמֵד אָז רָם־עִם־הַזְּמַן עַל חוֹף יָם.

And I, their good son, am like a lyre
whose radiant melody has been stopped,
as I stand, towering with Time, on the
seashore.

וְיֵשׁ : עֶרֶב הוֹלֵךְ לְלִבִּי עִם הַיָּם . .
וַאֲנִי — הוֹלֵךְ אֶל הַיָּם.
כְּלִשׁוּלֵי שָׁמַיִם נִקְרֵאתִי לַחֲזוֹת :
מִזֶּה וּמִזֶּה לְגַלְגַּל הַחַמָּה
הַשּׁוֹקַעַת
נִרְאֶה וְנִרְאֵית :
אָבִי מִיָּמִין וְאִמִּי מִשְּׂמֹאל ;
וְתַחַת כַּפּוֹת רַגְלֵיהֶם הַיְחֵפוֹת
זוֹרֵם הַיָּם הַבּוֹעֵר — —

And at times the evening and the sea
run into my heart, and I run to the sea.
I am summoned, as if to the rim of the
heavens, to behold: on either side of
the sinking globe of the sun, he is seen,
she is seen: my father to the right and
my mother to the left; and beneath
their bare feet flows the burning sea.

בְּלֵיל גֶּשֶׁם בִּירוּשָׁלַיִם

ON A NIGHT OF RAIN IN JERUSALEM

עֲצֵי מְעַט בֶּחָצֵר הוֹמִים כַּעֲצֵי יַעַר,
כִּבְדֵי נְהָרוֹת עֲנָנִים מְרָעֲמִים,
מַלְאֲכֵי הַשָּׁלוֹם לִמְרַאֲשׁוֹת יְלָדַי
בַּהֲמִיַּת הָעֵצִים וְחַשְׁרַת הַגְּשָׁמִים.

The few trees in the yard moan like a
forest. The thunderous clouds are
heavy with rivers. The Angels of Peace
stand at the head of my sleeping
children, as the trees moan and the
heavy rains pour down.

בַּחוּץ — יְרוּשָׁלַיִם : עִיר מַסַּת הוֹד הָאָב
וַעֲקֵדַת בְּנוֹ בְּאַחַד הֶהָרִים :
הָאֵשׁ־מִשַּׁחֲרִית עוֹד דּוֹלֶקֶת בָּהָר
הַגְּשָׁמִים לֹא כִבּוּהָ : אֵשׁ בֵּין הַבְּתָרִים.

Outside: Jerusalem, city of the Father's[1]
glorious trial, where he bound his son
on one of the hills. That fire, kindled
at dawn, still burns on the hill, the
rains have not put it out: it is the fire
between the sacrificial pieces.[2]

1. Abraham.   2. Genesis 15.17.

'אִם אֵל יְצַוֵּנִי כָעֵת כְּשֶׁצִוָּה
לְאָבִי הַקַּדְמוֹן – אֲצַיֵּת בְּוַדַּאי',
רָן לִבִּי וּבְשָׂרִי בְּלֵיל הַגֶּשֶׁם הַזֶּה
וּמַלְאֲכֵי הַשָּׁלוֹם לִמְרַאֲשׁוֹתֵי יְלָדָי !

'If God were to command me now, as
once He did my ancient Father, I
would surely obey,' sing my heart and
my flesh on this night of rain, as the
Angels of Peace stand at the head of
my sleeping children!

מַה מֵּהוֹד מַה מָּשָׁל לְזֶה רֶגֶשׁ פְּלָאִי
חַי מִקֶּדֶם שַׁחֲרִית עַד כָּעֵת אֶל הַר מוֹר:
מִתְרוֹגֵן דַּם הַבְּרִית בְּגוּף אָב תְּפִלִּי
נָכוֹן לְקָרְבַּן הַר הַבַּיִת עִם אוֹר !

What can equal this glory, this
wondrous zeal – alive since that ancient
dawn to this very moment – for the
Mount of Moriah? The blood of the
covenant sings on in the father's
fervent body. He is prepared to offer
his sacrifice on the Temple Mount at
dawn.

בַּחוּץ – יְרוּשָׁלַיִם .. וְהֶמְיַת עֲצֵי יָהּ
שֶׁכְּרָתוּם הָאוֹיְבִים בָּהּ מִכָּל הַדּוֹרוֹת ..
עֲנָנִים כִּבְדֵי נְהָרוֹת: בָּם בְּרָקִים
וּרְעָמִים, שֶׁהֵם לִי בְּלֵיל גֶּשֶׁם – בְּשׂוֹרוֹת
מִפִּי הַגְּבוּרָה עַד סוֹף הַדּוֹרוֹת.

(1954)

Outside: Jerusalem, and the moaning
of the Lord's trees, cut down by her
enemies in every generation; clouds
heavy with rain, lightnings in them and
thunders which, for me, on this night
of rain, are tidings from the mouth
of the God of Might to endless
generations.

כְּרִיתַת כָּנָף

THE SEVERING OF THE
WING

לְפֶתַע וּלְפִתְאוֹם בְּבֹקֶר לֹא עָבוֹת
וְרֵיחַ כָּל הַצּוֹמֵחַ נָדָף
וְכָל הַצִּפֳּרִים עָפוֹת בְּמִין כָּנָף אַחַת ..
אַלְלַי לְכָל רוֹאָן בְּכָךְ וְהוּא לֹא נָטַל בְּיָדָיו
אֶת עִנְבֵי עֵינָיו וְלֹא סָחַט !

So very suddenly, one cloudless
morning, the fragrance of growth filling
the air, and all the birds were flying
with some sort of single wing . . . Woe
to the man who, seeing them thus, did
not pluck the grapes of his eyes and
crush them with his hands!

גַּם הַצִּפֳּרִים עַצְמָן אֵינָן יוֹדְעוֹת מִי קִצֵּץ לָהֶן כָּנָף
לְפֶתַע וּלְפִתְאוֹם הֵן עָפוֹת כָּךְ בָּאֲוִיר
נוֹטוֹת אֶל צַד..
וְאַף דָּם אֵינוֹ נוֹטֵף וְאֵין הֶכֵּר כִּי לְכָל צִפּוֹר
הָיוּ שְׁתֵּי כְנָפַיִם לְהַעֲבִיר

Even the birds, they themselves, do not
know who cut off their wing. So very
suddenly, and they were flying through
the air, thus, tilted to one side. And no
blood drips, and there is no sign that
every bird once had two wings, to
carry

לְבָבוֹת דִּכְסִיפִין מֵהָכָא לְהָתָם —
עַכְשָׁו אֵין יוֹתֵר לְהָתָם.
בִּדְבַר אֱלֹהִים כְּמוֹ בַחֲלוֹם נֶחְתְּכָה כָנָף
וְעַל מְקוֹם הַחִתּוּךְ חָתַם.

yearning hearts from over-here to
over-there. Now over-there is no more.
By the word of God, as if in a dream,
the wing was cut off, and then He
sealed up the gash.

(1955)

מַעֲשֶׂה בְּאֶחָד שֶׁיָּצָא מִמִּנְעָלָיו

THE MAN WHO STEPPED OUT OF HIS SHOES

עָמַדְתִּי וּשְׁתֵּי עֵינַי רָאוּ
לֹא יָדַעְתִּי מִי הָאִישׁ וּשְׁמוֹ מַהוּ
וּמָה הֵם סִבְכֵי מְאֹרָעָיו,
הָיָה זֶה בֹּקֶר שֶׁכֻּלּוֹ זָהָב
וּבָא הָאִישׁ עֲדֵי עַמּוּד חַשְׁמַל
כְּאֶל מְקוֹם הַגְּבוּל שֶׁבּוֹ בָחַר
וְשָׁם יָצָא מִמִּנְעָלָיו
וְהִשְׁאִירָם לַעֲמֹד שָׁם כְּאֶל סַף
וְהֵחֵל לִפְסֹעַ בְּרַגְלַיִם יְחֵפוֹת
אֶל מֵעֵבֶר זֶה מְקוֹם הַסּוֹף
אֱלֵי בְרֵאשִׁית אֵין קֵץ הַרְחֵק:
בְּלִי בַיִת בְּלִי מִשְׁכָּב בְּלִי חֵיק:
בְּלִי כִכַּר לֶחֶם בְּלִי צַפַּחַת...קַל וָרֵיק.

I stood, and my two eyes saw this: I
didn't know who the man was, his
name, or his tangled history. It was a
morning all of gold, and this man
marched up to the electric pole as if to
a borderline that he had chosen, and
there he stepped out of his shoes, and,
leaving them behind, as if on a
threshold, he began walking barefoot,
to somewhere beyond this final point,
towards an endless beginning far in the
distance . . . without house, or bed, or
bosom, without a loaf of bread or a jar
of water . . . light and empty-handed.

אֲנִי רָאִיתִי אֶת רַחֲבוּת כְּתֵפָיו
קוֹמַת גּוּפוֹ וּמִצְעֲדֵי גַבְרוּת
הוֹלֵךְ הוֹלֵךְ מִכָּאן אֶל מֶרְחַקָּיו
בְּלִי זֵכֶר מִנְעָלָיו פֹּה. מְחַכָּיו.

I saw his broad shoulders, his high
stature, his manly steps, going away,
going from here to his distances,
without the memory of his shoes, which
wait for him here.

שִׁמְעוֹן הַלְקִין

Simon Halkin

דִּין־אֱמֶת

THE TRUE JUDGE

שֶׁאֵין אֶלָּא חַיִּים הַלָּלוּ, כָּאן נִשְׁנִים עַל אֲדָמָה
שְׁחוֹרָה,
אֱמֹר אֱמֹר עִם שֶׁמְּבָרֵךְ אַתָּה דַּיַּן־אֱמֶת לְאוֹר בְּרָקוֹ
שֶׁל דִּין מוֹרִיק בִּטְרִיז כּוֹכַב־הָעֶרֶב.

That there is nothing but this life,
repeated here on the black soil, say it,
say it as you bless the True Judge by
the light of judgement's sudden flash,
shining green in the wedge of an
evening star.

וְכָאן בָּרֵךְ דַּיַּן־אֱמֶת עִם שֶׁמְּנַשֵּׁק אַתָּה פִּי אֵם
שֶׁמֵּתָה,
שֶׁמֵּתָה וְלֹא תָשׁוּב וּפִיהָ שָׁב וְחַי בְּנֵכֶל אַהֲבָה
לְאוֹר בְּרָקָיו כְּחֻלִּים שֶׁל שַׂר־הַלַּיְלָה.

And, here, bless the True Judge, as you
kiss the mouth of a dead mother, who
died, never to come back, but whose
mouth comes to life again and again, in
love's duplicity, by the light of the
Prince of Night's blue lightnings.

לְאוֹר גְּשָׁמִים הַלָּלוּ כָּאן, שְׁחוֹרִים וְגַם כְּחֻלִּים
לְעֵת הַלַּיְלָה
כְּאָז בִּכְפַר־מוֹלֶדֶת, מְזַדַּמְזֵם בַּצַּפְצָפוֹת בְּעַד חַלּוֹן
בִּבְרַד חִפּוּשִׁיּוֹת טְרוּפוֹת־הַחֵשֶׁק,

By the light of these rains here, black,
blue, when the night – as in my native
village – drones in the poplars by the
window, in a hail of beetles frenzied
with desire,

בָּרֵךְ דַּיַּן־אֱמֶת בְּזִיעַ, חָשָׁה־לֹא־הֵבִינָה אִם שֶׁמֵּתָה,
תָּחוּשׁ־וְלֹא־תָבִין אוֹהֶבֶת צוֹפִיָּה סוּמָה לְזֶרַע
הַלַּיְלָה –
בָּרֵךְ דַּיַּן־אֱמֶת הָרָה לָנֶצַח.

bless the True Judge with the tremor
which the dying mother felt and did
not understand, which your love,
blindly looking for the seed of night,
feels and does not understand – bless
the True Judge eternally conceiving.

533

אַבְרָהָם שְׁלוֹנְסְקִי   *Abraham Shlonsky*

[עָמָל]   [TOIL]

הַלְבִּישִׁינִי, אִמָּא כְּשֵׁרָה, כְּתֹנֶת פַּסִּים לְתִפְאֶרֶת
וְעִם שַׁחֲרִית הוֹבִילִינִי אֱלֵי עָמָל.

Dress me, good mother, in a glorious
robe of many colours,[1] and at dawn
lead me to [my] toil.

עוֹטְפָה אַרְצִי אוֹר כַּטַּלִּית,
בָּתִּים נִצְּבוּ כַּטּוֹטָפוֹת,
וְכִרְצוּעוֹת תְּפִלִּין גּוֹלְשִׁים כְּבִישִׁים, סָלְלוּ כַּפַּיִם.

My land is wrapped in light as in a
prayer shawl. The houses stand forth
like frontlets; and the roads paved by
hand, stream down like phylactery
straps.

תְּפִלַּת שַׁחֲרִית פֹּה תִּתְפַּלֵּל קִרְיָה נָאָה אֱלֵי בּוֹרְאָהּ.
וּבַבּוֹרְאִים – בְּנֵךְ אַבְרָהָם,
פַּיְטָן־סוֹלֵל בְּיִשְׂרָאֵל.

Here the lovely city says the morning
prayer to its Creator. And among the
creators is your son Abraham, a road-
building bard of Israel.

וּבָעֶרֶב בֵּין הַשְּׁמָשׁוֹת יָשׁוּב אַבָּא מִסִּבְלוֹתָיו
וְכִתְפִלָּה יִלְחַשׁ נַחַת:
– הַבֵּן יַקִּיר לִי אַבְרָהָם,
עוֹר וְגִידִים וַעֲצָמוֹת –
הַלְלוּיָהּ.

And in the evening twilight, father will
return from his travails, and, like a
prayer, will whisper joyfully: 'My dear
son Abraham, skin, sinews and bones –
hallelujah.'

הַלְבִּישִׁינִי, אִמָּא כְּשֵׁרָה, כְּתֹנֶת פַּסִּים לְתִפְאֶרֶת
וְעִם שַׁחֲרִית הוֹבִילִינִי
אֱלֵי עָמָל.

Dress me, good mother, in a glorious
robe of many colours, and at dawn lead
me to toil.

---

1. Genesis 27.3.

ABRAHAM SHLONSKY

קֵץ אֲדָר   LATE ADAR[1]

כְּאֶצְעָדוֹת־הַזָּהָב אֲשֶׁר לִזְרוֹעוֹת הַבֶּדְוִיָּה,
יַעַנְדוּ הָרֵי הַגִּלְבֹּעַ לְעֵמֶק יִזְרְעֶאל
אֶת צְמִידֵיהֶם
בִּשְׁעוֹת הַזָּהָב אֲשֶׁר לְעַרְבֵי קֵץ־אֲדָר.
אָז תֵּצֶאןָ הַשּׁאָבוֹת הָעַיְנָה,
וְהָיוּ הַכַּלָּנִיּוֹת כְּאֶצְעָדוֹת לְרַגְלֵיהֶן.

Like the golden bangles on the arms of
a Bedouin woman, the hills of Gilboa
bind their bracelets about the valley of
Jezreel in the golden hours of late Adar
evenings. Then do the women go down
to the spring to draw water, and the
anemones are like bangles around their
feet.

הַטִּי, הַטִּי־נָא אֶת כַּדֵּךְ,
וְנִשְׁתֶּה מֵימֵי־עַיִן קָרִים, נוֹזְלִים,
וְהָיוּ לְחִכֵּנוּ כַּיַּיִן הַטּוֹב.

Please lower your jar, now, so that we
may drink the cool flowing waters of
the spring, and they will be like spiced
wine on our tongues.

כִּי יָרַד הָאֲדָר לִגְוֹעַ מִתְּנוּבָה,
כַּאֲשֶׁר יָמוּתוּ הַבֶּדְוִים אֲשֶׁר לְשֶׁבֶט עַזְרָא
מִנִּי אַהֲבָה.

For Adar has come down to expire of
luxuriance as the Bedouins of the tribe
of Asra die of love.[2]

אָז הָיִינוּ שְׁמֵי־הַשְּׁקִיעָה
אֲשֶׁר לְעַרְבֵי קֵץ־אֲדָר.

Then we became the sunset skies of the
evenings in late Adar.

שָׁלֹשׁ זְקֵנוֹת   THREE OLD WOMEN

בָּעֶרֶב הָאָפֹר עַל יַד הַבַּיִת הַלָּבָן
יוֹשְׁבוֹת שָׁלֹשׁ זְקֵנוֹת וְצוֹפִיּוֹת אֶל נִכְחָן.
וְהַס סָבִיב.
כְּאִלּוּ בִּמְעוּפוֹ קָפָא פִּתְאֹם הָעַיִט.
שָׁלֹשׁ זְקֵנוֹת יוֹשְׁבוֹת עַל יַד הַבַּיִת.

In the grey evening, beside the white
house, three old ladies sit, gazing
straight ahead. And stillness all around.
As if the eagle had suddenly frozen in
flight. Three old ladies sit beside the
house.

1. The Hebrew month roughly corresponding to March.
2. A reference to a well-known Arab legend, also found in Heine's lyric 'Der Asra': '. . . my kinsmen
are those Asra / who die when they love'.

וּמִי־שֶׁהוּא דּוּמָם סוֹרֵג מֵעַל רֹאשָׁן
פֻּזְמָק כָּחֹל בַּנֻּסָּח הַיָּשָׁן.
צְנֶפֶת זָהָב בָּאֹפֶק מִתְגּוֹלֶלֶת.
שָׁלֹשׁ זְקֵנוֹת רָאוּ לְפֶתַע יֶלֶד.

And someone, silently, above their
heads, knits a blue stocking in the old
style. A golden skein unravels on the
horizon. Three old ladies suddenly saw
a child.

שָׁלֹשׁ זְקֵנוֹת הִתְעוֹרְרוּ פִּתְאֹם
וְנֶאֶנְחוּ: מִסְכֵּן ... וַדַּאי יָתוֹם ...
וְאַחַר כָּךְ נִגְּשׁוּ. לְטָפוּהוּ עַל הַלֶּחִי.
הַיֶּלֶד הִתְבּוֹנֵן — וְהִתְפָּרֵץ בִּבְכִי.

Three old ladies woke with a start and
sighed: 'Poor thing . . . an orphan,
probably . . .' And then went over.
Patted him on the cheek. The child
looked, and burst into tears.

וְאַחַר כָּךְ בָּא לַיְל, כְּיֶלֶד לֹא־מוּבָן,
שָׁלֹשׁ זְקֵנוֹת חָמְקוּ אֶל תּוֹךְ הַבַּיִת הַלָּבָן.
וְהַס סָבִיב.
רַק אֵיזֶה עֶלְבּוֹן עוֹד הִתְחוֹגֵג כְּעַיִט
מֵעַל לְדַף סַפְסָל, שֶׁנִּתְרוֹקֵן עַל יַד הַבַּיִת.

And then night came, like a baffling
child. Three old ladies slipped away
into the white house. And stillness all
around. Only a kind of humiliation still
circled like an eagle above the wooden
bench, empty now, beside the house.

נְאֻם פְּלוֹנִי עַל שְׁכוּנָתוֹ:

SAID JOHN DOE OF HIS NEIGHBOURHOOD

בֵּית־מְגוּרַי הוּא בֶּן 5 קוֹמוֹת, —
וְכָל חַלּוֹנוֹתָיו מְפַהֲקִים אֶל שֶׁכְּנֶגֶד,
כִּפְנֵי הַנִּצָּבִים אֶל מוּל רְאִי.

The house I live in is 5 floors high, and
all its windows yawn at their opposites,
like the faces of those standing before
a mirror.

70 קַוֵּי אוֹטוֹבּוּסִים בְּעִירִי,
וְכֻלָּם עַד מַחֲנָק וְעַד סִרְחוֹן הַגּוּפִים.
הֵם נוֹסְעִים
הֵם נוֹסְעִים
הֵם נוֹסְעִים אֶל לֵב הַכְּרָךְ,
כְּאִלּוּ אִי־אֶפְשָׁר לִגְוֹעַ מִשִּׁעֲמוּם גַּם כָּאן, —
בִּשְׁכוּנָתִי שֶׁלִּי.

There are 70 bus routes in my city, all
chock-full, stifling with the stench of
bodies; travelling, travelling, travelling
deep into the heart of the city, as if one
couldn't die of boredom right here, in
my own neighbourhood.

536

שְׁכוּנָתִי שֶׁלִּי הִיא קְטַנָּה מְאֹד,
אַךְ יֵשׁ בָּהּ כָּל הַלֵּדוֹת וְהַמִּיתוֹת,
וְכָל שֶׁבֵּין לֵדָה לְמָוֶת
שֶׁיֵּשׁ בְּכַרְכֵּי הָעוֹלָם, –
אֲפִלּוּ תִינוֹקוֹת, הַמְּסוֹבְבִים לְהַפְלִיא
צַלַּחַת־מְעוֹפֶפֶת,
וּ־3 בָּתֵּי־קוֹלְנוֹעַ.
לוּלֵא הִסְתַּפַּקְתִּי בַּשִּׁעֲמוּם שֶׁיֵּשׁ לִי בְּבֵיתִי,
הָיִיתִי הוֹלֵךְ לְאֶחָד מֵהֶם.

My neighbourhood is very small, but
within it are all the births and deaths,
and all there is from birth to death,
that you find in the world's great cities
– even tots, who twirl 'flying saucers'
marvellously, and 3 cinemas. If I
weren't content with the boredom in
my own house, I would go to one of
them.

בֵּית־מְגוּרַי הוּא בֶּן 5 קוֹמוֹת, –
זוֹ שֶׁקָּפְצָה מִן הַחַלּוֹן שֶׁכְּנֶגֶד
נִסְתַּפְּקָה בְּ־3 בִּלְבַד. –

The house I live in is 5 floors high –
that woman who jumped from the
window opposite contented herself
with 3.

יוֹכֶבֶד בַּת־מִרְיָם

Yokheved Bat-Miriam

עֲגוּרִים מֵהַסַּף

CRANES FROM THE
THRESHOLD

מֵאַחֲרַי אַתְּ נִשְׁאַרְתְּ עַל הַדֶּרֶךְ,
וְרוֹנֵן צַעֲדִי הַנִּזְכָּר.
אֲלֻמָּה זְהֻבָּה וּמְהֻרְהֶרֶת,
עֲגוּרִים, עֲגוּרִים עַל הַסַּף!

You remained on the road behind me
and my footsteps sing, remembering.
A golden, pensive sheaf, cranes, cranes
on the threshold!

אֶכָּשֵׁל בְּעָנָן כְּבָאֶבֶן,
אֶכָּשֵׁל בְּיוֹמִי כְּבַחֵטְא.
יִשָּׂאֵנִי בֵּין כָּחֹל וְכוֹכֶבֶת
תֹּם גִּמְגּוּמֵךְ הַמַּרְטֵט!

I trip on a cloud as on a stone, I trip
on my day as on a sin. The innocence
of your quivering stammer lifts me
between the blue and a star.

כִּי הָיִית, כִּי הִקְרַנְתְּ מִבֶּכִי,
כִּי נָחַנְתְּ עַל גַּל מְצֻיָּר,
נוֹשְׁמָה, מַפְלִיגָה וְהוֹלֶכֶת
נִשְׁמַת חוֹף לֹא־נִרְאָה וְנִסְעָר.

Because you were, because you shone with tears, because you leaned over a painted wave, breathing, as you sailed on and on, the breath of an invisible and stormy shore.

מְטַפְּחִים אֵלָיו וְאֵלַיִךְ
(הַסְּגוּרָה בְּמֶרְחַקּוֹ הַזָּהֹב !),
מְטַפְּחִים מִשְׁתַּפְּכִים יָמַי לִי
וְשָׁרִים חֲלוֹמֵךְ הָאָהוּב.

My days are pounding toward the shore and toward you (who are enclosed within its golden distance!), pounding, pouring themselves out and singing your beloved dream.

זְהָרִים וּדְמִי לְלֹא־שַׁחַר,
זְהָרִים וּתְכֵלֶת אֵין־שֵׁם ;
יְחִידָה הַשָּׁעָה הַצּוֹמַחַת
וּמֵעֵבֶר לְעֵינַי תֵּעָצֵם.

Splendours and silence without meaning, splendours and azure without name; this hour that rises is alone and will be closed beyond my eyes.

יְחִידָה אֶל הַסַּף וְהָאֶבֶן,
שֶׁבָּדוּ אַגָּדָתֵךְ בְּרֹן,
יוֹלִיכוּנִי כְּאוֹת הַזּוֹהֶבֶת,
כְּשֵׁם עַל דַּפֵּךְ הָרִאשׁוֹן.

Alone, to the threshold and the stone that devised your legend in song, the splendours will lead me like a golden initial, like a name on your first page.

אָבוֹת יְשׁוּרוּן   *Avot Yeshurun*

[מִכְתָּבִים]   [LETTERS]

1   *1*

יוֹם יָבוֹא וְאִישׁ לֹא יִקְרָא מִכְתָּבִים שֶׁל אִמִּי.
יֵשׁ לִי מֵהֶם חֲבִילָה.
לֹא שֶׁל מִי
וְלֹא מִלָּה.

> There will come a day when no one
> will read my mother's letters. I have a
> whole pack of them. Not whose they
> were and not a clue.

יוֹם יָבוֹא וְאִישׁ לֹא יִקַּח אוֹתָם לַיָּד.
יֵשׁ מֵהֶם צָרוּר וְהוֹתֵר.
יֹאמְרוּ: נְיָר פְּסָת
וְלֹא יוֹתֵר.

> There will come a day when no one will
> touch them. There's a bundle of them,
> and to spare. They'll say: paper, a
> sheet of, and that's it.

בַּיּוֹם הַהוּא אֲבִיאֵם אֶל מְעָרַת בַּר-כּוֹכְבָא
לְהַעֲלוֹתָם בָּאָבָק. הָעוֹלָם הַקֹּדֵם
לֹא יַחְקֹר בָּהּ
שְׂפַת אֵם.

> On that day I'll take them to Bar-
> Kokhba's cave to lay them in the dust.
> That bygone world won't research the
> cave for a mother-tongue.

5   *5*

בִּקַּשְׁתִּי אֲנִי מִכְתָּבִים שֶׁל אִמִּי לִשְׁכֹּחַ.
אַף עָשִׂיתִי שֻׁלְחָנִי נָקִי.
מוֹסִיפִים עַצְמָם לִשְׁלֹחַ,
אֵלַי נוֹגְעִים:

> I did my best to forget my mother's
> letters. I even tidied up my desk. They
> go on mailing themselves, reaching out
> for me:

פִּנִּיתָ הַשֻּׁלְחָן מִכֹּל נְיָרוֹת שֶׁלְּךָ מְבֻלְבָּלִים,
סָגַרְתָּ בַּתִּיקִים אֶחָד לְאֶחָד

> [The Dead:] 'You've cleared your desk
> of all your cluttered papers. You've
> locked away in files, one by one, the

מִכְתָּבִים אַף הַבּוּלִים;
וְאוֹתָנוּ בַּצַּד.

letters, and the stamps; and put us
aside.

תִּקְרָא אוֹ לֹא תִקְרָא. עוֹשֶׂה עַצְמוֹ כְּאִלּוּ...
כְּהַיּוֹם שֶׁהִכְנַסְתָּ סֵדֶר בַּתִּיקִים,
יֵשׁ עִנְיָן אֲפִלּוּ
בְּמִכְתְּבֵי מֵתִים.

'Yes, you'll read, no you won't; putting
on airs as if . . . Now that you've set
your files in order, even letters by the
dead compel attention.'

22

22

קִבַּלְתִּי מִכְתַּבְכֶם וּבוֹ לָאָח הַבְּכוֹר.
מָה רָחַקְתָּ כָּכָה מָה?
מִלָּה וְלֹא חַמָּה
וְלֹא אוֹמֶרֶת.

[The poet to his mother:] 'I received
your letter with my younger brother's
message:[1] "Why have you become so
distant, why? One word, not warm,
and saying nothing.

לְאַחַר תִּקְוָה – מִכְתָּב. קָטֹן מִכְּתָב.
קָטָן מֵאוֹת וְרַב מִתּוֹךְ.
וְעוֹד אַתָּה אוֹמֵר
וּכְבָר גּוֹמֵר.

After hope – a letter. Too tiny for the
name. Tinier than a [Hebrew] character,
though crammed inside. You've hardly
begun to speak, before you're done.

מַלֵּא דַּפִּים שְׁלֵמִים כְּמַחַט יַחַד,
כְּאֵשׁ הַמִּתְנַפֶּלֶת עַל הַגָּאז
וְכַשַּׂק עַל הָאֵשׁ,
וּבִלְבַד שֶׁתִּקְרַב.

Fill up whole pages, tightly pinned
together, like a flame hurling itself upon
gas, or like a sack upon flames. Just be
sure to come close."'

---

1. Lit. 'and in it to the eldest brother', i.e. to me.

540

פְּרֶיילוּד עַל מוֹת הַתּוּת / PRELUDE TO THE DEATH OF THE MULBERRY TREE

גִּשְׁמֵי הַזַּעַף הָיוּ מְלֻוִּים רוּחַ סְעָרָה.

The heavy rain was accompanied by a stormy wind.

בְּרֹאשׁ הָרְחוֹב בְּרֹאשׁ הָעֵץ עָמַד צִפּוֹר,
עוֹרֵב שָׁחוֹר, וּמִתְקָרֵא, וּמִתְקָרֵא. מִדְּבָרָיו יוֹצֵא,
שֶׁאָחוּז נִכָּר שֶׁל הַבְּרוֹשִׁים 'מֵתוּ זְקוּפִים'.

At the top of the street, at the top of the tree stood a bird, a black crow, and screeching, and screeching. He said, in so many words, that a large percentage of cypresses 'die on their feet'.

הָעִתּוֹן בְּתַלְמֵי מִקְוֶה מַבִּיעַ צַעַר בְּמִיָחָד
עַל הָאֵיקָלִפְּטוּס: מִי הָיָה חוֹשֵׁד כִּי בְּשָׁרְשֵׁי
עֲנָק זֶה מִסְתַּתֶּרֶת פִּטְרִיָּה שֶׁתָּבִיא עָלָיו כְּלָיָה.

The newsletter of Talmey Mikveh[1] expresses deep sorrow over the [fate of] the eucalyptus: who would suspect that in the roots of this giant lurks a fungus that brings about its downfall?

הָעִתּוֹן אוֹמֵר, כִּי רֹב הָעֵצִים מַתְחִילִים לְהִתְנַגֵּן
אַחֲרֵי יוֹבֵל שָׁנִים, בִּגְלַל הָעֵצָה הָרַךְ שֶׁמַּתְחִיל
לְהִתְפָּרֵק. וְזֶה מַה שֶּׁקָּרָה לַעֲצֵי הָאִזְדָּרֶכֶת
וַעֲצֵי הַתּוּת.

The newsletter says that most trees begin to deteriorate after fifty years because the soft pith begins to decompose. And that's what happened to the Persian lilacs and the mulberries.

טוֹב.

All right.

עַל מוֹת הַתּוּת / ON THE DEATH OF THE MULBERRY TREE

לֹא אָמַרְתִּי יָפְיָם שֶׁל בָּתִּים הֲרוּסִים, כְּגוֹן רַבִּי,
לִפְנֵי מִלְחָמָה הָיָה קַפְּדָן וּמַעֲנִישׁ,
וְאַחֲרֵי מִלְחָמָה הָיָה רַךְ וְהָלַךְ.
לֹא דִבַּרְתִּי עַל עֵצִים שֶׁנֶּעֶקְרוּ בִּרְחוֹב
בֶּרְדִּיצֶ'בְסְקִי. עֵץ הַתּוּת שֶׁעָמַד אַרְבָּעִים

I haven't said the beauty of ruined houses, such as my Rabbi: before the War[2] he had been harsh and punitive but after the War he went soft and passed away. I haven't spoken of the trees that were pulled out on Berditchevsky Street.[3] A mulberry tree that stood there for forty years, and nobody

---

1. A weekly bulletin issued by the agricultural school in Mikveh Yisrael.
2. The First World War. 3. A side street in Tel Aviv.

שָׁנָה, וְאִישׁ לֹא יָדַע נָטַע אוֹתוֹ מִי מָה מוּ. עָמַד
עַל מִדְרָכָה בְּלִי כְּבִישׁ, לְיַד
חֲנוּת מַכֹּלֶת. יְלָדִים טִפְּפוּ בַּחוֹל וְטִפְּסוּ עַל
הָעֵץ. פְּרִי הַתּוּת דָּמָה לָאֵבָרִים
הַקָּשִׁים וְהַחִוְּרִים שֶׁל הַמִּין אֵצֶל יְלָדִים.
מִשֶּׁעָשׂוּ כְּבִישׁ וְהִנְהִיגוּ תּוּת־בּוֹנְבּוֹנְיֶרָה־
בְּקַרְטוֹן, אִישׁ לֹא זָכַר שֶׁהָעַצְלָנָה גָּעָלְמָה מִן
הָעֵץ. הָיָה מְעֻסָּק בָּאַחֲרוֹנָה לְיַד
חֲנוּת מַכֹּלֶת, לִתְמוֹךְ גַּג שֶׁל סְמַרְטוּט עַל
הַיְּרָקוֹת וְהַפֵּרוֹת. עֲקָרוֹת הַבַּיִת,
בְּבָרְרָן אֶת הַפֵּרוֹת וְהַיְּרָקוֹת, מִתְכּוֹפְפוֹת, לָאוּ
עִם הַפָּנִים אֶל הָעֵץ.
קָרְאוּ לָעִירִיָּה לָבוֹא לַעֲקֹר אוֹתוֹ. אָמְרָה
הָעִירִיָּה: לֹא הִיא נְטַעָתּוּ. אָמְרוּ: אִם
לַנְּטִיעָה, הֵם גַּם לֹא נְטָעוּהוּ.

knew who planted it, or gave a damn.
Stood on a sidewalk, without a road,
next to the grocery. Children hopped
in the sand and climbed the tree. The
berries looked like the hard, pale
genitals of children. After a road was
paved and they began selling berries in
fancy candy boxes, no one remembered
that the tree had lost its foliage. Lately
it was employed, next to the grocery, in
supporting an awning of rags over the
vegetables and fruits. The housewives,
picking out fruits and vegetables, bent
down, their backs to the tree. They
called city hall to come and pull it out.
City hall said: it didn't plant it. Well,
they said, as far as that goes, they
didn't plant it either.

בָּאָה עֶגְלַת גּוּמִי, הוֹרִידוּ חֶבֶל, כָּבְלוּ אֶת הָעֵץ,
נִסְּרוּ לִשְׁנַיִם. אָדוֹן בְּדֹלַח
זָרַק אַחֲרָיו קְלִפָּתוֹ.
מְעַט אֲנָשִׁים עָמְדוּ: צַלָּם שֶׁבַּסָּמוּךְ, נַהַג טַקְסִי
שֶׁמִּנֶּגֶד וְאִישׁ שֶׁבָּא, מִן הַמִּשְׂרָד,
נִכְנַס לַחֲנוּת קֹדֶם.

A cart came with rubber wheels. They
lowered a rope, tied the tree, sawed it
in two. Mr Crystal threw its bark into
the cart. A handful of people stood
around: the next-door photographer,
the taxi-driver from across the street,
and a man, from some office, who had
come before and stepped into the store.

הַגְּבֶרֶת בְּדֹלַח מְסַפֶּרֶת: 'יוֹם אֶחָד עָמְדָה
וְהִתְחִילָה מִתְנוֹדֶדֶת. וְהָעֵץ מִתְנוֹדֵד'.
הָאָדוֹן בְּדֹלַח אוֹמֵר: 'נָתַן לוֹ סְחִיבָה, וְזֶה נָפַל'.

Mrs Crystal tells her story: One day,
standing there, she began to rock back
and forth. And the tree rocked, too. Mr
Crystal says: He gave it a shove and it
fell.

הָעִתּוֹן בְּתַלְמֵי מִקְוֶה כּוֹתֵב: 'הָעֵצִים מְהַוִּים
מְקוֹם קִנּוּן וּמַחֲסֶה לְאַלְפֵי צִפֳּרִים,
לְשִׂמְחַת חוֹבְבֵי הַשִּׁירָה, אַךְ לֹא לַיּוֹגְבִים וְלַיַּרְקָנִים'.

The newsletter of Talmey Mikveh
writes: 'Trees serve as a nesting-place
and shelter for thousands of birds, to
the delight of poetry-lovers, but not of
farmers and greengrocers.'

טוֹב. אָנוּ מְנַתְּקִים אוֹתְךָ מִכָּל חֶבְרָה, אָנוּ
מְבַקְשִׁים מִמְּךָ סְלִיחָה. עַל כַּפַּיִם יִשָּׂאוּנְךָ.
גַּלְגַּלֵּי גּוּמִי. לֹא שׁוֹמְעִים.

All right. We hereby sever you from all
society, we beg your forgiveness. They
will lift you on their hands.[1] Rubber
wheels. Not a sound.

חַיִּים לֶנְסְקִי   *Hayim Lenski*

[הַיּוֹם יָרַד]   [THE DAY CAME DOWN]

הַיּוֹם יָרַד בְּמַדְרֵגוֹת הָאֶבֶן
אֶל תְּכֹל מֵימֵי הַיְאוֹר לִרְחֹץ וּבְטֶרֶם
כָּלָה לִטְבֹּל צָלַל פִּי תְהוֹם. וְתֶלֶם
גַּלִּים עָבַר בְּתַהֲלוּכַת אֵבֶל.

The day came down the stone steps to
bathe in the blue waters of the river,[2]
but it had scarcely immersed itself
when it plunged into the depths. And a
furrow of waves passed by in funeral
procession.

יָרְדָה דְּמָמָה שְׁלֵמָה וַחֲצִי אֹפֶל,
וַעֲגֻלָּה, מוּפֶזֶת וּמַזְהֶרֶת,
שָׁקְעָה כִּפַּת אִיסָאקִי תּוֹךְ הַזֶּרֶם
כְּפַעֲמוֹן אֲמוֹדַאי מְשֻׁלְשָׁל חֶבֶל.

Then complete silence and half-
darkness descended; and round, gilded,
glowing – the dome of St Isaac[3] sank
into the stream like a diving-bell
lowered by a cable.

וּכְמוֹ כַּדּוּר זָהָב מְגַשֵּׁשׁ בַּמַּיִם
חֹד גַּג הָאַדְמִירַלְיָה. בַּעְבּוּעַ.
שׁוֹטֵף הַיְאוֹר בְּזֹהַר בֵּין עַרְבַּיִם.

And like a ball of gold, the roof of the
Admiralty,[4] spires and all, gropes
through the water. A gurgle. The river
flows in the twilight glow.

הֹעֲלָה הַמֵּת, הִנֵּהוּ הַטָּבוּעַ;
אָרֹךְ, לְבֶן פָּנִים וּכְחֹל שְׂפָתַיִם.
'הַלַּיְלָה הַלָּבָן' – כֹּה יִקְרָאוּהוּ.

Now the corpse has been hauled up,
here is the one who drowned: long,
white-faced and blue-lipped. 'The
White Night' – that is how he's known.

---

1. 'We hereby sever, etc.' These phrases are taken from various parts of the funeral service.
2. The Neva, in Leningrad.
3. The cathedral.
4. The Admiralty building overlooking the Neva.

יוֹנָתָן רָטוֹשׁ   *Yonatan Ratosh*

אֶת נִשְׁמַת   THE SOUL OF

צֶדֶק לְפָנָיו יְהַלֵּךְ	Justice goes before him, clearing a
יְפַלֵּס אָרְחוֹ מִישׁוֹר	level path for him, shield-bearing
צֶדֶק בַּמָּגֵן לְפָנָיו בָּאַשְׁמַנִּים	Justice before him in the darkness,
צֶדֶק לְפָנָיו יְהַלֵּךְ	Justice goes before him,

אֶל אֱלֹהֵי רוּחוֹת יָם	to the god of the sea-winds,[1] deep
קֶרֶב אֲפִיק תְּהֹמוֹתַיִם	within the bed of the twin abysses,[2]
אֲשֶׁר בִּכְנָפוֹ מַעֲרִיב עֲרָבִים	who, with his wing, brings on evenings,
שֵׂיבַת זְקָנוֹ עוֹלָה קֶצֶף	whose white beard surges like foam.

עִם גֵּרַת אֵלִים עָלִיתָ	You rose with the lamp of the gods,
גַּם תָּבוֹא	now you shall set with it, with the
עִם גֵּרַת אֵלִים הַשֶּׁמֶשׁ	lamp of the god, the sun, where it goes
בַּמָּבוֹא	down

אֶל סוֹף כָּל מַיִם רַבִּים	to the end of all the mighty waters, to
אֶל רֹאשׁ עַפְרוֹת כָּל אָרֶץ	the fountainhead of all the world's dust,
רֹאשׁ כָּל דֶּרֶךְ הוֹלֶכֶת שָׁמַיִם	the head of all roads leading to heaven,
רֹאשׁ כָּל דֶּרֶךְ יוֹרֶדֶת שְׁאוֹל	the head of all roads descending to
	Sheol,

אֶל אֱלֹהֵי רוּחוֹת יָם	to the god of the sea-winds, to the
קֶרֶשׁ מֶלֶךְ אַב שָׁנִים	timbered tabernacle of the King, Father
אֲשֶׁר בְּיָדוֹ נֶפֶשׁ כָּל בָּשָׂר	of all years, in whose hand are the souls
לִפְעָמָיו יִשְׁתַּחֲווּ כָּל חָי	of all flesh, at whose feet all the living
	prostrate themselves.

---

1. Also, 'the spirits of the West'.   2. Heaven and earth.

זֶה הַגֶּבֶר
רָאָה עֳנִי וְשִׁבְטוֹ
זֶה הָאִישׁ חָדַל מִמַּעַשׂ
‏– לְבֵיתוֹ

This man has known affliction and its rod. This man no longer provides for his home.[1]

צֶדֶק לְפָנָיו יְהַלֵּךְ
יְפַלֵּס אָרְחוֹ מִישׁוֹר
צֶדֶק בַּמָּגֵן לְפָנָיו בָּאַשְׁמַנִּים
צֶדֶק לְפָנָיו יְהַלֵּךְ

Justice goes before him, clearing a level path for him, shield-bearing Justice before him in the darkness, Justice goes before him.

קֶרֶב אָפִיק תְּהֹמֹתַיִם
קֶרֶשׁ מֶלֶךְ אַב שָׁנִים
אֲשֶׁר מִיָּדוֹ גֵזֶר בַּעַל
אֲשֶׁר מִיָּדוֹ עֹז עֲנָת
אֲשֶׁר מִיָּדוֹ חָכְמַת כּוֹשָׁר
אֲשֶׁר מִיָּדוֹ טוּב אֲשֵׁרָת
אֲשֶׁר מִימִינוֹ קֶרֶן בַּעַל
אֲשֶׁר מִשְּׂמֹאלוֹ כֶּבֶד מוֹת

into the bed of the twin abysses, the timbered tabernacle of the King, Father of all years, from whose hand – the diadem of Ba'al, from whose hand – the might of Anat, from whose hand – the wisdom of Koshar, from whose hand – the bounty of Asherat, at his right – the prowess of Ba'al, at his left – the weight of Mot.

אֵל אַדִּיר אֲבָרוֹת
מֵצֵל כַּנְפֵי עוֹלָם
הָעוֹשֶׂה מִשְׁפָּט בִּתְהוֹמָיו
בָּרֵךְ אֶת הַבָּא אֶל עַמָּיו

O El of the mighty pinions, who overshadow the ends of the earth, who administer justice in your abysses, bless the one who is going to his father's kin,

אֶת נִשְׁמַת
עַבְדְּךָ
שֶׁהָלַךְ
‏– לְעוֹלָמוֹ

bless the soul of your servant who has gone to his rest.

---

1. Or, 'This man has come to the end of his deeds. He is going home.'

צֶדֶק לְפָנָיו יְהַלֵּךְ
יְפַלֵּס אָרְחוֹ מִישׁוֹר
צֶדֶק בַּמָּגֵן לְפָנָיו בָּאַשְׁמַנִּים
צֶדֶק לְפָנָיו יְהַלֵּךְ

Justice goes before him, clearing a level path for him, shield-bearing Justice before him, in the darkness, Justice goes before him.

נָתָן אַלְתֶּרְמָן

Nathan Alterman

הָאֲסוּפִי

THE FOUNDLING

הִנִּיחַתְנִי אִמִּי לְרַגְלֵי הַגָּדֵר,
קְמוּט פָּנִים וְשׁוֹקֵט. עַל גַּב.
וָאַבִּיט בָּהּ מִלְּמַטָּה, כְּמוֹ מִן הַבְּאֵר, —
עַד נוּסָהּ כְּהַנָּס מִן הַקְּרָב.
וָאַבִּיט בָּהּ מִלְּמַטָּה, כְּמוֹ מִן הַבְּאֵר,
וְיָרֵחַ עָלֵינוּ הוּרַם כְּמוֹ נֵר.

My mother laid me at the foot of the fence, wrinkled and still, on my back. And I looked up at her, as if from a well – till she fled as one flees from a battle. And I looked up at her, as if from a well, and the moon was raised over us like a candle.

אַךְ בְּטֶרֶם הַשַּׁחַר הֵאִיר, אוֹתוֹ לֵיל,
קַמְתִּי אַט כִּי הִגִּיעָה עֵת
וָאָשׁוּב בֵּית אִמִּי כְּכַדּוּר מִתְגַּלְגֵּל
הַחוֹזֵר אֶל רַגְלֵי הַבּוֹעֵט.
וָאָשׁוּב בֵּית אִמִּי כְּכַדּוּר מִתְגַּלְגֵּל
וָאֶחְבַּק צַוָּארָהּ בְּיָדַיִם שֶׁל צֵל.

But that same night, before the break of dawn, I slowly rose, for the time had come. And I returned to my mother's house as a ball rolls back to the foot that kicked it. And I returned to my mother's house as a ball rolls back, and clasped her neck with hands of shade.

מֵעָלֵי צַוָּארָהּ, לְעֵינֵי כֹּל יָכוֹל,
הִיא קְרַעֲתַנִי כְּמוֹ עֲלוּקָה.
אַךְ שָׁב לַיְלָה וְשַׁבְתִּי אֵלֶיהָ כִּתְמוֹל,
וַתִּהְיֶה לָנוּ זֹאת לְחֻקָּה:
בְּשׁוּב לַיְלָה וְשַׁבְתִּי אֵלֶיהָ כִּתְמוֹל
וְהִיא לַיְלָה כּוֹרַעַת לַגְּמוּל וְלָעֹל.

In the sight of the Almighty, she picked me off her neck like a leech. But when night returned, I returned to her as on the day before, and this became our binding rule: when night returns I return to her as on the day before, and every night she bows down to the retribution and the yoke.

וְדַלְתוֹת חֲלוֹמָהּ לִי פְּתוּחוֹת לִרְוָחָה
וְאֵין אִישׁ בַּחֲלוֹם מִלְבַדִּי.
כִּי נוֹתְרָה אַהֲבַת־נַפְשׁוֹתֵינוּ דְּרוּכָה
כְּמוֹ קֶשֶׁת, מִיּוֹם הִוָּלְדִי.
כִּי נוֹתְרָה אַהֲבַת נַפְשׁוֹתֵינוּ דְּרוּכָה
וְלָעַד לֹא נִתֶּנֶת וְלֹא לְקוּחָה.

And the gates of her dream are wide
open to me, and there is no one in that
dream but myself. For the love of our
souls has remained bent as a bow, ever
since I was born. For the love of our
souls has remained bent, and can never
be given or taken away.

וְעַל כֵּן עַד אַחֲרִית לֹא הֵסִיר אוֹתִי אֵל
מֵעַל לֵב הוֹרָתִי הַצּוֹעֵק
– וַאֲנִי – שֶׁנֻּתַּקְתִּי מִבְּלִי הִגָּמֵל –
לֹא נִגְמַלְתִּי וְלֹא אֶנָּתֵק.
וַאֲנִי שֶׁנֻּתַּקְתִּי מִבְּלִי הִגָּמֵל
נִכְנָס אֶל בֵּיתָהּ וְהַשַּׁעַר נוֹעֵל.

And therefore, till the very end, God
did not dislodge me from my parent's
wailing heart, and I, who had been torn
away unweaned, have never been
weaned and shall never tear away. And
I, who had been torn away unweaned,
now enter her house and lock the gate.

הִיא זָקְנָה בְּכִלְאִי וַתִּדַּל וַתִּקְטַן
וּפָנֶיהָ קֻמְּטוּ כְּפָנָי.
אָז יָדַי הַקְּטַנּוֹת הִלְבִּישׁוּהָ לָבָן
כְּמוֹ אֵם אֶת הַיֶּלֶד הַחַי.
אָז יָדַי הַקְּטַנּוֹת הִלְבִּישׁוּהָ לָבָן
וָאֶשָּׂא אוֹתָהּ בְּלִי לְהַגִּיד לָהּ לְאָן.

She grew old in my prison, she
shrivelled and shrank, and her face
became wrinkled like mine. Then my
little hands dressed her in white, like a
mother dressing her living child. Then
my little hands dressed her in white,
and I carried her off without telling her
where.

וָאַנִּיחַ אוֹתָהּ לְרַגְלֵי הַגָּדֵר
צוֹפִיָּה וְשׁוֹקֶטֶת, עַל גַּב.
וַתַּבֵּט בִּי שׂוֹחֶקֶת, כְּמוֹ מִן הַבְּאֵר,
וַנֵּדַע כִּי סִיַּמְנוּ הַקְּרָב.
וַתַּבֵּט בִּי שׂוֹחֶקֶת כְּמוֹ מִן הַבְּאֵר,
וְיָרֵחַ עָלֵינוּ הוּרַם כְּמוֹ נֵר.

And I laid her at the foot of the fence,
watchful and still, on her back. Then
she looked at me, laughing, as if from
a well, and we knew that the battle was
done. Then she looked at me, laughing,
as if from a well, and the moon was
raised over us like a candle.

[בְּעוֹד עֶרֶב יוֹרֵד]   [IN THE MARKET PLACE]

אִישׁ צוֹעֵק עַל דּוּכָן: עַרְמוֹנִים קְלוּיִים —
וּמְלַבֶּה בְּחַלֵּי אֵשׁ בְּמְנִיפָה שֶׁל פָּח.
אִישׁ חַי הוּא. נִגְזַר מֵאַרְצוֹת הַחַיִּים
וְכֻסָּה אַדְמַת פּוֹלִין וְשָׁב־וְנָח.

A man, hawking at his stall: 'Roasted chestnuts!' – and blowing the embers with a tin fan. He is a living man. He had been cut off from the land of the living and covered with Polish soil, yet he broke out, came back.

אִישׁ מוֹזֵג יֵין חָבִית וּבַלֵּיל לֹא יִישַׁן
עַד אַחֲרוֹן הַמְאַחֲרִים מִדֶּלְפֵּק יָסוּף.
אִישׁ מוֹזֵג שֶׁהָיָה לְעַמּוּד עָשָׁן
וְחָזַר וְהָיָה לְגוּף.

A man pouring wine from a keg. He does not sleep at night until the last, loitering drinker quits the counter. A vintner, who had become a column of smoke, then became a body again.

אִישׁ נַפָּח. בְּיָדוֹ פַּטִּישׁוֹ מוּנָף
וּסְבִיבוֹ גִּצֵּי אֵשׁ לָרֹב.
כְּאִישׁ חַי יִתְנוֹעֵעַ, יִזְדַּקֵּף וְיִכַּף
וּבְיָדוֹ הַבַּרְזֶל יָכֹף.

A man, a smith; his hammer raised in his hand, sparks of fire flashing about him. Moving like a living man, he straightens up, and bends, and twists the iron with his hand.

אִישׁ כְּלִי זֶמֶר שֶׁקָּם מִשָּׁכְבוֹ עַל גַּב
מְנַגֵּן מַנְגִּינָה תַּמָּה
וּסְבִיבוֹ בְּעִגּוּל נִצָּבִים שׁוֹמְעָיו
שֶׁהָיוּ עִם יוֹרְדֵי דוּמָה.

A man, a minstrel, who had been down on his back but arose, now playing a simple tune, and about him, in a circle, stand his listeners, those who had gone down into silence.

אִישׁ עֶגְלוֹן. הוּא מִגַּל אֲבָנִים
קָם וַיֶּחִי. וְהִנֵּהוּ פֹּה
מַעֲמִיד שְׁנֵי סוּסָיו הַלְּבָנִים,
קוֹשֵׁר לָהֶם שַׂק הַמִּסְפּוֹא.

A man, a wagoner. He rose from under a heap of stones, and lived. And now he's here, reining his two white horses, tying on their feedbags.

אִישׁ סוֹפֵר שֶׁקָּרְבוּ עַצְמוֹתָיו
וַתִּחְיֶינָה אַחֲרֵי כִּלָּיוֹן

A man, a writer, whose bones fitted themselves together and came to life

יוֹשֵׁב בַּזָּוִית, קַו לָקָו
כּוֹתֵב דְּבָרִים עַל גִּלָּיוֹן.

after extinction, now sits in a corner, little by little putting things down on paper.

אִישׁ אוֹהֵב שֶׁהוּשַׁב מֵעָפָר
סָר בַּשּׁוּק אֶל דּוּכָן אוֹ שְׁנַיִם,
קוֹנֶה עֲגִילֵי עִנְבָּר
לְאִשְׁתּוֹ שֶׁהוּשְׁבָה מִמַּיִם.

A man, a lover, brought back from the dust, pauses in the market by a stall or two, buys amber earrings for his wife, who was brought back from water.

בְּרֵיחוֹת שֶׁל קָלִי וְנָזִיד,
תַּחַת שְׁמֵי עֲנָנִים עָטִים,
כֹּה טְרוּדָה וְכָל כָּךְ מַעֲשִׂית
וְנִפְלָאת כֹּה תְּחִיַּת הַמֵּתִים.

Amidst the odours of roasting grain and broths, under a sky of sweeping clouds, so bustling and so business-like, so wondrous is the resurrection of the dead.

גֵּר בָּא לָעִיר

A STRANGER COMES TO THE CITY

הָעִיר נְצוּרָה מִבּוֹא וּמִצֵּאת.
וַאֲנִי אֶעֱבֹר לָבֶטַח.
אֲנִי הַזּוֹכֵר, הֶעָנִי־כָּמֵת,
אֶעֱמֹד עַל שְׁנָתֵךְ בַּפֶּתַח.

The city is under siege, none comes in, none goes out, but I shall pass through unscathed. I the rememberer, the pauper as good as dead, I shall stand in the gate, and guard your sleep.

וּבְאֶפֶס־כַּפּוֹת אֲחוֹנֵן,
וּכְאֵשׁ וַחֲנִית אָגוֹנֵן,
וּבְטֶרֶם־אָבְדָן אֲאַמְּצֵךְ לַמּוֹעֵד,
אֲנִי הַזּוֹכֵר, אֲנִי הָעֵד.

And, without hands, I shall give you comfort, I shall protect you like fire and spear; and before all is lost, I shall brace you for the time, I the rememberer, I the witness.

יוֹם־יוֹם אֶתְפַּלֵּל שֶׁתִּכְלִי כְּמוֹ נֵר
שֶׁאֵלַי תֵּרָדְפִי בַחֶרֶב.
וְיוֹם־יוֹם בַּעֲדֵךְ עַל פְּתָחִים אֲחַזֵּר,
לְמַעַן תִּחְיִי עוֹד עֶרֶב.

Each day I shall pray that you waste away like a candle, that you be driven to me by the sword. And each day, for your sake, I shall beg from door to door, that you may live to see another evening.

פַּת לָךְ אָבִיא אַחֲרוֹנָה
בְּשֵׁם לָךְ אֶקְרָא רִאשׁוֹנָה.
הַחֵמֶת אַגִּיעַ אֶל פִּיךְ שֶׁחָרֵב,
אֲנִי הַדּוֹאֵג, אֲנִי הַשָּׂב.

I shall bring you the last crumb of
bread, I shall be the first to call out
your name. I shall hold the water-skin
to your parched mouth, I the worrier,
I the greybeard.

כִּי הִנֵּה לֹא יוֹשִׁיעַ הַחַי אֶת הַחַי,
וָאָבוֹא כַּסּוֹתֵךְ אַהֲבָה כַּמַּיִם,
אַהֲבָה לֹא סוֹלַחַת, נָכְרִית לְאַחַי,
גְּלוּיָה כְּשֹׁד בַּצָּהֳרַיִם.

For the living can never save the living.
Therefore I have come to cover you
with love as if with water, a merciless
love, alien to my brothers, as brash as
plunder at high noon.

וְאַתְּ בֵּאלֹהִים הִשָּׁבְעִי,
כִּי אוֹנִים מִצָּרָה תִּשְׁאָבִי,
וּבְהַגִּיעַ עַד נֶפֶשׁ, תָּרִימִי קוֹל,
אֵלַי הָאַחֲרוֹן, הָאַחֲרוֹן לַכֹּל.

And you, now swear by God that you
will draw strength from your miseries,
and when they rise up to your neck,
you will cry out, to me, the last, the
very last of all.

כִּי הָעִיר נְצוּרָה מָבוֹא וּמֹצָאת,
וַאֲנִי אֶעֱבֹר לָבֶטַח.
בַּעֲדֵךְ, בַּעֲדֵךְ, אָמַר הַמֵּת,
שִׁבְעָתַיִם אָמוּת בַּפֶּתַח.

For the city is under siege, none comes
in, none goes out, but I shall pass
through unscathed. For you, for you,
said the Dead, I shall die sevenfold in
the gate.

וּכְאֵשׁ וַחֲנִית אֲחוֹגֵן,
וְכֹחַ לֹא־אִישׁ בָּךְ אֶתֵּן,
וּבְטֶרֶם אָבְדָן אֲכַבֵּךְ כְּמוֹ נֵר,
אֲנִי הַנָּכְרִי, אֲנִי הַגֵּר.

And like fire and spear I shall give you
comfort, I shall fill you with inhuman
strength. Then, on the verge of
destruction, I shall snuff you out like a
candle, I the alien, I the stranger.

הָאִשָּׁה   THE WOMAN

אָמְרָה הָאִשָּׁה: אֱלֹהַי,
שֶׁמְתַּנִי מֵאָז קַדְמַת עֵת
לִהְיוֹת נוֹפְלָה לְרַגְלֵי הַחַי
וְלִהְיוֹת נִצָּבָה לִמְרַאֲשׁוֹת הַמֵּת.

The woman said: My God, You have
appointed me since days of old to fall
at the feet of the living, and to stand at
the head of the dead.

הַכִּבְשָׂה   THE LAMB

גָּזַל אֶת כִּבְשַׂת הָרָשׁ,
כִּסָּה דָמָהּ בְּאָבֶן.
בְּשָׂרָהּ אָכַל, חֶלְבָּהּ שָׂרַף,
לֹא הִשְׁאִיר כִּי אִם בְּדַל צֶמֶר.

He robbed the poor man of his lamb,
covered its blood with a stone. Ate its
meat, burnt its fat, left nothing but a
shred of wool.

מִן הַצֶּמֶר הַזֶּה נִטְוָה הַחוּט
שֶׁבּוֹ אָחַז הַגֵּץ
שֶׁבָּא כִדְלֵקָה פֶּתַח בֵּית הָאִישׁ
וְנִכְנַס כְּכִבְשָׂה שֶׁל אֵשׁ.

This is the wool of which the thread
was woven, which was gripped by the
spark, which came as a flame to the
door of his house and went in as a lamb
of fire.

הַיְצִיאָה מִן הָעִיר   THE EXIT FROM THE CITY

בַּעַל־בַּיִת אֶחָד בָּא חֲדָרָיו,
סָגַר הַדֶּלֶת אַחֲרָיו.
לְאוֹר הַמְּנוֹרָה מָנָה כַסְפּוֹ,
מָנָה שׂוֹנְאָיו. מֵעַל לוּחַ לִבּוֹ
אַחַר־כָּךְ מָחָה אֶת הַשֵּׁמוֹת כֻּלָּם,
הִשְׁאִיר שֵׁם אֶחָד לְשָׁמְרוֹ לְעוֹלָם.

A certain man of means retreated into
his inner rooms, shutting the door
behind him. By the light of the lamp
he counted his money, counted his
enemies, then blotted out all the names
from the tablet of his heart, left one
single name to keep it forever. Then he

אַחַר־כָּךְ עָמַד וְכִבָּה הָאוֹר,
צָמַח נוֹצָה, כְּנָפַיִם וּמַקּוֹר,
עַל אֶדֶן הַחַלּוֹן נִתֵּר עָלָה,
חָלַף עַל הָעִיר כְּצִפּוֹר גְּדוֹלָה.

got up and put out the light, grew
feathers, wings, and a beak, hopped up
and mounted the window sill, crossed
over the city like a giant bird.

לֵאָה גּוֹלְדְּבֶּרְג

Lea Goldberg

מִבֵּית אִמִּי

FROM MY MOTHER'S
HOUSE

מֵתָה אִמָּהּ שֶׁל אִמִּי
בַּאֲבִיב יָמֶיהָ. וּבִתָּהּ
לֹא זָכְרָה אֶת פָּנֶיהָ. דְּיוֹקְנָהּ הֶחָרוּט
עַל לִבּוֹ שֶׁל סָבִי
נִמְחָה מֵעוֹלָם הַדְּמֻיוֹת
אַחֲרֵי מוֹתוֹ.

My mother's mother died in the spring
of her days. And her daughter did not
remember her face. Her image,
engraved upon my grandfather's heart,
was erased from the world of figures
after his death.

רַק הָרְאִי שֶׁלָּהּ נִשְׁתַּיֵּר בַּבַּיִת,
הֶעֱמִיק מֵרֹב שָׁנִים בְּמִשְׁבֶּצֶת הַכֶּסֶף.
וַאֲנִי, נֶכְדָּתָהּ הַחִוֶּרֶת, שֶׁאֵינֶנִּי דּוֹמָה לָהּ,
מַבִּיטָה הַיּוֹם אֶל תּוֹכוֹ כְּאֶל תּוֹךְ
אֲגַם הַטּוֹמֵן אוֹצְרוֹתָיו
מִתַּחַת לַמַּיִם.

Only her mirror remained in the house,
grown deeper with age within its silver
frame. And I, her pale granddaughter,
who do not resemble her, look into it
today as if into a lake that hides its
treasures beneath the water.

עָמֹק מְאֹד, מֵאֲחוֹרֵי פָּנַי,
אֲנִי רוֹאָה אִשָּׁה צְעִירָה
וְרֻדַּת לְחָיַיִם מְחַיֶּכֶת.
וּפֵאָה נָכְרִית לְרֹאשָׁהּ.

Deep down, behind my face, I see a
young woman, pink-cheeked, smiling.
She is wearing a wig. Now she is

הִיא עוֹגֶדֶת
עָגִיל מָאֲרָךְ אֶל תְּנוּךְ אָזְנָהּ. מַשְׁחִילַתְהוּ
בְּנֶקֶב זָעִיר בַּבָּשָׂר הֶעָנֹג
שֶׁל הָאֹזֶן.

hanging a long earring from her ear
lobe, threading it through the tiny
opening in the dainty flesh of her ear.

עָמֹק מְאֹד, מֵאֲחוֹרֵי פָּנַי, קוֹרֶגֶת
זְהוּבִית בְּהִירָה שֶׁל עֵינֶיהָ.
וְהָרְאִי מַמְשִׁיךְ אֶת מָסֹרֶת
הַמִּשְׁפָּחָה:
שֶׁהִיא הָיְתָה יָפָה מְאֹד.

Deep down, behind my face, glows the
clear golden speck of her eyes. And the
mirror carries on the family tradition:
that she was very beautiful.

תֵּל־אָבִיב 1935

TEL AVIV 1935

הַתְּרָנִים עַל גַּגּוֹת הַבָּתִּים הָיוּ אָז
כְּתָרְנֵי סְפִינָתוֹ שֶׁל קוֹלוּמְבּוּס
וְכָל עוֹרֵב שֶׁעָמַד עַל חֻדָּם
בִּשֵּׂר יַבֶּשֶׁת אַחֶרֶת.

The masts on the housetops then, were
like the masts of Columbus' ships, and
every raven that perched on their tips
announced a different shore.

וְהָלְכוּ בָּרְחוֹב צִקְלוֹנֵי הַנּוֹסְעִים
וְשָׂפָה שֶׁל אֶרֶץ זָרָה
הָיְתָה נִנְעֶצֶת בְּיוֹם הַחַמְסִין
כְּלַהַב סַכִּין קָרָה.

And the kit-bags of the travellers
walked down the streets, and the
language of an alien land was plunged
into the *hamsin*-days like the blade of
a cold knife.

אֵיךְ יָכוֹל הָאֲוִיר שֶׁל הָעִיר הַקְּטַנָּה
לָשֵׂאת כָּל כָּךְ הַרְבֵּה
זִכְרוֹנוֹת יַלְדוּת, אֲהָבוֹת שֶׁנָּשְׁרוּ,
חֲדָרִים שֶׁרוֹקְנוּ אֵי־בָזֶה?

How could the air of the small city
support so many childhood memories,
loves that were shed, that were stripped
somewhere?

כִּתְמוּנוֹת מַשְׁחִירוֹת בְּתוֹךְ מַצְלֵמָה
הִתְהַפְּכוּ לֵילוֹת חֹרֶף זַכִּים,
לֵילוֹת קַיִץ גְּשׁוּמִים שֶׁמֵּעֵבֶר לַיָּם
וּבְקָרִים אֲפֵלִים שֶׁל בִּירוֹת.

Like pictures turning black inside a
camera, they all turned inside out: pure
winter nights, rainy summer nights of
overseas, and shadowy mornings of
great cities.

וְקוֹל צַעַד תּוֹפֵף אַחֲרֵי גַבְּךָ
שִׁירֵי לֶכֶת שֶׁל צָבָא נֵכָר,
וְנִדְמָה – אַךְ תַּחֲזִיר אֶת רֹאשְׁךָ וּבַיָּם
שָׁטָה כְּנֵסִיַּת עִירְךָ.

And the sound of steps behind your
back drummed marching songs of
foreign troops; and – so it seemed – if
you but turn your head, there's your
town's church floating in the sea.

הִסְתַּכְּלוּת בִּדְבוֹרָה

OBSERVATION OF A BEE

א

A

בְּרִבּוּעַ חַלּוֹן מוּאָר –
עַל שִׁמְשָׁה, מִבַּחוּץ,
צְלָלִית שֶׁל דְּבוֹרָה
כִּמְעַט אֵין לִרְאוֹת אֶת כְּנָפֶיהָ.

In the square of a lit window, on the
pane, from the outside, the silhouette
of a bee; her wings are hardly visible.

הֲפוּכָה.
גּוּף צַר.
שֵׁשׁ רַגְלַיִם דַּקּוֹת –
בְּגִלּוּי עֶירֹם,
בְּאִיּוּם מְכֹעָר
זוֹחֶלֶת דְּבוֹרָה.

Upside down. Narrow body. Six thin
legs – baring her nakedness, with an
ugly threat, the bee crawls.

אֵיךְ נַכְתִּיר אוֹתָהּ בְּדִבְרֵי שִׁירָה!
אֵיךְ נָשִׁיר וּמָה ?
יָבוֹא יֶלֶד קָטָן וְיֹאמַר:
הַמַּלְכָּה עֵירֻמָּה.

How shall we crown her with song!
How shall we sing and what? A little
boy will come along and say: 'The
queen is naked.'

ב

בַּשֶּׁמֶשׁ הִיא הָיְתָה עָלֶה זָהָב נוֹפֵל,
בַּפֶּרַח הִיא הָיְתָה טִפָּה שֶׁל דְּבַשׁ אָפֵל,
וְאֶגֶל טַל בְּנַחִיל שֶׁל כּוֹכָבִים –
וּפֹה הִיא צֵל.

מִלָּה אַחַת שֶׁל שִׁיר בַּנַּחִיל הַמְצַלְצֵל,
בְּשׁוֹרַת רָצוֹן נִמְרָץ בְּתוֹךְ שָׁרָב עָצֵל,
תְּנוּעַת הָאוֹר בְּאֵפֶר דְּמוּמִים –
וּפֹה הִיא צֵל.

ג

מִדְּבָשֵׁךְ? מִי יִזְכֹּר אֶת דְּבָשֵׁךְ?
הוּא שָׁם, הָרְחֵק, בַּכַּוֶּרֶת.
כָּאן, בְּשִׁמְשָׁה מוּאָרָה, גּוּפֵךְ, רֹאשֵׁךְ –
כֻּלָּךְ עֹקֶץ, שִׂנְאָה אֵין־אוֹנִים עֲלוּבָה וְעִוֶּרֶת.
הַפַּחַד הוֹרֵג.
הִשָּׁמְרִי לְנַפְשֵׁךְ.

B

In the sun she was a falling golden
leaf, in the flower she was a drop of
dark honey, and a dewdrop in the
swarm of stars – and here she is
shadow.

One word of song in the humming
swarm, a message of keen will in the
languid heat, a movement of light in
the ashen twilight – and here she is
shadow.

C

Your honey?[1] Who will remember your
honey? It is there, far away, in the
hive. Here, in the lit window-pane,
your body, your head – you are all
sting, impotent hate, pathetic and blind.
Fear kills. Take good care!

גַּבְרִיאֵל פְּרַיִל

Gabriel Joshua Preil

מִצָּהֳרַיִם עַד עֶרֶב קָטָן

FROM NOON TO A SMALL
EVENING

בְּצָהֳרֵי יוֹם־רוּחַ פִּתְאוֹמִי
מַצְלִיף בְּשֶׁמֶשׁ יְרֵחִית
שׁוֹרֵק כְּרוֹעֶה לַעֲדָרָיו
וּמַעֲבִיר בָּאָפָר הַשָּׂעִיר
סַכִּין אַחַר סַכִּין –

In the noon of a sudden wind-swept
day that lashed the moon-like sun,
whistling like a shepherd to his flocks,
running knife after knife over the hairy
meadow,

---

1. An allusion to a Hebrew saying: 'One says to the bee: "I want neither your honey nor your sting."'

נִתְלֵיתִי בְּעַנְפֵי עֵץ הַשֵּׁנָה הַגְּדוֹלָה
וּבְצִלּוֹ אָמַרְתִּי לָנוּחַ – אַבְשָׁלוֹם חָדָשׁ
יְדוּעַ אֵלֶם פּוֹרֵחַ, מְחַסֵּל כָּל עֶבְדָּה.

I held fast to the boughs of the tree of great sleep, resolved to rest in its shadow – a new Absalom[1] addicted to blossoming silence, annihilating all facts.

וַדַּאי הָיָה מִי שֶׁרָאַנִי מְנַצֵּחַהּ שֶׁל יְקִיצָה
עַד שְׁקִיעָה-שֶׁעָמוּם יָרְדָה מֵעַל הָר,
הָיָה עֶרֶב קָטָן, עָלָה
כּוֹכָב בִּלְתִּי מֻזְמָן, –
וַאֲנִי פָּקַחְתִּי אֶת עֵינַי.

Surely someone saw me as I triumphed over awakening until a tedious sunset came down from a mountain. It was a small evening, an uninvited star rose – and I opened my eyes.

עָבִים, בִּרְקֵי יָם   CLOUDS, SEA-LIGHTNINGS

מֵחַלּוֹן בֵּית-הַדֹּאַר רָאִיתִי אֶת הֶעָבִים
מְלַבְלְבִים בַּעֲצֵי אֲפַרְסֵק וּשְׁלַחְתִּים
כִּגְלוּיוֹת מְצֻיָּרוֹת, לְאַרְצוֹת קֹר מַחֲרִיף,
זָר לָהֶן טִיב-בַּסְתָּן עַל מַפַּת קַיִץ.

From the post-office window I saw the clouds blossoming like peach trees and I mailed them as picture postcards to countries of wintering cold, that have no notion of an orchard on summer's map.

טוֹב אֶעֱשֶׂה בְּצָהֳרַיִם מְאֻחָרִים אֵלֶּה
אִם אֶלְבַּשׁ חֲלִיפָה מְגֻוֶּנֶת יוֹתֵר
וְאָשִׂים עַצְמִי מְפַקֵּחַ עַל בַּיִת יָשָׁן:
אֲבַקֵּשׁ בּוֹ צַעֲצוּעֵי בֹּקֶר תָּם
אָבְדוּ בִּתְהוֹמוֹ שֶׁל רְאִי שַׁכְחָן.

I would be well advised, on such a late afternoon, to wear a more colourful suit and to appoint myself caretaker of an old house. I would search it for toys of an innocent morning, that were lost in the depths of a forgetful mirror.

בְּחַיִּים אֲחֵרִים – הִסְתַּכַּלְתִּי מְקַוֶּה
בִּזְכוּכִית הֵכִילָה-הֶחֱזִירָה
כָּל בְּרָקָיו שֶׁל יָם;
הַפֵּרוֹת שֶׁבְּיָדִי אָז שָׁרוּ שִׁיר-תְּהִלָּה
מוּל כָּל הֶעָבִים.

In another life, I gazed hopefully at a glass that held and reflected all the sea's lightnings. The fruits in my hands then sang a song of praise, in the sight of all the clouds.

---

1. The allusion is to Absalom hanging from the oak (2 Samuel 18.9 ff).

זֶלְדָּה *Zelda*

אָז תִּצְעַק נִשְׁמָתִי THEN MY SOUL CRIED OUT

אָז תִּצְעַק נִשְׁמָתִי :
שְׂפָתַיִם חֲרוּכוֹת
אַתְּ מִן בְּצַד אֶחָד
וְהָעוֹלָם בַּצַּד הַשֵּׁנִי
וְכָל הָעוֹלָם בַּצַּד הַשֵּׁנִי.

Then my soul cried out: scorched lips,
you are on the one side, and the world
is on the other, the whole world is on
the other side.

כִּי
בְּאוֹתוֹ חֶדֶר מוּצַף שֶׁמֶשׁ
עָמַדְתִּי
כֹּה קָרוֹב אֵלֶיהָ
שֶׁפִּי נָגַע בְּפָנֶיהָ
אֲשֶׁר שֻׁנּוּ בְּחֶבְלֵי מָוֶת.
הִיא בִּטְאָה אֶת שְׁמִי
בְּקוֹל
שֶׁשָּׁן עַל קַרְקַע הַיָּם,
בְּקוֹל רָחוֹק וּמְעֻמְעָם
שֶׁנִּפֵּץ לִרְסִיסִים אֶת מַרְאוֹת
הַכֶּסֶף
אוֹתְחוּ אֶת שְׁמִי
שְׂפָתֶיהָ הָעֲשֵׁנוֹת.

For in that sun-drenched room, I stood
so close to her, that my mouth touched
her face, which was disfigured by the
pangs of death. She uttered my name
with a voice that dwelt on the ocean's
floor; in a far-away, muffled voice,
which splintered the silver mirrors, her
smouldering lips formed my name.

לְכָל אִישׁ יֵשׁ שֵׁם — EACH MAN HAS A NAME

לְכָל אִישׁ יֵשׁ שֵׁם
שֶׁנָּתַן לוֹ אֱלֹהִים
וְנָתְנוּ לוֹ אָבִיו וְאִמּוֹ
לְכָל אִישׁ יֵשׁ שֵׁם
שֶׁנָּתְנוּ לוֹ קוֹמָתוֹ וְאֹפֶן חִיּוּכוֹ
וְנָתַן לוֹ הָאָרִיג
לְכָל אִישׁ יֵשׁ שֵׁם
שֶׁנָּתְנוּ לוֹ הֶהָרִים
וְנָתְנוּ לוֹ כְּתָלָיו
לְכָל אִישׁ יֵשׁ שֵׁם
שֶׁנָּתְנוּ לוֹ הַמַּזָּלוֹת
וְנָתְנוּ לוֹ שְׁכֵנָיו
לְכָל אִישׁ יֵשׁ שֵׁם
שֶׁנָּתְנוּ לוֹ חֲטָאָיו
וְנָתְנָה לוֹ כְּמִיהָתוֹ
לְכָל אִישׁ יֵשׁ שֵׁם
שֶׁנָּתְנוּ לוֹ שׂוֹנְאָיו
וְנָתְנָה לוֹ אַהֲבָתוֹ
לְכָל אִישׁ יֵשׁ שֵׁם
שֶׁנָּתְנוּ לוֹ חַגָּיו
וְנָתְנָה לוֹ מְלַאכְתּוֹ
לְכָל אִישׁ יֵשׁ שֵׁם
שֶׁנָּתְנוּ לוֹ תְּקוּפוֹת הַשָּׁנָה
וְנָתַן לוֹ עִוְרוֹנוֹ
לְכָל אִישׁ יֵשׁ שֵׁם
שֶׁנָּתַן לוֹ הַיָּם
וְנָתַן לוֹ
מוֹתוֹ.

Each man has a name, given him by God, and given him by his father and mother. Each man has a name given him by his stature and his way of smiling, and given him by his clothes. Each man has a name given him by the mountains and given him by his walls. Each man has a name given him by the planets and given him by his neighbours. Each man has a name given him by his sins and given him by his longing. Each man has a name given him by his enemies and given him by his love. Each man has a name given him by his feast days and given him by his craft. Each man has a name given him by the seasons of the year and given him by his blindness. Each man has a name given him by the sea and given him by his death.

אָמִיר גִּלְבֹּעַ *Amir Gilboa*

וְאָחִי שׁוֹתֵק

AND MY BROTHER SAID NOTHING

אָחִי חָזַר מִן הַשָּׂדֶה
בְּבֶגֶד אָפֹר.
וַאֲנִי חָשַׁשְׁתִּי שֶׁמָּא חֲלוֹמִי יִתְבַּדֶּה
וְהִתְחַלְתִּי מִיָּד אֶת פְּצָעָיו לִסְפֹּר.
וְאָחִי שׁוֹתֵק.

My brother came back from the field
dressed in grey. And I was afraid that
my dream might prove false, so at once
I began to count his wounds. And my
brother said nothing.

אַחַר חִטַּטְתִּי בְּכִיסֵי הַסַּגִּין
וּמָצָאתִי אִסְפְּלָנִית שֶׁיָּבֵשׁ כְּתָמָהּ.
וּבִגְלוּיָה שְׁחוּקָה אֶת שְׁמָהּ
תַּחַת לְצִיּוּר שֶׁל פְּרָגִים.
וְאָחִי שׁוֹתֵק.

Then I rummaged in the pockets of
the trench-coat and found a field-
dressing, stained and dry. And on a
frayed postcard, her name – beneath a
picture of poppies. And my brother
said nothing.

אָז הִפַּרְתִּי אֶת הַצְּרוֹר
וְהוֹצֵאתִי חֲפָצָיו, זֵכֶר אַחַר זֵכֶר.
הֵידָד, אָחִי, אָחִי הַגִּבּוֹר,
הִנֵּה מָצָאתִי אוֹתוֹתֶיךָ!
הֵידָד, אָחִי, אָחִי הַגִּבּוֹר,
אָשִׁיר גַּאֲנָה לִשְׁמֶךָ!
וְאָחִי שׁוֹתֵק.
וְאָחִי שׁוֹתֵק.

Then I undid the pack and took out his
belongings, memory by memory.
Hurrah, my brother, my brother, *the
hero*, now I've found your decorations!
Hurrah, my brother, my brother *the
hero*, I shall proudly hymn your name!
And my brother said nothing. And my
brother said nothing.

וְדָמוֹ מִן הָאֲדָמָה זוֹעֵק.

And his blood was crying out from the
ground.[1]

---

1. See Genesis 4.10: 'Your brother's blood cries out to me from the ground.'

יִצְחָק ISAAC

לִפְנוֹת בֹּקֶר טִיְלָה שֶׁמֶשׁ בְּתוֹךְ הַיַּעַר
יַחַד עִמִּי וְעִם אַבָּא
וִימִינִי בִּשְׂמֹאלוֹ.

At dawn, the sun strolled in the forest together with me and father, and my right hand was in his left.

כִּבְרָק לַהֲבָה מַאֲכֶלֶת בֵּין הָעֵצִים.
וַאֲנִי יָרֵא כָּל־כָּךְ אֶת פַּחַד עֵינַי מוּל דָּם עַל הֶעָלִים.

Like lightning a knife flashed among the trees. And I am so afraid of my eyes' terror, faced by blood on the leaves.

אַבָּא אַבָּא מַהֵר וְהַצִּילָה אֶת יִצְחָק
וְלֹא יֶחְסַר אִישׁ בִּסְעֻדַּת הַצָּהֳרַיִם.

Father, father, quickly save Isaac so that no one will be missing at the midday meal.

זֶה אֲנִי הַנִּשְׁחָט, בְּנִי,
וּכְבָר דָּמִי עַל הֶעָלִים.
וְאַבָּא נִסְתַּם קוֹלוֹ.
וּפָנָיו חִוְּרִים.

It is I who am being slaughtered, my son, and already my blood is on the leaves. And father's voice was smothered and his face was pale.

וְרָצִיתִי לִצְעֹק, מְפַרְפֵּר לֹא לְהַאֲמִין
וְקוֹרֵעַ הָעֵינַיִם.
וְנִתְעוֹרַרְתִּי.

And I wanted to scream, writhing not to believe, and tearing open my eyes. And I woke up.

וְאָזְלַת־דָּם הָיְתָה יַד יָמִין.

And my right hand was drained of blood.

מֹשֶׁה MOSES

נִגַּשְׁתִּי אֶל מֹשֶׁה וְאָמַרְתִּי לוֹ:
עֲרֹךְ אֶת הַמַּחֲנוֹת כָּךְ וְכָךְ.
הוּא הִסְתַּכֵּל בִּי
וְעָרַךְ לְפִי שֶׁאָמַרְתִּי.

I stepped up to Moses and said to him: Station the troops in such and such a manner. He looked at me, then stationed them as I said.

וּמִי לֹא רָאָה אָז בִּכְבוֹדִי!
הָיְתָה שָׁם שָׂרָה מִן הַיַּלְדוּת
שֶׁעַל שְׁמָהּ תִּכַּנְתִּי לִבְנוֹת עִיר.
הָיְתָה שָׁם אֲרֻכַּת־הָרַגְלַיִם מֵחַוַּת־הַפּוֹעֲלוֹת.
הָיְתָה מֶלְוִינָה מֵרַבַּת אֲשֶׁר בְּמַלְטָה.
דִּינָה מֵהַגְּבוּל הָאִיטַלְקִי־הַיּוּגוֹסְלָבִי.
וְרִיָּה מֵהַשִּׁפְלָה שֶׁבַּצָּפוֹן.

And who did not see me then in my glory! Sarah was there, Sarah from my childhood, in whose name I had planned to build a city. And the long-legged girl was there, from the cooperative training farm. There was Melvina, from Rabbat in Malta. Dina, from the Italo-Yugoslav border. And Ria, from the northern lowlands.

וְגֵאֶה מְאֹד מִהַרְתִּי אֶל מֹשֶׁה
לְהוֹרוֹתוֹ הַדֶּרֶךְ הַנְּכוֹנָה
וְהָחֲוַר לִי לְפֶתַע
כִּי זוֹ אֲשֶׁר בְּתוֹךְ שְׁמִי
חֲרוּתָה וּנְכוֹנָה —
אֵינֶנָּה.

And, very proud, I hurried over to Moses, to show him the right way, when suddenly I realized that she who is engraved and fixed in my name – she was not there.

מֹשֶׁה מֹשֶׁה הַנְחֵה אֶת הָעָם,
רְאֵה, אֲנִי כָּל־כָּךְ עָיֵף וְרוֹצֶה לִישֹׁן עוֹד
אֲנִי עוֹדֶן נַעַר.

Moses, Moses, go lead the people. Please, I'm so tired and I'd like to sleep some more. I'm still a child.

פְּנֵי יְהוֹשֻׁעַ

THE FACE OF JOSHUA

וִיהוֹשֻׁעַ מֵעַל אֶל פָּנַי מַבִּיט. וּפָנָיו זָהָב
שָׁחוּט. חֲלוֹם קַר. חֲלוֹם חָנוּט.
וּלְרַגְלַי הַיָּם מַכֶּה נְצָחִים אֶל הַחוֹף.
אֲנִי חוֹלֶה נְהִיָּתוֹ. דוֹמֶה, אֲנִי עוֹמֵד לָמוּת.
אַךְ מֻכְרָחֲנִי, מֻכְרָחֲנִי לְחַכּוֹת חַי
אֵל־תָּמִיד.
אָחִי מֵעַל פָּנָיו עוֹלִים בָּעָב
לְהַגִּיד עִקְּבוֹתַי בַּחוֹל הַנִּשְׁטָף.

And Joshua, from above, looks at my face. And his face is beaten gold. A cold dream. A shrivelled dream. And at my feet, the sea beats eternities against the shore. I am sick with its wailing. It seems I am about to die. Yet I must, oh I must wait alive, everlastingly. My brother's face, above, rises in the cloud to reveal my footprints in the sea-swept sand.

561

הַיָּם מַכֶּה וְנָסוֹג. מַכֶּה וְנָסוֹג.
מִלְחָמוֹת אֵיתָנִים מַתְנוּת בָּחֹק.
אֲנִי. בָּרוּחַ. אַחֵר. בּוֹרֵחַ. רָחוֹק.
גַּם יְהוֹשֻׁעַ עַכְשָׁיו נָח מִמִּלְחָמוֹת.
שֶׁהִנְחִיל נַחֲלָה לְעַמּוֹ,
אֲבָל קֶבֶר לֹא חָצַב לוֹ
בְּהָרֵי אֶפְרָיִם.
עַל כֵּן לַיְלָה לַיְלָה הוּא יוֹצֵא
לָשׁוּחַ בַּשָּׁמַיִם.
וַאֲנִי חוֹלֶה, דּוֹמֶה עוֹמֵד לָמוּת
מְיַחֵף בְּחוֹל יָרֵחַ קַר
בְּשׁוּלֵי הַמַּיִם
וְהוֹמֶה בִּי, הוֹמֶה בִּי סוֹף
הַמַּכֶּה לְרַגְלַי אֶת מוֹתִי
גַּל אַחַר גַּל —

עַל פְּנֵי חַיִּים רַבִּים
יִתְרוֹמַם וְיִתְגַּדָּל.

The sea beats and withdraws, beats and
withdraws. Elemental warfare fixed by
law. I. In the wind. Different. On the
run. Far away. Now Joshua, too, is
resting from wars. For he gave a
patrimony to his people, but did not
hew himself a grave in the hills of
Ephraim. And, therefore, night after
night he goes forth to roam the skies.
And I am sick, it seems, about to die,
bare-footed in the cold moon-sand at
the water's edge, and within me moans,
within me moans the end that beats
my death at my feet, wave upon wave –

upon the many lives, be it extolled and
glorified.[1]

בָּעֲלָטָה

IN THE DARKNESS

אִם יַרְאוּנִי אֶבֶן וְאֹמַר אֶבֶן יֹאמְרוּ אֶבֶן.
אִם יַרְאוּנִי עֵץ וְאֹמַר עֵץ יֹאמְרוּ עֵץ.
אַךְ אִם יַרְאוּנִי דָם וְאֹמַר דָּם יֹאמְרוּ צֶבַע.
אִם יַרְאוּנִי דָם וְאֹמַר דָּם יֹאמְרוּ צֶבַע.

If they show me a stone and I say stone
they say stone. If they show me a tree
and I say tree they say tree. But if they
show me blood and I say blood they
say paint. *If they show me blood and I
say blood they say paint.*

---

1. The final phrase is taken from the *Kaddish* (mourner's doxology), where it refers to the name of God.

[לְבַסּוֹף אֲנִי הוֹלֵךְ] [FINALLY, I GO]

לְבַסּוֹף אֲנִי הוֹלֵךְ אֶל הָאִישׁ שֶׁהִצִּיב מַלְכּוֹדוֹת
לַצִּפֳּרִים
מְבַקֵּשׁ סְלִיחָתוֹ, שֶׁבִּקַּשְׁתִּי לְטָרְדוֹ מִלְּשַׂחֵק
בְּחַיֵּי אֲחֵרִים
מְקַלֵּל סִכְלוּתִי, שֶׁלֹּא נָאֶה לִטֹּל מִשִּׂמְחַת יְצָרָיו
שֶׁהִקְפִּיד לְשָׁמְרָם דְּרוּכִים בְּכָל עֵת
וּמַה גַּם שֶׁהַצִּפֳּרִים כְּבָר הִתְעוֹפְפוּ וְדוֹמֶה
שֶׁמְּצַפְצְפוֹת וּמְלַהֲגוֹת לְעֻמָּתִי מֵרוּמֵי מַעֲלָה
מֵעַל לְרֹאשִׁי
וַדַּאי לָהֶן, גַּם לִי מַלְכּוֹדוֹת יָדַי מַלְכּוֹדוֹת
וּלְעוֹלָם לֹא תִּנַּחַתְנָה בְּכַפּוֹתַי הַפְּשׁוּטוֹת לִקְרָאתָן.

Finally, I go to the man who sets
snares for birds and beg his forgiveness
for having tried to deter him from
toying with the lives of others. I curse
my stupidity, how indelicate to deny
him the joy of his appetites which he
took great pains to keep on the alert at
all times, and especially as the birds
have already flown away and it seems
that they are twittering and chattering
at me from the upper heights above my
head. They know for certain that I,
too, have snares, my hands are snares,
and they will never alight on my palms,
which are stretched out towards them.

אַבָּא קוֹבְנֵר *Abba Kovner*

[אֲחוֹתִי יוֹשֶׁבֶת] [MY SISTER]

אֲחוֹתִי יוֹשֶׁבֶת שְׂמֵחָה אֶל
שֻׁלְחַן חֲתֻנָּה. הִיא לֹא בּוֹכָה.
אֲחוֹתִי לֹא תַעֲשֶׂה כָּזֹאת
מַה יֹּאמְרוּ הַבְּרִיּוֹת!

My sister sits happy at her bridegroom's
table. She isn't crying. My sister
wouldn't do such a thing. What would
people say!

אֲחוֹתִי יוֹשֶׁבֶת שְׂמֵחָה אֶל
שֻׁלְחַן חֲתֻנָּה. לִבָּהּ עֵר.
עוֹלָם שָׁלֵם שׁוֹתֶה
מְרַק עוֹף כָּשֵׁר:

My sister sits happy at her bridegroom's
table. Her heart is awake. The whole
company is sipping kosher chicken
broth:

הַכֻּפְתָּאוֹת מִקֶּמַח מַצּוֹת הֵן
מַעֲשֵׂה חֲמוֹתָהּ. מִשְׁתָּאֶה הָעוֹלָם
וְטוֹעֵם מִמִּרְקַחַת הָאֵם.

The dumplings of unleavened flour were made by her mother-in-law. The whole company admiringly tastes the mother's marmalade.

אֲחוֹתִי כַלָּה יוֹשֶׁבֶת וּלְיָדָהּ
קַעֲרִית הַדְּבַשׁ. כַּמָּה עַם רָב!
אֶת צַמּוֹת הַחַלָּה

My sister-bride sits with the bowl of honey beside her. Such a huge crowd! The braids of the *halah*

קָלַע הָאָב:

were twisted by father:

אָבִינוּ אֶת לַחְמוֹ רָדָה בָּרוּךְ הַשֵּׁם
מ׳ שָׁנִים מִתַּנּוּר אֶחָד. לֹא שִׁעֵר
שֶׁיָּכוֹל עַם שָׁלֵם לַעֲלוֹת בַּתַּנּוּרִים
וְהָעוֹלָם בְּעֶזְרַת הַשֵּׁם מִתְקַיֵּם.

For forty years, praise God, our father took out his bread from the same oven. He never suspected that an entire people could go up in [the smoke of] ovens, while the world, with God's help, endures.

אֲחוֹתִי בְּהִינוּמָה יוֹשֶׁבֶת לַשֻּׁלְחָן
לְבַדָּהּ. מֵחֲבִיוֹן אֲבֵלִים
קוֹל חָתָן קָרֵב.
בִּלְעָדַיִךְ נַעֲרֹךְ הַשֻּׁלְחָן
הַכְּתֻבָּה בָּאֶבֶן תִּכָּתֵב.

My sister, in her bridal veil, sits at the table alone. From the covert of the mourners, the voice of the bridegroom draws near. We shall set the table without you, [my sister], the marriage-contract will be written in stone.

חַיִּים גּוּרִי · *Ḥayim Gouri*

יְרֻשָּׁה · HERITAGE

הָאַיִל בָּא אַחֲרוֹן.
וְלֹא יָדַע אַבְרָהָם כִּי הוּא
מֵשִׁיב לִשְׁאֵלַת הַיֶּלֶד,
רֵאשִׁית־אוֹנוֹ בְּעֵת יוֹמוֹ עָרָב.

The ram came last of all. And Abraham
did not know that it came to answer the
boy's question[1] – first of his strength
when his day was on the wane.

נָשָׂא רֹאשׁוֹ הַשָּׂב.
בִּרְאוֹתוֹ כִּי לֹא חָלַם חֲלוֹם
וְהַמַּלְאָךְ נִצָּב –
נָשְׁרָה הַמַּאֲכֶלֶת מִיָּדוֹ.

The old man raised his head. Seeing
that it was no dream and that the angel
stood there – the knife slipped from his
hand.

הַיֶּלֶד שֶׁהֻתַּר מֵאֵסוּרָיו
רָאָה אֶת גַּב אָבִיו.

The boy, released from his bonds, saw
his father's back.

יִצְחָק, כַּמְסֻפָּר, לֹא הֹעֲלָה קָרְבָּן.
הוּא חַי יָמִים רַבִּים,
רָאָה בַּטּוֹב, עַד אוֹר עֵינָיו כָּהָה.

Isaac, as the story goes, was not
sacrificed. He lived for many years, saw
what pleasure had to offer, until his
eyesight dimmed.

אֲבָל אֶת הַשָּׁעָה הַהִיא הוֹרִישׁ לְצֶאֱצָאָיו.
הֵם נוֹלָדִים
וּמַאֲכֶלֶת בְּלִבָּם.

But he bequeathed that hour to his
offspring. They are born with a knife in
their hearts.

---

1. [Isaac:] 'Here are the fire and the wood, but where is the young beast for the sacrifice?' (Genesis 22.7).

[יֵשׁ לִי קְרוֹבֵי מִשְׁפָּחָה]　　[RELATIVES]

יֵשׁ לִי קְרוֹבֵי מִשְׁפָּחָה,
לְבָבוֹת מִפֶּחָם וְשִׁנַּיִם מִכֶּסֶף.
עֲטוּפֵי מְעִילִים.
מְעַשְּׁנִים סִיגָרִיּוֹת לְלֹא בַּנְדֵּרוֹלָה.
אוֹרְחִים לֹא־קְרוּאִים
בְּעִיר שֶׁלֶג.

I have relatives, hearts of coal and
teeth of silver. Wrapped in overcoats.
Smoking cigarettes without banderoles.
Uninvited guests in a city of snow.[1]

קְרוֹבֵי מִשְׁפָּחָה רְחוֹקִים.
לְסָתוֹת מִפְּלָטִינָה.
רַגְלַיִם שֶׁל אֵשׁ.
יָדַיִם שֶׁל מַיִם.
מַבִּיטִים בִּי שָׁעוֹת אֲרֻכּוֹת
בְּעֵינֵי צִיאָן־קָלִי.

Distant relatives. Jaws of platinum.
Feet of fire. Hands of water. Looking
at me, for hours on end, with cyanide
eyes.

קְרוֹבֵי מִשְׁפָּחָה אֲצִילִים.
זִכָּרוֹן לֹא נוֹרְמָלִי.

Aristocratic relatives, they have a
terrific memory.

מַזְכִּירִים לִי סֵפֶר שֶׁבּוֹכֶה בּוֹ מֶלֶךְ
רָחוֹק, יְרוּשַׁלְמִי,
רַק גַּבּוֹ אֶל רוֹאֵהוּ,
עַד לַיְלָה.

They remind me of a book in which a
king, long ago, in Jerusalem, his face
turned to the wall, weeps until night
falls.

---

1. This refers to refugees in Vienna, shortly after the Holocaust.

טוּבִיָה רִיבְּנֶר *Tuvia Ruebner*

שָׁם, אָמַרְתִּי

THERE, I SAID

יָצָאתִי מִבֵּיתִי הָאַרְעִי לְהַרְאוֹת לְבָנַי אֶת
מְקוֹם מוֹצָאִי.
שָׁם, אָמַרְתִּי, שֶׁכַבְתִּי עַל הָאָרֶץ
אֶבֶן לִמְרַאֲשׁוֹתַי נָמוּךְ מִן הָעֵשֶׂב
כַּעֲפַר הָאָרֶץ
הַכֹּל שָׁם נִשְׁמַר.

I set out from my temporary home to
show my sons the place that I came
from. 'There,' I said, 'I lay on the
ground with a stone for a pillow, lower
than the grass, like the dust of the
earth; everything has been preserved
there.'

עָבַרְנוּ בֶּהָרִים וּבַיְּעָרוֹת וּבֶעָרִים שֶׁהָיוּ
מְעָרוֹת וְהַמַּיִם נִקְווּ בַּדֶּרֶךְ וְהַכְּבִישִׁים הָיוּ רָעִים.
הַמְּכוֹנִית דִּלְּגָה עַל הַבּוֹרוֹת.

We passed through mountains, forests
and cities that were caves, and water
gathered in pools on the way and the
roads were bad. The car bumped over
the ditches.

מָה הָאֲוִיר הַמָּתוֹק הַזֶּה? שׁוֹאֲלִים בָּנַי.
מָה הַטִּיחַ הַנּוֹפֵל מֵהַקִּירוֹת?

'What is this sweet air?' ask my sons.
'What is this plaster peeling from the
walls?'

אֵין דָּבָר, הִגִּידָה הַיְּשִׁישָׁה בַּחַלּוֹן.
כָּאן גַּם הֶעָתִיד עָבָר. וְסָגְרָה אֶת עֵינֶיהָ הַיְּבֵשׁוֹת
כְּעוֹף הָעוֹלֶה וְקוֹפֵל אֶת כְּנָפָיו וְצוֹלֵל.

'Nothing at all,' pronounced the old
woman in the window. 'Here even the
future is past.' And she shut her eyes
like a bird that soars, folds its wings
and dives.

כָּאן נוֹלַדְתִּי, אָמַרְתִּי לְבָנַי.
הוֹרַי וּזְקֵנַי נוֹלְדוּ כָּאן קָרוֹב.
נוֹלָדִים. כָּאן הָיָה בַּיִת
אָמַרְתִּי לְבָנַי וְהָרוּחַ עָבְרָה
בֵּינִי לְבֵין הַמִּלִּים.

'I was born here,' I said to my sons.
'My parents and grandparents were
born nearby. Everybody is born
[somewhere]. There was a house here,'
I said to my sons, and the wind came
between me and the words.

יָצָאתִי לְהַרְאוֹת לְבָנַי אֶת מְקוֹם מוֹצָאִי, וּמָתַי
נֹאכַל, שׁוֹאֲלִים בָּנַי, וְאֵיפֹה
נָלוּן?

I set out to show my sons the place that
I came from, 'And when will we eat,'
ask my sons, 'and where will we sleep?'

יְהוּדָה עַמִּיחַי   *Yehuda Amichai*

[אָבִי הָיָה]   [MY FATHER]

אָבִי הָיָה אַרְבַּע שָׁנִים בְּמִלְחַמְתָּם,
וְלֹא שָׂנֵא אוֹיְבָיו וְלֹא אָהַב.
אֲבָל אֲנִי יוֹדֵעַ, כִּי כְּבָר שָׁם
בָּנָה אוֹתִי יוֹם־יוֹם מִשַּׁלְווֹתָיו

My father took part in their war for
four years, and he didn't hate his
enemies or love them. But I know that
already there, day after day, he was
forming me out of his few – so very
few –

הַמְּעַטּוֹת כָּל־כָּךְ, אֲשֶׁר לָקַט
אוֹתָן בֵּין פְּצָצוֹת וּבֵין עָשָׁן,
וְשָׂם אוֹתָן בְּתַרְמִילוֹ הַמְמֻרְטָט
עִם שְׁאֵרִית עוּגַת־אִמּוֹ הַמִּתְקַשָּׁה.

tranquillities, which he scraped up
between bombs and smoke, then put
them in his tattered pack, together with
the scraps of his mother's hardening
cake.

וּבְעֵינָיו אָסַף מֵתִים בְּלִי שֵׁם,
מֵתִים רַבִּים אָסַף לְמַעֲנִי,
שֶׁאַכִּירֵם בְּמַבָּטָיו וְאֹהֲבֵם

And in his eyes he gathered the name-
less dead, a great many dead he
gathered for my sake, that I might
recognize them in his look and love
them

וְלֹא אָמוּת כְּמוֹהֶם בַּזְּוָעָה...
הוּא מִלֵּא עֵינָיו בָּהֶם וְהוּא טָעָה:
אֶל כָּל מִלְחֲמוֹתַי יוֹצֵא אֲנִי.

and not die, as they did, in such horror
... He filled his eyes with them, and
he was mistaken: I must go out to all
my wars.

חֲבָל. הָיִינוּ אַמְצָאָה טוֹבָה   A PITY. WE WERE A GOOD
INVENTION

הֵם קָטְעוּ
אֶת יְרֵכַיִךְ מִמָּתְנַי.
לְגַבֵּי הֵם תָּמִיד
רוֹפְאִים. כֻּלָּם.

They amputated your thighs from my
hips. As far as I'm concerned they are
always M.D.s. All of them.

הֵם פֵּרְקוּ אוֹתָנוּ
זֶה מִזּוֹ. לְגַבֵּי הֵם מְהַנְדְּסִים.
חֲבָל. הָיִינוּ אַמְצָאָה טוֹבָה
וְאוֹהֶבֶת: אֲוִירוֹן עָשׂוּי מֵאִישׁ וְאִשָּׁה,
כְּנָפַיִם וְהַכֹּל:
מְעַט הִתְרוֹמַמְנוּ מִן הָאָרֶץ,
מְעַט עַפְנוּ.

They dismantled us from each other.
As far as I'm concerned, they are
engineers. A pity. We were a good and
loving invention: an aeroplane made of
a man and a woman, wings and
everything: we rose a little off the
ground, we flew a little.

מִשְּׁלֹשָׁה אוֹ אַרְבָּעָה בַּחֶדֶר

OUT OF THREE OR FOUR
IN A ROOM

מִשְּׁלֹשָׁה אוֹ אַרְבָּעָה בַּחֶדֶר
תָּמִיד אֶחָד עוֹמֵד לְיַד הַחַלּוֹן.
מֻכְרָח לִרְאוֹת אֶת הָעָוֶל בֵּין קוֹצִים
וְאֶת הַשְּׂרֵפוֹת בַּגִּבְעָה.
וְכֵיצַד אֲנָשִׁים שֶׁיָּצְאוּ שְׁלֵמִים
מֻחְזָרִים בָּעֶרֶב כְּמַטְבְּעוֹת עֹדֶף לְבֵיתָם.

Out of three or four in a room, there is
always one who stands at the window.
Compelled to see the injustice between
the thorns and the fire on the hill. And
how people who had gone forth whole
are brought back to their homes, in the
evening, like small change.

מִשְּׁלֹשָׁה אוֹ אַרְבָּעָה בַּחֶדֶר
תָּמִיד אֶחָד עוֹמֵד לְיַד הַחַלּוֹן.
שְׂעָרוֹ הָאָפֵל מֵעַל לְמַחְשְׁבוֹתָיו.
מֵאֲחוֹרָיו הַמִּלִּים.
וּלְפָנָיו הַקּוֹלוֹת הַנּוֹדְדִים בְּלִי תַּרְמִיל,
לְבָבוֹת בְּלִי צֵידָה, נְבוּאוֹת בְּלִי מַיִם
וַאֲבָנִים גְּדוֹלוֹת שֶׁהוּשְׁבוּ
וְנִשְׁאֲרוּ סְגוּרִים כַּמִּכְתָּבִים שֶׁאֵין
לָהֶם כְּתֹבֶת וְאֵין מְקַבֵּל.

Out of three or four in a room, there is
always one who stands at the window.
His dark hair over his thoughts.
Behind him the words. And before him,
voices that are straying without packs,
hearts without provisions, prophecies
without water and large stones which
were returned and remained sealed like
letters with no address and no one to
receive them.

מַחֲצִית הָאֲנָשִׁים בָּעוֹלָם

מַחֲצִית הָאֲנָשִׁים בָּעוֹלָם
אוֹהֲבִים אֶת הַמַּחֲצִית הַשְּׁנִיָּה,
מַחֲצִית הָאֲנָשִׁים
שׂוֹנְאִים אֶת הַשְּׁנִיָּה,
הַאִם בִּגְלַל אֵלֶּה וְאֵלֶּה עָלַי
לָלֶכֶת וְלִנְדֹּד וּלְהִשְׁתַּנּוֹת בְּלִי הֶרֶף,
כַּגֶּשֶׁם בַּמַּחֲזוֹר, וְלִישֹׁן בֵּין סְלָעִים,
וְלִהְיוֹת מְחֻסְפָּס כְּגִזְעֵי זֵיתִים,
וְלִשְׁמֹעַ אֶת הַיָּרֵחַ נוֹבֵחַ עָלַי,
וּלְהַסְווֹת אֶת אַהֲבָתִי בִּדְאָגוֹת,
וְלִצְמֹחַ כָּעֵשֶׂב הָרָהוּי בֵּין פַּסֵּי הָרַכֶּבֶת,
וְלָגוּר בָּאֲדָמָה כַּחֲפַרְפֶּרֶת,
וְלִהְיוֹת עִם שָׁרָשִׁים וְלֹא עִם עֲנָפִים,
וְלֹא לְחַיֵּי עַל לְחִי מַלְאָכִים,
וְלֶאֱהֹב בַּמְּעָרָה הָרִאשׁוֹנָה
וְלָשֵׂאת אֶת אִשְׁתִּי תַּחַת חֻפַּת
הַקּוֹרוֹת הַנּוֹשְׂאוֹת אֲדָמָה,
וּלְשַׂחֵק אֶת מוֹתִי, תָּמִיד
עַד הַנְּשִׁימָה הָאַחֲרוֹנָה וְהַמִּלִּים
הָאַחֲרוֹנוֹת וּבְלִי לְהָבִין,
וְלַעֲשׂוֹת בְּבֵיתִי עַמּוּדֵי דְגָלִים לְמַעְלָה
וּמִקְלָט לְמַטָּה. וְלָצֵאת בַּדְּרָכִים
הָעֲשׂוּיוֹת רַק לִשִׁיבָה וְלַעֲבֹר
אֶת כָּל הַתַּחֲנוֹת הַנּוֹרָאוֹת —
חָתוּל, מַקֵּל, אֵשׁ, מַיִם, שׁוֹחֵט,
בֵּין הַגְּדִי וּבֵין מַלְאַךְ־הַמָּוֶת ?

HALF THE PEOPLE IN THE WORLD

Half the people in the world love the
other half, half the people hate the
other half. Must I, because of those
and the others, go and wander and
endlessly change, like rain in its cycle,
and sleep among rocks, and be rugged
like the trunks of olive-trees, and hear
the moon bark at me, and camouflage
my love with worries, and grow like the
timorous grass in between railway
tracks, and live in the ground like a
mole, and be with roots and not with
branches, and not rest my cheek upon
the cheek of angels, and make love in
the first cave, and marry my wife under
the canopy of beams which support the
earth, and act out my death, always to
the last breath and the last words,
without ever understanding, and put
flag-poles on top of my house and a
shelter at the bottom. And set forth on
the roads made only for returning, and
go through all the terrifying stations –
cat, stick, fire, water, butcher – between
the kid and the angel of death?[1]

---

1. A reference to a well-known song which concludes the Passover Haggadah. The last stanza reads:
'Then came the Holy One, blessed be He, and destroyed the angel of death, that slew the butcher, that
killed the ox, that drank the water, that quenched the fire, that burned the stick, that beat the dog, that
bit the cat, that ate the kid, that father had bought for two *zuzim*.'

מַחֲצִית הָאֲנָשִׁים אוֹהֲבִים,
מַחֲצִיתָם שׂוֹנְאִים.
וְהֵיכָן מְקוֹמִי בֵּין הַמַּחֲצִיּוֹת הַמֻּתְאָמוֹת כָּל-כָּךְ,
וְדֶרֶךְ אֵיזֶה סֶדֶק אֶרְאֶה אֶת
הַשִּׁכּוּנִים הַלְּבָנִים שֶׁל חֲלוֹמוֹתַי,
וְאֶת הָרָצִים הַיְחֵפִים עַל הַחוֹלוֹת
אוֹ לְפָחוֹת אֶת נִפְנוּף
מִטְפַּחַת הַנַּעֲרָה, לְיַד הַתֵּל?

Half the people love, half the people
hate. And where is my place between
these halves that are so well matched?
And through what crack shall I see the
white housing-projects of my dreams,
and the barefoot runners on the sands
or, at least, the fluttering of the girl's
handkerchief, by the hill?

[בְּיוֹם כִּפּוּר]

[ON THE DAY OF ATONEMENT]

בְּיוֹם כִּפּוּר בִּשְׁנַת תַּשַׁכַּ״ח לָבַשְׁתִּי
בִּגְדֵי חַג כֵּהִים וְהָלַכְתִּי לָעִיר הָעַתִּיקָה בִּירוּשָׁלַיִם.
עָמַדְתִּי זְמַן רַב לִפְנֵי כּוּךְ חֲנוּתוֹ שֶׁל עֲרָבִי,
לֹא רָחוֹק מִשַּׁעַר שְׁכֶם, חֲנוּת
כַּפְתּוֹרִים וְרֻכְסָנִים וּסְלִילֵי חוּטִים
בְּכָל צֶבַע וְלַחְצָנִיּוֹת וְאַבְזָמִים.
אוֹר יָקָר וּצְבָעִים רַבִּים, כְּמוֹ אֲרוֹן-קֹדֶשׁ פָּתוּחַ.

On the Day of Atonement in 1967, I
put on my dark holiday suit and went
to the Old City in Jerusalem. I stood,
for some time, before the alcove of an
Arab's shop, not far from Damascus
Gate, a shop of buttons and zippers
and spools of thread in all colours, and
snaps and buckles. A glorious light and
a great many colours like a Holy Ark
with its doors ajar.

אָמַרְתִּי לוֹ בְּלִבִּי שֶׁגַּם לְאָבִי
הָיְתָה חֲנוּת כָּזֹאת שֶׁל חוּטִים וְכַפְתּוֹרִים.
הִסְבַּרְתִּי לוֹ בְּלִבִּי עַל כָּל עֲשָׂרוֹת הַשָּׁנִים
וְהַגּוֹרְמִים וְהַמְּקוֹרִים, שֶׁאֲנִי עַכְשָׁו פֹּה
וַחֲנוּת אָבִי שְׂרוּפָה שָׁם וְהוּא קָבוּר פֹּה.

I told him in my heart that my father,
too, had such a shop of threads and
buttons. I explained to him in my
heart all about the tens of years and the
reasons and the circumstances because
of which I am now here and my
father's shop is in ashes there, and he
is buried here.

כְּשֶׁסִּיַּמְתִּי הָיְתָה שְׁעַת נְעִילָה.
גַּם הוּא הוֹרִיד אֶת הַתְּרִיס וְנָעַל אֶת הַשַּׁעַר
וַאֲנִי חָזַרְתִּי עִם כָּל הַמִּתְפַּלְּלִים הַבַּיְתָה.

By the time I had finished, it was the
hour of 'the locking of the Gates'[1]. He
too pulled down the shutter and locked
the gate, and I went back home with
all the worshippers.

---

1. Ne'ila, the evening prayer, which concludes the Day of Atonement. See p. 241.

[הָעִיר שֶׁבָּהּ נוֹלַדְתִּי]

הָעִיר שֶׁבָּהּ נוֹלַדְתִּי נֶהֶרְסָה בְּתוֹתָחִים.
הָאֳנִיָּה שֶׁבָּהּ עָלִיתִי, טֻבְּעָה אַחַר כָּךְ, בַּמִּלְחָמָה.
הַגֹּרֶן בַּחֲמַדְיָה שֶׁבּוֹ אָהַבְתִּי, נִשְׂרַף.
הַקִּיּוֹסְק בְּעֵין גֶּדִי פָּצַץ בִּידֵי אוֹיְבִים,
אֶת הַגֶּשֶׁר בְּאִיסְמָעִילִיָּה שֶׁעָבַרְתִּי
בּוֹ הָלוֹךְ וָשׁוֹב בְּעֶרֶב אַהֲבוֹתַי
קָרְעוּ לִקְרָעִים.

חַיַּי נִמְחָקִים אַחֲרַי לְפִי מַפָּה מְדֻיֶּקֶת.
כַּמָּה זְמַן יַחֲזִיקוּ הַזִּכְרוֹנוֹת מַעֲמָד?
אֶת הַיַּלְדָּה מִיַּלְדוּתִי הָרְגוּ וְאָבִי מֵת.

לָכֵן אַל תִּבְחֲרוּ בִי לְאוֹהֵב אוֹ לְבֵן,
לְעוֹבֵר גְּשָׁרִים וּלְדַיָּר וּלְאֶזְרָח.

[THE CITY IN WHICH I WAS BORN]

The city in which I was born was destroyed by cannon. The ship by which I emigrated was later sunk, during the war. The barn in Hamadiya[1] where I loved was burnt down. The kiosk in Ein-Gedi[2] was blown up by enemies. The bridge by Ismailiyeh,[3] which I crossed and recrossed on the evening of my love, was ripped to pieces.

My life is being wiped out behind me according to a precise map. How long will the memories hold out? The little girl of my childhood was killed, my father died.

Therefore do not choose me as a lover or a son, as a bridge-crosser, tenant or citizen.

אַבְנֵר טְרֵינִין

Avner Treinin

מַפָּה

A MAP

לוּ תֻרְשַׁם מַפַּת אֶחָד־עַל־אֶחָד,
וְהַקַּוִּים יָחֵלּוּ הֱיוֹת אֶת אֲשֶׁר הֵם בֶּאֱמֶת;
וּדְרָכִים מִסּוּג אָלֶף וּבֵית,
סִימָנִים, כְּתָמִים בְּכָל גּוֹנֵיהֶם,
הָעֲקֻמּוֹת הַמִּצְטַפְּפוֹת אֶל שִׂיאָן –

Let a map be drawn on a scale of one-to-one and the lines will begin to be what they really are. Class A and B roads, signs, multicoloured patches, contours crowding towards their summits – everything will be what it

---

1. A kibbutz south of the Sea of Galilee.
2. A kibbutz on the shore of the Dead Sea.
3. A city on the Suez Canal.

הַכֹּל אֶת אֲשֶׁר הוּא בֶּאֱמֶת:
שְׁבִיל עָמוּס בְּצֹאן
מוֹבִיל אֶל הַשְּׁקָתוֹת,
עָפָר כָּבוּל אֶל הַמִּדְרוֹן
בְּחִשּׁוּקֵי טֶרָסוֹת מַדְרִיגוֹת.

really is: a path, heavy with sheep,
leading to the troughs and earth
clamped to the slope by the hoops of
graded terraces.

לוּ יַעַל הַנְּיָר חֶלְקַת אַסְפֶּסֶת מוֹרִיקָה,
וְאִישׁ בְּחֶרְמֵשׁוֹ צוֹעֵד וּמֵרִיקָה,
וְסֵבֶר פְּנֵי הָאֵם הַמֵּינִיקָה,
וְאֶת עֶגְלַת הַתְּאוֹמִים הַמְּעִיקָה.
וְהָרִיחוֹת לוּ יַדִּיף,
בְּהַקְטֵר פְּרְחֵי הַבָּר,
וְעַל פָּנֶיךָ מְשִׁי הַשֵּׂעָר.
וּבְקוֹלוֹת לוּ יָצִיף:
קְדִיחַת בְּאֵר מִבֹּקֶר אוֹר,
קִילוֹן חוֹרֵק עַל פִּי הַבּוֹר,
וּבַכָּחֹל סִירַת מוֹטוֹר,
שִׁכְשׁוּךְ הַנְּעָרוֹת עִם שַׁחַר.

Let the paper bring forth a green plot
of lucerne, a man with a scythe stepping
through it, mowing, the look on the
face of a mother nursing her child and
the baby-carriage laden with twins.
And let it pour forth fragrances, wild
flowers perfuming with incense and
silken hair upon your face. And let it
flood [the air] with sounds: the drilling
of a well from daybreak, the creak of a
water-hoist over a cistern, and in the
blue – a motor-boat, the splashing of
girls at dawn.

וְהַבָּתִּים לוּ יִזָּרְעוּ בִּמְקוֹמָם,
סֻכּוֹת הַפַּח הַצּוֹחֲקוֹת בַּשֶּׁמֶשׁ,
וַאֲלֻמּוֹת הַמַּיִם מוּכָסוֹת בָּרוּחַ,
וְהַגֶּרָנְיוּם עַל הָאֶדֶן,
וְהָאִישׁ הַמַּחְזִיק בָּעִתּוֹן,
וְהָאִשָּׁה מְבַּצֵּד לְחַלּוֹנָהּ
רוֹאָה אֶת יְלָדֶיהָ בִּשְׂדֵרָה
גּוֹבֶלֶת בֵּית עָלְמִין צְבָאִי
לְיַד הַדֶּרֶךְ הָרָאשִׁית.

And let houses be sown in their places,
tin sheds laughing in the sun, sheaves
of water flattened by the wind, the
geranium on the window sill, a man
holding a newspaper, a woman by the
window watching her children in the
lane that borders the military cemetery,
next to the highway.

> הוֹ, לוּ תְהֵא זוֹ הַמַּפָּה לִפְנֵי הַקְּבַרְנִיט
> וְלִפְנֵי הַמַּצְבִּיא הָרָכוּן עַל דִּגְלוֹנָיו —
> שֶׁיִּנְעָצֵם, שֶׁיִּנְעָצֵם עַד זוֹב
> בַּבָּשָׂר הַחַי.

O let this be the map [set] before the head of state and the general bent over his little flags – let him stick them in, stick them in till they draw blood from the living flesh.

דָּן פָּגִיס — *Dan Pagis*

אַחֲרוֹנִים

THE LAST ONES

> אֲנִי כְּבָר נָדִיר לְמַדַּי. זֶה שָׁנִים
> שֶׁנִּגְלֵיתִי רַק פֹּה וָשָׁם
> בְּשׁוּלֵי הַגַּ׳וּנְגֶל הַזֶּה. גּוּפִי הַמְגֻשָּׁם
> מֻסְוֶה יָפֶה בֵּין קְנֵי הַסּוּף וְנִצְמָד
> אֶל הַצֵּל הַלַּח מִסָּבִיבוֹ.
> בִּתְנָאֵי תַרְבּוּת בִּכְלָל לֹא הָיִיתִי מַחֲזִיק מַעֲמָד.
> אֲנִי עָיֵף. רַק הַשְּׂרֵפוֹת הַגְּדוֹלוֹת
> עוֹד מְגָרְשׁוֹת אוֹתִי מִמַּחֲבוֹא לְמַחֲבוֹא.

I am already quite rare. For years now I have appeared only here and there at the edges of this jungle. My ungainly body is nicely camouflaged among the bulrushes and clings to the damp shadow around it. Under civilized conditions, I would never have been able to hold out. I am tired. Only the great fires still drive me from one hiding-place to another.

> וּמָה עַכְשָׁו? תְּהִלָּתִי הִיא רַק בַּשְּׁמוּעָה
> שֶׁמֵּעֵת לְעֵת
> וַאֲפִלּוּ מִשָּׁעָה לְשָׁעָה
> אֲנִי הוֹלֵךְ וּמִתְמַעֵט.
> אֲבָל נָכוֹן שֶׁבָּרֶגַע הַזֶּה מִישֶׁהוּ
> עוֹקֵב אַחֲרָי. בִּזְהִירוּת אֲנִי זוֹקֵף
> אֶת כָּל אָזְנַי וּמַמְתִּין. הַצַּעַד
> כְּבָר בֶּעָלִים הַמֵּתִים. קָרוֹב מְאֹד, מְרַשְׁרֵשׁ. זֶהוּ?
> אֲנִי הוּא? אֲנִי.
> כְּבָר לֹא אַסְפִּיק לְפָרֵשׁ.

And now, what? My fame rests only on the rumour that from one day to the next, and even from hour to hour, I am wasting away. But it is true that at this very moment someone is tracking me. Cautiously, I prick up all my ears and wait. The step is already in the dead leaves. Very close, rustling. Is that it? Is it I? I. Too late for me to explain.

574

DAN PAGIS

סוֹף הַשְּׁאֵלוֹן / THE END OF THE QUESTIONNAIRE

תְּנָאֵי מְגוּרֶיךָ: מִסְפַּר הָעַרְפִלִּית וְהַכּוֹכָב.
מִסְפַּר הַקֶּבֶר.
הַאִם אַתָּה לְבַד, אוֹ לֹא.
אֵיזֶה עֵשֶׂב צוֹמֵחַ לְמַעְלָה
וּמִנַּיִן (לְמָשָׁל מִבֶּטֶן, מֵעַיִן, מִפֶּה וְכָךְ הָלְאָה).

Your housing conditions: the number
of the galaxy and of the star. The grave
number. Are you alone, or not. What
grasses grow above and where from
(e.g. from the stomach, eye, mouth,
and so on).

מֻתָּר לְךָ לְעַרְעֵר.

You have the right to appeal.

וּבַמָּקוֹם הָרֵיק לְמַטָּה צַיֵּן
מִמָּתַי אַתָּה עֵר וּמַדּוּעַ הֻפְתַּעְתָּ.

In the blank space below specify how
long you have been awake and why you
were taken by surprise.

כָּתוּב בְּעִפָּרוֹן בַּקָּרוֹן הֶחָתוּם / WRITTEN IN PENCIL IN THE SEALED FREIGHT CAR

כָּאן בַּמִּשְׁלוֹחַ הַזֶּה
אֲנִי חַוָּה
עִם הֶבֶל בְּנִי
אִם תִּרְאוּ אֶת בְּנִי הַגָּדוֹל
קַיִן בֶּן אָדָם
תַּגִּידוּ לוֹ שֶׁאֲנִי

Here, in this carload, I, Eve, with my
son Abel. If you see my older boy,
Cain, the son of Adam, tell him that I

הַפּוֹרְטְרֶט / THE PORTRAIT

הַיֶּלֶד
אֵינֶנּוּ יוֹשֵׁב בִּמְנוּחָה,
קָשֶׁה לִי לִתְפֹּס אֶת קַו לְחָיָיו.
אֲנִי רוֹשֵׁם קַו אֶחָד

The child is not sitting still. It's hard
for me to catch the line of his cheeks.
I draw one line and his wrinkles

575

NATHAN ZACH

וְקִמְטֵי פָּנָיו מִתְרַבִּים,
אֲנִי טוֹבֵל מִכְחוֹל
וּשְׂפָתָיו מִתְעַקְּמוֹת, שְׂעָרוֹ מַלְבִּין,
עוֹרוֹ הַמַּכְחִיל מִתְקַלֵּף מֵעַל עַצְמוֹתָיו. אֵינֶנּוּ.
הַזָּקֵן אֵינֶנּוּ וַאֲנִי
אָנָה אֲנִי בָא.

multiply, I dip the brush and his lips
become twisted, his hair goes grey, his
skin, turning blue, peels from his bones.
He is gone. The old man is gone, and
I, what am I to do.

נָתָן זַךְ — *Nathan Zach*

רֶגַע אֶחָד — A MOMENT

לאסיה — for Assia

רֶגַע אֶחָד שֶׁקֶט בְּבַקָּשָׁה. אָנָּא. אֲנִי
רוֹצֶה לוֹמַר דְּבַר מָה. הוּא הָלַךְ
וְעָבַר עַל פָּנַי. יָכֹלְתִּי לָגַעַת בְּשׁוּלֵי
אַדַּרְתּוֹ. לֹא נָגַעְתִּי. מִי יָכוֹל הָיָה
לָדַעַת מַה שֶּׁלֹּא יָדַעְתִּי.

Quiet for a moment. Please. I'd like to
say something. He went away and
passed in front of me. I could have
touched the hem of his cloak. I didn't.
Who could have known what I didn't
know.

הַחוֹל דָּבַק בִּבְגָדָיו. בִּזְקָנוֹ
הִסְתַּבְּכוּ זְרָדִים. כַּנִּרְאֶה לָן
לַיְלָה קֹדֶם בַּתֶּבֶן. מִי יָכוֹל הָיָה
לָדַעַת שֶׁבְּעוֹד לַיְלָה יִהְיֶה
רֵיק כְּמוֹ צִפּוֹר, קָשֶׁה כְּמוֹ אֶבֶן.

There was sand stuck to his clothes.
Sprigs were tangled in his beard. He
must have slept on straw the night
before. Who could have known that in
another night he would be hollow as a
bird, hard as a stone.

לֹא יָכֹלְתִּי לָדַעַת. אֵינֶנִּי מַאֲשִׁים
אוֹתוֹ. לִפְעָמִים אֲנִי מַרְגִּישׁ אוֹתוֹ קָם
בִּשְׁנָתוֹ, סַהֲרוּרִי כְּמוֹ יָם, חוֹלֵף לְיָדִי, אוֹמֵר
לִי בְּנִי.
בְּנִי. לֹא יָדַעְתִּי שֶׁאַתָּה, בְּמִדָּה כָּזֹאת, אִתִּי.

I could not have known. I don't blame
him. Sometimes I feel him getting up
in his sleep, moonstruck like the sea,
flitting by me, saying to me my son.
My son. I didn't know that you are, to
such an extent, with me.

576

טַלִיתָא קוּמִי TALITHA CUMI[1]

טַלִיתָא קוּמִי, אֲנִי מְבַקֵּשׁ,
אַתְּ אָדָם אִינְטֶלִיגֶנְטִי, קוּמִי.
אוּלַי טָעִיתִי. וַדַּאי לִי שֶׁלֹּא רָאִיתִי.
זְמַן רַב עָבַר מֵאָז. קוּמִי,
לֹא לְכָךְ נִתְכַּוַּנְתִּי, כֵּן, אוּלַי,
אֲנִי מוֹדֶה, אֲבָל קוּמִי,
טַלִיתָא קוּמִי.

Talitha, cumi, I beg of you. You're an intelligent person, get up. Perhaps I was mistaken. I'm certain that I didn't see. It's been a long time since then. Get up, this isn't what I intended, yes, perhaps, I admit it, but get up, *Talitha, cumi.*

אֵלִי, לָמָה שְׁבַקְתָּנִי, שֶׁפֵּרוּשׁוֹ
לָמָה עֲזַבְתָּנִי. אֵלִי, לָמָה
עָשִׂיתָ לִי כָּזֹאת, שֶׁפֵּרוּשׁוֹ מַדּוּעַ.
מַדּוּעַ לֹא מָנַעְתָּ בַּעֲדִי, שֶׁפֵּרוּשׁוֹ
מַיִם שֶׁפֵּרוּשָׁם רוּחַ.

Eli, lama shevaktani, which means, why have you left me.[2] My God, what made you do such a thing to me, which means, why. Why didn't you stop me, which means water which means wind.

הִתְכַּוַּנְתִּי אַךְ לְטוֹב. רָאִיתִי שֶׁהִיא מְחַיֶּכֶת.
חָשַׁבְתִּי שֶׁעוֹד אַהֲבָה לֹא תוֹסִיף
לְחֶשְׁבּוֹנָהּ יוֹתֵר מִשֶּׁהִיא מוֹסִיפָה
לְחֶשְׁבּוֹנִי. לֹא יָדַעְתִּי עַד כַּמָּה הִטְרַדְתִּי
אוֹתְךָ בִּדְבָרִים בְּטֵלִים, קוֹנִי. בַּטֵּל אוֹתִי, אֲדוֹנִי. לֹא
יָדַעְתִּי עַד כַּמָּה אַתָּה מְבַטֵּל אוֹתִי, אֲדוֹנִי,
בִּרְעֲבוֹנִי. טַלִיתָא קוּמִי.

I only intended to do good. I saw that she was smiling. I thought some more love would not add to her account more than it adds to mine. I didn't realize how greatly I troubled you with trivialities, my Maker. Make me null and void, my lord. I didn't realize how little you made of me, my lord, in my hunger. *Talitha, cumi.*

---

1. 'Taking her hand he said to her: "*Talitha, cumi,*" which means, "Little girl, get up".' (Mark 5.41)
2. 'At that time Jesus cried in a loud voice, "*Eli, Eli, lama sabachthani?*" which means, "My God, my God, why have you forsaken me?".' (Mark 15.34)

דָּלְיָה רָבִיקוֹבִיץ׳   *Dalia Ravikovitch*

בֻּבָּה מְמֻכֶּנֶת   MECHANICAL DOLL

בַּלַּיְלָה הַזֶּה הָיִיתִי בֻּבָּה מְמֻכֶּנֶת
וּפָנִיתִי יָמִינָה וּשְׂמֹאלָה, לְכָל הָעֲבָרִים,
וְנָפַלְתִּי אַפַּיִם אַרְצָה וְנִשְׁבַּרְתִּי לִשְׁבָרִים
וְנִסּוּ לְאַחוֹת אֶת שְׁבָרַי בְּיָד מְאֻמֶּנֶת.

On that night I was a mechanical doll
turning right and left, in all directions,
and I fell flat on my face and was
broken to bits, and they tried to put my
parts together with skilful hands.

וְאַחַר־כָּךְ שַׁבְתִּי לִהְיוֹת בֻּבָּה מְתֻקֶּנֶת
וְכָל מִנְהָגִי הָיָה שָׁקוּל וְצַיְתָנִי,
אוּלָם אָז כְּבָר הָיִיתִי בֻּבָּה מִסּוּג שֵׁנִי
כְּמוֹ זְמוֹרָה חֲבוּלָה שֶׁהִיא עוֹד אֲחוּזָה בְּקְנוֹקֶנֶת.

And after that I again became a proper[1]
doll, and my bearing, at all times, was
poised and submissive. But by then I
was already a different sort of doll, like
an injured twig, still held fast by a
tendril.

וְאַחַר כָּךְ הָלַכְתִּי לִרְקֹד בְּנֶשֶׁף הַמְּחוֹלוֹת
אַךְ הִנִּיחוּ אוֹתִי בְּחֶבְרַת חֲתוּלִים וּכְלָבִים
וְאִלּוּ כָּל צְעָדַי הָיוּ מְדוּדִים וּקְצוּבִים.

And afterwards I went to dance at a
ball, but they put me in the company
of cats and dogs, yet all my steps were
measured and fixed.

וְהָיָה לִי שֵׂעָר זָהָב וְהָיוּ לִי עֵינַיִם כְּחֻלּוֹת
וְהָיְתָה לִי שִׂמְלָה מִצֶּבַע פְּרָחִים שֶׁבַּגַּן
וְהָיָה לִי כּוֹבַע שֶׁל קַשׁ עִם קִשּׁוּט דֻּבְדְּבָן.

And I had golden hair and I had blue
eyes and I had a dress the colour of
garden flowers and I had a straw hat
with an ornamental cherry.

---

1. The word also means 'repaired'.

DALIA RAVIKOVITCH

מִיּוֹם לְלַיְלָה   FROM DAY TO NIGHT

כָּל יוֹם אֲנִי קָמָה מֵחָדָשׁ מִן הַשֵּׁנָה
כְּמוֹ בְּפַעַם אַחֲרוֹנָה.
אֵינֶנִּי יוֹדַעַת מָה מְצַפֶּה לִי
וְאוּלַי מִסְתַּבֵּר מִתּוֹךְ זֶה
שֶׁלֹּא מְצַפֶּה לִי דָּבָר.
הָאָבִיב שֶׁבָּא הוּא כְּמוֹ הָאָבִיב שֶׁעָבַר.
אֲנִי יוֹדַעַת מַהוּ חֹדֶשׁ אִיָּר
אֲבָל אֵין דַּעְתִּי נְתוּנָה לוֹ
אֵינֶנִּי מַבְחִינָה בַּגְּבוּל שֶׁבֵּין הַיּוֹם לְבֵין הַלַּיְלָה.
רַק שֶׁהַלַּיְלָה קַר יוֹתֵר
וְהַשֶּׁקֶט שָׁוֶה לִשְׁנֵיהֶם.
בַּבֹּקֶר אֲנִי שׁוֹמַעַת קוֹלוֹת שֶׁל צִפֳּרִים
אֲנִי נִרְדֶּמֶת בְּקַלּוּת
מֵרֹב חִבָּה אֲלֵיהֶן.
מִי שֶׁיָּקָר לִי אֵינוּ נִמְצָא פֹּה
וְאוּלַי בִּכְלָל אֵינוּ נִמְצָא.
אֲנִי עוֹבֶרֶת מִיּוֹם לְיוֹם
מִיּוֹם לְלַיְלָה
כְּמוֹ נוֹצָה
שֶׁאֵין הַצִּפּוֹר מַרְגִּישָׁה בָּהּ כְּשֶׁהִיא נוֹשֶׁרֶת.

Every day I wake up again as
though for the last time. I don't know
what to expect and perhaps that means
that nothing is expecting me. The
spring that has come is like the spring
that has gone. I know what May is, but
I do not give it a thought. I can't
perceive the border between day and
night. It's only that the night is colder,
and both are equally quiet. In the
morning I hear the voices of birds. I
doze off easily, being so fond of them.
The one who is dear to me is not here,
and perhaps he simply is not. I pass
from day to day, from day to night, like
a feather which the bird is unaware of
when it falls off.

SELECT BIBLIOGRAPHY

THE following bibliography is limited to works in English. The reader is referred to the relevant entries in the *Encyclopaedia Judaica* (Keter Publishing House, Jerusalem, 1972), and especially to 'Genizah, Cairo', 'Hebrew Literature, Modern', 'Kabbalah', 'Literature, Jewish', 'Piyyut', 'Poetry' and 'Prosody, Hebrew'.

GENERAL

Ginzberg, L., *The Legends of the Jews*, 7 vols., Jewish Publication Society, Philadelphia, 1909. A shorter, one-volume version was published by Simon & Schuster, New York, 1956.

Zinberg, I., *A History of Jewish Literature* in 12 vols.: Vols. 1-3, The Press of Case Western Reserve University, Cleveland and London, 1972-3; Vols. 4-9, Hebrew Union College Press, Cincinnati, Ktav Publishing House, New York, 1974-7.

BIBLICAL POETRY

Driver, S. R., *An Introduction to the Literature of the Old Testament*, 9th edn, 1913; reprinted by the World Publishing Company, Cleveland and New York, 1961.

Eissfeldt, O., *The Old Testament: an Introduction*, Harper & Row, New York, 1965.

Fohrer, G., *Introduction to the Old Testament*, S.P.C.K., 1970.

Gevirtz, S., *Patterns in the Early Poetry of Israel*, University of Chicago Press, 1963.

POST-BIBLICAL POETRY

Dead Sea Scrolls

Gaster, T. H., *The Dead Sea Scriptures*, rev. edn, Doubleday & Company (Anchor Books), New York, 1964.

Vermes, G., *The Dead Sea Scrolls in English*, Penguin Books, 1962.

Liturgy and Talmudic Poetry

Birnbaum, P. (ed.), *Daily Prayer Book*, Hebrew Publishing Company, New York, 1949.

Birnbaum, P. (ed.), *High Holyday Prayer Book*, Hebrew Publishing Company, New York, 1951.

Gaster, T. H., *Festivals of the Jewish Year*, William Sloane Associates, New York, 1964.

Heinemann, J., *Prayer in the Talmud*, Walter de Gruyter, Berlin, New York, 1977.

Heinemann, J., with Petuchowski, J. J., *Literature of the Synagogue*, Behrman House Inc., New York, 1975.

Idelsohn, A. Z., *Jewish Liturgy and its Development*, Schocken Books, New York, 1967.

Perath, M. J., *Rabbinical Devotion*, Prayers of the Jewish Sages, Van Gorcum Ltd, Assen, 1964.

Hekhalot Hymns

Scholem, G. G., *Jewish Gnosticism, Merkabah Mysticism, and Talmudic Tradition*, 2nd edn, Jewish Theological Seminary of America, New York, 1965.

Scholem, G. G., *Major Trends in Jewish Mysticism*, 3rd rev. edn, Schocken Books, New York, 1964.

General and Criticism

Ashtor, E., *The Jews of Moslem Spain*, Jewish Publication Society, Philadelphia, 1973.

Baer, Y., *History of the Jews in Christian Spain*, 2 vols., Jewish Publication Society, Philadelphia, 1960, 1966.

Bargebuhr, F. P., *The Alhambra, A Cycle of Studies on the Eleventh Century in Moorish Spain*, Walter de Gruyter & Co., Berlin, 1968.

Davidson, I., *Maḥzor Yannai*, Jewish Theological Seminary of America, New York, 1919.

Davidson, I., *Parody in Jewish Literature*, Columbia University Press, New York, 1907.

Habermann, A. M., 'The Beginning of Hebrew Poetry in Northern Europe and France', *The World History of the Jewish People – the Dark Ages*, C. Roth (ed.), Massadah Publishing Company, Tel Aviv, 1966, pp. 267-73.

Kahle, P., *The Cairo Geniza*, 2nd edn, Oxford University Press, 1959.

Schechter, S., 'Safed in the Sixteenth Century: A City of Legists and Mystics', *The Jewish Expression*, J. Goldin (ed.), Bantam Books, New York, 1970, pp. 258-321. Reprinted from S. Schechter, *Studies in Judaism*, 2nd series, Jewish Publication Society, Philadelphia, 1908.

Schirmann, J., 'Hebrew Liturgical Poetry and Christian Hymnology', *Jewish Quarterly Review*, N.S., XLIV, Philadelphia, 1953-4, pp. 123-61.

Schirmann, J., 'The Beginning of Hebrew Poetry in Italy', *The World History of the Jewish People – the Dark Ages*, C. Roth (ed.), Massadah Publishing Company, Tel Aviv, 1966, pp. 249-66.

Schirmann, J., '*The Ephebe in Mediaeval Hebrew Poetry*', *Sefarad*, XV, 1955, pp. 55-68.

Schirmann, J., 'The Function of the Hebrew Poet in Medieval Spain', *Jewish Social Studies*, XVI, 1954, pp. 235-52.

Sharf, A., *Byzantine Jewry*, from Justinian to the Fourth Crusade, Routledge & Kegan Paul, 1971.

Spiegel, S., *The Last Trial*, On the legends and lore of the command to Abraham to offer Isaac as a sacrifice: the *Akedah*, translated by J. Goldin, Jewish Publication Society, Philadelphia, 1967.

Spiegel, S., 'On Medieval Hebrew Poetry', *The Jewish Expression*, J. Goldin (ed.), Bantam Books, New York, 1970, pp. 174-216. Reprinted from *The Jews: Their History, Culture and Religion*, L. Finkelstein (ed.), Vol. 1, Harper & Brothers, New York, 1960.

Stern, S. M., *Hispano-Arabic Strophic Poetry*, Oxford University Press, 1974.

Anthologies

Glatzer, N. N. (ed.), *Language of Faith*, A Selection from the Most Expressive Jewish Prayers, Schocken Books, New York, 1967.

Goldstein, D., *The Jewish Poets of Spain*, Penguin Books, 1965.

Halper, B. Z., *Post-Biblical Hebrew Literature*, Vol. 2 (English translations), Jewish Publication Society, Philadelphia, 1921.

Nemoy, L., *A Karaite Anthology*, Yale University Press, 1952.

Individual Authors

Lewis, B., *The Kingly Crown by Solomon Ibn Gabirol*, Vallentine Mitchell, 1961.

Salaman, N., *Selected Poems of Jehudah Halevi*, Jewish Publication Society, Philadelphia, 1924 (1974, paperback).

Solis-Cohen, S., *Selected Poems of Moses Ibn Ezra*, Jewish Publication Society, Philadelphia, 1934 (1974, paperback).

Wallenstein, M., *Some Unpublished Piyyutim from the Cairo Genizah* by Samuel Hashelishi, Manchester University Press, 1956.

Weinberger, L. J., *Jewish Prince in Moslem Spain: Selected Poems of Samuel Ibn Nagrela*, University of Alabama Press, 1973.

Zangwill, I., *Selected Religious Poems of Solomon Ibn Gabirol*, Jewish Publication Society, Philadelphia, 1932 (1974, paperback).

MODERN POETRY

Bibliography and Criticism

Alter, R., *After the Tradition*, E. P. Dutton & Company, New York, 1969.

Goell, Y., *Bibliography of Modern Hebrew Literature in English Translation*, Israel Universities Press, Jerusalem, London, New York, 1968.

Goell, Y., *Bibliography of Modern Hebrew Literature in Translation*, Institute for the Translation of Hebrew Literature, Tel Aviv, 1975.

Halkin, S., *Modern Hebrew Literature, Trends and Values*, Schocken Books, New York, 1950.

Silberschlag, E., *Saul Tschernichowsky*, East and West Library, Cornell University Press, Ithaca, 1968.

Spiegel, S., *Hebrew Reborn*, Macmillan Company, New York, 1930; paperback reprint, Schocken Books, New York, 1962.

Anthologies

Anderson, E. (ed.), *Contemporary Israeli Literature, TriQuarterly 39*, Northwestern University, Evanston, 1977. Published in hardback by the Jewish Publication Society, Philadelphia, 1977.

Burnshaw, S., Carmi, T., and Spicehandler, E. (eds.), *The Modern Hebrew Poem Itself*, Holt, Rinehart & Winston, New York, 1965. Reprinted in paperback by Schocken Books, New York, 1966.

Friend, R. (guest ed.), *Modern Poetry in Translation, Israel*, London, 1974.

Silk, D. (ed.), *Fourteen Israeli Poets*, André Deutsch, 1976.

Individual Authors

Alterman, N., *Selected Poems*, bilingual edition, trans. Robert Friend, Hakibbutz Hameuchad, Tel Aviv, 1978.

Amichai, Y., *Selected Poems*, trans. A. Gutmann and H. Schimmel, Penguin Books, 1971.

Amichai, Y., *Songs of Jerusalem and Myself*, trans. H. Schimmel, Harper & Row, New York, 1973.

Amichai, Y., *Amen*, trans. by the author and T. Hughes, Harper & Row, New York, 1977.

Ben Yitzhak, A., *Poems*, trans. I. M. Lask, Youth and Hehalutz Department of the Zionist Organization, Jerusalem, 1957.

Carmi, T., *The Brass Serpent*, trans. D. Moraes, André Deutsch, 1964.

Carmi, T., *Somebody Like You*, trans. S. Mitchell, André Deutsch, 1971.

Carmi, T., and Pagis, D., *Selected Poems*, trans. S. Mitchell, Penguin Books, 1976.

Gilboa, A., *The Light of Lost Suns*, trans. S. Kaufman with S. Rimmon, Persea Books, New York, 1979.

Goldberg, L., *Selected Poems*, trans. R. Friend, Menard Press and Panjandrum Press, 1976.

Kovner, A., and Sachs, N., *Selected Poems*, Kovner's poems trans. S. Kaufman and N. Orchan, Penguin Books, 1971.

Kovner, A., *A Canopy in the Desert*, trans. S. Kaufman with R. Adler and N. Orchan, University of Pittsburgh Press, 1973.

Pagis, D., *Selected Poems*, trans. S. Mitchell, Carcanet Press, 1972.

Ravikovitch, D., *A Dress of Fire*, trans. C. Bloch, Menard Press, 1976.

Vogel, D., *The Dark Gate*, trans. A. C. Jacobs, Menard Press, 1976.

Zach, N., *Against Parting*, trans. the author and others, Northern House Pamphlet Poets, 1967.

ACKNOWLEDGEMENTS

FOR permission to reprint poems in copyright, thanks are due to the following:

ACUM LTD, for poems by Ḥayim Naḥman Bialik, Jacob Fichman, Jacob Steinberg, David Vogel, Israel Efrat, Uri Zvi Greenberg, Simon Halkin, Abraham Shlonsky, Yokheved Bat-Miriam, Yonatan Ratosh, Nathan Alterman, Lea Goldberg, Zelda (Mishkovsky), Amir Gilboa, Abba Kovner, Ḥayim Gouri, Tuvia Ruebner, Yehuda Amichai, Avner Treinin, Dan Pagis, Dalia Ravikovitch;

THE BIALIK INSTITUTE, for poems by Gabriel Joshua Preil;
DR M. SPITZER (TARSHISH BOOKS), for poems by Avraham Ben Yitsḥak;
AM OVED LTD, for the poem by Hayim Lenski;
DVIR PUBLISHING HOUSE, for poems by Saul Tchernikhovsky;
AVOT YESHURUN, for his poems;
NATHAN ZACH, for his poems.

GLOSSARY

ALL words are in Hebrew unless otherwise noted. Terms followed by an asterisk are discussed in the Note on Medieval Hebrew Genres (pp. 51-5). Explanations of italicized words in the definitions may be found elsewhere in the Glossary.

Aggadah (or *haggada*). The sections of the Talmud and Midrash containing homiletical expositions of the Bible, stories, legends, folklore or maxims.

*Ahava** (pl. *ahavot*, 'love'). A *piyut* inserted in the *Shema*, originally part of a *yotser* sequence.

Akeda (pl. *akedot*, 'binding'). (1) The binding of Isaac in Genesis 22. (2) A *seliha* on the theme of Isaac's sacrifice.

*Amida** (pl. *amidot*, 'standing'). The main obligatory prayer, recited in the daily services.

Amora (pl. *amora'im*). Jewish scholars in Palestine and Babylonia in the third to sixth centuries, whose discussions are recorded in the Talmud.

Ashkenazi. (1) The rites and liturgy of German Jews. (2) German, West-, Central-, or East-European Jews and their descendants.

Ashkenazit. Hebrew pronunciation used by Ashkenazi Jews.

*Avoda** (pl. *avodot*, 'service'). Poem describing the sacrificial service of the High Priest in the Temple.

Bar Kokhba. Leader of Palestinian rebellion against the Romans between 132-135 C.E.

Bet Din. Rabbinic court of law.

Dayan ('judge'). Member of a rabbinic court of law.

Diwan [Arabic]. A collection of poems or literary works by one author.

Essenes. Ascetic sect usually associated with the Dead Sea Scrolls.

Gaon (pl. *ge'onim*, 'eminence'). Title of the heads of rabbinic academies, especially in Babylonia, from the sixth to the eleventh century.

Genizah. Depository for used and damaged Hebrew manuscripts and books.

*Geula** ('redemption'). A *piyut* inserted in the *Shema*, originally part of a *yotser* sequence.

Halakhah. The sections of rabbinic literature concerned with religious, ethical, civil and criminal law.

Hasid (pl. *hasidim*). Adherent of the religious movement founded in the early eighteenth century in Eastern Europe.

Hasidey Ashkenaz. Pietistic movement in medieval Germany.

Havdala ('division'). (1) Ceremony marking the close of the Sabbath. (2) A poem, usually in praise of the Sabbath, for the *havdala* service.

Ḥazan. Synagogal prayer-leader or cantor.

Hekhalot ('palaces'). (1) Term employed by early mystics to describe the seven heavens. (2) The writings of these mystics.

Kabbalah. Jewish mystical tradition, originating in Provence in the thirteenth century.

Karaites. Schismatic sect, originating in the eighth century, which accepts only the biblical tradition and rejects rabbinic authority.

Kedusha* ('sanctification'). (1) The prayers describing the angelic choirs, based upon Isaiah 6.3 and Ezekiel 3.12. (2) The hymn concluding a *kedushta* sequence. (3) A *piyut* celebrating the sanctification of God.

Kedushta*. A type of *kerova* for the *Amidot* of Sabbaths and Holydays, which include the *Kedusha* prayer.

Kerova* (pl. *kerovot*). A poem sequence related to the benedictions of the *Amida*.

Kharja [Arabic]. The concluding lines, usually a couplet, of a *muwashshaḥ*.

Kina (pl. *kinot*, 'lament'). Dirges recited on days of mourning.

Knesset. Israel's parliament.

Ladino. Spanish-Jewish dialect.

Maḥzor. Holiday and festival prayerbook.

Maqama [Arabic]. Narrative in rhymed prose, interspersed with metrical poems.

Me'ora* (pl. *me'orot*, 'light'). A *piyut* inserted in the *Shema*, originally part of a *yotser* sequence.

Merkava ('chariot'). In mystical tradition, the Divine Throne.

Midrash (pl. *midrashim*). Rabbinic method of biblical exegesis, also collections of such homiletical interpretations or legal discussions.

Mishnah. Earliest codification of Jewish Oral Law, edited by Judah Hanasi (d. 225 C.E.), which forms the basis of the Talmud.

Mustajab [Arabic]. A type of *seliḥa* composed of unmetrical four-line stanzas with a biblical refrain.

Muwashshaḥ [Arabic]. Metrical strophic poem ('girdle poem') which regularly alternates lines with separate rhymes and others with common rhymes.

Ofan* (pl. *ofanim*, 'wheel'). Angelical *piyut* inserted in the *Shema*, based on Ezekiel's vision (Ez. 1.15 ff.); originally part of a *yotser* sequence.

Paytan (pl. *paytanim*). Liturgical poet.

Piyut (pl. *piyutim*). Liturgical poem.

Pizmon ('chorus'). Strophic *seliḥa* with a refrain.

Qasida [Arabic]. Non-strophic poem, employing quantitative metre and uniform rhyme.

Reshut (pl. *reshuyot*, 'permission'). Lyrical prelude to a prayer.

Sefirot (sing. *sefira*). In the Kabbalah, the ten powers that constitute the manifestations and emanations of God.

Seliha (pl. *selihot*, 'supplication'). Penitential verse.

Sepharadit. Hebrew pronunciation used in Palestine and Israel.

Sephardic. (1) The rites and liturgy of the Jews of Spain and Portugal. (2) Spanish and Portuguese Jews and their descendants.

Shekinah. Divine Presence, God's 'immanence' or 'indwelling' in the world.

*Shema** ('hear!'). (1) Liturgical affirmation of the unity of God. (2) The cluster of benedictions, prayers and biblical passages which compose the 'Reading of the *Shema*'.

Sheol. Underworld.

Shofar. Ram's horn blown on the New Year and the Day of Atonement.

*Siluk** ('conclusion'). Climactic section of a *kedushta* sequence, usually in rhymed, rhythmical prose, which introduces the *Kedusha*.

Talmud. Collection of rabbinic discussions completed *c.* the sixth century which forms the basis of Jewish Oral Law.

Tanna (pl. *tanna'im*). Rabbinic teacher in the Mishnaic period.

Tokhaha. Poetic rebuke.

Tosafist. Medieval Talmudic commentator, mainly from France and Germany.

Tsahot ('purity'). Rhetorical ideal of Spanish Hebrew poetry.

Yeshiva (pl. *yeshivot*). Traditional academy for the study of rabbinic literature.

*Yotser** (pl. *yotserot*). A poem sequence related to the benedictions of the *Shema* prayers in the morning service.

Zohar ('splendour'). Medieval mystical commentary written in Aramaic, which became the central Kabbalistic text.

*Zulat**. A *piyut* inserted in the *Shema*, originally part of a *yotser* sequence.

INDEX OF FIRST WORDS

INDEX OF POETS